THE VISUAL HISTORY OF
BRITAIN

FROM 1900 TO THE PRESENT DAY

THIS IS A CARLTON BOOK

Text and design copyright © Carlton Books Limited 2006

First published in in 2006 by
Carlton Books Limited
20 Mortimer Street
London W1T 3JW

A CIP catalogue for this book is available from the British Library

ISBN-10 1-84442-153-8
ISBN-13 978-1-84442-153-4

Executive Editor: Stella Caldwell
Art Editor: Emma Wicks
Book Design: Michelle Pickering
Picture Research: Stephen O'Kelly
Production: Lisa Moore

Printed and bound in Dubai

THE VISUAL HISTORY OF
BRITAIN

FROM 1900 TO THE PRESENT DAY

R.G.GRANT

FOREWORD BY JOHN HUMPHRYS

CARLTON
BOOKS

CONTENTS

One way of telling that you are getting old, says a friend of mine, is when you bend over to tie your laces and you wonder if there's anything else you can do while you're down there. I prefer a different test. It's when you are talking to some bright young people, clutching their shiny new degrees and buzzing with ambition, and you happen to mention the "winter of discontent" or swinging Britain or what it was like driving to London before there were any motorways. The eyes glaze over and you realize you might as well be talking to your long-dead grandparents about the latest MP3 player.

Memories still fresh in your mind are ancient history to them. It is inevitable and sad in roughly equal measure — not least because history has never moved so fast as it has in the lifetimes of our oldest generation. A foolish notion, you may say, since time moves at a constant speed. Yes, but change does not.

I was born during the last World War and my parents were born only a few years before the first. My childhood years were not so very different from theirs. The welfare state had yet to emerge and if my father had no work he would go from door to door trying to find some. There was no television at home and the working class did not go "abroad" — except to wage war. Holidays consisted of a week in a boarding house in Weston-super-Mare and to get there we crossed the Bristol Channel by paddle steamer. Men doffed their caps to ladies and stood up when they came into the room. We feared policemen and accorded teachers great respect. Nobody had heard of computers. In the closing years of my father's life he would often ask me what exactly they did. I always found it surprisingly difficult to answer.

My youngest child was born as the century turned and could tap out his name on a screen long before he could laboriously write it out on a page. His childhood bears as much relationship to mine and my parents' as a laptop does to an abacus. He may not know it yet, but the world he was born into is a much less certain place — even though, thank God, he is unlikely to see another war of the sort that ripped the world apart when I was the age he is now. But global warming threatens the planet in a way that Adolf Hitler never did. Does it matter that the years through which his parents and grandparents lived will seem so strange to him? Of course it does.

At the most fundamental level, he needs to know how we got to where we are now. He needs to know why so many of his fellow citizens, only a couple of generations removed from him, sacrificed their lives in the face of a terrible threat. A very small child, exposed to the banality of modern television with its gratuitous violence, believes war is a game and he needs to know it is not. He needs to know why we were so careless with the environment. He needs to understand the great social, economic, commercial,

FOREWORD
BY JOHN HUMPHRYS

cultural and industrial transformations through which this country has passed in such a brief span. Has ever one century delivered such change? No. And he needs to understand that.

He will get some of that understanding, I hope and expect, from the massive store of information that is, quite literally, at his fingertips on the Internet. But I hope he will get most of it from reading books. Yes, I know his books will arrive on paper-thin screens and he will be able to download an entire library to slip into a jacket pocket as he boards a space craft that will take him to Mars. And that's fine. But I hope he will also sometimes stagger under the weight of real books with real photographs that will bring history to life for him.

I have been a journalist for almost half a century. Using the oldest cliché of my trade, I have enjoyed the privilege of a ringside seat at history. I hope, in some minuscule way that I have contributed to the first draft of history. Cynics say that journalists observe only one law: first simplify, then exaggerate. Well maybe, but the best journalism does at least provide a narrative with which future historians can make sense of events.

I cherish books like this that make no judgements but tell a story and let us decide for ourselves what to make of it. It helps, of course, when a story has a beginning and an end. Not that history comes to an end – in spite of what eminent thinkers such as Francis Fukuyama may have said

– but if ever a century provided neat book ends for the story of a nation, it was the one that has just ended.

It helps, too, that photography became ubiquitous during the last century and we have so many powerful images to inform the narrative. Academics may scoff a little, but the pictures matter. You learn a lot from seeing the resignation in the eyes of a miner defeated by the collapse of the General Strike or the fear in the eyes of a mud-caked soldier in the First World War trenches or the joy in the eyes of a crowd celebrating victory. Those are defining moments in the history of this nation. But you learn a lot, too, when you compare the innocent sauciness of a line of chorus girls from the 1920s with the knowing sophistication of a young teenager with her pierced navel on display in the 1990s.

I hope my small boy will leave his computer screen long enough to read books like this. I hope they will help show him where the nation has been, how we got here from those days of Empire only a century ago, and offer some hint at where we might be going in the future.

John Humphrys

1900–1919

At the start of the twentieth century, Britain ruled the largest empire the world had ever seen, covering over a fifth of the land area of the globe. Its possessions included Canada, Australasia, the Indian subcontinent and substantial parts of Africa. The City of London was the undisputed financial hub of the world economy and a large proportion of world trade was carried in British ships. The rise of other industrial powers, notably Germany and the United States, meant that Britain was no longer the undisputed superpower that it had been in the mid-nineteenth century, but most British citizens still regarded their country as being at the pinnacle of civilization.

The new century soon saw the death of Queen Victoria: a symbolic transition away from the moral austerity that characterized her reign. Her affable successor, Edward VII, personified the relative relaxation and jollification of the era that bears his name. Edwardian Britain was certainly a self-confident society, yet it was far from being tranquil or self-satisfied. There were serious concerns about the abject poverty that afflicted a large part of the population, in stark contrast to the conspicuous consumption of the wealthy elite.

The rate of technological change that the new century brought was impressive. In little more than a decade, city streets once dominated by horse-drawn transport were crammed with motor-buses, electric trams and automobiles. Moving pictures grew from a novelty into a craze – by 1917 there were an estimated 4,500 cinemas in Britain. Aviation developed from a risky sport and novelty entertainment into an essential arm of warfare. Yet it should perhaps have troubled Britons that in none of these areas was their nation at the forefront of either invention or innovation.

Britain experienced political conflicts in this period, often acute. Troops were deployed on the streets to counter striking workers, while militant suffragettes, seeking votes for women, smashed windows, bombed property and assaulted government ministers. The Labour Party was on the rise, espousing its own brand of democratic socialism. From 1905 a Liberal government laid the foundation stones of a welfare state equipped with old age pensions and national insurance, and took on the House of Lords in a major constitutional crisis. Ireland, then an integral part of the United Kingdom, produced – as so often – the most extreme political confrontation. Protestant Ulstermen armed themselves to resist a measure of limited Irish self-government, but Irish nationalists went further, staging a rebellion against British rule in 1916.

The overwhelming shock to British life delivered by the First World War led to the early part of the century being looked back upon nostalgically as a time of peace and tranquillity. Until 1914 Britain had not been involved in a major European war for almost 100 years. But the rise of German military power under Kaiser Wilhelm II had frightened Britain and driven the country into a closer relationship with France. When war erupted on the continent, the British government and people felt they could not safely stand aside.

The four years that the war lasted changed Britain for ever. The psychological trauma of the loss of three-quarters of a million young men in trench warfare – a hideous nightmare of poisoned gas, barbed wire and mud – marked British society for a generation. A certain sense of confidence and security was never fully regained. The emotions generated by the war found scant resolution in a subsequent peace that produced neither a satisfying feeling of victory nor a sense of justice and reconciliation. The war left Britain relatively impoverished and diminished as a world power, haunted by the prospect of imperial decline.

- The population of the United Kingdom is around 38 million
- The British Empire covers more than a fifth of the surface of the Earth and includes some 400 million people
- Books published this year include *Lord Jim* by Joseph Conrad
- First performance of Edward Elgar's oratorio *The Dream of Gerontius*
- The *Daily Express* newspaper is founded
- The Wallace Collection in London is opened to the public

JANUARY
- Southern and Northern Nigeria become British protectorates
- Death of writer and social reformer John Ruskin

FEBRUARY
- In South Africa, Boer sieges of Kimberley and Ladysmith are lifted by British forces

MARCH
- British authorities in India organize relief as hundreds of thousands die of starvation

APRIL
- A 16-year-old anarchist, Jean-Baptiste Sipido, tries to assassinate Edward, Prince of Wales, in Brussels
- Bury beats Southampton 4–0 in first FA Cup final of the new century, played at Crystal Palace

BIRTH OF BRITAIN'S LABOUR MOVEMENT

The British labour movement took a major step forward in its aim of achieving parliamentary success on February 28, 1900. The Labour Representation Committee (LRC) was established following cooperation between the Independent Labour Party (founded in 1893) and the Trades Union Council (founded in 1868). The first secretary of this body was the Scotsman James Ramsay MacDonald, who had already stood unsuccessfully as a parliamentary candidate in 1894.

The work of social reformers such as Robert Owen and the Chartists during the mid-nineteenth century had already done much to improve the plight of British workers, but in the 30 years since they had won the right to vote, the movement had been too fragmented to offer a viable alternative to successive governments formed by the Tories (Conservatives) and Whigs (Liberals). The LRC sought to unite the disparate elements that made up the labour movement and to end the widespread antipathy that the working class showed towards a system of government which had largely ignored their interests.

On the far left was the hardline Social Democratic Federation, led by Henry Hyndman. A prominent Marxist, Hyndman in 1881 had published *England For All*, the first socialist document to be produced in Britain since the Chartist era. Although a major influence on other British socialists, Hyndman was disliked by Karl Marx who felt that Hyndman had taken too much credit for his own ideas. Also vocal were the more moderate Fabian Society, a group of intellectuals whose aim was to establish a democratic socialist state through social reform within the law rather than through Marxist revolution.

The LRC formally changed its name to the Labour Party in 1906, but would have to wait a further 18 years for a first brief glimpse of parliamentary power.

▲ **Ramsay MacDonald, the first secretary of the Labour Representation Committee.**

BRITON UNEARTHS NEW CIVILIZATION

▲ **The throne room of the palace of Knossos, the centrepiece of Sir Arthur Evans's remarkable discovery on the island of Crete.**

On March 16, 1900, excavations by the British archaeologist Sir Arthur Evans uncovered one of the most remarkable finds ever from the ancient world. Evans had discovered the ruins of the Minoan city of Knossos on the Aegean island of Crete.

The curator of the Ashmolean Museum in Oxford, Evans had already suggested that the Mycenaean civilization of mainland Greece had its origins in Crete. In 1886 he purchased a tract of land near Heraklion, the modern-day Cretan capital, which included the site of Knossos. His findings astonished the archaeological world, and provided clear evidence that a highly developed Bronze Age civilization had thrived on the island, a culture Evans dated to between 3000 and 1100 BC.

Evans continued to excavate the site for the next 25 years, unearthing numerous artefacts which provided crucial new data on the development of civilization. His later work concentrated on attempting to interpret the "Linear B" script found on more than 3,000 clay tablets dug up at the site. Evans died in 1941.

RELIEF OF MAFEKING

Britain had been at war since 1899 with Transvaal and the Orange Free State, the two independent Boer states of southern Africa. The ostensible cause of the conflict was the refusal of Transvaal President Paul Kruger to grant full citizenship rights to non-Boer immigrants (largely British), although Transvaal's gold mines made the territory an attractive proposition for takeover.

To the consternation of the patriotic British public, an undermanned British army suffered major defeats in the early stages of the war. The gallant resistance of some 1,200 British soldiers and local troops besieged by Boers at Mafeking became a focus for imperial pride,

▲ Colonel Robert Baden-Powell sits upon his horse, rifle in hand. He has gone down in history as the "Defender of Mafeking".

making their commander Colonel Robert Baden-Powell a national hero. Popular newspapers fed the public with daily accounts of the gallantly endured deprivations of the garrison. One besieged

English lady recounted that "breakfast consisted of horse sausages; lunch minced mule and curried locusts".

The tide of war turned and, on May 17, 1900, British troops lifted the siege, which had lasted 216 days. When news of the relief of Mafeking spread, the celebrations which ensued in Britain were unbridled and often aggressive – mobs smashed the windows of houses occupied by known pro-Boers and stopped trams in the street, only allowing them to continue if all the occupants sang "God Save the Queen". The rejoicings on "Mafeking night" led to the invention of the verb "to maffick" to describe such extreme public outbursts of jingoism.

THE BOXER REBELLION

In the summer of 1900, while heavily committed to the war in South Africa, British armed forces faced a fresh challenge in China. In May a sect known to the Chinese as the "fists of righteous harmony", and to westerners as the Boxers, began an uprising against foreign influence in the country. China's ruling Empress-Dowager Cixi gave them her support and, the following month, churches and other foreign buildings in Beijing were razed. The foreign legations in the city also came under siege.

A powerful international relief force led by British Admiral Sir Edward Seymour advanced from the coast towards Peking but was forced to turn back when the Boxers cut its lines of communication to the rear. After hard fighting in which British, Japanese, German, French, Italian, American, Austrian

▲ A group of British officers "inspect" the gates of Peking.

and Russian forces co-operated fully, the major city of Tianjin was taken by the relief force. The international force, under General Alfred Gaselee, eventually entered Beijing on August 14, putting the Boxers to flight.

Convinced that their military victory was a triumph of civilization over barbarism, Britain and other

foreign powers imposed harsh conditions on the Chinese imperial government. In a peace treaty signed in Beijing in September 1901, the foreign powers were granted the right to station troops at key points in China, while the Chinese had to pay a large indemnity for the harm caused to foreign citizens and property.

- The Shah of Persia sells a 60-year oil concession to William D'Arcy, whose company later becomes British Petroleum (BP)
- The first petrol-engined motorcycles appear in Britain
- The Royal Navy launches *Holland*, its first submarine
- The Imperial Tobacco Company founded
- Books published this year include *The First Men in the Moon* by H G Wells and *Kim* by Rudyard Kipling

JANUARY
- Death of Queen Victoria; her son succeeds as Edward VII
- Edward VII gives his nephew, Kaiser Wilhelm II of Germany, the rank of Field Marshal in the British Army

FEBRUARY
- Funeral of Queen Victoria
- Edward VII opens the first parliament of his reign
- Germany and Britain agree the boundary between German East Africa and Nyasaland

APRIL
- Non-League side Tottenham Hotspur win the FA Cup

MAY
- Edward VII escapes injury when his racing yacht *Shamrock II* is damaged in a squall off the Isle of Wight
- The British government rejects a proposal to seek an alliance with Germany to escape diplomatic isolation over the Boer War

THE END OF A MAGNIFICENT ERA

▲ **Queen Victoria, who ascended the throne when she was just 18, photographed at the age of 80, two years before her death.**

January 22, 1901, saw the death of Britain's longest-reigning monarch, Queen Victoria. She was 81 years old.

Victoria acceded to the throne in 1837, following the death of her uncle, King William IV. Although William had fathered a number of illegitimate children, the two daughters of his marriage had died in infancy.

Born on May 24, 1819, at Kensington Palace, London, Alexandrina Victoria was the only child of Edward, Duke of Kent. Her father died a year after her birth and a dominant figure of her early life was her uncle Leopold, later King of the Belgians.

Early in her reign Victoria enjoyed a close relationship with the Whig Prime Minister, Lord Melbourne. He remained her principal political influence until she married her cousin, Prince Albert of Saxe-Coburg-Gotha, in 1840. At a time when the sovereign still played a decisive role in everyday affairs of state, Albert emerged as one of the key figures of nineteenth-century British politics. Stricken with grief at Albert's premature death in 1861, the Queen never fully recovered from her loss and the years that followed were marked by a personal austerity.

Victoria's reign was contradictory in that although she always sought an active role in running the country and its empire, hers was an era that saw a gradual shift towards an increasingly neutered "figurehead" monarch. Popular among her subjects, Victoria's greatest legacy may well have been that, following the tainted reigns of George IV and William IV, she brought a level of dignity and respectability to the monarchy that would allow this somewhat anachronistic establishment to thrive in the democratic twentieth century.

A passionate and strong-willed woman to the very end, Victoria's death was accompanied by an unprecedented level of public mourning.

▲ **Thousands of mourners pay their final respects to Queen Victoria as the funeral cortege passes along The Mall.**

DAWN OF THE RADIO AGE

The first ever transatlantic telegraphic transmission was successfully made on December 12, 1901, by the physicist Guglielmo Marconi.

Marconi had begun his experiments in his native Bologna, Italy, in 1894 where he successfully transmitted signals to a receiver 3 km (2 miles) away. After failing to interest the Italian government in his work, he moved to England where he won the support of Sir William Peace, the Postmaster General. By the

▲ **Guglielmo Marconi gives a demonstration of his pioneering wireless telegraphy apparatus.**

end of the century, Marconi had patented his idea and successfully managed a 50-km (30-mile) transmission across the English Channel.

Marconi still had his doubters, some scientists believing that the curvature of the Earth would limit the distance over which transmissions could be made. Marconi proved them wrong when a signal sent from a 50-m (164-ft) transmitter in Poldhu, Cornwall, was received across the Atlantic Ocean in St Johns, Newfoundland – a distance of 3,500 km (2,232 miles).

Marconi's work played a crucial role in the development of radio communications over the next 50 years.

BRITAIN'S CONCENTRATION CAMPS

On June 14, 1901, Sir Henry Campbell-Bannerman, the leader of the opposition Liberal Party, made a powerful speech denouncing the "methods of barbarism" being used by Britain in its war in South Africa. He was referring to the mistreatment of Boer women and children, which had become widely known through the efforts of welfare campaigner Emily Hobhouse.

Engaged in a bitter struggle against Boer fighters who had turned to guerrilla warfare, the British Army under Lord Kitchener had resorted to burning Boer farms and clearing the countryside of Boer civilians. Around 77,000 of them, almost exclusively women and children, along with 21,000 of their black servants, were moved to "concentration camps" – a term first used at this time. Using her political and social connections, Hobhouse obtained permission to visit the camps and her reports threw light on the unspeakable conditions prevailing there. With people herded into overcrowded, unsanitary accommodation, and in the absence of adequate medical care, diphtheria, typhoid and measles were rampant. Some 4,000 women and 16,000 children died in the camps.

Campbell-Bannerman's moral stance won welcomed by many Liberals, including the fiery young Welsh radical David Lloyd George, but a group led by Lord Rosebery insisted on undivided support for the war effort. The Conservative

▲ **Boer prisoners were held in unspeakable conditions by the British, leading to the first use of the term "concentration camps".**

government naturally rejected allegations of mistreatment. The issue embittered British political life, with pro-imperialists adopting an aggressive attitude towards the allegedly unpatriotic critics of the war. In December Lloyd George was attacked by a mob in Birmingham, escaping with his life only by disguising himself as a policeman.

THE SCANDAL OF POVERTY

▲ **A crowded room interior shows a British family living in severe poverty at the turn of the century.**

In 1901 a book written by Seebohm Rowntree drew Britain's attention to the scandalous persistence of mass poverty in the heart of an increasingly wealthy country. Rowntree was born into a family that had grown rich through chocolate manufacture. In 1899 concern for the lives of workers in the family firm led him to carry out a survey of living conditions in his native city of York. His findings, published in 1901 in *Poverty: A Study of Town Life*, were enough to shock the hardest conscience.

Rowntree maintained that more than a quarter of the city's population were living in abject poverty. He described overcrowded housing – seven or eight people existing in a two-room dwelling, with "walls, ceiling and furniture filthy" and "children pale, starved looking, and only half-clothed". A dreary diet of bread, dripping and tea was relieved only by an occasional rasher of bacon. Every Monday morning children were sent to the pawnshop to pawn the family's Sunday clothes, which would be redeemed the following Saturday night. Many people were in poor health: around half of men who volunteered to join the army in York were rejected as unfit to serve.

The impact of Rowntree's book was underlined within two years when the social reformer Charles Booth published *Life and Labour of the People in London*, a massive study documenting a similar state of extreme poverty in the empire's capital. The problem of poverty was firmly established as a central item on the political agenda.

JUNE
- Liberal MP David Lloyd George denounces the high death rate among Boer civilians in concentration camps

JULY
- In the Taff Vale case the House of Lords rules that a trade union can be held responsible for financial losses sustained by a company as a result of strike action

AUGUST
- The Royal Titles Act adds the words "and of the British Dominions beyond the Seas" to Edward VII's titles

SEPTEMBER
- A smallpox epidemic begins in London; over the following months it kills several thousand people

NOVEMBER
- Hay-Pauncefote Treaty between Britain and the United States allows the construction of a canal across the Isthmus of Panama

DECEMBER
- Britain forms an alliance with Japan, recognizing common interests in China and Korea
- British engineers complete the Uganda railway between Mombasa and Lake Victoria

- A J Balfour's Education Act provides for publicly funded secondary education in England and Wales
- A Royal Commission is set up to investigate the scale and effect of Jewish immigration into Britain recommends immigration controls
- English physiologists William Bayliss and Ernest Starling discover hormones
- Ernest Rutherford and Frederick Soddy identify the cause of radioactivity as the disintegration of atoms
- Triumph Cycle Company builds its first motorcycle
- Fish and chips begins to be a popular meal
- Books published this year include *Heart of Darkness* by Joseph Conrad, *The Hound of the Baskervilles* by Arthur Conan Doyle, the *Just So Stories* by Rudyard Kipling, *The Wings of the Dove* by Henry James and *The Tale of Peter Rabbit* by Beatrix Potter
- J M Barrie's play *The Admirable Crichton* opens in London

FEBRUARY

- Women textile workers petition parliament to grant women the right to vote

MARCH

- The British Army decrees that soldiers are permitted to wear glasses

END OF AN EMPIRE BUILDER

On March 26, 1902, Cecil Rhodes, the towering figure of the British imperial presence in Africa, died.

Rhodes was born in 1853 in Bishop's Stortford, Hertfordshire. His early ambitions had shown a leaning towards law or the clergy, but his early education was seriously impeded by a lung condition. At the age of 17 he joined his brother in South Africa. Together, they gravitated towards Kimberley, the world's diamond mining capital. Over the next decade Rhodes accrued considerable wealth in South Africa while intermittently returning to England to complete his studies at Oxford. He continually expanded his claims, and by 1890 the company he founded, De Beers Consolidated Mines, was believed to own more than 90 per cent of the world's diamond deposits.

Above all, however, Rhodes was a man of the Empire. His dream was to see an African continent unified under British rule. During the 1880s he became actively

▲ Cecil Rhodes, the relentless imperialist who sought an African continent under British rule.

engaged in the politics of the region. At his behest the British South Africa Company was formed with a government charter to create a new territory and extend British control to the north, to encourage trade and colonization and to secure mineral deposits.

In 1890 his "Pioneers" marched northwards through Matabeleland, establishing a base that they named Salisbury, after the current British Prime Minister. Five years later, this territory was formally renamed Rhodesia.

In 1890 Rhodes became Prime Minister of the Cape Colony. A dictatorial figure, his rule was dominated by a fierce personal rivalry with Paul Kruger, President of the Transvaal. His political downfall came in December 1995 when he tacitly authorized the disastrous Jameson Raid, an attempt to invade the Transvaal that did much to damage the already fractious relationship between the two states.

Cecil Rhodes died with a considerable fortune to his name. Much of this was channelled into setting up Rhodes Scholarships, which continue to offer gifted students from outside Great Britain the opportunity to study at Oxford University. Among the recipients of this award have been US President Bill Clinton.

PEACE IN SOUTH AFRICA

▲ Thousands gather around London's Mansion House to celebrate Britain's victory over the Boers in South Africa.

The signing of the peace of Vereeniging in Pretoria on May 31, 1902, brought to an end the costly hostilities between Britain and the Boer republics of Transvaal and the Orange Free State. By June 1900 Britain had effectively won the Boer War, having deployed almost half a million troops to engage barely 80,000 Afrikaners. But for nearly 18 months after their loss of Johannesburg and Pretoria, Boer forces continued to carry out bold, destructive commando raids on British bases, until a brutal war of attrition conducted by British commander

Lord Kitchener eventually forced them into submission.

News of the war's end reached London on the afternoon of Sunday, June 1. Throughout that evening large crowds gathered in the streets, waving flags and singing the national anthem. However, *The Times* observed that "there were none of those disorderly scenes witnessed on 'Mafeking night'".

The war had cost the lives of more than 20,000 British soldiers, two-thirds of them victims of disease rather than combat. More than 30,000 Boers died in the conflict and 15,000 nonwhites. The war might have been expected to leave a permanent legacy of bitterness between Afrikaners and the British, but in 1906 the Liberal government granted self-rule to Transvaal. Four years later,

the Boers voluntarily joined in the creation of the Union of South Africa within the British Empire. South African troops fought alongside the British in the First World War. The price paid for this remarkable reconciliation was the exclusion of nonwhites from any share in political power in South Africa, an injustice in which Afrikaners and British South Africans found common cause.

CORONATION OF EDWARD VII

On August 9, 1902, King Edward VII was crowned in Westminster Abbey at the age of 60. His long wait for a coronation, through the seemingly interminable reign of his mother Queen Victoria, had been further prolonged at the last moment by an attack of appendicitis. This caused the postponement of the ceremony – originally planned for June 26 – while the king underwent emergency surgery in a hastily improvised operating theatre at Buckingham Palace.

The delay meant that many of the dignitaries from overseas who had come to participate in the event in June had gone home by the time the postponed ceremony took place. The delay also had the odd result that a film of the coronation, made by French director Georges Méliès – using a laundryman to play the king and cardboard sets to represent the Abbey – was available for viewing before the event actually happened.

Despite the king's convalescent state, the day was carried off in style. The sun shone and crowds lined the streets to cheer the new king and his wife, Danish-born Queen Alexandra. The ceremony in the Abbey was somewhat curtailed

▲ **King Edward VII and his Danish-born wife, Queen Alexandra, at the coronation ceremony in London.**

in deference to the king's health, although it was the ageing Archbishop of Canterbury, Frederick Temple, who could not take the strain, fainting after swearing allegiance on behalf of the Church.

A notable feature of the celebrations was the provision of dinner at the king's expense to almost 500,000 of the London poor, who were invited to halls, chapels and churches across the city. Teams of entertainers, including the music-hall favourite Marie Lloyd, were employed to keep the diners happy during their meal. The menu included rump

steak, veal and ham pies, boiled beef and fruit tarts.

Edward was expected to bring a very different tone to public life following the moral austerity of the Victorian era. He had always been noted for his hedonistic tastes and his affairs with attractive mistresses, although his life had never sunk to the depths of raffish immorality suggested by hostile rumour. As king, he proved an able diplomatist, playing an important role in improving relations between Britain and France, and he showed a common touch that his mother had singularly lacked.

APRIL
- More than 20 people die and several hundred are injured when a stand collapses at Ibrox Stadium, Glasgow, during a Scotland–England football international
- The Barbican area of London is devastated by a major fire

MAY
- An appeal court rules that women can work behind the bar in Glasgow pubs, reversing an earlier ruling banning barmaids on moral grounds
- Australia's cricketers are bowled out for 36 at Edgbaston, their lowest ever innings in a Test against England
- The signing of the Peace of Vereeniging ends the Boer War

JUNE
- A Colonial Conference agrees a preferential trade policy ("Imperial Preference") between Britain and other countries in the Empire

JULY
- Lord Salisbury, Prime Minister since 1895, retires and is succeeded by his nephew Arthur Balfour

SEPTEMBER
- More than 20,000 people take part in demonstrations in Dublin against the state of emergency imposed by the British government in Ireland

NOVEMBER
- German Kaiser Wilhelm II makes a state visit to Britain

DECEMBER
- British engineers complete the Aswan Dam in Egypt

- Women's Social and Political Union founded by Emmeline Pankhurst to campaign for female suffrage
- Introduction of a 20 mph speed limit for motor vehicles on British roads
- Establishment of the Royal Naval College at Dartmouth
- The Catholic Westminster Cathedral is completed in London
- The *Daily Mirror* is founded by Alfred Harmsworth as a newspaper for "gentlewomen"
- Books published this year include *The Way of All Flesh* by Samuel Butler, *The Riddle of the Sands* by Erskine Childers and the final part of *Life and Labour of the People in London* by Charles Booth

JANUARY
- Edward VII is proclaimed Emperor of India at a durbar held outside Delhi
- A fire at a mental hospital at Colney Hatch, near London, kills 51 people

FEBRUARY
- A Royal Commission is set up to investigate the problem of traffic congestion in London

MARCH
- The Sokoto caliphate in Nigeria is conquered by British forces

ANTARCTIC EXPEDITION BREAKS RECORD

In the winter of 1902–03, members of the British National Antarctic Expedition (organized by the Royal Geographical Society) travelled closer to the South Pole than anyone had done before.

Led by Commander Robert Falcon Scott, a Royal Navy officer, the expedition set off for Antarctica in 1901 aboard the *Discovery*, a wooden-hulled vessel purpose-built to resist the crushing force of ice floes. The record-breaking overland journey southward began in November 1902. A party led by Scott – including Irish merchant navy officer Ernest Shackleton – set off from *Discovery* on dog-sledges. Disastrously, the wrong food had been brought for the dogs, which sickened and died. Scott's men

▲ **Members of Scott's British National Antarctic Expedition celebrating Christmas.**

were then forced to pull the sledges themselves.

Undergoing numerous hardships, the group reached 82º 17' south – 857 km (533 miles) from the South Pole – at the start of January 1903, before the decision was taken to turn back. On the return journey some of Scott's men experienced snow blindness and all were seriously undernourished. Shackleton was in especially poor condition by the time they reached *Discovery*. Suffering from scurvy, he was sent back to Britain at the earliest opportunity. Scott and the rest of the expedition returned in early 1904.

Although the expedition had enjoyed mixed fortunes, it set in motion the idea of a race to be first to reach the South Pole, an obsession which would cost Scott his life in 1912.

▲ **A young Winston Churchill, one of the politicians opposed to the protectionism advocated by Joseph Chamberlain.**

TRADE DISPUTE SPLITS THE GOVERNMENT

On May 15, 1903, Joseph Chamberlain, the Colonial Secretary, and one of the most respected elder statesmen in British politics, delivered a provocative speech in which he called for preferential treatment for imports from countries within the Empire. The speech caused a sensation because the system of "imperial preference" advocated by Chamberlain would involve imposing tariffs on goods imported from outside the Empire. This protectionism ran counter to the principle of free trade which had become almost a religion to the British – the foundation on which the nation's prosperity was believed to have been built.

Chamberlain's stance precipitated a crisis within the government, which was split between dedicated advocates of free trade and supporters of imperial preference. In September Chamberlain resigned from the government to devote himself single-mindedly to the cause of tariff reform. The Prime Minister, Arthur Balfour, was determined to hold his Conservative and Unionist Party together and keep his government in power. He responded to Chamberlain's resignation with a Cabinet reshuffle in which a number of key supporters of free trade lost their posts – in effect balancing the departure of the leading advocate of protectionism. This subtle manoeuvre succeeded temporarily in maintaining the government in power, although at the cost of systematically evading further debate on free trade in the House of Commons.

In the longer term, the grave split in the Unionist Party was damaging and insoluble. Politicians and voters who were opposed to protectionism – including the young Winston Churchill – were tempted to switch to the solidly free trade Liberals, while the government continued to come under attack from Chamberlain and the "tariff reformers" because of its lukewarm and evasive stance. The split opened the way for the Liberal dominance of British politics from 1906 until the First World War.

BRITAIN OFFERS JEWS AN AFRICAN HOMELAND

In April 1903, the British Colonial Secretary Joseph Chamberlain suggested to Theodor Herzl, founder of the World Zionist movement, that the Jews could be given a homeland in British-ruled East Africa.

▲ The Hungarian founder and leader of the Zionist movement, Theodor Herzl.

The British government had become interested in Herzl's campaign for a Jewish homeland because it offered a solution to the problem of Jewish immigration to Britain. Jews fleeing persecution and poverty in Eastern Europe were arriving in unprecedented numbers, rapidly changing the character of some areas of British cities, such as the East End of London and fuelling fears about cheap immigrant labour. A Royal Commission had been set up in 1902 to investigate the problem of "alien immigration" and the government had introduced immigration controls. Herzl's proposed homeland would take the pressure off Britain's cities by offering Jews an alternative destination.

After some hesitation, Herzl accepted the British offer of an unpopulated area of Uganda measuring 15,000 sq km (5,800 sq miles). But a majority of Zionists rejected it at their next congress, insisting that the only possible Jewish homeland was Palestine. In any case, British settlers in East Africa reacted with horror to the idea of thousands of Jews arriving in their midst and would probably have scotched the plan. British interest in backing the Zionist project would eventually lead in 1917 to the offer of a homeland in Palestine.

RIDDLE INSPIRES GERMAN INVASION SCARE

One of the bestselling books of 1903 was *The Riddle of the Sands*, which has been described as the first spy novel. Written by Erskine Childers, an Anglo-Irish veteran of the Boer War, it narrates the daring exploits of two British secret agents who succeed in stealing a copy of "a confidential memorandum to the German government embodying a scheme for the invasion of England by Germany".

Childers wrote his novel specifically to alert the public to the risk that Britain ran through the unpreparedness of its armed forces in the face of increasing German military might. Its success marked a decisive step in changing British attitudes, so that Germany, rather than France, came to be viewed as the most potent threat to the nation's freedom. According to Winston Churchill, *The Riddle of the Sands* was directly responsible for the Royal Navy's decision to create new bases at Invergordon, the Firth of Forth and Scapa Flow to guard against a possible attack by the German Navy across the North Sea.

Childers later regretted the part he had played in triggering an arms race between Britain and Germany. A committed Irish nationalist, after 1918 he joined Sinn Fein in its armed struggle against British rule. He was shot by an Irish Free State firing squad in 1922, during the civil war that followed the granting of independence to southern Ireland.

▲ Republican author Erskine Childers (right) aboard his yacht, the *Asgard*, which he used to run guns for the Irish Volunteers.

1904

- First mainline electric train in Britain runs between Liverpool and Southport
- The largest ship yet built, the British liner *Baltic*, goes into service
- Ebenezer Howard founds Letchworth Garden City
- The royal park at Richmond is opened to the public
- Books published this year include *Nostromo* by Joseph Conrad and *The Napoleon of Notting Hill* by G K Chesterton
- New plays include J M Barrie's *Peter Pan* and George Bernard Shaw's *John Bull's Other Island*
- The Abbey Theatre is opened in Dublin
- Charles Rennie Mackintosh designs the Willow Tea Rooms, Glasgow

FEBRUARY
- British consul Roger Casement submits a report denouncing atrocities committed by Belgian colonial authorities in the Congo
- Britain declares itself neutral as war erupts between Russia and Japan

MARCH
- A Royal Navy submarine is sunk when it is struck by a liner in the Solent

APRIL
- Britain and France settle their colonial disputes in Egypt, Morocco and Madagascar as part of the Entente Cordiale
- A new law permits peaceful picketing by trade union strikers

BRITISH MILITARY ACTION IN TIBET

Tibet, a mountainous landscape between India and China, was virtually independent by 1900. In July 1903 British forces sent a military expedition to the region in order to investigate reports of a Russian presence there. The action took advantage of Russia's involvement in conflict with Japan and was intended to curb its ambitions in the area.

The British force set out from India under the command of Sir Francis Younghusband (1836–1942) with the intention of reaching the sacred capital of Tibet, Lhasa. Once there, they forced Tibet's spiritual leader, the Dalai Lama, to grant Britain trading posts in the country and not to concede territory to other foreign powers.

In March 1904 British troops under Brigadier General Macdonald encountered more than 2,000 Tibetan soldiers on the Guru road. Although the defenders put up a strong battle, they were no match for the superior arms of the enemy and soon found themselves outflanked and outmanoeuvred. Tibetan losses reached 300, including one of their generals, and the road to Guru was cleared.

Within six months, the British forces reached Lhasa and the Tibetan leaders acceded to their demands. Despite Britain's

▲ **Brigadier General Macdonald, leader of the British expedition, forces the Tibetan lamas to provide grain for his troops.**

declared aim of preventing Russian incursions into Tibet, in fact no Russian forces were encountered during this campaign.

AGREEMENT BETWEEN BRITAIN AND FRANCE

▲ **Pierre Paul Cambon, the French ambassador to Great Britain and one of the signatories of the "Entente Cordiale".**

The phrase *"entente cordiale"* came into common use with the agreement signed by France and Britain on April 8, 1904, that resolved the differences between the two nations, bringing them closer together.

The term was actually first used in the 1840s to describe a friendly period between the two powers but the 1904 agreement also indicated Britain's move away from isolation following the Boer War. The agreement was a great progression from the atmosphere of autumn 1898, when a colonial dispute in Africa brought France and Britain to the brink of war at Fashoda in the Sudan.

The 1904 agreement changed much between the two nations: fishing rights in Newfoundland were settled, as were ongoing territorial disputes – Britain relinquished parts of West Africa and maintained control of Egypt, while France was given access to the Suez Canal and a free hand in Morocco, effectively ending that country's independence. Some of these issues dated back centuries and the negotiations had taken months. It was signed by Paul Cambon on behalf of the French Minister for Foreign Affairs and Lord Lansdowne, the British Foreign Secretary.

▲ **Lord Lansdowne, Henry Charles Keith Petty-Fitzmaurice, Britain's Foreign Secretary during the negotiations with France.**

The initiative for the move was attributed by some to the British monarch, Edward VII, who had visited Paris the previous year. Others were more cynical, suggesting that his role was limited to a willingness not to take affront at the Republican attitude he had discovered during his stay.

But beyond the physical agreements of the Entente Cordiale was the division of the major European powers into rival systems: France establishing closer ties with Britain – and both nations moving away from Germany.

ROLLS MEETS ROYCE

▲ A 1905 20-horsepower Rolls-Royce. Seated at the back is Charles Rolls, who co-founded the company with Henry Royce.

On May 4, 1904, Charles Stewart Rolls met Henry Royce in the Midland Hotel, Manchester – a pivotal moment in the development of the British motor industry. The two men were from sharply contrasting backgrounds. Rolls was born into money and educated at Eton and Cambridge. In contrast, Royce had grown up in poverty, succeeding through sheer hard work in founding and expanding an electrical engineering company in Manchester. What they shared was a fascination with automobiles.

Rolls was running a business selling foreign cars in Britain, while also building up a formidable reputation as a driver. In 1903, he had set a new world land speed record of 149 km/h (93 mph) in Phoenix Park, Dublin. Rolls drove and sold cars manufactured abroad, since they were far superior to any existing British designs. But as a patriotic Englishman, he was on the lookout for a home-grown vehicle of suitable quality. He found what he wanted in a 10-horsepower automobile that Royce had built for himself, in a departure from his company's usual line of work.

The meeting between Rolls and Royce was a total success. An agreement was struck for Royce to manufacture cars that Rolls would sell under their joint name. The full merger that created Rolls-Royce Ltd was not completed until 1906, but a motoring legend had been born.

RUSSIAN FLEET SINKS
BRITISH TRAWLERS

On the night of October 21–22, 1904, warships of the Russian Baltic Fleet inadvertently sailed into the midst of a group of British trawlers which were peaceably fishing the Dogger Bank in the North Sea. Commanded by Admiral Rozhdestvensky, the fleet was making the long voyage to the northern Pacific to join the war raging there between Russia and Japan.

The Russian sailors were in a nervous state, fearing a surprise attack by the Japanese navy – although the likelihood of this happening in the North Sea was infinitesimal. Finding themselves suddenly surrounded by unidentified vessels, the Russian warships opened fire with their powerful guns. One of the trawlers had been sunk and two British fishermen killed before the Russians realized their mistake and the firing stopped. The Baltic Fleet steamed on, failing to halt to aid the trawlermen.

Britain was outraged by the incident. Although the Tsar sent a message to Edward VII "regretting" the fishermen's deaths, his statement fell short of an apology. The Russian admiral absurdly insisted that Japanese torpedo boats had been hidden among the fishing vessels. For a short time Britain and Russia teetered on the brink of war, but level heads on both sides realized that conflict was in neither country's interests.

Russia agreed to submit to the judgement of an international tribunal, which ruled her responsible for the incident. In 1905 Russia paid Britain £65,000 in compensation.

▲ Russian warships open fire on defenceless British fishing boats during the notorious Dogger Bank incident.

NEWS IN BRIEF

- Trade union membership in Britain rises to 1,997,000
- Lord Curzon, Viceroy of India, divides Bengal into East and West Bengal; this offends many Bengalis and stimulates political opposition to British rule
- Cardiff is granted the status of a city; new city hall is opened
- Aspirin is marketed for the first time
- Books published this year include *The Scarlet Pimpernel* by Baroness Orczy and *The Return of Sherlock Holmes* by Arthur Conan Doyle
- First performance of George Bernard Shaw's plays *Man and Superman* and *Major Barbara*
- British film producer Cecil Hepworth releases a seven-minute feature, *Rescued By Rover*

MARCH

- The government announces a tripling of the Royal Navy budget as Britain embarks on building dreadnought-class battleships
- The Wright brothers, American inventors of heavier-than-air flight, offer to provide the British Army with an "aerial scouting machine"
- A disaster at a Cambrian pit in the South Wales coalfields kills 32 miners
- Britain is struck by gale-force winds, causing the deaths of at least 23 people

SUFFRAGETTES JAILED AS CAMPAIGN FOR VOTE MOUNTS

On October 14, 1905, Christabel Pankhurst and Annie Kenney, members of the Women's Social and Political Union (WSPU), were sent to prison after disrupting a Liberal Party meeting at the Free Trade Hall in Manchester. It was the first imprisonment of women agitating for female suffrage and heralded a major escalation in the WSPU's campaign.

The WSPU had been established by Emmeline Pankhurst and her daughters Christabel and Sylvia in 1903. This formidable family brought a fresh energy and extremism to the campaign for women's suffrage, which had been pursued by other groups in a more genteel fashion for many years. The granting of the vote to women in New Zealand in 1893 and Australia by 1902 had increased pressure on British

▲ **A group of suffragette women with English, French and German placards condemn the British government.**

politicians to recognize the logic of women's suffrage. But the Pankhursts were convinced that progress would only come through radical action.

The police had been called to the Free Trade Hall after Pankhurst and Kenney had refused to stop heckling speakers at the Liberal meeting. The women

spat in the faces of police officers who tried to restrain them and were finally arrested for "causing an obstruction" outside the hall. In court they were offered the option of paying fines, but chose prison instead – seven days for Pankhurst and three days for Kenney.

Pankhurst told the court: "My conduct … was meant as a protest against the legal position of women to-day. We cannot make any orderly protest because we have not the means whereby citizens may do such a thing; we have not a vote; and so long as we have not votes we must be disorderly." This was a position that was to lead the "suffragettes" – as they would soon be called – to pursue a campaign of mounting violence in the years up to 1914.

▲ **The inauguration of the London electric tram system, attended by the Prince and Princess of Wales in 1903.**

In 1905 public transport in British cities was in a state of flux, as the long-established dominance of horse-drawn omnibuses and steam trains was challenged by new electric trains and trams. In London, where transport problems

LONDONERS TRAVEL ELECTRIC

were most acute – with perhaps 300,000 people every workday commuting from the suburbs – only the electric revolution prevented the progress of commerce from grinding to a halt.

The most spectacular development was the expansion of underground railways. The first underground line had opened in 1863, but the use of steam engines meant that tunnels had to be near the surface to allow ventilation, and passengers emerged from their journey blackened with soot. In the first decade of the twentieth century,

a network of deep "tubes" was built, exploiting the cleaner energy of electricity. Construction of these immense tunnels was phenomenally expensive – much of the early expansion was financed by an American entrepreneur, Charles Tyson Yerkes. But the electric trains were cheap to run and underground tickets cost only a few pence. The new services were immensely popular – 37,000 passengers travelled on the Bakerloo line on the day it opened in 1906.

The first electric tramway in London was built in 1901, from

Shepherd's Bush to Southall. The electric trams were quicker, cleaner and cheaper than horse-drawn transport. By 1905 tram lines stretched as far as outer the suburbs, such as Twickenham and Uxbridge. But the challenge from petrol-driven vehicles was already growing. The first motor-buses and a handful of motor-taxis were already operating in 1905. Horses, motor vehicles and electric trams would jostle for space on the streets up to the First World War.

SHAW BRINGS "SALLY ARMY" TO THE STAGE

In November 1905 George Bernard Shaw's *Major Barbara* had its first performance at the Royal Court Theatre in London. The play confirmed the Irish writer's reputation as the most intelligent and stimulating dramatist to emerge since the heyday of Oscar Wilde.

Born in Dublin in 1856, Shaw made a name for himself as a journalist and a socialist before taking the theatrical world of the Edwardian years by storm with a profusion of witty, intellectual comedies. *Major Barbara* tells the story of a rich arms manufacturer whose daughter joins the Salvation Army. This was a subject of pressing contemporary interest, as General William Booth was at the time leading a highly publicized Salvation Army crusade against poverty.

Shaw's play ironically argued that the powerful capitalist, with his morally dubious source of wealth, was more likely to improve the lot of the poor than Booth's followers, inspired by religion and the love of humanity. Whatever they thought of Shaw's conclusion, theatre audiences acknowledged that he was raising probably the most important social issue in Edwardian Britain: what was to be done about the poor?

▲ An actor playing a Salvation Army musician with a drum in George Bernard Shaw's *Major Barbara*.

BALFOUR QUITS DOWNING STREET

▲ Arthur Balfour was the Conservative Prime Minister from July 1902 until his resignation in December 1905.

On December 4, Prime Minister Arthur Balfour resigned because of irreconcilable differences within his party over free trade. The schism had undermined a parliamentary majority of around 140 won by the Unionists – the Conservatives and their political allies – at the 1900 general election.

Balfour's decision to resign rather than call a general election may have been based on a guess that the main opposition party, the Liberals, would fall apart under the strain of trying to form a government. They were split between supporters of Sir Henry Campbell-Bannerman, a severe critic of the Boer War, and the imperialist Lord Rosebery. On December 5, the king invited Campbell-Bannerman to form a government, but he was not able to assemble a quorum of ministers until December 11. The new government then belatedly set off for Buckingham Palace – a journey achieved with some difficulty as the ministers spent an hour feeling their way along The Mall in an impenetrable fog.

Strangely, Campbell-Bannerman became Britain's first official Prime Minister. Previous incumbents of 10 Downing Street had formally held the post of First Lord of the Treasury. It was only now that the king agreed to the creation by royal warrant of an official post of Prime Minister.

1906

- The term "suffragette" is coined by popular newspapers
- The Trade Disputes Act protects unions against being held responsible for companies' losses sustained as a result of strike action
- The Rolls-Royce Silver Ghost is launched
- A new city hall is opened in Belfast
- The Ritz hotel opens in London
- The King Edward VII Bridge opens over the River Tyne
- In cricket Yorkshire all-rounder George Hirst establishes a record by taking over 200 wickets and scoring more than 2,000 runs in a season
- Everyman's Library, cheap editions of the classics, are launched by Joseph Dent
- Books published this year include *A Man of Property* by John Galsworthy, the first volume of the Forsyte Saga
- New plays include George Bernard Shaw's *The Doctor's Dilemma*

JANUARY

- The Liberals win a landslide victory in the general election; the former Prime Minister, Arthur Balfour, loses his seat
- In Liverpool a tram accident kills 30 people
- Foreign Secretary Sir Edward Grey approves "military conversations" between Britain and France

THE LIBERAL PARTY TAKES POWER

It was the resignation of the Conservative Prime Minister Arthur Balfour in December 1905 that made Henry Campbell-Bannerman, leader of the Liberal Party, Britain's Premier. The general election that followed on January 13, 1906, brought about a massive majority for the Liberals.

Long established as the principal opposition to the Tories, the Liberals had thrived in the nineteenth century, establishing a reputation as the party of reform under the dominant figure of William Gladstone. Towards the end of the Gladstone era, the party was weakened by the defection of the Unionist element who opposed his ideas for giving Ireland home rule.

After a lengthy period in the political doldrums, the Liberals, at the 1906 election, were able to take advantage of the Conservative Party's divisions on the matter of tariff reform. The scale of the Liberal victory was massive – a parliamentary majority of over 100 seats. The newly formed Cabinet included two future Prime Ministers, Herbert Asquith and David Lloyd George.

The election was also notable for the promising showing of the Labour Representation Committee who, following a pre-election pact with the Liberals, secured 54 seats. Adopting Keir Hardie as their leader, five days after the election they re-christened themselves the Labour Party.

The Liberal Party remained in government for the next 11 years, a period of reform that saw the first seeds of Britain's welfare system being sown. It would be the last time that a Liberal government ruled outside of a coalition.

▲ A future Prime Minister, David Lloyd George held a Cabinet post in the 1906 government.

DREADNOUGHT LAUNCHES NAVAL RACE WITH GERMANY

On February 10, 1905, Edward VII launched HMS *Dreadnought*, the first of a new class of battleship,m at Portsmouth. *The Times* described the scene as the ship was released down the slipway as "one of those moments when thousands of people thrill with a common emotion … Every eye was fixed on the great vessel as, slowly at first, but every instant increasing in speed, she glided over the well-greased ways with the ease and grace of a bird".

The Dreadnought class were by far the most powerful naval vessels ever seen, floating fortresses weighing 18,000 tons,

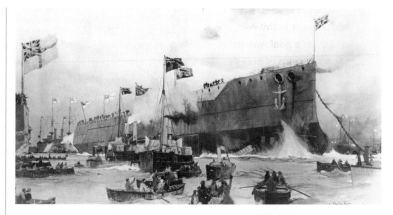

▲ The most powerful battleship in the world, HMS *Dreadnought*, at its launch by King Edward VII in Portsmouth.

with 28-cm (11-in) thick armour. Their main armament consisted of ten 12-in guns, backed up by 24 smaller guns and torpedoes.

These turbine-powered ships were very fast for their size and were capable of making 39 km/h (21 knots). *Dreadnought* briefly made every other warship in the world obsolescent.

Dreadnought was a splendid focus for patriotic pride, but she was also a portent of storms ahead in international relations. Britain's aim in building up a fleet of dreadnoughts – four a year were initially planned – was to maintain what was called the "two-power standard", that is that the Royal Navy was to be more powerful than any other two navies put together. British schoolchildren learnt that it was this naval superiority that had preserved Britain's freedom since before the time of Nelson. But Germany, too, had embarked on a naval construction programme, launching its own equivalent of the

dreadnoughts, and by 1908 it appeared to outstrip Britain. Comparison of the number and size of warships between the two countries became a focus of anxiety over national security and of competition for international status – much like American anxieties over the "missile gap" with the Soviet Union and competition in the space race of the early 1960s.

In the years leading up to the First World War, the naval race with Germany not only increased international tension, but also stoked up political pressures within the Liberal government. Many Liberal ministers balked at the scale of spending involved, which would drain off money needed for

social welfare programmes, but Sir John Fisher, the First Sea Lord, was a passionate advocate of naval expansion. He found allies in the Tory press, which by 1909 was demanding a programme of eight new battleships a year with the catchy slogan: "We want eight and we won't wait!"

By the end of 1914, despite compromises for budgetary reasons, the Royal Navy had built 24 dreadnoughts or super-dreadnoughts, far outnumbering Germany's equivalent warships. Ironically they proved of limited effect during the First World War, when submarines and mines successfully challenged the battleships' claim to rule the waves.

BADEN-POWELL PROPOSES "BOY SCOUTS"

In 1906, Lieutenant-General Sir Robert Baden-Powell, hero of the defence of Mafeking during the Boer War, circulated a document entitled *Boy Scouts: A Suggestion*. Sent to leading figures in public life, it suggested setting up an organization that would encourage boys to take part in healthy outdoor activities.

Baden-Powell's goal was no less than the reform of society through improvement of the young, who had in his view been corrupted by urban society. As he wrote in *Scouting for Boys*, published in 1908, city life had produced boys and young men who were "pale, narrow-chested, hunched up, miserable specimens, smoking endless cigarettes, numbers of them betting". Baden-Powell believed such boys would grow into "men who shirk their duties and responsibilities to the State and to others". The scouting

▲ **Robert Baden-Powell, founder of the Boy Scout movement, at a rally of Boy Scouts at Chatham.**

experience was intended to turn them into "good citizens or useful colonists".

Baden-Powell led the first week-long scout camp on Brownsea Island, Dorset, in August 1907. In line with his aspirations to overcome social differences, it included both boys from Eton and Harrow and youngsters from London's East End. The movement

sparked genuine enthusiasm in young people and its rapid growth over following years was driven largely by a rush of volunteers rather than through any organized recruiting effort on Baden-Powell's part. By 1910, when the Guides movement was formed under Baden-Powell's sister Agnes, there were over 100,000 Boy Scouts in Britain.

- Britain's first airship, *Nulli Secundus*, flies
- Vauxhall Motors car company is formed
- Methodist groups combine to form the United Methodist Church
- The first houses in Hampstead Garden Suburb are completed
- South African cricketers play their first Test series in England
- The English Rugby Union buys a site for a stadium at Twickenham
- Books published this year include *The Secret Agent* by Joseph Conrad

JANUARY

- Secretary for War Richard Haldane unveils plans to reform the army, including the creation of a general staff and a territorial army reserve
- An earthquake devastates the British colony of Jamaica
- The opening of J M Synge's play *The Playboy of the Western World* causes riots at Dublin's Abbey Theatre

FEBRUARY

- Clashes occur between suffragettes and police
- The British government's programme includes a proposal for Irish Home Rule
- Death of war correspondent Sir William Howard Russell
- New Criminal Courts at the Old Bailey are opened by the king

THE WOMEN'S PARLIAMENT

The evening of February 13, 1907, saw the women's suffrage movement take a violent turn as a large crowd of suffragettes attempted to storm the Houses of Parliament to hand in a petition to the British government.

The women had declared their own self-styled "parliament" earlier in the day, after which over 100 members of the Women's Social and Political Union (WSPU), the most prominent campaigners for women's suffrage in Britain, marched through the streets of Westminster to the House of Commons. Emmeline Pankhurst, the founder and leader of the WSPU, had already been jailed for issuing a pamphlet inciting women to "rush the House of Commons".

It took a battalion of mounted policemen five hours to quell the demonstration. In all, 57 women were arrested, although 15 suffragettes did manage to break into the Commons building. In Holloway prison the following day, one of the captives, Pankhurst's daughter Christabel, showed no remorse and described the event as a "great day for our movement".

The main target of WSPU activity had been the Liberal Party, which they saw as actively impeding the progress of women's suffrage. Up until the storming of Parliament, their protests had largely been nonviolent, a situation that now looked very certain to change.

▲ **Emmeline Pankhurst and her daughter Christabel, pioneers of the women's suffrage movement in Britain, in prison garb.**

CHANNEL TUNNEL PLAN ABANDONED OVER DEFENCE FEARS

In 1907 a private member's bill was introduced into Parliament proposing construction of a Channel tunnel linking England and France. Promoted by Sir Francis Fox in Britain and Albert Sartaux in France, the project envisaged the building of an electrified railway to run under the sea from Calais to Dover.

There was nothing new about the idea of a cross-Channel link.

Since the mid-nineteenth century, railway companies had been calculating the possible profits to be made from a direct line between Britain and mainland Europe. Digging of a tunnel actually began in 1880, but it was abandoned in 1883 because the British Army objected, claiming it would lay Britain open to invasion from France.

By the early twentieth century, the invention of electric railways as an alternative to steam had made the project even more feasible, removing the need for elaborate ventilation schemes to stop passengers choking on smoke. But the problem of national

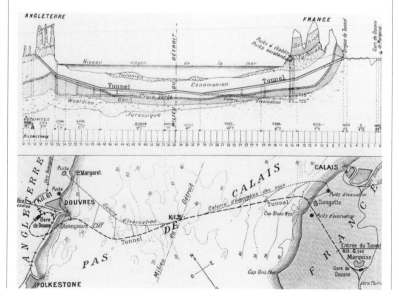

◀ **A French diagram and map of the proposed Channel tunnel between England and France.**

security remained an insuperable objection. Both Prime Minister Campbell-Bannerman and the War Office argued that building the tunnel would require a large increase in defence spending to give Britain an army capable of repelling an enemy land invasion. The vision of swarms of foreign soldiers spewing out of the tunnel at Dover and marching up to London was too much for British opinion. The bill was withdrawn in April, and the project had to wait for almost 90 years to be realized.

RIVALRY ON THE HIGH SEAS

At the end of 1907, the two new sister ships of the British Cunard line, the *Lusitania* and the *Mauretania*, began a series of record-breaking transatlantic voyages, with each new journey seemingly creating a new benchmark for ocean-going speed.

The *Lusitania* made her maiden voyage on September 6, 1907. Sailing from Queenstown on the Irish coast, she arrived in Sandy Hook, New Jersey, having made the fastest-ever crossing in just five days and 54 minutes. This achievement wrested the Blue Riband, awarded for speed of transatlantic travel, from the German liner *Deutschland*. Carrying a crew of 650 and 1,200 paying passengers, the *Lusitania* averaged a speed of 24 knots. The record was shattered the

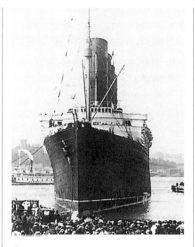

▲ The *Lusitania*, winner of the Blue Riband in 1907, was later sunk by a German U-boat during the First World War.

following month on her return journey, which took just four days and 20 hours.

On November 16 Cunard launched the *Mauretania*. With improved turbines, she was capable of even greater speeds than her sister ship. During her maiden voyage to New York, she achieved 635 knots in a single day – almost 20 knots faster than the *Lusitania*.

During a long life, the *Mauretania* became known as the "Grand Old Lady of the Atlantic", retaining the Blue Riband for speed until 1929. Interrupted only by the First World War, during which she was decommissioned as a hospital ship, the *Mauretania* made 269 two-way transatlantic crossings until her farewell in 1934. She was broken up for scrap a year later.

The fate of the *Lusitania* was more dramatic. Her sinking by a German submarine on May 7, 1915, was one of a string of events that drew the United States into the First World War.

KIPLING WINS NOBEL PRIZE

In 1907 Rudyard Kipling, the bard of the British Empire, was awarded the Nobel Prize for Literature. Born in Bombay in 1865, Kipling was sent to England for his education, but returned to India as a young man. It was to stories based on his Indian experiences – especially *The Jungle Book* (1894) and *Kim* (1901) – that he owed his fame.

Kipling's writings were far from a celebration of the pomp and glory of imperialism. His vision was of a responsible empire subject to law and duty. He reserved his highest admiration for the humble soldiers and civil servants who stoically bore the burden of empire without enjoying its benefits. He famously celebrated the soldier's life in his *Barrack-Room Ballads* (1892). His work was tinged with respect for and curiosity about the exotic subject peoples in his work, as well as with an undoubted vein of racism.

In 1899 Kipling settled in England, after which his inspiration gradually faded. He never recovered from the blow of

▲ Rudyard Kipling, the English short-story writer, novelist and poet, celebrated the heroism of British colonial soldiers.

the death of his son in the First World War. With cruel irony, it fell to him to compose the epitaph written on the war graves of unidentified soldiers: "A Soldier of the Great War Known unto God". Kipling died in 1936.

1908

- A Children Act abolishes the death penalty for minors
- The National Farmers Union is founded
- Port of London Authority established
- The Rotherhithe tunnel in London opens
- Sir Edward Elgar's *First Symphony* is performed to critical and popular acclaim
- Lord Northcliffe buys *The Times*
- Ernest Rutherford, a New Zealand-born scientist working at Cambridge, wins the Nobel Prize for Chemistry for his work on radioactivity
- Books published this year include *A Room with a View* by E M Forster, *The Old Wives' Tale* by Arnold Bennett, *The Wind in the Willows* by Kenneth Grahame, and *The Autobiography of a Supertramp* by W H Davies

JANUARY
- The Labour Party decides to adopt socialism

MARCH
- British colonial police shoot rioters dead in India

APRIL
- Herbert Asquith replaces Campbell-Bannerman as Prime Minister
- The fourth Olympic Games open in London

ASQUITH IS NEW PM

On April 3, 1908, Prime Minister Sir Henry Campbell-Bannerman resigned after suffering a series of heart attacks. Herbert Asquith, chosen to succeed him, had to travel for royal confirmation of his appointment to Biarritz in southern France, where Edward VII was holidaying. Campbell-Bannerman was still in occupation of 10 Downing Street when he died on April 22.

Asquith's government contained a galaxy of individual talents. The selection of David Lloyd George, an outspoken radical, as Chancellor of the Exchequer held promise of a vigorous programme of social reform. The "Welsh wizard" did not disappoint, quickly introducing an old age pension of up to five shillings a week for single men over 70 and seven shillings and sixpence for married couples – a move confidently denounced by Conservatives as bound to bankrupt the country. Sir Edward Grey was confirmed in place at the Foreign Office, as was Viscount Haldane at the War Office. There was a first Cabinet post for Winston Churchill, as President of the Board of Trade. He would soon be promoted to Home Secretary.

Asquith's premiership lasted until 1916, through a stormy period in British politics that would

▲ A typical scene in a London post office as an elderly man collects his payment after the introduction of an old age pension.

see constitutional conflict between the House of Commons and the Lords, near civil war over Irish Home Rule, and finally the outbreak of the First World War.

CONTROVERSY AT THE LONDON OLYMPICS

▲ Marathon runner Pietri Donado of Italy is aided across the finishing line by an official. This helping hand led to his later disqualification.

The 1908 Olympic Games, the fourth such event of the modern era, had originally been scheduled to take place in Rome. Financial difficulties, including the cost of a spectacular eruption of Mount Vesuvius in 1906, caused Italy to pull out, and the venue was hastily moved to the newly built Shepherd's Bush stadium in London.

The 1908 Olympics were the first to begin with a formal opening ceremony. Not for the last time, this became a forum for symbolic political protest. The athletes from Finland, protesting at Russian rule, refused to carry the Russian flag. Prevented by the Olympic Committee from carrying their own standard, the Finns pointedly marched flagless. It was also the first Olympics in which the Anglo-Irish problems reached a world stage, a number of Irish athletes with republican sympathies refused to take part in the Games rather than compete under the British team flag.

The Games were also unfortunately noteworthy for the continual squabbling between Britain and the United States. The controversy started at the opening ceremony when the US flag bearer, shot-putter Ralph Rose, refused to dip his flag in salute as he passed King Edward VII. Thereafter, British officials and US athletes clashed a number of times. Events reached a climax with the final of the 400 m race, in which the American winner John Carpenter was disqualified for unfairly blocking the path of Britain's Wyndham Halswelle. Officials ordered the final to be rerun, the other qualifiers refused to take part, and Halswelle won the gold medal by a walkover – the only time this has happened in Olympic history.

Featuring over 2,000 athletes from 22 nations, the 1908 Olympics were the biggest and most successful to date. As in the previous games, American athletes dominated most of the disciplines, although their successes also brought about charges of "professionalism". One of the stars of the 1908 Olympic Games was US athlete Ray Ewry, who took gold medals in all three standing jump categories, giving him a total of ten gold medals in three Olympic Games.

W G GRACE RETIRES FROM CRICKET

In September 1908, W G Grace, a towering figure in cricket's early history, retired from the game at the ripe age of 60. Born into a cricketing family in Downend, Bristol, in 1848, Grace entered first-class cricket in 1865. Playing for Gloucestershire and England, he was outstanding in all departments of the game, but particularly excelled as a batsman. Although much of his career spanned a time when pitches were poor and there were no fours or sixes for boundaries all runs actually had to be run – he scored more than 54,000 runs in first-class cricket. In one eight-day period in 1876, he made 839 in three innings, including a career-best 344 and another score of 318.

Grace's status was so high that he was sometimes described as the most famous living Englishman. He is credited with transforming cricket into the first sport to attract a mass paying public. Although officially an amateur – making his living as a doctor – he in fact earned large sums from his cricketing appearances. His tricks and wiles were legendary. He is said on one occasion to have refused to leave the crease when given out, on the grounds that the public had come to see him, not the umpire. Although contrary to the cricketing tradition of "fair play", such stories served only to enhance his reputation as one of the great characters of sport.

▲ **The legendary English cricketer William Gilbert Grace scored more than 54,000 runs in his first-class cricket career.**

KAISER INTERVIEW SHOCKS BRITAIN

GUILLAUME II SUR SON NOUVEAU CHEVAL DE BATAILLE.

ZEPPELIN 1908

... NOTRE AVENIR EST EN L'AIR !
(GARE ATOI LA LUNE ...)

▲ **A French satirical cartoon shows Kaiser Wilhelm soaring aloft on his new warhorse, a German zeppelin.**

On October 28, 1908, the *Daily Telegraph* published an interview in which German Kaiser Wilhelm II made a series of extraordinary statements about Britain. He described the English as "mad, mad, mad as March hares" because of their suspicions of Germany's territorial ambitions. While proclaiming his commitment to peace, he sounded both unstable and arrogant. He described Britain's rejection of his "repeated offers of friendship" as a personal insult. "The people of England refuse my proffered hand," he said, "and insinuate that the other hides a dagger." The Kaiser bizarrely claimed credit for Britain's victory over the Boers, alleging that this military success was based on a plan Germany had sent to the British government. He praised himself for refusing to join an international alliance that would have served to "humiliate England to the dust".

The interview appeared shortly after reports in the British press of a public meeting in Berlin at which Rudolf Martin, a retired German civil servant, called for the construction of a fleet of 10,000 airships for an airborne invasion of Britain. Nothing in Kaiser Wilhelm's comments was well judged to reassure a British public increasingly paranoid about German intentions.

- Mohandas Gandhi calls for Indian Home Rule
- Shackleton expedition gets to within 160 km (100 miles) of the South Pole
- Wages in "sweatshops" are regulated under the Trade Boards Act
- Girl Guides established in Britain
- The Victoria and Albert Museum opens in London
- The *Daily Sketch* newspaper appears, a tabloid costing a halfpenny
- Selfridges department store opens in London
- Motor-taxis outnumber horse-drawn cabs in the capital

JANUARY
- Around 400,000 people over 70 draw their first old age pension
- Opening of a telegraphic link between Britain and India
- Two Latvian anarchists are shot dead by police in London after hijacking a tram at gunpoint

FEBRUARY
- A Royal Commission calls for a reform of the poor laws, with children no longer to be sent to workhouses

MARCH
- Britain accelerates the naval race with Germany with approval of a naval bill, to build six more dreadnoughts
- Death of Irish dramatist J M Synge

BLERIOT CROSSES THE CHANNEL

▲ Aviation pioneer Louis Blériot, the first man to fly an aircraft across the English Channel. Engine failure prevented his rival, Hubert Latham, taking his place in the record books.

On July 25, 1909, Frenchman Louis Blériot made aviation history, becoming the first man to fly an aircraft the 34 km (21 miles) across the English Channel.

Taking off from Calais, France, at 5 am, Blériot made a clumsy but successful landing 37 minutes later in a field outside Dover. His achievement won him a prize of £1,000 which had been put up by the *Daily Mail* to reward the first cross-Channel flight. The newspaper also invited the aviator to a glittering celebration dinner at the Savoy hotel. On his arrival in London, Blériot was mobbed by cheering crowds. The *Daily Mail* asserted enthusiastically that the flight marked "the dawn of a new age for man".

Despite their generous response to the Frenchman's historic flight, many British observers were aware that no British aircraft had been in the running for the prize. Not only was Britain clearly behind in the development of aerial technology, but the existence of aircraft was becoming a threat to British national security, traditionally dependent on naval power. Command of the seas no longer made Britain invulnerable to attack from abroad.

SECRET SERVICE TO COUNTER GERMAN SPIES

In July 1909, a subcommittee of the Committee of Imperial Defence proposed the setting up of a Secret Service Bureau "to deal both with espionage in this country and with our own foreign agents abroad". This was to be the origin of both MI5 and MI6 (or SIS, as it is more properly known). The subcommittee also recommended increasing police powers to crack down on aliens in Britain and to improve the defence of key installations against possible sabotage.

The background to these decisions was an outbreak of "spy fever" in Britain, promoted by the popular press. Reports circulated that a hidden army of 66,000 German soldiers was living secretly in Britain – disguised as innocent civilians – and that a cache of 50,000 rifles was concealed "within a quarter of a mile of Charing Cross". On the day war broke out, this underground army would seize control of the British capital. Serial publication of a novel, *Spies of the Kaiser* by William Tufnell Le Queux, further stoked public anxieties. When a newspaper offered £10 to any reader who spotted a German spy, there was unsurprisingly a flurry of spurious sightings. Many people also reported German Zeppelins flying over Britain, although no airship had yet crossed the sea.

The wave of spy fever abated after the summer of 1909, but the counter-espionage organization that would become MI5 was up and running by 1910. Although its head, Captain Vernon Kell, had only a single-room office and a filing cabinet under his command, he set up a vigorous surveillance of Germans resident in Britain. By 1914 Kell held files on 16,000 aliens, 11,000 of them German.

▲ British Army officer Sir Vernon George Waldegrave Kell, who became the first head of MI5.

FORCE-FEEDING OF SUFFRAGETTES AROUSES FIERCE DEBATE

In October 1909 Laura Ainsworth, a suffragette, brought an action in the High Court to protest at her treatment in prison. She had been jailed for two weeks after taking part in a demonstration during a visit to Birmingham by Prime Minister Herbert Asquith. Once in Winson Green prison, she had gone on hunger strike. The prison authorities responded by force-feeding Ainsworth. She described the horror of the procedure: "I was forced into a seated position and a tube about two feet long was brought out. My mouth was opened with a steel instrument. I felt like I was going to choke and a gag was placed between my teeth to keep my mouth open."

Force-feeding was a serious embarrassment for the government, which stood accused of brutal mistreatment of women, many of whom were of "good family". On the other hand, it was not possible to let suffragettes starve themselves to death in custody. Nor could the government avoid jailing them, as their protests became ever more extreme, including blowing up buildings and physical attacks on politicians. It was not until 1913 that a partial solution to hunger strikes was found through the "Cat and Mouse Act", which allowed the authorities to release prisoners temporarily on health grounds, and then rearrest them once they were well.

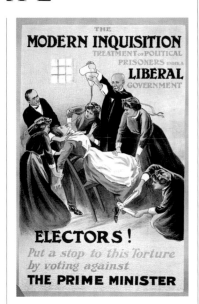

▲ A militant poster shows a suffragette being force-fed under the Liberal government.

PEOPLE'S BUDGET BRINGS CLASH WITH LORDS

▲ Winston Churchill listens attentively to the Chancellor of the Exchequer, David Lloyd George, on Budget Day.

On November 30, 1909, the House of Lords definitively rejected the budget drawn up by Chancellor of the Exchequer David Lloyd George, and thereby precipitated a major constitutional crisis. The "People's Budget" proposed large increases in income tax for the well-off, a rise in death duties, tax on unearned income from land, and a new tax on cars and petrol. The revenue was to pay for naval expansion – the building of dreadnoughts – and for measures to attack poverty, such as old age pensions and unemployment insurance.

The Liberal government had a massive majority in the House of Commons, but the Lords were overwhelmingly Conservative. They saw the budget as a direct attack on their wealth and privilege. Lloyd George railed against the power of an upper house consisting of "500 men, ordinary men, chosen accidentally from among the unemployed", but the Lords had the right to veto legislation and they used it. Refusing to back down on the budget, the government called a general election in which the main issue was who should govern the country, the elected Commons or the unelected Lords.

The Liberals won the election in January 1910, although with a much-reduced majority. They then introduced a Parliament Bill, under the terms of which the Lords would only be able to delay legislation, not veto it, and would have no power over finance bills. But this bill itself could not become law without passing through the Lords. For a year-and-a-half there was stalemate, as the upper house refused to vote for the diminution of its own powers. The Lords were finally persuaded to pass the new law in August 1911, when Asquith threatened to create enough new Liberal peers to swamp the upper house's Tory majority.

- A Post-Impressionist painting exhibition is organized by Roger Fry in London
- Singer and comedienne Gracie Fields makes her debut
- The Palladium (from 1934 the London Palladium) opens
- Books published this year include *Clayhanger* by Arnold Bennett and *Howard's End* by E M Forster
- First London performances of Frederick Delius's opera *A Village Romeo and Juliet* and Ralph Vaughan Williams's *First Symphony*
- First rugby union Five Nations championship is held

JANUARY
- The Liberals are returned to power in the general election, but now depend on the support of Labour and Irish Nationalist MPs for a majority

FEBRUARY
- The first labour exchanges are opened for the unemployed
- Edward Carson becomes leader of the Ulster Unionists
- Winston Churchill is appointed Home Secretary at the age of 35

NATION MOURNS DEATH OF EDWARD VII

▲ After a nine-year reign, Edward VII lies in state with a ceremonial guard at Westminster Hall in London.

Late on the evening of May 6, 1910, Edward VII died of bronchitis at Buckingham Palace, after reigning for only nine years.

Respected for his good sense and loved for his good humour, Edward had been a popular monarch. About 350,000 people filed past his coffin as it lay in state in Westminster Hall, and more than 3 million turned out on May 20 to line the route of the funeral procession, as his body was carried to rest in the royal vault at Windsor. The fashionable Ascot race meeting held shortly afterwards is remembered as "Black Ascot", because all the Society ladies were decked out in huge mourning hats and bows.

Edward's funeral was the last mass gathering of European royalty, with eight monarchs following the coffin, along with some 40 other lesser members of royal families. Within less than a decade, many of them were to lose their thrones and some even their lives.

The pomp surrounding Edward's death was in some ways alien to his nature. He had declared himself happiest "when I can forget I am Your Royal Highness; when I can smoke a really good cigar and read a good novel on the quiet".

ROLLS IS FIRST BRITISH AIR-CRASH VICTIM

On July 12, 1910, Charles Rolls, the co-founder of the Rolls-Royce motor company, was killed in an air crash. He was the first Englishman to die while flying a heavier-than-air powered aircraft.

Rolls was an experienced aviator, who had successfully flown nonstop across the English Channel and back just the month before his death. The fatal accident occurred during an air show at Bournemouth. Rolls was piloting a Wright biplane to which he had added an experimental rear elevator. The elevator splintered as Rolls was coming into land, causing the plane to plummet vertically into the ground from a height of 50 m (165 ft).

Rolls's death highlighted the dangers of the aviation craze that was then sweeping Europe. He was one of more than 60 pilots killed in an 18-month period in 1910–11, at a time when there

▲ The debris of air pioneer Charles Stewart Rolls's Wright biplane after the crash that claimed his life.

were probably no more than 600 airmen in the world. Yet nothing could dampen the appeal of flight, which attracted both wealthy amateurs like Rolls and ambitious young working-class men out to make their fortune.

Between 1910 and 1914 aviation began to develop towards practical uses, rather than as mere sport and spectacle. During the celebrations for George V's coronation in 1911, aircraft carried 130,000 letters and postcards between Hendon and Windsor in a trial demonstration of airmail. The British Army and the Royal Navy were also now taking a serious interest in the military potential of airships and aeroplanes.

DR CRIPPEN OUTWITTED BY MARCONI WIRELESS SYSTEM

On July 31, United States-born dentist, Dr Hawley Harvey Crippen, and his mistress, Ethel Le Neve, were arrested on board the SS *Montrose* by Inspector Walter Dew of Scotland Yard for the murder, some months previously, of his wife, the music-hall singer, Belle Elmore. It was a triumph for the Marconi wireless installed on the ship and ended a life on the run for Crippen.

Returning from a party on January 31, Dr Crippen gave his wife a dose of hyoscin hydrobromide. It was enough to kill her. Once his wife was dead, Crippen carved up her body, and buried the remains in the cellar. He told anyone who asked that his wife had gone to the United States.

Shortly afterwards he, brought to his house, as secretary, 27-year-old Ethel Le Neve, and told the increasingly suspicious friends of Belle Elmore that his wife had died while on her trip. By July, when Inspector Dew came to investigate

▲ **Dr Crippen (far right) is led from the SS *Megantis*, the ship that returned him to England, where he was tried and hanged.**

her disappearance, Dr Crippen and Ethel Le Neve were deeply in love. A few days after his first visit, Inspector Dew returned with a search warrant and found that the couple had vanished. The remains of Belle Elmore were found in the cellar and a warrant was issued for Dr Crippen's arrest.

The couple had fled to Belgium, disguised as Mr Robinson and his son: Crippen had shaved off his moustache and discarded his glasses, and Ethel Le Neve had dressed herself as a boy. At

Antwerp they boarded the SS *Montrose*, sailing to Quebec, Canada. The ship's captain, Henry Kendall, was immediately suspicious of the pair. He observed them closely over the next two days, then sent a radio message to Liverpool: "Have strong suspicions that Crippen London cellar murderer and accomplice are among saloon passengers".

Alerted, Inspector Dew boarded the faster White Star liner, *Laurentic*; off Canada, he radioed that he would board the *Montrose* from the St Lawrence, disguised as a river pilot. Once he was on board Captain Kendall invited "Mr Robinson" to his cabin to meet the "river pilot". As the two shook hands, Inspector Dew revealed himself and made the arrest.

On October 22 Dr Crippen was found guilty of poisoning his wife and sentenced to death; his mistress was acquitted. Crippen was hanged, protesting his innocence, on November 23 in Pentonville.

THE TONYPANDY RIOTS

In the autumn of 1910, miners in the South Wales coalfields went on strike in a pay dispute with the pit owners of the Cambrian Combine. On November 7 there were serious clashes between police and strikers, who were picketing the single mine in the area that had remained open. Captain Lionel Lindsay, the Chief Constable of Glamorgan, asked for troops to be sent in to reinforce the police. His request was turned down by Home Secretary Winston Churchill, who instead sent contingents of the Metropolitan Police. On November 8 further clashes erupted, centred

on the town of Tonypandy. Rampaging strikers smashed almost every shop window in the town, allegedly sparing only a store run by a former Welsh rugby international player. In all, some 80 police and 500 other people were injured in the course of the riots.

Churchill eventually did send a cavalry detachment into Tonypandy, but it arrived after the situation had calmed. He was then denounced by the left for sending troops against workers, and by the right for failing to send troops when they were needed. The whole event displayed the

▲ **Strikers sleeping on the floor of the powerhouse at Glamprgan Colliery during the 1910 Tonypandy coal strike.**

embittered state of industrial relations in Britain, which led to further, much more large-scale, violence the following year.

- The Official Secrets Act is passed, making it illegal for civil servants to reveal classified information
- Ford Motor Company begins manufacturing cars in Britain
- The Copyright Act establishes copyright in a work for 50 years after an author's death
- The last horse-drawn bus in London is retired
- First escalator is introduced, at Earl's Court underground station
- Books published this year include *The White Peacock* by D H Lawrence and *In a German Pension* by Katherine Mansfield
- Sir Edward Elgar's *Second Symphony* has its first performance
- The Camden Town group of artists, led by Walter Sickert, holds its first exhibition

FEBRUARY
- Ramsay MacDonald is appointed chairman of the Labour Party

APRIL
- The House of Commons rejects a referendum on the Parliament Bill reforming the House of Lords

MAY
- The House of Commons passes the Parliament Bill
- The government tables a National Insurance Bill to protect workers against sickness and unemployment
- Death of librettist Sir William Gilbert
- The liner *Titanic* is launched

ANARCHISTS DIE IN SIDNEY STREET SIEGE

▲ **Police issued with rifles by order of the Home Secretary, Winston Churchill, during the Sidney Street Siege.**

In January 1911 London's East End became the scene of dramatic events known as the "Siege of Sidney Street". The police had learnt that a group of anarchists of Latvian origin were living in a room on the second floor of 100 Sidney Street, in Stepney. The anarchists, believed to include a certain "Peter the Painter", were wanted for killing three unarmed policemen in Houndsditch the previous month.

Early on the morning of January 3, the house was surrounded by about 50 armed police. The two anarchists inside opened fire from upstairs windows, severely wounding a detective sergeant and forcing the rest of the police to take cover. By mid-morning the police presence had swollen to 750 officers, who were joined by a contingent of the Scots Guards, bringing a machine gun with them. Home Secretary Winston Churchill also arrived on the scene, unable to resist joining in the action.

Field artillery was being brought in when, at around 1 pm, fire broke out in the besieged building. Churchill backed the police chief's decision to stop the fire brigade from putting out the flames. Both the of anarchists, later tentatively identified as William Solokov and Fritz Svaars, were burned to death.

Churchill came under criticism for improperly taking personal charge of the operation. The Liberal government was also attacked for having failed to crack down on alien immigration, which it was claimed had permitted foreign anarchists to find a haven for their activities in Britain.

CORONATION OF GEORGE V

On June 22, 1911, at the beginning of an exceptionally hot summer, George V was crowned "King of the United Kingdom of Great Britain and Ireland and of the British Dominions beyond the seas, Defender of the Faith, Emperor of India" at Westminster Abbey in a ceremony that lasted seven hours.

Heads of state from throughout the Empire attended the moving service, while thousands of less elevated subjects stood outside the Abbey and lined the streets to watch the procession following George V and Queen Mary. The death of the expansive, worldly, sociable and charming Edward VII had also marked the end of an extravagant, optimistic and glamorous era. His shy, modest and anxious son was crowned in the middle of a constitutional crisis amid growing unrest at home and abroad.

The down-to-earth George V was to preside over more complex and difficult times than his much-loved father and he would earn respect and popularity from the manner in which he handled them.

▲ **George V photographed with his wife, Queen Mary, at Westminster Abbey on the day of his coronation.**

SUMMER OF CRISIS AT HOME AND ABROAD

In the summer of 1911 Britain experienced a diplomatic confrontation with Germany and an unprecedented wave of industrial unrest, events that between them set nerves on edge and put fingers dangerously on triggers.

The international crisis was over Morocco. It brought Europe closer to a major war than at any time in the previous 40 years. Germany had its sights upon establishing a naval base on Morocco's Atlantic coast, which would aid its longer-term goal of creating a global empire – winning "a place in the sun". Early in July a German gunboat, the *Panther*, arrived at the port of Agadir, officially to guarantee the safety of German citizens during a Berber uprising. A larger warship, the *Berlin*, soon took the place of the *Panther*, training its guns upon the Moroccan town. French opinion was outraged, regarding Morocco as clearly within France's sphere of influence. The French asked Britain for support, which was readily forthcoming.

On July 21, speaking at the annual Lord Mayor's dinner at the Mansion House, Chancellor of the Exchequer David Lloyd George delivered a clear and explicit warning to Kaiser Wilhelm. If peace could only be preserved by allowing Britain to be treated "as if she were of no account in the Cabinet of Nations", Lloyd George declared, "peace at that price would be a humiliation intolerable for a great country like ours to endure". It was a speech that virtually amounted to the announcement of a Franco-British alliance against Germany.

Through the first two weeks of August, as Britain sweltered in

▲ **Striking dockers rally in London's Trafalgar Square; some 20,000 men were refusing to work.**

one of the hottest summers on record and the menace of war hung in the air, a series of major strikes threatened to bring the entire country to a standstill. A dock workers' strike that had begun in May then spread until some 20,000 men were refusing to work. Carters, vital for supplying shops with provisions and factories with raw materials, also came out. The last straw was a national railway strike, which began on August 18. Railways were essential not only for maintaining fuel and food supplies, but also for national defence. Winston Churchill, as Home Secretary, therefore took the view that the strikes must be suppressed for the sake of national security.

On August 15 troops sent to Liverpool to confront rioting transport workers fired on a crowd which was attempting to release prisoners from a police van, killing two people. Soldiers were deployed to defend stations and trains from picketing strikers. Yet the momentary impression of a revolutionary uprising in Britain was quickly dissipated. Lloyd George used his remarkable negotiating skills to persuade the railwaymen to go back to work by August 21. Other strikes were settled by piecemeal deals on wages and conditions.

The international crisis took somewhat longer to resolve, but France and Germany reached agreement over Morocco in November. Meanwhile, a little shaken by the Home Secretary's excessively warlike response to strike action, Prime Minister Asquith shifted Churchill to the Admiralty, where his pugnacity could be more suitably deployed.

- The British Army forms the Royal Flying Corps
- Thomas Sopwith sets up the Sopwith Aviation Company
- The Post Office takes over the burgeoning telephone service
- A craze for ragtime songs sweeps Britain
- The England touring cricket team defeats the Australians 4–1 to regain the Ashes
- Britain wins 10 gold medals in the Stockholm Olympics
- The *Daily Herald* is launched as a Labour newspaper
- Charles Dawson claims to have found the skull of the humanoid Piltdown Man in Sussex, now known to have been a hoax
- The British Board of Film censors is set up
- Hit songs of the year include "It's a Long Way to Tipperary"
- Frst Royal Command Performance is held at the Palace Theatre; Harry Lauder tops the bill

JANUARY
- The Ulster Unionists decide to reject the authority of any Irish Home Rule parliament
- Scott's expedition reaches the South Pole

FEBRUARY
- The coal miners strike begins

SCOTT DIES IN POLAR TRAGEDY

On January 18, 1912, a five-man party led by Captain Robert Falcon Scott reached the South Pole – five weeks after Norwegian explorer Roald Amundsen. The Norwegian won the race and also came back safely, but Scott's party perished.

▲ The flag planted by Norwegian explorer Roald Amundsen flies over the South Pole.

Scott had relied on motor-sledges and ponies, rather than dog teams, to cross the Antarctic wastes. The sledge motors soon broke down and the ponies, unfortunately, had to be shot when the weather got too cold. The worst part of the journey – 240 km (150 miles) from the final depot to the Pole and back – had to be done on foot.

On their way back the five men encountered blizzards and worsening cold, forcing them to travel more slowly and to survive on less and less food. The entry in Scott's diary dated March 19 makes agonizing reading: "We have two days' food but barely a day's fuel. All our feet are getting bad … Amputation is the least I can hope for now … The weather doesn't give us a chance."

▲ **The final entries of Captain Scott's diary tell the desperate story of a heroic but doomed struggle for survival.**

His last diary entry is dated March 29, but it was not until February 1913 that a relief party found the five men's bodies and only in April 1913 did the expedition's ship, the *Terra Nova*, reach New Zealand with the dreadful news that they had all perished.

DISASTER STRIKES THE "UNSINKABLE" TITANIC

Twenty minutes before midnight on April 14, 1912, the *Titanic*, the largest liner in the world, pride of the White Star line, struck an iceberg in the freezing waters of the Atlantic off Newfoundland. Just two hours and 40 minutes later, the 270-m (885-ft), 47,070 ton luxury steam ship – proclaimed by its owners to be virtually unsinkable – foundered with the loss of 1,523 passengers and crew. Only 705 people survived the disaster.

It had taken 11,000 men at the Belfast shipyards of Harland and Wolff a year to build the splendid SS *Titanic*, which was the second of three luxurious ocean giants planned by White Star to operate the route between Southampton

▲ The *Titanic* heads away from the port of Belfast for a final sea-going trial before her fateful maiden voyage.

and New York in competition with the – slightly less impressive – Cunard transatlantic ships. The massive liner boasted a restaurant with French walnut panelling, sumptuous ballroom, swimming pool, gymnasium, Turkish bath, Parisian-style café and indoor gardens. It also featured a double

bottom for extra protection and a hull comprised of 16 watertight compartments, each transversed by a bulkhead. Doors in the bulkheads could be closed by a flick of a switch on the bridge of the ship. So, in theory, if the hull was damaged in one place any flooding that occurred could be contained within the compartment affected. The ship was designed to continue to float if damage to the hull affected two separate compartments, or if as many as the first four compartments were flooded.

A record number of icebergs had been sighted in the north Atlantic during 1912, and Captain Edward J Smith was well aware of the high possibility of encountering some of them. In the early afternoon of April 14, the *Titanic*'s Marconi wireless operators received an ice warning from the White Star liner *Baltic*, which they passed to Captain Smith. That night there was no moon, although the skies were clear, and the two lookouts posted in the crow's nest would have found it difficult to discern icebergs in the smooth, inky ocean, especially as they had no binoculars. Despite this, Captain Smith gave no order to reduce speed from 22 knots. Later that evening, another ice warning – of heavy pack ice and large icebergs

– was received in the wireless room from the Atlantic Transport Line steamer *Mesaba*. Tragically, this message was never passed to the bridge.

The *Titanic* was almost upon the iceberg when the lookout rang the bell to alert the officers on the bridge. The ship was moving too fast to turn away quickly enough and at 11.40 pm the *Titanic* collided with the iceberg. Five compartments at the front were damaged – more than the ship could stand. As the *Titanic* dipped into the ocean, water flowed over the top of each of the bulkheads in turn, flooding

▲ **The disaster made headline news all over the world. In all, 1,523 lives were lost as the "unsinkable" liner went down.**

one compartment after another. The ship was lost.

Uncovering, loading and launching the lifeboats was a chaotic affair – the crew were unfamiliar with the equipment and the planned lifeboat drill had been cancelled just a few days before. Only 18 of the 20 lifeboats were launched and most of them were only partially filled (mainly with wealthy first- and second-class passengers), resulting in the unnecessary loss of 500 lives.

At 2.20 am the ship plunged to the bottom of the ocean, leaving hundreds of passengers and crew floundering in the icy waters. Most of them died within minutes, although a handful were picked up by two of the lifeboats that returned to the scene.

At 4.10 am the Cunard liner *Carpathia* picked up the first of the lifeboats. It took four hours to complete the rescue operation of the 705 survivors of this terrible tragedy – a testament to human pride and complacency.

ULSTER DEFIES HOME RULE

In September 1912 more than 470,000 Ulster Protestants signed a "solemn covenant" pledging to resist Home Rule, a limited measure of self-rule for Ireland proposed by the Liberal government. The Protestants feared that Home Rule would put them under the control of Irish Catholics.

During the nineteenth century, the Liberals had made two efforts to pass a Home Rule Bill, but on each occasion the Conservative-dominated House of Lords had thrown the legislation out. Now the Parliament Act of 1911 had ended the power of the Lords to veto legislation; and the upper house could now only block bills

for two years. At a stroke, the road to Home Rule was open.

The Conservatives responded with extraordinary vehemence to the very mild Home Rule Bill introduced in the House of Commons in 1912. Their leader Andrew Bonar Law stated: "I can imagine no length of resistance to which Ulster can go in which I should not be prepared to support them." In April 80,000 members of the Ulster Volunteer Force (UVF), a militia formed by Ulster Protestants, were reviewed by senior Tories, including the lawyer Sir Edward Carson, who became the UVF's chief spokesman. The Liberal government wanted to avoid

a confrontation over Home Rule, but they were trapped by the need for support in the House of Commons from Irish Nationalist MPs.

Irish support depended upon Home Rule going ahead. As expected, the House of Lords rejected the Home Rule Bill, but their veto could only last until 1914. A trial of strength between the government and Ulster Protestants appeared inevitable.

▲ **Unionist Lord Londonderry and other Ulster Protestants sign a covenant opposing the Third Home Rule Bill.**

- Emigration from Britain tops 450,000 people a year; Canada and Australia are prime destinations
- A report by schools' medical officer says one in three pupils are so dirty as to be a threat to health
- Emily Duncan is the first woman magistrate appointed in England
- A speed limit of 10 mph is imposed on traffic at Hyde Park Corner, London
- HMS *Queen Elizabeth* is launched, the first battleship powered by oil
- An aeroplane carries 10 people into the air at Hendon
- The *New Statesman* begins publication
- Robert Bridges becomes Poet Laureate after death of Alfred Austin
- Architect Edward Lutyens designs government buildings in New Delhi
- Bloomsbury artists set up the Omega Workshop
- The foxtrot is the latest dance craze

JANUARY
- The Irish Home Rule Bill is passed by the House of Commons but rejected by the Lords
- Suffragette demonstrations in London against the withdrawal of the bill for women's franchise

APRIL
- Suffragette leader Emmeline Pankhurst is jailed for involvement in a bomb explosion at Lloyd George's villa in Surrey

MARCONI SCANDAL TARNISHES GOVERNMENT

In June 1913 Chancellor of the Exchequer David Lloyd George and a number of other government ministers were cleared of corruption over their dealings in shares of the Marconi Wireless Telegraph Company. However, the affair was widely considered to have left their reputations tarnished.

Marconi had received a lucrative government contract to provide radio stations throughout the British Empire. It was alleged that, aware of this deal, Lloyd George and Attorney General Rufus Isaacs had bought shares in Marconi, hoping to profit by a rise in their value. Postmaster General Herbert Samuel was also implicated. The involvement in the scandal of Isaacs and Samuel, both Jewish, gave to the allegations an unpleasant anti-Semitic twist.

In the event, a report by a select committee showed that the shares had been bought in Marconi's American company, not the British arm that would benefit from the government contract. The ministers had in fact failed to make any money on the share dealing. A minority report accused them of "grave impropriety", but the majority on the committee exonerated all concerned.

Revealed as someone who speculated in shares, however, Lloyd George never quite recovered his earlier reputation as a fiery radical and a man of the people. Later, as Prime Minister from 1916 to 1922, he would face further accusations of corruption connected with the sale of official honours. A taste

▲ **Although cleared of corruption, David Lloyd George's reputation was tarnished by accusations of shady dealings in Marconi shares.**

for financial peculation seems to have been a part of Lloyd George's complex nature, as was lechery – throughout his career he ruthlessly exploited his undoubted sexual magnetism.

NOVELIST IS MINER'S SON

▲ **The working class novelist D H Lawrence pushed himself to the forefront of the British literary scene.**

In 1913 David Herbert Lawrence published his autobiographical novel *Sons and Lovers*, pushing himself to the forefront of the contemporary literary scene.

Lawrence came from outside the charmed circle of the cultivated middle and upper classes who dominated cultural activity in Britain. He was born in 1885, the son of a Nottinghamshire coalminer. His mother ensured that he received a decent education and Lawrence worked as a schoolteacher until the success of his first novel, *The White Peacock* (published in 1911), emboldened him to take up writing full time.

Lawrence was patronized by the aesthetes of the Bloomsbury set and married a German aristocrat, Frieda von Richthofen, but always regarded himself as an intruder into polite society. *Sons and Lovers* had an emotional energy and a sensuous engagement with the physical world that brought a new note to English fiction.

The exploration of sexual experience in *Sons and Lovers* stayed within the bounds of acceptable taste, but Lawrence's next novel, *The Rainbow* (1915), led to a prosecution for obscenity. He also came under suspicion during the First World War because of his German wife and antiwar views. From 1919 he abandoned Britain, living in Italy, Mexico and elsewhere. His novel *Lady Chatterley's Lover*, published abroad in 1928, was banned in Britain for over 30 years. Lawrence died of tuberculosis in 1930.

THE DEATH OF
A SUFFRAGETTE

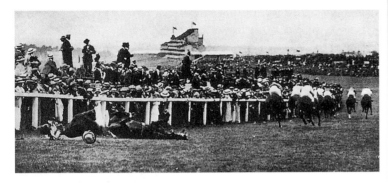

▲ Epsom racegoers look on in horror as women's suffrage campaigner Emily Davison throws herself under the king's horse.

When Emily Wilding Davison threw herself in front of the king's horse at Epsom on Derby Day (June 4) 1913, she epitomized the courage and desperation of an increasingly militant suffragette movement. Often heard to say that one should be prepared to die for the cause, this 40-year-old Oxford graduate died four days later from the terrible injuries she had received. She was buried on June 14 in the family vault at Morpeth, Northumberland, at the end of a day which had begun with an impressive funeral procession – thousands of women marched across London from Victoria to King's Cross station in a display of suffragette colours, carrying banners and distributing leaflets.

The suffragette movement had been growing in militancy ever since the Liberals won the election in 1906. Many Liberal MPs sympathized with the suffragettes who were hopeful of gaining a limited suffrage for women after the Liberal victory. However, the government was split on the issue, and nothing happened to progress the women's cause.

Angry and disappointed, leaders of the suffragette movement (embodied in the Women's Social and Political Union formed by Mrs Emmeline Pankhurst) pursued an increasingly militant policy. They organized demonstrations in places where demonstrations were forbidden in order to invite arrest. Then, given the option of paying a fine or going to prison, they chose prison in order to maximize the amount of publicity won for their cause.

They also harassed government ministers, interrupting meetings and picketing their houses. When imprisoned, they immediately went on hunger strike, gaining much publicity and some public sympathy when prison doctors began to force-feed them via tubes inserted into their mouths and nostrils.

In 1910 the government passed the Conciliation Bill, and, once again, the suffragettes became hopeful. However, the Bill was soon shuffled into

parliamentary oblivion, and in March 1912 Mrs Pankhurst stepped up the militancy of the campaign.

Groups of suffragettes smashed shop windows with hammers in the West End; they threw stones through the windows of the House of Commons, Downing Street and in Kensington; they dropped flaming rags through ministers' letter boxes and planted bombs in their houses when they were away. In short, the suffragettes waged war on the establishment and the prisons filled with suffragettes on hunger strikes.

To avoid the practice of force-feeding, which had attracted a great deal of negative publicity for the government, Home Secretary Reginald McKenna introduced the Prisoners (Temporary Discharge for Ill-Health) Act, dubbed the "Cat and Mouse Act". Instead of force-feeding prisoners, they were released, then, after a few days, arrested again – that is, if they could be found. It was under this Act that Mrs Pankhurst was arrested just as she was about to climb into her carriage behind Emily Davison's hearse.

Although the suffragettes continued their militant campaign until the outbreak of the First World War, they still had not then achieved their goal. The Representation of the People Act of 1918 gave married women over 30 the vote. It was the first step on the road to votes for all women.

▲ Attended by thousands of fellow suffragettes, the funeral of Emily Davison became a rallying point for the suffrage movement.

1914

NEWS IN BRIEF

- Britain enters the Great War; casualties by the end of December total around 100,000
- Legislation obliges local authorities to provide school meals for children
- Ernest Shackleton sets out on an Antarctic expedition
- George Bernard Shaw's play *Pygmalion* has its first performance
- Books published this year include *Dubliners* by James Joyce and *Chance* by Joseph Conrad
- Wyndham Lewis launches the Vorticist movement in art
- First performances of *On Hearing the First Cuckoo in Spring* by Frederick Delius and *A London Symphony* by Ralph Vaughan Williams

JANUARY

- Northern and Southern Nigeria join to become the British protectorate of Nigeria

MARCH

- Suffragette Mary Richardson slashes Velazquez's painting known as the "Rokeby Venus" at the National Gallery, London
- The Curragh Mutiny by British Army officers in Ireland

APRIL

- The Ulster Volunteer Force lands large quantities of arms at Larne
- George V and Queen Mary make a state visit to Paris

▲ **A meeting of Ulster Unionists who wanted to block Home Rule entirely or to split off Ulster from the rest of Ireland.**

Had war not broken out in Europe in August 1914, Britain might well have descended into civil war over Ulster. The opposition Conservative Party had made it clear that it would support an armed rebellion by Protestant Ulstermen to resist the imposition of Irish Home Rule.

The Liberal government's Home Rule Bill – originally introduced in 1912 – envisaged a severely limited devolution of powers to an Irish parliament in Dublin. English diplomat Sir Harold Nicolson commented that the devolved parliament would be no more than "a glorified county council". But it would inevitably be dominated by Ireland's Catholic majority. Protestants, however, formed a majority in four of the nine counties of Ulster. Most importantly, they were dominant in Belfast, Ireland's main industrial city. Determined not to be ruled by Catholics, they plotted to block Home Rule altogether or to separate Ulster from the rest of Ireland, threatening to use their armed militia, the Ulster Volunteer Force (UVF), to this end.

The Home Rule Bill was twice passed by the House of Commons and twice rejected by the House of Lords. In 1914 the Lords veto was set to run out. However, many senior British Army officers were strongly pro-Unionist and openly declared that the army could not be expected to force Ulster Protestants to accept rule by Irish Papists.

Through 1914 the crisis deepened. Winston Churchill, the Liberal First Lord of the Admiralty, raised the temperature in March by publicizing the movement of a battle squadron to the west coast of Scotland. At the same time, the government decided to strengthen defences at armaments depots in Ireland. Ulster Protestants feared that a military crackdown was on its way.

Doubts about the reliability of the British Army in Ireland now came to a head. Many officers were Ulstermen or had Ulster connections. The Third Cavalry Brigade, stationed at the Curragh outside Dublin, was at that time commanded by General Sir Hubert Gough, a fervent Ulsterman.

On March 21 the general and 70 of his 90 officers announced that they would rather be

▲ **Irish Springtown Volunteers preparing to oppose the Ulster Volunteer Force, the paramilitary arm of the Ulster Unionists.**

dismissed than fight the UVF. Emboldened by this "Curragh Mutiny", the UVF took temporary control of the Ulster port of Larne in April, and unloaded an estimated 30,000 rifles and three million rounds of ammunition from two steamers. The British authorities made no attempt to intervene. Meanwhile, nationalists in southern Ireland flocked to join their militia, the Irish Volunteers.

In the third week of July, an all-party conference on Home Rule was held at Buckingham Palace. For the first time, the Liberal Prime Minister, Herbert Asquith, proposed that six of the nine counties of Ulster might be excluded from Home Rule altogether. But the Conservatives found even this unacceptable.

On July 26 the Irish Volunteers smuggled in a quantity of arms through Howth. The incident was followed by a confrontation between British soldiers and local people in Dublin. Three civilians were shot dead and many more wounded. Civil war in Ireland seemed imminent.

Then came war with Germany, dwarfing all other concerns. The Home Rule Bill was passed, but its implementation was postponed until after the end of the war. The Ulster Volunteers were, at their request, integrated into the British Army. Many of the Catholic Irish Volunteers also joined up, but thousands stayed in Ireland, vowing to continue the fight for Home Rule. Asquith promised the Ulster Protestants they would never be made to accept Home Rule against their will. The stage was set for the next act of the Irish tragedy.

THE SLIDE INTO WAR

▲ Archduke Franz Ferdinand, heir to the throne of the Austro-Hungarian Empire: his murder sparked the "war to end all wars".

On June 28, 1914, Archduke Franz Ferdinand, heir to the Austro-Hungarian throne, and his wife were assassinated by a Serb nationalist in Sarajevo, Bosnia-Herzegovina. This single act of violence triggered a long-expected conflict between the two armed camps into which Europe was divided: France and Russia on one side; Germany and Austria-Hungary on the other. As Europe slid inexorably into war – Austria-Hungary declaring war on Serbia on July 28, Germany declaring war on Russia on August 1 and on France on August 3 – the question remained whether Britain would fight or not.

Britain had traditionally stood aside from European entanglements, but the growing industrial and military might of Germany had alarmed the British public and British statesmen. As a result, Britain had engaged in a naval arms race with Germany and formed an entente with France. Although this fell short of a full alliance, plans had been developed for military cooperation in case of war. These amounted to a British commitment to aid in the defence of France. Most notably, in 1912

the two countries' navies had agreed a division of duties, with the French Navy patrolling the Mediterranean and the Royal Navy controlling the North Sea and the English Channel. If Britain failed to support the French in a war against Germany, the German fleet would have a free hand to attack France's northern coastline.

The diplomatic and military policies that committed Britain to support France had been developed by Foreign Secretary Sir Edward Grey without consulting most of his government colleagues. When, as the European crisis mounted, the extent of British involvement with France became clear to the whole Liberal government, many ministers were horrified. The Liberal Party had a strong tradition of opposition to war and some government members were in effect pacifists. As late as July 28, the Cabinet was evenly split between supporters and opponents of war, with Lloyd George the most prominent of the "peace party". Four antiwar ministers resigned over the following days as Prime Minister Herbert Asquith, Foreign Secretary Grey and First Lord of

▲ A soldier bids farewell to a loved one at London's Victoria Station, as he leaves for the fighting on the Front.

▲ Two men conscripted to the British Army undergoing a medical check-up at Marylebone Grammar School in London.

the Admiralty Winston Churchill pressed for a commitment to fight.

On August 4 the Germans saved the British government from its paralysis by sending troops into neutral Belgium, a necessary move in the German army's plan for the invasion of France. Britain was a guarantor of Belgian neutrality. At last prowar ministers had a persuasive argument that Britain's honour required her to fight. Lloyd George switched sides and an ultimatum was sent to Germany, demanding the withdrawal of its forces from Belgium. At 11 pm on August 4, the ultimatum expired and Britain declared war.

Britons had for many decades been schooled in the military virtues of courage and self-sacrifice for the homeland. But although cheering, flag-waving crowds packed Trafalgar Square, the British people's response to the declaration of war was far from uniformly jingoistic. Even Sir Edward Grey, who had done so much to take Britain into the war, realized that it marked the end of an era. Standing at a window in Whitehall as dusk fell, he reportedly said: "The lamps are going out all over Europe. We shall not see them lit again in our lifetime."

MAY
- Emmeline Pankhurst and other suffragettes are arrested after clashes with police outside Buckingham Palace

JUNE
- Building workers, railway workers and miners take part in a wave of strikes in Britain
- Archduke Franz Ferdinand is assassinated in Sarajevo

JULY
- A conference at Buckingham Palace, chaired by the king, fails to resolve differences over Irish Home Rule
- British troops kill three rioters in Dublin as Irish Volunteers attempt to smuggle arms into the country

AUGUST
- Britain declares war on Germany and, a week later, on Austria-Hungary
- Lord Kitchener is appointed Secretary of State for War
- Defence of the Realm Act gives the government emergency powers
- Most suffragettes, led by Emmeline and Christabel Pankhurst, agree to abandon militancy and support the war effort
- The British Expeditionary Force (BEF) dispatched to Belgium, fights Battle of Mons
- Reports of an angel appearing to British troops at Mons are widely believed
- The French and British capture Douala in German-controlled Cameroon, West Africa

THE WESTERN FRONT

The British soldiers who embarked for the front in August 1914, amid scenes of patriotic enthusiasm, were almost instantly thrown into a series of battles more bloody than any previously experienced in European warfare.

Unlike France and Germany, which could call on mass armies of conscripts numbering in the millions, Britain had only a small professional army, backed up by part-time Territorials. In line with prewar planning, a British Expeditionary Force (BEF), consisting of one cavalry division and four infantry divisions, embarked for France on August 9 – two more infantry divisions were sent later in the month. The force took up position at the northern end of the French line, on France's border with Belgium. This was expected to be a quiet sector, with the fiercest fighting taking place much further south, where France and Germany had a common border. Instead, the British troops found themselves directly in the path of the main German advance.

Marching across Belgium, on August 23, the grey-clad hordes of the German Army ran into the British at the Mons Canal. Although the BEF was desperately short of machine guns, the rapid and accurate rifle fire of the superbly trained British regulars took a heavy toll of the German attackers. Heavily outnumbered, however, the BEF was soon in headlong retreat, as were the French on their right. It seemed that nothing could stop the German steamroller crushing all in its path.

By the end of August, the pace of the advance, on foot over hundreds of kilometres, had exhausted the German infantry. In early September the French, commanded by General Joseph Joffre, counter-attacked at the Battle of the Marne. The BEF, whose demoralized commander Sir John French had been contemplating evacuating his forces to Britain, joined in the counter-offensive, and the Germans were forced to retreat.

Hopes of turning this victory into a rout soon faded, as the Germans established a defensive line along the Aisne River. British infantry who attempted to break through by advancing into the fire of enemy machine guns with bayonets fixed learnt a lesson that was to be repeated endlessly over the following years – the superiority of defence over attack when troops were dug in to trenches.

At this stage of the war, there was still room for armies to manoeuvre. In a series of actions known as the "Race to the Sea", German and Allied forces tried to outflank one another in open country between the Aisne and the Channel coast. These manoeuvres ended in Flanders, near the Belgian town of Ypres. There, between mid-October and mid-November, a series of brutal engagements was fought, in which the British Army heroically resisted a German breakthrough at great cost.

With winter approaching, the armies dug in. Two parallel lines of trenches stretched without a break from the Channel to Switzerland. With no more flanking movements possible, the only way forward for either side was a frontal assault in the face of overwhelming firepower. For the next three years, the armies on the Western Front would barely move.

The human cost of the first five months of the war was astounding. About 90 per cent of the original BEF were casualties by the end of the year, with 10 per cent of them killed. Britain was now committed to fighting a long war of attrition on the Western Front.

▲ **Men removing harnesses from horses wounded at the battle of Aisne at Soissions, France.**

KITCHENER CALLS FOR VOLUNTEERS

▲ **Lord Kitchener features in an army recruitment poster which threatens conscription if there are not enough volunteers for the forces.**

On August 3, 1914, the government appointed Lord Kitchener as Secretary for War. Kitchener was the much-celebrated victor of wars in Sudan and South Africa, a symbol of empire and patriotic fervour.

Enigmatic and monosyllabic, Kitchener could easily come across as foolish, yet he had a shrewd instinct in military matters was shrewd. While almost everyone else expected the fighting to be bloody, but swift – "all over by Christmas" – the new Secretary for War warned the Cabinet to plan for a conflict that would last at least three years and requiring an army numbering millions.

Kitchener proposed to create a "New Army" of 70 divisions. The government rejected conscription as contrary to the principles of British freedom, so the New Army was raised by voluntary recruitment. Soon Kitchener's finger was pointing out of the world's most famous recruitment poster, calling on British men to serve their country. The response was staggering. Around 175,000 men volunteered in the first week of September, and a total of 750,000 had come forward by the end of the month. Enlistment continued to run at around 125,000 a month up to the middle of 1915.

Voluntary recruitment had its drawbacks. Many of those who enlisted were men in vital jobs, whose skills were needed by industry. The decision to allow men to join up in "Pals' Battalions", serving alongside friends and colleagues from civilian life, meant that if a particular unit suffered heavy casualties it was a tragedy for a whole village or town. But the scale of volunteering left no possible doubt about the patriotic enthusiasm of the British people.

CHRISTMAS TRUCE SHOCKS GENERALS

On Christmas Day, 1914, soldiers at many points along the trench lines on the Western Front instituted an informal and spontaneous truce. After singing Christmas carols in their trenches and exchanging shouted greetings, men emerged into no-man's-land between the lines to shake hands and exchange gifts of tobacco and chocolate. In some places football matches were staged; in others, soldiers took the opportunity to retrieve corpses for burial.

The scale of fraternization appalled senior officers on both sides. British commanders gave strict orders that no such scenes should be allowed to occur again. Officers were ordered in future to shoot any soldier making contact with the enemy.

In reality, fears that the truce would turn into a general revolt against the war proved groundless. Once Christmas was past, the soldiers returned to the business of killing the enemy and trying to preserve their own lives. Serious problems with morale would take another two years to develop.

▲ **British and German troops observe a Christmas and New Year truce in the trenches of the Western Front.**

- Employment of women increases by 2 million in the year
- Pub opening hours are restricted and buying rounds is made illegal
- Canadian-born magnate Lord Beaverbrook buys the *Daily Express*
- The Shackleton Antarctic expedition faces disaster as its ship *Endurance* is trapped in ice
- First Women's Institute (WI) is founded
- The Last FA Cup match is played for the duration of the war
- The song of the year is "Pack Up Your Troubles in Your Old Kit Bag"
- Books published this year include *The Rainbow* by D H Lawrence, *The Thirty-Nine Steps* by John Buchan, and *1914 and Other Poems* by Rupert Brooke

JANUARY
- Women begin to be employed as munitions workers

FEBRUARY
- Engineers on Clydeside strike for higher wages
- German U-boats start an unrestricted campaign against merchant shipping around Britain

MARCH
- A British offensive at Neuve Chapelle fails
- Allied warships fail to break through the Dardanelles in Turkey

DEATH FROM THE SKY

Britain suffered the first air raid in its history on the night of January 19–20, 1915. Although the damage caused was relatively small, the attack was the prelude to a three-year air offensive that eventually killed more than 1,000 British civilians.

The air strike was delivered by Zeppelin airships of the German Navy. Three Zeppelins took off from Hamburg, intending to attack targets around the Humber. One got into difficulties, however, and had to turn back, while the other two, bearing the designations *L3* and *L4*, drifted off course.

At 8.20 pm, *L3* reached the English coast at Great Yarmouth, and dropped its load of six high-explosive bombs and seven incendiaries. *L4*, hopelessly lost, ranged over the Norfolk countryside terrorizing various small villages before flying over King's Lynn, which it bombed. The raid of January 19–20 killed four people and injured 16 others. Many thousands more were terrified by this completely new experience of total war.

▲ Houses in the East Anglian town of King's Lynn were destroyed by an unexpected new threat from the skies: the Zeppelin.

SINKING OF THE LUSITANIA

On May 7 a Cunard ocean liner, the *Lusitania*, bound for Liverpool from New York, was sunk by a German U-boat 13 km (8 miles) off the south coast of Ireland. A total of 1,198 people drowned, 128 of them US citizens.

The *Lusitania* was one of the elite transatlantic liners that in prewar years vied for the Blue Riband, awarded to the vessel making the fastest Atlantic crossing. Its passengers included many figures from the highest circles of society, including US millionaire Alfred Vanderbilt.

The barbarism of the sinking of a passenger ship without any warning brought widespread condemnation. It was not generally known at the time that, as well as passengers, the *Lusitania* was carrying munitions, making it arguably a valid military target.

A week before the liner sailed from New York, the German embassy had included it in a published list of vessels on which US citizens should avoid travelling.

When the news of the sinking broke in Britain, rioters took to the streets, attacking German-owned shops – or shops with German-sounding names – in Liverpool, Manchester, London's East End and other cities.

Once the mob was loosed, other "aliens" soon came under attack, including Jews and Chinese. In Liverpool troops had to be sent in to restore order. A government promise to intern enemy aliens eventually managed to calm the "*Lusitania* riots". Although there was no comparable violent popular response in the United

▲ Paintings such as this enabled newspapers to portray the sinking of the *Lusitania* as "a crime that staggered humanity".

States, the sinking of the *Lusitania* played a huge part in turning US public opinion against Germany, preparing the way for the United States's eventual entry into the war.

▲ **The hidden terror of the seas, the German U-boat campaign created havoc amid Allied shipping.**

GALLIPOLI

In January 1915 the British government tried to get the war moving with a bold attack against Germany's ally, Turkey. Chiefly at the instigation of the First Lord of the Admiralty, Winston Churchill, the British planned to send a naval force through the Dardanelles, the narrow waterway that leads from the Mediterranean to the Turkish capital, Istanbul.

With the grudging support of France, a fleet of mostly outdated warships was assembled. But a full-scale attempt to break through the Dardanelles on March 18 failed after three battleships were sunk by mines.

The British decided that the navy could only get through after a landing force had captured the shores of the waterway.

The troops available in the eastern Mediterranean included volunteers of the Australia and New Zealand Army Corps (ANZAC), who had reached Egypt on their way to the Western Front. The site chosen for the landings was the Gallipoli peninsula. At dawn on April 25, British, French and ANZAC troops arrived off the Turkish shore aboard some 200 merchant vessels. Lacking specialist landing craft, most of the men went ashore in lines of rowing boats. Their officers had no idea of the terrain they were to face, nor of Turkish troop dispositions.

▲ **Troops from the Australian and New Zealand Army Corps come ashore during the unsuccessful Gallipoli campaign.**

The Australians and New Zealanders missed their designated landing beach, instead coming ashore at a small cove backed by steep ridges. The troops were soon stuck a mile inland, precariously hanging on to positions dominated by Turkish fire. The British and French landings had no more success.

By early May the stalemate of the Western Front had been reproduced at Gallipoli, with Allied troops holding on to their small enclaves, blocked by Turkish trenches. The British attempted another landing at Suvla Bay in August, but it, too, was bogged down and faltered.

Although the Allied troops fought with great courage and endurance, by Christmas their commanders had decided to cut their losses. Over the following weeks the survivors slipped away to sea – by far the most successful operation in the whole fiasco.

The Allies suffered 265,000 casualties at Gallipoli. For Australia and New Zealand, it was an experience never to be forgotten – one that encouraged a nascent national pride, and bred an enduring suspicion of the British authorities.

APRIL
- In the Second Battle of Ypres, the Germans use poison gas
- Allied landings at Gallipoli
- The *Daily Mail* denounces the government for shortage of artillery shells
- Death of poet Rupert Brooke, en route to Gallipoli

MAY
- Asquith brings leading Unionists and one Labour Party member into the government
- Churchill quits the Admiralty, blamed for the Gallipoli fiasco
- The liner *Lusitania* is sunk by a U-boat
- Around 225 people are killed in a collision involving a troop train at Quintinshill, Scotland.
- The Germans carry out the first Zeppelin raid on London

JUNE
- A Ministry of Munitions is created, headed by David Lloyd George
- Statistics show prices have risen more than 30 per cent since the start of the war

JULY
- Suffragettes demonstrate for the "right to serve" in the war effort
- Welsh miners strike in defiance of a new law banning strikes in war-related industries

SEPTEMBER
- Anglo-Indian troops take Kut-al-Amara in Mesopotamia
- Death of Labour leader Keir Hardie

OCTOBER
- Nurse Edith Cavell is executed by the Germans

DECEMBER
- Sir Douglas Haig is appointed commander of the BEF
- Allied troops begin withdrawal from Gallipoli

- The British Army suffers unprecedentedly heavy casualties on the Western Front
- The Military Service Act introduces conscription in Britain
- Conscientious objectors are allowed to argue their case for exemption from army service in front of military tribunals
- A National Savings movement is launched to help pay for the war
- Steeply rising food prices lead to protests by trades unions
- Official campaigns attack waste and extravagance, such as motoring for pleasure and the employment of large numbers of servants
- The lifetime of parliament is extended to avoid holding an election in wartime
- A government Department of Scientific and Industrial Research is established
- Plastic surgery develops in response to war wounds
- Doctors warn of an epidemic of sexually transmitted diseases, with one in ten of Britain's urban population infected
- The British Museum and Natural History Museum are closed for the duration of the war
- School of African and Oriental Studies founded in London
- British Summer Time first introduced as a "daylight saving" measure to save fuel
- Publication of James Joyce's *A Portrait of the Artist as a Young Man*
- Hit song of the year is "If You Were the Only Girl in the World"

BATTLE OF JUTLAND

▲ HMS *Queen Mary* perishes during the Battle of Jutland in which more than 7,500 British and German sailors lost their lives.

Dreadnought battleships were the most advanced fighting machines of the early twentieth century. To the British public, an encounter between the German High Seas Fleet and the British Grand Fleet was anticipated as the climactic moment of the Great War. But when that battle came, at Jutland on May 31, 1916, it proved disappointingly indecisive.

Commanded by the aggressive Admiral Reinhard Scheer, the German fleet had begun to make sorties into the North Sea, hoping to inflict damage before the Royal Navy's main force of dreadnoughts could arrive, steaming south from Scapa Flow. Due to the cracking of German naval codes, however, the British had immediate warning when the High Seas Fleet set out to sea at the end of May. The British commander, Admiral Sir John Jellicoe, steamed to meet them.

In all, more than 250 warships headed for a showdown in grey, squally weather. With 28 Dreadnoughts and nine battlecruisers to the Germans' 16 dreadnoughts and five battlecruisers, the Royal Navy had every expectation of victory.

When the British battlecruisers made contact with the enemy, they soon turned north, drawing the Germans after them towards the British dreadnoughts. The ploy worked, and for five minutes the world's top battleships slugged it out. Then the Germans turned away and escaped the British pursuit in failing light.

Both sides claimed a victory. The Germans had lost only 11 ships and 2,551 men, compared with the Royal Navy's 15 ships and 6,094 men. On the other hand, the German High Seas Fleet was once more forced back into port, and had little effect on the further course of the war.

"A TERRIBLE BEAUTY IS BORN"

Although as many as 100,000 southern Irish enlisted to fight for Britain in the Great War, some Irish Nationalists were still determined to act on the saying: "England's extremity is Ireland's opportunity." The Irish Republican Brotherhood, led by Padraic Pearse and James Connolly's Citizen Army, planned an armed uprising for Easter 1916. The nationalists established contact with Germany, which agreed to supply arms.

On Good Friday a merchant vessel, the *Aud*, flying the Norwegian flag, arrived off the Irish coast carrying 20,000 German rifles. Owing to a misunderstanding, however, no rebels turned up to take the weapons ashore, and the ship was scuttled.

Despite the incident, on Easter Monday, April 24, the uprising went ahead. About 1,800 rebels, armed with a mix of rifles, shotguns, pickaxes and sledgehammers, took over key buildings in Dublin. One of them, the General Post Office, became the headquarters of the rebellion. Pearse read out a proclamation establishing a "Provisional Government of the Irish Republic" and declaring that "Ireland, through

▲ British infantrymen snipe from behind a barricade of empty beer casks during the 1916 Easter Rising in Dublin.

us, summons her children to her flag and strikes for her freedom."

The rebels had, in fact, very little popular support in Ireland. The British response was severe and heavy-handed. Artillery was used extensively to dislodge the rebels, causing large-scale damage to property and considerable civilian casualties. In all, about 500 people died and more than 2,000 were wounded during a week of intense fighting. Finally, with the General Post Office gutted by fire, the insurgents surrendered.

The British commander, General Sir John Maxwell, used his powers under martial law to send over 2,000 people to prison camps in Britain. At secret court martials 90 rebels were sentenced to death; 15 were actually executed, including Pearse and Connolly. Among those spared – because he held a United States passport was future Irish President Eamon de Valera.

The executions, carried out over a ten-day period, completely altered public sentiment in Ireland. The unpopular rebels were transformed into national heroes by their blood sacrifice – a metamorphosis captured by the Irish poet W B Yeats's *Easter 1916*, in which the leaders of the uprising are said to have been "changed, changed utterly: /A terrible beauty is born".

▲ Dublin's General Post Office, destroyed by a bombardment of British shells that put an end to the rebellion.

LORD KITCHENER LOST AT SEA

The Secretary for War, Lord Kitchener, was drowned when the ship on which he was sailing, HMS *Hampshire*, struck a mine in the North Sea within two hours of leaving Scapa Flow on June 5, 1916. Kitchener had been on his way to visit the Tzar to ascertain the true state of affairs in Russia. Lloyd George, who was to have accompanied him, was called to Ireland at the last moment: the Irish negotiations saved his life.

A veteran of the Boer War, Lord Kitchener was idolized by the public who had rallied to his first recruiting appeal for 100,000 volunteers to join the army – a plea immortalized by the poster in

▲ The eternal image of Britain's great war veteran Lord Kitchener appealing for volunteers to enlist in the army.

which the words: "Your country needs you" were accompanied by a picture of him pointing his finger at the reader.

At the outbreak of the war, Kitchener had fiercely opposed the common view that the conflict would be over by Christmas, believing that it would be long and difficult. Unfortunately, his effectiveness as Secretary for War was diminished by politicians who gave him little room for manoeuvre. Winston Churchill wrote of his death: "The sudden onrush of the night, the deep waters of the North, were destined to preserve him and his renown from the shallows."

CASEMENT HANGED AS TRAITOR

On August 3, 1916, Roger Casement, a former British diplomat and knight, was hanged for treason at Pentonville prison, London, for his involvement in the Easter Uprising in Ireland.

Born outside Dublin in 1864 and raised in Ulster, Casement worked as a young man in the Belgian Congo, where he witnessed at first hand atrocities committed against the native population by the colonialists. He subsequently joined the British diplomatic service, and in 1904 he prepared an official report on conditions in the Congo. His outspoken condemnation of Belgian rule there caused an international sensation and earned him a reputation as a liberal humanitarian. He was knighted in 1911.

Casement's deepest commitment, however, was to Irish nationalism. Before the start of the First World War he joined the predominantly Catholic Irish Volunteers, and once war broke out he took on a personal mission to win German support for Irish independence. Casement travelled clandestinely to Germany, negotiating for the supply of arms to the Irish rebels and attempting unsuccessfully to recruit a nationalist army from Irish soldiers held in German prisoner-of-war camps.

In 1916 he arranged a shipment of German rifles to Ireland, but the arms ship was intercepted by the British. Casement himself was carried to Ireland on board a German submarine, but was arrested soon after reaching shore. Stripped of his knighthood, he was tried in June and sentenced to hang.

Several prominent figures, including George Bernard Shaw, campaigned for the sentence to be commuted. To ensure that sympathy did not swing in Casement's favour, the British secret service circulated a copy of his "Black Diary" to the king and other leading establishment figures. The diary – which may have been a forgery, but was most probably genuine – recorded a life of promiscuous homosexuality. Offending contemporary prejudices, it ended any chance of a reprieve for Casement.

▲ Irish patriot Sir Roger Casement is escorted to the gallows of Pentonville prison after being found guilty of treason.

BATTLE OF THE SOMME

On July 1, 1916, the British army – with French support – launched a major offensive on the Western Front at the Somme. The operation led to slaughter unprecedented in British military history, for only the most limited of gains.

The original plan for a Somme offensive, drawn up in late 1915, had envisaged equal roles for the French and British. But in February 1916 the Germans launched a huge assault against the French Army at Verdun. As France battled to prevent a German breakthrough, the Somme offensive was modified to become a primarily British operation, designed to take the pressure off their allies. The initial attack would be made by 11 British divisions, commanded by General Sir Henry Rawlinson, and supported by five French divisions south of the Somme.

▲ British troops stand ready to charge over the top on the first day of the Battle of the Somme on July 1, 1916.

The offensive was to be the first major test of Britain's New Army, the mass of volunteers raised, trained and equipped since the outbreak of war. Sir Douglas Haig, the British Commander-in-Chief, relied heavily on his enormously expanded artillery arm, which included just over 2,000 artillery pieces. In an eight-day preliminary bombardment, 1,732,873 shells were fired, sufficient, the British High Command thought, to destroy the German defences. But the British did not have enough heavy-calibre guns: nearly a third of the shells fired were defective; and the German dug-outs proved more shell-proof than expected. Although mines were also dug under the German lines and packed with explosives, none of these preparations weakened the German power of resistance sufficiently.

On the morning of July 1, the British infantry went "over the top" in perfect order, walking across no-man's-land in accordance with Haig's order to "push forward at a steady pace in successive lines …" Well-directed German artillery and machine-gun fire cut them down in waves. In the first day's fighting, there were 57,000 casualties out of an attacking force of 100,000 British; nearly 20,000 of them killed.

The British attack was virtually stopped in its tracks, although over on the right flank the tactically more sophisticated French did manage to make some gains.

Although a terrible setback for the British, July 1 was only the first day of the great summer offensive, which was to continue until November. Lessons were learnt and more flexible approaches adopted.

▲ **Field Marshal Haig's handling of the battle of the Somme was criticized by the future British Prime Minister, Lloyd George.**

A successful dawn attack on July 14 demonstrated what the "New Armies" were capable of doing and represented a marked improvement in British staff work. But every attack soon became bogged down in desperate trench warfare, especially as the Germans operated a policy of vigorous counter-attacks; the commander of the German Second Army, General von Below, instructed his men "to hold our present positions at any cost. The

enemy should have to carve his way over heaps of corpses."

On September 15 tanks were thrown into the battle, but after some small local gains the hopes invested in them were also dashed. The last phase of the battle ended with the capture of Beaumont Hamel on November 13, when cold and rain had turned the battlefield into a sea of freezing mud, making effective operations impossible.

The first great British offensive of the war ended in disappointment, although the British Army had proved itself a valiant and capable fighting force. The 142-day offensive of the Somme produced 415,000 British casualties; the French lost over 200,000. German casualties ranged from between 400,000 and 600,000 men. For great loss of life and scant territorial gains, Verdun and the Somme personified the horror of trench warfare on the Western Front.

LLOYD GEORGE BECOMES PRIME MINISTER

On December 7, 1916, David Lloyd George became Prime Minister of Britain. His appointment followed a series of articles hostile to the Prime Minister, Asquith, that appeared in the press, including *The Times*, owned by Lord Northcliffe, and the *Daily Express* and *Daily Chronicle*, both greatly influenced by Lord Beaverbrook.

The papers increasingly favoured Lloyd George, Secretary of State for War, who, for a month, had battled with Asquith over the formation of a streamlined War Committee. Lloyd George proposed to run the committee, from which the Prime Minister would be excluded.

On the evening of December 5, Asquith went to Buckingham Palace to tender his resignation.

The king recorded in his diary that he accepted his resignation with "great regret". He then summoned Colonial Secretary Bonar Law, asking him to form a government.

The next day a conference was held at Buckingham Palace between the king, Asquith, Balfour, Lloyd George, Henderson and Bonar Law. The latter stated that he would lead a government only if Asquith agreed to join the government under him. It was agreed that Asquith should consider this proposal and that should he decline, the commission would be passed to Lloyd George.

After several hours' thought Asquith declined a subordinate position, and so Bonar Law refused the King's commission,

which was immediately passed to Lloyd George. Within 24 hours Lloyd George informed the king that he was able to form an administration, and he was duly appointed Prime Minister and First Lord of the Treasury.

▲ **David Lloyd George became Prime Minister after Herbert Asquith refused to serve under Bonar Law.**

1917

- The British royal family changes its name from Saxe-Coburg-Gotha to Windsor; the related Battenbergs adopt the name Mountbatten
- Chequers becomes a country residence for Prime Ministers
- The "bob" is a fashionable haircut for women
- Leonard and Virginia Woolf found the Hogarth Press
- P G Wodehouse publishes *The Man With Two Left Feet*, the first Jeeves stories

JANUARY
- British naval intelligence intercepts the "Zimmerman telegram" in which Germany calls on Mexico to attack the United States

FEBRUARY
- Germany warns that its U-boats will sink American ships trading with the Allies

MARCH
- Revolution overthrows the Tsarist regime in Russia and establishes a provisional government.
- British troops occupy Baghdad in Mesopotamia

APRIL
- The United States enters the war against Germany
- Canadian forces capture Vimy Ridge on the Western Front
- The government proposes Home Rule for Ireland, but excluding six counties of Ulster
- German U-boats sink nearly a million tons of Allied shipping

THE HELL OF PASSCHENDAELE

▲ **British casualties litter the churned-up battlefield outside the town of Passchendaele during the Third Battle of Ypres.**

On July 31, 1917, British Field Marshall Haig launched another major offensive on the Western Front, this time in Flanders. Officially called the Third Battle of Ypres, in popular memory it will always be known by the emotive name of Passchendaele.

Haig, who regarded himself as "a tool in the hands of Divine Power", was convinced that German morale was near breaking-point and that a fresh offensive could win the war. Prime Minister David Lloyd George did not share Haig's optimism, but reluctantly gave the go-ahead to the operation because he saw a chance that it might lead to the capture of U-boat bases on the Flanders coast.

As at the Somme, Haig put his faith in a massive preliminary bombardment, raining some four million shells down on the German trenches over 15 days. But once again, this failed to soften up the enemy to any sufficient degree. After some limited initial gains, British and Commonwealth troops became bogged down in low-lying country churned to an impassable sea of mud by a combination of torrential rain and heavy artillery.

The hellish nature of the conditions the troops experienced, as a wet summer turned into a wetter autumn, surpassed anything seen in the rest of the war. Heavily laden men who slipped off the duck-boards laid across the sodden ground sank without trace in deep mud. Wounded men drowned as water filled the shell holes in which they sheltered. Tanks could not be used and coherent manoeuvre was nearly impossible.

With impressive stubbornness, and irrationally convinced that the enemy was "faltering" and that a "decisive result" was almost within reach, Haig kept the offensive going into early November. By the time Canadian troops seized Passchendaele village on November 6, the offensive had cost over 300,000 casualties for an advance of a few kilometres.

BRITAIN PROPOSES JEWISH STATE

On November 2, 1917, Britain's Foreign Secretary Arthur Balfour declared: "His Majesty's government views with favour the establishment in Palestine of a national home for the Jewish people, and will use their best endeavours to facilitate the achievement of this object, it being clearly understood that nothing shall be done which may prejudice the civil and religious rights of existing non-Jewish communities in Palestine." In doing so he hoped to secure Zionist support for the Allies.

The Balfour Declaration shocked the Arab world. Only the previous year, with the help of Hussein Ibn Ali, ruler of the Hejaz and guardian of Mecca, the Allies had defeated the Turks, securing Palestine for Britain.

In return, Britain had pledged to help realize the independence of most of the Arab world. In addition, Muslims in Palestine outnumbered Jews by ten to one, and Arabs could conceive of no grant of rights that did not include self-determination for this majority.

▲ **Arthur Balfour (right), architect of a "Jewish homeland". His proposal caused consternation throughout the Arab world.**

WOMEN'S ROLE IN THE FIRST WORLD WAR

▲ **With eligible young men on active war service in France, women took on increasingly significant roles at home.**

During 1914 and 1915, as more and more men answered Lord Kitchener's recruitment appeals, labour came to be in short supply, especially in the engineering trades. By June 1915, one-fifth of the men working in engineering had enlisted, at a time when the army desperately needed supplies. Wages rose dramatically – a shipyard riveter, for example, saw his wage double between 1914 and 1919 – and conditions at work improved, not least in the introduction to the factories of canteens that provided workers with nutritious meals at low prices. Still, demand for workers in almost every field, especially munitions, was greater than supply.

Many women were eager to enter the workforce, suffragette Mrs Dacre Fox voicing the opinion of many when she said: "We believe women can be employed in almost any capacity of intellectual or physical work." In July 1915 30,000 women marched down Whitehall behind suffragette Christabel Pankhurst, carrying banners bearing the words: "We demand the right to serve." Their demand was granted, as was their demand for "equal pay". And with the beginning of conscription on March 2, 1916, the government itself instigated a drive to recruit women to fill the places of those who had been conscripted.

Women flooded the market, taking on traditional male work roles, such as carrying sacks of coal, working on the land or making shells in the armaments factories, as well as joining other women in more traditional women's fields, such as nursing and teaching. Between 1915 and 1918 more than a million women embarked on some form of paid work for the first time in their lives. Nearly 800,000 women were recruited to the engineering and munitions industries; 100,000 became bus and tram drivers and conductors, railway porters, guards and inspectors. Government departments gained almost 200,000 women, and women employed in clerical work rose in numbers from 33,000 to 102,000. The female shorthand typist had taken the place of the male clerk with his quill pen for ever. More than 150,000 women joined the auxiliary branches of the armed forces.

This newfound independence increased women's confidence and changed their habits. It became usual to see women dine without a male chaperone, buy their own drinks in pubs and smoke cigarettes. Women took to dressing with a growing fashion confidence and a greater deference to practicality: they favoured shorter skirts that finished above the ankle, some wore trousers, even out of work, and hat styles were less flamboyant. Hair styles changed, too, with women preferring short, neat cuts.

After the war, women's worthy contribution to the nation was recognized; the passing of the Fourth Reform Act in July 1918 gave those over the age of 30 the vote.

Although many women had to give back their jobs to the returning men, many continued to work, and wider employment opportunities remained open to women. In 1919 the Sex Disqualification (Removal) Act provided that no person should be disqualified from any job because of sex or marriage. The status of women in society had changed for good.

▲ **"Land Girls" engage in tough agricultural work. Female labour was vital to the economy during the war years.**

- Passage of the Representation of the People Act gives women over 30 the right to vote
- An Education Act proposes increasing the school leaving age to 14
- Food rationing is introduced
- Books published this year include *Eminent Victorians* by Lytton Strachey and *Married Love* by Marie Stopes
- First performance of Gustav Holst's *The Planets* suite

JANUARY
- Restaurants are ordered not to serve meat on two days of the week

FEBRUARY
- Jericho falls to Australian forces

MARCH
- A massive German offensive on the Western Front drives the Allies into retreat towards Paris

APRIL
- The Army's Royal Flying Corps and the Royal Naval Air Service combine to form the Royal Air Force
- Allied forces in France are put under unified command, with the French General Foch as Commander-in-Chief
- British naval raid on the German submarine base at Zeebrugge, Belgium

THE "FINAL PUSH": THE GREAT ALLIED OFFENSIVE

After the failure of the Germans to break through in the spring of 1918, the Allies went over to the offensive. The British Army spearheaded the attack, which began on August 8, a date Ludendorff would call "the black day of the German Army". General Rawlison's Fourth Army, comprising British, Australian and Canadian troops, opened the Battle of Amiens. The initial success was gained by a devastating bombardment by British artillery (using the advanced techniques of "predicted shooting") and supported by the advance of more than 400 tanks, whose presence had been masked by dense fog.

By August 11 the British had taken 30,000 prisoners and a great hole had been punched into the German line. The importance of the victory at Amiens lay in the effect it had on German morale. For the first time since the war began, whole German divisions had fallen back without a fight, while thousands of men were captured with little or no resistance. The decline in morale

▲ The Great War draws to its inevitable close as thousands of German soldiers are left with no choice but to surrender.

was also felt at the top, so that at a conference with his generals held at Avesnes on August 11, the Kaiser was forced to concede: "I see that we must strike a balance. We have nearly reached the limit of our power of resistance. The war must be ended."

The British Fourth Army now began to approach the shattered landscapes of the Somme battlefields of 1916 – a formidable obstacle – and Field Marshal Haig was determined that the advance should not become

bogged down in this area. Consequently, the axis of attack was progressively extended northwards. General Byng's Third Army was brought into the attack on August 21 (Battle of Albert), and General Horne's First Army on August 26 (Battle of the Scarpe). To the south, the French attacked at Noyen, and on September 12 the Americans fought and won their first great battle at St Miheil.

The climax of the Allied offensive came in late September: the British began their assault on the Hindenburg Line; the French and Americans pushed forward in the Argonne; and a combined Belgian-British-French force attacked in Flanders.

On September 29 the British broke through the formidable Hindenburg Line, a magnificent feat of arms which brought them 35,000 prisoners and 380 guns. This marked the beginning of the end, for on this day the German High Command concluded that they must make an immediate approach to President Woodrow Wilson to ask for an armistice.

THE WAR ENDS

▲ Celebrations take place all over Europe and the United States as Armistice Day signals the official end of the war.

By October 1918 Germany and Austria-Hungary were losing on the battlefield, and at home the political authority of their governments was collapsing. Reluctantly admitting that they could not continue the war, the German High Command sought an armistice. They hoped that US President Woodrow Wilson would guarantee them favourable treatment, but Germany's enemies inevitably insisted on terms that would render the Germans incapable of resuming the war once the fighting had stopped. Britain demanded the surrender of the German fleet into its hands, while France insisted on military occupation of the Rhineland.

Having no alternative, German representatives signed an armistice at 5 am on November 11, 1918, in a railway carriage in the forest of Compiègne. The armistice came into effect six hours later – at the eleventh hour of the eleventh day of the eleventh month. The First World War was over.

In cities across Britain and the Empire, there were scenes of unbridled jubilation. In London all work stopped when the news was announced. Crowds of servicemen on leave and cheering civilians thronged the streets, provoking various degrees of disorder. Less eye-catchingly, thousands of people packed into churches to welcome peace with prayers and remembrance of the dead. In towns and villages across the

▲ **Jubilant Britons celebrate victory outside Buckingham Palace in London. They were later greeted by George V.**

country, church bells were rung and in many places there were improvised street parties. But even as the celebrations greeted peace, there were still people who were receiving the official telegrams telling of the loss of a son or brother at the Front. The family of the poet Wilfred Owen were among them.

Three-quarters of a million British people had lost their lives in the war, almost all of them young men serving at the Front. About 200,000 men from the British Empire had also been killed, more than a fifth of them were from the Indian subcontinent.

There was a determination that the soldiers' sacrifice should not be forgotten. At 11.00 am on the first anniversary of the armistice, a two-minute silence was observed. throughout Britain and its Empire, a custom meticulously followed for many years. The Cenotaph was erected in Whitehall as a focus for an annual remembrance ceremony. The wearing of artificial red poppies began in 1921. As memorials sprang up in Britain's towns and villages, the cost of war was insistently brought home. Britons would never again welcome a war with flag-waving enthusiasm.

KILLER 'FLU STRIKES BRITAIN

In 1918–19 the world was swept by an influenza epidemic that is now believed to have killed at least 40 million people – far more than died in the First World War. Although Britain was not as severely hit by the disease as some countries, around 228,000 British people died in the pandemic.

The origins of the influenza outbreak are obscure, but the deadly mutant strain of the virus may have struck first in an American Army camp in January 1918. Its ravages were publicized when it reached Spain the following May – hence its popular name, "Spanish 'Flu". Cases of the disease were identified in Glasgow that same month, and by the late summer it was raging among British troops at the Front and civilians at home.

The Spanish 'Flu was abnormal because it struck down people aged 20 to 40 more than children or the elderly. Many of those who contracted the disease died within a day, although the virus was not

virulent enough to kill the majority of those who contracted it. All efforts to limit the spread of the disease – by spraying public transport with chemicals or wearing face masks – failed totally and there was no effective treatment. The epidemic exhausted itself by natural means in the course of 1919.

▲ **Precautions against the devastating influenza epidemic which hit the postwar world included anti-flu spray for London buses.**

1918 EFFECTS OF THE GREAT WAR

The war of 1914–18 was a crucial experience for most British people who lived through it. Those who did not actually serve in the armed forces were none the less emotionally involved through grieving for lost friends or relatives. The impulse to memorialize the war dead found expression in the annual Remembrance Day, the creation of shrines such as the Tomb of the Unknown Warrior and the Cenotaph, and the work of the War Graves' Commission, which created and tended the monumental cemeteries for the war dead in France and Belgium. The rituals of respect were universally observed in the years after the war – men doffed their hats or caps on walking past the Cenotaph and, for the two minutes' silence on November 11, traffic halted and pedestrians stood stock still in the streets.

The human cost of the war included, as well as three-quarters of a million dead, more than two million wounded. About 65,000 former soldiers diagnosed as suffering from "shell shock" received pensions on psychiatric grounds. But the loss and suffering were not, on the whole, seen as a futile sacrifice. The bitter left-wing view that this had been a capitalist war in which workers were sent to die in the interests of their bosses convinced only a minority – after all, proportionally the heaviest casualties were suffered by junior officers, all drawn from the middle or upper classes. Although in the immediate aftermath of war the stresses of demobilization and fluctuations in the economy provoked scattered riots and a

▲ Despite Lloyd George's promise of a "land fit for heroes", the return of many men from the war to long-term unemployment and poverty created a sharp sense of injustice.

virtual workers' uprising on Clydeside, there was never a serious risk of the British social fabric tearing apart during or after the war.

In fact, the Great War tended overall to increase social solidarity. In the course of the conflict, Britain's rulers acknowledged that victory could only be obtained with the wholehearted support of all classes of society, and of both sexes. There was a broad feeling that since all had contributed to the war, all should benefit. This impulse found its most obvious expression in the extension of the franchise at the end of the war, which gave the vote not only to women over 30, but also to large categories of men previously

excluded. The Great War made Britain a democracy.

Although inevitably much of the generous sentiment felt by the ruling classes during the war evaporated once peace came, the average British working-class family benefited materially from changes wrought by the war and in its aftermath. Unemployment insurance was extended to the overwhelming majority of the working population and governments recognized a responsibility to provide decent affordable housing, even if Lloyd George's promise of "Homes Fit for Heroes" was notoriously not fulfilled in the immediate post-war period. The wages of low-paid workers rose sharply relative to

inflation and progressive taxation reduced social inequality – tax on higher incomes increased from 8 per cent before the war to around 30 per cent in the 1920s.

In some ways, the effects of war were less dramatic than might have been expected of such a titanic conflict. It is a myth, for example, that the losses of young men in the war left a generation of spinsters and widows. In fact, a higher percentage of women over 15 were married in the 1920s and 1930s than had been before the war. Nor did the war transform the relationship between women and work. A slightly higher proportion of women were in paid employment in the 1920s than before the war, but the difference was not spectacular. The war did not even have much impact on the size of the British population. Before the war emigration had been running at over 250,000 a year, greater than the annual losses in the trenches during the war years. Since emigration virtually stopped during the war and never returned to pre-war levels, the conflict may actually have led to an overall population gain.

Some relatively trivial innovations of wartime became fixtures of everyday life for decades after, and a few have endured to the present day. For example, the patriotic practice of playing the national anthem in cinemas and theatres at the end of a performance, adopted during the war, was not abandoned until the 1960s. Curtailed pub licensing hours, imposed in 1915 to increase workers' productivity, remained in force until the 1980s. Summer Time, originally known as daylight saving, was brought in during the war and is still with us, as is the compulsory use of passports when travelling abroad.

Changes in personal behaviour and attitudes are less easy to pin down, but it seems clear that the war turned the smoking of cigarettes into an almost universal male habit. Wartime probably also introduced many men for the first time to the use of contraceptives, and it may even have been responsible for the "f-word" becoming a standard form of strong swearing. At a deeper level, the shocking experience of the Great War probably contributed to the sharp decline in formal religious belief in Britain in the course of the twentieth century.

The clearest consequence of the war was the decline of the British economy. The cost of the struggle forced Britain to liquidate overseas assets and contract heavy debts to the United States. The dominant position that Britain had held in world capitalism was lost. Even worse was the impact upon trade and industry. Britain's competitors on the world market had taken advantage of the war years to strengthen their position at Britain's expense. The textile industry, shipbuilding and coal would never regain many of their export markets. Workers in these industries, once at the hub of world manufacturing, found they were struggling for jobs in failing factories, pits and yards. It was the return of men from the war to long-term unemployment that created the sharpest sense of injustice.

Even when the onset of an even larger conflict saw the Great War renamed as "World War One", it was never forgotten, occupying an indelible place in the folk memory of the British people.

▲ **Thiepval Memorial to the missing of the Somme is the largest memorial to Britain's war dead.**

▲ **Londoners and traffic come to a standstill at Piccadilly Circus as the first anniversary of the armistice is marked on November 11, 1919. The rituals of respect were universally observed in the years after the war.**

- Britain's national debt stands at almost £6 billion
- Ernest Rutherford, working at Manchester University, splits the atom
- British scientific expeditions observing the solar eclipse confirm Einstein's Theory of Relativity
- First air service between London and Paris
- The Church of Wales is disestablished
- Books published this year include *The Economic Consequences of the Peace* by J M Keynes and *The Moon and Sixpence* by Somerset Maugham
- First performance of Sir Edward Elgar's *Cello Concerto*
- The American all-white Original Dixieland Jazz Band brings jazz to Britain

JANUARY
- The peace conference opens at Versailles
- Sinn Fein MPs form a parliament (the Dáil Eireann) in Dublin and proclaim an Irish Republic
- Striking workers across Britain demand a 40-hour week

FEBRUARY
- A national industrial conference attempts to resolve differences between unions and employers

BITTER PEACE AT VERSAILLES

▲ **The leaders of Britain and France, Lloyd George and Clemenceau, and US President Wilson in Paris in 1919.**

In January 1919 the victorious Allies staged a peace conference in the glittering setting of the Palace of Versailles, outside Paris. Although delegations arrived from as far afield as China, Japan and Siam, all the key decisions at the conference were taken by three men: Prime Minister Georges Clemenceau of France, US President Woodrow Wilson, and British Prime Minister David Lloyd George.

Lloyd George had just won a general election in which his determination to punish Germany had been a vote-grabbing theme. The popular press insisted that the former Kaiser Wilhelm II – now a refugee in the Netherlands – should be tried as a war criminal and that the Germans should be made to pay for the war, which had left Britain heavily in debt to the United States. Lloyd George was privately sceptical about both these policies. But although calls to "hang the Kaiser" were abandoned after the Netherlands refused to hand him over, the pressure to make Germany pay reparations to Britain soon became irresistible.

The conference turned into an almost clichéd confrontation between Old World cynicism and New World idealism. Wilson sought to build a new Europe based on democracy and national self-determination. Clemenceau wanted to ensure that Germany, temporarily down, remained that way. Lloyd George deviously charted as moderate a course as he could, while satisfying hardliners in his government and in the press.

The Germans and other defeated powers were not invited to negotiate. Peace terms were decided between the victors and then imposed on the losers. Whether the terms Germany eventually had to accept were excessively onerous has been a matter of dispute ever since. The main ones included the return of Alsace-Lorraine to France, the loss of other territory to newly independent Poland, severe restrictions on the size and nature of German armed forces, and the loss of Germany's overseas empire – much of it snapped up by Britain. The decision to demand economic reparations was to cause most problems. It was justified by blaming the Germans for starting the war – the "war guilt" clause included in the peace treaty. German opinion was

▲ **Street parties were held across Britain to mark peace in July 1919. By the end of the year, however, the celebratory mood was disappearing.**

▲ **Georges Clemenceau affixes his signature to the peacy treaty at the historic scene in the Hall of Mirrors at Versailles.**

outraged by this clause more than any other element in the treaty.

The German government would have refused to sign the terms but for the dire predicament in which it found itself. Britain was still maintaining its wartime naval blockade, which had reduced much of the German population to near starvation. On June 21, 1919, in protest at the peace terms, German sailors scuttled the German fleet, which had been interned at Scapa Flow since the end of the war. But a week later, the German delegation signed the peace treaty in the Hall of Mirrors at the Palace of Versailles.

After the conference, Lloyd George was criticized by the right for treating Germany too leniently and by the left for being punitively harsh. The Labour Party opposed the treaty and it was also attacked by intellectuals such as economist John Maynard Keynes, whose book *The Economic Consequences of the Peace* savaged reparations as wrong and unworkable. Already by the end of 1919, Britain was rapidly losing any feeling of self-satisfaction it might have felt at winning the war.

ALCOCK AND BROWN FLY ATLANTIC

At 1.58 pm on June 14, 1919, two former RAF pilots, Captain John Alcock and Arthur Whitten-Brown, took off from St John's in Newfoundland, Canada in a bid to fly nonstop across the Atlantic. The newspaper baron Lord Northcliffe had put up a £10,000 prize for the first person to achieve the feat.

The aircraft the pilots used was a First World War Vickers Vimy bomber with two Rolls-Royce engines. Apart from a radio, the aircraft's equipment was primitive. The cockpit was open, giving the pilots no protection against the elements and exposing them to the noise of the engines, which made conversation impossible.

▲ Captain John Alcock and Arthur Whitten-Brown (centre), the first men to fly the Atlantic Ocean non-stop.

After 16 hours in the air, Alcock and Brown were cold, hungry, exhausted and rapidly losing hope. Then, through the grey mist, they saw the darker hue of land. The aircraft flew in over the Galway coast and landed in a marshy bog, which tipped the plane over on its nose. They had flown 2,735 km (1,700 miles) in 16 hours and 28 minutes.

Both men were consequently knighted for their exploit, but Alcock had little chance to enjoy his triumph; he died in an air crash in France later that year.

MALE MONOPOLY OF PARLIAMENT ENDS

The 1918 Representation of the People Act at last gave British women the vote, although not on an equal basis with men – only women over 30 were judged rational enough to go to the polls. The general election that followed in December 1918 showed that female suffrage would not necessarily give women a share of political power.

One woman was elected to the House of Commons – Countess Markiewicz (Constance Gore-Booth), who represented a Dublin constituency. But she was a member of Sinn Fein, whose MPs did not take their seats in Westminster, instead proclaiming themselves the parliament of an Irish Republic.

It was not until 1919 that the House of Commons saw its first female MP. The honour fell to an American-born Conservative, Nancy Astor. She was the daughter of a Virginia tobacco auctioneer, and the wife of William Waldorf Astor, MP for Plymouth. After his father's death in 1919, Astor became Viscount Astor and was elevated to the House of Lords.

Lady Astor inherited his position as Plymouth Tory candidate and duly won a by-election, taking her seat in the Commons.

Despite coming to parliament through her husband's influence, Lady Astor was to prove a vigorous and effective MP, with an active interest in women's rights and social problems.

▲ American-born Lady Nancy Astor, the first woman to take her seat in the British parliament.

APRIL
- British troops open fire on protestors at Amritsar, in the Punjab region of India, killing at least 400 people
- The Irish Dáil elects Eamon de Valera as its President
- British and French troops fight Russian Bolshevik forces at Archangel

MAY
- British aircraft bomb tribesmen in Afghanistan

JUNE
- Alcock and Brown fly across the Atlantic
- The German fleet is scuttled at Scapa Flow in the Orkneys
- Peace is signed with Germany in Versailles
- A government commission recommends nationalization of the coal industry

JULY
- The British airship R-34 flies from Scotland to New York and back

AUGUST
- A police strike leads to an outbreak of lawlessness in Liverpool

SEPTEMBER
- The Irish parliament, the Dáil, is banned by the British authorities

OCTOBER
- The British War Cabinet is dissolved
- Lloyd George rejects nationalization of the coal industry

NOVEMBER
- Nancy Astor, the first woman MP to take up her seat in parliament, is elected

DECEMBER
- Lord French, Lord Lieutenant of Ireland, narrowly escapes assassination by the Irish Republican Army in Dublin

1920–1939

Britain emerged from the First World War fundamentally weakened. The country was heavily in debt to the United States and some of its major industries were no longer able to cope with foreign competition. In the 1920s and 1930s, mass unemployment blighted the lives of millions in the old industrial and mining areas. Yet the story of Britain in these two decades is far from one of unrelieved gloom and decline. Despite economic problems, the British people were on the whole better off than ever before, with surplus time and cash to devote to leisure activities. Cinemas and dance-halls flourished, and sports events attracted huge crowds.

Technological progress and social development continued at a rapid pace. The wireless introduced the first broadcast news and entertainment to British households, while mass-produced motor cars brought a new mobility – at least to the better-off. The petrol station became a familiar feature of the British scene, along with the electricity pylon and the telephone box. Housing improved as government-backed schemes for slum clearance rehoused thousands of the poor on new council estates, while semi-detached owner-occupied suburban houses spread remorselessly from the outskirts of cities into the countryside.

British political life was characterized simultaneously by a desire for peace and security, and by aspirations to fundamental social change. The first aspect was embodied in Conservative Prime Minister Stanley Baldwin, whose appeal to the British electorate lay in his unruffled complacency – a colourless demeanour seeming to guarantee the country against shocks or sudden changes. Yet this was also the era of the General Strike, of hunger marches by the unemployed and of battles between fascists and communists on city streets. British society and the British political system proved capable, as so often, of absorbing and taming the impulse to revolt. The Labour Party, in theory committed to socialism, took over from the Liberals as the leading party of the left. But instead of challenging the capitalist system, Labour twice formed governments of impeccable respectability.

As Britain's economic power and moral authority waned, its imperial rule was inevitably contested. Full independence for the Dominions – Australia, Canada, New Zealand and South Africa – was amicably agreed, smoothly transforming Britain's Empire into a Commonwealth of equals. Elsewhere, things were not so trouble-free. Southern Ireland was the first region to mount a successful revolt against British rule, even if the Irish rebels had to accept that six counties in Ulster would remain within the United Kingdom under Protestant rule. British forces were active sporadically in the Middle East, especially in the hotly disputed territory of Palestine. But it was India that became the focus of the most dispute and bitter controversy. Under the leadership of Mohandas Gandhi, Indian nationalists kept a sustained pressure upon the British imperial authorities, who had accepted the need to give India a measure of self-government, but baulked at granting effective independence.

Colonial disputes were overshadowed, however, by the rapid descent of Europe in the course of the 1930s towards another major war. A renewal of armed conflict between the great powers was exactly what the peacemakers had sought to prevent with their arrangements at the end of the First World War, especially by the creation of the League of Nations. But the rise to power of Adolf Hitler's extreme nationalist Nazi Party in Germany set a challenge in the face of which the League's principle of "collective security" shattered. Leading a country whose people overwhelmingly desired to preserve peace, successive British governments were slow to rearm and reluctant to confront German aggression with threats of a military response. The policy of appeasement of Hitler eventually succeeded only in weakening Britain's position by the time war at last became unavoidable.

Britain went into the Second World War with its social fabric still largely intact and with its Commonwealth still ready to provide the mother country with military support. This was a fortunate situation for a nation about to undergo its time of greatest peril.

1920

- Unemployment rises to over one million in the post war slump
- Unemployment insurance is extended to cover most working people
- The Communist Party of Great Britain is founded
- The government sets a target to build 100,000 new houses – "homes fit for heroes"
- Women students are given equal status with men at Oxford University
- Surrey batsman Percy Fender scores a century in 35 minutes, the fastest 100 ever made
- British runner Albert Hill wins two gold medals at the Antwerp Olympics
- Marie Rambert founds the Rambert dance school in London
- Bernard Leach establishes his pottery at St Ives, Cornwall
- The Imperial War Museum opens in London
- Books published include *Bliss* by Katherine Mansfield and *Collected Poems* by Wilfred Owen (posthumously)

JANUARY
- British war veterans, known as "Black and Tans", enlist to fight the IRA

FEBRUARY
- The League of Nations meets for its second session in London

LONDON HOSTS LEAGUE OF NATIONS MEETING

On February 11, 1920, the second meeting of the Council of the League of Nations took place at St James's Palace, London. Proposed at the Paris peace conference by US President Woodrow Wilson, the League was a project of high idealism, intended to end the era of war between sovereign states and begin a new age of cooperation and the rule of law in international affairs.

The League of Nations Council was made up of delegates from eight nations: Britain, Italy, France, Japan, Belgium, Spain, Brazil and Greece. The United States was absent as the US Congress had refused to ratify the agreements negotiated by Wilson, finding the degree of commitment to foreign entanglements implied in the League's Covenant too much to stomach.

Britain was an active and enthusiastic participant in the

▲ **Delegates from eight nations meet for the inauguration of the League of Nations. The purpose of its existence was to prevent a recurrence of the horrors of the First World War.**

League from the start. It took seriously Article 8 of the Covenant, which called for the reduction of national armaments "to the lowest point consistent with national safety". It also placed considerable faith in "collective security" – the commitment of all member states of the League to defend any member that fell victim to aggression. In practice, though, general disarmament never happened and the principle of collective security proved utterly ineffective when challenged by German, Italian and Japanese aggression in the 1930s.

OXFORD GRANTS EQUAL STATUS TO FEMALE STUDENTS

The University of Oxford, Britain's oldest body of higher learning, began to align itself with the prevailing wind of change in the early twentieth century when on October 7, 1920, the first 100 female students were admitted as full members of the university. It has a history that can be traced back to the twelfth century, when it came into being as a result of English students being barred from the University of Paris in 1167. Since then, it has schooled many of the world's most noted scientists and political leaders.

◀ **Female students at Oxford University gather in preparation for a visit from the Queen. Women had not been allowed full membership of the university before 1920.**

Like its counterpart at Cambridge, Oxford has always operated on the collegiate system under which the university as a whole comprises a series of semi-autonomous colleges. The first women's college, Lady Margaret Hall, was established in 1878, but it was not until 1920 that it was considered appropriate to accept women on an equal par with male students. This had previously meant that although women might have received tuition from one of the most reputable universities in the world, they would not be rewarded with a degree for their efforts.

While this may not have had a particularly great impact on women as a whole – a university education at this time was still realistically only available to the privileged few – it was yet another indication that the British establishment was finally beginning to recognize and acknowledge the demands for a new role for women in the twentieth century.

"BLOODY SUNDAY" IN IRELAND

▲ **Eamon de Valera inspects members of the Western division of the IRA at Six Mile Bridge, County Clare, during the Sinn Fein rebellion.**

On Sunday, November 21, 1920, the Irish Republican Army (IRA) murdered 11 British Army officers in Dublin and British paramilitaries fired on a crowd of Irish civilians. It was the climax of a year of worsening atrocities as Ireland descended into a vicious spiral of terror and counter-terror.

Irish nationalists had declared Ireland a republic in 1919, and Eamon de Valera soon became President of its parliament. Britain refused to recognize Irish independence and sent troops to enforce its rule. The IRA, armed with the help of sympathizers in the United States, began a campaign of assassination against the Royal Irish Constabulary, British soldiers and the British civilian authorities.

Britain pushed ahead with plans for Home Rule, which would establish separate parliaments in Dublin and Belfast with limited self-government. But this was firmly rejected by Irish nationalists, who demanded full independence for a united Ireland.

Unable to cope with the deteriorating security situation, the British government recruited ex-servicemen to form a paramilitary police force, known as the Black and Tans after the colour of their uniforms. In the summer of 1920, these were further augmented by the recruitment of another body of paramilitaries, the Auxiliaries. Both the Black and Tans and the "Auxies" soon earned a reputation for extreme brutality, terrorizing the Catholic population.

In the autumn of 1920, the Irish republican leadership identified a number of British officers working as undercover agents in Dublin. Michael Collins, the effective leader of the IRA terror campaign, decided to wipe them out in a single spectacular coup. At exactly 9 am on November 21, at a series of locations across the city, the British officers were dragged from their beds by armed IRA men and shot in cold blood, some of them in front of their families.

Retaliation was immediate. Three men in British custody – two of them IRA leaders and the other an innocent acquaintance of theirs – were tortured and killed "while attempting to escape". Members of the Auxiliaries planned a more random revenge. That afternoon some 10,000 people gathered at Croke Park to watch a Gaelic football match between Dublin and Tipperary. Auxiliaries armed with rifles and a machine gun entered the stadium and fired into the crowd. Fourteen people died and 70 were injured in the gunfire and the terrified stampede that followed. The dead included women and children.

Bloody Sunday has been described as the day that broke British rule in Ireland. The British government had no stomach either for the losses the fighting entailed or for the terror they themselves had unleashed. The following month they sought negotiations with their Irish enemies.

- A census estimates the population of Britain at 42,769,000
- Females outnumber males by 1,750,000, partly as a result of war deaths
- Government control of food, rail and coal industries, assumed during the war, ends
- More than 2 million workers are unemployed as the slump worsens
- 85 million working days are lost to strikes and lock-outs in the year
- Poplar borough councillors, led by George Lansbury, are jailed for refusing to set a rate they think unfair to the poor
- The first female barrister practises as professions are opened to women
- The British Legion is founded to care for ex-servicemen
- Books published this year include *Women in Love* by D H Lawrence, *Crome Yellow* by Aldous Huxley and *The Mysterious Affair at Styles* by Agatha Christie
- Filmgoers flock to see Charlie Chaplin in *The Kid*

JANUARY
- First Indian parliament meets

MARCH
- British and other Allied troops occupy the Ruhr as Germany refuses to pay reparations
- Bonar Law resigns the leadership of the Conservative Party on grounds of ill-health
- Marie Stopes opens a birth-control clinic
- Coal mines return to private ownership

STRIKE FAILS AS BRITAIN SLUMPS

▲ **By December 1921 almost one in five of the British workforce was unemployed, causing union leaders to halt plans for a general strike.**

On March 31, 1921, Britain's coal mines, which had been taken over by the government during the war, were returned to private ownership. The following day, all pits closed as miners refused to accept pay cuts of between 10 and 40 per cent imposed by the owners. The miners union called for the support of two other national trade unions, those of the railway workers and the transport workers. This union "Triple Alliance" threatened a general strike that would bring the country to a halt. Many observers, both on the right and left of politics, saw this as the possible prelude to a socialist revolution.

Trade union militancy had been on the rise since the end of the war. Union action had mostly been channelled into pressure for shorter working hours and higher wages during a short-lived postwar economic boom. But this militancy also had a political edge. The fact that the railways and the mines had come under government control in the war gave weight to calls for outright nationalization of these major industries – a policy embraced by the Labour Party. In 1919 a Royal Commission had declared in favour of the nationalization of coal mines, horrified by accounts it received of the poor conditions under which miners were forced to work. But the government was determined to restore all sectors of the economy to private hands.

As the railways and mines were returned to the private sector in 1921, Britain was entering a severe economic depression. The slump, caused by the long-term decline of key British industries and aggravated by a combination of short-term factors, saw the number of unemployed rise to 1.4 million by March and over 2 million by December, almost one in five of the total workforce. This was an economic background that made union leaders hesitate. It was one thing to strike when money and jobs were plentiful, quite another to risk income and security when hard times threatened.

The general strike was set to begin on Friday, April 15. At the last minute, the leaders of the rail and transport workers – J H Thomas and Ernest Bevin – pulled out. Condemned as a betrayal by the miners, the day became known to left-wing socialists as "Black Friday". The miners held out alone until July, when they were forced to return to work on terms even worse than originally offered.

INDIA SEEKS SELF-RULE

On November 17, 1921, the Prince of Wales landed in Bombay at the start of a state visit to India. However, instead of demonstrating the loyalty of India's population to the British Raj, the visit revealed the depth of Indian nationalist sentiment. Widespread protests were orchestrated by a British-educated lawyer, Mohandas Gandhi.

The modern movement for Indian independence began with the formation of the Indian National Congress in 1885. For the first three decades of its existence, the Congress's campaigns had been largely

▶ **A symbol of peaceful resistance, Mohandas Gandhi took the struggle for independence to India's peasant villagers.**

ineffectual. In 1917, however, in a spirit of gratitude for the service of Indian troops in the First World War, the British government committed itself to "the gradual development of self-governing institutions" in India. This move seriously boosted nationalist aspirations. The British also inflamed Indian opposition by an exceptionally brutal act of oppression in April 1919, when the authorities fired on protestors at Amritsar, in the Punjab, killing at least 379 people.

In 1920 Gandhi emerged as the figurehead of Indian nationalism, leading a campaign of noncooperation with the authorities. He ordered a boycott of imported British textiles and declared all British-run institutions invalid, including courts and schools. In January 1921, in fulfilment of the policy of advancing self-government, the British established a Central Legislative Assembly, a Chamber of Princes and a Council of State in Delhi.

Gandhi, however, continued his implacable resistance.

Gandhi rejected violence in any form, but he was still, in the eyes of the British authorities, a dangerous subversive, since his noncooperation campaign created chaos. In March 1922 he was tried and given a six-year jail sentence for sedition. Gandhi was not to be so easily disposed of: within a decade he would be negotiating with British statesmen as the acknowledged leader of the Indian people.

MAY
- Sinn Fein wins a landslide victory in elections in southern Ireland
- Germany agrees to begin paying reparations
- Anti-British nationalist riots in Egypt

JULY
- Miners forced to return to work
- A truce ends fighting between republicans and the British in Ireland

AUGUST
- The British install King Feisal as ruler of Iraq
- A Muslim revolt in India is suppressed

NOVEMBER
- Riots in Bombay during a visit to India by the Prince of Wales
- Widespread rioting in Belfast as Catholics resist Protestant Northern Ireland government
- Britain and Afghanistan sign a treaty of friendship

DECEMBER
- The Anglo-Irish Treaty founds the Irish Free State
- Britain, the United States, Japan, France and Italy sign the Washington Treaty limiting the size of their navies

IRELAND DIVIDED

▲ **The Dublin Customs House goes up in flames during the violent protests that preceded the first Anglo-Irish Treaty.**

On December 6, 1921, British and Irish nationalist negotiators signed a treaty to end the independence war that had ravaged Ireland since 1919. The British and the Irish republicans had agreed a truce in July so that formal negotiations could begin. Both sides wanted an agreement, since the IRA was exhausted by its struggle with the British Army and paramilitaries, while the British government was not prepared to face the huge military effort that would be required to subdue the Irish rebels.

Led by Michael Collins, the Irish negotiators reluctantly accepted that six counties of Ulster, to be known as Northern Ireland, would remain under British rule. Britain had already established an autonomous parliament and

government there, dominated by the six counties' Protestant majority. The only concession the British were prepared make was that a border commission would be set up to ensure that areas of Northern Ireland with a Catholic majority might later be transferred to southern Ireland (in fact no transfers of territory were ever made).

Collins and his colleagues also wanted complete independence as an Irish Republic, something the British would not concede. A compromise was struck that gave southern Ireland full independence in practice, but retained some symbols of British rule. One of these was that members of the Irish parliament would have to swear an oath of allegiance to the king.

The Anglo-Irish Treaty was ratified by the Irish parliament (the Dáil). British troops were withdrawn from southern Ireland and the Irish Free State duly came into existence in December 1922. By then, however, Ireland was in the grip of a civil war between those nationalists who accepted the treaty and hardliners, led by Eamon de Valera, who rejected both the division of the island and the oath to the king.

Southern Ireland eventually became a republic, with little fuss, in 1949. But the division into Protestant-dominated north and Catholic south would generate political conflict and periods of armed strife until the end of the twentieth century.

▲ **The Anglo-Irish Treaty split the republican community, although it received the backing of these Sinn Fein supporters.**

- The Labour Party replaces the Liberals as the party of the left
- The RAF bombs villages in Iraq to suppress a revolt
- The British Broadcasting Company (BBC) makes its first radio broadcast
- The Austin Seven is introduced, Britain's first mass-market motor car
- Books published this year include *The Waste Land* by T S Eliot, and *Ulysses* by James Joyce
- First performance of Ralph Vaughan Williams's *Pastoral Symphony*

JANUARY
- Death of polar explorer Sir Ernest Shackleton off South Georgia on his fourth expedition to Antarctica

FEBRUARY
- Britain officially grants Egypt independence under King Fuad, but retains a military presence in the country
- A committee chaired by Sir Eric Geddes proposes swingeing pay cuts for teachers and other civil servants and for the armed forces

MARCH
- Irish nationalists riot in Belfast
- Britain and Egypt take joint control of Sudan
- Gandhi is jailed by the British

MARIE STOPES ADVOCATES BIRTH CONTROL

▲ **Marie Stopes's controversial stance on the need for birth control led to a nationwide debate on the subject.**

Birth-control campaigner Marie Stopes was one of the most controversial figures of 1920s Britain. A notable palaeobotanist in her early years, Stopes's life was transformed by the experience of a failed first marriage between 1911 and 1914. Remarried in 1918 to wealthy aircraft manufacturer Humphrey Verdon Roe, she published *Married Love*, a somewhat gushing but, for its day, daringly explicit sex guide. Her aim was to dispel the abysmal ignorance about sex that she believed blighted many, if not most, marriages – and to counter the assumption that "nice women" did not have sexual impulses and needs.

Married Love was a bestseller, as was its sequel, *Wise Parenthood*, which provided information on contraception. In March 1921, funded by her husband, Stopes opened Britain's first clinic to offer free birth-control advice for working-class women, in Holloway, London.

In 1922 Halliday Sutherland, a Catholic doctor of medicine at Edinburgh University, called for Stopes's imprisonment, expressing astonishment that her "monstrous campaign on birth control should be tolerated by the Home Secretary". Stopes reacted to Sutherland's description of her books as "obscene" by suing him for libel. The court case that resulted from Stopes's suit against Dr Sutherland led to nationwide debate on the topic of birth control.

Stopes lost her case in the first court, won it on appeal, then lost on further appeal to the House of Lords. But the tide of opinion was with Stopes, not against her. Throughout the 1920s, birth rates in Britain fell, largely because of the refusal of women to serve as breeding machines. Whereas in the first decade of the century one in four British women had had five children or more, by 1930 only one in ten had such large families.

There was a darker side to Marie Stopes's thinking. Like many progressive intellectuals of her day, she believed in eugenics – the improvement of human genetic stock through selective breeding. She declared herself in favour of the sterilization of half-castes, the insane and other undesirables. Indeed, one of the main impulses behind her birth-control campaign was the desire to reduce the size of working-class families, considered to be of less good stock than their social betters. "Family planning" was in fact already standard practice among middle- and upper-class couples.

IRISH LEADER ASSASSINATED

On August 22, 1922, the Irish nationalist leader Michael Collins, one of the architects of the new Irish Free State, was killed in an ambush. His death was a direct result of a split in the ranks of republicanism that followed the signing of the Anglo-Irish Treaty in 1921.

Collins, along with former President Arthur Griffith, had been sent to London by Eamon de Valera to negotiate a peaceful settlement to the Irish crisis. The resulting treaty brought about the split between north and south. Although Collins considered the treaty the best that could be achieved at that time, de Valera and many other hardline republicans saw it as an unacceptable compromise.

The disagreements ultimately resulted in a state of civil war, sparked off by the seizure by republican rebels of the Four Courts building in Dublin on June 29, 1922. Collins, in spite of his relative youth – he was 31 years old – was a notable military strategist and took control of the Irish National Army. Following the death of Arthur Griffith earlier in August, Collins also became head of the government. It was while on his way to a troop inspection that his assassins – presumed to be a republican group – shot him dead.

▲ **Draped with the flag of the Irish Republic, the coffin of assassinated nationalist leader Michael Collins is paraded through the streets of Dublin.**

TUTANKHAMUN'S TREASURES REVEALED

▲ Carefully wrapped and carried in a cardboard box, a life-size effigy of Tutankhamun's queen is carried from the pharaoh's tomb.

On November 4, 1922, British Egyptologist Howard Carter made one of the most amazing finds of the age when, after years of persistent research, he discovered the burial place of Pharaoh Tutankhamun in the Valley of the Kings near Luxor. Carter's financial sponsor, the Earl of Carnarvon, was alongside him as he entered the tomb a few weeks later.

Untouched for more than 3,000 years, Tutankhamun's tomb contained an unimaginable wealth of priceless treasures, including exquisitely hand-carved chariots inlaid with precious jewels, gold statues of the pharaoh and a magnificent gold face mask. Over 1,700 items were eventually taken from the tomb and put on display at the Egyptian Museum in Cairo.

The discovery unleashed an unprecedented level of interest in Egyptology, a fascination reflected in the Egyptian decorative details found in many public buildings – especially cinemas – erected in Britain during the 1920s and 1930s. A number of supposedly mysterious deaths of those associated with the excavation, especially that of the Earl of Carnarvon the following year, led to speculation about an "ancient curse" that further fuelled popular interest in the spectacular discovery. Carter, however, lived until 1939, devoting the rest of his life to unearthing, cataloguing and transporting Tutankhamun's treasures.

▲ Howard Carter kneels in front of the doors of the fourth shrine in the tomb; here, Tutankhamun's sarcophagus was found.

WIRELESS OFFERS DAILY NEWS

In November 1922 the British Broadcasting Company (BBC), under licence from the Post Office to build radio stations and transmit programmes, began transmissions. The project was financed by a ten-shilling receiving licence that all listeners had to buy.

The BBC was formed by companies who manufactured wireless sets, foreseeing large profits from sales of their equipment. Daily broadcasts of concerts, talks and news had attracted 125,000 people to purchase licences by March 1923, although many more were believed to be listening unlicensed on homemade sets.

Radios were at first too expensive for any but the well-off middle classes and even they listened mostly with headphones, since a loudspeaker added significantly to the cost. Also, there were at first restrictions on the content of programmes – the powerful newspaper lobby successfully promoted a ban on the broadcast of news before 7 pm and live commentaries on sports events were not permitted. But the popularity of the wireless grew regardless. By 1927, when the BBC was taken into government control as the British Broadcasting Corporation, there were over two million licensed listeners.

▲ George Robey and Alma Adair recording for an early wireless review programme, "You'd be Surprised".

- The birth rate in Britain falls below 20 per thousand
- Women gain equality in divorce suits in Britain, with wives given the right to petition over a husband's adultery
- Railway ownership is reorganized into four companies: Great Western; London; Midland and Scottish; London and North Eastern; and Southern
- The Indian National Congress embarks upon a campaign of civil disobedience
- The FA Cup final is held at Wembley Stadium for the first time
- Surrey and England opener Jack Hobbs becomes the third batsman to score 100 centuries in his career
- The sale of alcohol to under-18s is banned by law
- The Charleston dance craze sweeps the country
- *Façade*, with words by Edith Sitwell and music by William Walton, is first performed in London
- Books published this year include *Antic Hay* by Aldous Huxley and *Tractatus Logico-Philosophicus* by Ludwig Wittgenstein
- Irish poet W B Yeats wins the Nobel Prize for Literature
- Song of the year is "Who's Sorry Now"

MARRIAGE OF A FUTURE KING AND QUEEN

On April 26, 1923, Prince Albert, second son of King George V, married Lady Elizabeth Bowes-Lyon at Westminster Abbey. The couple were given the titles of Duke and Duchess of York.

The prince first met Lady Elizabeth at a ball in 1920. He proposed to her twice before being accepted at the third attempt. The daughter of the Earl and Countess of Strathmore, Elizabeth was technically a commoner, the first to marry into the royal family for several centuries. She was, however, of royal lineage, since her family claimed descent from Robert the Bruce, king of Scotland. The bride's royal blood, or lack of it, was not a matter of great account even to traditionalists since, as a

▲ Lady Elizabeth Bowes-Lyon leaves her home for her marriage to the Duke of York, the future George VI.

younger brother, the Duke of York was never expected to succeed to the throne.

Although a courageous and athletic young man – he had served in the forces in the First World War and was good enough at tennis to play at Wimbledon – the Duke had an anxious nature that had responded badly to the strict upbringing imposed by his father. The result was a nervous stutter and desperate shyness. Generally shunning the limelight, he was glad to immerse himself in family life. The couple's first child, Elizabeth, was born three years after the wedding.

By a quirk of fate, the abdication of his brother Edward in 1936 gave the Duke of York a throne he had never wanted. As George VI, he was to reign through the Second World War, while his wife, the Queen Mother, lived to see the start of the twenty-first century.

MOUNTED POLICEMAN SAVES FIRST WEMBLEY FINAL

▲ Mounted policemen, including PC George Scorey on his white mount Billy, control the crowds before the FA Cup final at Wembley Stadium.

On April 28, 1923, the FA Cup final was held for the first time at the newly constructed Empire Stadium at Wembley. The event was very nearly a major disaster.

The official capacity of the new ground was a massive 127,000, but more than 200,000 spectators turned up to see the match. Climbing walls or vaulting turnstiles, tens of thousands of fans flowed into the already packed stadium. It was impossible to start the match as a dense mass of spectators was forced to spread out from the terraces on to the pitch. The game looked likely to be abandoned, but the police finally succeeded in squeezing fans back behind the touchlines. Widely credited with working this miracle was Police Constable George Scorey, whose snow-white mount Billy shone out against the dark-clad crowd.

Finalists Bolton Wanderers and West Ham United succeeded in playing out the game under difficult conditions. The crowd was packed so close to the field of play that it was impossible to run up when taking a corner. The two sides remained on the pitch through the half-time interval, believing that if once they went off the field they would never get back on. The result, almost incidental to the drama of the "white horse final", was a 2–0 victory for Bolton.

POLITICAL INSTABILITY

▲ Andrew Bonar Law makes his final exit from 10 Downing Street, the traditional home of the Prime Ministers of Britain. Terminal illness caused his resignation.

By the middle of 1922, the coalition government in Britain, led by David Lloyd George since the end of the war, finally seemed to be running out of steam. A combination of the continuing Irish problem, a scandal regarding the sale of honours and a political incident which brought Britain and Turkey to the brink of war had raised doubts among the Conservative backbenchers. When Lloyd George, a Liberal, proposed that a further election be called to approve a continued coalition, a Conservative revolt ensued. Andrew Bonar Law, a former Conservative member of the War Cabinet who had retired from politics a year earlier through ill-health, called for a party vote. A majority of 2:1 came out against continuing the coalition. Instead, the rebel majority pledged to fight an election independently under Bonar Law and Stanley Baldwin.

On October 20, 1922, Lloyd George had no choice but to tender his resignation: the Conservatives in the Cabinet followed suit. The general election, which took place in November, duly resulted in a comfortable majority for the Tories.

During 1923, the relationship between Bonar Law and his Chancellor, Baldwin, was uneasy, and he came close to resignation over a number of disagreements with his party. However, it was ill-health that forced his final resignation. Suffering from an incurable cancer of the throat, on May 20, 1923, he handed over leadership to Baldwin; he died six months later.

Although Stanley Baldwin had been a Member of Parliament for 15 years, he was a relatively unknown quantity. His avowed aim was to bring stability to government, but his task was not an easy one. Most of the senior influential Tories of the coalition government were now in the political wilderness (Churchill had described the Bonar Law Cabinet as the "second team"). Additionally, Britain's economy was stagnant and unemployment was rising.

Baldwin's controversial insistence on seeking the introduction of import duties, contrary to the principle of free trade which was sacred to many Conservatives and Liberals, led him to seek a fresh popular mandate. Despite enjoying a substantial majority in parliament, Baldwin called a general election for December 1923. It was a serious error of judgement, as senior figures within his party told him at the time. Although in terms of votes cast the election brought only a limited change from November of the previous year, measured by the distribution of seats in the House of Commons there was a substantial upheaval. The Conservatives lost 86 seats overall, around 40 of them to the Liberals and 50 to the Labour Party.

The Conservatives were still the largest single party, but together the Liberals and Labour – with 159 and 191 seats respectively – had 91 more MPs. Among the Liberal MPs, supporters of Lloyd George were far outnumbered by followers of Herbert Asquith. Using the authority that this position gave him in the party, Asquith led the Liberals to agree to support a minority Labour government rather than prop up the Conservatives. Thus on January 24, 1924, 57-year-old Scotsman Ramsay MacDonald became Britain's first ever Labour Prime Minister.

▲ An unknown quantity, Stanley Baldwin had had a largely undistinguished political career before he came to the fore in 1922.

- First Labour government is in power from January to October
- British athletes Eric Liddell and Harold Abrahams win gold medals at the Paris Olympics
- Huddersfield Town win the Football League trophy for the first of three consecutive years
- Books published this year include *A Passage to India* by E M Forster and *The Inimitable Jeeves* by P G Wodehouse
- George Bernard Shaw's *St Joan* has its first London performance
- Sir Edward Elgar is appointed Master of the King's Musick

JANUARY
- Prime Minister Stanley Baldwin resigns; Labour takes power under Ramsay MacDonald

FEBRUARY
- Britain establishes diplomatic relations with the Soviet Union

MARCH
- Imperial Airways is formed by a merger of four British companies

APRIL
- Britain takes control of Northern Rhodesia
- The British Empire Exhibition opens at Wembley

MAY
- Britain and Turkey negotiate over control of a disputed area of northern Iraq

THE ZINOVIEV LETTER

▲ **Grigory Zinoviev: did he write the Zinoviev letter? Timed to coincide with the general election, the scandal contributed to the downfall of the Labour government.**

On February 1, 1924, a week after the first Labour government came into office, Britain officially recognized the Soviet Union. This was a diplomatic upheaval, since the previous Conservative government had regarded the Russian Communists as outlaws who flouted all norms of civilized behaviour.

Talks with the Soviet Union made limited progress, but in August treaties were signed on trade and on the thorny issue of Russia's prerevolutionary obligations to Britain. The British government also proposed a loan to aid Soviet economic recovery. These measures sparked rumours that the Labour administration, despite its impeccably conventional and moderate domestic polices, was secretly advancing the communist cause.

Ramsay MacDonald headed a tenuous minority government, and it came as no surprise when on October 9, having lost a vote of censure, the Prime Minister was forced to call the second general election within 10 months. Many powerful figures on the right of British politics were determined that the election would see the Labour government turned out of office.

Britain's internal security service, MI5, now came into possession of a document that became known as the "Zinoviev letter". This purported to be a message from Grigory Zinoviev, the head of Comintern, the Soviet organization that had been set up to coordinate the work of communist parties worldwide.

Addressed to the Central Committee of the British Communist Party, the letter advised in practical terms how a workers' revolution could be achieved in Britain, including the infiltration of the armed forces.

In the last week of the election campaign, the Zinoviev letter was leaked to the press. Its effect was to provoke a "red scare" that turned voters away from the Labour Party, associated with communism, and into the arms of Stanley Baldwin's Conservatives. Labour lost 40 seats, while the Liberals who had passively supported them in power did even worse, losing 118 MPs. The Conservatives were returned to power with a large majority.

The Zinoviev letter is widely believed now to have been a fake, although spreading world revolution was certainly part of the Soviet agenda. Leaking it to the press was unquestionably a deliberate manoeuvre – most probably by the secret service – to influence the election result.

CLIMBERS LOST ON EVEREST

On June 6, 1924, two British climbers, 37-year-old George Leigh Mallory and 22-year-old Sandy Irvine, set out from their camp at 7040 m (23,100 ft), intending to become the first men to conquer Mount Everest.

Mallory had taken part in two previous Everest expeditions, in 1921 and 1922. Equipped only with solid tweeds and knitted sweaters, climbers had found it impossible to tackle the rarefied air of the final slopes. Irvine had developed an experimental oxygen apparatus, which Mallory hoped would make the third expedition succeed where others had failed.

KILLED ON HIS THIRD ATTEMPT TO REACH THE SUMMIT OF EVEREST THE LATE MR. GEORGE LEIGH MALLORY.

KILLED DURING THE LAST ATTEMPT TO CLIMB MOUNT EVEREST: THE LATE MR. A. C. IRVINE.

Yet he was full of foreboding, as seven sherpas had been killed by an avalanche as the 1922 expedition made its attempt on the summit.

◄ **George Mallory and Sandy Irvine were equipped only with tweeds and knitted sweaters on their fatal attempt to climb Mount Everest.**

On June 8 Mallory and Irvine were spotted by another member of their party, Noel Odell, heading towards the 8,848-m (29,029-ft) peak. Then snow began to fall, obliterating the view. The two climbers were never seen alive again. Whether they were in fact the first men to reach the summit of Everest will probably never be known. Mallory's body was not found until 1999, when it was discovered at around 8,400 m (27,500 ft).

OLYMPIC GOLDS FOR BRITAIN

At the Paris Olympics in summer 1924, two British runners, Eric Liddell and Harold Abrahams, won gold medals in a seeming triumph for something more than simple athletic prowess.

Liddell was a strict Scottish Presbyterian, whose faith prohibited running on the sabbath. He withdrew from the 100 m, which he had stood a good chance of winning, because one of the heats was scheduled for a Sunday. Abrahams, of Lithuanian Jewish origin, had no such problem with Sunday heats. In part inspired to prove his worth by resentment of anti-Semitism, he won the 100 m final in 10.6 seconds – equalling the Olympic record – with Liddell watching from the stands.

Liddell's turn came on July 11, when he competed in the 400 m final. With his unorthodox arm-flapping style, the Scot was considered far better at a short sprint than over a longer distance, yet he won the event in a world record time of 47.6 seconds.

▲ **Eric Liddell, a theological student from the University of Edinburgh, wins gold in the 400 m final at the Paris Olympics.**

DEATH OF A LITERARY MASTER

▲ **One of the great exponents of the English language, Polish-born Joseph Conrad (Jozef Teodor Konrad Korzeniowski) could speak little English until he reached his twenties.**

Joseph Conrad, one of the greatest authors of the period, died on August 3, 1924.

Born Jozef Teodor Konrad Korzeniowski in Poland in 1857, Conrad moved with his family to the north of Russia when his father, the poet Apollo Korzeniowski, was exiled for leading an insurrection against Russian rule. Sent to school in Switzerland following the death of his father, Conrad was unable to adapt to his education and left to join the French merchant navy. His transfer to the British ship *Palestine* in 1881 changed his life and, later, provided the inspiration for many of his greatest novels, such as *Lord Jim*, which he wrote in 1900.

Conrad spent a further 16 years as a merchant sailor, a time that included his greatest adventure – his command of a steamboat sailing up the River Congo into the heart of Africa. The trauma he experienced during four years in the Congo – at the time a private colony of Leopold II, king of the Belgians – where greedy European traders brutally exploited the native tribes, was conveyed in the most troubled of his works, the story *Heart of Darkness*. It was a title that not only symbolized the journey into "the dark continent", but also the evil and darkness within man.

Settling in England, Conrad found the life of an author difficult; not only did he and his young family live in near poverty, but the gout he had contracted in the Congo plagued him intermittently for the rest of his life. It was only in his last decade that he achieved widespread literary recognition.

Conrad is still widely viewed as one of the greatest writers of the English language. This is impressive in that English was not his native tongue, but astounding when we learn that at the age of 21 his vocabulary barely stretched to a dozen words.

- In the Locarno Treaties, Britain guarantees the existing borders between France, Belgium and Germany
- Britain and Australia join to provide loans to encourage Britons to emigrate Down Under
- The Contributory Pensions Act reduces the pension age for insured workers to 65 and extends pensions to widows and orphans
- First BBC long-wave transmitter goes into operation
- Pilot Alan Cobham flies from London to Cape Town, South Africa
- The Modernized Great West Road opens at Chiswick
- Books published this year include *Mrs Dalloway* by Virginia Woolf and *Politicians and the Press* by Lord Beaverbrook
- George Bernard Shaw wins the Nobel Prize for Literature
- Song of the year is "Show Me the Way to Go Home"

JANUARY
- Britain and China sign the Treaty of Peking

FEBRUARY
- England cricketers record their first Test victory over Australia in 12 years

MARCH
- Britain refuses to sign the Geneva Protocol
- Plans are announced to build a major naval base at Singapore
- Death of British statesman Lord Curzon

CHURCHILL GOES FOR GOLD

On April 28, 1925, in his Budget speech to the House of Commons, Conservative Chancellor of the Exchequer Winston Churchill announced that the value of sterling was to be pegged to gold – a return to the pre-First World War "Gold Standard".

It is debatable which was more surprising – the economic decision or the name of the man who was making it. Churchill had deserted the Conservative Party for the Liberals in 1904, earning the unflattering sobriquet "the Blenheim rat". Twenty years after that desertion, he was elected MP for West Essex, formally as an independent but actually with Conservative support. Churchill apologized for his opportunism with the quip: "Anyone can rat, but it takes a certain amount of ingenuity to rerat." As soon as he was back in the Tory fold, Prime Minister Stanley Baldwin put him in charge of the nation's finances, although Churchill had a poor head for figures and no knowledge of economics.

The decision to return to the Gold Standard had the approval of almost all economic experts. It harked back to the stability of prewar days, when the fixed value of the pound had been the foundation stone of international trade and capital investment. Declaring a return to the Gold Standard was an announcement that normal life had resumed after the interruption of the war.

In practice, though, the British economy was no longer strong enough to sustain such a high value for sterling. In order to keep to the Gold Standard, interest rates had to be raised, while British exports were rendered too

▲ Winston Churchill, Chancellor of the Exchequer, leaves 11 Downing Street on his way to present the Budget.

expensive by an artificially inflated exchange rate. Instead of boosting economic growth, the Gold Standard added impetus to Britain's apparently inexorable industrial decline.

Churchill was himself later to comment: "Everybody said I was the worst Chancellor of the Exchequer there ever was … and I am now inclined to agree with them."

DEATH TOLL RISES AS MOTORING SOARS

In 1925 the number of private cars on British roads exceeded the number of motorcycles for the first time. With a new Austin Seven available for little over £200, the middle classes were beginning to discover a means of transport previously restricted to

◀ In 1925 anyone over 16 could drive, and the speed limit was largely ignored; unsafe conditions led to a steep rise in accidents.

the rich. In 1919 there had been around 100,000 cars in Britain; by 1930 there would be over a million. The age of mass motoring was arriving.

An unwanted consequence of the motoring boom was a steep rise in road-accident fatalities. Anyone over 16 could drive – there was no test of any kind. In principle, a speed limit of 20 mph was in force, but it was universally ignored. Until the end of the decade, traffic lights were rare and there were few road markings of

any kind. With little or no regard for the risk to pedestrians or cyclists, "road hogs" roared along highways and byways that had been built for horses and carts, and where, moreover, the children of the poor were in the habit of playing unsupervised.

As a result of these unsafe conditions, road deaths ran at more than 4,000 a year in the mid-1920s. By the early 1930s, this figure would rise to over 7,000. This was far higher than the average of around 3,600 road deaths a year for Britain in the first decade of the twenty-first century, when the volume of traffic was so much greater.

COWARD SPEAKS FOR THE DECADE

On June 8, 1925, Noël Coward's *Hay Fever* opened at the Ambassador's Theatre in London's West End. Once described as "a comedy of bad manners", the play's hilarious portrayal of the unconventional Bliss family confirmed its author's status as the most fashionable theatrical personality of the day.

Coward was a "bright young thing". His first hit play, *Vortex*, had opened in the West End on December 16 the previous year – the author's 25th birthday. He spoke for a generation determined not to take the world seriously. His scripts were laced with cheeky references to drugs and homosexuality, lacerating dull pomposity and lauding the pursuit of pleasure.

It was ironic that this was the year when George Bernard Shaw was awarded the Nobel Prize for Literature. Despite his deserved reputation for wit, Shaw's plays displayed a philosophical weightiness and seriousness of purpose that seemed totally out of date when compared with Coward's sparkling superficiality and intentional frivolity. Witty, camp and apolitical, he fitted perfectly into the world of cigarette-smoking "flappers", jazz and the Charleston. In him the 1920s had found one of its most characteristic cultural voices.

▲ A scene from Noël Coward's play *Hay Fever* starring Graham Brown and Marie Tempest at London's Ambassador's Theatre in 1925.

HOBBS IS THE CRICKETING MASTER

▲ Jack Hobbs pictured shortly after he scored his record-breaking 126th century in first-class cricket.

On August 18, 1925, at Taunton, Somerset, Surrey's opening batsman Jack Hobbs broke W G Grace's record of 126 centuries in first-class cricket. Known as "the Master" because of his serenely dominant style and unsurpassable run-making ability, Hobbs scored 16 hundreds in the summer of 1925, totalling 3,024 runs at an average of more than 70 an innings.

Born in 1882, Hobbs played his first first-class match for Surrey in 1905 – ironically against a side that included W G Grace. It was not until after the First World War, however, that his talent reached full maturity. His partnership with Herbert Sutcliffe as England openers, begun in 1924, was the stuff of legend. In the 1924–25 Ashes series in Australia, Hobbs scored three centuries in consecutive Tests, Sutcliffe three centuries in consecutive innings.

Hobbs continued playing first-class cricket until 1934, when he retired, aged 51. He had scored a total of 61,237 runs at an average of 50.65 an innings, including 197 centuries – half of them made after the age of 40. His gentle charm made him one of the best-loved players ever to grace the game, and there was general satisfaction when he was knighted in 1953 for his services to cricket.

- Imperial Chemical Industries (ICI) is formed
- The Central Electricity Board is set up to create a National Grid
- The Tube is extended to Morden, making this section the world's longest tunnel at 27 km (17 miles)
- Newspapers are banned from publishing transcripts of divorce cases
- Marie Rambert founds the Rambert dance company in London
- First British greyhound racing track opens at Belle Vue, Manchester
- Books published this year include *The Seven Pillars of Wisdom* by T E Lawrence, *Winnie-the-Pooh* by A A Milne, and *The Murder of Roger Ackroyd* by Agatha Christie
- Alfred Hitchcock directs his first film, *The Lodger*, starring Ivor Novello
- Song of the year is "Bye Bye Blackbird"

JANUARY
- John Logie Baird demonstrates wireless images

APRIL
- Huddersfield Town wins the Football League title for the third consecutive season
- Princess Elizabeth is born, daughter of the Duke and Duchess of York

JOHN LOGIE BAIRD INVENTS THE TELEVISION

On January 27, 1926, members of London's Royal Institution were given the first successful demonstration of the transmission of a moving image by wireless. The inventor of the system was a 38-year-old Scottish engineer named John Logie Baird, who coined the phrase "television" to describe the process. It was the first stage in the development of a communication system which was to revolutionize life in the second half of the twentieth century.

The scientific principle on which television works is based around the workings of the human eye.

Every image we see is retained momentarily after it hits the retina. If sections of a picture are shown fast enough on a screen, the brain is able to interpret a fully assembled image. In the same way as cinema projection or animated film works, continuously changing the picture at a speed of up to 30 images per second creates the effect of movement.

For his groundbreaking demonstration, Baird built an electric camera that was able to convert the moving image of the inventor holding a pair of ventriloquist's dummies into electrical signals. These were transmitted in the same way as a radio signal and picked up and displayed independently by mechanically scanning a narrow beam of electrons in a series of lines on to the back of the cathode-ray picture tube. Baird's prototype scanned 240 horizontal lines, which produced a relatively crude, but nonetheless recognizable image.

Baird's mechanical system was updated by subsequent work by Isaac Shoenberg, who pioneered electrical scanning, and suggested that picture quality would be improved by increasing the number of lines that made up the picture: his 405-line standard became the norm in Europe until the 1970s when the use of ultra high frequency (UHF) transmissions allowed for improvements to 625 lines.

The impact of television on modern society has been incalculable, altering every aspect of human communication from the dissemination of news and popular culture to the dynamics of the family.

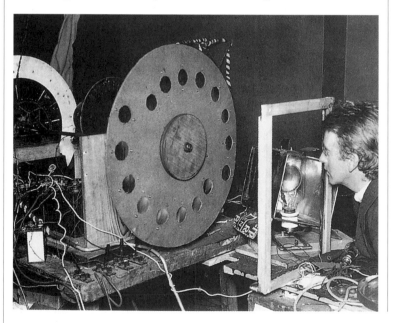

◄ A "transmitting disc" sends the image of a human face which is then scanned by a beam of electrons. John Logie Baird called his invention "wireless vision".

BRITAIN'S GENERAL STRIKE

Following the end of the First World War, the great British coal mines of Wales and Yorkshire – crucial to Britain's economy – were in decline. The revival of the mining industry in Germany following the destruction of the war had led to a collapse in the price of British coal. The situation was exacerbated when Winston Churchill, the newly appointed Chancellor of the Exchequer, restored Britain to the Gold Standard, causing deflation and further unemployment. The government attempted to support the coal industry with a series of subsidies. However, when Prime Minister, Stanley Baldwin announced that these were to be withdrawn in early 1926, the mine owners took measures to prevent a further slump in profits: they reduced the wages of their employees. The Miners Federation, the trade union that represented mine workers, unsuccessfully lobbied the government to intervene. The outcome was inevitable: on May 1,

◄ In spite of the General Strike, buses were still able to operate along London's Oxford Street. Police protection was given to the volunteer strike-breakers who helped maintain public services.

1926, more than a million of Britain's miners went on strike.

The miners took their case to the Trades Union Congress (TUC), an association governing all of Britain's trades unions. The TUC had created a General Council in 1921 as a way of offering resistance to employers who sought to drive down wages in the uncertain economic climate. With a significant national membership of more than 5 million, the trade union movement was now a powerful force in Britain. It was also one that made the British establishment uneasy: the birth of the TUC was hardly shrouded in bloody revolution, but many on the political right considered it part of a wider Red threat.

At the request of the Miners Federation, the TUC voted to back the miners' dispute and called for a general strike. It was, perhaps, the first opportunity for Britain's trade union movement to flex its muscles.

So it was that on May 3, 1926, 3 million workers went on strike. In addition to the coal mines, Britain's railway and tram systems, docks, and iron and steel works were all paralyzed.

Under the influence of Winston Churchill, the government took a firm line against the strike, resisting any form of negotiation while it was in progress. With all of the national newspapers frozen, Churchill – well-known as a writer outside of politics – edited an emergency newspaper, the *British Gazette*. His zeal for bombastic propaganda that would be so valuable to his country 20 years later helped turn public opinion against the strike. Calls for volunteers to keep Britain moving were met with enthusiasm. Creating a wartime atmosphere, Churchill was able to draft servicemen and university students in to man crucial positions.

A week into the conflict, the TUC, realizing that the strike was failing, attempted to negotiate a compromise. This was rejected by the miners. On May 12, 1926, with no hope of victory, the TUC instructed its members to return to work. Out on a limb, the miners continued their strike for a further seven months, but by winter the strike funds had run out. They were forced to return to the mines on lower wages and longer hours. The union movement had been firmly defeated.

For all the drama surrounding the nine days of the General Strike, it had no long-term impact on the economy. It was to be Britain's first and only general strike and one that set back the workers' movement in Britain. It would be another 40 years before the trade union movement would feel able to take on the might of the British government.

▼ A convoy of armoured cars assembles at Hyde Park Corner in London as troops are called in to maintain Britain's food supply.

1927

NEWS IN BRIEF

- By royal charter, the British Broadcasting Company becomes the British Broadcasting Corporation
- The Trades Disputes Act makes any future general strike illegal
- Imperial Airways opens a desert air mail service from Cairo to Basra
- Imperial Airways launches a scheduled air service from Britain to India
- Supermarine S5 seaplane wins the Schneider Trophy race in Venice
- Road accidents kill 5,329 people in the year
- Archaeologist Leonard Woolley makes important discoveries at the site of the ancient Mesopotamian city of Ur
- Books published this year include *To the Lighthouse* by Virginia Woolf and *Tarka the Otter* by Henry Williamson
- Eric Gill creates the sculpture *Mankind*

JANUARY
- First commercial transatlantic telephone link established
- First educational radio broadcasts are made, to schools in Kent

FEBRUARY
- Malcolm Campbell sets a world land speed record of 280 km/h (174 mph)

TELEPHONE LINKS UK TO AMERICA

On January 8, 1927, Sir Evelyn Murray, the Secretary of the General Post Office, held a telephone conversation from London with the President of the American Telegraph and Telegraph Company, Walter S Gifford, in New York. Their chat officially inaugurated the first transatlantic telephone link open for public use. A long-wave radio transmitter was used to bridge the ocean, providing perfectly adequate reception for a clear two-way conversation. But communication was by no means secure as amateur radio enthusiasts could listen in. A more secure short-wave system was introduced a year later in 1928.

The original tariff for transatlantic calls was prohibitively high at £15 for three minutes – at a time when the weekly old age pension for a married couple was £1. In general, telephones for home use were still a luxury confined to the distinctly well-off. But new telephone exchanges were opened every year and rising numbers of telephone boxes were put up on city streets. The famous red cast-iron kiosks designed by architect Sir Giles Gilbert Scott made their appearance in 1927.

The British government, as always with an eye to imperial and strategic concerns, insisted on securing the new international communications under its control.

▲ **An early telephone exchange with switchboard and operators. In 1925 home telephones were still very much a luxury.**

In 1929 Imperial & International Communications – the forerunner of Cable & Wireless – was set up as a semi-public utility to run both overseas telephone and overseas cable services.

BRITAIN EXPELS SOVIET "SPIES"

On May 12, 1927, several hundred police officers – some of them armed – raided the London premises of Arcos (the All-Russian Cooperative Society) seeking evidence of Soviet espionage activities in Britain. They also searched the offices of the Soviet Trade Delegation, housed in the same building, which should have enjoyed diplomatic immunity.

The police raid followed information from MI5 that classified material would be found in the building. MI5 knew this because they had themselves provided the Soviets with a classified document – namely, an RAF training manual – through a double agent. Embarrassingly, however, the manual was not found, and other documents seized were of only limited use to the British authorities.

The Conservative government had backed the Arcos raid and used it as a pretext to break off diplomatic relations with the Soviet Union. The government wanted to make this gesture because it believed the Soviets were guilty of stirring up trouble throughout the British Empire, especially in India where communists were blamed for the spread of nationalist agitation.

When the raid drew a blank, Prime Minister Stanley Baldwin instead publicized extracts from Soviet diplomatic telegrams that had been intercepted and decoded by British intelligence. This material was sufficient to incriminate the Soviet Union in involvement with subversion and was used to justify expelling all Soviet diplomats from Britain.

British intelligence services were furious at the government's use of decoded material, since this alerted the Soviets to the fact that their codes had been broken. More secure codes consequently adopted by the Soviet Union defied British intelligence up to the Second World War. The spy scandal was also unfortunate for a number of Soviet citizens, who, in retaliation, were tried and executed for allegedly spying for Britain.

◀ **Sir Austen Chamberlain, a member of Stanley Baldwin's government which used decoded material to expel Soviet spies.**

BRITISH AIRCRAFT IS FASTEST

On September 26, 1927, at Venice in Italy, a Supermarine S5 seaplane piloted by RAF Flight-Lieutenant Sidney N Webster won the coveted Schneider Trophy race at an average speed of 282 mph (453 km/h). A sleek high-powered monoplane, the S5 outperformed the American and Italian competitors – the failure of the latter a profound embarrassment for Italian dictator Benito Mussolini who was hosting the event.

Air racing was a popular craze in the interwar years, attracting large crowds, and it was also a focus for serious international competition between governments. Developing the world's fastest aircraft had implications not only for national prestige but also, more crucially, for national defence. The British government supported development of the Supermarines – another S5 took second place – and provided a team of RAF pilots to fly the British entrants.

The victory of the S5 was a triumph for its designer, Reginald Mitchell. Over the following years Mitchell developed his aircraft into the S6, which won the biennial event in 1929 and 1931, in the process becoming the first aircraft to top 640 km/h (400 mph). After three consecutive wins, Britain was awarded the Schneider Trophy outright and the competition ended. Mitchell used the experience gained in designing racing seaplanes to create an even more famous Supermarine aircraft in the 1930s – the Spitfire.

▲ The Supermarine S5 seaplane outperformed American and Italian competitors to win the coveted Schneider Trophy race in Venice.

QUOTA BACKS BRITISH FILMS

By the mid-1920s cinema going was an established part of life in British towns and cities. However, the vast majority of the films that audiences saw were American. So great was the dominance of Hollywood that by 1926, less than one movie in 20 of those shown in Britain was a home-grown product. The British had no lack of talent, but performers with the right skills followed the path beaten by Charlie Chaplin to fame and fortune in California.

In 1927 the British government reacted to American dominance of film production and distribution by introducing the Cinematograph Films Act, often known as the Quota Act. This established the principle that British movie houses would be legally obliged to show a fixed percentage of British films. When the Act first came into force in 1928, this quota was set at 7.5 per cent.

In a way, the act was a straightforward example of economic protectionism, designed to foster a national industry by protecting it against foreign competition. But it also reflected concerns about the Americanization of popular culture, a phenomenon seen as a threat to British traditions and cultural values.

The quota system devised unquestionably achieved its basic objective. The British film industry expanded, even if much of its output consisted of cheap "quickies" rushed out so that distributors could meet their quota target. By the mid-1930s almost 200 British films were being produced every year.

▲ Talented British actors, such as Charlie Chaplin (above), were often lured away to the bright lights of Hollywood.

1928

- First £1 and ten-shilling banknotes are issued
- *The Flying Scotsman* rail service is inaugurated between London and Edinburgh
- Professor Alexander Fleming discovers penicillin
- An official report states that the average Briton smokes 1.5 kg (3 lb 4 oz) of tobacco a year
- Elastoplast sticking plasters are first manufactured
- First payment of pensions to 65-year-olds who belong to the state contributory scheme
- *The Oxford English Dictionary* is completed after 70 years' work
- The Quota Act stipulates that at least 7.5 per cent of films shown in British cinemas must be British-made
- The West Indies cricket team tours England for the first time, losing all three Tests
- Books published this year include *Decline and Fall* by Evelyn Waugh, *The Well of Loneliness* by Radclyffe Hall and *Point Counter Point* by Aldous Huxley
- D H Lawrence's novel *Lady Chatterley's Lover* is printed privately in Florence
- Henry Moore and Barbara Hepworth stage their first sculpture exhibitions in London

JANUARY
- Flooding in London kills 14 people and damages paintings in the Tate Gallery
- Deaths of writer Thomas Hardy and First World War commander Field Marshal Douglas Haig

CONSERVATIVES GIVE THE VOTE TO "FLAPPERS"

In April 1928 the Conservative government introduced a bill to give women equal political rights with men. Since 1918, women over 30 had been able to vote. Now that right was extended to women over 21, the same qualifying age as for men.

This radical measure, fulfilling at last the aspirations of the prewar suffragettes, was proposed and carried with remarkably little fuss or public notice. In the Cabinet, only Winston Churchill and Lord Birkenhead opposed it. The Act was not introduced in response to public pressure, since there had been no significant suffragette agitation since 1914. It was not even based on a calculation of political advantage, although Labour suspected that women might be more inclined than men to vote Conservative. The Home Secretary, Sir William Joynson-Hicks, in fact committed the administration to giving "flappers" the vote in a rather casual way at a public meeting, and the rest of the government felt obliged to do what he had promised.

The cumulative effect of the 1918 and 1928 electoral reforms was radical. In 1906, although Britain broadly regarded itself as a democracy, 7.3 million people had been eligible to vote – which was 58 per cent of adult males, and only 27 per cent of all people over 21. By the time of the 1929 general election, the registered electorate included almost the entire adult population, numbering around 29 million people, 15.2

▲ A "flapper", provocatively dressed and holding a cigarette, challenges society's expectations of women in the 1920s.

million of them women. For obscure and archaic reasons of university or business privilege, about half a million people still enjoyed two votes, a situation not rectified until 1948. But Britain had truly become a democracy.

▲ The prolific Everton Football Club goal-scorer, Dixie Dean, pictured before a match against West Ham United.

DIXIE DEAN SCORES 60 GOALS

On May 1, 1928, Everton Football Club clinched the First Division championship with a victory and, predictably, a goal from centre-forward Dixie Dean. It was Dean's sixtieth goal of the season, a scoring record still unbeaten in England's top league.

Born in Birkenhead in 1907, William Ralph Dean played for Tranmere Rovers before joining Everton for a £3,000 transfer fee in 1925. His nickname Dixie was based on his dark curly hair, which reminded fans of the then current stereotype of the black American minstrel. Dean disliked the name, preferring to be known as Bill.

Dean was almost lost to football in 1926 when he suffered serious injuries in a motorcycle accident. He returned the following season to score his celebrated 60 goals in 39 of Everton's 42 League games. He led Everton to another League championship in 1932, followed by an FA Cup triumph in 1933. His overall scoring record at the club was a remarkable 383 goals in 433 games.

Like all players of his day, Dean eventually left the sport with very little money to his name, subsequently earning a living as a publican and later as a Littlewoods security manager. He died in 1980 at Goodison Park football ground, watching an Everton home derby match against Liverpool.

BRITAIN SIGNS PACT TO END ALL WARS

On August 27, 1928, an international agreement was signed which claimed to consign war to the dustbin of history. The Kellogg-Briand Pact, also known as the Pact of Paris, was immediately accepted by representatives of 15 countries, including Britain and Germany. Over the coming months almost all the major countries in the world – 62 in all – added their signatures.

Negotiated by French Foreign Minister Aristide Briand and US Secretary of State Frank B Kellogg, the pact was originally intended as a bilateral treaty between France

▲ Aristide Briand (left) and Frank B Kellogg (right), declared that peace was preferable to war. Sixty-two countries agreed.

and the United States renouncing war between the two countries – an unlikely eventuality. Kellogg suggested turning it into a multilateral treaty through which all countries would, in the words of the preamble to the pact, make "a frank renunciation of war as an instrument of national policy".

The pact represented a moment of optimism in international relations, when durable peace and disarmament seemed real possibilities. However, it was utterly ineffectual once aggressive militarist governments took power during the 1930s in Japan, Germany and elsewhere. But the pact has remained a point of reference in international law and its provisions are broadly enshrined in the UN Charter.

ACCIDENTAL DISCOVERY LEADS TO PENICILLIN

In September 1928 an accidental occurrence in a London medical laboratory led to one of the most important discoveries of the twentieth century – the crucial antibiotic drug penicillin.

While working at St Mary's Medical School in London, bacteriologist Alexander Fleming noticed that during a series of experiments with the bacteria *Staphylococcus aureus* an area on the dish had accidentally become contaminated with a green mould – spores of *Penicillium notatum*. He observed that the bacteria was unable to grow on these contaminated areas, which led him to believe that something within the mould – which he called penicillin – was in fact killing the bacteria. Carrying out further tests led Fleming to the amazing discovery that penicillin prevented the growth of many

of the common bacteria active in human infection.

Fleming's frustrating problem was that he lacked the chemical expertise needed to isolate the active ingredient. Thus he was aware that he had made a discovery of potentially staggering importance, but at that time was unable to develop a practical application.

It was left to others to take up his work, notably the biochemist Ernst Chain and the pathologist Howard Florey. Researchers at Oxford University, they managed to isolate and purify penicillin in 1940. Following this breakthrough, they went on to carry out the first human clinical trials. The results showed that penicillin was the most potent nontoxic antibiotic yet discovered.

In 1945 the importance of Fleming's, Chain's and Florey's work was acknowledged when they were awarded the Nobel Prize for

Medicine. Although some human bacteria have now developed an immunity to it, the various forms of penicillin continue to play an important role in modern medicine.

▲ Bacteriologist Sir Alexander Fleming's discovery of penicillin turned out to be one of the most significant medical developments of the century.

- Margaret Bondfield is the first woman appointed to the Cabinet
- First "green belt" area protected from development is designated
- The Post Office introduces Bakelite telephone handsets, one of the first major uses of plastics
- Imperial and International Communications (Cable & Wireless from 1934) is founded to handle Britain's overseas communications
- Presbyterian churches in Scotland unite to form the Church of Scotland
- The Metropolitan Police Flying Squad is given radio cars
- England win Test series in Australia by four matches to one
- Alfred Hitchcock's *Blackmail* is the first British film with full sound
- First performance of the play *Journey's End* by R C Sherriff
- Books published this year include *Goodbye To All That* by Robert Graves and *A Room of One's Own* by Virginia Woolf
- John Grierson makes the documentary film *Drifters* for the Empire Marketing Board
- First performance of Constant Lambert's suite *The Rio Grande*
- Song of the year is "Tip-toe Through the Tulips"

FEBRUARY
- Death of Lily Langtry, actress and mistress of Edward VII

MARCH
- The Grand National is won by 100–1 outsider Gregalach

LABOUR BACK IN POWER

Conservative Prime Minister Stanley Baldwin called a general election in the spring of 1929 after almost five years in office. The Baldwin government had been solid, unspectacular and unimaginative. These were the qualities it proposed to the electorate, campaigning under the slogan "Safety First". The Labour Party, led by Ramsay MacDonald, was also primarily concerned to reassure voters that it would not rock the boat if elected. MacDonald firmly slapped down left-wingers in the party, promising there would be "no monkeying" with the economy – in other words, no socialism.

The only excitement and innovation in the election campaign came from the Liberals, led by David Lloyd George. Employing intellectuals, such as economist John Maynard Keynes, Lloyd George drew up a radical new economic policy, explained in a document entitled *We Can Conquer Unemployment.* This recommended increased government borrowing to finance public works projects and invest in industry, thereby stimulating economic growth and creating jobs. It prefigured the New Deal policies that President Roosevelt would introduce in the United States in the 1930s. To the British electorate, it appeared far too risky and revolutionary.

In the election of May 30, 1929, the Conservatives actually won the largest share of the popular vote. They attracted 8.3 million votes compared with 8.4 million for Labour. The Liberals lagged behind with 5.1 million. As usual, the quirks of the British constituency system meant that voting figures translated into a quite different distribution of seats in the House of Commons. Labour found themselves the largest party, with 287 seats against 260 for the Conservatives and a mere 59 for the Liberals.

Ramsay MacDonald formed a government with Arthur Henderson as his Foreign Secretary and Philip Snowden as Chancellor of the Exchequer. All of these men were Labour veterans, men born in the 1860s who had grown up in the Victorian era. Any socialist ardour that they may once have possessed had been dimmed by an unshakeable attachment to political respectability. They settled firmly into government, determined to prove that they could rule as sensibly and efficiently as any Conservative government. It was to be their great misfortune, however, to run straight into the worst economic crisis of the twentieth century.

▲ **The new Labour Prime Minister, Ramsay MacDonald (left), and his Chancellor of the Exchequer, Phillip Snowden, outside 10 Downing Street.**

DOLE QUEUES LENGTHEN AFTER WALL STREET CRASHES

On October 24, 1929, share value on the American stock market began to collapse as a wave of panic selling enveloped Wall Street. The crash only affected a small number of British investors, but it marked the onset of a world economic Depression that would plunge Britain into an era of mass unemployment.

Since the end of the First World War, unemployment in Britain had never fallen below a million – around one in ten of the workforce. The problem was concentrated in the industrial and mining regions of northern England, south Wales, Scotland and Northern Ireland. In these areas cotton mills, ship-building

yards, pits and foundries – once the powerhouses of the British Empire – had fallen fatally behind foreign competitors, leading to closures that deprived entire communities of their livelihood.

The onset of the Depression was a body-blow to industries already in serious trouble. British exports almost halved between

▶ **Unemployed ship workers parade through the streets of Plymouth, as Britain is plunged into an era of mass unemployment.**

1929 and 1931 as world demand slumped. By July 1930 unemployment in Britain had risen above 2 million and was still increasing. By 1932 almost two-thirds of ship-building workers were out of a job, along with almost half of all coal miners and steel workers.

The response of the Labour government to the Depression was entirely in line with orthodox economic thinking of the day. The Chancellor of the Exchequer, Philip Snowden, insisted on keeping the budget balanced by raising taxes and reducing government expenditure – measures that in fact tended to reduce demand further and increase unemployment.

One junior Labour minister, Oswald Mosley, proposed an imaginative scheme for planned economic development, government control of industry, and cheap credit to stimulate economic growth. When his views were rejected by the Cabinet, he resigned. Mosley famously went on to become the leader of British fascism in the 1930s.

WRITERS RETURN TO THE TRENCHES

In the late 1920s a flood of books, plays and films were produced reflecting on the experience of the First World War, now more than a decade in the past. Cumulatively, these significantly altered attitudes to the war, emphasizing its horrors and questioning its purpose.

The suffering and death of the young men in the trenches had until then been widely respected as a noble, if tragic, sacrifice. In the words of Archbishop of Canterbury Cosmo Lang, speaking in 1928, their bravery had "kept the honour of the nation's pledged word and preserved its freedom". But now the war was represented as futile slaughter – in the words of war veteran Siegfried Sassoon, "a dirty trick which had been played on me and my generation".

The most influential of the wave of antiwar books in 1929 was German author Erich Remarque's *All Quiet on the Western Front*, an instant bestseller in English translation and the basis for an Oscar-winning Hollywood film of 1930. Britain's contribution included Robert Graves's war memoirs *Goodbye To All That*, Frederick Manning's *Her Privates We*, and Richard Aldington's novel *Death of a Hero*. The hit play of 1929 was R C Sherriff's tear-jerking trench drama *Journey's End*, which ran at London's Savoy Theatre for more than 500 performances and was broadcast by BBC radio on the evening of Armistice Day.

Those who, instead of listening to their wireless on Armistice Day, attended the British Legion's "Festival of Empire and Remembrance" at the Albert Hall encountered a quite different view of the war. The Legion thoroughly

▲ **Poet and novelist Siegfred Sassoon is famous for his bitter antiwar poems; he described the war as a "dirty trick".**

indulged nostalgia and patriotic sentiment, from the singing of "Tipperary" to a tableau of Britannia and her Empire, and a rousing reception for the Prince of Wales. But the tide of educated opinion was increasingly set firmly against simplistic patriotism and the celebration of military valour. Antiwar sentiment was to remain an important factor in British political life to the present day.

APRIL
• The RAF Fairey monoplane flies nonstop from Britain to India

MAY
• Labour win the general election; 13 women MPs are elected

JUNE
• A Labour government is formed under Ramsay MacDonald
• Britain and other Allies agree the Young Plan to settle German reparation payments
• Bentley cars take the first four places in the Le Mans 24-hour race

JULY
• Paintings of nudes by novelist D H Lawrence are seized by police from a London gallery
• The Kellogg-Briand Treaty comes into force

AUGUST
• Clashes between Arabs and Jews in British-ruled Palestine lead to more than 200 deaths

SEPTEMBER
• Britain wins the Schneider Trophy air race with a Supermarine S6 seaplane

OCTOBER
• Britain resumes diplomatic relations with the Soviet Union
• British airship makes its maiden flight
• Shares crash on Wall Street

DECEMBER
• A hurricane sweeps Britain, causing more than 20 deaths
• Seventy-one children are killed at the Glen cinema in Paisley on New Year's Eve, when a small fire causes panic

- Infant mortality in Britain is 67 per thousand births, compared with 142 per thousand in 1900
- Almost 6,500 people are killed on British roads in the year
- A Housing Act provides funds for slum clearance
- Newspaper magnate Lord Beaverbrook promotes the United Empire Party
- Youth Hostel Association is founded
- Australian cricketer Don Bradman scores a record 974 runs in a Test series against England, including one score of 334
- BBC Symphony Orchestra is founded under conductor Sir Adrian Boult
- Books published this year include *Vile Bodies* by Evelyn Waugh, *Ash-Wednesday* by T S Eliot and *Poems* by W H Auden
- Noel Coward's play *Private Lives* opens in London

JANUARY
- Indian National Congress demands complete independence from Britain

MARCH
- Mohandas Gandhi leads a "march to the sea" in protest against the British-imposed salt tax in India
- Unemployment in Britain rises above 1.5 million
- Deaths of writer D H Lawrence and former Prime Minister Arthur Balfour

AMY JOHNSON FLIES SOLO TO AUSTRALIA

At dawn on May 5, 1930, 26-year-old amateur pilot Amy Johnson took off from Croydon Airport in the south of England with the declared intention of flying solo to Australia, a distance of 17,500 km (11,000 miles). Understandably, few people took her seriously, since her longest previous flight had only been from London to Hull.

Johnson was one of the small, but growing, band of adventurous women who were elbowing their way into the male-dominated field of aviation. She was working as a secretary when she joined the London Aeroplane Club in 1928. After obtaining a flying licence the following year, she sought in vain for a job as a professional pilot, finding all avenues blocked by sexist prejudice. It was this that led her to prove her worth by joining the current craze for record-breaking long-distance flights. In 1928 Australian pilot Bert Hinkler had flown solo from England to Australia in 15 and a half days. Johnson decided she would beat his record.

Johnson got financial backing from oil baron Lord Wakefield, who helped pay for an aircraft and fuel along the route. Her aeroplane was a De Havilland Gipsy Moth, a single-engine open-cockpit biplane with a top speed of 145 km/h (90 mph). She christened it *Jason*. Johnson covered the 6,500 km (4,000 miles) to Karachi in six days, easily beating Hinkler's time, but a crash when landing at Rangoon cost her three days and put the record time out of reach. Nonetheless, by the time she reached Darwin on May 24, 19 and a half days after leaving Croydon, she had become an instant celebrity.

▲ Amy Johnson and the Gipsy Moth in which she made her 19-day solo flight to Australia.

While in Australia, Johnson met fellow pilot Jim Mollison, who she married. She performed many other long-distance flights, either solo or with Mollison, but interest in record-breaking flights declined in the later years of the decade and her marriage fell apart. She never lost her place in the hearts of the British public, and her death while flying on military duties in 1941 was widely mourned.

CREATOR OF SHERLOCK HOLMES DIES

▲ Sir Arthur Conan Doyle, the creator of the greatest sleuth of them all, Sherlock Holmes. He remains one of Britain's most popular authors.

Sir Arthur Conan Doyle, the Scottish-born writer best known for his colourful tales of the exploits of fictional detective Sherlock Holmes, died in Crowborough, Sussex, on July 7, 1930, at the age of 71. Born in Edinburgh on May 22, 1859, Conan Doyle graduated from the University of Edinburgh, where he studied medicine, before practising as a doctor until 1891. It was while he was studying at the University of Edinburgh that he chanced upon a lecturer, renowned for his deductive reasoning, who was to provide the inspiration for the character of Sherlock Holmes.

The world's most famous detective first appeared in print in 1887 in a story called *A Study In Scarlet*. Conan Doyle contributed regular short stories about the exploits of Sherlock Holmes to *Strand Magazine* from 1891 onwards. These stories also featured the fictional detective's good friend Dr Watson, the kindly if occasionally slightly dim companion who followed Holmes on his many adventures. Dr Watson's character was in stark contrast to that of Holmes's sworn enemy, the evil criminal mastermind Professor Moriarty.

Although the stories proved to be enormously popular with

readers, Conan Doyle soon tired of his creation and killed him off in 1893. Such was the outcry from the public, however, that Conan Doyle was forced to bring Sherlock Holmes back from the dead by means of an unlikely plot twist.

Sherlock Holmes continues to be a popular character and versions of Sir Arthur Conan Doyle's work have been presented as radio plays, animations and

▲ "Holmes was working hard over a chemical investigation." An 1893 colour plate from Sir Arthur Conan Doyle's adventure story, *The Naval Treaty.*

films. New stories featuring Holmes, Watson and Moriarty have been written, principally for the screen, since Conan Doyle's death. The character of Holmes has also assumed cult status with the formation of the Sherlock Holmes Society in London, the Baker Street Regulars in New York (Holmes lived in Baker Street in London) and similar groups of enthusiasts in other countries around the world.

BRITISH AIRSHIP CRASHES IN FRANCE

On October 4, 1930, the giant British airship *R101* embarked on its inaugural flight from Britain to India. Those on board included the Secretary of State for Air, Lord Thomson, and the Director of Civil Aviation, Sir William Sefton Brancker. The flight ended in disaster.

Britain had watched with envy the success of Germany's *Graf Zeppelin*, which carried passengers on a round-the-world air cruise in 1929. Britain's Air Ministry was determined to see its own airship fleet flying routes across the Empire. *R101* was built by the government Royal Airship Works. A leading advocate of airships, Lord Thomson gave it his particular attention. He would brook no delay in completing the project, despite serious difficulties encountered in the airship's design and construction. The result was a flawed, overweight machine short of lift that was not truly fit to fly. Thomson, however, insisted that the India flight scheduled for October should go ahead, publicly declaring that the airship was "as safe as a house".

R101 was in trouble soon after taking off from Cardington, Bedfordshire. The weather was

bad, with wind and heavy rain. Forced down to low altitude, the airship crossed the Channel pitching and rolling dangerously. Around 2 am on October 5, *R101* went out of control and dived into a hillside outside Beauvais in northern France, bursting into flames. Forty-six of the 54 people on board were killed, including Thomson and Brancker.

The disaster brought an abrupt end to Britain's airship programme. Another airship, *R100*, had been built for the government by the private company Vickers and was a far more airworthy design, successfully flying to Canada and back. Nonetheless, it was sold for scrap, fetching £504, a tiny fraction of the money it had cost to build.

▲ The remains of the *R101* airship after it crashed in France; 46 people were killed including the Secretary of State for Air, Lord Thomson.

* The Statute of Westminster confirms the independence of the Dominions as "freely associated members of the British Commonwealth of Nations"
* A "means test" is introduced as the basis for welfare payments
* Ford opens a car-making plant at Dagenham, Essex
* The Road Traffic Act abolishes the 20 mph speed limit and makes third-party insurance compulsory
* The use of traffic lights is generalized after successful trials in London
* A Supermarine seaplane becomes first aeroplane to exceed the 640 km/h (400 mph)
* Books published this year include *Afternoon Men* by Anthony Powell and *The Waves* by Virginia Woolf
* William Walton's oratorio *Belshazzar's Feast* premieres

JANUARY
* Gandhi is released from jail to negotiate with the British authorities in India
* Winston Churchill resigns from the shadow cabinet in protest at the policy of allowing India progress towards self-rule

FEBRUARY
* India's Viceroy, Lord Irwin, meets Gandhi for the first time
* Malcolm Campbell sets a new world land-speed record of 394 km/h (246 mph)
* Former Labour minister Oswald Mosley forms the New Party, declaring it will "save the nation"

YEAR OF CRISIS IN BRITAIN

▲ **Unemployed demonstrators march to a rally in Hyde Park, London. Britain had been thrown into economic crisis by a worldwide Depression.**

In the summer of 1931, a financial crisis threw British politics into disarray. The key to the crisis was the insistence of the Labour government, and in particular of its Chancellor of the Exchequer, Philip Snowden, on obeying the orthodox financial principles of the day. These laid down the government's duty to balance income and expenditure, and to keep the value of the pound stable by maintaining the Gold Standard.

In February 1931 a committee headed by Sir George May was set up to inquire into the state of government finances. It reported at the end of July that drastic action was needed to balance the budget. Since 1929, Britain had been severely affected by the onset of a worldwide Depression. Economic activity was falling while unemployment was rising. As a consequence, government revenues from taxation had fallen while expenditure on unemployment benefit had risen sharply. The May committee recommended tax rises and sharp expenditure cutbacks. In particular, it wanted to see unemployment benefit cut by 20 per cent.

On August 11 the influential bankers of the City of London weighed in to back the call for spending cuts. At an emergency meeting with the Prime Minister, they warned the government that foreign investors had lost confidence in the soundness of British finances. If nothing were done to restore confidence, there would be a "run on the pound" and sterling would have to be devalued, coming off the Gold Standard.

On August 23, after days of acrid debate within the Cabinet, Snowden and Prime Minister Ramsay MacDonald insisted on a package of spending cuts, including a 10 per cent cut in unemployment benefit and similar reductions in the wages of all government employees, including the armed forces, teachers and the police. This direct assault on the living standards of working people and the jobless was too much for many within the government to swallow. Nine Labour ministers resigned.

Instead of resigning himself, as was expected, MacDonald responded by forming a coalition National Government with the Conservatives and Liberals to pass the necessary budget changes. The National Government was intended to be an all-party coalition, but although MacDonald remained Prime Minister and Snowden stayed at the Exchequer, the Labour Party as a whole moved into opposition. The former Labour leaders were denounced as "traitors" and expelled from the party.

If the principal objective of the spending cuts was to preserve the value of the pound, they failed miserably. There was widespread popular discontent as the reductions went into effect. On September 15 sailors of the Atlantic Fleet at Invergordon in Scotland refused duty in protest at the scale of their pay cut. News of this "mutiny" in the Royal Navy panicked foreign holders of sterling, who imagined the country plunging into a communist revolution. Although the mutiny was quickly settled by minor concessions, the feared "run on the pound" became a reality. On September 20 Britain was forced to abandon the Gold Standard. The pound plummeted, losing almost a third of its value on foreign exchanges.

Devaluation brought none of the predicted dire consequences. Indeed, by making British exports cheaper for foreigners to buy it gave the economy a much-needed stimulus. The political result of the crisis was a disastrous setback for the Labour Party. At a general election in October, MacDonald and his National Government allies – primarily the Conservatives – took more than 60 per cent of the popular vote and 521 seats in parliament. Labour was left with a mere 52 seats and consigned to the opposition benches for the rest of the decade.

BBC BROADCASTS OVERSEAS

Television broadcasting history was made on May 8 when the BBC (British Broadcasting Corporation) broadcast overseas from London as part of a seven-year programme of experiments and investigations into the new technology. At this time the BBC had been investigating the possibility of making regular broadcasts using a system devised by the Scottish engineer and inventor John Logie Baird.

Baird had given the first successful demonstration of television in 1926, when he used his primarily mechanical approach

▲ Alexandra Palace, the original home of the British Broadcasting Corporation. Television would play an increasingly important role in communications during the twentieth century.

to scan moving images, transmitting them electronically as a series of moving pictures on a small screen. The pictures were made up of only 30 lines, which were scanned around 10 times per second. Although the results were understandably very crude, they still provided a practical demonstration that the new technology would work. But unfortunately for Baird, the BBC ultimately opted for a superior system devised by the Marconi Company and began regular broadcasts from Alexandra Palace in London in 1936.

GANDHI IN LONDON TALKS

On September 8, 1931, the second Round Table Conference on the future of India opened at St James's Palace in London. Present as the sole representative of the Indian National Congress, the principal Indian nationalist movement, was Mohandas Gandhi.

The first Round Table Conference – held the previous year – had been boycotted by Congress. In the spring of 1931, however, Gandhi had negotiated a pact with the Viceroy of India, Lord Irwin, agreeing to suspend his campaign of civil disobedience in return for the release of political prisoners.

Winston Churchill, the principal spokesman of the India Defence League, dedicated to preserving British rule in the subcontinent, derided as "alarming and also nauseating" the sight of Gandhi, a seditious Middle Temple lawyer, now posing as a fakir of a type well known in the East, striding half-naked up the steps of the Viceregal Palace." Gandhi's appearance certainly made an

▲ Attired in his customary dress, and making no concessions to the British climate, Gandhi left an indelible impression on London.

indelible impression on his visit to London. Making no sartorial concessions to the climate or to British convention, he wore his scanty wrap and loincloth even when taking tea with the king at Buckingham Palace.

The Round Table Conference was not a success. It broke up on December 1 without agreement. On his return to India at the end of the year, Gandhi relaunched the campaign of passive resistance and was soon back in jail.

- One in four of the British workforce is unemployed
- The atom split mechanically for the first time
- Battersea Power Station, designed by Sir Giles Gilbert Scott, approaches completion
- The BBC opens new headquarters in Portland Place, London
- Three Methodist churches combine to form the Methodist Church of Great Britain and Ireland
- Ramblers begin "mass trespasses" to open up the countryside to public access
- The Southern Electric railway operates a third-rail system on the London to Brighton main line
- Hungarian-born film director Alexander Korda founds London Films
- Books published this year include *Brave New World* by Aldous Huxley, *Black Mischief* by Evelyn Waugh, and *Stamboul Train* by Graham Greene
- Novelist John Galsworthy wins the Nobel Prize for Literature
- Conductor Thomas Beecham founds the London Philharmonic Orchestra

JANUARY
- Civil disobedience resumes in India; the Indian National Congress is outlawed; Gandhi and other leaders are arrested
- Troops quell riots at Dartmoor prison
- Death of *Manchester Guardian* newspaper editor C P Scott

RECTOR DEFROCKED AFTER NATIONAL SCANDAL

On July 8, 1932, a Church court found Harold Davidson, rector of the parish of Stiffkey in Norfolk, guilty on five charges of misconduct. It was the conclusion of a scandalous case that enthralled readers of popular newspapers across Britain and made the rector one of the celebrities of the decade.

Born in 1875, Davidson had been a professional entertainer before entering the Church. In the 1920s, after his wife became pregnant by another man, the rector's life started to go off the rails. In 1925 he was prosecuted for debt and declared bankrupt. He also began to neglect his parish duties in order to work for the salvation of "fallen women" in London's Soho district.

Davidson's unorthodox activities eventually attracted the critical attention of the Church authorities and, more damagingly, the curiosity of investigative journalists. It was in order to forestall publication of articles about the rector in the *Daily Herald* that ecclesiastical court proceedings were opened.

Davidson defended himself vigorously, claiming to have saved large numbers of young women from prostitution, partly by exploiting his show business connections to find them acting jobs. But sensational evidence was presented of his excessive personal involvement in his work, including the testimony of a 16-year-old Lyons Tea House waitress he had fondled and a photograph in which he appeared with a naked 15-year-old.

Found guilty and defrocked, Davidson returned to his original career as a performer, doing his best to exploit his notoriety to financial advantage. He died in

▲ Harold Davidson's unorthodox activities enthralled readers of popular newspapers, and made the rector a leading celebrity.

1937 in a macabre incident at a Skegness amusement park. Performing in a cage with two lions, he accidentally trod on one of the animals' tails and was mauled in the ensuing fracas, dying two days later.

UNEMPLOYED MARCH AGAINST MEANS TEST

▲ The women's contingent of a hunger march on their way from Holloway in north London to Hyde Park.

In September and October 1932, "hunger marches" organized by the National Unemployed Workers' Movement (NUWM) ended in clashes between protesters and police in London, Belfast, Manchester and elsewhere. The NUWM's predominantly communist leadership was seeking to mobilize the resentment felt by jobless workers and to publicize their plight. With almost 3 million unemployed, and cuts in benefits in operation since the previous year, there was no shortage of discontent.

The NUWM's 1932 campaign was focused on the recently introduced and much hated "means test". Unemployment benefit – the "dole" – could only be drawn as a right for 26 weeks. After that, officials investigated the financial situation of jobless families and the benefit was withdrawn if they were deemed sufficiently well-off to support themselves. The process was resented as humiliating and intrusive, even when it did not lead to a cut in benefit.

The "hunger march" tactic adopted by the NUWM was highly effective in publicizing their cause. Groups of jobless people trudged from depressed industrial areas to major cities, passing through every town and village along the way. The marches made unemployment visible and won a sympathetic response – marchers were fed from soup kitchens set up by local volunteers and allowed to sleep in schools or village halls. It was only when the different marches came together at their destination, meeting up with hardline political activists assembled to greet them, that rioting was liable to break out.

Overall, the NUWM had limited impact. Its members never numbered more than 100,000 out of the jobless millions. Its connection with the Communist Party meant it received no support from the Labour movement. The reaction of most unemployed people to their fate was bitter apathy rather than militant action.

NOT-SO-BRAVE NEW WORLD

In 1932 Aldous Huxley, one of the leading literary intellectuals of his day, published his famous vision of a dystopic future, *Brave New World*. From a distinguished family of scientists, Huxley was well placed to satirize a future in which science and technology have abolished sorrow and suffering – along with every other truly human experience.

In the New World of Huxley's novel, war has been abolished by a World State; feel-good drugs and easy sex keep citizens in a mindless state of hedonistic self-satisfaction; children are produced in test-tubes and brought up without family ties; and subhuman clones take care of manual labour. Everyone is happy all the time, but at the cost of everything that makes human life worth while: love, poetry and freedom.

Huxley's vision appeared at odds with the driving issues of the 1930s, such as poverty, unemployment and the rise of militarist dictatorships. But by the

▲ Huxley's unique vision of a world free of suffering and sorrow was at odds with the issues of the day, such as poverty and unemployment.

end of the century his prescience was acknowledged, in forecasting a society driven mad by an unholy alliance between technological progress and the pleasure principle.

COCKCROFT AND WALTON SPLIT THE ATOM

1932 was the year that saw two Cambridge University-based physicists, Britain's John Cockcroft and Ireland's Ernest Walton, succeed in their efforts to split atoms of lithium. By

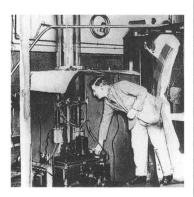

▲ Dr John Cockcroft makes an adjustment to the pump of his "Atom Splitter". His work with Ernest Walton had a dramatic impact on life in the twentieth century.

bombarding the nuclei, or cores, of the lithium atoms using a very high-voltage particle accelerator, the two scientists were able to transform the atoms of lithium into atoms of helium. This was the first time that a nuclear reaction was achieved by means of artificially accelerated particles.

Cockroft's and Walton's pioneering work with their particle accelerator made their device an essential tool of any physics laboratory, putting it on a par with the microscope and the spectrometer as a means of examining the material world. The particle accelerator, a device which accelerates subatomic particles – known as elementary particles – generates up to 800,000 volts of electricity. This was used to blast a high-energy beam of protons at a group of lithium atoms. The impact of the protons altered the atomic structure of the lithium, turning it into atoms of helium. Although transmutation, as the process is called, had long been the aim of alchemists, who dreamed of turning lead into gold, this was the first time that such a feat had been achieved.

The two scientists were able to construct their particle accelerator with the support of the eminent scientist and peer Lord Rutherford, plus a much-needed £1,000 grant from Cambridge University. In recognition of their remarkable achievement, Cockcroft and Walton were jointly awarded the Nobel Prize for Physics in 1951.

FEBRUARY
• A disarmament conference opens in Geneva, with Britain among 60 countries attending
• Death of bestselling author Edgar Wallace

MARCH
• Eamon de Valera is elected President of the Irish Free State
• The BBC begins transmissions from its new Broadcasting House

APRIL
• In the Irish Free State, MPs vote to drop the oath of allegiance to the British crown

JUNE
• Indian cricketers play their country's first Test match against England

SEPTEMBER
• Liberals quit the National Government over the introduction of tariffs on imports, as does former Labour Chancellor of the Exchequer Viscount Snowden

OCTOBER
• Sir Oswald Mosley forms the British Union of Fascists
• Riots break out when hunger marchers reach London

NOVEMBER
• The Northern Ireland parliament buildings at Stormont open
• The third India Round Table Conference opens in London

DECEMBER
• Britain, France, Germany and Italy sign a declaration renouncing the use of force to resolve differences
• George V makes the first royal Christmas broadcast on BBC radio

1933

- ICI markets the first synthetic detergent
- England cricketers win the "Bodyline" Test series in Australia 4–1
- The London Passenger Transport Board takes over underground railways, buses and trams in the capital
- A schematic London Tube map, designed by Harry Beck, is introduced
- The Odeon cinema chain is founded
- Charles Laughton stars in Korda's *The Private Life of Henry VIII*
- British Film Institute established
- Kenneth Clark is appointed head of the National Gallery
- Books published this year include *Down and Out in Paris and London* by George Orwell, *Love on the Dole* by Walter Greenwood and *Testament of Youth* by Vera Brittain
- The Duke Ellington jazz orchestra makes its first tour of Britain
- Sales of the *Daily Express* newspaper top 2 million a day
- Songs of the year are "Stormy Weather" and "Smoke Gets in Your Eyes"

JANUARY
- Death of novelist John Galsworthy

FEBRUARY
- Oxford students declare they will not fight "for king and country"

OXFORD WON'T FIGHT "FOR KING AND COUNTRY"

On February 9, 1933, students at the Oxford Union, the prestigious university's debating forum, passed by a majority of 275 to 153 a motion stating that "This House will under no circumstances fight for King and Country." The vote caused a sensation, for it suggested that the elite of the younger generation had abandoned patriotism and converted to pacifism.

The controversial debate came at an important turning point in international affairs, less than a fortnight after Nazi Party leader Adolf Hitler had been appointed head of the German government. Trouble was also brewing in the Far East, where Japan had invaded Manchuria in 1931. The British government was torn between preparing to respond to German and Japanese militarism and international disarmament.

Public opinion in general, like the opinion held by the Oxford undergraduates, was clearly strongly opposed to war. Britain was a sincere participant in the world disarmament conference that had opened in February 1932. At the same time, the government was aware that war might best be avoided by building up armaments to deter aggression. This was the view for which Winston Churchill, now a backbench Tory MP, would become the leading spokesman through the 1930s.

In October 1933 Hitler pulled Germany out of the disarmament conference and the League of Nations. The British government announced the strengthening of the armed forces, although the actual scale of the build-up was to be quite small. At the same time, a Labour candidate, John Wilmot, who campaigned strongly for Britain to take the lead in "general disarmament", carried off a stunning by-election victory at

▲ Hitler and Goebbels are saluted by Nazi followers in Berlin; pacifist feeling in Britain ran high, as shown by the Oxford debate.

East Fulham, winning by almost 5,000 votes in a constituency the government had previously held with a majority of 14,000.

There is no evidence that – as was later asserted – the Oxford vote encouraged Hitler by making him believe the British had lost the will to fight. But evidence of pacifist feeling, such as the Oxford debate and the East Fulham by-election, did weaken the government's will to rearm in the face of mounting international danger.

THE "BODYLINE" TOUR

The English have a long tradition of dismissing unsporting behaviour as "simply not cricket". Unfortunately, the good name of cricket itself, the very embodiment of all that is gentlemanly and honourable was dragged through the mud in January by the touring English team, who disgraced themselves with their behaviour on the field in Australia during a series of Test matches. A cable sent to the MCC by the Australian Cricket Board of Control complained of unsportsmanlike behaviour on the part of the English team, who had been applying a technique known as "bodyline" bowling – with the frighteningly quick Harold Larwood the chief exponent – to the formerly genteel game of cricket. The technique was developed essentially to intimidate the Australian batsman by bowling short-pitched deliveries at his body with a ring of close fielders on the leg side ready to catch the ball. However controversial bodyline proved – one English bowler refused to embrace the tactics – it helped England win the Ashes four Tests to one.

▲ Australian batsman H M Woodful ducks to avoid another delivery by Harold "The Wrecker" Larwood. In spite of the presence of the great Don Bradman, Australia lost the Ashes.

LONDON ECONOMIC SUMMIT FAILS

On July 23, 1933, a World Monetary and Economic Conference that had been convened in London to try to confront the problems of the Depression was abandoned with nothing achieved. The delegates of 66 nations had failed to reach agreement on any significant issue.

The slump in industrial and agricultural production and the rise of mass unemployment since 1929 had brought out the worst in a world of nation states which lacked any sense of common purpose or shared interests. Like the rest, Britain had ended up by adopting protectionism – that is, imposing heavy tariffs on imported goods – and by allowing its currency to devalue. These were "beggar-my-neighbour" policies, which could only benefit one nation's economy at the expense of the others. Because all countries did the same, all suffered from a downward spiral of trade. Between 1929 and 1933, world trade declined by 60 per cent – a disaster for Britain's dockers, merchant seamen and ship builders.

▲ **Delegates attending the economic summit in London which sought to stabilize Europe's financial position.**

The aim of the World Economic Conference was to negotiate a return to international cooperation based on stable exchange rates and relatively free trade. The US Secretary of State Cordell Hull spoke of achieving an end to "wild competition" between states that was a menace to "peace and commerce". But mutual suspicions between countries were far too strong to be overcome. After much futile bickering, the Conference was effectively ended by a telegram from the new US President Franklin D Roosevelt, in which he made it clear that he had no intention of returning the dollar to a fixed rate against gold. As a result of the failure to achieve international cooperation, the "global economy" of classic capitalism effectively ceased to exist.

HENRY VIII LEADS UK FILM REVIVAL

The British film industry fought back against Hollywood domination in 1933 when *The Private Life of Henry VIII* proved a popular success both in the United States and the UK. Directed and produced by Hungarian immigrant Alexander Korda, the film starred Charles Laughton in a gross and supercilious impersonation of the famous Tudor monarch.

Korda's London Films was the must successful British production company of the 1930s, both commercially and artistically. Michael Balcon, head of Gainsborough Pictures and Gaumont-British, was another producer who waved the flag for Britain, especially through backing the young Alfred Hitchock to make movies such as *The Thirty-Nine Steps* and *The Man Who Knew Too Much*.

Another area of outstanding achievement in the 1930s was British documentary filmmaking. John Grierson, first as head of the Empire Marketing Board Film Unit and then with GPO backing, put Britain among the world leaders in this genre. Documentaries such as *Song of Ceylon* (1934) and *Night Mail* (1936) have rarely, if ever, been surpassed.

▶ **Charles Laughton portrays the famous Tudor monarch in the popular British film *The Private Life of Henry VIII*.**

1934 DIVIDED BRITAIN – CLOTH CAPS AND COSMETICS

▲ For many communities the 1930s was a period of extreme poverty and unveiled misery; here a family is forcibly evicted from their home.

▲ The vanguard of a long line of unemployed and hunger marchers at a mass demonstration in Hyde Park, London.

In 1934, author J B Priestley published an *English Journey*, a record of his observations while travelling around the country the previous autumn. Many of the areas he visited matched the cliché of 1930s Britain as a place of unemployed men in cloth caps hanging about the streets of derelict boarded-up towns. But Priestley also identified another country altogether: "the England of arterial and by-pass roads, of filling stations and factories that look like exhibition buildings, of giant cinemas and dance-halls and cafés, bungalows with tiny garages, cocktail bars, Woolworths, motor-coaches, wireless, hiking, factory girls looking like actresses…"

The truth is that, if for many communities in Britain the 1930s was a decade of unrelieved misery, for far more people it was a time of rising prosperity and widening horizons. To a large degree, this depended on where you lived. In the industrial and mining zones of northern England, south Wales, Northern Ireland and Scotland, the impact of economic decline was grim in the 1920s and worse in the decade that followed. Many towns or regions had once thrived around a single industry – ship building, textiles, coal mining, iron and steel. When these industries declined irreversibly, whole communities were impoverished, with unemployment rates in the worst-hit areas at times reaching 70 per cent.

Because of the National Insurance scheme introduced in 1911 and extended after the First World War, unemployment meant life on the "dole". In return for "signing on" as available for work at a labour exchange, a jobless worker received roughly one-third of the average wage. Even this might be taken away after 26 weeks of unemployment, when a "means test" came into play and benefit was only given on proof of desperate poverty.

Although unemployment was particularly demoralizing, it was far from the sole cause of poverty. Wages in some jobs were actually lower than the dole – both agricultural labourers and workers in sweatshops in London's East End were notoriously badly paid.

Poverty manifested itself in diseases such as rickets and tuberculosis, caused by poor nutrition and unsanitary housing. Social investigators such as George Orwell, author of *The Road to Wigan Pier*, found people existing on a diet of bread,

▲ While for many the 1930s was a time of crippling poverty, for others it was a time of rising prosperity, as this new Art Deco cinema in London suggests.

▲ Industries such as those producing electrical consumer goods boomed in the 1930s, while older industries collapsed.

potatoes, tea and jam, and living in dark, damp, cramped accommodation.

Yet even at its worst, poverty was rarely as bad as it had been in the Edwardian era. An unemployed man on the dole in the 1930s was probably as well-off as his father would have been in work in the prewar period. Like the rest of the population, the poor benefited from the paradoxical advantage of a depressed world economy: prices were low and tended to fall. If an individual could get hold of any money at all, life's necessities and small luxuries came remarkably cheap.

The explosion of leisure activities between the wars embraced rich and poor alike. Bolton, a largely working-class northern town with a population of 260,000, boasted 14 cinemas. A survey of young unemployed men showed that four out of five went to see a film at least once a week. Dance-halls were equally popular and accessible at a price almost all could afford. Thanks to cheap clothes and cosmetics provided by rapidly expanding chains of department stores – Woolworths, Marks & Spencer, Boots – young working-class people could dress for an evening out in a fair imitation of real style. As Orwell wrote: "... for two pounds ten on

the hire-purchase a youth can buy himself a suit which, for a little while and at a little distance, looks as though it had been tailored in Savile Row. The girl can look like a fashion plate at an even lower price."

These developments took place throughout Britain, but were most keenly felt in areas which experienced economic growth rather than recession in the 1930s. In the Midlands and a strip of southern England from London to Bristol, industries such as car manufacture, aircraft building and the production of electrical consumer goods – radios, vacuum cleaners, irons – boomed while the older industries went bust. These new industries were housed in clean, light factories sparkling with plate glass and chrome, seemingly a world away from the smoke-blackened mills of the industrial past. They paid good enough wages to give their workers a chance of a truly comfortable existence.

For the middle classes and the more prosperous sections of the working class, a good life was available on the cheap. There was a boom in building of both council houses and private housing. With around 300,000 new homes a year coming on the market, prices were low. A £25 deposit was sufficient to secure a pebble-dashed suburban semi on easy repayment terms. Not surprisingly, such offers were snapped up. The 1930s set the British on the road to becoming a nation of owner-occupiers. These new homes would almost certainly be connected to the electricity grid, which was ending the era of gas and oil lighting. There would be a radio for home entertainment, a Hoover for cleaning, and a daily newspaper by the armchair – 10 million daily newspapers were sold in the 1930s, more than double the circulation 20 years earlier.

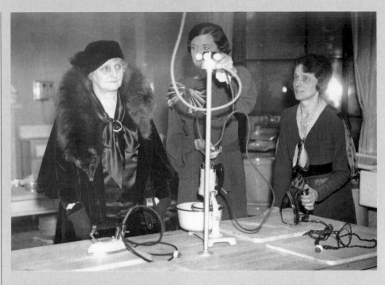

▲ Electrical goods such as irons became widely available, but they were still considered luxury items in a nation divided by poverty.

One of the keys to this real if modest prosperity was the fall in the size of families. The overwhelming majority of couples had three children or less, a significant change from the large broods of the Edwardian period, when families with five children were commonplace. Married women as a result were healthier, had more spare time, and kept their looks better. Among the significant growth areas of the period were women's magazines and hairdressers.

The problems of poverty and unemployment were a major preoccupation of the 1930s, attracting the attention of the government and local authorities, radical politicians of both left and right persuasions, journalists and photographers. But the direction the future would take was clearly visible in the neon sign on the local Odeon, the leafy streets of the newly-built suburban sprawl, and the cut-price luxury of the Woolworths cosmetics counter.

▲ Wide streets of middle class suburban houses constructed at Ilford in Greater London.

1934

- Road deaths for the year total 7,300
- The Road Traffic Act imposes a 30 mph limit in built-up areas and introduces pedestrian crossings
- The Mersey road tunnel opens between Liverpool and Birkenhead
- The first season of opera is staged at Glyndebourne, Sussex
- Women tennis players at Wimbledon are permitted to wear shorts
- Books published this year include *I, Claudius* by Robert Graves, *A Handful of Dust* by Evelyn Waugh and *An English Journey* by J B Priestley
- British films this year include Alexander Korda's *The Scarlet Pimpernel*, Basil Wright's documentary *Song of Ceylon* and Alfred Hitchcock's thriller *The Man Who Knew Too Much*
- Labour politician Arthur Henderson is awarded the Nobel Peace Prize for his work in promoting disarmament

JANUARY
- Sir Oswald Mosley calls for a fascist uprising in Britain

FEBRUARY
- Death of composer Sir Edward Elgar

APRIL
- Gandhi suspends the civil disobedience campaign in India

DEATH OF SIR EDWARD ELGAR

Sir Edward Elgar, widely regarded as the greatest British composer since Purcell, died on February 23, 1934.

Born in a Worcestershire village in 1857, Elgar was to find inspiration for most of his best music in a sensitive response to the changing moods of the English countryside. He was a self-taught musician who for many years scraped a precarious living – for a time he was employed as bandmaster at a lunatic asylum.

In 1899 the first performance of his *Enigma Variations* brought him fame and fortune, confirmed by the success of his *Pomp and Circumstance Marches* in 1901. One of these he unwisely allowed to be set to words and turned into the enduring patriotic song "Land of Hope and Glory". In the context of Edwardian England, it was inevitable that Elgar would be celebrated as Britain's answer to the traditionally dominant German and Austrian composers. His *First Symphony* was performed over 100 times in the year after its first appearance in 1908, carrying Elgar to the peak of his renown.

The experience of the First World War darkened Elgar's personal mood and destroyed his music's fashionable appeal. As opinion turned against jingoistic patriotism, he was unfairly dismissed as the pompous composer of "Hope and Glory". Elgar expressed his own reaction to the war in the sombre,

▲ Edward Elgar composing in his later years. He will for ever be associated with the patriotic song "Land of Hope and Glory".

agonized *Cello Concerto*, his last important work.

Elgar once described the joyful ease he found in composing: "There is music in the air, music all around us, the world is full of it and you simply take as much as you require." But after the death of his wife in 1920, his mighty talent fell silent.

MOSLEY FASCISTS FIGHT FOR POWER

On June 7, 1934, fighting broke out at Olympia in London, where Sir Oswald Mosley was addressing a meeting of his British Union of Fascists (BUF). Mosley's blackshirted bodyguards

▲ Training a nation of warriors. Under Mussolini's guidance, a regiment of young, rifle-carrying Italian fascists provide a public display of their enthusiasm as they march through the streets of Rome.

ejected hecklers with excessive violence and battled with left-wing and Jewish antifascist protestors in the streets outside.

A well-connected aristocrat and war veteran, Mosley had been a Conservative MP and then a minister in the Labour government, before setting up his own party in 1931. Violence was an essential element of the BUF's political style, which Mosley modelled on Mussolini's Italian fascists and the German Nazi Party. His aim was to establish a dictatorship which would use emergency powers to solve Britain's economic and social problems. This would incidentally involve driving Jews out of public life.

Mosley had the support of Lord Rothermere's *Daily Mail* and of many right-wing Conservatives.

▲ The founder of the British Union of Fascists, Sir Oswald Mosley, addresses a fascist rally in London.

BUF membership never exceeded 20,000, however, and it had no chance of electoral success. Mosley therefore concentrated on public demonstrations designed to provoke conflict with his political opponents. He hoped that mounting disorder would fuel calls for strong leadership, giving him the chance to step forward as the man who could do the job.

In fact, instead of proving itself the force of the future, the BUF lost impetus after 1934. Mosley was far too closely identified with the Nazis – Hitler was a guest at his wedding – to attract widespread popular support. In 1936 the government attacked the fascist movement by banning political uniforms after a BUF incursion into the predominantly Jewish East End resulted in the famous "Battle of Cable Street". Mosley's party caused little trouble after that.

Mosley was arrested along with other Nazi sympathizers in 1940. He was released three years later on health grounds and returned to active right-wing politics in the 1950s. He died in 1980.

SUMMER OF SPORTING SUCCESS

▲ Henry Cotton on his way to vistory at the British Open championship at Royal St George's, Sandwich.

The Wimbledon tournament of July 1934 brought double success to British tennis, with victories for Fred Perry in the men's singles and Dorothy Round in the women's singles. Perry's victory in the final – in straight sets over Australian Jack Crawford – ended a period of 25 years since the last Englishman had won the title. Round, who had been the defeated finalist the previous year, also won the women's doubles with Ryuki Miki.

These Wimbledon successes followed the victory of golfer Henry Cotton in the British Open championship at Royal St George's, Sandwich, the previous month. He was the first British golfer to take the trophy in 11 years. Cotton entered the last day of the championship with a record 10-shot lead, which was fortunate as a stomach upset ruined his last round. Despite recording a poor 79, he fought through to win by a five-stroke margin.

England's cricketers failed to make it a hat-trick of sporting successes, allowing the Australian tourists to regain the Ashes after the traumas of the previous year's Bodyline series. Once again, Don Bradman was England's undoing, scoring 304 and 244 in consecutive innings. Australia won the final Test match at the Oval by a resounding 562 runs to take the series 2–1.

MOUNT EVEREST CLAIMS ANOTHER VICTIM

Hopes of a successful ascent of Mount Everest were dashed on July 19 when mountaineer Maurice Wilson died during a solo attempt to reach the peak. Wilson was not the first climber to die on Everest nor was he to be the last. To many climbers, Mount Everest, was the Holy Grail of their sport and represented the pinnacle, in every sense, of achievement within their field.

The mountain forms part of the Great Himalayan Range in Asia, and at 8,848 m (29,028 ft), the peak of Everest is the highest point on Earth, reaching two-thirds of the way up through the Earth's atmosphere. Lack of oxygen at this altitude, combined with powerful winds and extremely low temperatures found on the upper slopes of Everest defeated many early climbers, including British mountaineering legend George Mallory.

Many believe that Mallory reached the summit in June 1924 before dying on the descent. He was last seen by colleagues close to the summit and "going strongly". His body, well preserved by ice, was found in 1999.

▲ Lost on the slopes of Everest, British climber Maurice Wilson failed to tame the world's highest peak. This feat would continue to elude adventurers until 1953.

- The Peace Pledge Union agitates against rearmament
- A mandatory driving test is introduced
- The British government announces plans to expand the RAF three-fold in the next two years
- The Hawker Hurricane monoplane fighter makes its maiden flight
- First practical aircraft detection radar developed
- The restriction of Ribbon Development Act attempts to stop burgeoning suburbs encroaching on the countryside
- "Cat's eyes" glass reflectors come into use as an aid to night driving
- British films of the year include Alfred Hitchcock's *The Thirty-Nine Steps*
- First performances of T S Eliot's *Murder in the Cathedral* and Emlyn Williams's *Night Must Fall*
- Books published this year include *Mr Norris Changes Train* by Christopher Isherwood and *The Seven Pillars of Wisdom* by T E Lawrence
- Sidney and Beatrice Webb give a glowing account of life in Stalin's Russia in *Soviet Communism: A New Civilization?*
- Publisher Victor Gollancz establishes the Left Book Club; Allen Lane launches Penguin Books
- Songs of the year include "Cheek to Cheek" and "Red Sails in the Sunset"

BRITAIN CELEBRATES SILVER JUBILEE

▲ **Thousands line the streets to cheer the royal procession as it makes its way through London for the Silver Jubilee celebrations.**

On May 6, 1935, George V and Queen Mary celebrated a quarter of a century on the throne with a service at St Paul's Cathedral. Thousands lined the streets to cheer the royal procession through London, which was enlivened by the antics of a stray mongrel that insisted on accompanying the royal carriage, defeating all efforts by the military guard to drive him off.

The declaration of a Silver Jubilee had been a calculated move by the government to stimulate loyalty and patriotism. Celebratory street parties were held across the country in a somewhat surprising show of popular enthusiasm for a dutiful but unbending monarch who had made little effort to ingratiate himself with his people. His subjects may have remembered his frequent visits to wounded soldiers during the First World War, or perhaps they felt a closer link to the sovereign since hearing him address them on the radio at Christmas, a tradition begun in 1932.

George V was already in poor health, his lungs affected by life-long smoking, and he survived the Jubilee by only eight months. His later years were darkened by regret at the behaviour of his elder son, the Prince of Wales, of whose affairs with married women he deeply disapproved. Shortly before his demise, the king made the startlingly accurate prophecy: "After I am dead, the boy will ruin himself in 12 months."

BALDWIN BACK TO FACE INTERNATIONAL CRISIS

On June 7, 1935, Conservative leader Stanley Baldwin began his third term of office as Prime Minister, taking over from Ramsay MacDonald. It was failing health that caused MacDonald to step down, but his authority as leader of the National Government was in any case fading. Despite the presence of National Labour and National Liberal members, the government was a Conservative administration in all but name, supported by a Conservative majority in the House of Commons.

The most pressing issue confronting Baldwin was defence. As militarist dictatorships in Nazi Germany and fascist Italy flexed their muscles, Britain was torn between disarmament or rearmament, support for the "collective security" of the League of Nations or traditional reliance

▲ **Stanley Baldwin poses for an official portrait after his return to power following the resignation of Ramsay MacDonald.**

on its own armed forces. Matters came to a head in the autumn of 1935 when Mussolini sent Italian forces to attack Abyssinia, a League of Nations member. According to the principle of collective security, Britain and other the members of the League were duty-bound to come to Abyssinia's defence. They denounced Italy as an aggressor and imposed economic sanctions, but took no military action.

In the midst of the crisis, Baldwin called a general election. The Labour Party campaigned against rearmament, while denouncing the government for not taking strong enough action against the Italian fascists. Baldwin promised to strengthen Britain's defences, while simultaneously reassuring voters that rearmament would be limited and there would be no war. In the vote on November 14, the electorate gave Baldwin a resounding mandate. The Conservatives attracted 11.1 million votes to Labour's 7.9 million, which translated into an overwhelming Tory majority in the Commons.

Baldwin was fortunate that the election was over by the time the Abyssinian affair reached its inglorious climax. In December Foreign Secretary Sir Samuel Hoare stitched together a deal, in conjunction with French Prime Minister Pierre Laval, that would give Italy the most fertile parts of Abyssinia but leave the country's emperor, Haile Selassie, on his throne. When the deal was announced, there was an outcry over this craven surrender to aggression. Hoare was forced to resign, his place taken by the relatively young Anthony Eden. Italy conquered Abyssinia the following year, driving Haile Selassie into exile in south London. With the policy of collective security in tatters, the Baldwin government found itself reluctantly committed to large-scale rearmament.

PENGUIN STARTS READING REVOLUTION

In the summer of 1935, the first Penguin paperback books appeared in their distinctive colours: green for crime, orange for fiction and blue for biography. They were the brainchild of publishing executive Allen Lane. Taking a train from Exeter to London, he was struck by the absence of any decent reading to be had at the station bookstall. He decided that Britain needed cheap editions of contemporary writing, to be sold at railway stations and chain stores, as well as by traditional bookshops.

The original Penguins were priced at sixpence – the cost of a packet of cigarettes. In 1936, Lane's new company sold over 3 million books, forcing other publishers to begin developing their own paperback lists. Previously, readers had mostly

accessed contemporary writing by borrowing hardbacks from subscription lending libraries. Now the spines of Penguins in their uniform colours lined up on their bookshelves.

Lane's project was based on his belief "in the existence in this country of a vast reading public for intelligent books at a low price". His success proved that such a public really did exist.

◀ **The new Penguin paperbacks fed a British public hungry for intelligent reading material at affordable prices.**

HITCHCOCK MASTER OF SUSPENSE IN THIRTY-NINE STEPS

In 1935 the resurgence of the British film industry was confirmed by the success of a new gripping thriller, *The Thirty-Nine Steps*, directed by Alfred Hitchcock. The movie was a product of Gaumont-British, under production director Michael Balcon, which was vying with Alexander Korda's London Films for recognition as Britain's top film production company.

It was Balcon who had given Hitchcock his first opportunity to direct movies in the 1920s. With *Blackmail* in 1929 – generally considered the first British-made full-length sound picture – Hitchcock had shown his talent for suspense, but for the next few years his career had drifted. Then, in 1934, he directed the box-office hit thriller *The Man Who Knew Too Much*. *The Thirty-Nine Steps*, a free adaptation of a spy novel by John Buchan, was even more successful with the public and critics, offering a delightful if implausible mix of nail-biting suspense and romantic comedy.

Hitchcock continued to work in Britain until 1939, when he made what was perhaps an inevitable move to the bigger stage of Hollywood.

▲ **Actors Robert Donat and Madeleine Carroll are directed by Alfred Hitchcock on the set of *The Thirty-Nine Steps*.**

JANUARY
• A housing Bill is introduced to limit overcrowding in accommodation

FEBRUARY
• Parliament passes a bill allowing for a degree of Home Rule in India
• Jack Hobbs retires from first-class cricket aged 53

MARCH
• A civil service White Paper advocates full-scale rearmament and the abandonment of reliance on collective security
• Britain protests as Nazi Germany renounces the disarmament clauses of the Versailles Treaty and introduces conscription

APRIL
• After a meeting at Stresa, Prime Ministers of Britain, France and Italy agree on joint action to oppose German rearmament
• Sheffield Wednesday win the FA Cup, defeating West Bromwich Albion 4–2

MAY
• George V celebrates his Silver Jubilee
• Arsenal are Football League champions for the third consecutive season
• Death of T E Lawrence, known as Lawrence of Arabia

1935

THE INVENTION OF RADAR

▲ The development and testing of radar, vital to Britain's defence strategy, took place under conditions of the greatest secrecy.

Perhaps the most vital invention to emerge during 1935, certainly as far as the British were concerned, was radar (an acronym for Radio Detection And Ranging). Although the principle of radar was understood back in the late nineteenth century, and radar systems were developed independently by the French, Germans and Americans, it is two British scientists working at the National Physical Laboratory, Robert Watson-Watt and A F Wilkins, who are credited with having first put the idea to practical use. Having learnt that passing aircraft could cause distortion to the reception of radio signals, the two men went to work on finding ways of locating aeroplanes using radio waves. Watson-Watt's earlier work as a meteorologist, during which he spent his time trying to create devices that could be used to warn of approaching thunderstorms, led him to apply a similar approach to finding aeroplanes.

Towards the end of 1935, the two men had developed a technique of firing radio waves at possible targets and then measuring the amount of time it took for the radio waves to bounce back. The time lapse between the outgoing and incoming signal was then measured and used to calculate the distance of the aircraft from the radio emitter. By the end of the year, their system was capable of locating aircraft up to 112 km (70 miles) away.

The work of Watson-Watt and Wilkins was used to develop the world's first practical radar defence system. This proved to be a vital weapon during the Battle of Britain, giving prior warning of German attacks from the air and enabling British fighter crews to become airborne before the enemy's aircraft had even reached the British coast. Robert Watson-Watt was knighted for his work in 1942.

LAWRENCE OF ARABIA DIES

May 19, 1935, saw the death of T E Lawrence, the man who wrote *The Seven Pillars of Wisdom* and who was more famously known in life and death as Lawrence of Arabia. A brilliant scholar, outstanding soldier and undoubtedly one of the bravest men to serve in the Middle East during the First World War, Thomas Edward Lawrence was the second of five sons born to Sir Thomas Chapman and Sara Maden. Lawrence's father had left his wife and two daughters in Ireland in order to set up home with Sara Maden, the children's governess. The new family eventually moved to Oxford, where they assumed the family name of Lawrence.

After graduating from Oxford University with a first class honours degree in history, Lawrence was recruited by British intelligence and sent

▲ **A brave and eccentric military genius, T E Lawrence was shunned by the establishment after refusing to accept honours from King George V.**

on a map-making expedition to north Sinai, on the border with Turkey. At the start of the First World War Lawrence was based in Cairo, where he continued to carry on with his intelligence duties. He soon became frustrated at the lack of progress being made against Turkey, Germany's ally in the region, and managed to persuade his superiors to let him set up a guerrilla force using Arabian tribesmen.

Lawrence's guerrillas proved to be remarkably effective, playing a key role in the Allied advance towards Jerusalem. Captured in November 1917, Lawrence was the victim of several severe homosexual assaults by Turkish troops before he was able to make his escape. The experience left him a changed man. During a reception with George V near the end of the war, Lawrence offended the monarch by refusing to accept the Order of the Bath and the DSO, thus cutting himself off from much of the British society that he had come to despise. In later life his behaviour appeared to become increasingly eccentric. Lawrence died as a result of a motorcycle accident that occurred on May 13.

CAMPBELL ZOOMS INTO THE RECORD BOOKS

The British driver Sir Malcolm Campbell caused a stir in Utah when he smashed the 483 km/h (300 mph) land speed barrier in *Bluebird*, his superfast, custom-built racing car. On September 3 Campbell revved up his vehicle and set off down the Bonneville Salt Flats in near-perfect conditions for an attempt on the land speed record. No one before Campbell had made a successful attempt on the 300 mph record under test conditions; Campbell and *Bluebird* were officially timed over the measured distance at precisely 584.85 km/h (301.337 mph).

Campbell first acquired a taste for speed while serving as a pilot in the Royal Flying Corps during the First World War. From flying he went into motor racing and in 1924 he achieved a very impressive 146.16 mph (235.17 km/h) in the first version of *Bluebird*. All of Malcolm Campbell's land speed cars and later hydroplanes were named *Bluebird*, after the play *L'Oiseau Bleu* by Belgian playwright Maurice Maeterlinck. Campbell eventually went on to establish land speed records on a further nine separate occasions up to 1935.

Having cracked the 300 mph barrier, Campbell set his sights on the world water speed record. In 1937 he took his hydroplane up to 208.36 km/h (129.5 mph), setting a new record. He managed to exceed this speed in 1938 and on August 19, 1939, Campbell set a world water speed record of 228 km/h (141.74 mph), which he still held at his death in 1948. Campbell's son, Donald, followed in his father's wake, setting records for speed on both land and water. He died in an attempt on the water speed record on Coniston Water in England in 1967.

▲ *Bluebird*, driven by Malcolm Campbell, was the first land vehicle to achieve a speed of 300 mph (483 km/h). The car became one of the great icons of the Art Deco era.

- A Midwives Act provides for the creation of a national system of salaried midwives
- The Supermarine Spitfire and the Wellington bomber make their maiden flights
- The number of cars on British roads exceeds 2.5 million
- London Transport begins phasing out trams, to be replaced by trolley-buses
- Gatwick airport opens in Sussex
- First Butlins holiday camp opens
- The BBC begins regular television broadcasts
- The telephone "speaking clock" service is introduced
- Pinewood film studios open in Buckinghamshire
- John Maynard Keynes's *General Theory of Employment, Interest and Money* advocates higher government spending to overcome unemployment
- Books published this year include *Eyeless in Gaza* by Aldous Huxley and *A Gun for Sale* by Graham Greene
- First performance of W H Auden's and Christopher Isherwood's *The Dog Beneath the Skin*
- Dame Laura Knight is the first woman artist appointed to the Royal Academy
- Alex Korda's film *Things To Come*, based on a novel by H G Wells, predicts the destruction of cities in an air war
- The documentary film *Night Mail* by John Grierson's GPO Film Unit has verse by W H Auden and music by Benjamin Britten

QUEEN MARY TAKES TO THE OCEAN

On May 27, 1936, the luxurious Cunard liner *Queen Mary* set sail from Southampton on its inaugural transatlantic voyage. Through the troubled history of its construction, the ship had become a potent symbol of triumph over the economic Depression of the 1930s.

Work on *Queen Mary* began at the John Brown shipyard in Clydebank in 1930, in an area already suffering from high unemployment. The bulk of the ship's hull was already towering impressively over the surrounding streets in December 1931, when construction had to be halted. Hard-hit by the recession, Cunard had run out of money. The laying-off of workers from the shipyard was a catastrophe for the local economy.

The ship was saved by a government-brokered deal in 1933. Cunard and the White Star Line – historic rivals – were

▲ The Cunard ocean liner *Queen Mary* sets sail from Southampton on her inaugural transatlantic voyage.

induced to merge by the offer of a government subsidy of £9.5 million, to be used to complete *Queen Mary* and build a sister ship, *Queen Elizabeth*. When work restarted in April 1934, Clydebank was hung with flags and pipers escorted the workforce back to the shipyard.

Carrying around 2,000 passengers at a cruising speed of 55.2 km/h (28.5 knots), *Queen Mary* was a worthy rival to the great French ship *Normandie* in the last golden age of the transatlantic liners. Transformed into a troop ship during the Second World War, it then resumed passenger service until its retirement in 1967. *Queen Mary* now serves as a tourist attraction in Long Beach, California.

BRITISH VOLUNTEERS FIGHT IN SPAIN

On July 17, 1936, Spanish generals, including General Francisco Franco, led a military revolt against their country's left-wing republican government. This precipitated a civil war that would last until 1939. Fascist Italy and Nazi Germany gave military support to the rebels with arms, aircraft, troops and pilots. The Soviet Union – somewhat later – provided military aid to the Republic. But Britain and France, above all intent on avoiding a widening of the conflict, adopted an impotent stance of "nonintervention".

Although the British government kept out of the Spanish Civil War, British public opinion was passionately involved, either for or against the Republic. Whereas

▲ Volunteer soldiers from the British Battalion of the Fifteenth International Brigade who fought for the republican cause.

right-wing newspapers horrified their readers with tales of church burnings and the rape of nuns by Spanish communists and anarchists, the British left denounced the atrocities of Franco's forces and called on the government to support the struggle against fascism with "arms for Spain".

An adventurous minority of Britons chose to risk their lives for their beliefs by volunteering to fight in the civil war. A small number fought for Franco, but a much larger contingent joined the republican side as part of the International Brigades. Organized by the communists, the Brigades were staffed by left-wing volunteers from all over Europe and North America. Of the more than 2,000 British volunteers, most were young working-class men and women, although a fair number of British intellectuals and artists took part in the fighting, including writer George Orwell and poet John Cornford.

Smuggled over the Pyrenees to beat the Anglo-French blockade imposed in the name of nonintervention, the International Brigade volunteers saw their first action in the heroic defence of Madrid in the autumn and winter of 1936. Cornford was among those killed in these desperate early encounters. Formed into the British Battalion of the Fifteenth International Brigade, the volunteers continued in action until September 1938, by which time around 500 had been killed and over a thousand seriously wounded. With the Republic facing certain defeat, the remnant was disbanded.

Historians reflecting upon the Spanish Civil War with the benefit of hindsight have argued that it was never a clear-cut fight against "fascism" – too many complex local issues were involved. Nor were the moral issues ever straightforward. After all, the International Brigades were organized by the Soviet-controlled Comintern at a time when Soviet dictator Joseph Stalin was massacring or imprisoning millions of his own people in a reign of terror. But nothing can detract from the honest idealism of those young volunteers who were prepared to die for a cause they believed to be just.

JARROW CRUSADE FOR JOBS

On October 5, 1936, some 200 jobless men from the Tyneside town of Jarrow, which had a long-term unemployment rate above 70 per cent, set off on a march to London. Led by local Labour MP Ellen Wilkinson, they intended to present a petition to parliament, in the hope of bringing new life to a town that had been "murdered" by the closure of local shipyards.

The Jarrow Crusade – as it was called on some of the marchers' banners – was in fact one of the smallest "hunger marches" of the period. But it received far more sympathetic treatment from the press and politicians, because it had been organized by highly respectable Labour and Conservative members of the town council. The Jarrow marchers shunned any connection with much larger marches run by the communist-led National Union of Unemployed Workers, which took place at the same time.

▲ **Men from Jarrow march to London in protest at long-term unemployment caused by the closure of local shipyards.**

The progress of the Jarrow marchers along the 450-km (280-mile) route was extensively covered by newspaper photographers and newsreel cameramen. The stages of the march were widely publicized in advance and crowds turned out to applaud the gallant contingent along the way. The marchers reached London on October 31 in pouring rain, to a warm and respectful reception.

Wilkinson presented their petition to parliament, but Prime Minister Stanley Baldwin, ignoring the obvious media benefits of a hypocritical display of public sympathy, refused to meet them.

For all their efforts, the Jarrow marchers achieved nothing but a place in the history books, where the name of their town is engraved for ever as a symbol of mass unemployment.

1936

THE BATTLE OF CABLE STREET

▲ A crowd of demonstrators flees as police break down a barricade in Cable Street during the protest against Oswald Mosley's BUF march.

On October 4, 1936, Oswald Mosley's British Union of Fascists (BUF) planned a march through Stepney in the East End of London. This was a deliberate provocation by the anti-Semitic BUF, since the area had a large Jewish population. Despite a petition signed by around 100,000 local residents, the government refused to ban the march. As a legal political demonstration, it was accorded a police escort.

Various antifascist groups, including Jews, communists and socialists, were determined to stop the march at any cost. Some 3,000 of Mosley's blackshirted followers participated in the march, with almost twice that number of police trying to clear the streets ahead of them. Soon, running fights broke out between police and thousands of antifascist demonstrators. At Cable Street the antifascists improvised barricades and successfully defended them by hurling missiles at the police. There were casualties on both sides. Eventually, the Police Commissioner decided that the march must be abandoned and the blackshirts were obliged to disperse.

Celebrated as a triumph by the antifascists, the riots provoked the government into long-overdue action to stop the BUF's incitement of disorder. The Public Order Act, rushed through parliament, banned the wearing of political uniforms and gave police greater powers to ban demonstrations that might lead to violence. Mosley's campaign never regained its momentum after this humiliating setback.

FIRE DESTROYS THE CRYSTAL PALACE

On the night of November 30, 1936, the Crystal Palace, one of London's most famous landmarks, was destroyed by fire. The conflagration, which broke out shortly after 8 pm, was one of the most spectacular ever witnessed in peacetime. Tens of thousands of Londoners packed buses, trains and cars in an effort to take a closer look at the blaze, which lit up the night sky for many miles around.

Designed by Joseph Paxton, a gardener by trade, the Crystal Palace was originally put up in Hyde Park for the Great Exhibition of 1851. Its revolutionary prefabricated glass and iron structure made such an impression on the British public that in 1854 it was reconstructed in Sydenham, south London, by popular demand. By the 1930s the building had fallen out of fashion and into a degree of disrepair. Used as a naval barracks during the First World War, in 1920 it had become the first home of the Imperial War Museum.

Despite the efforts of more than 500 fire-fighters, nothing was left of the building by the morning but a tangle of twisted metal and shattered glass. Today all that remains to recall the Crystal Palace's original splendour is a collection of somewhat fanciful Victorian life-size models of dinosaurs in the surrounding park.

▲ A view of the still-smoking ruins of Crystal Palace after it was raised to the ground despite the efforts of hundreds of fire-fighters.

EDWARD VIII PUTS LOVE BEFORE DUTY

On December 3, 1936, Britain's national newspapers revealed that Edward VIII wished to marry a twice-divorced American, Mrs Wallis Simpson. Although the rest of the world had been fully informed about the couple's blossoming relationship, *Daily Express* owner Lord Beaverbrook had marshalled the Fleet Street press into a conspiracy of silence on the issue, as a personal favour to the king. Once the situation became public knowledge, events proceeded with great speed towards the king's abdication.

Edward VII had succeeded to the throne in January 1936 on the death of his father, George V. He promised to be a popular monarch, possessing a glamour and charisma that his father had lacked. Some, on the other hand, thought him too inclined to interfere in political matters. His public statement, on a visit to the Welsh coalfields, that "something must be done" about unemployment was resented by the government, which felt a constitutional monarch had no business expressing views on such a sensitive topic.

Edward had met Mrs Simpson in 1931, while he was still Prince of Wales. Frequent meetings over a period of years had led eventually to love. In October 1936 Mrs Simpson divorced her second husband in preparation for marrying Edward. The king's love affair with Mrs Simpson had not been regarded as a serious issue, but when he made it clear in private that he intended to marry her, Britain was plunged into a constitutional crisis. Edward was head of the Church of England, which was firmly against divorce.

▲ **Edward VIII and Wallis Simpson are snapped holding hands as they disembark from his chartered yacht in Yugoslavia.**

He also found the royal family, the British government and the heads of Commonwealth governments united in opposition to such a marriage.

Prime Minister Stanley Baldwin presented Edward with a stark choice between marriage and the throne. Mrs Simpson herself left for the south of France, inviting the king to give her up, but he would not. Despite pro-Edward demonstrations outside Buckingham Palace and high-flown speeches by Winston Churchill, the king's most ardent supporter in parliament, the majority of opinion was solidly behind the government's stand.

On December 10 Edward signed the Instrument of Abdication, pronouncing his "irrevocable determination" to renounce the throne for himself and his descendants. The following day he addressed the nation in a moving radio broadcast, claiming that he would have been incapable of fulfilling his duties as king "without the help and support of the woman I love". He then embarked on a naval warship at Portsmouth to join Mrs Simpson in France. Edward's brother Albert was proclaimed king as George VI.

Contrary to expectations at the time, the abdication crisis had no effect on the popularity of the monarchy or the stability of the constitution. Given the title of Duke of Windsor, Edward finally married the woman of his choice on June 3, 1937.

- Ballerina Margot Fonteyn, aged 17, makes her first appearance in the title role of Giselle at Sadler's Wells
- Books published this year include *The Hobbit* by J R R Tolkien, *Spanish Testament* by Arthur Koestler and *The Road to Wigan Pier* by George Orwell
- First appearance of children's comic *The Dandy* and popular women's magazine *Woman* (price two pence)
- First Butlins holiday camp opens
- Alexander Korda abandons the problem-ridden filming of *I, Claudius*, directed by Josef von Sternberg and starring Charles Laughton

JANUARY
- Britain forbids its citizens to fight in the Spanish Civil War

FEBRUARY
- The Congress party wins most seats in Indian elections

MARCH
- Death of golfer Harry Vardon

APRIL
- The Government of India Act comes into force; Burma is separated from India
- The aircraft carrier HMS *Ark Royal* is launched

MAY
- George VI is crowned at Westminster Abbey
- Neville Chamberlain becomes Prime Minister after the resignation of Stanley Baldwin

A NEW KING AND A NEW PRIME MINISTER

In May 1937, George VI was crowned at Westminster Abbey and Neville Chamberlain moved into 10, Downing Street. It was a changing of the guard that marked the beginning of a new, perilous phase in British history.

The coronation on May 12 was a self-consciously exuberant exhibition of pageantry, reaffirming the anachronistic but reassuring splendour of monarchy following the undignified debacle of the abdication. From the fairytale golden coach that ferried the new king between Buckingham Palace and the Abbey to the splendid, if slightly absurd, fancy dress of the royal family and officials such as the Maltravers Herald of Arms Extraordinary, the occasion was as far removed from everyday reality

▲ The newly crowned George VI and his family greet their subjects from a balcony of Buckingham Palace.

as could practically be achieved.

The new king was ill-prepared for the role that had been sprung upon him and, on the face of it, singularly unsuited to rule. Nervous, stuttering and frail, he was the opposite of a born leader. But his elevated sense of duty and his devotion to family and country were exactly the qualities that Britain would require of a monarch in the difficult years of war that lay ahead.

Whether Neville Chamberlain possessed the right qualities to lead Britain at this point in its history is a matter of dispute. His predecessor Stanley Baldwin, who chose the aftermath of the coronation as a suitable moment to retire, had been a master of

▲ Neville Chamberlain, previously Chancellor of the Exchequer, conducts a radio broadcast after becoming Prime Minister.

inaction, a subtle political operator who chose to follow events rather than lead them. Chamberlain, previously Chancellor of the Exchequer, was an altogether brisker, more positive personality, a man who believed in taking the bull by the horns and getting things done. Aged 68, he was self-confident and contemptuous of the opinions of those who disagreed with him.

The goal that Chamberlain set himself was to avoid a second war with Germany. Faced with the threat of Nazi expansionism, he embarked on a bold policy of dealing with Hitler, intending to satisfy Nazi demands once and for all. This was the policy of appeasement. Its failure would stain his reputation for ever.

BRITAIN CAUGHT UP IN PALESTINE TURMOIL

In 1937 British troops in Palestine faced an Arab armed uprising intended to drive both them and the Jews out of the territory. Jewish groups had responded with their own terrorist campaign against the Arabs. Reporting on this

increasingly dangerous situation, a Royal Commission headed by Lord Peel in July recommended dividing Palestine into an Arab and a Jewish state, with Britain retaining control of an enclave that would include Jerusalem and Bethlehem.

Britain had administered Palestine under a League of Nations mandate since 1922. The British government was committed to implementing the 1917 Balfour Declaration, which pledged to create a national home for the Jewish people. Jewish immigration

▲ British troops stand guard along the Wailing Wall, a seemingly unending flashpoint for conflict between the Arab and Jewish communities of Palestine.

was, however, deeply unpopular with Palestinian Arabs. In 1929 tensions erupted into open violence, in which 133 Jews and over 100 Arabs died – the Jews mostly killed by rioting Arabs, the Arabs killed by the British bent on restoring order.

The rise of anti-Semitism in Europe from the early 1930s led to a huge increase in the number of Jews seeking to enter Palestine. The Jewish population grew to around 30 per cent of the total for the region. Britain attempted an impossible balancing act, seeking to limit Jewish immigration to a manageable level through a quota system, while reassuring the Arabs that their interests would be respected.

In November 1935 Arab leaders demanded an end to Jewish immigration and a freeze on any further land transfers to Jews. When these demands were not met, militant Arab nationalists rose in revolt, beginning a campaign of guerrilla warfare and terrorism.

The British were forced to adopt draconian measures to stifle the revolt, which nonetheless raged for three years. Jewish Zionists were no more content with British rule than the Arabs, resenting the limits Britain placed on immigration.

The Royal Commission's partition proposals, which would have given the Arabs about two-thirds of Palestine, were rejected by both sides. In any case, a British partition commission reported in 1938 that the Arab and Jewish communities were so inextricably entangled that politically, administratively, and financially, partition would be impossible.

In May 1939, as Britain's military forces brought the Arab uprising under control, the British government issued a White Paper declaring that Jewish immigration would be limited to 75,000 over five years and then stopped altogether. This was a gesture that alienated the Jews without reconciling the Arabs. The Palestine problem defeated the British, as it has confounded everyone else ever since.

ON THE ROAD TO WIGAN PIER

The most perceptive description of British life in 1937 appeared in a new book by socialist author George Orwell, *The Road to Wigan Pier*. An Eton-educated ex-colonial policeman, Orwell had made a speciality of sharing the life of the poor and reporting back on his experiences. The first part of his latest book was a predictable but powerful description of the grim hopelessness of existence in the towns of northern England, ravaged by poverty and unemployment.

But Orwell's honest eye also picked up elements of the contemporary scene which fitted less neatly with the socialist vision of a people groaning under capitalist oppression. He noticed that although millions were underfed, everyone had access to a radio. Such "cheap luxuries", he believed, were keeping the poor content. "It is quite likely," he wrote, "that fish-and-chips, art-silk stockings, tinned salmon, cut-price chocolate … the movies, the radio, strong tea and the Football Pools have between them averted revolution."

Orwell's readers in the Left Book Club were also expected to swallow some swingeing attacks

▲ George Orwell's impassioned account of poverty in the north of England is considered a milestone in modern literary journalism.

on their own fads. Orwell deeply regretted that socialism attracted "every fruit-juice drinker, nudist, sandal-wearer, sex-maniac, Quaker, 'Nature Cure' quack, pacifist, and feminist in England".

1938   THE MUNICH CRISIS

In 1938 an international crisis that had been brewing ever since Adolf Hitler's rise to power in Germany at last came to boiling point. Hitler had systematically overturned the terms of the Versailles Treaty, rebuilding German military forces in defiance of arms limitation clauses. In 1936 he marched his army into the demilitarized Rhineland. By 1938, the Nazi dictator was ready for the next step in his drive for the domination of Europe. He intended to create a "Greater Germany" that would bring millions of ethnic Germans currently living outside the country's borders within the Third Reich.

In March 1938, in a bloodless military takeover known as the *Anschluss*, Nazi Germany absorbed its German-speaking neighbour, Austria. Hitler's obvious next target for expansion was the Sudetenland region of Czechoslovakia. The predominantly ethnic German inhabitants of the region disliked being ruled by the Czechs and were easily stirred up

▲ Hitler is given an enthusiastic welcome as he makes a triumphant return to Austria, the country of his birth.

by Nazi propaganda to agitate against the Prague government. This provided the excuse for German military intervention.

Britain's reaction to Hitler's expansionism was confused. After the *Anschluss*, backbench Conservative MP Winston Churchill warned that Europe faced "a programme of aggression, nicely calculated and timed, unfolding stage by stage". Neville Chamberlain's government did not necessarily disagree with this assessment, but rejected Churchill's view that Britain should confront Hitler with the threat of force. Chamberlain was pushing through a programme of rapid rearmament, which concentrated particularly on the expansion of

the RAF and the improvement of the country's air defences. He was convinced that Britain was still militarily too weak in 1938 to face up to Germany. In any case, he was horrified at the prospect of war, an attitude he shared with most of the British people. He decided that instead of opposing German expansion, Britain should avoid war by seeing that Hitler's ambitions were satisfied without conflict.

This policy of "appeasement" enjoyed widespread support. The opposition Labour Party, while denouncing Hitler's dictatorship and all its works, was also dedicated to the cause of peace at almost any price. It was only as recently as 1937 that Labour had belatedly abandoned a position of total opposition to rearmament. The small group of MPs associated with Churchill – including Anthony Eden who resigned as Foreign Secretary in February over disagreements with Chamberlain – were almost alone in articulating consistent criticism of the government's appeasement policy.

In the summer of 1938, Britain and France put pressure on the Czech government to negotiate with Nazi leaders of the Sudeten Germans about alleged ill-treatment. This the Czechs reluctantly did, but no amount of concessions would

satisfy the Nazis. On September 13, the Sudeten Germans staged a revolt that the Czech authorities easily put down. Britain and its ally France feared that this was the moment Hitler would choose for an invasion. Chamberlain decided to seize the initiative and flew to Munich on September 15 for face-to-face talks with Hitler. This was a far more dramatic gesture then that it would be nowadays – it was in fact the first time the British Prime Minister had been in an aircraft.

Meeting Hitler at Berchtesgaden, Chamberlain promised to ensure that the Czechs handed over the Sudetenland to the Germans. This apparently abject surrender to the threat of German military might met with some criticism in Britain but was in general welcomed. To give the Sudeten Germans the right to decide which state they belonged to seemed in line with the principle of self-determination. The feeling that Germany had been hard done by at the end of the First World War – a view largely propagated by left-wing intellectuals – undermined opposition to Hitler's expansionism, which could be seen as the Germans taking what was rightfully theirs.

After being bullied and threatened by Britain and France, the Czech government agreed to negotiate the handover of the Sudetenland. On September 22, Chamberlain flew to Germany again, fondly believing the crisis was resolved. Instead, Hitler angrily raised his demands, insisting on the right to occupy the Sudetenland immediately, without further negotiation. Shocked by Hitler's evident hostility, Chamberlain returned to Britain and authorized preparations

▲ After meeting Adolf Hitler, British Prime Minister Neville Chamberlain claimed to have secured "peace for our time".

▲ Prime Minister Neville Chamberlain arrives in London waving the Munich agreement signed by Germany, Great Britain, France and Italy.

by the all-powerful Luftwaffe – everyone had heard of the devastation wrought upon Guernica by German bombers during the Spanish Civil War. Over 80 per cent of London parents applied for their children to be evacuated from the city.

On September 28, help arrived from an unlikely quarter. Italian dictator Benito Mussolini suggested a four-power conference to avert war. Hitler agreed. The following day Chamberlain flew to Germany for a third time. Meeting in Munich, Hitler, Mussolini, Chamberlain and French Prime Minister Daladier reached agreement on the German occupation of the Sudetenland. Czechoslovakia was not consulted.

Chamberlain arrived at Heston airport waving a document bearing Hitler's signature, pledging never to go to war with Britain. Later, addressing a cheering crowd in Downing Street, he claimed to have achieved "peace with honour … peace for our time". In the House of Commons, Winston Churchill was one of the few to sound a dissenting note, calling the Munich agreement "a defeat without a war".

In the initial relief after Munich, Chamberlain's popularity soared. But British opinion soon began to swing against appeasement. The German occupation of Prague in March 1939 showed that the Munich agreement had handed the Czechs to Germany bound hand and- oot. The predominant British attitude was then to swing from the pursuit of peace at any price to stopping Hitler at any cost.

for war. Trenches were dug in parks to act as air-raid shelters and anti-aircraft guns were trundled into position. The fleet was mobilized. Germany was officially warned that Britain, France and the Soviet Union would support Czechoslovakia if the country were attacked.

The British people viewed the military preparations with fear and consternation. The crisis had deepened too quickly and the nation was psychologically unprepared for war. It was considered a given that any conflict with Germany would open with the destruction of major British cities

▲ Schoolchildren at Harrow County School for Boys dig air-raid trenches around the playing field.

▲ As part of Britain's general preparations for war, London policemen wear gas masks in a training drill.

- The Holidays With Pay Act increases the number of workers with paid holidays from 3 million to over 11 million
- Unemployment is stable at 13 per cent of the workforce
- All schoolchildren are issued with gas masks
- The Supermarine Spitfire enters service with the RAF
- The *Queen Elizabeth* is launched, the world's largest ocean liner
- The record transfer fee for a footballer is £14,000, paid by Arsenal for Bryn Jones
- British hit film of the year is Alfred Hitchcock's *The Lady Vanishes*
- Books published this year include *Homage to Catalonia* by George Orwell, *Brighton Rock* by Graham Greene and *Scoop* by Evelyn Waugh
- The Magazine *Picture Post* and children's comic *Beano* appear for the first time

FEBRUARY
- Foreign Secretary Anthony Eden resigns; he is replaced by Lord Halifax

MARCH
- In the wake of Germany's take-over of Austria, Britain pledges to defend France and Belgium if they are attacked

MALLARD SETS STEAM SPEED RECORD

On July 3, 1938, an A4 Pacific locomotive of the London & North Eastern Railway registered the highest speed ever attained by a steam engine. The locomotive was *Mallard*, and on the footplate for the record run was its designer, Sir Nigel Gresley.

Through the 1920s and 1930s, Gresley had made a speciality of designing stylish, exceptionally powerful steam engines. With the A4 Pacific class, first introduced in 1935, he surpassed himself. Taking advantage of the latest development in wind-tunnel technology, Gresley gave the A4s a streamlined shape never before seen on British locomotives. Steam engines had traditionally exposed all their workings to view – boiler, valves, pipes and cylinders. Now all these were encased in a sleek metallic shell that was beautiful as well as efficient.

Gresley was a competitive man with a flamboyant streak. He wanted to show that his glamorous locomotives were the fastest in the world. The speed record was held by a German engine that had narrowly topped 200 km/h (125 mph). Gresley decided to take advantage of a brake test run with *Mallard*, his latest locomotive, to surpass this. Pulling seven coaches, *Mallard* eased through Grantham station and gathered speed. With driver Duddington and fireman Bray giving all they had, the locomotive reached 203 km/h (126 mph) down the slight incline at Stoke Bank.

Gresley died in 1941. *Mallard* retired from service in 1963, but it remains a star attraction at the National Railway Museum in York.

▲ The *Mallard* locomotive sits on railway sidings in London before being towed up to the York National Railway Museum.

HUTTON SCORES 364 IN CLASSIC TEST

▲ Len Hutton is congratulated on breaking Don Bradman's test score record of 334 during the fifth test of the Ashes series.

In August 1938, Yorkshire batsman Len Hutton was a promising 22-year-old competing to secure a regular place as an opener in the England Test team, when a single innings made him a cricketing legend and a national hero.

The fifth Test in an otherwise unexceptional Ashes series began at the Oval on August 20. England won the toss and elected to bat. On a placid pitch against a poor Australian bowling side, Hutton set about accumulating runs with unflinching seriousness and unwavering concentration. He gave one chance, when on 40, but otherwise eschewed all risk. He was still at the wicket at the end of the second day, by which time the England score was 634–5.

The progress of Hutton's innings was followed with mounting excitement by English cricket fans. The great question was whether the Yorkshireman could beat Australian batsman Don Bradman's record Test score of 334, made against England in 1930. To add spice to the contest, Bradman was captain of the Australian side at the Oval.

On the morning of the third day, Hutton took the record; Bradman was the first to step forward and shake his hand. The England opener was finally dismissed for 364 after 13 hours and 17 minutes at the crease. In some parts of the country, church bells were rung to celebrate his epic achievement.

England went on to score 903 before declaring and won the match by an innings and 579 runs, the biggest margin of victory ever recorded in a Test match.

DAWNING OF THE JET AGE

In 1938, a company called Power Jets Ltd demonstrated its latest invention before a far from interested group from the British Air Ministry. The company, which had been formed by Frank Whittle, a graduate of the RAF College at Cranbourne, had produced the first working prototype of the jet engine. Although the invention was confined to a workshop bench for the purposes of the demonstration, Whittle proposed that his new engine be fitted to the RAF's existing fighter planes in order to give them a speed advantage over other aircraft.

Whittle had little success in convincing the men from the ministry of the advantages of his invention until German engineers, working independently of Whittle, applied their version of the technology to one of their own aircraft. On August 27, 1939, the Heinkel-built He 178, powered by a jet engine designed by Hans von Obain, took to the skies over Germany, forcing the British to take Whittle's invention seriously.

▲ **Frank Whittle (right) explains the workings of the jet engine. It was fear of invasion by Nazi Germany that would later drive the development of jet aircraft.**

JEWISH REFUGEE CHILDREN ARRIVE IN BRITAIN

The extension of German Nazi rule over Austria in 1938 was accompanied by a vicious persecution of Jews. Hitler's regime had discriminated against people of Jewish origin from the outset, but it was now emboldened to acts of outrageous violence. On 9–10 November there were Nazi-orchestrated riots throughout Germany and Austria in which synagogues were burned, Jews were badly beaten and Jewish businesses looted. Thousands were rounded up and taken to concentration camps.

As life became unbearable under Nazi rule, Jewish people naturally sought to emigrate. The Nazis were at first happy for them to leave, as long as the regime could draw financial advantage from it. But nowhere in the world was keen to offer the Jews refuge. At an international conference on Jewish refugees in July 1938, the Australian representatives frankly stated that "as we have no racial problem, we are not desirous of importing one". Britain was set against admitting a new influx of Jews into Palestine, regarding the problems of Arab-Jewish conflict there as already bad enough. Nor did the British government want more Jews settling in Britain. Hostility to this prospect was shared by most of the British press – the *Evening Standard* stated that it was impossible "to contemplate permanent increased Jewish settlement in this country".

Coming under pressure from Jewish groups and their sympathizers, in November 1938 the government grudgingly agreed to allow Jewish children to come to Britain unaccompanied by adults, as long as refugee support organizations would guarantee to look after them. The first of the *Kindertransport* – trains carrying Jewish children – arrived in early December. On their arrival in Britain, the children were distributed to foster homes and orphanages across the country.

Thanks partly to a charitable fund promoted by former Prime Minister Stanley Baldwin, tens of thousands of Jewish children found refuge in Britain before the transports stopped at the outbreak of the Second World War. It was, of course, a desperately sad option for Jewish families. Most of the children never saw their parents again.

▲ **A group of more than 500 Jewish refugee children aged from five to 17, mainly from Vienna, after arriving in England.**

1939

- Around 1.5 million people are conscripted into the armed forces by the year's end
- British Overseas Airways Corporation (BOAC) is founded as a state airline
- ENSA is formed to entertain the forces
- Petrol rationing is introduced
- Tommy Handley's ITMA ("It's That Man Again") is a hit series on the radio
- Books published this year include *Finnegans Wake* by James Joyce, *Autumn Journal* by Louis MacNeice and *Goodbye to Berlin* by Christopher Isherwood
- First performance of William Walton's *Violin Concerto*
- Songs of the year include Flanagan and Allen's "The Washing on the Siegfried Line" and the Crazy Gang's "Run, Rabbit, Run"

JANUARY
- The IRA launches a bombing campaign in Britain
- Death of Irish poet W B Yeats

FEBRUARY
- Britain officially recognizes the nationalist government of General Franco in Spain

MARCH
- Hitler occupies Prague and demands Danzig and the "Polish Corridor" from Poland
- Britain and France commit themselves to the defence of Poland

IRA BOMBS COVENTRY

At around 2.30 pm on August 25, 1939, a bomb exploded in Broadgate, the main street in the centre of Coventry. It was a Friday afternoon and the pavements were crowded with shoppers. Glass shopfronts were shattered by the blast, which left a scene of devastation. Five people were killed, including a 21-year-old woman out buying the trousseau for her wedding. More than 50 people were injured, a dozen of them seriously. The bomb had apparently been left in the box of a tradesman's bicycle.

The bombing was the worst single incident in a campaign that had been waged by the Irish Republican Army (IRA) since the beginning of the year. In January the IRA issued a demand for the British to withdraw from Northern Ireland. They followed up this declaration with a flurry of attacks using incendiary and explosive devices, including two bombs left in London Underground stations that caused serious injuries. Targets ranged from electricity pylons and post offices to Madame Tussaud's and Hammersmith Bridge.

The IRA attacks were on a considerable scale. By June

▲ The wreckage in Broadgate, Coventry, after the explosion of an IRA time bomb which was apparently placed in a tradesman's bicycle basket.

official figures showed that there had been 127 incidents, in which one person had died and 55 had been injured. The IRA's devices lacked sophistication – some of the most simple devices consisted of acid bombs made out of party balloons – but the organization could call on a large pool of idealistic young Irishmen to maintain the momentum of the campaign. Arrests were frequent. Brought to court, the bombers typically spoke defiantly and

without regret of "the duty of every Irishman to overthrow British tyranny in Ireland".

The IRA campaign did not end with the outbreak of war with Germany. There were explosions at London railway stations in November 1939 which killed one person and injured more than 20. But the IRA's efforts were soon dwarfed from the sky by Luftwaffe bombing – in which, ironically, Coventry was to be one of the worst-hit targets.

EVACUATION OF CHILDREN

▲ Children from the Chelsea district of London are prepared for evacuation to the countryside.

On September 1, 1939, two days before Britain's declaration of war on Germany, the long-planned evacuation of children from its cities was set in motion. Mass evacuation was considered an essential measure to save the young from possible massacre by Luftwaffe bombers.

While infants travelled with their mothers, primary school children were evacuated with their teachers. Each child carried a gas mask and a small bundle of essential personal items. The child was labelled with its name, address and school number. Parents were not told where their children were going and, in any case, in the confusion many children did not end up where they were supposed to arrive. Still, by the evening of September 3, around 1.5 million children had been moved to reception areas in the countryside or in towns not expected to be targets for air attack.

The government had planned to evacuate 80 per cent of the children in major cities; in fact, less than 50 per cent moved out. By January 1940, when no air attacks had materialized, over 700,000 of the original evacuees had returned home.

BRITAIN DECLARES WAR

At 11.15 on the morning of September 3, 1939, Prime Minister Neville Chamberlain addressed the nation in a radio broadcast. Speaking in melancholy but dignified tones, he told the British people that the government had called on Germany to give an assurance that its invasion of Poland, begun two days earlier, would be stopped. No such assurance had been received. "Consequently," Chamberlain regretfully intoned, "this country is now at war with Germany."

The slide to war had proceeded inexorably during the preceding five months. In March, German troops occupied Prague and Czechoslovakia ceased to exist. Those who had argued that German dictator Adolf Hitler was a reasonable man, concerned only to undo the allegedly unjust Versailles Treaty, were confounded. The destruction of Czechoslovakia outraged British public opinion. Even Chamberlain, the architect of appeasement, felt duty bound to forestall any further German aggression. Poland was clearly Hitler's next target. At the end of March, Chamberlain committed Britain and France to go to war if the Poles were attacked.

Urged on forcefully from the backbenches by Winston Churchill – increasingly admired by the press and public as the man who had been right about Hitler –

Chamberlain hesitantly set in motion war preparations, including the introduction of conscription and advancing preparations for coping with air raids. Rearmament, already well under way, continued apace.

The British government and military chiefs were uncomfortably aware that their guarantee to the Poles was an empty gesture, as they had no practical means of coming to Poland's aid. Only the Soviet Union was capable of contesting a German advance. Chamberlain was extremely reluctant to ally himself with Soviet dictator Joseph Stalin, but in August a military mission was tardily sent to Moscow for talks. While Britain fumbled, Germany pounced. A Nazi-Soviet Pact was announced on August 23, clearing the way for a German invasion of Poland.

Despite Britain's unequivocal commitment to Poland, Chamberlain still hesitated over his decision. It was not until late on September 2 that, under pressure from parliament and the majority of the Cabinet, he agreed to send an ultimatum demanding a German withdrawal. After the declaration of war the following morning, he gloomily told the House of Commons: "Everything that I have worked for, everything that I have hoped for, everything that I have believed in during my public life, has crashed in ruins."

▲ **Winston Churchill returns to Admiralty House as First Lord of the Admiralty, a position he also held during the First World War.**

The man of the hour was Churchill. He was invited to rejoin the government as First Lord of the Admiralty, the post he had held at the outset of the First World War. Unlike Chamberlain, Churchill was assured. "I felt a serenity of mind," he later wrote, "and was conscious of a kind of uplifted detachment from human and personal affairs." Churchill was a war leader by nature and by destiny; Chamberlain decidedly was not.

1939

Just a few moments after Chamberlain's radio broadcast on September 3, 1939, in which he announced a state of war with Germany, the wail of air-raid sirens sounded in London. There was widespread panic, for this represented exactly what most people had expected and feared – instant mass air attacks on Britain's cities. Experts had confidently predicted a quarter of a million casualties in the first week of a war. But the air-raid warning was a false alarm. Hitler had no plans yet to bomb Britain, and the Luftwaffe was, in any case, fully occupied with the destruction of Poland.

Preparations for air attack nonetheless had a dramatic effect on British life. The mass evacuation of children from cities was the most obvious upheaval, affecting millions of people. Coping with evacuees from urban slums was a shock for many of their rural hosts, just as the encounter with the countryside was a shock for many of the evacuees. Objects were evacuated as well as people – the paintings in the National Gallery collection were evacuated from London, eventually ending up in a cave in Wales. Poisonous snakes at London Zoo were killed in case bomb damage to the reptile house gave them a chance to escape.

Structures known as Anderson shelters – after Home Secretary Sir John Anderson – sprouted in back gardens. Around 150,000 were distributed in kits of steel sheets, which the householder bolted together and partially buried to make a primitive but effective refuge from bombing. As it was assumed poisoned gas would be used in air raids, the

▲ The imposition of a blackout meant householders were obliged to devise ways of blocking any escape of light from windows or doors.

authorities attempted to make the carrying of gas masks compulsory. The tops of pillar-boxes were coated with gas-sensitive paint that would change colour in case of a gas attack.

The imposition of a blackout, rigorously enforced by an army of air-raid wardens, obliged householders to block any leakage of light from doors and windows. In the streets, this caused mayhem. Road-accident deaths soared to over 1,000 a month, until the situation was mitigated by the use of masked headlights and by the decline of private

motoring following the introduction of petrol rationing.

Although unemployment did not magically disappear with the onset of war, the armed forces had absorbed over a million conscripts by the end of 1939. Thousands of others signed up as auxiliary firemen, air-raid wardens or other civil defence personnel. Yet day followed day and week followed week with very little military action. The British people found themselves geared up for a war that – for its first seven months – simply failed to ignite. At first the British called this period the "funny

war" or the "bore war", later adopting the term the Americans used: the "phoney war".

As in the First World War, a British Expeditionary Force sailed for France once war was declared, but this time they did not have to face an immediate German onslaught. Hitler was preoccupied with his invasion of Poland and had neither the desire nor the capacity to fight simultaneously on two fronts. The French, for their part, settled into the defensive fortifications of their Maginot Line; they had no intention of attacking Germany. Once Poland was defeated – which took the Germans and their Soviet allies less than a month – Hitler grandiloquently offered peace. Prime Minister Chamberlain, although privately most unhappy to be at war with Germany, felt bound to turn the offer down without negotiation. Both sides settled down to sit out the winter.

Most of the action that did occur was at sea. A German U-boat sank the liner *Athenia* on the first night of the war. A steady trickle of bad news followed for First Lord of the Admiralty Winston Churchill to report. In October the battleship *Royal Oak* fell victim to a daring submarine raid while at anchor in the Royal Navy base at Scapa Flow. Other vessels were sunk by German magnetic mines.

Fortunately, December brought at least one heartening story for the navy. The pocket battleship *Admiral Graf Spee* had been one of the most effective German surface raiders, preying upon merchant shipping in the southern oceans. On December 13 three British cruisers, *Exeter*, *Ajax* and *Achilles* encountered *Graf Spee* off the coast of South America. In the best traditions of the Royal Navy, the outgunned British

▲ Over 200,000 volunteer air-raid wardens were recruited to help enforce the blackout and arrange aid should there be an air attack.

warships engaged the enemy. Although suffering heavy losses, they drove *Graf Spee* to take refuge in the port of Montevideo, where it was scuttled by its demoralized commander.

Apart from this naval engagement, there was little chance for bold action in any quarter – not that the British government was keen to take the initiative. The lack of martial spirit in the Cabinet was typified by Secretary for Air Kingsley Wood, who responded with outrage to a proposal to use incendiary bombs to burn down German forests: "Are you aware it is private property?" he cried. Chamberlain settled for the comforting fiction that a British naval blockade would suffice to bring Germany to its knees.

At the end of November 1939, the Soviet Union attacked Finland. The initial success of the Finns in defending their country won the admiration of the British people. Urged on by the French, the British government seriously considered sending a military expedition to aid Finland, thus adding a conflict with the Soviet Union to their war with Nazi Germany. Fortunately, the defeat of Finland in March 1940 put an end to the scheme.

The war in Finland had, however, focused Britain's attention on Scandinavia. Neutral Sweden was supplying Germany with iron ore through ports in neutral Norway. Churchill devised a plan to mine Norwegian territorial waters and possibly occupy Norwegian ports to stop this trade. In April 1940 the operation was set in motion. At exactly the same moment, Hitler launched his own invasion of Denmark and Norway. Quite unexpectedly, the phoney war was at an end and the real war had begun.

▲ A soldier bids farewell to his family. Soldiers who sailed for France after war had been declared in 1939 faced little action until the following year.

1940–1949

The early 1940s were perhaps the most dramatic period in British history. Driven out of mainland Europe but saved in the near-miraculous evacuation from Dunkirk, the British Army prepared to defend the country against a German invasion that never came. Instead, the Royal Air Force fought the world's first exclusively aerial battle in the skies over southern England. The Battle of Britain denied Germany command of the air but was followed by the Blitz, a nine-month campaign of night bombing of Britain's cities. The country emerged undefeated – though severely battered – from this ordeal. At the same time, U-boat attacks on merchant shipping threatened to starve Britain into submission.

In its hour of peril, Britain found the leader it needed. The war crisis transformed Winston Churchill from a washed-out Tory backbencher into Britain's greatest twentieth-century hero. Often irrational, obstructive of progressive social policies and plain wrong about war strategy, he nonetheless provided that unquantifiable but essential quality: leadership. It was because of Churchill's presence that no one in Britain seriously believed the country would give up when it stood alone against Germany in 1940–41.

Britain survived the Second World War only through devoting every human, economic and financial resource to the conflict. The state took unprecedented control over its citizens, dictating where they worked, what they ate and even what clothes they wore. At the same time, freedom of expression was upheld to a remarkable degree – the government never ceased to face sharp criticism of its conduct of the war in parliament and the press. Britain's rulers recognized that a war in which sacrifice and suffering were the lot of civilians as well as soldiers would be unbearable without the promise of a better world to be won by victory. While the war was still in progress, the Beveridge Report laid the foundations for a welfare state, and the Butler Education Act promised the reform of schooling. The landslide election of a Labour government in 1945 expressed the aspiration to social justice that the war years had inspired.

After the war, the British people could be forgiven for wondering if they had really won a great victory. The privations from shortages of food and fuel were greater in 1946–47 than in any year of the war. Yet the Labour government did surprisingly well in the face of an acute financial and diplomatic crisis. Playing with a hand that contained few trumps and no aces, the Attlee Cabinet managed to carry through fundamental changes – the National Health Service, nationalization of major industries – while upholding a dignified and responsible presence in a wider world where Britain's Empire still entailed vast responsibilities. The Indian subcontinent was given independence, arguably in disorder and in haste, but with a legacy of democratic institutions and enough goodwill to keep the successor states inside the Commonwealth. Palestine was abandoned in the face of uncontrollable conflict between Arabs and Jews. But elsewhere Britain clung on to its Empire, despite its sharply declining resources. The British government still acted like a major player on the world stage, but with military and economic power so reduced that it in practice acted as a subordinate ally of the Americans. The special relationship with the United States, in which Churchill had placed so much faith, proved a sham from the moment the war ended. Britain was given no special treatment by the Americans, who quickly withdrew financial support that the British desperately needed. Yet worsening relations with the Soviet Union and the development of the Cold War by the end of the 1940s left Britain tied to the United States for better or for worse.

The decline of Britain as a world power meant little to the majority of the population. Whereas the First World War had deeply troubled the national psyche, the British people emerged from the Second World War with a reinforced sense of national identity, based not on pride in Empire or martial valour, but grounded in a sense of quiet virtues that the British were deemed to share – decency, fairness, solidarity and endurance. Put to the most severe of tests, British society had held together, in war and in peace.

- Food rationing is introduced
- The defence budget rises to £3.9 billion, over 80 per cent of total government spending
- Old age pensions are paid to women over 60
- The Ministry of Labour is given power to direct "any person in the United Kingdom to perform any service required in any place"
- A government propaganda campaign warns that "careless talk costs lives"
- Railings around parks and gardens are torn up for scrap metal
- The George Cross is founded as an award for civilian bravery
- Writer J B Priestley's radio broadcasts attract an audience of millions
- Propaganda broadcasts from Germany are made by William Joyce ("Lord Haw-Haw")
- First flight of the Mosquito fighter-bomber
- Books published this year include *Portrait of the Artist as a Young Dog* by Dylan Thomas and *Darkness at Noon* by Arthur Koestler
- Paul Nash and Stanley Spencer are among painters appointed official war artists
- Britain's favourite singer is Vera Lynn, performing "We'll Meet Again" and "Faithful For Ever"

NAZI BLITZKRIEG IN NORWAY AND FRANCE

On April 5, 1940, Prime Minister Neville Chamberlain informed the House of Commons that Hitler had "missed the bus". The previous autumn, German forces might have caught Britain and France on the hop, but the delay through the winter had worked to the Allies' advantage. This complacent view was immediately put to the test in Scandinavia.

Three days after Chamberlain's speech, British warships sent to mine Norwegian territorial waters ran into a German invasion force on its way to occupy Norway. As battle raged at sea, an Allied expeditionary force was hastily dispatched across the North Sea. The fighting soon proved the clear superiority of German forces. On land they moved more quickly and fought more effectively than the British. At sea, German air power negated the strength of the Royal Navy, bombers taking a heavy toll of warships. By May 2, the Allies had been forced to abandon south and central Norway.

Defeat in Norway led directly to the fall of the Chamberlain

▲ **British soldiers advance through a Belgian town on May 17. The Germans drove them back to Brussels later that day.**

government. On May 8, after two days of acrimonious debate in parliament, almost 100 Conservative MPs voted against the government or abstained. Chamberlain had to go. His most obvious successor – from a Conservative point of view – was the Foreign Secretary, Lord Halifax. But Winston Churchill, the enemy of appeasement, had most support in the country. At a backroom meeting on May 9, Halifax revealed that he had no stomach for the job of wartime Prime Minister. Churchill welcomed the post as his destiny.

Churchill formed his War Cabinet on May 10. On the same day, Hitler's forces attacked Belgium and the Netherlands, as a prelude to the invasion of France. The campaign that followed was a masterclass in mobile warfare. Both Germany and the Allies had tanks and aircraft, but only the Germans had worked out how to use them in combination to devastating effect. Their *Blitzkrieg* (lightning warfare) won the war on the European mainland within a month.

The British Expeditionary Force (BEF), commanded by Lord Gort, played into German hands by moving into Belgium where the main thrust of the German offensive was expected. Instead, Germany's armoured forces advanced further south through the supposedly impassable Ardennes and punched a hole in the French line near Sedan. Without stopping to consolidate their position, they then swung north and drove towards the Channel ports. Threatened with being cut off, the BEF retreated in haste towards the coast.

Churchill put pressure on Gort and the French to organize a counter-attack. The very speed of the German armoured thrust should have left the enemy exposed. But the French Army was riddled with defeatism and the British had no answer to German command of the air. Allied air forces had suffered heavy losses, leaving the Luftwaffe's Stuka dive-bombers free to strike at will. On May 26 the British government abandoned all remaining hope of making a stand in France and authorized Gort "to evacuate the maximum force possible".

▲ **The wreckage of a German Heinkel bomber is searched by British soldiers after it was brought down by a British anti-aircraft battery in Belgium.**

DUNKIRK EVACUATION

Towards the end of May, British forces retreating from the German advance gathered on the beaches near the French Channel port of Dunkirk. Hitler, seeing an opportunity to destroy an enemy now trapped like rats with their backs to the sea, wasted no time in unleashing the full power of his air force against the stranded men. Wave after wave of bombers dropped their deadly cargo of explosives on to the overcrowded beach and harbour at Dunkirk. Meanwhile, back in London, plans were under way to get the British Expeditionary Force (BEF) back to England.

Aware that the Belgian army was about to collapse, the British Expeditionary Force was ordered to develop a bridgehead at Dunkirk from where it could be picked up by sea. On May 26 Operation Dynamo began with the removal of the first troops from Dunkirk. On the night of May 27, the first of the famous flotilla of small boats made its way across the Channel to rescue stranded troops. The effectiveness of the evacuation was greatly increased after Admiralty officers scoured

▲ In a remarkable military operation, troops from the British Expeditionary Force were evacuated from the beaches of Dunkirk.

boathouses looking for suitable craft to bring the soldiers home and later put out an appeal for assistance from boat owners across England.

By May 30, what remained of the BEF was believed finally to have arrived in Dunkirk. From an original armada of around 40 small vessels, the flotilla that rescued them grew to the point where over 400 small boats of every description were being piloted by volunteers who ferried troops from the bomb- and bullet-strewn beaches to larger ships waiting out in the Channel.

Between May 31 and June 1, 132,000 men were pulled out of Dunkirk in this way, but it was becoming clear that the BEF would not be able to keep the Germans at bay for much longer.

By June 2, despite the best efforts of the Royal Air Force, it was no longer possible to pull troops out of Dunkirk during daylight hours because of the activities of the Luftwaffe. It was decided to make one last effort to remove as many men as possible on the night of June 2, and to this end more ships than ever before were dispatched to Dunkirk under cover of darkness. Unfortunately, French forces caught up in fighting at the perimeter of the beachhead were left behind as dawn broke on June 3. In a remarkable display of courage, the flotilla returned the next night and, against impossible odds, removed over 26,000 French troops from Dunkirk.

At 2.23 pm on June 4, the British Admiralty declared that Operation Dynamo was over. More than 338,000 troops had been rescued from the Dunkirk beaches and would one day return to fight the Germans on the mainland of Europe.

▲ In a five-day period, Operation Dynamo rescued more than 300,000 Allied troops who were safely returned to mainland Britain.

THE BATTLE OF BRITAIN

The defeat of France in June 1940 left Britain to face the might of the triumphant German forces alone. On June 18, Prime Minister Winston Churchill told the House of Commons: "I expect that the Battle of Britain is about to begin ... The whole fury and might of the enemy must very soon be turned on us ... Let us therefore brace ourselves to our duties and so bear ourselves that, if the British Empire and the Commonwealth last for a thousand years men will still say, 'This was their finest hour.'"

If the British expected to face a German invasion, however, Hitler was sure that Britain would accept that it was beaten and give in. On July 19, he made an apparently magnanimous public offer of peace. The British government contemptuously brushed it aside. Only then did Hitler give the go-ahead for preparations for Operation Sealion, the invasion of Britain.

Hitler's plan required that the German Navy create a narrow corridor across the Channel, protected on each side by mines and U-boats, through which men and supplies would be ferried to the English coast. Given Britain's superior navy, this corridor would be devastatingly vulnerable to attack unless the Luftwaffe could first clear the Royal Air Force from the skies over the English Channel. So it was that Hermann Göring, head of the German Air Ministry, found himself with the job of destroying the RAF.

Flying from airfields in Belgium and France, German aircraft began preliminary strikes in July, clashing with RAF fighters over the Channel. The Luftwaffe's main onslaught –

▲ **RAF Spitfires on patrol over the English Channel during the Battle of Britain.**

attempting to fulfil Hitler's directive "to overcome the British air force with all means at its disposal and in the shortest possible time" – did not start until August 8.

In the desperate battle that then commenced, the RAF was entirely outnumbered. Against the Luftwaffe's 1,300 bombers and 1,400 fighter aircraft, the British could muster only 900 fighter planes. But Britain had the crucial advantage of the most sophisticated air-defence system in the world. This was a battle for which Britain had thoroughly prepared during peacetime. A chain of radar stations around the coast was linked to control centres where the movement of enemy aircraft could be plotted. Fighter pilots in constant readiness at airfields were "scrambled" at the approach of German aircraft

and directed by ground controllers to their targets. The Germans sent over large fleets of bombers in daylight, closely escorted by Messerschmitt fighters operating at the limit of their range. The RAF used its high-performance Spitfires to take on the German fighters, and Hurricanes to shoot down the bombers.

The head of Fighter Command, Hugh Dowding, adopted an intelligent strategy. His goal was to keep the RAF in existence as a fighting force. He hoarded his resources, keeping plenty of fighters in reserve at all times. Dowding was less worried about losing machines, because the British aircraft industry was quite capable of making up for losses with new aircraft coming off the assembly lines. Trained pilots, however, were in very short supply.

Britain was fortunate to be able to recruit fliers from around the world – including Canadians, New Zealanders, Australians, South Africans, Poles and Czechs. Even so, pilots were under instructions to bail out immediately if their aircraft was damaged, saving themselves and their valuable skills rather than trying to preserve the aircraft.

The Luftwaffe should have devoted its strength to the systematic destruction of Britain's air defences, picking off radar stations, bombing airfields and destroying aircraft factories. Instead, it was drawn into a war of attrition, with air battles involving hundreds of aircraft fought in the skies over southern England. The resistance of the RAF was at times stretched almost to breaking point, but German losses were themselves consistently heavy. It came as some relief to hard-pressed RAF pilots when, on September 7, on Hitler's orders, the Luftwaffe switched its attentions from attacks on airfields to bombing Britain's cities. Still, the scale of the aerial conflicts continued to mount. On September 15 – now celebrated as Battle of Britain Day – Luftwaffe fighters and bombers came in two waves, each numbering over 500 aircraft. The RAF's claim to have shot down 186 enemy aircraft that day are now largely discounted – around 60 is a more credible figure – but the Luftwaffe was evidently getting no closer to command of the air.

September 15 was in fact the latest date that Hitler had set for the completion of the first phase of Operation Sealion. Although mass daylight air raids continued until the end of the month, it was clear to all concerned that Germany was

▲ **RAF fighter pilots run to their planes during the Battle of Britain. Pilots had to remain in constant readiness and were "scrambled" at the approach of German aircraft.**

▲ **A German bomber drops its deadly cargo over England.**

in no position to launch a seaborne assault against the British coast that year. Although the RAF had lost more than 1,000 fighter aircraft during the Battle of Britain, they had managed to shoot down around 1,800 German fighters and bombers. Germany formally abandoned the planned invasion of Britain on October 12.

The Battle of Britain was not a clear-cut victory for the RAF, which had remained on the defensive throughout and was unable to prevent a German night-time bombing campaign devastating British cities through the winter of 1940–41. But to have stopped the Germans from winning was victory enough.

Summing up the contribution made to Britain's survival by the young fighter pilots of the RAF, Churchill made his memorable statement that "Never in the field of human conflict was so much owed by so many to so few."

CHURCHILL OFFERS "BLOOD AND TEARS"

In May 1940, Britain was fortunate to find the war leader it needed in Winston Churchill. His eloquent rhetoric and his unshakable dedication to victory held the country together in its darkest hour.

Churchill's appointment as Prime Minister was far from universally welcomed in political and diplomatic circles, but he immediately set his stamp on the war. Addressing the House of Commons on May 13, he offered nothing but "blood, toil, tears and sweat". He stated his war aims in a single word: "Victory – victory at all costs, victory in spite of all terror; victory, however long and hard the road may be." Such speeches, also broadcast on the radio, roused the mood of the nation to defiance.

Churchill set up a coalition government. As part of the deal that took him to Downing Street, he had to include the leaders of

▲ One of the grand old men of British politics, Winston Churchill's career reached its greatest peak as an inspirational war leader.

the Conservative "old guard", Chamberlain and Lord Halifax, in the War Cabinet, along with Labour leaders Clement Attlee and Arthur Greenwood. But he was able to assert his own preferences with imaginative appointments to key posts – trade union leader Ernest Bevin as Minister of Labour and newspaper magnate Lord Beaverbrook as Minister for Aircraft Production. By the end of 1940, Chamberlain was dead, Halifax had been sent as ambassador to Washington, and Churchill had become leader of the Conservative Party.

From the outset Churchill took on the role of Minister of Defence as well as PM, running the war through direct communication with the Chiefs of Staff. Despite the careful attention he paid to the formalities of parliamentary tradition, in practice he often acted more like a war dictator than a conventional Prime Minister. Churchill was to take some dubious decisions in the course of the war, but his presence at the top sent a current of energy coursing through the entire British war machine.

"DAD'S ARMY" READY TO FIGHT

▲ Members of the House of Commons Defence Committee watch Home Guards in training during a visit to a training camp.

On May 14, 1940, the government appealed for men over military age to come forward for unpaid part-time service as Local Defence Volunteers. A flood of more than 1.5 million volunteers joined an organization that was later renamed the Home Guard – and known affectionately as "Dad's Army".

After the Dunkirk evacuation, when Britain stood in daily expectation of a German invasion, it seemed that the Home Guard might well find themselves called into action. Yet they were in no fit state to fight. Home Guard units were lucky if they had one rifle between ten men. Carrying out night patrols on the lookout for German paratroopers, volunteers armed themselves with pickaxes, crowbars and knives. A shotgun was regarded as a very superior piece of equipment.

It was fortunate the German invasion never came, for the Home Guard would surely have been massacred. Volunteer duty turned out nonetheless to be a useful occupation for those too old for real fighting. They continued drilling, training and watching out for spies until the Home Guard was disbanded in December 1944.

THE BLITZ ON BRITAIN

▲ Surrounded by flames, the magnificent dome of St Paul's Cathedral stands defiantly above the smoke and rubble.

In the early stages of the war, the Luftwaffe showed the destruction it could visit upon cities with devastating attacks on Warsaw and Rotterdam, but the Germans made no attempt to bomb British cities. On August 24, 1940, a German aircraft that had gone off course unloaded its bombs over London. The following night, the RAF retaliated with a raid on Berlin. Incensed, Hitler ordered an all-out offensive against the British capital.

On September 7, the Luftwaffe carried out its first large-scale daylight raid on London. Daylight bombing, however, entailed heavy losses. In the autumn the Germans changed their tactics to night attacks, sending over fleets of bombers whenever weather permitted. Britain had no effective air defence against night bombing. From October 1940 to May 1941, the civilian population of London and other British cities – Liverpool, Belfast, Plymouth, Coventry, Cardiff and many more – found themselves exposed to the full terror of aerial bombardment. This became known as the Blitz.

By day, people on the whole did the best they could to continue with normal existence, although often struggling to reach work as bombing disrupted transport services. By night, those in areas under attack found what protection they could in individual or communal shelters. In London, Underground railway stations were a popular refuge. Almost 180,000 people were sleeping there each night when the raids on London were at their peak. In smaller provincial cities, thousands fled to the surrounding countryside when the bombers came.

The dropping of a mix of explosive and incendiary bombs severely challenged the emergency services, called out to cope with raging fires as death rained down from the sky. On occasion, the situation on the ground threatened complete breakdown. The terrible raid on Coventry on November 14–15, 1940, damaged or destroyed a third of the city's

▲ The aftermath – the heart of London's commercial district viewed from the gallery of St Paul's Cathedral.

▲ A milkman makes his daily deliveries through the debris, as Londoners try to carry on with life during the Blitz.

houses and killed or severely wounded over 1,400 people. On May 10, 1941, the worst night for London, there were more than 2,000 fires, every mainline railway station was put out of action, and over 3,000 people were killed or injured.

Yet the raids never came close to destroying Britain's ability to wage war or its will to continue the struggle. The highly publicized visits to bomb-damaged areas by Churchill and the King and Queen were hardly necessary to raise morale. In a few localities that had experienced an especially severe raid, there might be temporary signs of mass panic, but on the whole people dug into reserves of courage and coped with private fears and grieving as best they could.

The Luftwaffe's bombing campaign came to an abrupt end in May 1941, as Hitler switched his attentions to other theatres of war. Although Britain's cities would continue to be a target for sporadic raids by the German Air Force, the Blitz was over. Around 43,000 British civilians had been killed – far more deaths than had yet been suffered by the country's armed forces.

OCTOBER
- Chamberlain resigns because of ill-health; Ernest Bevin and Sir Kingsley Wood join the War Cabinet
- Churchill replaces Chamberlain as leader of the Conservative Party
- Princess Elizabeth, aged 14, broadcasts a radio message to child evacuees in the Dominions and the United States
- The passenger liner *Empress of Britain* carrying child refugees from Britain is sunk by a U-boat

NOVEMBER
- Aircraft from the Royal Navy carrier *Illustrious* cripple the Italian fleet at Taranto
- Coventry is devastated by a German air raid
- Bomber Command carries out an air raid on Hamburg
- Deaths of former Prime Minister Neville Chamberlain, newspaper proprietor Lord Rothermere, and of sculptor Eric Gill

DECEMBER
- The British Eighth Army launches an offensive against Italian forces in Libya
- Lord Halifax is made ambassador to the United States; Anthony Eden replaces him as Foreign Secretary and as a member of the War Cabinet
- Recently re-elected US President Roosevelt promises the US will be the "arsenal of democracy"
- The City of London is set alight by incendiary bombs in a post-Christmas air raid

- Conscription is extended to unmarried women aged 20 to 30
- A National Fire Service is established
- Double Summer Time is introduced to maximize use of daylight hours
- "Utility" styles conform to clothes rationing
- "V for Victory" campaign is launched by the BBC
- "The Brains Trust" becomes one of the most popular radio programmes
- Penicillin is first used as a practical medical treatment
- The Gloster jet aircraft makes its maiden flight
- P G Wodehouse, interned by the Germans, makes broadcasts that lead to accusations of aiding the enemy
- Books published this year include *New Year Letter* by W H Auden
- British films this year include Harry Watt's documentary *Target for Tonight*
- Noël Coward's play *Blithe Spirit* has its first performance
- Vera Lynn sings "The White Cliffs of Dover"

AMY JOHNSON DIES IN PLANE CRASH

On January 5, 1941, pilot Amy Johnson, "Queen of the Air" as far as the British press was concerned, drowned after her plane went down in the Thames Estuary.

Born in Hull on July 1, 1903, Johnson leaped to fame with a solo flight from England to Australia in 1930. Throughout her life, she encountered male prejudice that prevented her pursuing a straightforward career as a professional pilot.

In 1940, she enrolled in the Air Transport Auxiliary, taking on the unglamorous but satisfying job of ferrying aircraft between RAF airfields.

On the morning of January 5, Johnson took off from Blackpool airport in freezing fog. She was bound for RAF Kidlington in Oxfordshire, but became hopelessly lost. Four hours after take-off she was spotted parachuting into the sea. She had almost certainly abandoned her aircraft after running out of fuel. A naval vessel, HMS *Haslemere*, went to her rescue, but she was sucked under the ship's stern. The ship's captain also died after diving into the freezing water in an attempt to save her.

Many wild rumours circulated about the circumstances of Johnson's death, but it appears to have been a tragic accident.

▲ Amy Johnson before setting out on the 1930 solo flight from England to Australia for which she became famous.

DEATH OF JAMES JOYCE

▲ The great modernist writer James Joyce, arguably one of the most influential authors of the twentieth century.

The great innovative Irish novelist James Augustine Aloysius Joyce died in Zürich, Switzerland, on January 13. Born in Dublin, Ireland, in 1882, Joyce received his education at the hands of the Jesuits, both at school and later, at University College Dublin.

He studied languages at University College but chose to devote the majority of his time to exploring his growing interest in literary matters. During this time,

he managed to sell a number of reviews and short stories to various magazines. Flushed with success, Joyce resolved to make writing his occupation.

Among his best-known works are *Dubliners*, *A Portrait of The Artist as a Young Man*, a largely biographical work, and *Ulysses*, which was written in a style that would later be known as "stream-of-consciousness" and which is seen as a modern parallel to Homer's *Odyssey*.

WAR IN THE DESERT

The British Army's first victories of the Second World War came against the Italians in North Africa. Italy's entry into the war in June 1940 raised alarm over the security of the Suez Canal, as British and Commonwealth forces in Egypt, Sudan and Somalia were easily outnumbered by the Italians

in Libya, Abyssinia and Eritrea. But, under the command of General Sir Archibald Wavell, they inflicted defeats on Mussolini's troops on all fronts. On February 5–6, 1941, 7th Armoured Division – the Desert Rats – crushed General Graziani's army at Beda Fomm in Libya,

taking over 20,000 prisoners.

Hitler sent one his most successful tank commanders, General Erwin Rommel, to North Africa to rescue the Italians. Rommel's mastery of mechanized desert warfare soon earned him the title of "Desert Fox", as time and again he hammered the British with a combination of surprise, ingenuity and the superior quality of his Afrika Korps. On March 31, he attacked the British position at El Agheila. Over the next two days, the British were driven into retreat, creating chaos in their ranks that led to serious losses. In less than a fortnight, they were pushed back out of Libya, withdrawing even faster than their previous advance. A small force held out in the port of Tobruk while the rest regrouped on the Egyptian border.

A see-saw battle ensued, with fighting swaying back and forth across the Western Desert. By the end of 1941, British and Commonwealth forces were once more deep inside Libya and had relieved the siege of Tobruk. But Rommel was no ordinary tank commander. He counter-attacked and, by June 1942, had sent the British reeling back to El Alamein, within just 100 km (60 miles) of Cairo.

▲ **A Panzer division of Rommel's Afrika Korps advances rapidly through the Libyan desert.**

CRETE FALLS TO NAZIS

The fall of the Mediterranean island of Crete to the Germans in May 1941 was one of the lowest points of Britain's military fortunes in the whole war. What is worse, it was a wholly avoidable catastrophe.

In April 1941 German forces overran Yugoslavia and Greece in yet another lightning campaign. British and Commonwealth troops – mostly Australians and New Zealanders – who had been sent to aid the Greeks were hastily evacuated in the face of the irresistible German advance. Most of them ended up on Crete.

Because of the success of Britain's Enigma codebreakers in deciphering German communications, the Allied commander on Crete, New Zealand Major General Bernard Freyberg, was fully informed of German plans to attack the island. He knew that General Kurt Student planned an airborne assault in which parachute troops would seize airfields, allowing reinforcements to be flown in.

When the German 7th Airborne Division drifted down from the sky over Crete on May 20, Freyberg's troops were waiting for them. More than half of the paratroopers were killed or wounded before or shortly after reaching the ground. Yet, unaccountably, the defenders failed to prevent the Germans taking the airfield at Malame. Once transport planes with reinforcements and heavy equipment began to land there, the balance of forces quickly reversed.

Under attack from the Luftwaffe, which had complete command of the air, Freyberg's troops retreated across the mountains to Sphakia on Crete's south coast, from where around half were successfully evacuated to Egypt. The Royal Navy lost three cruisers and six destroyers in this desperate mini-Dunkirk. Some 12,000 troops left trapped on the island became prisoners of war.

Coming at the same time as some of the worst air raids of the London Blitz and Rommel's first triumphs in the desert war, the fall of Crete completed a dark and bitter springtime for the British people in 1941.

▲ **German paratroopers move forward past the bodies of British soldiers after their successful air invasion of Crete.**

JANUARY
- British forces take Bardia in Libya
- The aircraft carrier *Illustrious* is seriously damaged by Luftwaffe bombers while escorting a convoy to Malta
- The *Daily Worker*, newspaper of the British Communist Party, is suppressed for defeatism
- Italian forces retreat from Kenya
- British forces in Kenya invade Italian Somaliland
- Death of Boy Scouts founder Lord Robert Baden-Powell

FEBRUARY
- British troops occupy Benghazi and take El Agheila in Libya
- General Erwin Rommel arrives in Libya

MARCH
- Over 500,000 tons of merchant shipping are destroyed by German U-boats, surface raiders and bombers in one month
- A British offensive penetrates Italian-controlled Abyssinia
- Rommel drives back British forces from El Agheila
- British forces capture Keren in Eritrea from the Italians
- A British naval victory over Italy at the Battle of Cape Matapan in the Mediterranean
- The Lend-Lease Bill is approved in the United States
- German air raids hit many cities and ports, including Clydebank, Bristol, Cardiff and Portsmouth
- Death by suicide of author Virginia Woolf

1941

HESS LANDS IN SCOTLAND

On May 10, 1941, the 3rd Renfrewshire Battalion of the Home Guard arrested a German who had landed by parachute near the Scottish village of Eaglesham in Scotland. The man initially gave his name as Alfred Horn and demanded to see the Duke of Hamilton, whose residence was nearby. Taken into custody, "Horn" soon revealed his true identity to be Rudolf Hess, Hitler's right-hand man in the Nazi regime.

Hess had taken off from Augsburg in southern Germany, piloting a Messerschmitt Bf 110 fighter-bomber. He had successfully navigated a course of around 1,600 km (1,000 miles) to land close to Dungavel House, the Duke of Hamilton's estate. By his own account, Hess had come to negotiate a peace deal with Britain. He was certain that Hamilton and other British

▲ The wreckage of Rudolf Hess's plane. The deputy leader of the Nazi Party's secret mission to Scotland ended in his capture.

aristocrats whom he had met before the war favoured a rapprochement with Germany. He intended to urge George VI to unseat Churchill from power and install a government favourable to the Nazis. Britain and Germany could then form an alliance against the Soviet Union, which the Germans planned to invade the following month.

Astonished by Hess's arrival, Churchill ordered him locked up in a house outside London and kept under observation. No public mention was made of his peace proposal, possibly because the government feared it might have sounded too tempting to the British people, suffering under the Blitz and depressed by a string of military setbacks. Hess's initiative was in any case immediately disowned by the Nazi leadership, which declared him the victim of mental illness and hallucinations.

Hess remained a prisoner throughout the war and was then put on trial at Nuremberg. Convicted as a war criminal, he was incarcerated in Spandau prison in Berlin until his death in 1987.

SINKING OF THE BISMARCK

The German Navy's most powerful warship, the *Bismarck*, a supreme symbol of the might of the Third Reich, came to the end of its short but illustrious career on May 27.

At the time of its launch in 1939, it displaced more than 52,000 tons and had a top speed of 30 knots. Armed with eight guns capable of firing 15-in (38-cm) shells, the sight of the *Bismarck* sailing over the horizon caused many a British sailor to wish he was on dry land.

Its sighting off Norway in May by a reconnaissance plane sent the Royal Navy into a frenzy. Determined to sink this symbol of German naval power, the British sent most of its North Atlantic fleet into action. After an initial contact near Iceland with two British

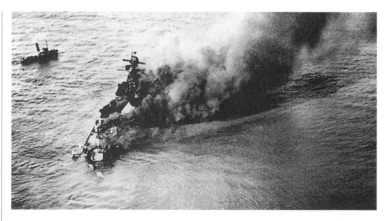

▲ Three torpedoes from HMS *Dorsetshire* send the *Bismarck*, flagship of the German navy, to its final resting place on the bed of the Atlantic.

cruisers, the mighty warship was attacked by the Royal Navy battleship *Prince of Wales* and the battle cruiser *Hood*.

After sinking the *Hood*, the *Bismarck* headed for open seas, but was spotted again on May 26. A torpedo attack destroyed the *Bismarck*'s steering gear and again it came under heavy attack from battleships in the area.

Finally, on the morning of May 27, the once invincible battleship was sent to the bottom of the sea by three torpedoes fired from the cruiser *Dorsetshire*.

CHURCHILL WELCOMES SOVIETS AS ALLIES

▲Churchill and Stalin at the Kremlin. Churchill placed Britain firmly on the side of Russia in the struggle against Nazism.

At dawn on June 22, 1941, Germany and its allies invaded the Soviet Union in Operation Barbarossa. That evening, Winston Churchill made a radio broadcast to the nation, placing Britain firmly on the side of the Soviets in the struggle against Nazism. "The cause of any Russian fighting for his hearth and home," he stated, "is the cause of free men and free peoples in every quarter of the globe."

This was a giant leap for Churchill, who had been one of the most consistent and outspoken enemies of Soviet communism. But victory over Hitler came before all other considerations. As Churchill had earlier remarked: "If Hitler invaded Hell I would make at least a favourable reference to the Devil in the House of Commons."

British military chiefs were dismissive of the Soviet armed forces and foresaw another easy triumph for German *blitzkrieg* tactics, but many British workers greeted the new ally with enthusiasm. Some factories were bedecked with Soviet hammer-and-sickle flags and "Uncle Joe" Stalin was turned into a popular hero.

The British government was unstintingly generous in its aid to the Soviets. By September hazardous Arctic convoys were carrying aircraft, tanks and other essential war material to Russia's northern ports. This was not enough for the British Communist Party and part of the British press, who raised the cry for a "second front" – a British invasion of Europe to take the strain off the hard-pressed Soviets.

Although long resisting second-front agitation, Churchill proved himself a loyal ally of Stalin throughout the war, never wavering in his commitment to the defeat of Hitler at any cost.

ATLANTIC CHARTER

The unofficial alliance between Great Britain and the United States took a step closer to becoming a formal agreement after the leaders of both countries issued a joint declaration on August 14.

Winston Churchill had travelled in great secrecy to meet President Franklin D Roosevelt at Placentia Bay in Newfoundland. During the meeting, the two men drew up the joint declaration which became known as the Atlantic Charter.

Essentially, the agreement was a statement of common aims that declared that neither nation sought aggrandisement, territorial or otherwise, nor did they seek territorial changes without the consent of the peoples involved. They also resolved to respect or restore all sovereign rights and to promote equal access for all to trade. They also pledged to improve labour standards, economic progress and social security. In addition, the two signatories stated that they would seek to keep the seas free and to disarm potential aggressors.

Admirable as these aims were, it was the statement contained within the declaration that the two countries would seek to carry out the first five aims of the charter "after the final destruction of the Nazi tyranny" that had the greatest impact.

For a country as powerful as the United States to be seen to be making such a declaration jointly with one of Hitler's few remaining undefeated enemies amounted to little more than a thinly veiled declaration of war which sent shock waves through the German High Command.

▲ US President Roosevelt and British Prime Minister Churchill bring their countries closer together with the signing of the Atlantic Charter.

1942

Although women had achieved full political rights in Britain by 1930, their social status was still determined by traditional patronizing attitudes towards the "second sex". Large numbers of women worked outside the home – more than a quarter of females over 14 were in paid employment in 1939. But most of those who worked were young and unmarried, and their jobs were considered of low status – primary school teaching, clerical and typing work, domestic service or light industry. Married women were generally expected to devote themselves to their domestic duties. The Second World War had some effect in opening up new opportunities for women, but it did little to alter ingrained attitudes to their position in society.

At the outset of war in 1939, around 43,000 women volunteered for the Women's Auxiliary Services – the WAAFS (Women's Auxiliary Air Force), the WRENS (Women's Royal Naval Service), the ATS (Auxiliary Territorial Service) and various nursing services. Otherwise, there was at first little change in the employment of women. It was not until the summer of 1940 that the mass unemployment of the 1930s came to an end and a labour shortage began to bite. By 1941, the competing demands of the army, civil defence and arms production left Britain facing a projected shortfall of about 1.5 million soldiers and workers. Such a shortage would clearly have to be made up by women.

Throughout 1941, increasing numbers of housewives were lured or pressured into taking jobs, while

▲ Although British women did not participate directly in the fighting, the Second World War had a profound impact on many women's lives. They encountered new experiences that were not forgotten in peacetime.

thousands of women already in employment were shifted into essential war work. In December the government reluctantly took the logical final step of introducing conscription for women, although only for those who were unmarried and aged 20 to 30. They were

▲ With Britain's men on active duty, the volunteers of the Women's Land Army were called upon to take on their roles.

given the choice between joining the armed forces or working in war industries.

By 1943, there were 8 million women in employment, about 2 million more than before the war. Around half a million of them were in the armed forces as members of the Women's Auxiliary Services or as nurses. This expansion of employment did not necessarily involve a change in women's status. While those employed in arms factories – numbering around 2 million by 1943 – were clearly doing jobs traditionally considered "men's work", many women still found themselves assigned to clerical or culinary duties, even when in the armed forces. Women were considered unsuitable for combat, although during the Blitz they did

staff anti-aircraft guns. The active role most commonly assigned to women in the services was as drivers.

As in peacetime, women were paid less than men, even when doing the same jobs. For example, women who worked in metalwork and engineering factories during the war received an average of £3/10s a week (£3.50) compared with £7 on average for male workers. Even so, more women than ever before found themselves with their own money in their purses or pockets.

Beyond the hard facts and figures, the individual experiences of women in the war varied greatly. Work in munitions factories was repetitive and exhausting, with shifts lasting from ten to 12 hours in harsh conditions. On the other hand, many of the 80,000 who joined the Women's Land Army have recorded enjoying working on farms, finding satisfaction in country life even if working hours were long and living conditions primitive. Some women were later to look back on their time in the armed services as a period of relative glamour and freedom in their lives; others found little but drudgery.

For women who remained at home, often bringing up children single-handedly with a husband away in the army, everyday life was exhausting and difficult. They had the complexities of food and clothes rationing to cope with and spent hours queuing to obtain the basic essentials for the family. Loneliness and anxiety were commonplace experiences of women in the war.

The general disruption of life inevitably led to some degree of breakdown in conventional sexual behaviour. The first year of the war brought a flood of marriages as sweethearts wed before being parted by military service. Many newly married women then spent years alone, separated from husbands with whom they may have lived just a few weeks. As well as an increase in marriages, the war brought a steep rise in the illegitimacy rate, with almost double the annual number of births outside marriage recorded in peacetime.

Unmarried pregnant women were cruelly treated. If they were in the armed services, they were thrown out the moment their condition was known. If they were housed in hostels – as many war workers were – they were frequently ejected on to the street. Married women who strayed from the straight and narrow while their husbands were away at the war did not suffer the physical hardships experienced by unmarried mothers. They would, though, perhaps understandably, face intense moral disapproval within their neighbourhoods.

The lack of any transformation in attitudes to sexual morality was mirrored by a general lack of change in men's view of women's place in society. For example, in 1946 William Beveridge, a man of notably liberal views and the architect of the welfare state, declared that a married woman should not have the same attitude to employment outside the home as a single woman, since: "Mothers have vital work to do in ensuring the adequate continuance of the British race."

This was not a view with which women actively disagreed. After the war, millions would return apparently contented – to the role of housewife and mother. It would take another two decades before the daughters and granddaughters of those who endured the Second World War marched in the streets demanding equal pay and equal opportunities as their right.

▲ Noncombatants they may be, but these women in uniform, a general nurse and a WRAF, are in the front line on the Home Front.

▲ The need for armaments brought women back into the munitions factories. Britain's war effort would have been unsustainable without them.

- A "Dig for Victory" campaign encourages British people to grow their own food
- Cheap self-service cafeterias are renamed British Restaurants
- Rationing is extended to soap, coal, sweets and chocolate
- The standard rate of income tax is 50 per cent; purchase tax is 66 per cent on many goods
- A government campaign publicizes the risks of venereal disease after the sharp rise in cases of syphilis and gonorrhoea
- The Avro Lancaster heavy bomber enters service with Bomber Command
- Navigational devices "GEE" and "OBOE" improve accuracy of night bombing
- The government threatens to shut down the *Daily Mirror* for criticizing the conduct of the war
- The ban on the communist *Daily Worker* newspaper is lifted
- Oxford Committee for Famine Relief, later known as Oxfam, is founded
- Books published this year include Evelyn Waugh's *Put Out More Flags*
- British films this year include Noël Coward's *In Which We Serve*, Alberto Cavalcanti's *Went the Day Well?*, Leslie Howard's *The First of the Few* and Michael Powell's *One of Our Aircraft Is Missing*
- Hit song of the year is Vera Lynn's "The White Cliffs of Dover"

FALL OF SINGAPORE ROCKS BRITISH EMPIRE

▲ **Despite outnumbering Japanese troops by two to one, the British attempt to defend Singapore ended in humiliating surrender.**

On February 15, 1942, General Arthur Percival, the British commander in Singapore, surrendered to Japanese General Tomoyuki Yamashita, despite possessing numerically superior forces and plentiful reserves of ammunition. It was the most humiliating day in the history of the British Army and a mortal blow to the prestige of the British Empire.

Britain had been helped when Japan attacked the American naval base at Pearl Harbor in December 1941, because it brought the United States into the war against Hitler. But in the short term, fighting alongside the Americans in the Pacific War only increased Britain's problem of severely overstretched resources. Within weeks of taking the offensive, the Japanese snapped up British-ruled Hong Kong and invaded the British colony of Malaya.

Singapore was Britain's major naval base in Asia and – in theory – an impregnable island fortress. Back in 1940, Churchill had dismissed the possibility that the Japanese would ever "embark on such a mad enterprise" as an attempt to take the base. Yet their rapid advance on foot and bicycle through the jungles of the Malay Peninsula brought Japanese troops to the mainland end of the causeway to Singapore by the end of January 1941.

The island was packed with British, Indian and Australian soldiers. Some had retreated there as the Japanese advanced through Malaya, while others were still being shipped in to join the fighting. They outnumbered Yamashita's troops by two to one. Yet General Percival could find no way of organizing them into a coherent defence. On February 9 the Japanese crossed Johore Strait and established a bridgehead on the island.

Churchill did his best to stiffen Percival's resolve, ordering a fight to the bitter end. He cabled the regional Commander-in-Chief General Wavell that "Commander and senior officers should die with their troops." But Percival and his Australian subordinate General Gordon Bennett were in no mood for a bloodbath. Unable to drive the Japanese from the island and under persistent artillery and aerial bombardment, they believed surrender to be the only sensible path.

Percival marched stiffly into the Japanese lines on the afternoon of February 15, carrying a furled Union Jack and accompanied by a staff officer with a white flag. Around 130,000 soldiers were delivered into the nightmare of Japanese captivity. General Bennett controversially slipped away on one of the last boats to escape from Singapore.

The British surrender to an Asiatic enemy rocked the foundations of an Empire based on the assumption of racial superiority. Most of the captured Indian troops joined a Japanese-formed Indian National Army to fight against the British. In Australia, where the abject surrender was deeply resented, the government ensured that henceforth Australian forces fought for the defence of their own country, rather than in the interests of Britain.

In truth, ever since the First World War, Britain had been trying to maintain an Empire that was beyond its resources to uphold. Now its bluff had been called, and a future of imperial withdrawal was inevitable.

AUSTERITY REIGNS UNDER CRIPPS

▲ A customer at a special parlour in Croydon saves her ration coupons by having stockings "painted" on to her legs.

In February 1942, Labour politician Sir Stafford Cripps joined the War Cabinet. He made himself the spokesman for "austerity", the deliberate denial of consumer choice and frivolous luxury. Perhaps surprisingly, this apparently killjoy policy was welcomed by most British people as necessary for the prosecution of the war and in line with a sense of fairness and social justice.

Rationing, imposed on such items as petrol, sugar, bacon and tea early in the war, was extended to an ever-widening range of goods, including soap, tinned salmon, chocolates and sweets. Some items were rationed by quantity – the cheese ration was initially a miserly one ounce a week. Others, such as clothes, worked on a points system – a pair of trousers cost eight coupons, a pair of shoes seven, and so on.

But austerity went far beyond simple rationing. A whole range of "utility" goods were produced in line with official regulations, intended to rationalize production and save resources. In utility clothing, limits were placed on the number of pockets and pleats in a garment and the length of socks and shirt-tails. There were utility versions of a host of other items, from tea cups – plain white – to tables, chairs and even pencils. Manufacture of objects considered purely frivolous, such as fruit machines and billiard tables, was banned altogether.

Of course, a black market flourished and wealth and power could always buy privilege – there was nothing austere about Churchill's wartime diet. But austerity appealed to a sense of shared sacrifice that helped hold Britain's social fabric together under the strain of war.

RAID ON DIEPPE

At dawn on the morning of August 19, 6,000 commandos drawn mostly from British and Canadian forces began a daring raid on the heavily defended French coastal port of Dieppe. Fighting was fierce all along the beach and the cost to Allied lives of attempting the landing and trying to bring heavy guns ashore was immense. Positions of a sort were created by the sea wall, although in reality most of the men who made it to the sea wall did so simply in order to shelter from the withering fire of the German guns.

Despite the hopelessness of their situation, the commandos fought on until, at around 2 pm,

they finally caved in. French citizens emerging from their shelters after the raid – they had been warned by the BBC to do nothing that might compromise their own safety – found a seafront in tatters, with bodies and damaged equipment lying everywhere. The Germans initially buried the almost 1,000 Allied dead in a mass grave but, in a rare display of respect for the fallen enemy, the Wehrmacht Graves Commission sent coffins to Dieppe and the dead commandos were reburied by the Germans with full military honours.

▶ The Allies lost tanks, aircraft, landing craft and other arms, as well as thousands of troops, either killed or taken prisoner, at Dieppe.

1942

RAF NIGHT RAIDS HIT GERMANY

In February 1942 Air Marshal Sir Arthur Harris was put in control of RAF Bomber Command. "Bomber" Harris, as he became appropriately known, sincerely believed that, given adequate resources, the bombing of German cities could win the war for Britain without the need for a costly invasion of Europe. His views chimed with those of Winston Churchill, who stated in 1940: "There is one thing that will bring Hitler down, and that is an absolutely devastating, exterminating attack by very heavy bombers … upon the Nazi homeland."

Bomber Command had begun the war with daylight raids against Germany, before unsustainable losses had forced it to switch to night attacks. The RAF's night bombing was so inaccurate that all thought of hitting precise industrial and military targets had to be abandoned. Instead, "area"

bombing was adopted, targeting nothing more precise than a whole urban zone. Harris argued that if such attacks were carried out on a sufficient scale, the German economy would crumble and German morale collapse.

There was definitely an element of revenge in the British decision to bomb enemy civilians. One bomber crew member recounted that when he and his colleagues were told they were going to bomb a German town indiscriminately, "a shout of agreement greeted the news, as most airmen came from towns that had suffered heavily from German air attacks." But in the British government's view, it was also a rational act of war, aimed at "the morale of the German civil population and, in particular, of the industrial workers".

After preliminary attacks on Lübeck and the Ruhr, in May and

▲ Hitler declared the RAF would never reach his capital, but Berlin and other German cities were in ruins by the war's end.

June 1942 Harris began mounting his famous "thousand-bomber raids" against German cities, notably destroying around a third of the entire city of Cologne in a single night. Bomber Command suffered heavy losses to German air defences, however, and Harris simply could not mount raids on this scale with any frequency.

In the second half of 1942, the daylight bombers of the US Air Force joined in the attack on Germany. There was to be no respite from then until the end of the war. The destruction of Hamburg in the summer of 1943, when incendiary bombs caused a fire-storm in which possibly 40,000 people died, showed what lay ahead for the German people. The devastation of their cities would far outstrip anything that the Luftwaffe inflicted on Britain.

▲ The crew of an RAF Lancaster bomber pose in front of their aircraft. Around 56,000 bomber crew members were killed in the war.

MONTY AND ROMMEL AT EL ALAMEIN

By the end of June 1942, Axis forces in North Africa led by General Erwin Rommel had driven British and Commonwealth forces back into Egypt – destroying many

of their tanks on the way. The British then succeeded in holding a defensive line at El Alamein. There the two armies remained as the months passed.

In August the British appointed a new general, Harold Alexander, to take command of its forces in the region and he in turn appointed General Bernard L Montgomery as

▲ General Bernard Montgomery – "Monty" to the men of the Eighth Army – the hero of the Allied campaign in North Africa.

his commander in the field. Montgomery delayed the counter-offensive against Rommel until he could be sure that the British Eighth Army was at full strength.

Allied air and submarine attacks in the Mediterranean made it difficult for Rommel to obtain fresh supplies and equipment at El Alamein. By the time that Montgomery was ready for battle, Rommel had only 80,000 men, 210 tanks and 350 aircraft with which to fight Montgomery's 230,000 men, 1,230 tanks and 1,500 aircraft.

At 10 pm on October 23, the Eighth Army went into action. Just two days later, half of Rommel's tanks had been destroyed, but on the next day he succeeded in stopping the British advance with antitank guns. For a week the British and Axis forces played a deadly game of cat and mouse, with the British taking by far the greater number of casualties. During the first week of fighting, the British lost four times as many tanks as the Axis forces. By November 2, however, it was obvious that Rommel had lost the battle. He headed back towards Libya, and from there was eventually forced back to Tunisia.

The victory at El Alamein made Montgomery a national hero. Churchill, with a mixture of caution and obvious satisfaction, described it as not "the beginning of the end" but perhaps "the end of the beginning". Celebratory church bells were rung across Britain for the first time in three desperate years of war.

▲ A worthy adversary, General Erwin Rommel – "the Desert Fox" – was held in the highest regard by his enemies.

THE YANKS ARE COMING

On January 26, 1942, seven weeks after the Japanese attack on Pearl Harbor brought the United States into the war, the first two ship-loads of American GIs landed at Belfast. By October there were more than 200,000 US military personnel in Britain.

The US forces brought with them a profusion of goods that were in short supply or unobtainable in Britain – razor blades, chocolate bars, good-quality soap, Lucky Strike cigarettes and nylon stockings. Much better paid than their British opposite numbers, and equipped with such valued items for barter, they found few problems in attracting girlfriends – hence justifying the famous quip about being "overpaid, over-sexed and over here".

▲ Sir Archibald Sinclair chats with the first US troops to arrive in the British Isles on January 26.

The Americans brought with them not just goods, but a way of life. They had their own social customs – including racial segregation – and their own newspapers, films and radio programmes. Their presence inevitably gave a boost to the Americanization of British culture, already recognized as a phenomenon of the 1930s. For example, young Britons gained access to the latest American jazz and swing bands, music otherwise available mostly in watered-down British imitations.

With 1.6 million US troops in Britain by spring 1944, it is hardly surprising that some jaundiced observers talked of "the American occupation".

- Labour shortages threaten the war effort
- A government White Paper, known as the Keynes Plan, advocates an international bank to create postwar economic growth and stability
- R A Butler, Minister of Education, draws up a plan for free secondary education for all children
- Launch of a National Savings campaign with the slogan "Wings for Victory"
- A Pay As You Earn (PAYE) income tax system is proposed
- The ban on ringing church bells – reserved for warning of an invasion – is lifted
- Official figures show the crime rate has risen 25 per cent compared with the last year of peace
- The Gloster Meteor – Britain's first jet fighter – makes its maiden flight
- Lord Nuffield creates the Nuffield Foundation for medical, scientific and social research
- Books published this year include T S Eliot's *Four Quartets*
- British films this year include Michael Powell's *The Life and Death of Colonel Blimp*, Humphrey Jennings's documentary *Fires Were Started*, and Roy Boulting's documentary *Desert Victory*
- First performance of Noël Coward's play *This Happy Breed*
- First performance of Benjamin Britten's *Serenade for Tenor, Horn and Strings*

BEVERIDGE REPORT SPLITS PARLIAMENT

On February 18, 1943, almost 100 Labour MPs voted against the government – which included leaders of their own party – at the end of a debate on the Beveridge Report on the reform of social security. It was a vote that set the agenda for Labour's election victory at the end of the war as the party of the welfare state.

Sir William Beveridge, director of the London School of Economics before the war, had chaired a government committee set up to consider the future of old age pensions, unemployment insurance and health insurance. Published in December 1942, his 300-page report offered a broad vision of a future Britain free from poverty and unemployment, where universal social security would guarantee every individual a reasonable standard of living and a National Health Service would offer free medical care for all. "The purpose of victory," Beveridge stated, "is to live in a better world than the old world."

Beveridge's vision of a welfare state met with an enthusiastic response from the public. More than 600,000 copies of the report and of a shorter official summary of its text were sold. But Churchill and most of his government ministers did not share this enthusiasm.

The debate on the report in the House of Commons opened on

February 16. It was soon obvious that although the government was officially proposing acceptance of Beveridge's plan, ministers held many reservations about its implementation. Beveridge had suggested the creation of a new Ministry of Social Security to press ahead with the necessary reforms; the government insisted that nothing should be done until after the war.

▲ **The economist Sir William Beveridge addresses an audience at a Liberal meeting at the Caxton Hall in London.**

The Labour MPs who voted against the government demanded a more enthusiastic embrace of the Beveridge plan and the policies proposed in it were broadly implemented by the post-1945 Labour government.

WINNING THE U-BOAT WAR

Britain's survival throughout the Second World War was dependent on the delivery of food and war material by sea. The Germans sought to cut this lifeline and reduce Britain to surrender through a blockade. Their most potent weapon was their U-boat

fleet, which at times came close to winning the war.

The German submarines first made serious inroads into merchant shipping when the defeat of France in June 1940 allowed them to sail from bases on the French Atlantic coast. Over the

next two and a half years, fortunes fluctuated in what became known as the Battle of the Atlantic. British and Canadian naval escort vessels, with a little help from the Americans, attempted to protect merchant convoys against the U-boat "wolf packs", deploying an ever-expanding array of sonar and radar detection devices and depth charges.

A secret intelligence war had a crucial influence on the Atlantic battlefield. Early on, the Germans cracked British naval codes and could decipher radio messages. British codebreakers at Bletchley Park struggled with mixed success to do the same to intercepted German naval messages encoded on Enigma machines.

The Battle of the Atlantic came to its climax in the spring of 1943. By late February the Allies were gaining the upper hand over the U-boats through successful decoding of intelligence intercepts and a cluster of other advances – improved radar, extensive air cover provided by long-range aircraft and escort carriers, and better-trained

and organized escort teams. But at the start of March, a change in the German naval codes suddenly foiled the British decoders. That month, sinkings of merchant shipping rose to almost the highest level of the whole war.

To the great relief of the Allies, there followed an even sharper downturn in shipping losses. By May the U-boats were facing the

▲ **Coast guards watch the explosion of a depth charge which destroyed a Nazi U-boat's hope of breaking into a large convoy.**

stark prospect of annihilation, as British intelligence and Allied sea and air power combined to destroy 41 submarines in a month. The U-boat fleet was withdrawn from the ocean to recoup. It never seriously threatened Britain's lifeline again.

JANUARY
- Churchill meets Roosevelt for a summit conference at Casablanca; unconditional surrender is adopted as a war aim
- A surprise Luftwaffe daylight raid kills 38 children when a bomb hits a school in Catford, south London
- The Eighth Army takes Tripoli in Libya
- The RAF bombs Berlin

FEBRUARY
- The Eighth Army reaches the Tunisian border
- Ceremonies in Britain celebrate Soviet armed forces on Red Army Day

MARCH
- More than 170 people are killed when panic breaks out in a crowded Underground shelter at Bethnal Green Tube station
- The German counter-attack in Tunisia fails
- Allied forces break through the Mareth Line in Tunisia
- Merchant convoys suffer heavy losses to U-boats in the Atlantic
- The RAF begin a large-scale bombing campaign against targets in the Ruhr

APRIL
- The Eighth Army links up with Allied forces under Eisenhower in Tunisia
- Death of socialist thinker Beatrice Webb

MAY
- Allied forces take Tunis; the German Army in Tunisia surrenders
- Churchill meets Roosevelt in Washington, DC; they agree to stage an invasion of Europe in May 1944
- Lancaster bombers breach the Ruhr dams
- U-boats are forced to withdraw from the Atlantic

THE WAR IN BURMA

▲ **The war in Burma saw British forces facing both a harsh climate and, in the Japanese, a formidable enemy.**

British forces fighting in Burma found themselves facing a Japanese army of considerable ability and determination. The Japanese interest in Burma had earlier led them to train a small guerrilla force of Burmese nationals, which was placed under the command of Aung San, and to promise them independence after the country was "liberated" from the British by Japanese forces.

The Japanese advanced into Burma in 1942 and by the end of the year had taken control of the entire country. Ba Maw, Burma's original Prime Minister under the

1939 constitution, was appointed head of state by the Japanese, while Aung San was given a position in the cabinet. In reality, however, Maw's government was little more than a front for the Japanese military.

When the British attempted to remove the Japanese from Burma, they found that the enemy had dug in well. Every attempt at an advance from India into Burma was met with the strongest possible response and soon the British began to despair of ever driving the Japanese out.

Against this desperate backdrop, Brigadier General Orde Wingate began to organize and train a small long-range specialist force. Known as the "Chindits", Wingate's troops were essentially a guerrilla army, which entered Burma from the west during February and May.

Having crossed the Chindwin River, they pressed further into enemy territory and began their

guerrilla campaign with attacks on the railway between Mandalay and Myitkyina, where they succeeded in cutting Japanese lines of communication.

From there they pressed on to the Irrawaddy River, all the time receiving supplies from the air. After crossing the river, they continued to disrupt Japanese communications but soon found that the terrain offered little cover or protection. Facing the possibility of capture, the Chindits were forced to return to India and the British were obliged to rethink the assault on Burma.

▲ **The "Chindit" army – Asian troops under the command of Allied officers – failed to rid Burma of the Japanese invaders.**

DAM BUSTERS TRIUMPH

Flying in a group of specially adapted Avro Lancaster bombers, Royal Air Force Wing Commander Guy Gibson and his team of "Dam busters" staged a series of daring raids in Germany on the night of May 16.

The aim of the raids was to strike a damaging blow at Germany's industrial military heartland in the Ruhr Valley by blowing up and breaching its three large dams. The dams, built in the valley, supplied water and hydroelectric power to Germany's vital armaments factories.

Previous attempts to blast the heavily defended dams had failed, either because the aircraft used for the attack had been intercepted before reaching their targets, or because the bombs they had dropped had proved relatively ineffective against the thick dam walls. Attempts on the dams using air-launched torpedoes were foiled by the antitorpedo nets that the Germans had placed in the water.

A British inventor, Barnes Wallace had, in the meantime,

▲ The Mohne Dam shatters, draining 134 million tons of water and crippling the Ruhr Valley's 300 hydroelectric power stations.

succeeded in demonstrating a new kind of bomb to an extremely sceptical group from the Ministry o of Defence.

Using the same principle that allows children to skim stones across the surface of a pond, Wallace's bomb could, if dropped at the right speed and from the correct height, bounce over the antitorpedo nets before coming to rest against the wall of the dam. Once there, it sank below the surface of the water and exploded.

The three targets for the raid were the dams on the Eder, the Mohne and the Scorpe. While the Scorpe dam was badly damaged during the raid on the night of May 16, the dams on the Eder and the Mohne were successfully breached, causing the Ruhr Valley below to flood and killing as many as 1,300 people in its wake.

To the Germans, the raid proved to be more of an inconvenience than a complete disaster, although the raid had successfully halted production until the dams were repaired.

ADVANCE THROUGH ITALY STALLS

▲ With a brief handshake, Italy's General Castellano (centre) gives his unconditional surrender to General Eisenhower (right).

Meeting at Casablanca in January 1943, British and American political and military leaders hotly debated their strategy for defeating Germany. The United States was keen to concentrate resources on an invasion of northern France; Churchill favoured an invasion of Italy, which would allow Allied forces to penetrate "the soft underbelly of Europe". In the end, Churchill got his way, but Italy was to prove far from a soft option.

The Italians themselves had little stomach for a fight. The

invasion of Sicily by Allied forces in July 1943 – with Montgomery commanding the British Eighth Army and General George Patton leading the US Seventh Army – brought about the downfall of the Italian dictator Benito Mussolini. In September, as the first Allied troops landed on the Italian mainland, Mussolini's successors surrendered and prepared to change sides. But the Germans had been preparing for the Italian betrayal, and when it came they were ready – if a little under strength – to step into the breach.

On September 9, a force of 170,000 British, US and other Allied troops landed at Salerno, south of Naples. The German Sixteenth Panzer Division was waiting for them, and succeeded in keeping them out of Naples

▲ **Inhabitants of the town of Reggio, grateful that their war is at an end, warmly welcome an invading Allied tank crew.**

until October 1. By the time the Italians declared war on Germany on October 13, German forces in Italy were being reinforced and had begun to consolidate their positions throughout the country, in particular along the Gustav Line, a series of defences ranged along the Garigliano and Sangro rivers that hinged on Monte Cassino.

General Sir Harold Alexander, the British Commander-in-Chief, found his troops – in his own words – "slogging up Italy". The narrow mountainous peninsula left no opportunity for flanking manoeuvres but offered plenty of natural defensive positions from which the Germans could resist frontal assaults. Four months after landing at Salerno, the Allied forces had advanced a mere 110 km (70 miles) northwards.

At the end of the year, Alexander's prestigious subordinate General Montgomery was transferred back to Britain to prepare for the invasion of France. The shifting of Montgomery revealed the true priorities of the war – the Italian campaign was in truth a costly sideshow

OCTOBER
• Allied troops enter Naples, Italy

NOVEMBER
• Churchill, Roosevelt and Stalin meet in Teheran
• The RAF begins a bombing campaign against the German capital, known as the Battle of Berlin
• Fascist leader Sir Oswald Mosley is released from prison on health grounds

DECEMBER
• The Royal Navy sinks the German battle cruiser *Scharnhorst*
• Ernest Bevin announces the conscription of young men into the coal mines
• A turkey shortage hits Christmas celebrations
• Death of children's author Beatrix Potter

BEVIN BOYS GO DOWN THE PITS

▲ **The drafting of one in ten boys of National Service age into coalmining was to prove a deeply unpopular measure.**

In 1943, Britain faced a severe labour shortage. The conflicting demands of the armed services, the armaments industries and ordinary production to meet civilian needs could not all be met. There were no more unemployed women to be drawn into the workforce and – because of the low birth rate in the 1920s – the numbers of young people leaving school were inadequate to compensate for the elderly retiring,

This problem fell to Minister of Labour Ernest Bevin, the blunt-spoken former trade unionist who had been one of Churchill's most inspired appointments. He faced a particular crisis in coalmining. Despite draconian measures by the government to keep miners and sons of miners in the pits, large numbers had found their way into the army or into less dangerous, better-paid jobs made available by the war. As coal production fell, Bevin decided upon drastic action to shift men from the armed services into the mines.

From December 1943, one in ten of all boys reaching the age for National Service was drafted into coalmining. The selection was done by random ballot, so many of those teenagers sent to pit villages were sons of the professional classes. The ballot was deeply unpopular. Almost any young man would prefer the prospect of being a soldier, sailor or airman to the equally dangerous but grim and unglamorous life of a miner.

Around 37,000 "Bevin Boys" worked in the pits in 1944–45. Experienced miners viewed them with amused contempt. As one miner wrote: "It would do the Bevin Boys no harm to see what the pits were like – but as for increasing production – a fat lot of difference they would make!"

- Wartime Allies agree to set up a United Nations Organization
- Britain plays the leading role in United Nations Bretton Woods Conference, which creates the World Bank and International Monetary Fund
- The Butler Education Act, introducing an 11-plus exam, is passed by parliament
- Children are again evacuated from London as German flying-bomb and rocket attacks cause heavy casualties
- "Austerity" restrictions on clothing styles are lifted
- Colossus, an electronic computer, comes into use for codebreaking at Bletchley Park
- British films this year include Laurence Olivier's *Henry V*, Carol Reed's *The Way Ahead* and Pat Jackson's documentary *Western Approaches*
- First performance of the oratorio *A Child of our Time* by Michael Tippett
- Books published this year include *The Horse's Mouth* by Joyce Cary, *For the Time Being* by W H Auden and *Full Employment in a Free Society* by William Beveridge
- First performance of Terence Rattigan's play *Love in Idleness*
- The Olympic Games, planned to be held in London, are cancelled because of the war

BAN ON TRAVEL TO IRELAND

▲ **A US marine, stationed at the Derry naval base in Northern Ireland, gets to know the locality.**

Concerned that information about the US naval base at Derry in Northern Ireland and Allied plans for the invasion of Europe might fall into the hands of Nazi supporters in the South, Britain introduced a general ban on travel to the Republic on March 12.

To a certain extent, the Irish Republic was a thorn in the side of those attempting to coordinate the defence of Britain. Despite declaring its neutrality early in the war, the Republic was still perceived by many in Britain as friendly to Hitler's Germany. In reality, this suspicion was born more of old enmities than of any concrete evidence of cooperation with the Nazis. While the Irish authorities did little to stop the Germans monitoring British communications from their consulate in Dublin, they did not actually encourage such activity and would probably have allowed the British to do the same thing had the situation been reversed.

The one area where Britain and Ireland may have clashed – over the use of Irish ports by British warships for the protection of its merchant fleet – was avoided by making arrangements elsewhere. Of this matter, however, Churchill later wrote, rather ominously: "if we had not been able to do without them we should have retaken them by force rather than perish by famine".

ALLIES STRUGGLE TO ROME

The start of 1944 found Allied forces in Italy stuck in front of the strongly defended Gustav Line at Monte Cassino. British General Sir Harold Alexander planned to exploit Allied command of the sea to outflank the enemy. On January 22, the Allies landed some 50,000 troops and 5,000 vehicles behind the Gustav Line at Anzio, 55 km (33 miles) south of Rome.

So unprepared were the Germans for the seaborne assault that at first they showed little resistance. Rather than press their advantage, however, the Allies wasted a great deal of time consolidating their bridgehead, giving the Germans time to mount a counter-attack. Churchill fumed, later writing: "I had hoped that we were hurling a wildcat on to the shore, but all we got was a stranded whale."

The Allies did ultimately break through at Monte Cassino in May, after controversially bombing the medieval monastery there. The Germans made an orderly retreat to positions north of Rome, allowing the Allies finally to enter the city on June 5, amid great celebrations. However, the Normandy landings in the same month put this success in perspective. The outcome of the war would not be decided in Italy.

▲ **Citizens give a hero's welcome to a British soldier after the Allies finally reached Rome on June 5.**

LONDON HAMMERED BY FLYING BOMBS AND ROCKETS

On June 13, 1944, Londoners were confronted with a terrifying new development in military technology when the Germans struck with their latest weapon – the V-1 flying bomb. Launched from sites in the Pas-de-Calais, northern France, the pilotless V-1s flew a steady course at around 580 km/h (360 mph) until their engine cut out, then plunged to the ground, detonating a warhead packed with almost 2,000 pounds of explosives.

Londoners soon learnt to recognize the approach of the deadly weapon by the dreaded characteristic sound of its primitive jet engine – which earned the V-1 the nicknames "buzz bomb" or "doodle bug". When the engine stopped, there were only 15 seconds in which to take cover. Arriving by day and night at a rate of around 100 each day, the flying bombs caused substantial devastation and great loss of life. When they scored direct hits on busy streets or crowded buildings, the carnage was hideous – there were over 200 casualties when a V-1 exploded at lunchtime in Aldwych in central London.

▲ Silent but deadly. With victory now slipping out of Hitler's grasp, the V-1 rocket was Germany's final attempt at terrorizing London

Coming under attack from flying bombs was in many ways more unnerving than the Blitz. Almost all those who could leave London did so – about 1.5 million people had quit the capital by the end of August. But gradually Britain's air defences brought the problem under control. The RAF's fastest aircraft – including a smattering of the new Gloster Meteor jets – patrolled the Channel, shooting down V-1s or tipping them off course with their wing-tips. Antiaircraft guns were moved down to the coast, forming a second barrier for the flying bombs to penetrate. Behind the guns, a line of barrage balloons blocked the path to London.

At the start of September, Allied forces overran the flying bomb launch sites in France, bringing the main phase of the V-1 attacks to an end. Of around 7,000 launched, around 2,300 had reached their target, killing 5,500 people. But no sooner had the V-1 menace been tamed than another secret weapon came into play.

On September 8, the first V-2 rockets hit Chiswick and Epping. Designed by Wernher von Braun, the V-2 was a ballistic missile, which travelled faster than sound, so that the noise it produced in flight was heard only after it had exploded on its target. Those who survived a V-2 strike reported a bang like a thunderclap followed by the sound of an express train. Through September and October, the rockets hit the London area at a rate of around five a day. Fearing panic, the government did not inform the public of the nature of the new weapon until mid-November.

Although there was no effective defence against the V-2s and they struck without warning, they never achieved the impact the Germans hoped for. Around 500 of them hit London, killing 2,700 people. To be really effective, a ballistic missile needed to cause a far more powerful explosion. If von Braun had had a nuclear warhead to attach to his V-2 rocket, the fate of London would have been very different.

▲ Clearing up after a V-2 rocket had hit became a frighteningly frequent task for England's defence workers in 1944.

JANUARY
- Allied forces in Italy assault German positions at Monte Cassino and land at Anzio
- The RAF carries out heavy bombing raids on Berlin
- Death of architect Sir Edwin Lutyens

FEBRUARY
- Heavy German air raids on London and southeast England (the "Little Blitz")
- Allied bombers carry out massive "Big Week" raids on German industrial centres
- In the House of Lords, the Bishop of Chichester, Dr George Bell, criticizes the RAF's area bombing of German cities
- Allied forces make a second assault on Monte Cassino
- The Pay As You Earn (PAYE) tax system is introduced

MARCH
- RAF Bomber Command loses 95 aircraft in a single raid on Nuremberg
- Allied forces make a third assault on Monte Cassino
- House of Commons vote in favour of equal pay for women school teachers is reversed after personal intervention by Churchill
- In India, British and Indian forces fight the Japanese as The Battle of Imphal-Kohima begins
- Death of Chindit commander Orde Wingate

APRIL
- The RAF targets roads, railways and other communications in France in preparation for the D-Day invasion
- More than 700 US servicemen are killed when German E-boats surprise an invasion rehearsal at Slapton Sands, south Devon

1944

THE NORMANDY LANDINGS

On June 6, 1944 – known as D-Day – the Western Allies opened their offensive against the Germans in Europe with the landing of a massive invasion force in Normandy. The operation, codenamed Overlord, was under the overall command of US General Dwight D Eisenhower, with General Montgomery as commander of land forces.

Preparations for the invasion had been lengthy and meticulous, turning southern Britain into a vast armed camp. Allied commanders considered the landings an immensely risky enterprise, with a serious chance of military catastrophe. The operation was almost abandoned at the last moment because of bad weather, but Eisenhower decided to risk sending the invasion fleet across the Channel during a brief break in the storms

Preceded by airborne troops dropped inland during the night, around 156,000 men were delivered on to the Normandy beaches by an armada of landing craft. British and Canadian troops came ashore on the eastern beaches codenamed Gold, Juno and Sword, while some 58,000 US troops doggedly fought their way on to the western beaches, Omaha and Utah.

The German High Command had been expecting an invasion for some time, but were undecided as to whether the Allies would strike in Normandy or the Pas-de-Calais. Rommel, in command of the coastal defences, was away from his office when the assault began, having been informed earlier that the weather in the Channel made an attack unlikely. By the end of the first day, the Allies had taken all five beaches, although at considerable cost.

The Allies enjoyed major advantages that helped them sustain and expand their foothold on the French coast. They had total command of the air and the sea. The technological wizardry of floating Mulberry harbours and PLUTO undersea oil pipelines enabled them to supply and reinforce their troops from across the Channel. But, as expected, the Germans fought back fiercely. The British and Canadian troops tasked to take the city of Caen were blocked by Panzer divisions for a month. Even when they entered the city on July 10 – after it had been flattened by the RAF – they could not push any further forward.

Montgomery came under criticism from US generals for his alleged failure to move quickly enough or with sufficient aggression, setting up tensions between Allied commanders that were to persist until the end of the war and beyond. Although Eisenhower handled the situation with great tact, there was inevitable friction as the British reluctantly accustomed themselves to the idea that the Americans had taken over the leading role among the Allies.

Friction in the Allied camp was as nothing to that on the German side, where a failed attempt on Hitler's life was made by a group of senior officers on July 20. By the end of the month, the Allies were able to break out of Normandy and begin a rapid advance across northern France. Although hard fighting lay ahead, from that point onward there could be little doubt that Germany faced ultimate defeat.

▲ **British troops wading ashore on D-Day.**

DEFEAT AT ARNHEM

▲ **Paratroopers and gliders taking part in Operation Market Garden drop behind German lines in this ill-fated operation.**

On September 17, 1944, massed Allied airborne forces embarked on a bold operation designed to win the war by Christmas. The brainchild of the usually staid and cautious General Montgomery, Operation Market Garden required British and US paratroopers to seize and hold a series of bridges that would open the way for British tanks to thrust through the Netherlands, progressing right into the industrial heart of Germany.

However, the weakest link in Montgomery's plan was the need for British paras to cling on to a bridge over the Rhine at Arnhem, which was far in advance of the starting point for the armoured column. By mischance, two SS Panzer divisions happened to be in the Arnhem area, changing the paras' task from a difficult one to an impossibility.

Under sustained attack from overwhelmingly superior German forces, the British paratroopers, led by Brigadier John Hackett, held on for nine days. The British forces crossed the Waal at Nijmegen, the last bridge before Arnhem, but their further advance was held up by stiffening German resistance. On the night of September 25–26, about 2,400 of Hackett's men escaped from Arnhem across the Rhine. They left behind more than 1,000 dead and almost 7,000 men taken prisoner by the Germans.

No one has ever fully understood why Montgomery gambled on such a risky operation, but it was at least partly related to his deteriorating relationship with his US colleagues. The British general had argued for a swift knock-out blow, concentrating all Allied resources – obviously under his own command – against the weakest point in the German defences. When he did not get his way, he set out to prove what he could do even with slimmer forces.

The failure of Operation Market Garden ensured that the war would last into the following year. A hard winter now lay between the Allies and ultimate victory.

OLIVIER'S HENRY V STIRS PATRIOTIC SPIRIT

It was probably only in wartime that a film of a Shakespeare history play could have had cinema-goers queuing round the block. This is what happened with Laurence Olivier's *Henry V* in 1944. Telling the story of a successful British invasion of France, its release could hardly have been more aptly timed.

Produced and directed by Olivier, as well as starring him in the title role, *Henry V* was an immensely ambitious project. It cost almost half a million pounds, making it the most expensive British film produced up to that date. It was filmed in neutral Ireland because Britain could not then spare enough people from the war effort to act as extras.

Stirring music by William Walton and saturated hues from Technicolor, as well as the glamour of Olivier himself, helped pull in the crowds. But Shakespeare's patriotic theme above all flattered the emotions of the British people, battered and worn by years of war, yet quietly proud of themselves and their country for winning through against the odds.

▲ **Laurence Olivier in the starring role of *Henry V*. Olivier also produced and directed this ambitious film.**

- The Second World War ends, with total British losses: 244,000 military dead; 60,000 civilians killed in bombing; 35,000 merchant navy seamen killed
- Rationing is tightened after the war ends as shortages of many essentials worsen
- Some 26,000 "GI brides", British women marrying US servicemen, leave Britain for the United States in 1945–46
- The De Havilland Vampire jet fighter aircraft goes into production
- The Arts Council is formed
- The Light Programme is a new entertainment and music channel on BBC radio
- British films of the year include Leslie Arliss's *The Wicked Lady*, David Lean's *Brief Encounter* and Carol Reed and Garson Kanin's documentary *The True Glory*
- First performance of Benjamin Britten's opera *Peter Grimes*
- Books published this year include *Animal Farm* by George Orwell, *Brideshead Revisited* by Evelyn Waugh and *Loving* by Henry Green

JANUARY

- British forces in Burma launch a new offensive
- Allies force the German Army to withdraw from gains made in the Battle of the Bulge
- Geoffrey Fisher is appointed Archbishop of Canterbury

THE YALTA CONFERENCE

Between February 4 and 11, 1944, Prime Minister Winston Churchill met US President Franklin D Roosevelt and Soviet dictator Joseph Stalin at Yalta in the Crimea to discuss plans for the defeat and occupation of Hitler's Germany.

The leaders had already decided that a defeated Germany would

▲ **The "Big Three" – Churchill, Roosevelt and Stalin – meet to discuss and decide the fate of a defeated Germany.**

be divided into "zones of occupation", which were to be administered separately by the victorious Allies. It was also agreed that Germany's war criminals would be brought to book before an international military tribunal. How to handle those countries in Eastern Europe which had been liberated or defeated by the Soviet Red Army was a much more contentious issue.

In essence, Churchill was prepared to allow Stalin to install pro-Soviet governments in Bulgaria, Romania and Hungary, but Czechoslovakia and – above all – Poland were a different matter. Britain had gone to war in 1939 in defence of Polish freedom. To see the country handed over after the war to Soviet domination and communist rule was hard to accept.

The meeting did not develop into a confrontation between the Western Allies and the Soviets. Indeed, Roosevelt in many ways felt more sympathy for the Soviet Union than for Britain – he had, like many Americans, a gut hostility to the British Empire. Left to press his case over Poland with little support from the US President, Churchill could extract only a few token concessions from Stalin. In any case, with the Red Army in control of Eastern Europe, there was little any other country could do to prevent Stalin having his way.

The conference ended in a faultless display of good-humoured friendship between the wartime Allies, but the waning influence of Britain on the world stage was becoming embarrassingly evident.

DRESDEN BLITZED

By February 1945, the Allies had virtually won the air war over Germany. Decimated by combat losses and inhibited by shortage of fuel, the Luftwaffe could no longer defend Germany's cities, which were devastated by bombing attacks day and night.

On the night of February 13–14, two waves of RAF bombers, totalling almost 800 aircraft, attacked the city of Dresden, dropping a mix of incendiary and high-explosive bombs. Soon the city was lit up by the flames of 1,000 out-of-control fires, which eventually combined to form a deadly fire-storm. The inferno sucked the oxygen from the atmosphere, suffocating thousands of people. Temperatures rose so high that the sewers ran with melted human fat. No one knows how many

people died that night and in the follow-up raid by the US Air Force the next day, but the death toll

▲ **Once one of Germany's most beautiful cities, in a single night's bombing Dresden was all but wiped off the map.**

was possibly as high as 60,000.

The destruction of Dresden provoked an outcry in Britain. The city was considered to be one of the most beautiful in the world, a treasure-house of outstanding architecture with some of the finest art galleries in the world. It was, critics of the bombing argued, of no significant military value. Churchill swiftly distanced himself from the operation, although he had been a determined advocate of strategic bombing throughout the war and had even suggested attacking German cities with poison gas. The Americans pretended they had had nothing to do with it. Full responsibility fell on the shoulders of Bomber Command chief Sir Arthur Harris, who was too honest to apologise for something he believed to be right.

▲ The people of Dresden work at clearing the rubble of their broken city; as many as 60,000 may have died in the bombing.

Controversy about the Dresden bombing has raged ever since. Supporters of Bomber Command have pointed out that the city was a valid military target as a communications centre just behind Germany's eastern front. They have also argued, more generally, that strategic bombing had a massive impact on Germany's ability to wage war. Critics of the air campaign have argued that it was generally ineffective and that the bombing of Dresden, in particular, amounted to a war crime.

After the defeat of Germany, Harris was ostracized – he was the only leading military commander not given a seat in the House of Lords in 1946. Bomber Command was not mentioned during the victory celebrations and no separate campaign medal was struck for its air crews. Whatever the rights or wrongs of the bombing campaign, this was shoddy treatment for a force that had lost 56,000 men fighting for their country.

GERMANY SURRENDERS

▲ Members of the Women's Royal Army Corps joyfully wave flags in London's Traflagar Square on VE Day.

By the time Winston Churchill announced victory in Europe to the British people, in a radio broadcast from Downing Street on May 8, 1945, it was already old news. Hitler had killed himself in Berlin on April 30. The document declaring the surrender of German forces in northwestern Europe had been signed at General Montgomery's headquarters on Lüneberg Heath on May 4. The unconditional surrender of all German forces was signed by General Jodl at a ceremony at General Eisenhower's headquarters at Reims on May 7.

The end of the war was naturally cause for great celebration. The centre of London was packed with revellers. Churchill led MPs to a special thanksgiving service in St Margaret's Church, next to Westminster Abbey, and then addressed crowds from a balcony overlooking St James's Park. The royal family made an appearance on the balcony of Buckingham Palace. After night fell, the sky was lit up with searchlights. Across the country bonfires were lit and fireworks let off – unknown excitements to children brought up in the war who had never seen a Guy Fawkes Night.

Festivities were nonetheless more restrained than in 1918, perhaps because everyone understood that the war was not yet over. Japan remained to be defeated, and no one knew how long that might take.

▲ One of the many thousands of street parties held throughout Britain to celebrate the Allied victory in Europe.

1945

LABOUR LANDSLIDE OUSTS CHURCHILL

When victory over Germany was achieved in May 1945, it was ten years since the British people had had a chance to vote in a general election. Prime Minister Winston Churchill was in no hurry to abandon the wartime coalition with Labour and the Liberals. He proposed postponing an election until the war with Japan was won – at the time thought likely to take another 18 months – and until a programme for postwar reconstruction was under way. But the rank and file of the Labour Party put pressure on their leaders to return to party politics. On May 23, Churchill formed a caretaker government without Labour, while elections were organized for July.

The Conservatives were confident that the British people would not vote against Churchill, the man who had won the war. They badly misjudged the mood of the electorate. For much of the British public, the Conservatives were still the party of appeasement, the men whose prewar mistakes – some said treachery – had exposed the country to such danger. The Tories were blamed for all the ills of the 1930s, to which the people wanted no return.

Labour had the inestimable advantage of leaders – Clement Attlee, Ernest Bevin and Herbert Morrison – who had been in government for five years.

▲ **Clement Atlee, the newly elected Labour Prime Minister, waves in celebration after a landslide victory.**

Churchill's aggressive election campaign, in which he suggested a Labour government would need a "Gestapo" to carry out its socialist programme, backfired on the Conservatives. It lacked all credibility when directed at men who had shown proof of patriotism, decency and fitness to rule throughout the war.

The election was carried out while millions of voters were still abroad in the armed forces. The process of collecting and counting service votes meant that, although election day was July 5, the result was not known until July 26. It was a landslide victory for Labour. With almost 48 per cent of the popular vote, they took 393 seats in parliament, compared with 213 for the Conservatives and their allies. This was a political earthquake.

As soon as Attlee had formed a government, he sprinted off to the Potsdam Conference, where the week before Churchill had been representing Britain in talks with the American and Soviet Allies. Attlee would never cut such a figure on the world stage as Churchill had. But what the British people were looking for now was action on the home front.

The King's speech on August 16 announced a programme of nationalization, social security legislation, and plans for the creation of a National Health Service. The government assembled to carry through this programme consisted mostly of experienced Labour stalwarts, including Ernest Bevin as Foreign Secretary and Hugh Dalton as Chancellor of the Exchequer, although the Ministry of Health was handed to fiery left-winger Aneurin Bevan.

When the new parliament opened, Labour MPs shocked traditionalists by singing "The Red Flag" in the House of Commons. Men such as Attlee and Bevin were an assurance that no red revolution was in fact going to take place, but the measures they proposed were radical enough to mark a sharp turning point in British social and economic life.

ATOM BOMBS END THE WAR

On August 6, 1945, the United States dropped an atomic bomb on the Japanese city of Hiroshima. Three days later, a second atomic device was exploded, destroying Nagasaki.

Because Britain had provided the United States with valuable research material at the outset of the atom bomb project, the British government in theory had a veto over the use of the weapon. But Britain's consent to the bombings was only sought – as a pure formality – at the last moment.

The dropping of the A-bombs was followed by the Japanese surrender on August 14. Although

naturally welcomed by the British government as the end of the war in Asia, this brought an immediate financial crisis. Britain was, in the words of the Treasury, "virtually bankrupt" as a result of the war. The United States had been willing to finance its ally as long as the war lasted. Now there was peace, and the Americans pulled the plug on Britain's life-support machine. Financial aid was abruptly cancelled on August 17.

Clement Attlee's government struggled to cope with both empty coffers and continuing worldwide military commitments. The Labour leaders were not ready to abandon Britain's pretensions to great power status. Attlee therefore took the decision to develop Britain's own atomic bomb, while also maintaining armed forces around the world. The dogma of high defence spending would eventually prove a millstone round the neck of the Labour government.

◀ **One of the defining moments of the twentieth century: a giant "mushroom" cloud rises over Hiroshima after the detonation of the atom bomb.**

OCTOBER
• Haganah, a Zionist militia organization, begins a sabotage campaign against British rule in Palestine
• The United Nations Organization formally comes into existence
• An unofficial dockers strike seeks introduction of a national minimum wage

NOVEMBER
• War crimes trials of leading Nazis open in Nuremberg, Germany
• The Gloster Meteor jet sets a world speed record of 970 km/h (606 mph)

DECEMBER
• John Maynard Keynes negotiates a massive American loan to keep British finances afloat, but on onerous terms

BRIEF ENCOUNTER
WARMS THE HEART

The British film industry came out of the Second World War brimming with talent and confident that movies with a very English flavour could be box-office successes. One of the cinematic hits of 1945 was *Brief Encounter*, based on a play by Noël Coward and directed by David Lean.

Lean and Coward had collaborated on one of the most famous wartime films, *In Which We Serve*. They now delivered an understated romance, with a lush Rachmaninov score to voice the suppressed emotions of its clipped English hero and heroine, played by Trevor Howard and Celia Johnson. Although the steamiest element in the film was a station buffet, the performances throbbed with inner passion.

Brief Encounter set the tone for many of the best British cultural products of the postwar period. Set in a socially restricted world of limited possibilities, where a visit to Lyons Corner House could be an adventure, it nevertheless gave its characters full dignity, viewing their struggles and emotions without irony.

▲ **Celia Johnson and Cyril Raymond suppress their emotions in the hit British romance, *Brief Encounter*.**

1945

When the soldiers, sailors and airmen of Britain's conscript armed forces exchanged their uniforms for state-provided "demob suits", they returned to a country altered in subtle but vital ways by the experience of six years of warfare. The bombsites that scarred most cities – the ruins already growing over with weeds – were obvious testimony to the impact of the conflict, but less obvious was the impact on people's minds and on the everyday life of society.

Around a third of a million British people had lost their lives in the war. Approximately 244,000 died on military service, less than a third of the number of servicemen who had been killed in the First World War. On the other hand, civilian casualties were far higher than in the previous war. Around 60,000 civilians were victims of bombing or missile attacks, and 35,000 merchant navy seamen perished in the desperate struggle to break the U-boat blockade – dangerous work

▲ Thousands of British women willingly surrendered to the charms of American GIs during the Second World War; many of these liaisons resulted in preganancies and marriage.

for which they received little recognition and no reward.

The scale of grieving and psychological shock in the wake of the Second World War was not comparable to the aftermath of the 1914–18 conflict. The legacy of physical destruction, on the other hand, was incomparably greater. Britain had lost around one-third of its merchant shipping. In London alone about 110,000 houses had been destroyed by enemy action and another million damaged to some degree.

The service personnel "demobbed" in 1945–46 were unlikely to have much trouble finding a job, but housing was a serious problem and would remain so for many years. One answer was the prefab, a bungalow made out of recycled metal and designed for swift assembly and a short life. About 125,000 of these had been built by 1949. More than half a million more permanent houses were constructed in the second half

of the 1940s, without solving the serious housing shortage.

Britain's national finances were in a similar state to its housing stock. The government had abandoned conventional financial management to pay for the war. As a result, the country was in debt to the tune of around £25,000 million. It had also sold off over £1,000 million of assets abroad, consequently reducing "invisible" earnings from overseas to less than half their prewar level. Exports in the immediate postwar period were also less than 50 per cent of the level in 1939. Once the hub of the world economy, Britain faced a long struggle to restore even basic financial viability.

Yet individually, many of the British people had not done so badly out of the changes wrought by the war. The ending of mass

▲ A Devon village turns out to greet a British soldier on his return from a prisoner-of-war camp.

▲ London children made homeless by the random bombs of the Nazi raids during the Blitz sit outside the wreckage of their former home.

▲ Partially prefabricated houses were built to meet high housing demand at the end of the war.

unemployment meant that over a million workers had jobs after 1945 who would not have done in the 1930s. This was achieved not through any revival of the old industries – coal, textiles and shipbuilding – but through the growth of new industries such as electronics, aircraft manufacture and chemical industries.

Rising wages during the war years, combined with a progressive income tax which weighed most heavily on the better-off, significantly shifted the balance of wealth. According to one calculation, the after-tax incomes of members of the working class rose about nine per cent in the course of the war, while after-tax middle-class incomes fell by seven per cent. Another set of estimates indicates that the purchasing power of poorer people may have increased by around a quarter during the war years.

The problem with purchasing power, both during the war and for years following it, was the absolute shortage of things to purchase. Although the wealthy always found ways around the regulations, for the vast majority rationing set tight limits on what could be eaten and worn. Fuel was in short supply

both for cars and for heating houses. The ration book, the coupon and the queue were a frustrating daily reality, although also a form of democracy and a shared sacrifice.

Of course, the war did not end class differences in Britain's obsessively hierarchical society, any more than it ended the inequality between the sexes. But there was evidence all around of a shift in the social balance of power. The presence of trade union leader Ernest Bevin in the War Cabinet was a practical symbol of recognition on the part of the governing class that working people's opinions had to be taken into account. Trade unionists would remain a significant power in the land from then on until the 1980s.

The concept of the "Blitz spirit", with people of all kinds and classes cheerily pulling together for the national good in wartime, has been attacked many times since the war as a propaganda myth. Yet, despite being an oversimplification, it did represent a certain reality. For Britain, the Second World War was in a real sense a "people's war". There was a widespread feeling that all the people should benefit from a

victory they had all worked hard to earn. The foundations of the welfare state were laid not by the postwar Labour government, but by Churchill's coalition government during the war.

The traumatic experiences that so many people had undergone during the war, both on service overseas and on the home front, seem to have imbued the wartime generation with a longing for

secure domesticity. A "baby boom" began immediately the war ended, in sharp contrast to the low birthrate after the First World War. Britain's declining status as a great power had very limited meaning for a population inclined above all to cultivate its own garden. What the British people really wanted, after two global conflicts in 40 years, was to be left in peace.

▲ London children enjoy a treat of newly imported bananas, a luxury after wartime restrictions.

1946

- A baby boom begins
- The National Insurance Act reforms social services
- Free school milk and dinners are introduced
- Bananas are available in Britain for the first time since 1939
- Heathrow airport opens
- The BBC establishes the Third Programme as a culture and classical music radio service
- The radio programme "Dick Barton: Special Agent" is a popular hit
- BBC television broadcasts resume after war interruption
- Books published this year include *A History of Western Philosophy* by Bertrand Russell, *Deaths and Entrances* by Dylan Thomas and *Alamein to Zem-Zem* by Keith Douglas
- British films this year include David Lean's *Great Expectations* and Michael Powell's *A Matter of Life and Death*
- First performance of *The Young Person's Guide to the Orchestra* by Benjamin Britten
- First performance of Terence Rattigan's play *The Winslow Boy*
- The New Bodleian Library opens in Oxford

JANUARY
- William Joyce ("Lord Haw-Haw") is hanged for treason
- The United Nations General Assembly meets for the first time in London

FEBRUARY
- Food rations are cut as the world food shortage worsens

FIRST SESSION OF UN HELD IN LONDON

The New Year began on a positive note when the first General Assembly of the United Nations opened on January 10,

▲ **Gunners from the Royal Artillery prepare place names for the first meeting of the United Nations.**

1946, at Westminster Central Hall in London. Delegates from 51 nations – representing around 80 per cent of the world's population – met with the aim of ensuring global peace. But their deliberations soon revealed how difficult it was going to be to achieve such a goal.

All UN members had agreed to a charter that committed them to the avoidance of war and respect for human rights. British Foreign Secretary Ernest Bevin had already made clear his view that the UN could guarantee world peace only if the great powers were "reasonably true to the promises which they have made in the charter". In

other words, if the United States or the Soviet Union followed aggressive policies, the UN would be powerless to stop them.

The first session of the UN assembly was marked by a sharp confrontation between Britain and the Soviet Union. Stung by criticism of their own behaviour in relation to Iran, the Soviets accused Britain of breaching the UN Charter through the presence of their troops in Greece and Indonesia. Bevin robustly rebuffed the Soviet attack, winning the debate in the assembly. But the evidence of Soviet hostility to Britain did not augur well for future East-West cooperation.

CHURCHILL DEFINES IRON CURTAIN

Speaking in Fulton, Missouri, in the United States on March 5, former Prime Minister Winston Churchill made his famous reference to the "iron curtain" between the capitalist West and the communist East. "From Stettin in the Baltic to Trieste in the Adriatic," he boomed, "an iron curtain has descended across the Continent."

The iron curtain to which he was referring was the ideological barrier between Stalin's Soviet Union and his neighbours in Europe and the rest of the world. Urging the United States to form an alliance with Britain to discourage any future expansion of the Soviet Union, Churchill went on to condemn Stalin's regime in words that sounded remarkably similar in tone to those he had used to describe Hitler's Germany some years earlier.

Churchill's speech was consistent with the views that he

had expressed privately to President Truman at the end of the Second World War. Worldwide reaction to the speech was, nonetheless, mixed. In London a leading article in *The Times* expressed the view that: "while Western democracy and communism are in many respects opposed, they have much to learn from each other." In the United States, however, Senator Robertson used public interest

▲ **Britain's wartime hero Winston Churchill coined the phrase that would forever describe the divide between East and West.**

in the speech to stress the continuing importance of close relations between Britain and the United States in order to curb the expansion plans of the Soviet Union.

Churchill's comments were born as much from up-close observations of Joseph Stalin as they were of the Soviet Union's actions after the end of the Second World War.

During the key meeting of the Allied powers at Potsdam in Berlin in July 1945, it had become apparent to Churchill that the interests of the West were no longer the same as those of Stalin and the Soviet Union. Despite assurances to the contrary, Stalin never did hand power back to those countries that came under Soviet control during the supposed interim period following the end of the conflict in Europe. This confirmed Churchill's worst fears as to Stalin's true intentions for postwar Europe.

JEWISH TERRORISTS BLOW UP KING DAVID HOTEL

On July 22, 1946, members of the Jewish terrorist organization Irgun blew up the King David hotel in Jerusalem, the hub of the British administration in Palestine. Ninety-one people were killed in this atrocity and 45 injured.

The British position in Palestine, already difficult before the war, had become impossible after 1945. The horror of the Holocaust, in which between 5 and 6 million European Jews were murdered, imbued Zionists with an implacable determination to found their own Jewish national state in Palestine. It also provoked a sharp rise in the number of Jews wanting to emigrate there.

The British authorities found themselves in the invidious situation of turning back desperate Jewish refugees from Palestinian

▲ **A young Jewish terrorist suspect is interrogated by British troops after the King David hotel was blown up in Jerusalem.**

ports, while British troops faced a mounting campaign of bombings, kidnappings and shootings by the Jewish Haganah militia and Irgun terrorists. At the same time, Arab nationalist sentiment was on the rise in Palestine and the Middle East generally. Any concessions to the Jews would provoke anti-British action by the Arabs.

The British government had neither the desire nor the financial resources to fight a lengthy campaign in Palestine. They handed the problem over to the United Nations, which decided in November 1947 that the country should be divided into separate Jewish and Arab states, with effect from no later than the following October. Unacceptable to both sides, the prospect of partition triggered mounting violence between Jews and Arabs.

British troops pulled out with relief in May 1948, leaving the superior Jewish forces free to establish the state of Israel and successfully defend it against intervention by surrounding Arab countries.

BRITONS ARE OUT FOR FUN

The immediate postwar years saw a boom in leisure industries, with crowds flocking to cinemas and sports events in numbers never equalled before or since. In 1946, one in three of the population went to the cinema once a week, while one in eight went twice a week. League football matches regularly attracted huge crowds.

The leisure boom was clearly in part accounted for by the release of tension after wartime: those who had survived intended to enjoy themselves. But the simple facts of ordinary people's finances were the real key. In 1946, almost every basic item was rationed, including clothing and most foods. Yet unemployment was low and wages for most people had risen

through the war. Rationing left workers with little to spend the contents of their well-filled wage packets upon except an afternoon at a sports ground or an evening at the cinema.

Holiday camps also entered their golden age. For the first time, ordinary working-class families could afford to go to Butlin's, previously the preserve of the lower-middle class. The organized group leisure that the camps provided appealed to a population that had become accustomed to "mucking in" together in the war.

The golden age of mass leisure pursuits was to fade away swiftly in the 1950s, vanquished by television and the different spending priorities of the new consumer society.

▲ **Holiday makers at Butlin's holiday camp in Clacton wave goodbye to troops. The camp was used as a military base during the war.**

1947

- Austerity measures tighten in a year of economic crisis
- Blackmarket "spivs" flourish
- Whale steaks are used as a substitute for scarce meat
- The birth rate rises to over 20 per thousand people, compared with 12 per thousand in the 1930s
- The number of divorces exceeds 50,000 a year
- The Town and Country Planning Act is passed
- The Government Economic Planning Council is set up
- The Agriculture Act guarantees farm prices
- The school leaving age is raised to 15
- Dior's New Look revolutionizes women's fashion despite clothes rationing
- The Edinburgh Festival of music and drama is founded
- Britain's first atomic reactor starts operating at Harwell
- Photo-finish cameras are introduced at horse races
- British national football associations rejoin FIFA
- The government imposes a prohibitive duty on the import of foreign films, effectively stopping distribution of Hollywood films in Britain
- British films this year include Michael Powell's Black Narcissus and Carol Reed's Odd Man Out
- Books published this year include Under The Volcano by Malcolm Lowry and Whisky Galore by Compton Mackenzie
- First performance of Benjamin Britten's opera Albert Herring

COAL INDUSTRY NATIONALIZED

▲ An experienced miner has some welcoming words for two young apprentices at the Lount Colliery in Leicestershire, opened in 1943.

The Labour Party was elected to power in 1945 on a platform of massive social reform and the nationalization of key industries and institutions. Nationalization was seen as the essence of socialism, giving control over the running of the economy to the state, instead of capitalist businessmen and financiers. Only state control, Labour believed, could avoid a repeat of the slump of the 1930s and enable the government to improve the rights and conditions of workers.

The Bank of England was nationalized with effect from March 1, 1946. On January 1, 1947, nationalization of the coal industry followed. A National Coal Board took over the running of the mines and the distribution of coal and related supplies. The board members were appointed by the Minister of Power and came under the chairmanship of Lord Hyndley. The National Coal Board's assets at the time included 1,647 mines, more than a million acres of land and around 100,000 miners' homes.

The coal mines had in the past been the focus for bitter industrial disputes – including the 1926 General Strike – and miners had long demanded nationalization as the solution to their problems. Many were disillusioned to find that being employed by the state was little different from employment conditions under private ownership. The government had no intention of allowing workers control of the industry, and kept power firmly in the hands of the bureaucrats appointed to run it. The mines remained a hot-bed of radical trade unionism for the next 40 years.

The nationalization of the Bank of England and the coal industry was not the end of the policy. Over time, the telephone industry, the airlines, the railways, the iron and steel industries and public utilities – including gas and electricity – would all be taken into public ownership.

COLDEST WINTER WORSENS PAIN OF SHORTAGES

The winter of 1946–47 was one of the harshest ever experienced in the British Isles. The fact that this coincided with a moment of national and international economic crisis created nightmarish conditions for the British people, remembered by some as worse than anything endured in wartime.

Throughout 1946, a combination of worldwide food shortages, lack of foreign currency to pay for imports and the continuing legacy of disruption from the war had forced the government to tighten rationing. Even bread – a commodity never subject to control during the Second World War – was rationed. Especially threatening, although invisible to the public, was a mounting fuel crisis. Coal production had slumped during the war and never recovered. By December 1946, Britain's coal-fired power stations were desperately short of stocks. As cold weather set in, some factories were forced on to short-time working to conserve power supplies.

The real crisis came at the end of January 1947. On the night of January 28, temperatures dropped to –20ºC in parts of eastern and southern England. A freeze set in that was to last until mid-March. During the coldest February ever recorded, the Thames froze at

Windsor and ice floes were spotted off Kent and Norfolk. During a period of 20 days, no sunshine at all was recorded in London. Oxford experienced a fortnight during which the temperature never rose above freezing, day or night. Blizzards blocked road and rail routes. Farms and villages, even medium-sized towns, were cut off; and tens of thousands of sheep and cattle froze to death.

Measures were in place to conserve fuel – householders were banned from switching on electric fires between 9 and 12 in the morning and 2 and 4 in the afternoon. But the freeze was too much for the system to bear. The

▲ Londoners skate on the frozen lake in St James' Park in the shadow of Buckingham Palace during the harsh winter of 1946–47.

newly nationalized mines were not producing enough coal, and the coal they did produce often could not be moved because of the snow. On February 7, Minister of Fuel and Power Emmanuel Shinwell announced a shutdown of some

power stations. For the following three weeks, much of British industry ground to a halt. Over two million workers were laid off in a brief return to mass unemployment. People were short of winter clothing, short of food and short of warmth. Cuts in gas and electricity supplies were frequent. Families huddled shivering by candlelight.

Seemingly interminable, the winter did eventually end, although the thaw in mid-March brought its own misery, with extensive flooding hitting 31 counties across the country. But there was no end to the shortages – of petrol, paper, clothes, food and fuel – which continued for the rest of the year.

MARSHALL AID TO THE RESCUE

In June 1947, some relief from Britain's economic gloom was offered by the prospect of American aid, when US Secretary of State George C Marshall proposed a plan for the rehabilitation of devastated European economies. By far the world's most powerful economy, only the United States was in position to kickstart European economic growth.

The Marshall Plan, properly called the European Recovery Programme, had both political and economic goals. The United States was increasingly committed to resisting the spread of communism worldwide. By restoring prosperity in Europe, Marshall hoped to encourage the survival of pro-Western liberal democracies. The Soviet Union and its satellite states rejected Marshall aid because it was quite evidently a measure aimed against communism.

The plan's economic goal was to revive industries and expand trade. After flirting with isolationism, the

United States had begun to realize that its own economic prosperity required a revival in Europe to provide markets and investment opportunities. An Economic Cooperation Administration was set up to distribute $13 billion of economic aid in the form of grants

and loans to help rebuild industry and agriculture.

When the Marshall Plan came on stream in 1948, it played a vital part in Britain's economic recovery. The country received a total of $2.7 billion in Marshall aid – although much of it was spent on overseas military commitments and developing an atom bomb rather than on industrial reconstruction.

▲ The first consignment of sugar arrives at Royal Victoria Docks in London under the terms of the Marshall Plan.

INDEPENDENCE FOR INDIA

▲ As the drive for independence continued, so did violence between India's Hindus and Muslims. (Insets: top, Nehru; bottom, Jinnah.)

British colonial rule in India came to an end in August with the enforcement of the Indian Independence Act. Under the Act, passed by the British parliament in July, a line of demarcation was to be drawn across India and the new Dominions of India and Pakistan established by midnight on August 14–15.

The British had tried for some time to establish a single administration in India to which all power could be transferred, but the complexities of Indian politics made the task almost impossible. The essential problem was that India was a country deeply divided along political and religious lines but united in its desire to see the British leave. (Mahatma Gandhi's "Quit India" campaign neatly expressed what the majority of people in India felt about the British presence on their soil.)

The two main political/religious groups in India were the Muslims, led by Mohammed Ali Jinnah, and the Hindus, led by Pandit Jawaharlal Nehru. The Sikh population of India, who had played so prominent a role in

the British Army, had naively assumed that their courage and loyalty would be rewarded in some way by the British. This proved not to be the case, of course, and their betrayal by the British left the Sikhs, led by Tara Singh, with little political influence in the country.

Civil war in India between rival Muslim and Hindu groups – which in 1946 had been particularly bloody – combined with the possibility of mutiny in the Indian

Army had led the British to seek a swift transfer of power. It was clear to all observers that the situation, rather than improving, would instead grow considerably worse.

In March 1947, Lord Mountbatten had taken over as Viceroy of India with the aim of returning the country to Indian rule by June 1948. He soon realized, however, that the situation was too dangerous for him to risk the lives of British troops still stationed in the country. Rather than see more lives lost to the civil war while protracted negotiations between both sides were played out, he resolved simply to divide Punjab and Bengal and hand over control to the Muslims (who got Pakistan) and the Hindus (who got India).

Gandhi could not accept the plan and was even prepared to put up with Jinnah, the Muslim leader, as Premier of a united India rather than face partition.

Nehru, however, had tired of the fight and finally, along with Jinnah, accepted the British plan for India. During the bloodshed triggered by the mass migrations that followed the partition, more than one million people are believed to have lost their lives.

▲ Lord Mountbatten sits between Nehru and Jinnah at one of the many negotiating sessions for Indian independence.

COMPTON'S GOLDEN SUMMER

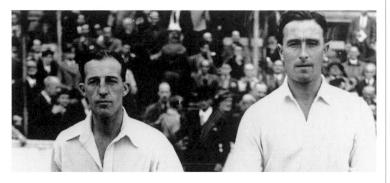

▲ **Denis Compton (right) and Bill Edrich walk out to open the batting for Middlesex at the Oval during Compton's golden summer of 1947.**

In the summer of 1947, still beset by rationing and recovering from an icy winter of fuel shortages and power cuts, Britain was in desperate need of cheering up. The hour produced the man: flamboyant Middlesex cricketer Denis Compton.

Born in 1918, Compton established himself as England's most exciting young batting talent in the late 1930s. A stylish and daring hitter of the ball, he was the season's top scorer in 1939 with 2,468 runs. He had begun his test career and was also tipped as a future England soccer international – he played for Arsenal and was to receive an FA Cup winner's medal in 1950.

The war was a cruel interruption of Compton's sporting career, but he came out of wartime service with his skill and his cavalier spirit undimmed. The batting performances he produced for Middlesex and England in the sunny summer of 1947 are the stuff of legend. Statistically they have never been equalled – 3,816 runs, including 18 centuries, at an average of 90.85 per innings. But figures can give no impression of the carefree style in which the runs were scored. Compton was never cautious, never cramped, always graceful and relaxed. For many Englishmen, watching Compton bat at Lord's in 1947 restored faith in cricket, England, and even life itself.

Compton could not maintain himself on the peak he had reached. Plagued by a troublesome knee, he displayed his best form only in fitful flashes over the following decade. His face was more often seen on advertisements for Brylcreem than on a cricket pitch. But the memory of his golden summer remained undimmed in the minds of millions of fans.

ELIZABETH MARRIES THE DUKE

On November 20, 1947, 21-year-old Princess Elizabeth, the heir to the throne, married 26-year-old Lieutenant Philip Mountbatten at Westminster Abbey. Cheering crowds lined the route between Buckingham Palace and the Abbey, above all keen for a glimpse of the young princess in her pearl-embroidered ivory dress, designed by Norman Hartnell.

The princess had first met her future husband on a visit to the Royal Naval College in Dartmouth when she was aged 13. The son of Prince Andrew of Greece, he was a great-great-grandson of Queen Victoria and thus Elizabeth's distant cousin. He was also the nephew of Lord Louis Mountbatten. Despite these credentials and respectable wartime service as a British naval officer, Philip was only accepted as suitable to marry the princess after renouncing his Greek inheritance. The bridegroom was created Duke of Edinburgh as a wedding gift from the king.

The wedding ceremony trod a careful line between royal pomp and the simplicity thought appropriate at a time of austerity and egalitarian sentiment. The royal couple's honeymoon took them no further than Hampshire. Their first son, Charles, was born almost exactly a year after the wedding.

▲ **Elizabeth's marriage to Lieutenant Philip Mountbatten trod a careful line between pomp and simplicity at a time of austerity.**

1948

NEWS IN BRIEF

- The National Health Service comes into operation
- Rationing of bread, jam and some other items ends
- Large-scale immigration from the West Indies begins
- The Citizenship Act gives all Commonwealth subjects the status of British citizens
- National Service – peacetime conscription – is extended from 12 to 18 months
- Women's Royal Army Corps and Women's Royal Air Force founded
- General Certificates of Education (GCEs) replace School Certificates
- Middlesex County Council introduces the first "comprehensive" schools
- The Morris Minor car enters production
- The Olympic Games are held in London
- Aged 12, Lester Piggott is the youngest jockey to win a race in Britain
- Poet T S Eliot wins the Nobel Prize for Literature
- Books published this year include *The Gathering Storm* by Winston Churchill, *The Heart of the Matter* by Graham Greene and *The Loved One* by Evelyn Waugh
- British films this year include Laurence Olivier's *Hamlet*, David Lean's *Oliver Twist*, Carol Reed's *The Fallen Idol*, Michael Powell's *The Red Shoes* and Charles Frend's *Scott of the Antarctic*
- First performance of Christopher Fry's *The Lady's Not for Burning* and Terence Rattigan's *The Browning Version*

THE TIDE OF NATIONALIZATION RISES

▲ **A Standard 80000 Class 2-6-4T steam locomotive, one of 12 standard steam designs introduced after the nationalization of Britain's railways.**

On January 1, 1948, the four British regional railway companies were taken into state ownership, creating a unified nationalized rail system. Later in the year, the generation and supply of electricity were nationalized, replacing a clutch of private companies with a single public corporation. A bill was also introduced for the nationalization of the iron and steel industries. These measures followed the earlier state takeover of the Bank of England and the coal mines.

In principle, the Labour government's nationalization campaign represented a revolutionary change in British society, which at least partly fulfilled the dream of a "Socialist Commonwealth" which had been promised in Labour's 1945 election manifesto. Labour was officially a socialist party and socialism, according to author George Orwell, meant "that the ownership of all major industry shall be formally vested in the State, representing the common people". The theoretical aim of state ownership was both to create a fair and efficient planned economy and to transform society – in Orwell's words "to eliminate the class of mere owners who live … by the possession of title-deeds and share certificates".

Attlee's government was, however, more pragmatic than idealistic. Coal, rail and electricity were all industries with a long history of state involvement, even under Conservative governments.

Both were industries in deep financial trouble that could not have fulfilled their vital role in the national economy after 1945 without a large injection of government money.

The wave of nationalizations created a "mixed economy", in which public and private ownership coexisted within the overall context of a capitalist free market. This was the dominant economic model not only in Britain but through much of Western Europe from the 1940s to the 1980s. It may have looked like socialism to American eyes, but in practice there turned out to be nothing revolutionary about it. Trade unions continued to oppose management – there were strikes in the nationalized coal mines as early as August 1947.

Nationalization proved an effective way of salvaging uneconomic but essential industries. This is why, with the exception of iron and steel, the Conservatives made no effort to reverse public ownership when they held power in the 1950s. Labour, on the other hand, lost its enthusiasm for state ownership as the road to a socialist commonwealth. A 1949 Labour policy document would state that "unless there is economic necessity, there is no reason for always socialising whole industries".

WEST INDIAN IMMIGRANTS ARRIVE ON WINDRUSH

On June 22, 1948, the steamship *Empire Windrush* docked at Tilbury on the Thames Estuary with almost 500 Jamaican passengers on board. It is an event that has since come to represent the beginning of large-scale West Indian immigration to Britain.

The *Windrush* had stopped at Kingston to pick up Jamaicans who were returning after leave from the British armed forces. These servicemen were joined by hundreds more young men who hoped either to enrol in the services or simply to chance their luck in a new country. Before the

Windrush even reached British waters, it became a public issue. Questions were asked in the House of Commons about these "coloured" immigrants and a government spokesman felt obliged to promise that those on board would stay for only a year.

All West Indians had the legal right of entry to the United Kingdom and the authorities did their best to cope with accommodating the new arrivals. Several hundred were temporarily housed in a deep shelter under Clapham Common, beginning a West Indian association with south London that has lasted to the present day.

West Indian immigrants had to face open racism as well as the unavoidable difficulties of building a life in a strange and alien land.

But in the 1950s, persistent labour shortages in Britain and the lack of decent jobs in the Caribbean created a situation in which mass immigration was more or less inevitable.

▲ **Jamaican immigrants aboard the *Windrush* pose with a newspaper before starting their new life in Britain.**

NHS REVOLUTIONIZES HEALTH CARE

On July 5, 1948, the National Health Service brought free comprehensive medical treatment to all British citizens for the first time. The Act founding the service was passed by parliament in 1946, but Health Minister Aneurin Bevan had to fight long and hard to win doctors' consent to the scheme.

Many in the medical profession feared a loss of status and independence that they believed would follow if they were turned into salaried civil servants. Some also feared the loss of lucrative revenue from private practice. Bevan was forced into a series of concessions, including allowing consultants to continue private practice alongside salaried work in hospitals. Even so, in February 1948 nine out of ten doctors in the British Medical Association voted to boycott the NHS.

Opposition belatedly crumbled in the face of Bevan's determination to introduce the scheme and of assurances that GPs would not become salaried government employees.

From the outset, the popularity of the NHS with the general public

▲ **Health Minister Aneurin Bevan fought long and hard to introduce the NHS; many in the medical profession feared a loss of status.**

was never in doubt. In the first year of its existence, 8.5 million dental patients were treated, 187 million free prescriptions written, and over five million pairs of spectacles dispensed.

Indeed, the popularity of the system quickly became its biggest headache. So many people wanted free treatment that the health budget soared. By 1951, a Labour Chancellor of the Exchequer, Hugh Gaitskell, had decided that free medicines, dentures and glasses were simply no longer affordable. Bevan was among those who resigned from the cabinet in defence of the principle of a totally free health service.

Despite its flaws, the introduction of the National Health Service is still the single measure for which the Attlee government is best remembered and most admired.

1948

BERLIN AIRLIFT TRIUMPH

In June 1948, deteriorating relations between the Soviet Union and its former wartime Allies Britain, the United States and France reached breaking point. The three western Allies, unable to agree with the Soviets on the future of Germany, took measures to combine their "zones of occupation" into a single body, which would eventually become West Germany. They also promoted an economic

▲ The "Berlin Airlift" carried out by the British and US Air Forces successfully foiled the Soviet attempt to isolate the city.

recovery in their area of occupation, introducing a new currency, the Deutsche Mark. In response, the Soviet Union decided to force the Western Allies out of Berlin, which was deep within the Soviet zone of occupation but administered jointly by the four Allied powers.

On June 24, the Soviets began a blockade of West Berlin – the British, French and American occupation zones within the city. All road and rail links to the west were cut. Two days later, on June 26, on the initiative of the RAF, the British and US Air Forces began to airlift food and other essentials into the besieged city. The Soviet Air Force made no attempt to block the airlift, but it still seemed unlikely that a population of 2.5 million people could be kept alive by aerial supply.

The RAF used Sunderland flying boats, which landed on lakes in the Berlin suburbs, and converted Lancaster bombers for their contribution to the airlift. With the technology available at the time, maintaining a dense

pattern of around-the-clock transport flights into the city was difficult and hazardous, especially when winter weather set in. More than 50 Allied airmen lost their lives in the operation.

The RAF was, of course, aware of the irony of flying supplies in to feed people whom five years earlier they had been trying to kill with bombs. Although not everyone was happy with helping the Germans in this way, the airlift did begin a change in the British perception of Germany. It encouraged identification with the former enemy, soon to become an ally, while transferring hostility to a former ally, the Soviet Union.

The Berlin blockade could easily have led to war. It did not, because neither side desired it. British and US airmen succeeded in keeping West Berlin supplied with food and fuel for 11 months until the Soviet Union lifted the blockade on May 12, 1949. The airlifts continued until the end of September, by which time well over two million tonnes of goods had been airlifted into Berlin.

LONDON STAGES AN AUSTERITY OLYMPICS

From July 29 to August 14, 1948, London hosted the summer Olympic Games. The last time the Games had been held was in Berlin 12 years earlier, with Adolf Hitler presiding over a spirit of Nazi triumphalism. This was a very different occasion – unpretentious, warm-hearted and generous in spirit.

At a time of postwar shortages, Britain had no resources with which to create new venues or an Olympic village. The Empire

Stadium in Wembley provided the main arena with the simple addition of a cinder running track. Visiting athletes were housed around the capital in military barracks and student dormitories. Because rationing was in force, foreign teams brought their own food with them as far as possible.

With wartime enmities still fresh, Germany and Japan were not invited to participate. The Soviet Union also did not take part, as it was not affiliated to

the International Olympic Committee. In all, 4,099 sportsmen and sportswomen from 59 countries participated.

The Olympic torch was brought from Athens across war-ravaged Europe – with a detour to avoid Germany – and carried into Wembley Stadium by proud Englishman John Mark. For the opening ceremony the stadium was dominated by a board displaying the motto of founder Baron de Coubertin: "The

important thing in the Olympic Games is not winning but taking part." This was just as well for the British, who did not win a single event in the stadium – although Britain did win two gold medals for rowing and one for yachting.

The crowds were happy to applaud the achievements of foreign heroes, including Emil Zátopek's first gold in the 10,000 m and the four gold medals of 30-year-old Dutch mother of two Fanny Blankers-Koen. The whole occasion was acknowledged as a great success, in its thrifty and amateurish way embodying the true Olympic spirit.

◀ **John Mark bears the Olympic flame at Wembley Stadium, brought from Athens to London across war-ravaged Europe.**

OCTOBER
• The government proposes nationalization of the iron and steel industry
• An official inquiry is set up into allegations of corruption at the Board of Trade

NOVEMBER
• Princess Elizabeth gives birth to a son, who will be known as Prince Charles
• Julie Andrews, aged 13, sings in front of the Goerge VI and Elizabeth at the Royal Command Variety Performance

DECEMBER
• Jam rationing ends
• US and British aircraft have carried 700,000 tonnes of supplies into Berlin by the year's end
• Lord Patrick Blackett wins the Nobel Prize for Physics

BRITONS MAKE HAPPY FAMILIES

By the late 1940s, postwar Britain was taking shape as a family-oriented society, centred on the home, where stay-at-home mothers looked after small broods of mostly healthy offspring.

Since the war there had been a "baby boom", with the birthrate peaking in 1947 at 20.5 per thousand of the population, compared with less than 15 per thousand in the late 1930s. But there was no return to the large families of the Edwardian era. More women were having babies, but they were having fewer babies each. In Edwardian times only half of women of child-bearing age had been married; by 1951 two-thirds of women aged 20 to 39 were married – which in most cases meant both having children and giving up paid work.

Earlier in the century, there had been widespread concerns about the low birthrate among the middle and upper classes, who were seen as being outbred by the working classes with their large families of ragged scamps. This pattern, too, had changed. By the late 1940s there was little difference between middle- and working-class family sizes.

The greatest gain to human happiness lay in the improvement in children's health.

Infant mortality was falling, heading below 50 per thousand births for the first time. That bare statistic represented the sparing of misery to millions of parents, who a generation or two earlier would have watched sons and daughters die of epidemic diseases or the effects of malnutrition and poor housing. With free school milk and school dinners, and access to the National Health Service, children were set to become still healthier in the years ahead.

▲ **Cinema-goers queue to see the film *Birth of a Baby*. By the late 1940s, Britain was taking shape as a strongly family-oriented society.**

- An act nationalizing the iron and steel industries is passed by parliament, but suspended until the 1950 general election
- The National Parks Act is passed by parliament
- Legal aid is established
- Official statistics show the divorce rate ten times the level of 1937
- The De Havilland Comet, the first jet passenger aircraft, makes its maiden flight
- First Badminton three-day horse-riding event held
- BBC television takes over Lime Grove studios in west London from Rank films
- Books published this year include *1984* by George Orwell, *The Heat of the Day* by Elizabeth Bowen and *The Concept of Mind* by Gilbert Ryle
- British films this year include Carol Reed's *The Third Man*, Robert Hamer's *Kind Hearts and Coronets* and Henry Cornelius's *Passport to Pimlico*
- Laurence Olivier's *Hamlet* is the first British film to win an Oscar for Best Picture

JANUARY
- A Royal Commission is appointed to inquire into capital punishment
- Death of water and land speed record contender Sir Malcolm Campbell

MARCH
- Clothes rationing ends after eight years in force

BRITAIN HELPS FORM NATO

On April 4, 1949, the North Atlantic Treaty was signed by the United States, Canada and 10 European countries, including Britain. When the treaty came into force on August 24, establishing the North Atlantic Treaty Organization (NATO), it was the fulfilment of a lengthy diplomatic effort by British Foreign Secretary Ernest Bevin.

In his four years at the Foreign Office, Bevin had become convinced that the Soviet Union was a potential aggressor, ready to use military force or political subversion to establish communist regimes in Western European states and absorb them into its sphere of domination. He believed that only an American commitment to the defence of Western Europe could deter Soviet aggression.

▲ **The signatures of the foreign secretaries and ambassadors of the 12 initial members of Nato.**

In March 1948, Britain signed a pact with France and the Netherlands – the Brussels Treaty. This agreement was a blueprint for a collective defence strategy against the Soviet Union. Bevin was aware that Britain and the other Brussels Treaty countries were in no position to offer serious resistance in the face of overwhelming Soviet forces in Eastern Europe. But under the banner of the Brussels pact, he led an approach to the United States, asking President Truman to join in the collective defence of Western Europe. The result was the North Atlantic Treaty.

The basic principle of NATO was that an armed attack on any member state "shall be considered an attack against them all". Its creation solidified the Cold War division of Europe into communist East and capitalist West. Bevin gave short shrift to critics in the Labour Party who disliked seeing Britain tied to the United States. NATO would "act as a deterrent", he declared, by making "aggression appear too risky" for an enemy to attempt. On the whole, the next 40 years proved him right.

COMET LEADS THE WORLD

▲ **The de Havilland Comet prototype flies over the English countryside; this revolutionary aircraft became the world's first passenger jet.**

On July 27, 1949, the prototype of the De Havilland Comet jet airliner made its maiden flight. This revolutionary aircraft became the world's first passenger jet and a symbol of the soaring ambition of the British aircraft industry in the postwar period.

Company chief Sir Geoffrey De Havilland, responsible for such famous aircraft as the Tiger Moth and the Mosquito, had the Comet developed in total secrecy so as to steal a march on its rivals, the US giants Boeing and Douglas. Capable of cruising at 400 mph (700 km/h), the jet would also fly higher than propeller-driven aircraft, giving a smoother ride above the level of the weather. It promised to put Britain at the forefront of a revolution in air travel.

The Comet proved what British technology was capable of, but there remained a question mark over the commercial sense of British companies. Another bold design unveiled in 1949 was the Bristol Brabazon, a giant airliner as big as the future Boeing jumbo jet. But the Brabazon was not an economic proposition for its day. No airlines placed orders, making the Brabazon a white elephant.

The Comet did better, entering service after lengthy trials in 1952. But it, too, was destined to lose out in the long run to US competition.

STERLING IS DEVALUED

On September 18, 1949, the British government slashed the foreign exchange value of sterling by 30 per cent. This drastic measure was in response to a mounting balance of payments crisis. Britain was importing far more from the United States than it exported, creating a "dollar gap" that undermined confidence in the currency. Devaluation was designed to restore confidence in sterling, to cut imports by making them more expensive and raise exports by making them cheaper.

Although a perfectly rational financial measure, rather tardily recognizing the strength of the dollar relative to the pound in the postwar world economy, devaluation was greeted by press, public and politicians as a grave setback for British prestige and evidence of the gross failure of government economic policies. This adverse view was in fact shared by Chancellor of the Exchequer Sir Stafford Cripps who – until the situation became unsustainable – had preferred a policy of renewed austerity.

In reality, Britain's economy was showing good signs of recovery by 1949. The number of items rationed was being reduced and shops were filling with goods for consumers to buy. The devaluation nonetheless left an impression of failure that weighed heavily on a government that faced a general election the following year.

▲ **A group of dealers make some impromptu deals outside the closed stock exchange following the devaluation of the British pound.**

EALING'S PASSPORT TO COMEDY

Ealing Studios enjoyed a golden year in 1949 with three successful comedies packing the cinemas: *Passport to Pimlico*, *Whisky Galore!* and *Kind Hearts and Coronets*.

The understated yet subversive humour of the Ealing comedies played perfectly upon the frustrations of people subjected to years of rationing and regulations. In *Passport to Pimlico*, an area of London declares itself independent of British rule; in *Whisky Galore!* the inhabitants of a Scottish island fight for the right to put shipwrecked alcohol to its proper use; while in *Kind Hearts and Coronets* a commoner triumphs over aristocracy by killing off an entire family to take a noble title.

The talents of many individuals contributed to the Ealing comedies, including those of director of production Michael Balcon, actors such as Alec Guinness and Margaret Rutherford, and screenwriters T E B Clarke and William Rose. But these charming films were above all a collective expression of a moment in British life, when a good-natured sense of community still prevailed and fantasies of rebellion were gentle in spirit, even when they ran to crime.

The Ealing comedy was a genre that kept its savour through to the mid-1950s, with classics such as *The Lavender Hill Mob* and *The Ladykillers*.

▲ **Richard Hearne (right) and Philip Stainton struggle over a stolen bicycle during the open-air filming of *Passport to Pimlico*.**

1950–1959

The catchphrase which more than any other characterized 1950s Britain was "You've never had it so good!" Adapted from a speech by Conservative Prime Minister Harold Macmillan, it encapsulated the materialism of a society in which self-satisfaction was based on nothing more complicated than purchase of a black-and-white television set and a small family car. It was in many ways a dull and complacent society, rebelled against by young people in search of excitement or an inspiring sense of purpose in life. The arrival of people of a different skin colour, through the influx of West Indians and other immigrants, brought out this society's worst characteristics – small-minded discrimination and rejection of anything challenging or "different". But, although intellectuals and moralists might hold that society needed higher goals, the British people were – on the whole – happy just to be free of wars, dole queues and ration books.

The most important reality for millions of Britons was that their living standards rose dramatically, since jobs were plentiful and wage rises far outstripped inflation. The political beneficiaries of this prosperity were the Conservatives, who had the good fortune to win a tightly contested election in 1951, just as Britain was turning the corner from postwar austerity. The Tories showed eminent good sense in embracing the new compromise system of welfare capitalism inherited from their Labour predecessors. The welfare state provided security while private industry delivered the consumer goods. The government tweaked and twiddled the financial controls to sustain demand and thus maintain full employment.

All was not well, however, with the British economy. Growth was inhibited by low productivity. Trade unions defended restrictive practices as a way of protecting jobs, while management was often no keener than the labour movement on innovation or investment in new machinery. The government struggled to stop price and wage rises getting out of hand and to narrow the "trade gap" between imports and exports. There was the beginning of what was to become a familiar pattern of "stop-go" economics, as Chancellors of the Exchequer alternately cut taxes and lowered interest rates to stimulate economic growth, and were then forced to slam on the brakes with spending cuts and rate rises as inflation took off. By the end of the decade, it was clear that Britain had lost out heavily in relative terms to countries with faster-growing economies such as West Germany and Japan.

Despite its waning power, Britain joined the elite club of nations with nuclear weapons. Even in this area, though, the government had by the end of the decade been forced to retreat from its insistence on possessing an independent nuclear deterrent and had instead to accept integration with NATO's nuclear forces, in subordination to the United States. For a minority of Britons, the risk of nuclear war loomed in the forefront of life, rather than – as it did for most people – forming a vaguely threatening background. The Campaign for Nuclear Disarmament became the most prominent protest movement of the decade, its highly publicized annual Aldermaston march as fixed a ritual of the British year as the University Boat Race or Ascot Week. The spirit of protest also found expression in campaigns for the abolition of the death penalty and for reform of the law on homosexuality. But, although important in their way, such issues were marginal to the major changes happening in society.

In the broadest historical perspective, the 1950s were most importantly the decade in which Britain gave up the attempt to maintain an Empire. Colonies proved a burden rather than an asset. A series of small, dirty wars – notably in Kenya and Cyprus – were fought in an attempt to hold on to colonial possessions, but the Suez fiasco of 1956 proved that the whole imperial project was untenable. By the last years of the decade, the Macmillan government had embarked on wholesale decolonization. Just as the retreat from empire gathered pace, however, Britain missed out on participation in the founding of the European Common Market. Meanwhile, the "special relationship" with the United States remained more of an aspiration than a reality. It did appear, as American Dean Acheson was to say in 1962, that Britain had "lost an Empire and not yet found a role".

1950

- Almost 17 million newspapers a day are sold in Britain (2005 figure: 12 million)
- A survey shows that fewer than half of British households have their own bathroom
- First package holiday is organized, flying to Corsica
- Ford Consul launched
- Sainsbury's opens Britain's first self-service store
- BBC television makes its first international broadcast live from France
- BBC radio broadcasts the children's programme "Listen With Mother" for the first time
- Francis Bacon paints Studies After Velazquez, often known as the "screaming popes"
- Books published this year include The Grass is Singing by Doris Lessing
- British films this year include Basil Dearden's The Blue Lamp and Jules Dassin's Night and the City
- Philosopher Bertrand Russell is awarded the Nobel Prize for Literature
- Sir Malcolm Sargent is appointed conductor of the BBC Symphony Orchestra
- Scottish National Orchestra is formed
- Frank Sinatra is mobbed by fans on his first visit to Britain

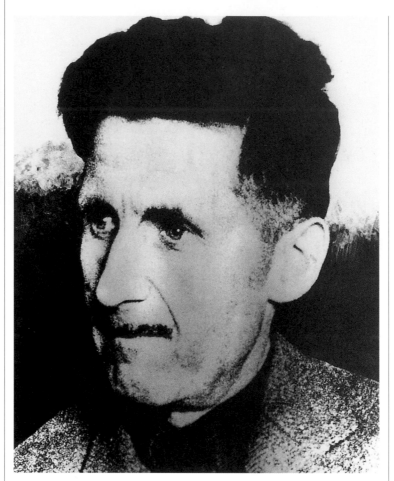

▲ Under the pen name of George Orwell, Eric Arthur Blair became one of the most popular British authors of the century.

Barely a year after the publication of his most famous work, *1984*, novelist and essayist George Orwell died on January 21, 1950.

Orwell was born Eric Arthur Blair in 1903 in Bengal, where his father was employed in the Indian Civil Service. He was brought up in the environment of impoverished snobbery that characterized the British colonial "Sahibs", whose attitudes he later pilloried, describing them as "landless gentry".

Educated in England, Blair turned down a university scholarship to join the Indian Imperial Police in Burma. Here he gained first-hand experience of the way in which the Burmese people were being abused by their colonial rulers.

Guilt-ridden for his own small contribution to these iniquities, he resigned his commission and returned to England, immersing himself in the slums and poverty of east London. As George Orwell – taking his surname from the East Anglian river – he published the semi-fictional work *Down and Out in Paris and London* (1933). The thrust of many of Orwell's early works aimed to highlight oppression and the emptiness of middle-class materialism.

Viewing himself as a socialist, Orwell set out much of his thinking in the autobiographical political essay *The Road to Wigan Pier* (1937), although the book betrayed his growing disillusionment with organized socialism. That same year found

Orwell, originally in Barcelona to report on the Spanish Civil War, fighting (and being wounded) on the side of the republicans. *Homage to Catalonia* (1938) grew out of his experiences in Spain.

In 1945 Orwell found wealth and fame with the political fable *Animal Farm*, which takes the story of Stalin's betrayal of the Russian Revolution and cleverly transposes it to a farm where the animals overthrow their human exploiters only to experience even greater oppression at the hands of a new ruling class of animals.

It was Orwell's final book for which he will be best remembered. *1984* (1949) warns against the perils of totalitarianism, be it communist or fascist. It describes a state in which the government distorts truth to its own ends and whose citizens, forbidden privacy, independent thinking or sexual pleasure, are under constant surveillance by "Big Brother". The book continues to find relevance wherever in the world abuse of government rule is identified.

▲ "Big Brother is Watching You". *1984*, George Orwell's most famous work, warned of the dangers of totalitarian rule.

LABOUR CLING ON TO POWER

On February 23, 1950, the British electorate was given the opportunity to pass judgement on the Labour government which had been voted into office with such a large majority five years earlier. Around 84 per cent of those eligible to vote turned up at the polling stations, the highest level of voter turnout recorded for 40 years.

Foreign journalists had flocked to Britain for the election campaign, sensing an epoch-making battle between the old war-horse Churchill and the fearsomely red socialists of the Attlee government. In fact, the campaign was a sedate and polite affair, conducted by politicians who respected one another and whose views on most issues were not radically opposed.

▲ **Clement Attlee's slim victory for Labour in the 1950 general election left him a lame duck Prime Minister.**

In terms of the popular vote, the election showed a remarkably small shift away from Labour, considering the difficulties that had beset the administration. The governing party attracted 46 per cent of the vote, compared with 48 per cent in 1945. But in terms of seats in parliament, the result was close to a triumphant

recovery for the Conservatives. With 40 per cent of the vote, they took 282 seats compared with 315 for Labour. With minor parties taken into account, the government was left with a barely workable overall majority of six.

Labour continued in government, but as a lame duck administration, unable to press forward with any controversial legislation. Their leaders were ageing. Two key figures, Foreign Secretary Ernest Bevin and Chancellor of the Exchequer Sir Stafford Cripps were in very poor health. A narrow defeat would probably have been better for Labour's future prospects, giving them a chance to recuperate their forces. As it was, they clung precariously to power for another 18 months.

ATOM SPY FUCHS IS JAILED

On March 2, 1950, German-born British scientist Klaus Fuchs was sentenced to 14 years in prison for passing atomic secrets to the Soviet Union. He had been arrested while working at the Harwell Atomic Energy Research Establishment in Berkshire.

A member of the communist party, Fuchs had fled Germany for Britain after Hitler took power in 1933. He was interned as an enemy alien early in the Second World War, but was soon released to take part in the development of an atomic bomb. A brilliant physicist, Fuchs contributed substantially to the atom bomb project, but he also passed all the information he possessed on the programme to the Soviet Union, both during and after the war.

Fuchs's arrest came at a time of acute paranoia in the West, following the testing of the first Soviet nuclear device in 1949. Unwilling to accept that Soviet scientists had sufficient know-how to have made the bomb all by themselves, the American intelligence services went in hot pursuit of spies that they held responsible for selling nuclear information to the communists. In reality, however, even if the information passed on by Fuchs and others was useful to the Soviet nuclear programme, it can only have been to a limited degree.

Fuchs served nine years of his sentence. On his release, he moved to communist-ruled East Germany, where he lived until his death in 1988.

▲ **Physicist Klaus Fuchs worked on Britain's atomic bomb project, but all the while he was passing secrets to his Soviet spymasters.**

ENGLAND SHAMED

▲ England's star striker Tom Finney is once again foiled during a brave performance from American goalkeeper Borghi.

June 29, 1950, was one of the darkest days in England's sporting history as the national football team, widely viewed as one of the greatest in the world, was dealt a severe and humiliating World Cup defeat at the hands of the United States.

Held in Brazil, this was the first World Cup to which England had accepted an invitation. They qualified for the finals as winners of the 1949–50 season's home international competition against Scotland, Wales and Northern Ireland. Scotland, runners-up to England, were also offered a place in the finals, but turned it down!

Drawn in the preliminary phase against Chile, Spain and the USA, England began with a promising 2–0 victory over the South American side. But England's stars Tom Finney and Stan Mortensen were unable to find a way past the tight American defence. In the end England went down 1–0 to a headed goal by Gaetjens. They were then eliminated from the tournament after a 1–0 defeat by Spain.

England had gone home by the time Uruguay took the trophy for the second time.

CALYPSO SUMMER

The successful West Indian cricket tour of England in the summer of 1950 was more than a mere sporting event. It announced the presence of West Indian culture as a new and vibrant strand in British life.

The West Indies had been playing Test cricket against England since the 1920s, but they had never won a Test match in England. In 1950 they won three, including the prestigious match at Lord's, and by crushing margins – 326 runs, 10 wickets, and an innings and 56 runs.

The key to West Indian success was the batting of the "three Ws" – Worrell, Weekes and Walcott – and the spin bowling of Sonny Ramadhin and Alf Valentine. These two young bowlers had played just two first-class matches each before the England tour. They bemused England batsmen with their subtle trickery, taking 59 wickets between them in a four-match series.

At the time there were only an estimated 15,000 West Indian-born immigrants in Britain. But even their numerically small presence at cricket grounds had a sensational impact. Singing, dancing, playing guitars and tin cans, they stood out vibrantly in what were then staid arenas ringing only to the sound of polite applause.

A calypso improvised by a Trinidadian immigrant captured the joyousness of the victory at Lord's. Beginning "Cricket lovely cricket", it ended by celebrating "those little pals of mine Ramadhin and Valentine". Although the cricketers went home after the match, but the West Indians were in Britain to stay.

▲ Sonny Ramadhin's devastating spin bowling helped the West Indies to their first test victory against England.

BRITAIN SENDS TROOPS TO KOREA

On August 29, 1950, two warships carrying British troops arrived in the port of Pusan in South Korea, where they were greeted by a Korean girls' choir and an all-black US military band playing "Tiger Rag". The soldiers were the first contingent of around 60,000 British infantry who were to serve in the Korean War.

The war had begun on June 25, when forces from communist North Korea invaded US-backed South Korea. The British government saw this as just the kind of naked aggression that the United Nations was meant to oppose. It fully supported the setting up of a United Nations force to defend South Korea. In practice, however, this amounted to legitimizing the actions of the US. The United Nations forces were in effect wholly under American command, deployed with only perfunctory reference to the United Nations.

The initial stages of the war consisted of a desperate struggle to prevent an outright North Korean victory. In September, however, after a seaborne operation to which the Royal Navy made a significant contribution, United Nations forces retook the South Korean capital Seoul. US General Douglas MacArthur then launched an invasion of North Korea.

From this point on, the war became increasingly controversial and uncomfortable for the Labour government. Its efforts to moderate the gung-ho spirit of the Americans failed and China, newly under communist government, was provoked into beginning sending its forces into North Korea in October 1950. The resulting debacle for UN

▲ British troops arrived in Korea to fight a war under UN auspices, but it became very much a US-directed operation.

forces led President Truman to make a barely veiled threat to use the atom bomb.

Attlee tried to persuade Truman to avoid the nuclear option and seek a peace agreement with the Chinese, but the United States made its own decisions without any reference to its allies – fortunately including the decision not to go nuclear. The British found themselves committed to fighting a war under US command with little or no say in how that war was conducted.

THEFT OF THE STONE OF SCONE

On Christmas Day, 1950, a group of Scottish nationalists made a defiant gesture of independence by breaking into London's Westminster Abbey and removing the Stone of Scone.

For centuries the Stone of Scone formed part of the crowning ceremony of the kings of Scotland. It was taken to England by the invading forces of Edward I in 1296. The stone is a small piece of sandstone marked with a simple Latin cross. According to legend, it was once set on the Hill of Tara, the crowning place of Irish High Kings. It was transported from Ireland to Scotland by the Celtic Scots who invaded the region

▲ The theft of the Stone of Scone from Westminster Abbey was a potent, symbolic gesture by Scottish nationalists.

from the sixth century and was subsequently encased in the seat of the royal coronation chair of Scotland. When the stone was brought south, it was set underneath the Coronation Chair in Westminster Abbey, thus symbolizing that whoever was crowned monarch of England was also the ruler of Scotland.

Four months after its theft, the Stone of Scone was found in Arbroath Abbey and returned to Westminster. The thieves were never discovered. In 1996, with the Scots having voted to have their independent parliament again, the Stone of Scone was formally returned to Scotland.

- A census records the UK population as 50.2 million
- A social survey showsthat the average British housewife works 15 hours a day
- Around 340,000 British households have television sets
- The nuclear reactor at Windscale (Sellafield) goes on line
- The Witchcraft Act of 1735 is repealed by the Fraudulent Mediums Act
- The Free Presbyterian Church founded by Ian Paisley in Northern Ireland
- GCE O' and A' Level exams are introduced
- Maiden flight of the Vickers Valiant jet bomber
- Books published this year include *The Day of the Triffids* by John Wyndham, *A Question of Upbringing* by Anthony Powell and *The Cruel Sea* by Nicholas Monsarrat
- Keith Douglas's *Collected Poems* is published posthumously
- British films this year include Charles Crichton's *The Lavender Hill Mob* and Alexander Mackendrick's *The Man in the White Suit*
- First performance of Benjamin Britten's opera *Billy Budd*
- Peter Walker and Peter Whitehead win the Le Mans 24-hour race in a C-type Jaguar

BEVAN QUITS GOVERNMENT

Internal conflicts in Clement Attlee's Labour government became uncontainable in April 1951, as Aneurin "Nye" Bevan, one of the most colourful figures in postwar British politics, resigned from his post as Minister of Labour. Two junior ministers, Harold Wilson and John Freeman, also resigned.

The specific pretext for the resignations was the introduction of charges for spectacles and dental care prescribed on the National Health Service. These charges, insisted upon by Chancellor of the Exchequer Hugh Gaitskell, were anathema to Bevan, the architect of the free NHS.

But the sources of friction within the Labour government went far deeper. The resignations were a protest at Attlee's programme of rearmament, announced in January, which was costing around £4.7 billion – at the expense of social welfare, left-wing critics claimed. And they were also a protest at the main cause of that rearmament, which was Britain's commitment to support the United States in the war in Korea. The left wing of the Labour Party had become increasingly unhappy with the US conduct of the war and with Britain's subservient attitude towards to the US.

The son of a Welsh miner, Bevan was well known as a left-winger and had at times been a thorn in the side of the moderate Labour leadership. He had been given the position of Minister of Health in Attlee's 1945 Labour government partly to keep the left of the party supporting the administration. With his razor-sharp wit and sometimes savage oratory – Churchill called him a "merchant of discourtesy" – Bevan would have been a dangerous man to have on the backbenches. His two great achievements were the creation of the NHS and the initiation of postwar housing programmes. He became Minister of Labour in January 1951, a position which he held for only three months.

Bevan was a figure of stature whom the government could not afford to lose at a difficult juncture. Sir Stafford Cripps, a veteran of the wartime coalition, had retired through ill-health in October 1950. Ernest Bevin, another pillar of the Attlee government, died in the same month as the Bevan resignation. Attlee himself was in hospital when Bevan resigned. His government was falling apart and literally ailing.

Labour was removed from power in the general election just months later. In opposition, Bevan remained the voice of the Labour left. In 1955, after Attlee's departure, he campaigned to become party leader, only to be defeated by his old enemy Gaitskell. He accepted the post of shadow Foreign Secretary. Bevan died in 1960, respected as one of the finest orators ever to enter parliament.

▲ One of the greatest political orators of the twentieth century, Nye Bevan was never one to shy away from verbal confrontation.

GLORY AT THE IMJIN RIVER

By April 1951, after 10 months of fluctuating warfare with heavy casualties inflicted on both sides, the front line in the Korean War had returned to almost precisely the place where the border between North and South Korea had been when the war began. There, British troops found themselves engaged in some of the most desperate fighting of the entire conflict.

On April 21 the Chinese Army launched an offensive with massed infantry against positions held by the British Twenty-Ninth Brigade on the Imjin River. The full brunt of the attack fell upon companies of the Gloucestershire Regiment – the "Glorious Glosters". Vastly outnumbered, the Glosters were soon encircled at a position that became known as Gloster Hill. They held the hill under sustained attack until April 25, when the few survivors were ordered to disperse and save themselves as best they could. The Glosters' resistance drew the sting of a Chinese offensive that soon ran out of steam through the massive losses it suffered.

By the following summer both sides in Korea were prepared to admit that a stalemate had been reached. The United States political leadership asserted its authority over the military by removing the aggressive United Nations commander General MacArthur. All talk of conquering North Korea was abandoned. The Chinese had suffered heavily and could no longer progress in the face of UN firepower. Peace talks between the two sides opened at Kaesong in July.

Tragically, it would take another two years before a formula for a ceasefire could be agreed, by which time the military and civilian death toll in the war had topped 4 million. British casualties in Korea were 1,078 killed and 2,533 wounded.

▲ **British troops took part in some of the most bitter fighting in Korea, most notably blunting a Chinese offensive on the Imjin.**

THE FESTIVAL OF BRITAIN

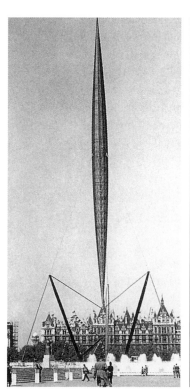

◀ **Like most of the exhibits, the Skylon was demolished by the incoming Churchill government who saw it as a shrine to socialism.**

May 4, 1951, saw the opening of the Festival of Britain, a science and technology fair that would attract over 8 million visitors during the summer.

The event had been announced in December 1947, Labour Minister Herbert Morrison telling the House of Commons that the government planned to mark the centenary of the Great Exhibition of 1851. Originally intended to be a "world fair", economic circumstances led to its being redesignated a national event. A grant of over £11,300,000 was provided to finance the project. Planned as a nationwide

celebration, the aim of the Festival was to "demonstrate Britain's contribution to civilization, to stimulate trade and to encourage creative effort in British national life". Although there were regional exhibitions throughout the country, the main attraction was built on a massive bomb site on the South Bank of the Thames.

The upstream section of the site was dominated by the Dome of Discovery and the impressive Skylon, both temporary exhibits designed to show off Britain's importance in the fields of science, technology, architecture and design. Also unveiled was the Festival Hall, one of the few buildings from the event still in use, as one of London's leading concert halls.

JANUARY
- A communist offensive in Korea retakes Seoul, but a UN counter-offensive is launched
- The government announces a £4.7 billion rise in defence spending
- Aneurin Bevan is appointed Minister of Labour
- The meat ration is cut as a result of British dispute with Argentina – a major meat exporter – over the Falklands

FEBRUARY
- England win a Test match against Australia for the first time since 1938, but still loses the series 4–1

MARCH
- Ernest Bevin resigns as Foreign Secretary; he is replaced by Herbert Morrison
- The Iranian parliament votes to nationalize the Anglo-Iranian Oil Company
- Death of composer and theatre producer Ivor Novello

APRIL
- Aneurin Bevan resigns from the Cabinet over NHS charges
- The government agrees in principle to withdrawal of British troops from the Suez Canal Zone
- The European Coal and Steel Community is created, without Britain
- In Korea, British troops are overrun by Chinese at the Imjin River
- Royal Navy submarine *Affray* sinks with the loss of its 75-man crew
- In the Grand National only three horses finish; the winner is Nickel Coin
- The Stone of Scone, stolen the previous Christmas, is found at Forfar
- Death of trade unionist and Labour politician Ernest Bevin

1951

PARTNERS IN CRIME

May 25, 1951, saw the start of an intriguing mystery that would take almost 30 years to unravel in full. It would reveal international espionage operating at the very heart of Britain's establishment. The story began with the sudden disappearance of two Foreign Office officials, Guy Burgess and Donald Maclean. They were next seen five years later in Moscow, where they announced their defection and longstanding allegiance to the Soviet Union.

Burgess and Maclean had met as students at Cambridge University in the early 1930s. They were both from "privileged" backgrounds – Maclean's father was a prominent Liberal MP and Burgess's was a naval officer. Communist sympathizers, like many other students of their day, they were both recruited as Soviet secret agents. Following graduation, the pair enjoyed rapid career success that allowed them to penetrate British intelligence. Burgess worked for MI6 during the Second World War, recruiting his Cambridge friend and fellow spy Kim Philby to the organization. Maclean rose through the Foreign

▲ With a background in MI6, Britain's secret intelligence service, Guy Burgess was well placed as a communist agent.

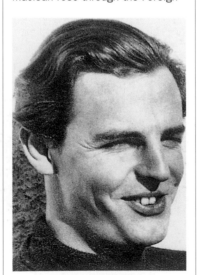

▲ Foreign Office high-flier Donald Maclean – one of the most infamous spies of the Cold War era.

Office, becoming First Secretary at the British embassy in Washington in 1944.

Maclean was able to pass especially valuable information on to his Soviet counterparts. As secretary of the Combined Policy Committee on Atomic Development, he had access to highly classified documents relating to the formation of NATO. In 1950 he was promoted further and engaged in work on high-level Anglo-American diplomacy at the start of the Korean War.

Both Burgess and Maclean were unstable personalities. After the war, Burgess was shifted from one Foreign Office job to another as his heavy drinking made him a liability to any department he worked for. Maclean was also prone to drinking bouts and by 1950 had been sent back to London to recuperate from what was diagnosed as a nervous breakdown. Meanwhile, Philby had been posted to Washington as principal liaison officer between British and American intelligence agencies. He was perfectly placed to discover that Allied counter-intelligence was close to identifying

a spy working at a prominent level in the Foreign Office – who was, of course, Maclean.

On May 25, 1951, British Foreign Secretary Herbert Morrison signed permission for Maclean to be pulled in for interrogation. The spies were ahead of the game. Burgess picked up Maclean from his Surrey home that evening and drove him to Southampton, where the pair took a ferry for France. They were not seen again for five years.

The swift disappearance of Burgess and Maclean indicated that there was at least one other person involved. The hunt for the "Third Man" was on. Philby was the most obvious suspect, but British intelligence chiefs refused to believe he was a traitor. Under pressure from the Americans – who were convinced of Philby's guilt – they sacked him, but he was not prosecuted.

The whole sorry tale of treachery continued to unravel over the next three decades, until not only Philby but also Sir Anthony Blunt, Keeper of the Queen's Pictures, had been revealed as a Soviet spy.

RETURN OF THE GREAT LEADER

October 26, 1951, saw Winston Churchill return to the pinnacle of British politics, succeeding Clement Attlee as Prime Minister at the age of 76. Many people, including Churchill's wife Clementine, thought he should have retired from active politics after the election defeat of 1945. But the Grand Old Man could not be content until he had avenged that humiliation.

The Conservative election victory was far less convincing than Churchill had hoped. In fact, Labour had increased its share of the popular vote, winning the support of almost 49 per cent of the electorate, a higher proportion even than in 1945. Yet the vagaries of the British electoral system meant that, with 44 per cent of the vote, the Tories took 302 seats to Labour's 295. With the support of the National Liberals, Churchill had a workable majority.

His personal prestige gave Churchill an unshakable claim to head any Conservative administration. Indeed, honours showered upon him – including the Nobel Prize for Literature, awarded in 1953 for his six-volume history of the Second World War. But many within his own party wished for a younger man to take his place once the election was won. The Foreign Secretary, Sir Anthony Eden, was the heir apparent, but Churchill made him wait.

The personal objective that Churchill set himself was to achieve reconciliation between East and West or at least to moderate the hostility of the emerging Cold War. But he never managed to organize the summit meeting between Stalin and Western leaders of which he dreamed.

In 1953 Churchill suffered a stroke. From then onwards he was increasingly incapable of conducting the business of government. He finally handed over to Eden in April 1955, leaving Downing Street at the age of 80.

▲ "V for Victory". First it was the defeat of Germany in 1945, six years later Churchill celebrated an election victory.

BRITAIN'S FIRST NATIONAL PARKS

▲ Dartmoor became one of the first National Parks, preserving an area of outstanding natural beauty for future generations.

In the course of 1951, four areas of Britain were designated as National Parks: the Peak District, the Lake District, Snowdonia and Dartmoor. It was the culmination of a long campaign for the protection of rural Britain and to allow access to the countryside for all.

Growing popular interest in rambling in the 1920s and 1930s, combined with an age-old popular hostility to large landowners, generated a movement for greater rural access and conservation. A government committee recommended the creation of a National Park Authority in 1931, but nothing was done. Pressure groups kept the issue alive, on occasion staging mass trespasses in beauty spots closed off by landowners.

It is to the credit of the postwar Labour government that it found time amid social reforms and financial crises for the National Parks and Access to the Countryside Act, which was passed with all-party support in 1949. The Pembrokeshire Coast and North York Moors were added to the list of National Parks in 1952, and by the end of the 1950s the Yorkshire Dales, Exmoor, Northumberland and the Brecon Beacons had also received protection.

- A report on the 1951 census reveals that one in three British households have no bath and one in 20 have no piped water
- Identity cards, introduced in 1939, are abolished
- British archaeologist Michael Ventris deciphers the Minoan Linear B writing
- The Austin and Morris car companies merge to form the British Motor Corporation
- The last tram is taken out of service in London (reintroduced in 2000)
- *New Musical Express* publishes Britain's first singles chart
- The Comet passenger jet begins commercial scheduled flights
- Maiden flight of the delta-wing Avro Vulcan jet bomber
- Books published this year include *Men at Arms* by Evelyn Waugh, *Excellent Women* by Barbara Pym and *The Common Pursuit* by F R Leavis
- British films include David Lean's *The Sound Barrier*
- *The Goon Show* begins on BBC radio
- *Bill and Ben, The Flowerpot Men*, appear on BBC television's children's programme *Watch With Mother*
- First performance of *Sinfonia Antarctica* by Ralph Vaughan-Williams
- Agatha Christie's *The Mousetrap* opens in London's West End
- Soprano Maria Callas makes a sensational first appearance at the Royal Opera House

DEATH OF THE KING

▲ **The coffin of George VI, Britain's war-time monarch, lies in state; his funeral procession route was lined by thousands of mourners.**

George VI, a man who had never aspired nor expected to become monarch of the British Empire, died on February 6, 1952.

Albert Frederick Arthur George was born on December 14, 1895, the second son of the future George V. In 1920, after a period serving in the Royal Navy and a year's study at Trinity College, Cambridge, Prince Albert was invested with the title of Duke of York. In April 1923, he married Lady Elizabeth Angela Marguerite Bowes-Lyon, the youngest daughter of the 14th Earl of Strathmore and Kinghorne (in later years the Queen Mother). The royal couple raised two children, the princesses Elizabeth (later to become Elizabeth II) and Margaret.

The Duke of York was proclaimed king on December 12, 1936, following the abdication of his brother Edward VIII who gave up the crown to marry Wallis Simpson, an American divorcee. The Duke of York took the title of George VI and was crowned in May 1937.

Before the start of the Second World War the king supported Prime Minister Neville Chamberlain's policy of appeasement towards fascist aggression from Germany and Italy. Throughout the war, he gave his firm support to the coalition government of Winston Churchill, even though he had called for the appointment of Lord Halifax to lead the war effort.

From 1948 onward, George VI's health deteriorated following treatment for lung cancer, which eventually claimed his life. His funeral procession on February 15 was attended by thousands of mourners – a testimony to a popular king who, against the wishes of his advisers, persistently refused to leave London during the Blitz.

▲ **Queen Mary, mother of the late king, is flanked by her daughter-in-law and granddaughter, Elizabeth II, at George VI's funeral.**

ELIZABETH BECOMES QUEEN

At the end of January 1952, 25-year-old Princess Elizabeth, the heir to the throne, and her husband Philip, Duke of Edinburgh, flew to Kenya on the first leg of a journey that was supposed to culminate in an official tour of Australia and New Zealand. The princess's parents, George VI and Queen Elizabeth, accompanied the young couple to Heathrow airport. It was the last time that Elizabeth saw her father alive.

The prince and princess went on safari in Kenya and were staying at the Treetops game lodge when news arrived that the king had died on February 6. Despite the king's

▲ **Elizabeth II arrives back at Heathrow following the death of her father. She had left for Kenya just a week earlier as a princess.**

ill-health, the suddenness of his death came as a shock. Elizabeth immediately flew back to England, arriving on February 7.

The following day, Elizabeth's accession to the throne was officially proclaimed at Castle Hill, Windsor. She was declared "Queen Elizabeth II by the Grace of God, Queen of the Realm, and Her other Realms and Territories, Head of the Commonwealth, Defender of the Faith, to whom Her Lieges do acknowledge all Faith, and constant Obedience with hearty and humble Affection."

Elizabeth had frequently represented the ailing king at the

Trooping the Colour ceremony and at state occasions at home and abroad. This was some preparation for the burden that now fell upon her young shoulders. In the summer, the royal couple, with their three-year-old son Prince Charles and two-year-old daughter Princess Anne, moved into Buckingham Palace. The coronation of Elizabeth II followed in June 1953.

FLASH FLOOD DEVASTATES LYNMOUTH

On the night of August 15–16, 1952, much of the north Devon seaside village of Lynmouth was destroyed in one of the worst flash floods ever to occur in Britain. In all, 34 people were killed in the flooding, most of them in Lynmouth itself or in neighbouring Barbrook.

Lynmouth lies at the confluence of the East and West Lyn rivers, which plunge down steeply from the heights of Exmoor. The first two weeks of August had been exceptionally wet, and the moor was already saturated when torrential rain began early on August 15. More than 22.5 cm (9 in) of rain fell in 24 hours –

people recalled that the downpour beat so hard it hurt their heads and faces – but no flood warning was given. The 450 village residents and some 700 holiday visitors went to bed in the riverside buildings without a qualm.

When the flash flood struck, a torrent of water carrying uprooted trees and boulders burst upon the village with terrifying force. Dozens of buildings were demolished, burying those inside. More than 100 vehicles were swept out to sea, as were many of the victims.

There have been persistent rumours that the flood was caused by military rainmaking experiments

– aircraft were allegedly being used to "seed" clouds to produce rain. But meteorologists are sure that nothing more than freak weather produced a disaster against which the village was defenceless.

▲ **When a massive flash flood struck the town of Lynmouth, buildings were simply demolished by the force of the raging torrent.**

THE MAU MAU REVOLT

▲ **More than 20,000 suspected Mau Mau terrorists were rounded up by the colonial authorities during the uprising.**

During 1952, British rule in Kenya had been under increasing threat from the Mau Mau movement, a nationalist antiwhite organization formed

among the Kikuyu, the predominant tribe in Kenya. The Mau Mau advocated violent resistance to British rule and a move towards unity among the tribes of Kenya that would eventually lead to independence from Britain.

On October 20, 1952, after a campaign of sabotage and assassination, the government in Kenya declared a state of emergency, after which a battalion of 800 British Lancashire Fusiliers were sent out to quell the uprising. What was first seen as a simple piece of military fire-fighting turned into four years of bitter guerrilla warfare which ended with the death of 11,000 rebels, 2,000 Kenyan loyalists and 100 British troops.

The conflict saw the widespread arrest of Kikuyu tribesmen, some

20,000 being placed in detention centres where numerous alleged tortures took place. In April 1953 Jomo Kenyatta, President of the Kenya African Union and known to his Kikuyu people as "Burning Spear", was tried on a charge of being a Mau Mau terrorist leader. While the British sought to present the trial as a simple criminal case, it was seen throughout the world as political repression. Although he always denied direct involvement with the Mau Mau, Kenyatta was imprisoned for seven years.

The Mau Mau became inactive after 1956. However, resistance and lobbying from the Kikuyu tribe continued and Kenya finally won independence in 1963. Jomo Kenyatta became the new nation's first Prime Minister.

BRITAIN EXPLODES ATOMIC BOMB

On October 3, 1952, Britain exploded its first atomic bomb. The test, which took place on a warship moored in the Monte Bello islands off the coast of Western Australia, was watched by servicemen on other vessels nearby, who were thereby casually exposed to radiation without protective clothing.

The British had first embarked on developing an A-bomb early in the Second World War, but their knowledge and personnel were then fed into the American Manhattan project. After the war, the United States was not keen to return the compliment by giving Britain full information about its nuclear technology. The British had to work out how

▲ The model shows the effect of a nuclear strike on a large town, an eventuality Britain's new nuclear deterrent was designed to prevent.

to build a bomb for themselves.

The formal decision to build a British atom bomb was taken by Labour Prime Minister Clement Attlee in January 1947. Parliament was not informed and the funding for the project was concealed

under other headings. Not even the whole government knew what was being done – Attlee restricted information to a special committee consisting of himself and six other ministers, including Ernest Bevin and Herbert Morrison.

When Winston Churchill's Conservative government came to power in 1951, it took to the atomic bomb project with enthusiasm. Having an "independent nuclear deterrent" fitted with the Conservatives' aim of maintaining Britain's status as a great power. From 1953 the country had a usable free-fall bomb that could be carried by Vulcan jet bombers. Nuclear tests continued, mostly in the Australian desert, through the 1950s.

HARROW RAIL TRAGEDY

October 8, 1952, saw the second-worst rail accident in British history as a three-train collision just north of London took the lives of 112 people and injured over 200 others.

The story began as commuters at Harrow station boarded the 08:19 train to take them into the centre of London. Before the train

had set off, a Perth–London overnight express ploughed into the back of it, demolishing four carriages and spreading debris over surrounding tracks. Less than a minute later, an outgoing express train from Euston collided with the wreckage. Within the space of a few minutes, three trains had been reduced to a pile

of wreckage, the smoke from which mushroomed 15 m (50 ft) into the air.

Emergency services from all over north London quickly arrived on the scene, but were overwhelmed by the carnage. Among the rescuers were US Air Force personnel from a nearby military base. Their expertise and prompt action was responsible for keeping the death toll down. Twelve hours after the accident, workmen were still cutting through the twisted debris, the hopes of finding survivors trapped inside diminishing by the hour.

Although an immediate investigation was launched into the tragedy, the outcome was inconclusive, with a dead train driver blamed for the accident, leading dissatisfied relatives of the victims to suspect the responsible parties were being protected by a cover-up.

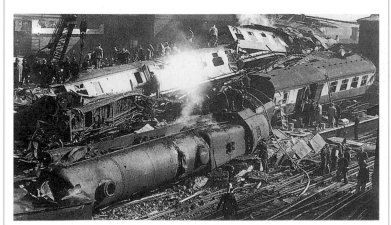

▲ The tangled wreckage of *The Night Scot* smoulders in the aftermath of a horrific three-way accident.

THE BENTLEY CASE

On November 2, 1952, 16-year-old Christopher Craig and 19-year-old Derek Bentley were surprised by police while breaking into a warehouse in Croydon, south London. In the ensuing gunfight on the roof of the building, one police officer was wounded and another, Constable Sidney Miles, was shot dead. Both Bentley and Craig were arrested and charged with murder. The resulting court case led to a notorious miscarriage of justice and gave a great impetus to the campaign for the abolition of the death penalty.

The case was heard by Lord Chief Justice Goddard, who exhibited a savage bias against the defendants. Craig had fired the gun, but was too young to hang. Bentley, however, was old enough for the gallows. Police

▲ Derek Bentley's hanging proved to be one of Britain's most notorious miscarriages of justice. His conviction was quashed in 1998.

witnesses claimed that Bentley had urged Craig to begin shooting at the police by crying: "Let him have it Chris!" On this basis it was argued that – although he

had no gun – Bentley was responsible for the murder.

The jury found both men guilty after a mere 75 minutes' deliberation. On December 11 the judge sentenced Bentley to death and Craig to indefinite imprisonment. Bentley's sentence aroused a storm of protest. His family made it known that the boy had a mental age of 11 and was prone to fits. Around 200 MPs petitioned for a reprieve, but Home Secretary Sir David Maxwell Fyfe was unmoved

Bentley was hanged at Wandsworth prison on the morning of January 28, 1953. Thousands gathered to make their protest outside the prison gates. Bentley's family campaigned against the murder verdict for the next 45 years, until it was overturned by the Court of Appeal in 1998.

LONDON SMOG KILLS THOUSANDS

▲ London's "pea-souper" smogs paralyzed the city. It is now estimated they caused thousands of deaths.

On December 5, 1952, London ground to a halt as a mixture of smoke and fog, known as "smog", reduced visibility to

almost zero. Smog was a familiar phenomenon in the capital, where coal was the main source of home heating and of the fuel for power

stations. But the thick noxious cloud that enveloped the city for the next four days was never equalled in its density or its deadly effects.

For most people the "pea-souper" was either an irritant or an amusing variant on daily life. Children were kept out of school for fear they would lose their way in the gloom. Buses crawled through the streets behind a man on foot with a torch. But for people with heart or respiratory diseases, the polluted air was a killer. Hospitals and morgues became the busy spots in the paralyzed city. It was reckoned at the time that around 4,000 people died as a result of the smog. Experts now estimate the number of excess deaths at nearer 12,000.

The great smog of 1952 drove the government to take action to limit the use of coal fires, leading to the passing of the Clean Air Act in 1956.

NOVEMBER
- Elizabeth II opens parliament for the first time
- The conservative government introduces a bill to denationalize the iron and steel industry
- Herbert Morrison defeats Aneurin Bevan in the Labour party deputy leadership election
- Kenyan nationalist leader Jomo Kenyatta is arrested and charged with heading the Mau Mau rebellion

DECEMBER
- Severe air pollution in the London smog causes thousands of deaths
- The Queen decides that next year's coronation ceremony in Westminster Abbey will be televised
- Derek Bentley is sentenced to hang
- British scientists Archer Martin and Richard Synge win the Nobel Prize for Chemistry

1953

- The discovery of the double helix structure of DNA announced by Cambridge scientists Francis Crick and James Watson
- Piltdown Man, found in southern England in 1912, is shown to be a fraud
- The Ford Popular is marketed as the cheapest family car at £390
- The royal yacht *Britannia* is launched
- The science fiction series *The Quatermass Experiment* is shown on BBC television
- Books published this year include *Casino Royale* by Ian Fleming and *Hurry On Down* by John Wain
- British films this year include Charles Frend's *The Cruel Sea* and the first Norman Wisdom comedy *Trouble in Store*
- Samuel Beckett's play *Waiting for Godot* premieres in Paris
- First performance of Benjamin Britten's opera *Gloriana*, written for the coronation
- Henry Moore completes *Screening Wall and Draped Reclining Figure* for the Time-Life Building in London
- Sir Arthur Bliss is appointed Master of the Queen's Musick

FREAK STORM KILLS HUNDREDS

On January 31–February 1 1953, Britain experienced one of its worst ever peacetime disasters. More than 400 people were killed as hurricane-force winds combined with a high tide to generate a storm surge around the coast of Scotland and eastern England.

The first victims were on board a car ferry, *Princess Victoria*, sailing from Stranraer in Scotland to Northern Ireland. Caught in exceptionally heavy seas off Belfast, the ferry sank on the afternoon of January 31, with the loss of 132 out of 172 passengers and crew.

The storm surge then swept down the east coast of Britain, with waves mounting ever higher. Lincolnshire and East Anglia caught the full force of the storm after darkness fell. Battered by 6 m (20-ft) waves, sea defences were breached in more than 1,000 places. Communications – in any case primitive by later standards – were disrupted by the high winds which had brought down telephone lines. There was consequently no warning given to residents in low-lying areas as the disaster then spread southward.

Forty-one people were drowned in Lincolnshire and 81 in north Norfolk, including 12 American servicemen. When the surge reached the Thames Estuary in the early hours of February 1, the sea wall at Canvey Island collapsed and caused the death of 58 people. Another 35 drowned in Clacton. In total, 307 people were killed along the English coast on that dreadful night – although England was lucky in comparison with the Netherlands, where more than 1,800 people died when dykes were breached by the same storm.

▲ The storm-surge which swept eastern England battered sea defences, leaving hundreds dead and extensive damage in its wake.

THE MATTHEWS FINAL

▲ Matthews was one of England's most gifted footballers; his dazzling display in the 1953 FA Cup final was a fitting climax to his career.

The 1953 FA Cup final, played between Blackpool and Bolton Wanderers in front of a 100,000 crowd at Wembley Stadium, is always remembered as "the Matthews final". Blackpool winger Stanley Matthews was England's best-loved footballer, but he had been on the losing side in both his previous Cup final appearances. He was now 38 years old, and millions of English football fans longed for him to succeed in almost certainly his last attempt at a winner's medal.

For the first hour of the match almost everything went wrong for Blackpool. Bolton comfortably outplayed them and built a deserved 3–1 lead. Then Matthews began to take the tiring Bolton defence apart. Repeatedly fed the ball by his colleagues, he swerved and darted through on the right, displaying dazzlingly swift changes of pace and direction.

A Matthews cross put Blackpool forward Stan Mortensen in for a goal at 68 minutes. Then, with two minutes of normal time remaining, Mortensen fired in another from a free kick equalizing the scores. Two minutes into stoppage time, Matthews cut through the Bolton defence for the umpteenth time and set up Bill Perry for the Blackpool winner.

The Bolton players must have been devastated, but they had the sportsmanship to congratulate Matthews on the most popular Cup final medal ever won.

CORONATION OF QUEEN ELIZABETH II

▲ **The advent of television allowed the coronation of Elizabeth II to be enjoyed in every corner of the Empire.**

June 2, 1953, saw Britain's greatest day of celebration since VE Day in 1945, as Elizabeth, the elder daughter of the late George VI, was formally crowned Elizabeth II.

The coronation ceremony took place at its traditional location, Westminster Abbey. The weather was unseasonably cold and wet, but nothing could dampen the enthusiasm of the estimated 3 million people who packed the streets of central London to witness the spectacle. Many had spent a night on the pavement to guarantee a prime viewing position.

Those seeing the event first-hand were far outnumbered, however, by television viewers. Over 20 million people – almost half the population – crowded around small black-and-white sets, sitting in darkened rooms with the curtains drawn. Many were watching television for the first time, and most watched in someone else's home – despite a rush to buy sets in the run-up to the event, less than 2 million households had sets.

The royal procession was cheered from Buckingham Palace to the Abbey, the young Queen travelling in a fairytale gold-encrusted coach. Inside the Abbey were 8,000 British and foreign dignitaries, and the ubiquitous television cameras, with Richard Dimbleby as commentator. The televising of the coronation ceremony itself was entirely the Queen's decision. She had been advised against it by the government and by experts in protocol, but she had overruled them, determined to share the event with her people.

So it was that, for the first time in history, most of the population saw a monarch take the orb, sceptre, rod and ring – the symbols of royal authority – and have St Edward's crown placed on her head by the Archbishop of Canterbury, Dr Geoffrey Fisher. The orchestration of the ceremony, with music by William Walton, was a triumph of pageantry, rich with colour and symbolic gesture.

Afterwards, the royal family returned to Buckingham Palace, where they waved to the crowds from the balcony. Across the

▲ **Flanked by her Maids of Honour, Elizabeth II makes her way along the nave of Westminster Abbey.**

country people emerged from their television rooms, many going on to celebrate in traditional style with street parties and fireworks.

The spectacle of the coronation undoubtedly had its comical aspects – notably the appearance of Winston Churchill in the startlingly archaic uniform of Lord Warden of the Cinque Ports. But it initiated the reign of the second Elizabeth on a note of genuine warmth and optimism.

▲ **Britain's most senior peer, the Duke of Norfolk, pays homage to Elizabeth II after her coronation.**

1953

EVEREST CONQUERED AT LAST

On May 29, 1953, New Zealander Edmund Hillary and the Nepalese mountaineer Tenzing Norgay became the first men to scale Mount Everest, at 8,848 m (29,028 ft), the world's highest mountain peak. Everest had long been revered by the local people of Tibet and Nepal as "Goddess Mother of the World", and its conquest was long prized as one of man's greatest challenges.

The earliest attempts to climb Everest began in 1920. Over the following 30 years, ten missions failed as man battled against some of the harshest natural elements on Earth. The successful expedition, led by Colonel John Hunt, was sponsored by the Royal Geographical Society. Hillary, a beekeeper by profession, had already been a part of a team of New Zealanders who had made a failed attempt in 1951. Tenzing, one of the mountain-dwelling

▲ In conquering the world's highest peak, Hillary and Tenzing achieved a feat that had long eluded mountaineers.

Sherpa people of Nepal, was one of the most experienced mountaineers in the region, and had been employed on most of the Everest expeditions since he assisted Sir Eric Shipton's failed mission in 1935.

The operation was planned and executed with military precision, making crucial use of oxygen maintenance systems, specially insulated clothing, and portable radio equipment. Eight interim

bases were set up along the way. The mission reached its successful climax at 11:30 on the morning of May 29. Tenzing planted the flags of Britain, Nepal, India and the United Nations at Everest's peak while Hillary photographed the event. They remained at the highest point on the Earth's surface for just 15 minutes before beginning their descent.

This incredible feat brought celebrity to both men, Hillary receiving a knighthood in July, 1953; Tenzing was awarded the George Cross. Hillary returned to the region in the late 1950s, where he played a major role in building schools and hospitals for the Sherpa people. Although he continued his life as a great adventurer, taking part in a successful trans-Antarctic crossing, it is for the conquest of the Earth's greatest peak that Sir Edmund Hillary and Sherpa Tenzing will always be remembered.

RILLINGTON PLACE MURDERS

The month-long trial of John Reginald Halliday Christie, the perpetrator of a series of notorious murders at 10 Rillington Place, London. took place in June 1953.

The saga began in 1949, when Timothy Evans, a barely literate van driver who lived in the top flat at 10 Rillington Place, walked into a police station claiming to have found the bodies of his wife and child, which he had then hidden down a drain. He later confessed to their murder but before he went on trial he accused "Reg" Christie of the murder. A tenant on a lower floor of the same house, Christie testified at the trial. Evans was

subsequently found guilty of murder and hanged.

In March 1953 Christie disappeared. Seeing that he had also emptied the flat, his landlord re-let it to another tenant, Beresford Brown. While attempting to put up a shelf on March 23, Brown discovered a woman's body buried behind the wall. When the police arrived and began a detailed search of the house, three more bodies were found, one of them that of Christie's wife Ethel. Christie was arrested a week later. Two further bodies were later found buried in the garden.

Christie admitted the killings; three of the women had been local

▲ Police evidence is removed from 10 Rillington Place.

prostitutes and his motive had been sexual. He had invited his victims into the flat where they were subdued with gas. They were then raped and strangled.

Convicted of murder on June 25, 1953, Christie was hanged at Pentonville prison on July 15. Although he always denied the Evans killings, the unlikely coincidence of two unrelated murderers living in the same building led to calls for a government inquiry, even though Evans had been hanged. Criticized by many as a whitewash, an inquiry that reported in July still found Evans to be the murderer. Evans's innocence was finally recognized in 1966, when he was granted a posthumous free pardon.

ENGLAND REGAIN THE ASHES AFTER 20 YEARS

On August 19, 1953, England's cricketers defeated the Australians at the Oval to win the coveted Ashes for the first time since the notorious Bodyline tour of 1932–33.

The series was gritty rather than flamboyant, but packed with drama. England were denied certain victory in the first test by rain, then saved from defeat in the second by an epic stonewall innings on the final day from Trevor Bailey. The third match was ruined by more rain, although not before England's bowlers had reduced Australia to 35–8, without a single batsman reaching double

▲ England waited two decades to recapture the Ashes from Australia. Although not a flamboyant win, their fans' joy was unbridled.

figures. A fourth draw at Headingley left everything to play for in the final Test at the Oval.

Narrowly ahead on the first innings, England were given the whip hand by their spin bowlers Jim Laker and Tony Lock, who between them bowled out Australia for 162 second time around. Only needing 132 to win, the English batsmen struggled but eventually got home comfortably enough with eight wickets to spare.

England's victory was not won in a cavalier spirit. Success hinged upon the accuracy of swing bowler Alec Bedser, who took 39 wickets, and Bailey's stroke-free occupation of the crease. But no England fan cared about the style. Just winning over the old rivals after two barren decades was sweet enough.

WELSH BARD DIES

On November 9, 1953, Dylan Thomas, one of Britain's best-known writers of verse and prose died in New York City. He was 39 years old. The Welshman was well known for a characteristic blend of humour and pathos which can be seen – and heard – in *Under Milk Wood*, his "play for voices" for which he is, perhaps, best remembered.

Thomas began writing at a very early age, contributing numerous pieces to his school magazine, which he also edited. In his general education, however, Thomas performed poorly, disregarding any subjects in which he was not interested. He left school at the age of 16 to become a local news reporter.

His first book was published in 1934. *Eighteen Poems*, many of which had been written in his late teens, was immediately hailed by literary critics. Although Thomas was widely published and acclaimed over the next decade he made little money during most of his life. His poor business acumen and legendary drinking exploits were as much to blame as his inability to reach a wide audience with his poetry.

By the beginning of the Second World War, Thomas also had a young family to support. Excused from military service because of an ongoing lung disease, he turned to scriptwriting as a way of making ends meet. Throughout the 1940s, he combined his literary career with working for the BBC, although even then he still struggled to survive.

In 1950, Thomas embarked on his first book tour of the United States, where he enjoyed a growing reputation. In 1952, *Collected Poems* was published to great acclaim on both sides of the Atlantic. For the first time in his life,

▲ Dylan Thomas struggled to make a living in the final three years of his life.

Thomas saw a book by him sell in large quantities; he failed to reap the rewards, much of which were lost to the British Inland Revenue.

He went to New York for the third time in 1953 to oversee the first production of *Under Milk Wood*. Suffering from depression, he survived such exhausting trips by indulging in increasingly heavy bouts of drinking. During this stay in New York he took a massive alcohol overdose, fell into a coma and died.

NOVEMBER
- In Uganda, the Kabaka of Buganda, Mutesa II, is deported by the colony's British governor
- England's footballers are thrashed 3–6 by Hungary at Wembley; it is England's first home defeat by a team from outside the UK
- The government announces plans for commercial television to compete with the BBC
- Death of Welsh poet Dylan Thomas

DECEMBER
- Iran restores diplomatic relations with Britain
- Sir Winston Churchill is awarded the Nobel Prize for Literature

- The Federation of Nigeria is formed as a step towards self-government
- The Anglo-Iranian Oil Company becomes British Petroleum (BP)
- The Independent Television Authority is formed
- The Atomic Energy Authority is founded
- Books published this year include *Under the Net* by Iris Murdoch, *Lord of the Flies* by William Golding, *Lucky Jim* by Kingsley Amis and *The Lord of the Rings* by J R R Tolkien
- Dylan Thomas's *Under Milk Wood* is broadcast on BBC radio's Third Programme
- British films this year include Michael Anderson's *The Dam Busters*, Ralph Thomas's *Doctor in the House* and Frank Launder's *The Belles of St Trinian's*
- First performance of Julian Slade's musical *Salad Days*
- The Roman Temple of Mithras is unearthed in the City of London
- "Teddy Boys" appear on the streets
- The myxomatosis virus threatens to wipe out British rabbits

COMET GROUNDED AFTER MYSTERY CRASHES

▲ **A series of crashes left Britain's pioneering Comet jet grounded and led to American companies taking the lead in jet airliners.**

On April 8, 1954, a South African Airways Comet bound from Rome to Johannesburg crashed in the Mediterranean off Naples, killing 14 passengers and seven crew. It was the fourth fatal crash for the De Havilland jet airliner in little over a year and all Comets were immediately grounded.

The entry of the Comet into service in 1952 had given Britain an enviable world leader in air passenger transport technology. Orders for the revolutionary new aircraft flooded in.

When a Comet crashed taking off from Karachi in March 1953, the disaster was shrugged off as due to pilot error. A second Comet crashed on take-off at Calcutta in May 1953. Then on January 10, 1954, another Comet, flown by BOAC, inexplicably broke up in the air off the Mediterranean island of Elba. Twenty-nine passengers and six crew were killed. After some hesitation, the authorities allowed Comet flights to continue, but the crash the following April left no alternative: the aircraft's certificate of airworthiness was withdrawn.

A lengthy investigation established that the problem lay in an apparently trivial decision about the shape of the aircraft's windows. These had been made square instead of round for aesthetic reasons. Pressure in flight concentrated at the corners of the windows, making them liable to buckle through metal fatigue.

It was four years before the Comet returned to service with rounded windows. By then, the American giants Boeing and Douglas had developed their own jet airliners and the Comet was no longer seriously competitive. Until the success of the European Airbus in the 1980s, most of the world flew in American-built jets.

FIRST FOUR-MINUTE MILE

On May 6, 1954, one of sport's most famous milestone barriers was broken as Roger Bannister, a medical student at Oxford University, achieved the unthinkable by running a mile in under four minutes.

For more than 20 years experts had argued over whether such a feat was physiologically possible. During the 1940s, the Swedish middle-distance runner Gunder Hägg – in whose dazzling career 15 world records were shattered – had gradually shaved the mile barrier to four minutes 1.3 seconds in 1945. In the nine

▲ **Roger Bannister crosses the finishing line as he completes his record-breaking run.**

years that followed, no athlete came near to bettering the record.

At the groundbreaking athletics meeting in Oxford, Bannister, already a British and European champion over 1,500 metres, had the additional impediment of strong 24 km/h (15 mph) cross winds. His winning time was three minutes 59.4 seconds. Bannister's achievement brought him overnight international celebrity. He wrote a successful account of his achievement, *The Four-Minute Mile*, then returned to his studies.

In 1963 Bannister earned a further medical degree and thereafter became a noted neurologist. He was knighted in 1979.

Surprisingly, Bannister's record was broken within six weeks when Australian athlete John Landy clocked a time of three minutes 58 seconds. Although a "sub-four" time is still regarded as commendable, top athletes over this distance regularly manage it. In July 1999 the Moroccan athlete Hicham El Guerrouj took the record down to an incredible three minutes 43.13 seconds. That time has yet to be bettered.

END OF RATIONING

▲ Rationing continued long after the end of the Second World War. Sweets continued to be rationed until 1953.

On July 2, 1954, the Conservative government announced the end of rationing, which had persisted through nine years of peacetime. In a few places ration books were burned – mostly for the benefit of news photographers – but the popular response was generally quiet relief and satisfaction, rather than celebration.

The last items to be taken off rationing were butter, margarine, cheese, condensed milk and, finally, meat and bacon. The meat and cheese rations had been especially stingy well into the 1950s – as late as 1952 the Conservatives had been forced to pare the cheese ration down to an ounce a week.

Although it inevitably gave rise to a flourishing black market, rationing had been widely accepted as a fair method of coping with shortages. But its abolition was an important symbolic step on the path to a normal peacetime economy and the Conservatives took the credit, earning a reputation as the party of prosperity and deregulation.

GOLDEN AGE OF RADIO COMEDY

Although television viewing was on the rise in the early 1950s, the new medium took time to supplant radio as the nation's favourite source of entertainment. With fewer than 4 million television sets in the country and a single Television channel transmitting just seven hours a day, radio series, such as *The Archers* and *Mrs Dale's Diary,* still had a far larger following than any of the television programmes.

The 1950s is remembered as a golden age of radio comedy, a reputation based mainly on two programmes: *The Goon Show* and *Hancock's Half Hour.* First heard on the air in 1951, the Goons were Spike Milligan, Harry Secombe, Peter Sellers and – in the early series – Michael Bentine. Anti-authoritarian and anarchic to the point of incoherence, the show took time to win its audience, but by 1954 it was becoming a national cult. Broadcast up to 1960, it established a new surreal tradition in British humour that would later flourish in the Monty Python television series.

Tony Hancock's depressed "little man", ever dreaming of escape from Railway Cuttings, East Cheam, was an acute embodiment of the frustrations of 1950s

▲ The Goons' anarchic brand of humour was at the forefront of a renaissance in British comedy during the 1950s.

Britain. More traditional than the Goons in its sit-com format, it was also more reliably funny thanks to the professional scriptwriting of Galton and Simpson and the perfect comic timing of Hancock and his foils, including Sid James. The series transferred effortlessly to television from 1956.

1955

EDEN WINS ELECTION AFTER CHURCHILL STEPS DOWN

On May 26, 1955, the Conservatives were confirmed in power at a general election called by their new leader, Sir Anthony Eden. Riding the crest of a wave of prosperity, they saw their overall majority in parliament increased to 60 seats.

The ageing Sir Winston Churchill had finally been pressured by his colleagues into resigning as Prime Minister at the start of April. Churchill had no confidence in Eden – he privately told one of his colleagues: "I don't think Anthony can do it." Yet the new leader at first looked set for a long period in office. Eden was personally popular with the electorate and his brand of Conservatism had broad appeal. He believed in a "property-owning democracy" and "welfare capitalism" – the combination of a free-market economy with the welfare state and full employment.

The Conservatives' embrace of the welfare state had blurred distinctions between the main parties. The lack of any sharp contrast between moderate Conservatives and Labourites led pundits to invent the term "Butskellism" for policies proposed by Chancellor of the Exchequer R A Butler and Shadow Chancellor Hugh Gaitskell. There remained

▲ **Anthony Eden's election victory in 1955 did him little good. The Suez crisis the following year fatally damaged his premiership.**

important nuances of difference – the Conservatives cut income tax, which Labour intended to raise. But consensus prevailed on the need to manage the economy to sustain full employment.

The Conservatives and their allies won almost 50 per cent of the popular vote in the general election, compared with 46 per cent for Labour. As turnout was down on 1951, however, the actual number of votes cast for the Tories actually fell. Commentators speculated that the key to the election was in fact that traditional Labour supporters had failed to go to the polls. With incomes rising and the welfare state secure, Labour's traditional appeal to socialism failed to press the right buttons.

Eden's popularity proved short-lived. Even before the Suez Crisis of 1956, an indecisive quality to his leadership had begun to earn him a bad press. Churchill's prophecy proved correct and his premiership lasted only 21 months.

A NEW ERA IN TELEVISION

On September 22, 1955, 188,000 television sets were tuned in to an event that would for ever change the face of broadcasting in Britain – the opening night of ITV, Britain's first independent television network.

Although the first broadcasts had been made in 1936, television in Britain only took off in earnest a decade later, following an end to the blackout of the war years. Until 1954 a Royal Charter had given the British Broadcasting Corporation (BBC) a total monopoly over television in the UK. It was during the early 1950s that the subject of providing commercial competition became widely debated in parliamentary circles. In spite of considerable establishment opposition, in 1954 parliament passed the Television Act creating the Independent Television Authority (ITA), a government body that was to be given responsibility for the regulation of a new channel financed by selling airtime to advertisers. The independent channel – called ITV – would be a national network of broadcasting organizations covering different regions of Britain.

On August 25, 1954, the ITA placed an advertisement in the British press, inviting "Applications from those interested in becoming programme contractors". Of the 25 organizations that applied, only four – Rediffusion, Granada, ATV and ABC – covering the majority of viewers in England, were initially deemed suitable.

The historic opening night of transmission saw viewers treated to live coverage of the annual Guildhall Banquet followed by Britain's first ever cash-prize quiz show. Although outwardly displaying little concern towards the ITV, the BBC upstaged its rival's opening night by killing off one of the main characters in the massively popular radio serial *The Archers*.

Nonetheless, with a schedule dominated by entertainment, the ITV network became an immediate success, reshaping the face of British television. With popular shows like *Sunday Night at the London Palladium* and *Coronation Street*, ITV quickly dominated the ratings.

By the end of the decade, advertising revenue had increased from an initial £2 million to approaching £100 million.

▲ **The opening night of ITV brought commercial television to Britain and gave viewers a choice of channels for the first time.**

SCIENTISTS' DIRE WARNING

On July 9, 1955, global leaders were given a dire warning of the potential consequences of nuclear war by some of the world's most eminent scientists. Led by the celebrated British political philosopher Bertrand Russell, a group of nine leading academics – among them seven Nobel Prize winners – called for the total renunciation of warfare, warning of a possible "utter and irretrievable disaster".

At a press conference held in London, Earl Russell stressed that the protest was opposed to war in general rather than specifically against nuclear conflict. It was also intended to be nonpolitical, with scientists of different persuasions coming from both sides of the Iron Curtain. In a lengthy statement published in many of the world's leading newspapers, Russell was unequivocal: "In view of the fact that in any future world war nuclear weapons will certainly be employed, and that such weapons threaten the continued existence of mankind, we urge the governments of the world to realize

▲ **Spokesperson for the scientific community, Bertrand Russell warns the world of the dangers of nuclear proliferation.**

and acknowledge publicly that their purposes cannot be furthered by a world war."

Russell had hoped to elicit a response from the three world powers with a nuclear capability – the United States, the Soviet Union and Britain – whose leaders were due to hold a summit meeting in Geneva, Switzerland, in mid-July.

The summit was significant as the first East–West meeting of heads of government since 1945, but President Eisenhower, Prime Minister Eden and Soviet Premier Bulganin failed to reach agreement on any significant issues. With Cold War loyalties now well-entrenched, the views of Russell and his eminent colleagues were politely ignored and the world arms race continued unabated.

JANUARY
• The Governor of Kenya announces an amnesty for Mau Mau rebels

FEBRUARY
• White transport workers in West Bromwich strike to block employment of "coloured" immigrants on buses
• England tourists win the Test series in Australia to retain the Ashes

MARCH
• A strike by electricians closes down national newspapers
• Death of British scientist Alexander Fleming

APRIL
• Prime Minister Winston Churchill resigns; Anthony Eden succeeds
• Newspapers reappear after a shutdown lasting almost a month

MAY
• Stirling Moss wins the prestigious Mille Miglia road race in Italy
• Chelsea are Football League champions for the first time
• Newcastle United beat Manchester City 3–1 in the FA Cup final
• A dock workers strike begins
• The Conservatives, under Anthony Eden, win the general election
• A railway strike begins; the government declares state of emergency to face rail and dock strikes

JUNE
• The amnesty offered to Mau Mau activists in January is withdrawn
• End of the railway strike
• Britain and the United States sign a deal on atomic energy
• EOKA terrorists are arrested in Cyprus

1955

JULY

- End of the dock workers strike
- Ruth Ellis is hanged, the last woman to be executed in Britain
- Stirling Moss wins the British Grand Prix
- Donald Campbell sets a world waterspeed record of 325 km/h (202 mph) on Ullswater
- Prime Minister Anthony Eden attends East-West summit conference in Geneva

AUGUST

- Pietro Annigoni's portrait of the queen is exhibited at the Royal Academy Summer Exhibition
- Revolts in southern Sudan; withdrawal of British and Egyptian troops is demanded
- A conference opens in London between Britain, Greece and Turkey, intended to solve the Cyprus issue
- A government committee on the impact of "coloured workers" advises against immigration controls

SEPTEMBER

- London talks on the future of Cyprus end without agreement
- The Foreign Office admits that Burgess and Maclean were Soviet spies
- Commercial television broadcasting begins in Britain
- EOKA stages a general strike in Cyprus

ELLIS HANGED FOR MURDER

▲ **Ruth Ellis, the last woman executed in Britain, is pictured with David Blakely, the racing car driver for whose murder she hanged.**

On July 13, 1955, 28-year-old Ruth Ellis was hanged for murder at Holloway prison, London. She was the last woman to be executed in Britain.

Ellis's crime was on the face of it clear-cut. On the evening of Easter Sunday, she waited outside the Magdala public house in Hampstead for her boyfriend, 25-year-old racing driver David Blakely, to emerge. When he left the pub, she drew a gun and fired, hitting him with her second shot. She then emptied four more shots into Blakely at point-blank range as he lay on the ground.

Ellis was a glamorous woman who inhabited the Soho nightclub scene and her case consequently attracted the attention of the popular press. Although she had other boyfriends beside Blakely – one had driven her to the Hampstead pub – she was on the whole sympathetically presented by journalists as a victim of Blakely's infidelity and brutality.

In court Ellis made no attempt to deny her action. Under cross-examination she declared: "It is obvious that when I shot him I intended to kill him." The jury took less than half an hour to find her guilty of murder, which carried a mandatory death penalty.

The verdict provoked a public outcry. This was partly because capital punishment had, since the Derek Bentley case in 1952, become a potent issue in British politics. It was also because the murderer was an attractive woman, and one whom many believed had been driven to her crime by her victim's behaviour.

Home Secretary Major Gwilym Lloyd George resisted all pressure for a reprieve. The execution was carried out by hangman Albert Pierrepoint at 9 am while a huge crowd stood in vigil outside the Holloway gates.

The following February, the House of Commons voted that "the death penalty for murder no longer accords with the needs of a civilized society". Because of resistance in the House of Lords, capital punishment was not abolished, but the Homicide Act of 1957 reserved the death penalty for specific categories of murder, including the killing of a police officer and murder while committing armed robbery.

PRINCESS MARGARET ENDS ROMANCE

After much speculation in the world's media, on October 31, 1955, Queen Elizabeth's sister, Princess Margaret, announced that her controversial two-year romance with Group Captain Peter Townsend was over, and that there would be no royal wedding.

The romance, between the handsome 40-year-old war hero and the lively, pretty 24-year-old princess, had captured the imagination of the British public. The only problem facing the couple was that Townsend had already been married and his divorce had not been sanctioned by the Church of England. This was not the first time such a dilemma had affected the royal family. Less than 20 years earlier, Princess Margaret's uncle, Edward VIII, had abdicated so that he could marry an American divorcee, Wallis Simpson. While her position in Britain's monarchy was minor by comparison, Margaret acted in accordance with her "royal duty" and ended the courtship.

Although she was married in 1960 to a commoner – the photographer Anthony Armstrong-Jones – there remained speculation that Princess Margaret was bitterly unhappy at having been deprived of her true love. The couple had two children, but the attractive young princess appeared increasingly dour and removed as she carried out her public duties.

By the time "Tony and Margaret" announced their divorce in 1978, they had long since been separated. The first divorce to come so close to the English throne, Princess Margaret thereafter became something of an embarrassment to the royal family, embarking on a jet-set lifestyle, smoking heavily and creating a tabloid scandal by her affair with the "toy boy" Roddy Llewellyn. After a series of health scares in the 1980s, Margaret overhauled her way of life and thereafter chose to keep a low public profile.

▲ **The glamorous face of the royal family, Princess Margaret opens a trade fair; Captain Townsend is pictured behind her.**

ATTLEE BIDS FAREWELL

▲ **One of the pivotal figures of Britain in the twentieth century, Clement Attlee, was never so grand that he would not travel on the Underground.**

On December 7, 1955, Clement Attlee resigned the leadership of the Labour Party, which he had held for 20 years. During that time he had served at the very pinnacle of British politics.

A former lawyer, Attlee had become Prime Minister following the 1945 election that ousted Winston Churchill and the Conservatives in favour of the Labour party. Attlee's premiership oversaw the birth of the National Health Service and the nationalization of numerous important industries. Abroad, he actively supported the move towards independence throughout the Empire and Commonwealth.

Although he returned to office in the 1951 election, Attlee's House of Commons majority was cut to only six seats, making his position extremely weak. His government crumbled as two very prominent ministers, Nye Bevan and the young Harold Wilson resigned from the Cabinet over the introduction of NHS charges. Later that year, after another election, the Conservatives were returned to power.

Serious ideological divides beset the Labour Party of the early 1950s. The main difficulty was the question of how socialism could fit into an affluent society. On the left of the party, "Bevanites" led by the outspoken Welshman Nye Bevan stood firmly by socialist policy and favoured a move away from dependence on the United States; "Revisionists" led by Hugh Gaitskell were opposed to the continued manifesto pledge towards further nationalization.

By 1955 Attlee, now 72, had become more of a figurehead than an effective leader of the Labour Party. He chose to stand down so that a new leader could be elected. Although Gaitskell won an easy victory, it would be nine years before Labour came to power again, led by Harold Wilson (Gaitskell having died in 1963). As the first Earl Attlee, Attlee continued a lower-profile career in the House of Lords until his death in 1969.

- Almost 30,000 West Indian immigrants enter Britain
- British troops face an EOKA terrorist campaign in Cyprus
- The antipollution Clean Air Act comes into force
- The government imposes a credit squeeze and spending cuts as inflation rises
- Premium Bonds are introduced by Chancellor of the Exchequer Harold Macmillan
- Third-class coaches are abolished on the railways
- First performance of John Osborne's play *Look Back in Anger*
- Books published this year include *My Family and Other Animals* by Gerald Durrell
- The *New Lines* poetry anthology, edited by Robert Conquest, presents the group of poets known as The Movement
- The "This Is Tomorrow" exhibition at the Whitechapel Gallery, London, makes Pop Art fashionable
- British films this year include Michael Powell's *The Battle of the River Plate* and Lewis Gilbert's *Reach for the Sky*
- "Teddy Boys" riot during performances of the film *Rock Around the Clock*
- Debut of Tommy Steele, Britain's first rock music star
- First Eurovision song contest is staged
- The Duke of Edinburgh's award scheme for young people is founded
- John Lennon, still at school, forms a group called The Quarrymen

CYPRUS EXPLODES

▲ **Royal Marines stationed on the island scour the mountain villages of Cyprus in search of EOKA strongholds.**

On January 10, 1956, the British government ordered a battalion of 1,600 paratroopers to the eastern Mediterranean island of Cyprus to deal with the growing number of guerrilla attacks on British military and police bases. The cause of the disturbances was the growing support on the island for an end to British rule.

Most of the political problems experienced in Cyprus have been a result of hostilities between the Greek and Turkish populations. From the 1930s onwards a growing movement emerged among Greek Cypriots for formal unification with Greece – *enosis*. Turkish Cypriots were still hostile to the idea. Even before the Second World War, rioting and fighting between the two sides was common in the capital, Nicosia.

In 1947 Britain's newly elected Labour government declared a move towards greater self-government for all of Britain's Crown Colonies, including Cyprus. The idea was strongly rejected by the Greek Cypriots. In 1955 Georgios Grivas ("Dighenis"), a Cyprus-born colonel in the Greek army, founded the National Organization of Cypriot Fighters (EOKA), believing that only by violent means could the island be rid of British rule. EOKA engaged in a campaign of bombings and assassinations of opponents of *enosis*, both Cypriot and British.

With British troops arriving on the island, the guerrilla war escalated, reaching a peak following the arrest and deportation of Archbishop Makarios III, the head of the Greek Orthodox Church in Cyprus, in March 1956. Protests also spread to mainland Greece, where crowds rioted outside the British embassy in Athens. In recognition of the severity of the situation, Britain recalled its ambassador from Greece.

The impact of EOKA alarmed the Turkish-Cypriot minority who, under the leadership of Fazil Küçük, began to voice demands for the partitioning of the island. The situation, in which the governments of Greece and Turkey had hitherto played little part, began to cause growing tensions between the two states.

In 1959, following the failure of the United Nations to broker any compromise between the two sides, Greece, Turkey and Britain agreed that Cyprus should become an independent republic, with neither Greece nor Turkey pressing any claims to sovereignty over the island. The first elections were therefore held in December 1959, with Archbishop Makarios achieving a majority vote to become the first President of Cyprus, his Turkish rival, Fazil Küçük, became Vice-President.

DRAMA AT THE NATIONAL

The Grand National run on March 24, 1956, saw the most dramatic finish in the history of the race.

The race leader Devon Loch – owned by the Queen Mother and ridden by Dick Francis – jumped the last fence in style and galloped for the finish a full five lengths clear of second-placed ESB. Francis later wrote: "Never had I felt such power in reserve, such confidence in my mount, such calm in my mind." The crowd was on its feet and cheering horse and rider home when, about 45 m (50 yards) short of the finish line, Devon Loch inexplicably lost its footing and went down on its stomach. Francis urged the horse back to its feet but the race was lost.

The jockey was inconsolable, striding away from his mount in tears. The Queen Mother's response was more philosophical: "That's racing!"

▲ Just strides from the finish, Devon Loch seemed unbeatable, but an inexplicable stumble cost jockey Dick Francis a Grand National victory.

THE DISAPPEARANCE OF BUSTER CRABB

On April 19, 1956, British diver Lionel "Buster" Crabb plunged into the waters of Portsmouth Harbour, where the Soviet cruiser *Ordzhonikidze* and two Soviet destroyers were moored. He was on a mission organized by the Secret Intelligence Service (SIS – also known as MI6), to examine special equipment below the waterline on the cruiser's hull. When Crabb failed to return from the mission, the government found itself facing an embarrassing political scandal.

The *Ordzhonikidze* had brought Soviet leaders Nikita Khrushchev

▲ Buster Crabb's disappearance while apparently spying on a Soviet warship caused a rupture in Anglo-Soviet relations.

and Nikolai Bulganin on an official visit to Britain. During eight days of talks with the British government and politicians, Khrushchev in particular had oozed charm and goodwill, appealing for "peaceful coexistence" between East and West. It was not a good moment for Britain to be caught spying on its visitors.

Crabb was quite a well-known figure, a Second World War hero who had already carried out a number of secret missions in the Cold War era. Although the secret services did their best to eradicate all trace of his stay in Portsmouth, journalists got wind of the affair a few days after Crabb vanished. The Soviets stirred the pot by reporting that they had seen a diver near one of their ships at Portsmouth.

Under pressure, the British Admiralty issued a statement confirming that Crabb had disappeared while diving, but placing the incident in Stokes Bay, well away from Portsmouth Harbour. This lie failed to staunch

a flood of press speculation. On May 4 the Soviet embassy in London issued a note in effect requesting that the British own up to espionage.

Prime Minister Sir Anthony Eden was forced to admit to the House of Commons that Crabb had indeed been diving near the Soviet ships. Eden described his action as "completely unauthorized" and expressed "regret" that it had taken place. Behind the scenes the Prime Minister was furious with SIS; its director-general, Sir John Sinclair, was kicked out of his job.

Exactly what happened to Crabb has remained a mystery. A body in a diving suit was later washed up near Chichester, but it could not be positively identified. Rumours circulated that Crabb had been captured by the Soviets and been "turned" to work for them. Another story alleges that Crabb was shot by a sniper from one of the Soviet ships. Or, as an ageing heavy drinker of declining fitness, he may simply have died in the water.

1956

THE SUEZ CRISIS

A major international crisis began on July 26, 1956, when Egypt's President Nasser announced that the Suez Canal, then owned and operated by the Anglo-French Suez Canal Company, was to be nationalized. It was a direct reprisal for the withdrawal of offers of financial support by Britain and the United States to fund the building of a new dam at Aswan. Nasser calculated that the tolls collected from ships passing through the canal – more than 50 a day at its peak – would pay for the construction of the dam within five years.

The Suez Canal was of crucial significance to Western Europe as the main route for transporting petroleum from the oil fields of the Gulf. Britain and France feared that Nasser might prevent their ships

▲ Thousands of ordinary citizens of Port Said were caught up in the heavy fighting as Anglo-French troops responded to President Nasser's decision to nationalize the Suez Canal.

from using the canal and so cut off their oil supplies. They also considered the radical Egyptian leader a troublemaker who might stir up opposition to their interests throughout the Arab countries of the Middle East. Their twin aims during the crisis were to secure control over the canal and to overthrow Nasser.

Britain's first response was to freeze Egyptian assets in Britain. Three days later, on August 1, 1956, emergency talks were held between Britain, France and the United States, with the Americans acting as a moderating force on their two allies. In secret, France and Britain also engaged in talks with the government of Israel, which was keen to attack the Nasser regime. Meanwhile, British forces were mobilized and stationed on Cyprus as a base for an invasion of Egypt.

Throughout August, the Western powers attempted to bring Nasser to the negotiating table, warning of an imminent invasion if he refused. In London members of states for whom the canal had strategic importance proposed the formation of the Suez Canal Users Association, agreeing that tolls would be paid to them rather than the Egyptian government.

With little progress being made, on October 29 ten Israeli brigades advanced into Egypt towards the Canal, easily overpowering Nasser's forces. Vetoing a call

▲ A salvage ship moves sunken vessels that block the Suez Canal, clearing the crucial route between the West and the Indian Ocean.

from the United States and Soviet Union for a ceasefire between Egypt and Israel, on 31 October British and French bombers launched a damaging raid on military targets within Egypt, destroying over 100 Russian-built fighter planes.

The bombing of Egypt caused outrage both in Britain and around the world. Britain and France were both condemned at an emergency meeting of the United Nations General Assembly. With the Soviet Union threatening to intervene on behalf of Egypt, there was a genuine fear that the conflict could escalate. In the British parliament, meanwhile, Prime Minister Anthony Eden was severely criticized by the Labour opposition leader Hugh Gaitskell, who called the action "a tragic folly". This attack in parliament was followed by a massive demonstration in London's Trafalgar Square demanding Eden's resignation.

November opened with Britain, France and Israel wholly out of step with international opinion. As the UN worked towards a peaceful solution, allied forces moved further into Egypt. On November 3, Israel invaded and claimed possession of the Gaza Strip. Two days later, Britain and France

launched an airborne invasion, taking Port Said and Port Fuad, thereby occupying the Canal Zone.

The outbreak of war led to a run on sterling, which threatened to plunge Britain into a financial crisis. The United States, which opposed the military action, made it clear that it would not support the British currency unless the invasion was ended. The British government was also under pressure in the UN and faced a lack of support at home. On November 6 Britain and France agreed to suspend their operation and a ceasefire was instituted. Although the UN demanded the swift withdrawal of the invading armies, Britain would not agree to evacuate its troops until a UN peacekeeping force was in place to secure free passage along the Suez Canal. A withdrawal was finally completed on December 22.

Although the Eden government tried to pass the operation off as a success, the Suez Canal adventure was a disaster for British foreign policy. Far from being driven from power, President Nasser emerged as the victor and a figurehead for an Arab and Egyptian nationalism prepared to take on the might of the Western world. The conflict also brought

▲ **The Franco-British bombing raids on Egyptian targets caused outrage and undermined possible international support for the Suez campaign.**

Egypt and the Soviet Union closer together, with Premier Khrushchev later agreeing to a loan to fund the Aswan High Dam. Before the campaign, Britain had been used to considering itself the dominant European power in the Middle East; by the beginning of 1957 its influence was all but a memory.

The Suez Crisis spelled the end of the political career of British Prime Minister Anthony Eden. It made his position untenable, and in January 1957 he resigned. Although he cited ill-health as his reason for standing down, he would most likely have been forced out of office had he not resigned. His successor, Harold Macmillan, found himself with the task of rebuilding Britain's relationship with the United States, which had suffered badly through the affair.

The failure at Suez represented a turning point in modern British history. The British government was forced to recognize that the country simply did not possess the resources to pursue an independent policy as an imperial power. One of Macmillan's first acts as Prime Minister was to initiate a defence review which would call for deep cuts in spending on conventional armed forces – precisely the kind of forces used to uphold British power in the old Empire. Instead, Britain would concentrate on its military contribution to the NATO alliance. The withdrawal from the Empire inevitably gathered pace after that. Within ten years of Suez, the vast majority of Britain's former colonies had been granted independence.

▲ **Prime Minister Sir Anthony Eden tells the people of Britain that the Suez campaign is "a matter of life and death to us all".**

JULY

- Egyptian President Nasser nationalizes the Suez Canal; Britain, France and the United States impose economic sanctions on Egypt
- England spin bowler Jim Laker takes 19 wickets in a Test match against Australia

AUGUST

- An anti-nuclear protest is held at Aldermaston weapons research centre
- The Dulles Plan for international control of the Suez Canal is proposed

SEPTEMBER

- Britain and France refer the Suez Canal crisis to the UN Security Council; France and Israel discuss military action against Egypt

OCTOBER

- The Soviet Union vetoes part of the Franco-British resolution on Suez at the UN
- They nuclear power station at Calder Hall is opened
- Railway workers stage a protest against the employment of nonwhite immigrants as train drivers
- Israeli forces invade Egypt; Britain and France issue an ultimatum for ceasefire in the conflict
- British and French aircraft bomb Egypt

ANGRY YOUNG MEN

▲ *Look Back in Anger* embodied the sense of rage and alienation against the establishment that was felt by many 1950s writers.

In May 1956 *Look Back in Anger*, a play by unknown 26-year-old dramatist John Osborne, was put on at the Royal Court Theatre by the newly formed English Stage Company. It came to typify more than any other single work the attitudes of writers of the 1950s caricatured by critics as the "Angry Young Men".

Osborne's play consisted almost entirely of a series of rambling rants by antihero Jimmy Porter. Understandably, most of its early audiences were puzzled, bored or offended. But Kenneth Tynan, the fashionable drama critic of the *Observer*, hailed it as an outstanding play that spoke to and for the young – that is, people between 20 and 30. Tynan summed up the play's specifically "contemporary" qualities as "instinctive leftishness, the automatic rejection of 'official' attitudes, the surrealist sense of humour ... the casual promiscuity, the sense of lacking a crusade worth fighting for".

This mix of disillusion with life and of anger against the establishment – a key term of the 1950s – was also found in highly praised novels of the period, notably John Wain's *Hurry On Down* (1953), Kingsley Amis's *Lucky Jim* (1954) and John Braine's *Room at the Top* (1957). These writers were distinguished from rebellious authors of the 1930s by their complete lack of interest in communism, socialism or the virtues and sufferings of the working class. Typically, Amis's hero Jim Dixon, trapped in a provincial world of dull phoneys and stuffed shirts, does not want to change the world – he is simply out to get the girl he fancies.

The "Angries" were at their best in their attacks on the stifling hypocrisy and small-mindedness of life in the British provinces. They were at their worst in their savage attacks on women, for a powerful strain of misogyny ran through almost all their works. Above all, they were men on the make who wanted their elders to move out of the way – and in this they expressed a brash go-getting impulse at the heart of 1950s British society.

LAKER'S MATCH

The Old Trafford Test match played between England and Australia in the last week of July 1956 is known as "Laker's match". On a turning pitch, the Yorkshire-born Surrey off-spinner Jim Laker took all 10 wickets in the Australian first innings – when they were bowled out for 84 – and nine wickets in the second innings. No other player has taken more than 17 wickets in any first-class match, let alone an England–Australia Test.

Laker's feat capped an exceptional period of English ascendancy over the Australians. Having regained the Ashes in 1953, England had retained them

▶ **Jim Laker tormented the Australian batsmen during their 1956 England tour. In one innings all ten wickets fell to his off-spin.**

with a series win in Australia in 1954–55. An innings victory in the Old Trafford Test, the fourth of the 1956 series, allowed England to win again by 2–1.

Laker was undoubtedly a fine bowler – accurate, subtle and achieving ferocious turn on a favourable pitch. But his dominance over the Australian batsmen was exceptional and uncanny. He had also claimed ten wickets in an innings against the tourists when they played Surrey earlier in the season – the only time a bowler has performed that feat twice in a season. In all matches he took 63 Australian wickets during the summer of 1956, at an average cost of around ten runs.

ROCK'N'ROLL AND TEDDY BOYS

In September 1956, cinema managers in Britain called on the police to control teenage "Teddy Boys" who were causing mayhem during showings of the American musical movie *Rock Around the Clock*. Trouble ranging from the slashing of seats to minor riots led to the film being banned in some cities and denounced by many councillors and politicians.

Teddy Boy youth gangs had been around for several years – the term may have been coined by the *Daily Express* in 1953. Wearing long jackets with velvet collar and cuffs, drainpipe trousers, bright socks and thin ties, they wore their hair greased and quiffed, with long sideburns. The Teds' style of youth revolt was associated with street crime and gang violence – fights with bicycle chains, slashing with razors. In 1956 they found their very own music in the newly emergent rock'n'roll.

"Rock Around the Clock" was a hit record for Bill Haley and the Comets. It was first used as the theme music for a film on juvenile delinquents, *The Blackboard Jungle*, and then taken as the title for a cheap quickie musical in pseudo-documentary style on the new rock'n'roll phenomenon. The *Rock Around the Clock* film made a small fortune for Hollywood and was an early indication to the big corporations that there was money

▲ Rock'n'roll music and youth gangs such as the Teddy Boys exemplified the energy and rebellious spirit of the new 1950s generation.

to be had in pandering to the youth market.

Rock'n'roll had, of course, a far wider appeal than just to Teddy Boys and other semi-delinquents such as leather-jacketed bike gangs. The rising prosperity of 1950s Britain put cash in the pockets of young people, who spent most of it on clothes and entertainment. As their elders increasingly stayed at home to watch "the telly", the young made up an ever-larger proportion of cinema audiences. The introduction of cheap 45-rpm singles had created the world of the juke-box and the hit parade. Although service in the armed forces through National Service had not been abolished, it did little to daunt the consumerist enthusiasm or rebellious ageism of youth.

When Bill Haley landed at Southampton for a tour of Britain in February 1957, he travelled to London in a special train chartered by the *Daily Mirror* and was mobbed by fans on arriving at the London terminus in what was dubbed "the second battle of Waterloo". By then Britain already had its first home-grown rock'n'roll star in Tommy Steele, but it would be years before any British performer could match the appeal of the American originals.

NOVEMBER
- British and French paratroopers and marines occupy the Canal Zone
- Under pressure from the United States, Britain and France agree a ceasefire in Suez conflict
- UN troops arrive in Egypt
- Hundreds of members resign from the British Communist Party in protest at the Soviet suppression of a workers' uprising in Hungary

DECEMBER
- Britons wins six gold medals at the Melbourne Olympic Games, including Chris Brasher in the 3,000 metres steeplechase and Terry Spinks in flyweight boxing
- British and French troops complete their withdrawal from Egypt

- EOKA continues its campaign for the union of Cyprus with Greece
- Britons own 6.9 million Television sets, up from 2.1 million in 1953
- UK exports total £3.5 billion (1948: £1.6 billion)
- The Queen's annual Christmas broadcast is televised for the first time
- The Rent Act removes many controls on landlords' exploitation of tenants
- Britain is hit by an Asian 'flu epidemic; it kills about a million people worldwide, including several thousand Britons
- In his book *The Uses of Literacy*, Richard Hoggart decries the impact of commercialized popular culture on working-class youth
- British films this year include David Lean's *The Bridge on the River Kwai* and Laurence Olivier's *The Prince and the Showgirl*
- Books published this year include *Room at the Top* by John Braine and *The Hawk in the Rain* by Ted Hughes
- Plays given their first production this year include Samuel Beckett's *Endgame* and John Osborne's *The Entertainer* (starring Laurence Olivier)
- Major sculptures include Henry Moore's *Reclining Figure* for the UNESCO Building in Paris and Jacob Epstein's *Christ in Majesty* for Llandaff Cathedral, Wales

CLOSING DOWN THE EMPIRE

On March 6, 1957, the British West African colony of the Gold Coast became the independent state of Ghana. The country's new leader, Kwame Nkrumah, declared that his people were casting off "the chains of imperialism". But ridding itself of colonies had come to seem a liberation to Britain as well.

When Harold Macmillan took over as Prime Minister in January 1957, he set his government the task of hastening the transition from Empire to Commonwealth, which was already well under way. In the wake of the Suez fiasco, the advantages of granting independence to the colonies in Africa, Asia and the Caribbean had become obvious from a British point of view. It would save large sums of money spent on administering the territories, avoid

▲ **Kwame Nkrumah, who led the British colony of the Gold Coast to independence as Ghana in 1957, was overthrown in a coup in 1966.**

costly and embarrassing colonial wars, and ward off international criticism from the United Nations and the United States.

Malaya became independent in August 1957. Jamaica and Trinidad followed suit in 1962. Independence was granted to a series of British-ruled African countries in the early 1960s – including Nigeria at the start of the decade, Tanganyika in 1961, Kenya in 1963, Zambia (formerly Northern Rhodesia) in 1964. The new leaders of these states were often individuals who had spent time in prison during British crackdowns on "nationalist agitation", yet the former colonies remained within the Commonwealth and on the whole maintained friendly relations with Britain.

BRITAIN STAYS OUT OF EUROPE

On March 25, 1957, the leaders of France, Belgium, Luxembourg, the Netherlands, Italy and West Germany put their signatures to the Treaty of Rome, establishing the European Economic Community (EEC), also known as the European Common Market.

Britain was notable by its absence.

In the immediate postwar period, leading Conservatives such as Winston Churchill and Anthony Eden had spoken strongly in favour of a united Europe, seen as a way of preventing a recurrence of the warfare that had torn the continent apart twice

in a space of 30 years. By the 1950s, however, their attitude had shifted. Speaking as Foreign Secretary in 1953, Eden stated that joining a federal Europe was "something which we know, in our bones, we cannot do".

Part of the problem was that, with vestiges of the great Empire of the nineteenth century still in working order, a British economic alliance with Europe would, inevitably, punish traders within the Commonwealth, especially those in Australia and New Zealand. Furthermore, Britain felt that too much involvement with the continent would damage its so-called "special relationship" with the United States.

Coming into effect on January 1, 1958, the Treaty of Rome was a diplomatic and economic setback for Britain. The British government had stood haughtily aside from the making of the EEC, but found itself feeling isolated once the Common Market was formed. British businesses were threatened with loss of access to key European

▲ **The German delegation at Rome, led by Chancellor Konrad Adenauer (centre), put their signatures on the treaty establishing the European Economic Community.**

▲ The Treaty of Rome, establishing the European Economic Community, was signed in Italy's capital on March 25, 1957.

markets at a time when the country desperately needed to boost its exports.

In 1960 Britain set up its own economic union, the European Free Trade Association (EFTA), with six smaller European nations: Austria, Denmark, Norway, Portugal, Sweden and Switzerland. But membership of the British-led "seven" was a poor substitute for joining with the Common Market "six". In 1961 Britain bit the bullet and applied to join the EEC. Having at first stayed out, however, the British were to find it took more than a decade to come in from the cold.

▲ As Foreign Secretary and, after 1955, as Prime Minister, Sir Anthony Eden expressed reservations about Britain becoming too closely involved in the affairs of Europe.

- Agatha Christie's *The Mousetrap* becomes Britain's longest-running play, passing 2,000 performances
- First edition of *The Sky At Night* on BBC TV and ITV's hospital soap opera *Emergency – Ward 10*
- The BBC popular music show *Six-Five Special* showcases young British performers

JANUARY
- Anthony Eden resigns as Prime Minister; Harold Macmillan succeeds, with R A Butler as Home Secretary

FEBRUARY
- American rock'n'roll star Bill Haley arrives for a UK tour

MARCH
- The Gold Coast becomes independent as Ghana – the first of Britain's African colonies to gain independence
- 22 people die when a British European Airways Vickers Viscount turboprop airliner crashes at Ringway airport, Manchester
- At a conference in Bermuda, Prime Minister Macmillan and President Eisenhower reaffirm the "special relationship" between Britain and the United States
- European Common Market is formed without Britain

APRIL
- Britain cedes the Simonstown naval base to South Africa
- The government announces that National Service is to end; the last call-up will be in 1960

MACMILLAN LOOKS ON THE BRIGHT SIDE

On July 20, 1957, Prime Minister Harold Macmillan told a Conservative Party rally in Bedford that "most of our people have never had it so good". It was a phrase that characterized the cheerful materialism of the 1950s and the upbeat tone of the early years of the Macmillan premiership.

Educated at Eton and Oxford, Macmillan was in many ways a traditional Tory figure, yet he played a key role in the rebranding of Conservatism after the Second World War. He was one of a group of Tory reformers who believed that the party had to shake off its association with the mass unemployment of the 1930s and appeal to working-class voters as well as the middle classes. The influence of Macmillan and other reformers – notably R A Butler and Ian Macleod – was predominant in the domestic policies of the Churchill and Eden governments from 1951 to 1956. They did not attempt to reverse the welfare state or nationalization, and aimed

▲ Harold Macmillan sought to run a reformist Tory administration. His optimism and a booming economy reaped electoral success.

to maintain full employment at any cost. As Minister for Housing, Macmillan was personally responsible for a substantial boom in council-house building.

When Eden's position as Prime Minister became untenable in late 1956 after the Suez Crisis, the obvious successor to the leadership was Butler. However, in behind-the-scenes discussions at Westminster, Macmillan emerged as the Conservatives' choice for the top position. Tory MPs correctly guessed that his air of unflappable optimism would be

what the party needed to recover from the Suez debacle.

Macmillan became Prime Minister on January 10, 1957. He set the tone for his administration by celebrating the appointment with a well-publicized meal of game pie and champagne at a London club. The following year, the Conservatives lost a number of by-elections, including one to the Liberals – the start of a new tendency for the third party to pick up protest votes, which has lasted to this day. But overall, morale was restored both within the ruling party and the country.

The strength of Macmillan's optimistic posture was that it represented a reality for most of the population. Between 1951 and 1959 average wages almost doubled, while the unemployment rate averaged less than two per cent. Macmillan spoke of "a state of prosperity such as we have never had in my lifetime – nor indeed in the history of this country". And, basically, he was right.

MAY

- Manchester United win the Football League championship, but lose 2–1 to Aston Villa in the FA Cup final after goalkeeper Ray Wood suffers a broken jaw in the sixth minute
- Petrol rationing, introduced because of closure of the Suez Canal, ends
- Britain tests a hydrogen bomb

JULY

- Derek Ibbotson sets a new world record for the mile, 3 minutes 57.2 seconds, in a race at White City
- Britain sends military aid to the Sultan of Oman, to help resist an insurrection against his rule

AUGUST

- Elections are held in preparation for self-rule in British Guiana
- The Malayan Federation becomes independent

SEPTEMBER

- The Wolfenden Report is published
- Chancellor of the Exchequer Peter Thorneycroft proposes major government spending cuts to counter inflation and raises the bank rate to 7 per cent

WOLFENDEN PROPOSES GAY LAW REFORM

In September 1957 a committee headed by Sir John Wolfenden, vice-chancellor of Reading University, published the findings of its three-year inquiry into the law relating to homosexuality and prostitution. Its chief recommendation was that "homosexual activity between consenting adults in private" should no longer be a criminal offence.

The imprisonment of homosexuals had been a public issue at least since Oscar Wilde had been sent to prison for the "crime" in the 1890s, but it was only in the 1950s that a current of liberal opinion finally swelled in favour of its decriminalization. A range of reactionary attitudes still prevailed within society – from the view that sinister homosexuals went around perverting "normal" men, to the comparatively benign categorization of homosexuality as a mental disease.

The Wolfenden Report was welcomed by the British Medical Association, the Archbishop of Canterbury and many groups campaigning for civil liberties. The government, on the other hand, rejected its findings on homosexuality, probably judging correctly that the British electorate was far less liberal on this issue than the educated elite. By contrast, another Wolfenden recommendation, that prostitutes should be driven off the streets, was swiftly implemented.

Despite the failure to produce immediate reform, the Wolfenden Report is rightly regarded as a turning point in attitudes to homosexuality in Britain. Its argument that it was "not the function of the law to intervene in the private life of citizens" inspired the eventual decriminalization of homosexual acts between men over 21 in 1967.

▲ The Wolfenden report marked a key stage in the improvement of the legal climate for homosexuality.

BEVAN BACKS THE BOMB

▲ Bevan's espousal of a British nuclear deterrent outraged Labour left-wingers, who had long looked to his moral leadership.

At the annual Labour Party conference in the first week of October, 1957, Shadow Foreign Secretary Aneurin Bevan eloquently declared his support for his party's official policy on nuclear weapons. He told Labour delegates that if they pressed ahead with their campaign to ban the British hydrogen bomb, they would "send a British foreign secretary naked into the conference chamber".

Bevan's speech caused a sensation because he was the acknowledged leader of the Labour left. Since 1951, the "Bevanites" had been a thorn in the side of the moderate party leadership. One of their main platforms had been opposition to Britain's development of a nuclear arsenal. They believed that nuclear weapons were intrinsically evil and that possession of such weapons would doom Britain to destruction by an enemy's nuclear bombs and missiles in any major future war.

Bevan's apostasy ensured a conference vote in favour of the British H-bomb and made it improbable that unilateral nuclear disarmament would be adopted as official Labour policy for the foreseeable future. The antinuclear movement instead grew outside the framework of party politics, in the activities of the Campaign for Nuclear Disarmament (CND) founded in 1958.

THE WINDSCALE FIRE

On October 8, 1957, a fire broke out in the graphite core of a nuclear reactor at the Atomic Energy Authority's Windscale plant in Cumberland. Although the fire was brought under control within three days, it was the world's worst nuclear accident until Chernobyl in 1986.

Windscale was producing plutonium for Britain's nuclear weapons programme. The fire started during routine maintenance, through a combination of human error and instrument failure. Hidden deep in the reactor's core, it was not noticed until two days later, when a rise in radioactivity was detected around Windscale. On October 10 a desperate struggle began to bring the fire under control. After all else had failed, water was poured into the reactor. This was a hugely risky experiment, which might have caused an explosion. Instead, it succeeded in controlling the fire, at the expense of releasing a cloud of radioactive steam that spread over a large swathe of central and southern England.

No emergency warning was given to the public during this crisis – it was later claimed that the authorities wished to avoid "unnecessary alarm". Sale of milk and other farm produce from an area of 500 sq km (200 sq miles) around the plant was banned for a month because of contamination with an iodine isotope. Much of the milk was poured away into rivers. No public mention was made of the radioactive steam-cloud.

A hasty public inquiry reassuringly concluded that the incident had "no bearing on the safety of nuclear power stations being built for the electricity authorities". Whether the radiation released – about 300 times less than from Chernobyl – caused any long-term health problems remains disputed.

▲ After fire broke out in the Windscale nuclear reactor, a catastrophic explosion was only narrowly averted.

LEWISHAM RAIL DISASTER

On December 4, 1957, two trains collided during the evening rush hour at Lewisham, south London, killing 90 people and injuring 173. It was one of Britain's worst ever rail disasters.

The collision occurred in thick fog – the Clean Air Act having failed as yet to rid London of its famous "pea-soupers". A steam express bound for Ramsgate ran into the back of an electric train heading from Charing Cross to Kent after running through at least one – and possibly three – stop signals. The impact drove part of one of the trains into a railway bridge support, bringing the metal bridge crashing down on top of the carriages.

The coaches were packed with commuters, hundreds of whom were trapped amid twisted metal and concrete. A third train travelling on the line that crossed the fallen bridge narrowly avoided plunging into the wreckage.

The Lewisham tragedy contributed to a total of over 300 deaths on Britain's nationalized railways in the 1950s. By comparison, fewer than a hundred people were killed in rail accidents in the 1990s.

◀ Twisted metal and crushed carriages mark the spot where 90 people died after an express train passed through a red light in fog.

OCTOBER
- The Labour Party conference rejects unilateral nuclear disarmament
- An accident at Windscale nuclear reactor
- Elizabeth II and Prince Philip pay an official visit to Washington, DC

NOVEMBER
- Jamaica gains internal self-government

DECEMBER
- The government rejects Wolfenden Report recommendations on the decriminalization of homosexuality
- A train crash in Lewisham kills 90 people
- Lord Alexander Todd wins the Nobel Prize for Chemistry
- Death of author Dorothy L Sayers

1958

- The Campaign for Nuclear Disarmament (CND) is founded, with Canon John Collins as its chairman
- After passage of the Life Peerages Act, the first women peers sit in the House of Lords
- Elizabeth II discontinues the presentation of debutantes at court
- The Public Records Act makes most government documents available to researchers after 50 years
- A report by the British Medical Association identifies smoking as the prime cause of lung cancer
- Scheduled transatlantic passenger jet services begin
- The expansion of Gatwick is airport completed
- Trunk lines allowing direct long-distance telephone calls come into operation in Britain
- Parking meters are introduced in central London
- The Austin Healey Sprite sports car goes on sale
- First hovercraft is built by Christopher Cockerell
- Books published this year include *The Bell* by Iris Murdoch, *Our Man in Havana* by Graham Greene, *Saturday Night and Sunday Morning* by Alan Sillitoe and *Collected Poems* by John Betjeman
- Films this year include Gerald Thomas's *Carry On Sergeant* (first of a series) and Terence Fisher's *Dracula*
- First performance of Harold Pinter's *The Birthday Party*
- The Lord Chamberlain bans performances of Samuel Beckett's play *Endgame* for alleged blasphemy

CRASH KILLS BUSBY'S BABES

February 6, 1958, is remembered as one of the darkest days in British sporting history. It was the day that the mighty Manchester United football team was destroyed by a plane crash that took the lives of 23, among them eight of United's first-team squad.

Britain's reigning League champions, Manchester United were returning from a triumphant European Cup encounter in Yugoslavia, which had seen them defeat Red Star Belgrade to reach the semi-finals of the competition. Having reached Munich in the south of Germany, their return flight to Manchester took off in snowy conditions. With visibility poor, the plane failed to clear a house close to the end of the runway. Seven of Britain's finest

▲ **The wreckage of the BEA Elizabethan airliner that crashed in flames shortly after taking off from Munich airport.**

▲ **Eight members of Manchester United's first team – "Busby's Babes" – perished in the Munich air crash.**

young players – Roger Byrne, David Pegg, Tommy Taylor, Eddie Coleman, Mark Jones, Billy Whelan and Geoff Bent – died instantly. Two weeks later, Duncan Edwards, still considered to be one of the greatest footballers England ever produced, also died from his injuries.

Although seriously depleted, United still reached the final of the FA Cup in May. In a highly emotional match for players and spectators at Wembley Stadium, they were unable to contain Bolton Wanderers, losing 2–0.

After a life-and-death struggle, manager and guiding light Matt Busby pulled through. He slowly rebuilt his side, finally achieving European glory in 1968, beating Portuguese side Benfica to take the European Cup. One of the goal-scorers in that match was Bobby Charlton, himself a survivor of the Munich disaster.

The passing of each anniversary is still mourned by fans at Old Trafford, Manchester United's home, even though most were not even born at the time of the tragedy. "Busby's Babes" – as the young side were popularly known – have passed into footballing legend, both for their mastery on the field and their cruel demise.

NUCLEAR PROTEST MOVEMENT

On Easter weekend in April 1958, the Campaign for Nuclear Disarmament (CND) staged a protest march from Trafalgar Square in London to the Atomic Weapons Research Establishment at Aldermaston in Berkshire. The event was such a success that it was repeated over following years, becoming an annual reminder to Britain's leaders that many of its people disagreed vehemently with the country's nuclear defence policy.

Through the 1950s, disparate groups of pacifists, Christians, left-wing Labour politicians and communists had expressed their deep concerns about Britain's development of nuclear weapons. These concerns became more acute as the government's commitment to nuclear deterrence hardened. In 1957 Britain exploded its first hydrogen bomb, vastly increasing the potential destructive power of its nuclear arsenal. In the same year, government defence policy was defined as reliance on "massive retaliation" to deter aggression. In February 1958 antinuclear groups coalesced in the formation of CND.

Among its leading members were philosopher Bertrand Russell, Canon John Collins, historian A J P Taylor and socialist Peggy Duff.

Several thousand protesters turned up for the CND-organized anti-nuclear rally in Trafalgar Square on Good Friday, April 4. A hard core of around 700 embarked on the 80-km (50-mile) march to Aldermaston, where, three days, later, a crowd variously estimated at 8,000 to 12,000 gathered at the gates of the research establishment to complete the peaceful protest.

The first Aldermaston march brought the nuclear arms issue to the top of the political agenda for the first time. CND's striking logo was soon to be seen daubed on walls and worn on badges across the land. The annual three-day march from 1960 starting at Aldermaston and ending in Trafalgar Square – offset the solemnity traditionally considered fitting for a serious moral protest,

with a carnival element supplied by jazz bands, folk singers and bizarrely dressed young "Beatniks". The style of the CND demonstrations foreshadowed the student protest movements of the 1960s.

By 1960 the body of Easter marchers had swelled to around 100,000. A survey at the end of the decade showed that CND had the support of around 30 per cent

of the British people. But the movement entered a difficult period in the early 1960s, when Russell and the Committee of 100 abandoned legal protest, instead encouraging mass civil disobedience. CND virtually disappeared from view for over a decade, before emerging with renewed force in the protests against the deployment of Cruise missiles in the 1980s.

▲ **Supporters of the Campaign for Nuclear Disarmament march from London's Trafalgar Square to RAF Aldermaston in Berkshire.**

BRITONS WIN OSCARS FOR RIVER KWAI

Stiff upper-lip Second World War dramas were the stock-in-trade of British cinema in the

▲ The *Bridge on the River Kwai* **questioned the uncritical celebration of British wartime successes portrayed in previous films.**

1950s. Films such as *The Dam Busters* and *The Battle of the River Plate* celebrated British wartime successes in an effectively understated style. But *The Bridge on the River Kwai*, which won the award for Best Picture and six other Oscars at the Hollywood Academy Awards in March 1958, was something different. The tale of a brave but blinkered British colonel who becomes obsessed with building a bridge for his Japanese captors, its message was overtly antiwar and implicitly critical of the British colonial mentality.

The popular success of *River Kwai* was undoubtedly a sign of shifting public attitudes. Its

success at the Oscars was a tribute to the rich vein of British talent that had been mined to make the film. David Lean was voted Best Director and Alec Guinness Best Actor, while other Britons carried off less high-profile awards, including composer Malcolm Arnold for Best Score and Jack Hildyard for cinematography.

Yet it was a sign of the financial problems facing the British film industry by the second half of the 1950s that the film was made by an independent American producer, Sam Spiegel, with American money. Britain had the actors, the technicians and the creative flair to make first-rate films, but mostly it no longer had the cash.

- First performances of the opera *Noye's Fludde* by Benjamin Britten and Michael Tippett's *Second Symphony*
- Debut of the children's programme *Blue Peter* on BBC television
- Singer Cliff Richard appears on new ITV music show *Oh Boy!*
- Long-haired bearded Beatniks appear in Britain

JANUARY
- Chancellor of the Exchequer Peter Thorneycroft resigns because Harold Macmillan refuses to cut spending as much as the Treasury believes necessary
- The West Indian Federation is formed by Britain's Caribbean colonies
- Turkish Cypriots riot after clashes with British troops

FEBRUARY
- An aeroplane carrying the Manchester United football team crashes in Munich
- Wales beat Israel to qualify for a place in the football World Cup finals

MARCH
- Antarctica is crossed for the first time by a British polar exploration team led by Dr Vivian Fuchs
- Death of suffragette activist Dame Christabel Pankhurst

APRIL
- CND stages the first Aldermaston march to protest against nuclear weapons
- The Maltese Prime Minister resigns over the terms for union with Britain

MAY
- British governor Sir William Luce declares a state of emergency in Aden after raids from Yemen
- Manchester United lose 2–0 to Bolton Wanderers in the FA Cup final
- Death of film actor Ronald Colman

RACE RIOTS HIT THE UK

Despite having a huge Empire, peopled by many different races, Britain itself had until the 1950s attracted relatively few immigrants of nonwhite ethnic groups. The British were used to observing the racial tensions of areas such as the southern United States with a patronizing feeling of superiority – it was something that "didn't happen here". All that changed when a series of race-inspired riots took place in London and Nottingham in the summer of 1958.

A large influx of black people into the UK, most of them hailing from Jamaica and other Caribbean islands, occurred in the mid-1950s. These immigrants relieved Britain's labour shortages, especially in transport and the National Health Service, and they created their own communities in some British towns and cities. Black people, however, found themselves the object of curiosity, suspicion and discrimination. They were also subject to attacks by white youth gangs – generically known as Teddy Boys – that roamed city streets after dark.

Tension spilled over into mob violence during 1958. On the evening of August 23, white youths and West Indian men clashed in the St Ann's district of Nottingham. These highly publicized, if relatively

▲ **Police arrest a demonstrator during the ugly race riots that hit London's Notting Hill during the summer of 1958.**

small-scale, encounters triggered violence on a far larger scale in London. On several nights between the end of August and the second week in September, white youths descended on London's Notting Hill, an area with a high immigrant population, looking for black people to attack. Members of Oswald Mosley's extreme-right Union Movement joined in inciting crowds to violence against the immigrant population. Street battles between whites, blacks and the police were fought with petrol bombs and milk bottles, razors, clubs and bicycle chains.

The violence, graphically covered by television cameras, shocked the government and the nation. Several prominent people publicly aired the view that a multiracial society was impossible and that immigration

should be stopped at once. Prime Minister Macmillan called for an inquiry, which was instituted by his Home Secretary, R A Butler. The tone of the ensuing report, by Lord Chief Justice Salmon, which may seem at the very least patronizing by today's standards, says much about the attitudes of the time.

Lord Salmon attributed the violence to the competitive jealousies of young white males, citing the attraction of white women to black males and the fact that black workers were seemingly happier to accept lower wages and a lower standard of living than their white counterparts. This, he continued, made unskilled labour cheaper to employ and led to increased rents as large groups of blacks were prepared to live in more confined spaces. Furthermore, he noted the unpopularity of black families in white neighbourhoods, claiming that Teddy Boys, formerly considered a public nuisance, were being turned into "local heroes" by engaging in violent acts against young blacks.

There was no admission by the government of the existence of any fundamental discrimination against immigrants. Indeed, at this time the plight of Britain's Caribbean community gave the establishment no real cause for concern on any matter other than public order.

JETTING ACROSS THE ATLANTIC

On October 4, 1958, the British Overseas Airways Corporation (BOAC) launched the first scheduled transatlantic passenger service by jet. The aircraft was the Comet IV. It was an improved and safety-guaranteed version of the Comet, which had been withdrawn

after there had been repeated crashes in 1954.

It speaks volumes for the lead Britain enjoyed in jet technology in the early 1950s that – after four years out of service – the Comet was still able to notch up this prestigious "first". But only

three weeks after BOAC's transatlantic service began, the American Boeing 707 also began scheduled flights to Europe. Able to carry twice as many passengers as the Comet, the 707 was set to dominate passenger air transport for the next decade.

Transatlantic air travel in propeller-driven aircraft had been increasing steadily since the Second World War – 1957 was the first year in which more people crossed the ocean by air than in ships. But the speed and comfort of jet airliners expanded the scale of air travel beyond any previous expectations. Over the following decade the number of air miles flown roughly quintupled.

For people living around major airports such as Heathrow, the new jets were a nightmare of noise pollution. But for those with money to spend, they brought an unprecedented ease of intercontinental travel. As one air executive boasted, "we have shrunk the world".

▲ The opening of the first scheduled transatlantic passenger service marked a revolution in air travel, now accessible to a mass market.

OCTOBER
• The British plan for joint Greek and Turkish administration of Cyprus is implemented with the backing of Turkey but not of Greece
• In Geneva, Britain, the United States and the Soviet Union begin talks on a draft treaty that would ban nuclear tests
• Driver Mike Hawthorn wins the Formula One world championship
• BOAC inaugurates the first passenger jet service between London and New York with Comet IV
• Death of birth control pioneer Marie Stopes

DECEMBER
• Britain's first stretch of motorway, the Preston bypass, later part of the M6, is opened

HAWTHORN AND MOSS DOMINATE MOTOR RACING

For British motor racing enthusiasts, 1958 was a year of triumph and tragedy. British drivers took all five leading places in the world championship, but the fierce competition on the circuits cost two of their colleagues their lives.

The contest for the world championship title was a close-fought battle between Mike Hawthorn in a Ferrari and Stirling Moss, driving for British constructor Vanwall. Moss was probably the superior driver and won four of the season's Grand Prix races to Hawthorn's one. But when the points for placings were added up, Hawthorne took the trophy with 42 points to Moss's 41. He was the first British driver to win the championship – a feat that would always elude Moss, despite his exceptional talent.

Hawthorn retired from racing at the end of the season, perhaps influenced by safety concerns. He had seen his Ferrari team mate Peter Collins die in an accident during the German Grand Prix in August and another British driver, Stuart Lewis-Evans, killed in the final Grand Prix of the year.

Ironically, Hawthorn lived for only three months after his retirement. In January 1959 he fatally smashed up his sports car while driving on the Guildford bypass in Surrey. He was 29 years old.

▲ Although he won four Grand Prix in 1958, Stirling Moss, Britain's best known Formula One driver, never actually won the world championship.

- Britain has its driest summer for 200 years
- Cinema admissions for the year total 601 million, down from 1,365 million in 1951
- The number of television sets has more than doubled since 1955, to 9.5 million
- The Obscene Publications Act is passed in response to concerns about the spread of pornography
- The Mini Minor car comes on the market
- The Mermaid Theatre opens in London
- Books published this year include *Cider With Rosie* by Laurie Lee and *Memento Mori* by Muriel Spark
- British films this year include John Boulting's *I'm All Right, Jack*, Tony Richardson's *Look Back in Anger* and Jack Clayton's *Room At the Top*
- Premieres of Shelagh Delaney's play *A Taste of Honey*, Harold Pinter's *The Caretaker* and Arnold Wesker's *Roots*
- Hit songs of the year include Cliff Richards's "Living Doll" and Adam Faith's "What Do You Want?"
- Ronnie Scott's jazz club opens in London

JANUARY

- Henry Cooper becomes British and Empire heavyweight boxing champion
- Death of British racing driver Mike Hawthorn

FEBRUARY

- England cricketers lose the Ashes to Australia after holding the trophy for six years

BMC MINI GOES ON SALE

▲ **The Mini's revolutionary compact design made it a firm favourite with motorists, combining cheapness, economy and manoeuvrability.**

In August 1959 the British Motor Corporation (BMC) unveiled its revolutionary new Mini car. A compact four-seater designed by Sir Alec Issigonis, the Mini was destined to become an icon of the 1960s and a quirky symbol of "Britishness" around the world to set alongside Big Ben and the bowler hat.

The Mini tackled head-on one of the crucial problems of Britain at the end of the 1950s: traffic congestion. Its compact size was ideal for towns and cities in which wholly inadequate roads and parking facilities were being swamped by the rising tide of car ownership.

By the end of the decade, there were around 10 million cars in Britain, more than double the 1939 figure. The reaction of public authorities to the car-ownership boom had been painfully slow. Britain's first full-length motorway, the M1, was at last opened in November 1959. Experiments were under way with yellow no-parking lines, parking meters and traffic wardens. But a small, competitively priced, stylish car like the Mini, ideal for nipping in and out of traffic jams and for parking in tight spaces, was assured of large sales.

TORIES CONTINUE WINNING STREAK

On October 8, 1959, the Conservatives scored their third consecutive general election victory. Led by Prime Minister Harold Macmillan – justifying his cartoon image as "Supermac" – they won 365 seats to 258 for Labour.

The prospect of a third Tory election win had looked unlikely to political commentators at the time of the British humiliation over Suez in late 1956 – although opinion polls at the time showed no switch of voters from Tory to Labour, the mass of the British public as usual proving indifferent to foreign affairs. Other problems had accumulated in the following years. Rising inflation and a worsening balance of trade had necessitated cuts in government spending and the tightening of credit during 1957–58. Growth in the British economy was falling well below that of West Germany, France and Japan.

Macmillan, however, handled electoral politics with consummate

▲ **A strong economy and a weakened Labour party handed Harold Macmillan a convincing election victory.**

skill. Briefly ignoring concerns about inflation, he gave away millions of pounds in tax cuts in the 1959 Budget. Playing upon memories of Labour as the party of austerity, the Tory election slogan was: "Life's better under the Conservatives; don't let Labour ruin it."

The Labour Party found itself with no clear message to offer. Low unemployment and the rise in prosperity for the better-off sections of the working class undercut the appeal of socialism. Labour leader Hugh Gaitskell felt the party could not regain electoral support without ditching nationalization and other policies from the socialist past, but much of the party rank and file vehemently disagreed with him.

In practice, as long as living standards continued to rise year on year, it would take a suicidal debacle within the Conservative Party to bring Labour back to power.

FIGHTING FOR FISHING RIGHTS

During the 1950s, competition between fishing fleets to exploit the food potential of the world's oceans first began to constitute a serious threat to fish stocks. British fishermen were only dimly aware of the difficulties that lay ahead for their industry, but one dispute brought the issue sharply into focus.

Iceland was a country whose economy was heavily dependent on fishing. In 1958, it extended the area around its coast preserved exclusively for its own trawlers from 7 km (4 miles) to 20 km (12 miles) offshore. This denied British fishing boats access to waters that they had traditionally fished. The announcement infuriated the British fishing industry and began an ongoing dispute that would not be resolved until the mid-1970s.

The first dangerously aggressive clashes took place in May 1959. Icelandic gunboats attempted to board British trawlers within the exclusion zone and fired blank shots across their bows. Over the coming months the Royal Navy regularly sent warships to support the trawlermen, while the government brought diplomatic pressure to bear on Iceland.

In February 1961 a temporary resolution of the dispute was achieved. A decade later, however, with catches falling rapidly through overfishing, Iceland extended its fishing limits far further from its coast, provoking a new round in what became known as the "Cod Wars".

▲ The Royal Navy in action in the north Atlantic, protecting Britain's fishing fleet. Such operations would be repeated in the 1970s.

CLIFF RICHARD IS A LIVING DOLL

In 1959 Britain discovered its answer to rock'n'roll king Elvis Presley in Hertfordshire teenager Harry Webb, better known as Cliff Richard. With his group the Shadows – originally known as the Drifters – he recorded a million-selling performance of Lionel Bart's song "Living Doll".

Richard was one of the first generation of British pop stars plucked out of the flourishing skiffle scene by ambitious television producers, agents and promoters such as Jack Good and Larry Parnes. These were thoroughly manufactured stars, with made-up names – Billy Fury, Marty Wilde,

Adam Faith – singing numbers composed by Tin Pan Alley tune-spinners. Young people with pretensions to art or authenticity stuck to jazz or the folk music scene. The British singers understandably had no impact on the United States, since they were all derivative imitations of successful American performers.

The cynical professionals running the music business expected their fame to be wholly ephemeral. The anticipated trajectory for all their careers was from a few promotional appearances on television shows such as *Six-Five Special* or *Oh Boy!*

to recording a couple of hit singles, roles in one or two movies, and rapid disappearance into oblivion.

But in reality, Richard's consolidation of his career in the early 1960s proved the cynics wrong, even before the revolution wrought by the Beatles changed every rule of the pop music game.

▲ Unlike many of the formulaic and copy-cat acts of the late 1950s, Cliff Richard's career was destined to last over four decades.

- Agreement is reached on independence for Cyprus, with a power-sharing government of Greek and Turkish Cypriots
- Prime Minister Harold Macmillan begins a visit to the Soviet Union
- A state of emergency is declared in Southern Rhodesia

MARCH
- Archbishop Makarios returns from exile to Cyprus
- Nationalist leader Hastings Banda is arrested in Nyasaland
- The deaths of 11 Mau Mau prisoners in Hola Camp, Kenya, provoke protests in Britain

MAY
- Britain protests to Iceland over "Cod War" violence

JUNE
- A printers strike begins in Britain
- Singapore becomes self-governing

JULY
- Hugh Carleton Greene is appointed director-general of the BBC
- Jamaica becomes self-governing

AUGUST
- Death of sculptor Jacob Epstein

SEPTEMBER
- Death of actress Kay Kendall

OCTOBER
- The Conservatives under Macmillan win the general election; Margaret Thatcher is elected MP for Finchley

NOVEMBER
- The M1 motorway opens
- Britain and six other European countries agree to form the European Free Trade Association (EFTA)
- A state of emergency in Kenya ends

DECEMBER
- Britain resumes diplomatic relations with Egypt and Syria
- Labour MP Philip Noel-Baker is awarded the Nobel Peace Prize
- Death of artist Sir Stanley Spencer

1960–1969

Writer Jonathan Green wittily summed up the popular image of the 1960s in Britain as: "Years of revolt, years of carefree, sinless excess, of drugs, music, revolution … when to be young was not only very heaven, but mandatory too." Conservative moralists have painted the decade in the same lurid colours, but demonized instead of idealized it. Thus Tory politician Norman Tebbit looked back on the 1960s as a time of disintegrating values: "To be clean was no better than to be filthy. Good manners were no better than bad. Family life was derided as an outdated bourgeois concept. …" Certainly, there was some evidence during the decade of damage to the social fabric – crime levels and divorce rates. rose – but for most people, life was getting better.

The consumer-led economic boom that had begun in the 1950s continued. This was the decade in which millions of Britons bought their first washing machine and refrigerator. By the end of the decade, telephones and central heating were becoming standard accessories of family homes. For the first time, many ordinary people could afford foreign holidays. Although unemployment rates rose higher than in the previous decade, they were still very low compared with prewar levels. And there was fun as well as relative prosperity. "Swinging London" was declared the cultural capital of the world, resonating to the music of the all-conquering Beatles. England won the football World Cup. British television was in its golden era,. Pop music and pop fashions brightened life for millions.

Faith in the future was strong, a fact reflected in high birth rates that produced a substantial "baby boom". The desire to leave the past behind did not have unreservedly good effects. Britain's cities were transformed by grandiose modernistic architectural projects, born of an unholy alliance between greedy developers and council planners. Redevelopment expressed the spirit of the times – to knock down what was old, in full confidence of replacing it with something better. But the consequence was to tear the heart out of Britain's Victorian cities.

The 1960s were famously the decade of liberation and protest. In Britain political agitation remained the preserve of a minority, with CND making a splash early in the decade, and student anti-Vietnam War protest towards the end. "Liberation" was often taken to mean a new freedom to use "bad" language and explore taboo topics. In the course of the decade, theatre censorship was abolished, television opened its doors to satirical lampoons, and nipples and pubic hair achieved a legal airing in magazines and films. Between 1964 and 1970 a Labour-dominated parliament carried through an impressive programme of social reforms, legalizing homosexuality and abortion, liberalizing divorce laws, lowering the voting age to 18 and abolishing the death penalty. Successive Conservative and Labour administrations felt the need to tighten controls on immigration, which during the decade switched from being predominantly of West Indian origin to Asian. But, to its credit, the Labour government also outlawed most forms of racial discrimination and segregation.

The retreat from Empire, begun in the 1950s, turned into a stampede in the 1960s. But attempts to switch policy from an imperial to a European focus stalled, as successive applications for membership of the EEC were blocked by the French. This would not perhaps have mattered had Britain's economy been flourishing, but it was not. British consumers benefited from a wave of economic growth sweeping the Western world, but in relative terms the British economy performed poorly. The political consensus held that the government should manage the economy by juggling with interest rates and public spending to keep unemployment low and growth high. But, by the early 1960s, this juggling act had failed. Growth rates were not high enough to justify the continuing rise in wage levels driven by workers' understandable desire to participate in the consumer boom. The struggle to maintain full employment while controlling inflation led to an ever more desperate use of the accelerator and break. The trade gap widened inexorably and overseas investors eventually had to be placated by a major devaluation of the pound. In the following decade these unresolved economic problems, and the confrontation with the unions that came in their wake, would dominate the political scene.

- The last call-up for National Service takes place
- The betting and Gaming Act allows legal off-course betting
- A heart pacemaker is developed by surgeons at Queen Elizabeth Hospital, Birmingham
- The last steam locomotive, *Evening Star*, is built for British railways
- D H Lawrence's novel *Lady Chatterley's Lover* is cleared of obscenity
- Books published this year include *The Country Girls* by Edna O'Brien, *This Sporting Life* by David Storey and *A Kind of Loving* by Stan Barstow
- British films this year include Karel Reisz's *Saturday Night and Sunday Morning* and Tony Richardson's *The Entertainer*
- The Royal Shakespeare Company is formed
- The review *Beyond The Fringe* debuts in Edinburgh
- First performance of Robert Bolt's play *A Man for All Seasons* and Lionel Bart's musical *Oliver!*
- *Coronation Street* first appears on television
- The *Manchester Guardian* newspaper is renamed the *Guardian*

JANUARY
- Prime Minister Harold Macmillan begins a visit to Africa
- Nationalist leader Kenneth Kaunda is released from prison in Southern Rhodesia
- The state of emergency in Kenya ends
- Death of author Nevil Shute

MACMILLAN'S "WIND OF CHANGE"

▲ Harold Macmillan's "Wind of Change" speech marked a definitive statement of Britain's intent to push decolonization forward in Africa.

On February 3, 1960, towards the end of a month-long tour of Africa, Prime Minister Harold Macmillan addressed the South African parliament in Cape Town. His message for the assembled MPs was that "the wind of change is blowing through Africa". Although he did not say so explicitly, the implication of Macmillan's speech was that South Africans must adapt to a new world in which assumptions of white racial superiority would have to be abandoned, or at least disguised diplomatically.

The wind of change speech was a landmark in Britain's relations with South Africa. It made clear to the white South Africans that if they continued to formalize their domination of the majority black population through the apartheid system, they would lose British support. But the speech was also a crucial moment in Britain's imperial history, and, if anything, created more of a stir in Britain than it did in South Africa. Macmillan was for the first time publicly declaring the British government's intention to hand over all of its African colonies to popularly elected black nationalist leaders. The Gold Coast had already become independent as Ghana in 1957, and Nigeria was slated for independence later in 1960. After Macmillan's Cape Town speech, there was no doubt that the other colonies would follow suit.

The South African government, headed by Hendrik Verwoerd, had no intention of listening to Macmillan's advice. Verwoerd responded by likening the British Prime Minister's attitude to black Africans to the appeasement of Hitler in the 1930s. If there was ever any doubt about the South African government's determination to uphold apartheid, these were dispelled six weeks after Macmillan's departure. On March 21, at the township of Sharpeville in the Transvaal, a large crowd of unarmed anti-apartheid protesters – the majority of them women and children – were fired on by police. Sixty-nine people were killed and over 180 injured. The following year, South Africa declared itself a republic and withdrew from the Commonwealth. There was to be no compromise between apartheid and Macmillan's "wind of change".

▲ The Sharpeville massacre saw the beginning of 30 years of political violence that preceded an end to apartheid.

INDEPENDENCE FOR CYPRUS

On August 16, 1960, the island of Cyprus became an independent republic after 82 years of British rule – and just six years after a British government had announced categorically that "Britain could never contemplate giving up sovereignty" over the island. The official British attitude had been changed by a resistance campaign that had made continued occupation of Cyprus too costly to contemplate.

As so often in colonial conflicts, the situation in Cyprus was far from simple. The population of the island was 78 per cent Greek. Rather than wanting independence, many of the Greek Cypriots aspired to *enosis* (union) with Greece.

The Greek government itself supported this aspiration, but it was flatly opposed by Turkey, who espoused the cause of the other 22 per cent of the island's population, the Turkish Cypriots. The fact that both Greece and

▲ Makarios's acceptance of a power-sharing deal between Cyprus's Turkish and Greek communities cleared the way for independence.

Turkey were Britain's allies in NATO did not make the situation any easier to resolve.

An armed campaign to drive the British out of Cyprus and achieve *enosis* was started by the *Ethniki Organosis Kyprion Agoniston* (EOKA) in April 1955. Led by the formidable General George Grivas, EOKA launched a series of guerrilla attacks that soon soaked up a large number of British troops in counter-insurgency operations.

Meanwhile, Archbishop Makarios, the Greek Cypriots' religious leader and chief spokesman, maintained political pressure for change. Makarios was deported in 1956,

but this did nothing to calm Greek Cypriot feelings.

The path to a compromise was found in 1958. The Greek Cypriots accepted that Turkey would never allow *enosis*, and settled instead for independence under a power-sharing deal that gave the presidency to Makarios. The vice-presidency was given to a representative of the Turkish community.

The British agreed to leave as long as they were allowed to retain bases at Dhekelia and Akrotiri. And so the Union flag ceased to fly in yet another corner of the British Empire.

THE TRIAL OF "LADY C"

Lifting the censorship of sexually explicit material was to be one of the great themes of the 1960s, starting with a sensational trial in the autumn of 1960. D H Lawrence's novel *Lady Chatterley's Lover* – banned when it was written in 1928 because it contained four-letter words and graphic descriptions of sexual acts between a gamekeeper and the lady of the manor – was finally cleared of the charge of obscenity.

The trial was a test case deliberately embarked upon by both sides. In 1959 the law on obscenity had been changed to allow a defence on the grounds of artistic or literary merit. Soon afterwards, Penguin Books announced that it intended to publish an unexpurgated paperback edition of Lawrence's banned classic. Consequently, the Director of Public Prosecutions rose to the bait and took Penguin to court.

The tone of the often farcical case was established at the outset by the prosecuting counsel, Mervyn Griffith-Jones. Asking the jury to consider: "Is it a book that

you would even wish your wife and servants to read?", Griffith-Jones felt safe in assuming that Britain was peopled by well-off patriarchs – people who regarded any description of adulterous sex as obscene, unless accompanied by a clear statement of disapproval supplied by the author.

To the prosecution counsel's evident astonishment, an array of

prominent people queued up to give evidence in favour of the book's literary merit, and the jury agreed with them.

The not-guilty verdict was pronounced on November 2. A week later, Penguin's *Lady Chatterley* appeared on shelves of bookshops. A total of 200,000 copies of the first print run were sold in just one day.

▲ After 32 years of censorship, the British public – "wife and servants" included – was free to read *Lady Chatterley's Lover*.

- A census puts the UK population at 52.8 million, up from 50.2 million in 1951
- Britain opens negotiations to join the European Economic Community (EEC)
- Amnesty International is founded
- Committee of 100 is founded to mount a campaign of civil disobedience in protest against nuclear weapons
- The oral contraceptive pill goes on sale in Britain
- The E-type Jaguar sports car is launched
- First betting shops open
- Denis Law is the first British footballer to be valued at £100,000, on his transfer to Torino in Italy
- Cellist Jacqueline du Pré makes debut in London, aged 16
- The destruction of a Victorian arch at London's Euston station focuses public attention on the need to preserve historic buildings
- Roman mosaics are discovered at Fishbourne
- University of Sussex is founded
- New Testament section of the New English Bible is published
- Books published this year include *A Severed Head* by Iris Murdoch and *The Prime of Miss Jean Brody* by Muriel Spark
- British films this year include Tony Richardson's *A Taste of Honey* and Basil Dearden's *Victim*
- The Young Contemporaries exhibition introduces a new generation of artists including David Hockney, Patrick Caulfield and R B Kitaj

SUBURBS HIDE SOVIET SPIES

▲ The "Canadian businessman" who called himself Gordon Lonsdale was really KGB officer Konon Trofimovich Molody.

An ordinary suburban house in Cranleigh Drive, Ruislip, north London, was revealed as the hub of a sophisticated Soviet spy ring in January 1961. The arrest of the so-called "Portland" spies caused a media sensation, stimulating fresh questions about the state of British security in the Cold War.

The investigation that cracked the spy ring began with a tip-off from an Eastern bloc defector, Michael Goleniewski, a senior officer in Polish military intelligence. Goleniewski told the CIA of an Englishman who had been recruited by the Soviets in Warsaw in the 1950s and was now working in a naval installation. The information was passed on to MI5, who identified the man as Harry Houghton, an employee of the top-secret Underwater Weapons Establishment, Portland.

Houghton and his mistress, Ethyl Gee, were put under surveillance and soon led their watchers to their Soviet contact. On a visit to London, they were observed handing over a package to a Canadian businessman, Gordon Lonsdale, who was living in a flat overlooking Regent's Park and enjoying a high-spending, playboy lifestyle. Lonsdale's true identity was established later: he was Konon Trofimovich Molody, an officer in the KGB.

In October 1960, after a spell abroad, Lonsdale/Molody changed his place of residence, moving into a house in Ruislip with a New Zealand couple, Peter and Helen Kroger, who were apparently harmless antiquarian booksellers. As with Lonsdale, their identities were elaborate fakes. They were later identified by the FBI as US citizens, Morris and Lona Cohen – long-established Soviet agents who had fled the United States in the 1940s.

On January 7 Special Branch arrested Lonsdale/Molody, Houghton and Gee outside the Old Vic Theatre, shortly after secret documents had been handed over to the Russian in a carrier bag. At the same time, other officers raided the house in Ruislip and arrested the "Krogers". The house was packed with fascinating espionage paraphernalia, including microdot equipment, a radio transmitter hidden under the kitchen floor and materials for invisible writing.

On the face of it, the arrests were a triumph for the British intelligence services. But, along with the later arrests of SIS double-agent George Blake and Admiralty clerk John Vassall, they fuelled Cold War paranoia, and created the impression that Britain's secret military establishment was riddled with Soviet spies.

THE SATIRE BOOM

In May 1961 the revue *Beyond the Fringe* opened in London's West End. Its success marked the beginning of the "satire boom" of the early 1960s that would leave a permanent mark on the British entertainment industry and British political life.

First aired at the previous year's Edinburgh Festival, the revue featured Peter Cook, Jonathan Miller, Dudley Moore and Alan Bennett. The witty, mildly anti-establishment sketches of these young Oxbridge graduates

lampooned the class system and traditional good taste. Their targets included the royal family, the Prime Minister and Shakespeare – all previously considered more or less out of bounds. Influential critic Kenneth Tynan described *Beyond the Fringe* as taking British comedy on "its first vital step into the second half of the twentieth century".

▲ *Beyond the Fringe* pushed the boundaries of British comedy, making difficult subjects fair game for satirical attack.

Beyond the Fringe launched four notable media careers. But beyond that, together with *Private Eye* magazine founded in the same year and the television programme *That Was The Week That Was* (first broadcast in 1962), it established a new tradition of humour based on the ridicule of prominent personalities and comment on contemporary events. From then on, British royals and politicians would have to survive being made to look silly, a corrosive form of attack that steadily ate away at the culture of respect for authority.

IMMIGRATION CONTROLS

▲ **Labour shortages made immigrants vital to the British economy, but the government eventually succumbed to political pressures to stem the tide of migration.**

By 1961 the rise in Britain's immigrant population of West Indian, Indian and Pakistani origin had become a hot political issue. The first legal restrictions on access to Britain for Commonwealth citizens soon followed.

During the 1950s, Conservative governments had on several occasions examined the possibility of limiting immigration from Commonwealth countries, but rejected it. They were well aware that labour shortages made the immigrants vital to Britain's expanding economy. After the Notting Hill disturbances in 1958, however, it became impossible to ignore the social strains that immigration was creating. In areas with large concentrations of immigrants, white racism flourished, fed by issues such as a shortage of housing and competition for jobs.

In 1960 the government made it clear that immigration controls were on the way. The immediate consequence was a sharp rise in immigration as people rushed to beat the ban. Immigration from the New (that is, nonwhite) Commonwealth grew from 21,550 entrants in 1959, to 58,300 in 1960. The figure more than doubled in 1961 to a record 125,400 entrants.

The Commonwealth Immigrants Bill, introduced into parliament in November 1961, proposed a work voucher system, ostensibly designed to ensure that immigrants were employable. It did not apply to the dependants of those already resident in Britain. The new measure became law in 1962.

The legislation was racist, in that it was not intended to apply to citizens of the white Commonwealth. It was also not accompanied by any measures to combat racial discrimination in Britain, which denied blacks and Asians access to housing, jobs and many clubs and pubs. Immigration continued, but no progress was made toward creating a truly integrated multiracial society.

- The revue *Beyond the Fringe* opens in London's West End
- Helen Shapiro is a pop music star at the age of 14; her hits include "Walking Back to Happiness"
- The Beatles first perform at the Cavern in Liverpool

JANUARY
- Arrest of "Portland" spies in Ruislip, north London

FEBRUARY
- CND stages a sit-down protest outside the Ministry of Defence on Whitehall
- Britain and Iceland settle their dispute over fishing rights

MARCH
- South Africa withdraws from the Commonwealth
- Protests take place at the US submarine base at Holy Loch, Scotland
- Deaths of conductor Sir Thomas Beecham and comedian George Formby

APRIL
- The British colony of Sierra Leone becomes independent
- Tottenham Hotspur win the Football League championship

MAY
- Anthony Wedgwood Benn, Viscount Stansgate, is refused the right to sit in the House of Commons despite winning a by-election
- Tottenham win the FA Cup to compete the Cup and League "double', the first team to achieve this feat in the twentieth century
- George Blake is sentenced to 42 years in prison for spying for the Soviet Union

ANTI-NUCLEAR PROTEST PEAKS

▲ 1961 saw a wave of antinuclear protests, including one in which the 89-year-old philosopher Bertrand Russell (left) was arrested.

During 1961, the protests against nuclear weapons that had begun in earnest with the founding of the Campaign for Nuclear Disarmament (CND) in 1958 reached their climax. At their centre was the 88-year-old philosopher Bertrand Russell, a figure of international renown with an unrivalled capacity for expressing the most extreme anti-nuclear position with concision and clarity.

The policy of the mainstream CND leadership was to mount peaceful, law-abiding protests, while focusing on the conversion of the Labour Party to their cause. They triumphed at the 1960 Labour conference when – thanks to a block vote by the Transport and General Workers Union – a motion in favour of unilateral nuclear disarmament was carried. The Labour leader Hugh Gaitskell was distraught, believing that no party committed to abandoning nuclear weapons could win a general election.

Despite this evidence of success for CND, the more extreme activists were unhappy with the movement's moderate leadership. They felt that the respect shown for CND by the authorities and the public was simply a sign that it was ineffectual. Russell agreed with them. With other intellectual celebrities and young activists, he founded the Committee of 100 to organize a campaign of illegal civil disobedience.

The first prominent action of the new campaign took place on February 18, 1961, when a mass sit-down protest was staged outside the Ministry of Defence building on Whitehall. The protest was peaceful, however, and was treated benignly by the authorities and the media. The venerable Russell stood out among the young student protesters. Asked by a TV journalist why he was there, he replied: "Because if the present policies of the Western governments are continued, the entire human race will be exterminated and some of us think that might be rather a pity."

The Committee of 100 remained convinced of the need to provoke a confrontation with the authorities. The committee's younger activists ensured that the 1961 Aldermaston march ended in violent clashes with police. Meanwhile, Russell raised the rhetorical temperature in a speech denouncing President Kennedy and Prime Minister Macmillan as "much more wicked than Hitler ... murderers ... the wickedest people that ever lived in the history of man".

By September, the authorities were beginning to take the Committee of 100 seriously. Russell and 36 others, including Russell's wife Edith, were charged with inciting a breach of the peace. Russell was sentenced to two months prison, reduced to a week on health grounds. He was in Brixton jail when, on September 17, the committee organized a sit-down protest by about 12,000 people in Trafalgar Square, despite a specific ban by the Home Secretary on political demonstrations. This time the gloves were off. There were mass arrests – those seized included playwright John Osborne and actress Vanessa Redgrave – and many protestors suffered violence at the hands of the police.

The fulfilment of the plans of the Committee of 100, however, only proved their miscalculation. A crackdown through the autumn saw several of the committee's younger hotheads given serious prison sentences of up to two years. But instead of sparking popular resistance to the authorities, the radicalization of protest only alienated public support. Gaitskell was easily able to reverse the unilateral disarmament vote at the Labour Party's autumn conference. Support for CND demonstrations the following year faded. The movement would not revive until the 1980s.

FOOTBALLERS FIGHT FOR FREEDOM

In a decade much associated with protest and freedom, one of the first groups to win a liberation struggle were footballers. The hero of the hour was Jimmy Hill, the chairman of the Professional Footballers' Association (PFA).

English football stars of the 1950s, such as Stanley Matthews and Tom Finney lived in a form of serfdom, tied to the club that employed them and limited to a maximum wage set by the Football Association (FA). By 1961, this wage was £20 a week, roughly the earnings of a skilled industrial worker, topped up by legal bonuses of a few pounds for winning matches. Inevitably, illegal payments flourished.

▲ Johnny Haynes became the first English player to earn £100 a week following the liberalizing of footballer's wages.

In 1960, the PFA won players a limited right of freedom of movement between clubs. The next target was the maximum wage. In 1961, Hill balloted players on strike action to break the wage-fixing agreement. Support for a withdrawal of labour was unanimous. The FA caved in, and the wage ceiling was abolished.

Some clubs were happy for the chance to raise the pay of their best players, who might otherwise have been attracted by higher wages to play on the Continent. Fulham proudly announced that their star Johnny Haynes was the first English player to earn over £100 a week.

WORKING-CLASS REBELS

The dominant trend in British films, plays and novels of the early 1960s was for gritty working-class dramas, sneered at by the cynical as the "kitchen-sink" school. Northern accents were de rigueur and the equation of the working class with raw sex was as fixed as in the days of D H Lawrence.

In the cinema, the key works of this New Wave were *Room at the Top* in 1959; *Saturday Night and Sunday Morning* in 1960; *A Taste of Honey* in 1961; *A Kind of Loving* in 1962; and *This Sporting Life* in 1963. The success of these serious, unglamorous movies – all based on novels or plays – was partly down to a talented raft of directors, including Tony Richardson, Lindsay Anderson and John Schlesinger. Even more was due to young actors such as Albert Finney, unforgettable as Arthur Seaton in *Saturday Night*, and Rita Tushingham, seemingly forever pregnant with an illegitimate baby.

But probably most was owed to the relaxation of the censorship code by the new secretary of the Board of British Film Censors, John Trevelyan. Audiences would pay for the novel experience of "strong" language, of previously taboo "adult themes" such as homosexuality and abortion, and of sex scenes more explicit than had previously been permitted.

▲ Actress Rita Tushingham and playwright John Osborne personified a new wave of dramas dealing with gritty, realistic and often sexual subjects.

- The government establishes the National Economic Development Council (NEDC) to advise on national production targets and wage levels
- The Commonwealth Immigrants Act comes into force
- First transatlantic television broadcasts are made via the *Telstar* satellite
- First "colour supplement" is published, by the *Sunday Times*
- The thalidomide drug is withdrawn from use in Britain because it has been found to cause birth defects
- Books published this year include *A Clockwork Orange* by Anthony Burgess, *The Anatomy of Britain* by Anthony Sampson and *The New Poetry*, an anthology edited by A Alvarez
- British films this year include David Lean's *Lawrence of Arabia*, the first James Bond movie *Dr No* and John Schlesinger's *A Kind of Loving*
- Musical premieres include the opera *King Priam* by Michael Tippett and Benjamin Britten's *War Requiem*
- New television series include *Z Cars, Steptoe and Son,* and *That Was The Week That Was*
- Ken Russell's acclaimed television documentary on Sir Edward Elgar is broadcast
- Hit records this year include The Tornados' "Telstar", Cliff Richard's "The Young Ones" and the Shadows' "Apache"

NEW CATHEDRAL OPENS WITH REQUIEM

▲ The tapestry of *Christ in Glory* is the crowning piece in Coventry Cathedral, itself a symbol of resurrection from wartime destruction.

On May 25, 1962, the new Coventry Cathedral was consecrated in the presence of Elizabeth II. Designed by Sir Basil Spence, the building had been erected alongside the ruins of the old cathedral, destroyed in the infamous German air raid on Coventry in November 1940. An uncompromisingly modernist structure, Coventry Cathedral was a treasure-house of contemporary British art, with a high altar tapestry by Graham Sutherland, a stained glass window by John Piper and – dominating the entrance – a magnificent statue of *St Michael and the Devil* by Jacob Epstein.

The conscious theme of the cathedral was international reconciliation and resurrection from wartime destruction. Benjamin Britten had been commissioned to write a piece for the consecration and his *War Requiem* was first performed in the cathedral on May 30. A powerful statement of the composer's hatred of war, it was one of the very few pieces of modern serious music to obtain a wide audience as well as critical praise.

TELSTAR FLASHES PICTURES ACROSS THE ATLANTIC

The first great step in the communications revolution of the 1960s was the launch of the satellite *Telstar* from Cape Canaveral on July 10, 1962. Described as "about the size and shape of a beachball", it permitted the first live television broadcasts between Europe and the United States.

Telstar was the first satellite owned and operated by a business corporation, the US communications giant AT&T. During its sixth orbit, images transmitted from Andover, Maine, were picked up successfully by a ground station at Pleumeur-Bodou in Brittany, and less successfully at Goonhilly Downs in Cornwall, where a technical fault meant the reception was blurred and foggy.

The following day, France and Britain transmitted television pictures to the United States – Yves Montand singing for the French, the test card for Britain.

After these initial experiments, the first live transatlantic programmes were broadcast by national networks on each side of the Atlantic on July 23.

Europe sent a 20-minute travelogue narrated by Richard Dimbleby – shots of Lapp reindeer farmers, a hovercraft on the Solent and the Sistine Chapel – while the United States responded with a baseball game, a speech by President Kennedy and Niagara Falls.

Although the content of these early broadcasts was disappointing, the technical leap forward towards what trendy Canadian academic Marshall McLuhan was already calling "the global village" was impressive. It certainly captured the popular imagination: the biggest hit single of 1962 was the Tornados' would-be futuristic instrumental "Telstar".

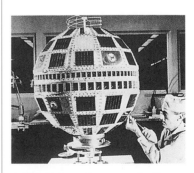

▲ The future of communication: the *Telstar* satellite was powered by solar panels that converted sunlight to electrical energy.

THE HOVERCRAFT GETS OFF THE GROUND

▲ The Vickers Armstrong hovercraft takes off from the beach at Rhyl, marking the start of the world's first passenger hovercraft service.

The development of the hovercraft showed Britain's determination to take its place at the cutting edge of technological innovation. First conceived in 1953 by English scientist Sir Christopher Cockerell, the cushioned aircraft became a reality through the support of the National Development Corporation A prototype crossed the English Channel in July 1959.

As with so many British inventions, however, commercial exploitation of a clever idea proved difficult. On July 20, 1962, the first passenger hovercraft service was initiated across the Dee Estuary, between Wallasey and Rhyl. The Vickers VA-3 carried 24 passengers on the 30-minute journey.

In August, another service, using a larger Westland SR-N2 model, was begun across the Solent between Southsea and Ryde on the Isle of Wight.

The aim of these experimental services was to see how money could be made out of hovercraft travel. Despite the high hopes raised by this new mode of transport, its commercial potential seemed likely to be limited by its inability to function in heavy seas, and by the small number of passengers it could carry compared with conventional ferries.

HANRATTY AND THE A6 MURDER

James Hanratty was one of the last men to die by the hangman's noose in Britain. Until quite recently, his conviction was widely believed to be a shameful miscarriage of justice.

The murder for which Hanratty was hanged took place on the night of August 22, 1961. Michael Gregsten and his lover Valerie Storie were in a Morris Minor car in a field near Slough when a man with a gun forced his way into the vehicle. He made Gregston drive to a lay-by on the A6 near Bedford. There he shot Gregston dead, and raped and shot Storie. She survived, but was left paralyzed for life.

Hanratty – aged 25 – was arrested in October. Police established that he had stayed in a hotel room where ammunition from the murder weapon had been found. He was also identified by Storie, on the basis of his voice rather than his appearance. Hanratty protested his innocence, claiming to have been 325 km (200 miles) away in Rhyl at the time of the murder. But the jury did not believe him. He was sentenced to hang and was executed at Bedford prison on April 4, 1962.

Opponents of capital punishment were quick to point out flaws in the evidence upon which Hanratty had been convicted. For decades after his execution, books and articles

▲ Despite doubts about Hanratty's hanging for a brutal double murder, subsequent DNA tests confirmed that he was indeed guilty.

appeared asserting his innocence. Yet in 2002, comparison of Hanratty's DNA with traces on exhibits from the trial appeared to prove beyond all reasonable doubt that he was after all guilty as charged.

- "Trad" jazz is in fashion, with clarinettist Acker Bilk and trumpeter Kenny Ball both topping the singles charts
- The Beatles release their first record, "Love Me Do"
- Pop group The Rolling Stones perform for the first time

JANUARY
- England cricketers lose a Test series against India for the first time

FEBRUARY
- Six members of the Committee of 100 are found guilty of offences under the Official Secrets Act

MARCH
- Liberal candidate Eric Lubbock scores a sensational victory in the Orpington by-election, overturning a Conservative majority of 14,760

APRIL
- James Hanratty is hanged for the A6 murder
- Driver Stirling Moss is seriously injured in a crash at Goodwood

MAY
- Managed by Alf Ramsay, Ipswich Town win the Football League championship
- The IRA declares an end to a sporadic six-year campaign of bombings and assassinations in Northern Ireland
- The West Indies Federation is dissolved

FOUR MINUTES FROM DOOM

▲ **The "golf ball" at Fylingdales Early Warning Station was part of a radar system intended to give Britain warning of a nuclear strike.**

In October 1962 the world came closer to full-scale nuclear war than at any time before or since. A Soviet attempt to station nuclear missiles on Cuba led to a confrontation with the United States that could easily have triggered a global conflict.

The face-off between the Soviets and the Americans did not concern Britain directly and was handled by US President Kennedy with only the most cursory reference to his allies. Yet there was no doubt that had nuclear war broken out, the British people would have been in the frontline, since Britain was home to bases for US nuclear-armed aircraft and submarines. Nothing could have demonstrated more clearly the impotence of the British government to control its country's destiny. The nation's fate was tied to that of the United States, for better or for worse.

Britons were well acquainted with the risks of nuclear war. Crude television graphics showed the probable effect of the Soviets' largest nuclear device, which could have devastated an area from central London to Reading. Giant "golf ball" installations appeared at Fylingdales in Yorkshire, part of a radar system that would give Britain four minutes' warning of a nuclear strike. School-children were asked to write essays about what they would do with their four minutes of life.

Considering the scale of the crisis, the level of antiwar demonstrations in Britain was not impressive. Only a small minority responded to Bertrand Russell's call to take to the streets in protest against the Americans, who were blamed exclusively for the crisis by Russell and others on the left. Most people followed the course of events on television and kept their fingers crossed.

The successful resolution of the crisis in late October earned President Kennedy great prestige, and it ushered in the beginnings of detente. During the next two years, a "hotline" was set up between the Kremlin and the White House, and a treaty was signed banning all except underground nuclear tests. The crisis also, paradoxically, lessened popular concern over nuclear war. Nuclear deterrence appeared to have worked and expectations of a Third World War – once considered almost inevitable – lessened. Those who had campaigned so vehemently against the Bomb looked around for other causes.

SCREEN DEBUT FOR BOND

The first James Bond film, *Dr No*, appeared in cinemas in October 1962. Made on a relatively low budget and released with minimal publicity, it was a box-office hit in both Britain and the United States, laying the foundations for an enduring film franchise. Its success across the Atlantic, alongside that of David Lean's *Lawrence of Arabia*, suggested Americans were heading for a bout of Anglophilia.

Bond was already a familiar figure to readers of pulp fiction, who had lapped up Ian Fleming's sado-masochistic spy fantasies since the early 1950s. He found an unsurpassed screen incarnation in Sean Connery, a Scottish actor already in his early 30s, whose career was heading nowhere special when he was picked for the role.

Directed by Terence Young, *Dr No* oozed sex, exoticism and pseudo-sophistication. Whereas

▲ Sean Connery takes on a tarantula in a scene from *Dr No*, the first James Bond movie.

British films had tended to represent warm-hearted domestic virtues or gritty realism, in contrast to Hollywood violence and glamour, the Bond series took on American cinema on its own terms. In its way, it contributed to the redefinition of Britishness in the 1960s – when the British proved they could give their own twist to American popular culture and sell it back to the United States.

NOVEMBER
• British businessman Greville Wynne is arrested by the Soviets as a spy
• Britain introduces a new constitution in Southern Rhodesia
• Britain and France agree to develop the Concorde supersonic passenger jet

DECEMBER
• Tanganyika becomes a republic within the Commonwealth, with Julius Nyerere as head of state
• At the Nassau Conference in the Bahamas, US President Kennedy agrees to provide Britain with Polaris nuclear missiles for its submarines
• Britain accepts the right of Nyasaland to cede from the Central African Federation
• Racing driver Graham Hill wins the Formula One world championship for BRM, ahead of fellow Britain Jim Clark
• British scientists Max Perutz and John Kendrew win the Nobel Prize for Chemistry; Francis Crick and Maurice Wilkins share the Nobel Prize for Medicine with American James Watson
• Death of British actor and director Charles Laughton

THAT WAS THE SHOW THAT WAS

In November 1962, satire stormed the bastions of British television with the launch of the topical late-night BBC show *That Was The Week That Was*. Fronted by the youthful David Frost and produced by Ned Sherrin, it put enough bite into its sallies against pompous politicians, sexual hypocrisy and accepted canons of good taste to infuriate conservative opinion and attract a weekly audience of 12 million.

Known as *TW3* for convenience, the show was technically innovative, as the first programme to allow the studio to appear in full view, cameras and all. Performed live in front of a studio audience, much of it was improvised and none of it was wellrehearsed. But it was the content rather than the form that caused a sensation. Sketches scripted by talented writers such as Keith Waterhouse, John Mortimer and Dennis Potter drove a cart and horses through the established convention that religion, royalty and the government were out of bounds for television comedy – the programme escaped the rules by being officially classified as current affairs, rather than light entertainment. Comedian

William Rushton's impersonations of Prime Minister Harold Macmillan were a regular feature. So was journalist Bernard Levin's vitriolic weekly slot in which he tore a studio guest to shreds, the first example of hostile interviewing on television.

"TW3" stirred up a furore in parliament and the press. As Levin wrote, newspapers were "crowded with fury against the filth, sedition and blasphemy that, to many viewers, the programme consisted of almost entirely". Most offence was caused by

irreverent items such as a consumer guide to religion and by savage attacks on politicians such as Home Secretary Henry Brooke. But critics struck home when they focused on the softer target of the schoolboy "dirty jokes" that constituted one of the programmes less successful elements. "TW3" had the support of BBC director-general Sir Hugh Carlton Greene, but he could not save it once accusations of peddling "smut" became rife. Despite still attracting large audiences, the programme was killed off at the end of 1963.

▲ *TW3* struck its targets once too often, and, despite attracting huge audiences, political pressure caused the satirical show's axing.

- Britain has its coldest winter since 1740, with snow on the ground from late December 1962 into early March 1963
- Almost 90 per cent of British households own a television; less than 30 per cent own a refrigerator
- Unemployment tops 450,000, provoking protests by the jobless
- The British Railways Board, headed by Dr Richard Beeching, proposes axing a third of the country's rail network
- The Robbins Report recommends a massive expansion of university education
- The malpractices of slum landlord Peter Rachman are exposed
- The Peerage Act allows hereditary peers to renounce their titles
- Continental-style road signs are introduced
- First one-day cricket tournament is played in England, a knock-out competition sponsored by Gillette
- Books published this year include *The Spy Who Came in from the Cold* by John Le Carré
- British films this year include Tony Richardson's *Tom Jones*, Terence Young's *From Russia With Love* and Lindsay Anderson's *This Sporting Life*
- The National Theatre stages its first performances
- The musical *Oh! What A Lovely War* opens in London

DE GAULLE SAYS NON! TO BRITAIN

▲ **Suspicious of Britain's close ties with the United States, French president De Gaulle vetoed the British application to join the EEC.**

In January 1963, French President Charles de Gaulle vetoed Britain's application to join the European Economic Community (EEC). It was a slap in the face for the Macmillan government, which had pushed for entry into Europe despite vociferous domestic opposition.

The reversal of government policy on Europe was motivated by the realization that Britain was facing economic decline and the end of its role as an imperial power. British businesses were appalled at the prospect of losing out in major European markets. On the other hand, many Britons –

probably a majority – viewed closer association with continental Europe with suspicion or downright hostility. They felt it was incompatible with Britain's ties with the Commonwealth and its "special relationship" with the United States. It was also feared that entry into the EEC would involve a loss of national independence.

Negotiations between Britain and the six EEC states began in November. They were conducted with skill and enthusiasm by Edward Heath, a convinced pro-European. But Britain's determination to maintain links with the Commonwealth and the United States acted as a red rag to de Gaulle, who was especially concerned to exclude American influence from Europe.

In a press conference on January 14, de Gaulle described Britain as neither thinking nor acting like a European nation – the most Britain deserved was some form of associate status. The door had been slammed in Britain's face and would remain firmly closed as long as de Gaulle remained in power.

GAITSKELL DIES, WILSON LABOUR LEADER

On January 18, 1963, Labour Party leader Hugh Gaitskell died at the age of 57, after a sudden illness. The man elected by Labour MPs to succeed him was 46-year-old Harold Wilson.

For the full seven years of his tenure of the party leadership, Gaitskell had been distracted from the task of opposing the government by the need to fight left-wingers within the Labour movement who were opposed to his moderate policies. He had attempted but failed to have the commitment to wholesale

▲ **Hugh Gaitskell (centre) led Labour for seven years, but was never able to adopt an electorally successful reformist agenda.**

nationalization removed from the party constitution, but he had succeeded in persuading the party to abandon unilateral nuclear disarmament as party policy.

Internal party disputes helped ensure that Gaitskell never became Prime Minister. He was a decent and honourable man who understood the difficulties Labour faced – chiefly the rising prosperity of the mass of voters under Conservative rule and the shrinking numbers of the industrial working class, the party's traditional core constituency. But, faced with these problems, he had failed to find a clear message to set against the Tories' mantra of "never had it so good".

Wilson nailed new colours to the mast. Once associated with Aneurin Bevan and considered a left-wing Labour man, he now presented himself instead as the champion of modernization. Under him, Labour was going to be the party of technological progress and efficient economic planning – this was a strong suit to play against the ageing Conservative leaders drawn from the landed aristocracy.

PROFUMO SEX SCANDAL

▲ **Disgraced Minister for War John Profumo; revelations about his private life contributed to the downfall of the Tory government.**

In 1963, a scandal involving two potent taboo areas of British life – sex and the secret service – blew the lid off the political establishment and struck a mortal blow to the Conservative government. The trouble began in June 1961, when the Minister for War, John Profumo, met 19-year-old Christine Keeler by Lord Astor's swimming pool.

Keeler was living under the protection of society osteopath Steven Ward, who had introduced her to the sleek world of upper-class vice. Her looks made her immediately welcome at the sex clubs and orgies, where the more raffish members of the establishment took their pleasures. She slept with a lot of men, and Profumo was one of them.

Unfortunately for Profumo, another of Keeler's bedfellows was Eugene Ivanov, a naval attaché at the Soviet embassy. Keeler had been pushed in Ivanov's direction by MI5, who hoped to use sexual entrapment to extract secrets from the attaché. This plot completely backfired, as Ivanov began to question Keeler about details of her pillowtalk with Profumo.

On March 22, 1963, as rumours about the affair began to surface in the press, Profumo vowed to the House of Commons: "There was no impropriety whatsoever in my acquaintanceship with Miss Keeler."

It was a lie that could not be sustained; stories about Keeler, her friend Mandy Rice-Davies and their numerous male companions were recounted in the press in detail. On June 5, Profumo resigned from the government, forced to admit to a sexual relationship that had put Britain's secrets at risk.

The establishment took its revenge by having Steven Ward arrested on a trumped-up charge of pimping. The trial offered more sensational newspaper copy, giving Mandy Rice-Davies the chance to produce the retort "He would, wouldn't he?" when she referred to a man of standing who had denied her allegations of sexual impropriety. For Ward, however, it was a tragedy. Unable to face a prison term, he committed suicide.

The Profumo affair had a massive impact largely because its public revelations of the pompous and hypocritical establishment chimed with a widespread mood of irreverence, expressed by the new satirical media, such as the magazine *Private Eye* and its television equivalent *That Was The Week That Was*.

In October, the Prime Minister, Harold Macmillan, resigned, and Sir Alec Douglas-Home succeeded him. A year later, Labour came to power after 13 years of Tory government – in part, at least, thanks to the charms of Christine Keeler.

▲ **The revelation of John Profumo's relationship with Christine Keeler forced the Minister of War to resign.**

COOPER FLOORS CLAY IN BOXING CLASSIC

On the evening of June 18, 1963, Wembley was the scene for a boxing classic, when British and Commonwealth heavyweight champion Henry Cooper squared up to the rising star of American boxing, Cassius Clay.

Cooper was a brave-hearted fighter with a heavy left-hook and a fatal tendency to cut above the eyes. Clay was a phenomenon unlike anything seen before. Turning professional after winning an Olympic light-heavyweight gold medal in 1960, he had won 18 fights in a row. Dancing around the canvas with his gloves lowered, he defied traditional musclebound bruisers to lay a punch on him. His loud-mouth taunting style in and out of the ring had made him the most talked about boxer in the world.

There were 35,000 fans in Wembley Stadium, worked up to fever pitch by Clay's arrogant prediction of victory in five rounds.

The fight opened with Cooper in aggressive mood, crowding Clay and drawing blood from his nose. Soon, though, Clay was dancing around Cooper, openly toying with the slower-moving boxer, laying enough punches to open up the familiar cuts above his eyes.

Infuriated by the deliberate humiliation Clay was inflicting, at the end of round four Cooper unleashed a mighty left hook to Clay's jaw and landed him on the canvas. The American staggered to his feet – clearly dazed – and was saved by the bell. The crowd were naturally wild with excitement, but Cooper's triumph was short-lived. Clay stood up for the fifth round slow and flat-footed but punching like a demon. The Englishman's cuts were pumping blood as blows rained on his face. The fight had to be stopped.

Clay went on to take the world heavyweight championship the following year and, as Muhammad Ali, grew into a sporting legend. Cooper had to be content with the status of a British folk hero, remembered above all for a fight that he lost.

▲ Henry's Cooper's flooring of Cassius Clay was a short-lived triumph; by the fifth round it was the American who had demolished Cooper.

PHILBY WAS THE "THIRD MAN"

At the start of July 1963, the British government was forced to make the embarrassing admission that former senior intelligence officer Harold "Kim" Philby had been a spy for the Soviet Union.

Like his fellow spies Donald Maclean, Guy Burgess and Anthony Blunt, Philby was an undergraduate at Cambridge in the 1930s. A convert there to communism, he was recruited by Soviet intelligence before the Second World War. Once war broke out, he slipped effortlessly into the British secret service and by 1944 was head of anti-Soviet counter-intelligence.

Philby's successful career as a Soviet "mole" was compromised by his association with Burgess and Maclean. When they fled the country in 1951 to avoid Maclean being arrested, Philby was implicated. He stood up well to interrogation, however, and no hard evidence could be found against him. To the disgust of the American CIA, which was convinced of Philby's guilt, in 1955 the British government officially cleared him of being the "Third Man" in the Burgess-Maclean affair. He was relegated to the status of a lowly intelligence officer in the field, and sent to

▲ Although his fellow spies defected to the USSR in 1951, Philby skilfully avoided implication until he fled to Moscow in 1963.

Beirut with a cover role as an *Observer* journalist.

During 1962, new evidence emerged against Philby from a woman he had attempted to recruit as a Soviet agent. Still unwilling to prosecute one of their own, British intelligence offered him immunity if he would provide full details on Soviet agents and operations. Instead, on January 23, 1963, he slipped away from Beirut on board a Soviet merchant ship, resurfacing in June in Moscow.

The revelation of Philby's treachery was an embarrassment not only for the government and the secret service but for the entire establishment. That members of the Oxbridge elite should have so spectacularly betrayed their country created the impression that the traditional ruling class was rotting away from within.

For his part, Philby never ceased to be a committed communist. His autobiography, *My Silent War* (published in 1968), was as good a book on espionage as the novels of John Le Carré, which it in many ways resembled. He continued to serve the Soviet regime and, at the time of his death in 1988, was an active supporter of the reforms of the Soviet system under Mikhail Gorbachev.

THE GREAT TRAIN ROBBERY

Around 2 am on August 8, 1963, a gang stopped the Glasgow to London Royal Mail train near Cheddington in Buckinghamshire. The raiders stole 120 mailbags holding £2.5 million in used bank notes. The daring operation was immediately dubbed "The Great Train Robbery".

Although the robbers were all essentially smalltime criminals, their operation was efficiently planned and executed. Using a false red stop light, they halted the train and took over the engine, coshing driver Jack Mills. One of the gang, himself an engine driver, took the train further down the track to where a lorry was waiting. In the meantime, other members of the gang broke into the sorting carriages and seized the mailbags. By the time the alarm was raised, they had made off into the night. However, the robbers' escape was far less efficient than their ambush; most of them were soon under arrest.

The authorities were astonished to discover that, as journalist

Bernard Levin wrote, the British public "regarded the train robbers as folk heroes, and viewed their crime with glee, their enterprise with admiration, and their fate with sympathy". Indeed, Southampton University students went as far as electing Bruce Reynolds, mastermind of the operation, an honorary life member of their union.

The courts imposed extravagant sentences of 30 years on most of those involved in the crime. Charlie Wilson, the first to be tried and charged, managed to escape from prison in 1964, but was rearrested in Canada in 1968. Buster Edwards fled to Mexico, but later gave himself up. Ronnie Biggs, a marginal late-comer to the scheme, escaped in 1965, and fought a memorable campaign against extradition from Brazil. Suffering from ill-health, he returned to Britain in 2001 at the age of 70 and was sent back to jail. The stolen money was never found.

▲ Scene of the crime: the Great Train Robbers, in particular Ronnie Biggs, later achieved a kind of folk-hero status.

SEPTEMBER
• Scottish driver Jim Clark wins the Formula One drivers' championship in a Lotus; Graham Hill is runner-up
• Death of cartoonist Sir David Low

OCTOBER
• Ill-health causes the resignation of Prime Minister Harold Macmillan
• Lord Home succeeds as Prime Minister, renouncing his peerage to become Sir Alec Douglas-Home

NOVEMBER
• The Beatles star in the Royal Variety Command Performance
• BBC governors decide to take satirical show *That Was The Week That Was* off the air
• Death of author Aldous Huxley

DECEMBER
• Christine Keeler is jailed for perjury and perverting the course of justice
• Zanzibar gains independence from Britain
• Kenya gains independence from Britain; Jomo Kenyatta is President
• Central African Federation is dissolved

1964

THE BEATLES CONQUER THE WORLD

In the history of popular culture, 1964 is the year when Britain invaded the United States. From the moment that the Beatles touched down at Kennedy Airport, New York, on February 7, the United States surrendered without a fight. The Fab Four were soon to become, in the words of John Lennon: "more popular than Jesus Christ".

As for any successful invasion, careful planning had been the key. The US record company Capitol pulled out all the stops to promote the Beatles' single, "I Want To Hold Your Hand", released in the United States in December 1963. It was already top of the American charts by the time the Beatles arrived for a short visit built around two appearances on the immensely popular *Ed Sullivan Show*.

The television broadcast of their airport arrival, complete with mobs of screaming teenagers and

▲ The Beatles, performing here on the *Ed Sullivan Show*, were the first British band to achieve real commercial success in the US.

▼ A Beatles concert in Manchester in 1963, the year the group had their first number one single.

a live press conference, fuelled American curiosity to fever pitch.

Their first *Ed Sullivan* appearance on February 9, was watched by a record estimated audience of 73 million. By April, the Beatles held all five top places in the Hot 100 singles chart.

Although the Beatles could never have achieved success on a global scale without skilful commercial promotion, they were not a manufactured band created by marketing men. They were the product of a genuine creative upsurge among British youth in revolt against the stifling dullness of life in the Britain of the early 1960s. Clubs and art colleges had spawned a flourishing culture centred on pop music and fashion. British bands reinterpreted American music in an inventive style, using it to express their own frustrations and aspirations.

The Beatles were a product of the especially vibrant Liverpool scene, although they had acquired their professionalism and their haircuts during a spell in Hamburg. By 1962 they were the most popular group on Merseyside. Under the management of a local businessman, Brian Epstein, they eventually secured a recording contract with Parlaphone.

The Beatles had their first number one single in April 1963, and by the end of that summer Beatlemania was in full swing.

Near-riots broke out at their concerts, where the screams of adolescent girls drowned the music. The country was deluged in Beatles wigs, brooches, collarless jackets and magazines.

Eager not to be square, grown-ups leaped on the bandwagon.

▲ Ringo Starr gets acquainted with female fans on a Florida Beach during the Beatles' American tour.

By the autumn, a *Sunday Times* music critic had called Lennon and McCartney "the greatest composers since Beethoven".

They topped the bill on the mainstream television show *Sunday Night at the London Palladium* in October and starred at a Royal Command Performance the following month – the occasion for Lennon's famous crack: "Will people in the cheaper seats clap your hands. The rest of you rattle your jewellery."

Their album *With the Beatles*, released on the day President Kennedy was shot, sold a quarter of a million copies in advance.

It is hard to appreciate the impact of the Beatles phenomenon retrospectively, because so many aspects of it have since become commonplace. For example, it is hard to recall that, until the Beatles, the "serious" press had never paid any attention to pop music as art.

The sudden appearance of articles by musicologists analyzing the Beatles' use of harmony had no precedent. Nor did the irreverent style of interview that they gave, dominated by John Lennon's caustic and surrealist-tinged wit. And nor did the fact that they wrote their own songs. Pop singers had traditionally been a carefully groomed front for the hack Tin Pan Alley tune-spinners.

The transatlantic breakthrough in 1964 transformed the whole scale of the Beatles phenomenon – and of pop music generally. Until then the Beatles had been still touring hard like any other band, appearing at local Gaumonts and Odeons throughout Britain. The members of the band were not fabulously rich, but when they visited the United States for the second time, in the autumn of 1964, they played huge venues such as the Hollywood Bowl and Chicago's International Amphitheatre. Their concert in Cleveland, Ohio, was stopped by a police chief who claimed the emotional frenzy of the audience posed a health risk.

Other British pop groups – the Animals, the Dave Clark Five, and the Rolling Stones – swarmed in to the United States to expand the bridgehead the Beatles had created. The Stones were marketed by their manager, Andrew Loog Oldham, as the anti-Beatles – loutish, inarticulate and offensive, compared to the Beatles more pleasing image. But they too had talent and a staying power beyond anything that would have been predicted at the time.

Even more surprising than the scale of the Beatles' success was the way they were able to develop their music and style in intelligent and inventive ways. Their first film, *Hard Day's Night*, directed by Richard Lester and released in 1964, was a piece of Pop Art, full of avant-garde cinematic tricks. It was a world away from the movies that Elvis Presley or Cliff Richard had done to extend their careers.

For the rest of the 1960s, the Beatles remained central to the evolution of the new youth culture that connected, at different points, to avant-garde art, political protest, and experiments with mind-altering drugs.

Britain's dominance of the US pop charts in 1964 was transient and partial, but it triggered a massive change in perceptions of Britain worldwide. The land of the bowler hat and Queen Victoria was reinvented as the home of the mini-skirt and the electric guitar.

▲ The Beatles arrive back in Britain after a tour that triggered a wave of British pop music successes in the USA.

- The birth rate peaks at 18.8 per thousand people
- The Forth Road Bridge is opened in Scotland
- The new Birmingham Bull Ring is opened
- The *Sun* newspaper begins publication
- A third television channel, BBC2, goes on the air
- First broadcast of BBC television's *Top of the Pops*
- Books published this year include *The Whitsun Weddings* by Philip Larkin and *In His Own Write* by John Lennon
- British films this year include Richard Lester's *A Hard Day's Night* and Joseph Losey's *The Servant*
- Theatre productions include Peter Hall's Shakespeare series *The War of the Roses* and Peter Brook's *Marat-Sade*
- First performance of Peter Shaffer's play *The Royal Hunt of the Sun*
- Hit songs include "Can't Buy Me Love" and "I Feel Fine" by the Beatles, and "House of the Rising Sun" by the Animals

JANUARY
- British troops quell army mutinies in Tanganyika, Uganda and Kenya

FEBRUARY
- The Beatles make their first tour of the United States

MODS AND ROCKERS CLASH

At the English seaside, 1964 was the year of the bank holiday riots. At the Easter, Whitsun and August bank holiday weekends, Mod and Rocker youth gangs descended upon resorts such as Clacton, Brighton, Margate and Hastings, fighting one another and terrorizing everyone else. Although blown out of all proportion by the press, these clashes did dramatize as public spectacle the feverish excitement and rebellious energy of the youth subcultures of the early 1960s.

Mods and Rockers were natural enemies. The term Mod had first been applied to a small London clique favouring stylish men's clothing and modern jazz. By 1964 Mods were found in every town and city. The boys wore sharp suits with parkas over the top and the girls crewneck sweaters. They rode Italian scooters decked out with mirrors, danced to ska and rhythm and blues, and got high on amphetamines. With their hair neat and their general turnout smart, they were employable as well as trendy.

To stylish Mods, the Rockers were born losers, neanderthals. With their leather jackets and flying boots, long greased hair and ton-up motorbikes, they could only hope for the most menial of jobs and were hopelessly out of touch with the trendy cutting-edge of youth culture. *Ready, Steady, Go!* presenter Cathy McGowan, dubbed the "Queen of the Mods", sneered at the Rockers as having "little fashion taste". Worst of all for her, they idolized "Elvis Presley, who is desperately old-fashioned".

Being stylish did not mean that Mods were soft. Many carried flick-knives or coshes to match the Rockers' bicycle chains. But most of the bank holiday fighting was strictly ritualized, with only a handful of significant injuries. The gangs went on the rampage, throwing stones and bottles at police, setting fire to deckchairs, and smashing the occasional window. The following day a few dozen were hauled in front of magistrates and given a fine or a brief prison sentence. All that was left of the events was a mess to clear up and a crop of sensational newspaper headlines.

▲ **A group of Mods on the look out for their Rocker rivals in Brighton, a traditional venue for Bank Holiday confrontations between the two gangs.**

WILSON PM AFTER TORY RULE CRUMBLES

On October 16, 1964, Labour leader Harold Wilson entered 10 Downing Street as Prime Minister, ending 13 years of Conservative rule. Labour had scored a narrow election victory, winning 317 seats in parliament compared with 304 for the Conservatives and their allies, and nine seats for the Liberals. This gave Wilson a barely workable overall majority of five.

That Labour had achieved even this degree of success was in large part attributable to the self-destruction of the Conservative Party. The Profumo scandal in 1963 had profoundly shaken the Tories. Conservative peer Lord Hailsham memorably stated that "a great party is not to be brought down because of a squalid affair between a woman of easy virtue and a proven liar". But if not "brought down", the Conservative Party was certainly wounded by the scandal.

▲ Harold Wilson's assurance and energy contrasted sharply with the aristocratic demeanour of his Tory opponent, Alec Douglas-Home.

This damage was compounded when the illness of Prime Minister Harold Macmillan triggered a savage struggle for the succession in October 1963. In unseemly manoeuvrings behind closed doors, Macmillan succeeded in shutting out the most obvious candidate for the premiership, R A Butler, at the cost of installing the most unlikely candidate, the fourteenth Earl of Home. Although he resigned his peerage to become an MP as Sir Alec Douglas-Home, the new Prime Minister remained an embodiment of the landed aristocracy – intelligent, thoroughly decent, but always faintly bemused in front of television cameras and – by implication – in the face of the modern world.

Home in fact did a remarkably good job of restoring the Conservatives' stability in his year in office. His guileless sincerity played quite well with the public against Wilson's media-savvy sharpness and pushiness. But with the economy performing poorly – the deficit in the balance of trade widening unsustainably and output stagnant – it was always unlikely that the Tories would succeed in holding on to power.

Wilson had promised to forge a new Britain in the "white heat" of a scientific revolution. In practice, little came of this, despite the creation of a Ministry of Technology headed by trade unionist Frank Cousins. Economic planning was another watchword, yet Labour's approach to Britain's economic problems was not essentially different from that of their predecessors. The new government sought to persuade workers to limit wage claims and foreign financiers – dubbed by Wilson the "gnomes of Zurich" – to keep their money in Britain.

Despite the absence of striking novelty, the Wilson government on the whole displayed an energy and panache that impressed voters. In 1966, Wilson became the first Labour Prime Minister to increase his majority in a general election.

POP TURNS TO OP

In October 1964, the term Op Art was coined for the works of painters such as Britain's Bridget Riley, which used bold abstract patterns to create an unsettling illusion of depth and movement. The coinage was a direct reference to Pop Art, until then by far the trendiest artistic movement of the 1960s.

In Britain both Pop and Op Art belonged to a broad tendency for artists to become less solemn and more involved in popular culture and fashion. In a previous generation "serious" writers, painters and composers – whether full of angst and alienation like artist Francis Bacon or high-minded like poet T S Eliot – had been seen as standing in stark opposition to the triviality of commercial culture. Now, in the words of Pop Art painter Richard Hamilton, art aspired to be "transient, expendable, low-cost, mass-produced, young, witty, sexy, gimmicky, glamorous".

Riley's black-and-white Op Art designs were almost immediately taken up by fashion designers such as Mary Quant for clothes and accessories. Pop Art painters such as Hamilton and Peter Blake went on to design album covers for pop groups. The fundamental distinction between "high" and "low" culture had broken down.

▲ Bridget Riley was a leading figure in "Op Art", which relied on abstract patterns and forms to create a sense of depth and movement.

- The Race Relations Act bans discrimination in public places and establishes the Race Relations Board
- The government implements wage and price controls in an attempt to improve the worsening trade deficit
- The Greater London Council (GLC) replaces the London County Council
- Oil is found in the North Sea
- The death penalty is abolished
- The government asks all local authorities to move towards comprehensive schools for secondary education
- The Universities of Kent, Warwick and Ulster are founded
- Britain accepts the jurisdiction of the European Court of Human Rights
- The Confederation of British Industry (CBI) is founded
- Elizabeth Lane is the first woman to sit as a High Court judge
- Cheap package holidays to Greece and Spain are increasingly popular
- British films this year include Richard Lester's *The Knack … and How to Get It*, John Schlesinger's *Darling*, David Lean's *Doctor Zhivago*, Sidney Furie's *The Ipcress File* and Roman Polanski's *Repulsion*
- Mary Whitehouse founds the National Viewers' and Listeners' Association
- The BBC television programme *The War Game*, showing the effects of nuclear war, is not broadcast because it is considered too disturbing

CHURCHILL MEETS HIS MAKER

▲ **Winston Churchill received the first state funeral for a non-royal since the Duke of Wellington in 1852.**

Sir Winston Churchill, Britain's pugnacious leader during the Second World War, died of a stroke at his London home, 28 Hyde Park Gate, on January 24, 1965. He was 90.

The son of a raffish English aristocrat, Lord Randolph Churchill, and American heiress Jennie Jerome, Sir Winston fought in imperial wars in Sudan, India and South Africa before entering politics in 1900.

He was a member of the reforming Liberal government before 1914, but later reverted to his father's Toryism. Becoming Prime Minister in 1940, in the darkest days of the war, he scorned defeatism and inspired resistance to Hitler with his lofty rhetoric. Churchill was also a prolific author, winning the Nobel Prize for Literature in 1953.

Elizabeth II had long made known her wish that Churchill should be honoured with a state funeral – the first accorded to a subject since the death of the Duke of Wellington in 1852. Sir Winston's body lay in state in Westminster Hall for three days, during which time over 300,000 people filed past to pay their last respects. The funeral was held on January 30. Watched by a crowd of thousands that lined the streets and by millions on television, the coffin was carried on a gun carriage to St Paul's Cathedral. After the service, it was ferried by barge down the Thames to Waterloo station, and carried by train to Oxfordshire. Churchill had asked to be buried alongside his parents in Bladon churchyard, near Blenheim Palace where he had been born.

Many commentators at the time attributed the emotional response to Churchill's death to a mourning for Britain's lost Empire. Most people, however, were almost certainly mourning the passing of a remarkable individual.

One of Churchill's own comments on his death, delivered on his 75th birthday, encapsulated the humour and courage that made him so well loved: "I am ready to meet my Maker," he quipped. "Whether my Maker is ready for the great ordeal of meeting me is another matter."

MODERNIZING BRITAIN

In May 1965 the British government made a statement of intent that the country would eventually switch to the metric system. With a typical British sense of compromise, however, the change would only be made gradually and both metric and imperial systems would coexist for many years.

Going metric was in line with Labour's commitment, elected in 1964, to modernization and technological progress.

The Labour Prime Minister Harold Wilson had spoken of a new Britain being forged "in the white heat of the technological revolution". The government was introducing a "planned economy". This was considered a scientific step forward from the old-fashioned laissez-faire economics of the Conservatives. It would also endow the Concorde supersonic airliner project with a high profile.

Furthermore, adopting the metric system was also an acknowledgement that Britain's future lay in forging closer links with Europe – still an intention despite the fact that British membership of the European Common Market had been vetoed by the French President Charles de Gaulle in 1963.

▲ **British Prime Minister Harold Wilson; his Labour government was dedicated to the "white heat" of technological progress.**

RHODESIA DECLARES UDI

Britain's withdrawal from its African colonies in the late 1950s and early 1960s was generally a smooth process, involving a polite handover to a friendly black African government content to maintain a special relationship with the former colonial power within the Commonwealth.

In 1963, the British-ruled Central African Federation, comprising Northern and Southern Rhodesia and Nyasaland, was dissolved into its component parts. The following year, Northern Rhodesia became independent as Zambia and Nyasaland as Malawi. However, in Southern Rhodesia, a smooth transition to independence was blocked by resistance from its white settlers.

Southern Rhodesia had a white population of 220,000. Although they were far outnumbered by the approximately 4 million black Africans, they had put down roots and regarded the country as theirs. In a sense, the country *was* theirs since they owned all the best land and were used to exercising a monopoly of political power under vague British tutelage.

Many whites were profoundly apprehensive at the prospect of coming under the rule of a black government, as would happen if Britain organized independence under a democratic constitution.

In 1961, a former Second World War RAF fighter pilot, Ian Smith, born and bred in Rhodesia, created the Rhodesian Front. Its programme was to resist the imposition of black majority rule. To the astonishment of the colony's moderate political establishment, Smith's extremist organization triumphed in the elections of 1963.

During lengthy negotiations, the British insisted that a large

▲ **Rhodesia's Prime Minister Ian Smith declared unilateral independence from Britain rather than accept black majority rule.**

measure of democracy must be a necessary precondition for granting independence. In April 1964, Smith became the colony's Prime Minister, and made clear his readiness to declare independence himself if the British would not back down. In a referendum that was held in Southern Rhodesia the following November, the white population wholeheartedly backed Smith's stance.

The election of a Labour government in Britain, somewhat more resolutely committed to the principle of "One Man One Vote" than its Tory predecessors, made the failure of negotiations ultimately inevitable.

On November 11, 1965, Smith made a Unilateral Declaration of Independence (UDI). The British government responded by denouncing Smith and his followers as rebels, but quickly decided against attempting military action to regain control of the colony. Instead, economic sanctions were imposed, which British Prime Minister Harold Wilson fondly prophesied would bring down the Smith regime in weeks. However, since Rhodesia's neighbours, white-ruled South Africa and the Portuguese colonies of Mozambique and Angola, supported UDI, sanctions were ineffectual. They were, in any case, covertly evaded by major multinational corporations, including oil companies. As the collapse of the Rhodesian regime failed to materialize, the British government made desperate efforts to lure Smith into renouncing UDI.

In December 1966, Wilson met Smith for talks on board a British warship, the *Tiger*; another meeting followed in 1968. Although Britain was now prepared to accept the token presence of a few black Africans in the Rhodesian government as a sufficient concession to the principle of majority rule, Rhodesia refused to budge.

Smith used draconian emergency powers to suppress any political opposition among the black majority. Consequently, in the years that followed, the white population of Rhodesia, as it was now called, enjoyed prosperity and security.

It was not until 1975 when Portuguese rule collapsed in Mozambique and Angola that military pressure from black guerrillas would begin to undermine the UDI regime.

- Edward Bond's play *Saved*, in which a baby is stoned to death, opens at the Royal Court Theatre despite being banned by the Lord Chamberlain
- Mini-skirts come into fashion
- Songs of the year include "It's Not Unusual" by Tom Jones, "Help" and "Yesterday" by the Beatles and "Satisfaction" by the Rolling Stones
- A new aviary at London Zoo, designed by Lord Snowdon, opens

JANUARY
- Stanley Matthews is the first footballer to be knighted
- Deaths of statesman Sir Winston Churchill and poet T S Eliot

FEBRUARY
- The Gambia gains independence from Britain
- Goldie the eagle temporarily escapes from London Zoo

MARCH
- 26-year-old Liberal David Steel wins a by-election, becoming Britain's youngest MP
- Death of Labour politician Herbert Morrison

APRIL
- The Greater London Council (GLC) comes into existence
- Julie Andrews wins the Best Actress Oscar for her part in the film *Mary Poppins*
- In a deflationary Budget, Chancellor of the Exchequer James Callaghan introduces a 30 per cent capital gains tax
- The TSR-2 supersonic military aircraft project is cancelled as too expensive

MOORS MURDERS SHOCK BRITAIN

MAY

- Manchester United win the Football League championship and Liverpool win the FA Cup; Leeds United are runners-up in both competitions
- The Rhodesian Front Party under Ian Smith wins general election in Southern Rhodesia
- A memorial to assassinated President John F Kennedy is dedicated at Runnymede
- Death of aircraft designer Geoffrey de Havilland

JUNE

- The four Beatles are awarded MBEs; some holders of the honour return their insignia in protest

JULY

- University lecturer Gerald Brooke is jailed for espionage in the Soviet Union
- Conservative Party leader Sir Alec Douglas-Home resigns and is replaced by Edward Heath, who is the first Tory leader elected by fellow MPs
- Death of former light-heavyweight boxing world champion Freddie Mills

AUGUST

- Cigarette advertisements are banned from British television
- Scottish driver Jim Clark wins the world motor racing championship ahead of Graham Hill and Jackie Stewart
- A government White Paper proposes limiting immigration from the "New Commonwealth" to 8,500 a year
- Photographer David Bailey marries actress Catherine Deneuve

▲ Ian Brady was influenced by authors such as the Marquis de Sade, viewing his sadistic murders as the acts of a superior being.

The serial killings known as the "Moors murders" shocked the British public more than any other crime of the twentieth century. The oldest of the five known victims was 17 and the youngest, Lesley Ann Downey, only ten years old.

The perpetrators were 27-year-old Ian Brady and his lover, 23-year-old Myra Hindley. Police searched their Manchester home on October 7, 1965, after Hindley's brother-in-law, David Smith, reported witnessing a murder there. In one of the bedrooms they found the body of 17-year-old Edward Evans, who had been killed the previous day with an axe.

Smith told the police that the couple had bragged of burying their victims on Saddleworth Moor. A grim search of the moor over the following fortnight turned up the bodies of Downey and a 12-year-old boy, John Kilbride.

Downey had gone missing in December 1964, Kilbride in November 1963. Police also found a left-luggage ticket among Hindley's possessions that led them to a suitcase containing nude photos of Downey and a harrowing tape-recording of her being tortured before she was killed. The police were convinced that the couple were also responsible for the disappearances of 16-year-old Pauline Reade in July 1963 and 12-year-old Keith Bennett in June 1964, but they were not charged with these murders because of lack of positive evidence.

Brady and Hindley protested their innocence, cynically attempting to pin responsibility for the crimes upon Smith. At their trial in Chester in April 1966, however, both were found guilty – Brady of all three killings and Hindley of two. As the death penalty had been abolished the previous year, they were jailed for life, with a recommendation that they serve at least 30 years.

The murders provided ample material for moralists who believed that something was going seriously wrong with British society in the 1960s. Brady, a product of the Glaswegian slums, had developed an ideology of crime based on his reading of authors hostile to the "bourgeois" morality of straight society, including the Marquis de Sade, whose works had become available through the relaxation of censorship. He and Hindley saw themselves as superior individuals who did what others only fantasized about. For them, murder was the "supreme pleasure".

An attempt on the back of the case to whip up support for a

▲ Repeatedly denied release from prison, Myra Hindley had served over 30 years for her part in the Moors murders when she died.

reimposition of strict censorship got nowhere. But some people committed to the liberalization of 1960s Britain accepted that the Moors murders posed a dilemma. If you advocated the principle of free expression of desire and fantasy, where could you draw the line? Counter-culture author Jeff Nuttall wrote in 1967: "We had all, at some time, cried 'Yes, yes' to Blake's 'Sooner murder an infant in its cradle than nurse an unacted desire.' Brady did it."

In the 1980s, both Brady and Hindley confessed to involvement in all five murders. Hindley, however, consistently claimed that her role had been secondary and up to her death in 2002 campaigned unsuccessfully to be released. The only release Brady sought was the right to starve himself to death, which has been continuously denied.

WHITEHOUSE CAMPAIGNS TO CLEAN-UP TELEVISION

In the view of traditionalists, 1960s Britain was drowning in a flood of filth peddled by proponents of "permissiveness". No organization was more the target of their wrath than BBC, which under director-general Sir Hugh Carlton Greene had been transformed from a bastion of the establishment into a showcase for cultural innovation. To moral campaigner Mary Whitehouse, Greene and his cohorts had turned television into a destructive medium threatening the moral collapse of the nation.

By 1965, when she founded the National Viewers' and Listeners' Association, Whitehouse was already a household name. Ironically, like her fellow scourge of permissiveness, journalist Malcolm Muggeridge, she proved to be a perfect television

personality, with her practised impersonation of a "normal housewife". There is no doubt that her concerns about sex and bad language were widely shared – she obtained 5 million signatures for a petition to clean-up television.

▲ Mary Whitehouse's 35-year campaign to clean up television proved ultimately ineffective, as one taboo after another was broken.

The programmes Whitehouse objected to were very tame by later standards. There were Ken Russell dramatized documentaries, for example, which created eroticism out of hints at naked flesh, but full-frontal nudity was still unthinkable on television. So was the use of the expletive "fuck" – a taboo broken just once, to general consternation, by critic Kenneth Tynan on a late-night chat show.

In Johnny Speight's comedy series *Till Death Us Do Part*, which Whitehouse loathed, the bigoted Alf Garnett declared himself one of her fans, with the priceless line: "She's concerned for the bleedin' moral fibre of the nation!" Despite Whitehouse's ability to muster popular support, she had no more chance of turning back the tide than Canute.

RICHARD DIMBLEBY DIES

On December 22, 1965, broadcaster Richard Dimbleby died of cancer, aged 52. He had played a founding role in British radio and television journalism, setting the standard by which all those who followed him would be judged.

Dimbleby joined BBC radio in 1936 and at the outbreak of the Second World War became the corporation's first war correspondent. His dispatches from the frontline captured the harsh reality of the conflict – he was the first reporter to broadcast from the death camp at Belsen.

After the war he switched to television, then still in its infancy. His commentary on the coronation in 1953 established him as the voice of state occasions, which he

covered up to the funeral of Sir Winston Churchill in January 1965. He also hosted the influential current affairs programme *Panorama* from 1955.

Dimbleby founded a broadcasting dynasty – his sons Jonathan and David, in their turn, also becoming leading current affairs presenters.

▲ Richard Dimbleby began his career during the Second World War, and became one of the most respected voices in television journalism.

1966

In April 1966, the cover story of the American news magazine *Time* was devoted to a celebration of "Swinging London". According to a *Time* journalist, "In this century every decade has its city ... and for the Sixties that city is London." As usual with such "discoveries" by mass-market journalism, the story was well behind the march of events. But it served to consecrate the newly established international reputation of London – and Britain as a whole – as a paradise of permissive sexuality and a powerhouse of popular culture.

The reinvention of Britain was an extraordinary triumph of style over substance. In many ways, the state of the nation was dire. The economy was fixed in permanent crisis and the decline of Britain as a world power in the postimperial era was approaching its nadir. Yet even symbols of past glory could be exploited ironically to promote the country's new youthful image. Union Jacks decorated everything from carrier bags to knickers. Thanks to the internationally successful television series *The Avengers*, the bowler hat and brolly, rapidly disappearing from the City of London, were rebranded as attributes of a trendy secret agent.

To foreigners, Britain in the mid-1960s meant above all pop music. There seemed no end to the original and exciting sounds that British youth could invent – much of the innovation stemming from graduates of art colleges, which were, in the words of musician George Melly, "a refuge for the bright but unacademic, the talented, the nonconformist ... all those who didn't know what they

▲ Carnaby Street became the headquarters of a British cultural renaissance, at the very core of "Swinging London".

wanted but knew it wasn't a nine-till-five job". Art school products included John Lennon, Eric Burdon (Animals), Pete Townshend (The Who), Keith Richard (Rolling Stones) and Eric Clapton (Yardbirds and Cream).

Apart from music, to foreigners Britain meant actors, fashion models and photographers. Fashion designer Mary Quant had defied the world of haute couture in the first half of the 1960s, imposing youth fashions and putting the mini-skirt on the mass market, leaving traditionally

fashionable Paris struggling to catch up. In hairstyles Vidal Sassoon headed the pack, inventing the "unisex" hair salon and many of the most striking cuts of the time, such as the "bob". The most talked-of model of the first half of the Sixties was Jean Shrimpton ("the Shrimp"), fashionably nonvoluptuous.

What foreigners could not see was the grimmer reality of British life in the early 1960s that gave urgency and edge to the drive for freedom and fun. Despite the progress of the consumer society,

most young people in Britain grew up in dreary surroundings, with limited prospects. It was a world in need of colour and life. Even outside the pockets of genuine poverty that persisted, average homes had few consumer durables. Only one in three had a refrigerator and one in five a telephone. The majority of young people – being workingclass – had to assert themselves not only against adults and their "old-fashioned" values, but also against a system that automatically consigned them to the bottom of the social pile.

The worlds of pop music and fashion opened up a potential road of escape for young working-class individuals who were talented and ruthless enough to seize their opportunities. Photographer David Bailey, who himself exemplified this category, released a set of 30 portraits called a "Box of Pin Ups", which was described as "making a statement about London life in 1965" with photographs of those who had "gone all out for the immediate rewards of success: quick money, quick fame, quick sex – a brave thing to do". Although the style and manners of the day were resolutely "classless" – at Bailey's wedding to actress Catherine Deneuve jeans were *de rigueur* – strict hierarchies of money, celebrity and even old-fashioned class still operated. Alongside the working-class upstarts, a remarkable number of the leading players in Swinging Britain were products of good public schools who had the social connections and the cash to make things happen.

The stars of Swinging London represented a small clique of the successful and therefore privileged, but the changes associated with music and fashion were a widespread phenomenon that to some degree involved the majority of the young. Mary Quant clothes were mass-market. Mini-skirts were a near-universal style and so was possession of a record collection. Hundreds of

▲ Photographer David Bailey and actress Catherine Deneuve after their wedding sealed an alliance between two 1960s cultural icons.

▲ Mary Quant, designer of the mini-skirt, provided a female mass-market with a very appealing sense of style and liberation.

thousands experienced their own version of liberation. One London girl later remembered how, banned by her parents from listening to the Rolling Stones, riding on the back of scooters and being alone with a boyfriend, she did all three in one evening and "screwed him in his house before going home". It was the spirit of the times.

The Swinging London of the first half of the 1960s was materialistic, modernistic, sharp and predatory, fuelled by amphetamine pills. By 1966, though, a shift in style was becoming very evident. Carnaby Street, where Mods had come to buy their sharp suits, was already well on the way to transformation into a tourist attraction. The tide of fashion had moved on to shops such as Biba and Granny Takes a Trip where "hippie" clothes were taking shape. Cannabis and LSD were replacing amphetamines on the drug scene. The "underground" bands such as Pink Floyd and Soft Machine made their first appearance. Swinging London's trendiness would be replaced by that of "the Summer of Love".

- *Time* magazine declares London the "swinging city" of the Sixties
- Unemployment rises above half a million
- The first British credit card, Barclaycard, is introduced
- The Post Office begins introduction of postcodes
- The football World Cup finals are staged in England and won by the home nation
- Canadian press magnate Lord Thomson buys *The Times*
- "Underground" magazine *International Times (IT)* is launched
- Hawker-Siddeley unveils the Harrier, the world's first vertical take-off jet
- Centre Point skyscraper is completed in London's West End
- Ultra-thin model Twiggy is declared the "face of 1966"
- Books published this year include *Wide Sargasso Sea* by Jean Rhys, *The Magus* by John Fowles and *Death of a Naturalist* by Seamus Heaney
- British films this year include Lewis Gilbert's *Alfie*, Silvio Narizzano's *Georgy Girl*, Michael Anderson's *The Quiller Memorandum* and Fred Zinnemann's *A Man for All Seasons*
- *Till Death Us Do Part* and *Thunderbirds* debut on television
- BBC television drama *Cathy Come Home* provokes an outcry over homelessness
- Joe Orton's play *Loot* opens in London

PACKAGE TOURS TAKE OFF

▲ **Freddy Laker set up Britain's first budget airline, an experiment that was doomed to failure in the face of resistance by mainstream operators.**

On February 8, 1966, Freddie Laker, managing director of British United Airways, announced that he was setting up his own budget airline, Laker Airways. As a bright entrepreneur, Laker could see that the future lay with cheap flights.

The British were taking to foreign holidays on a scale never before seen. In the 1950s holidays abroad had still attracted only the educated classes. In 1951 only around one in 14 of Britons' holidays was spent abroad, and even in 1961 the figure was only one in nine. The vast majority of British people had never flown and of those who had, most had done so during military service.

From around 1963, however, the habit of taking cheap "package" holidays by air began to make inroads into the working classes, sick of dismal English weather and bad-tempered boarding-house landladies. Spain – sunny and cheap – was the destination of choice.

There was no sudden revolution. By 1971 Britons still spent five holidays in their home country for every one holiday abroad. But the trend was set and Laker was rewarded for his far-sightedness with a fortune and status as the country's most popular entrepreneur.

WILSON WINS AGAIN

In the general election held on March 31, 1966, Harold Wilson led Labour to a striking victory over the Conservatives, winning what the Prime Minister termed "a clear mandate", after 18 months governing with a wafer-thin majority in parliament.

Labour won 363 seats against 253 for the Conservatives and 12 for the Liberals. The Tories had hoped for better under their new leader, Edward Heath. But the Wilson government had clearly impressed many voters with its energy and confidence, even if a solution to Britain's endemic economic crisis remained elusive.

The Labour-dominated parliament was to push ahead with important social reforms, including the legalization of abortion and the decriminalization of homosexual relations between consenting adults. The government also embarked on major cuts in Britain's overseas defence commitments, another decisive step in the retreat from empire. But its efforts to cope with economic pressures brought confrontation with groups of workers, headed either by shop stewards or trade union leaders, who resisted attempts to limit wage rises. One of the first crises after the election was a strike by merchant seamen.

Wilson's long-term aim was to establish Labour as the "natural party of government" – since it theoretically represented the interests of the majority of the population against the privileged minority. In this he was to fail, despite eventually winning four out of the five elections he contested as party leader.

▲ **Wilson's general election victory was the first time an incumbent Labour government had increased its parliamentary majority.**

DYLAN'S ELECTRIC TOUR

▲ **Many of Dylan's fans reacted angrily when the singer started using electric guitars, an act they regarded as a betrayal of his roots.**

American singer-songwriter Bob Dylan's 1966 tour of Britain is a music legend because of the hostility the performer faced from his audiences.

Born Robert Zimmerman, Dylan came to prominence in the early 1960s as the unique voice of self-righteous radical protest. With his acoustic guitar, harmonica and edgily subversive lyrics, he characterized everything that folk fans – mostly students – thought distinguished their music from "mindless" commercial pop.

But by 1965, Dylan had come to feel that the new versions of songs that he had written or performed, currently being played by pop groups such as the Animals ("House of the Rising Sun") sounded far more exciting than the acoustic originals. After one half-rock album, *Bringing It All Back Home*, he went fully electric with the single "Like a Rolling Stone" and the album *Highway 61 Revisited*.

Deaf to the radical inventiveness of Dylan's folk-rock fusion, traditional folk music fans felt betrayed. At the Albert Hall, London, in May 1966, much of the audience walked out as soon as the electric guitars went into action in the second-half set. Travelling around the country, Dylan was booed and heckled with depressing regularity. At the Manchester Free Trade Hall, one disillusioned fan shouted "Judas!", to which the singer called back "You're a liar!", before heading into a superb rendition of "Like a Rolling Stone".

The controversial tour illustrated the intensity with which musical fashions were followed in Britain in the constant flux of Sixties popular culture. While folk fans denounced Dylan, more young people turned to his music than ever before. "Like a Rolling Stone" far surpassed any of Dylan's acoustic numbers in popularity. In a wider cultural perspective, the contrast between CND-supporting folk fans and pop-consuming scooter-riders was rapidly sliding into oblivion.

CAINE IS HIT AS ALFIE

One of the hit movies of 1966 was *Alfie*, starring young British actor Michael Caine in the title role. It was inspired casting, for both Caine and Alfie were, in their slightly different ways, representative figures of British Sixties manhood.

As the son of a market porter and a cleaning lady, Caine was a working-class boy made good, With his "classless" accent and blend of roughness and sensitivity, he was an ideal type for the times, in the same vein as photographer David Bailey or fellow actor Terence Stamp.

The character Alfie, created by author Bill Naughton, is also working class, though instead of working in a factory or mine he lives by his wits off the surplus cash floating around – for example, as a chauffeur or a street photographer.

Above all, he is the predatory male who plagued the women of the liberated Sixties. He does not beat women up or rape them, but he enjoys the sexual pleasures they have to offer with an absolute resistance to commitment or emotional engagement.

Alfie was a mirror in which the emerging "permissive society" could see its reflection. Implicitly hostile to traditional morality, the film nonetheless recognized an emotional emptiness at the core of the fun and the freedom that were changing the image of Britain.

▲ **Michael Caine's portrayal of rough diamond Alfie in the eponymous film placed a mirror to the moral vacuum embodied in the "permissive society".**

- Peter Brook stages his antiwar play *US* in which actors with bags on their heads stumble into the audience
- American singer Bob Dylan faces abuse at British venues for singing with an electric band
- The Beatles release their innovative album *Revolver*
- Songs of the year include the Beatles' "Eleanor Rigby", the Kinks' "Sunny Afternoon" and Tom Jones's "Green Green Grass of Home"

JANUARY
- At the Commonwealth Conference, Prime Minister Harold Wilson rejects military action against Rhodesia and suggests economic sanctions may end the rebellion in "weeks rather than months"

MARCH
- John Lennon speculates that The Beatles are more popular than Christ
- Race horse Arkle wins the Cheltenham Gold Cup for the third consecutive year
- The Jules Rimet trophy – the football World Cup – is stolen in London but found by dog Pickles
- Labour increases its majority at the general election

MAY
- The Budget introduces a selective employment tax, which penalizes employment in service industries in favour of manufacturing

APRIL
- First scheduled hovercraft service across the English Channel begins
- Death of author Evelyn Waugh

1966

ENGLAND WINS THE WORLD CUP

▲ One of the great "gentlemen" of British football, the late Bobby Moore celebrates the greatest day in English football.

In July 1966, the football World Cup finals were held in England for the first, and so far only, time. The event had an inauspicious prelude in March, when the Jules Rimet trophy – the World Cup itself – was stolen from an exhibition in Westminster Hall. It was fortunately found in a London garden by an inquisitive dog called Pickles.

The tournament itself was marred by some outrageous foul play and violence. Pelé, the world's most famous footballer, was kicked out of the competition, and after England's victory over Argentina in a fierce quarter-final match, manager Alf Ramsey acrimoniously described the Argentinians as "animals".

Portugal, with their star striker Eusebio, was one of the best teams in the finals. So, more surprisingly, were North Korea, who beat Italy and went 3–0 up against Portugal, only to lose 5–3. But England appeared increasingly strong as the tournament progressed. By the time they beat Portugal 2–1 in the semi-finals, the players, such as Bobby Charlton, Geoff Hurst, Alan Ball, Martin Peters and captain Bobby Moore, were looking the equal of any in the world.

The final took place at Wembley on July 30. England's opponents were West Germany, a team hinged around the formidable Franz Beckenbauer. Germany scored first, but goals from Geoff Hurst and Martin Peters seemed to have given England victory when, with seconds to go to the final whistle, Germany equalized.

Early in extra time, a shot from Hurst hit the underside of the crossbar and appeared to bounce out of the goal. The Russian linesman, however, ruled that the ball had crossed the line and England were ahead. At the end of extra time, with spectators running on to the pitch and BBC commentator Kenneth Wolstenholme intoning "They think it's all over ...", Hurst completed his hat-trick to leave England 4–2 winners.

▲ Was it or wasn't it? Geoff Hurst's shot easily beat the German goalkeeper, but some still believe the ball did not fully cross the line.

DISASTER IN ABERFAN

One of Britain's worst peacetime disasters occurred at the Welsh mining village of Aberfan on October 21, 1966. It was 9.15 am and the children at the village's Pant Glas Junior and Infants School were just settling down to lessons after morning assembly – at which they had sung "All Things Bright and Beautiful" – when they heard a sound like thunder and felt the ground begin to shake.

Like many Welsh pit villages, Aberfan was dominated by a tip of waste from the nearby colliery. Heavy rain had destabilized the tip, and that morning it slid on to the village in a fatal avalanche. The school lay full in its path and within seconds it was buried under a tide of black slurry.

Local people, including miners from the local Merthyr Vale colliery, rushed to the scene. Reverend Kenneth Hayes, whose son was among the victims, later recalled: "I went up the road and turned the bend. I could see nothing but a mountain of black waste."

Joined by the emergency services, people frantically began trying to dig children out. But there were only five survivors. In total, 116 children and 28 adults lost their lives. The impact was especially extreme in such a self-contained, tight-knit community. The few surviving children led isolated lives – one poignantly pointed out that there were no longer enough local children even to play a game of football.

Local people felt particular bitterness against the National Coal Board, which adamantly avoided taking responsibility for the tragedy – the tip had been sited on top of a natural spring.

▲ More than 100 children lost their lives when a slag heap in the Welsh mining village of Aberfan collapsed following heavy rain.

The disaster was a tragic reminder of the harsh reality of life in Britain's declining industrial areas in the 1960s. It was a life far removed from the superficial glitter and glamour of "Swinging London". In Aberfan, the accumulated waste of Britain's industrial past had buried the generation of the future.

SPY GEORGE BLAKE ESCAPES FROM PRISON

On October 22, 1966, Soviet double-agent George Blake escaped from Wormwood Scrubs prison, where he was serving the sixth year of a sentence for espionage. The escape, made in amateurish fashion using a rope ladder with knitting needles as rungs, was a profound embarrassment to the British authorities.

Born in the Netherlands, Blake had become an officer in the British Secret Intelligence Service (SIS). During the Korean War, he was taken prisoner by the North Koreans. He emerged from captivity a committed communist. Returning to work for SIS, he acted as a double-agent on behalf of the Soviet Union, causing untold damage to Western intelligence operations in Berlin. Unmasked in 1959, two years later he was given an unprecedented 42-year sentence.

Blake's escape was organized by an unlikely trio he encountered in prison: Sean Bourke, Michael Randle and Pat Pottle. Bourke was an IRA man serving time for a bombing attempt. Pottle and Randle were members of the antinuclear Committee of 100, jailed for conspiring to infiltrate a US military base. Released from prison at the end of their sentences, they concocted a straightforward plan to spring Blake.

The Soviet spy broke out of his cell at night. His accomplices parked a getaway car outside the prison and threw the rope ladder over the outer wall. Although Blake broke his wrist coming down to the ground, they were able to drive him away before the alarm was raised.

The authorities had no idea who was behind the escape and thus had little notion where to look for the escapee. He was eventually smuggled out of the country in December. Pottle and Randle concealed him in the bottom of a campervan, which they drove on a family holiday to East Berlin. Once on the communist side of the Berlin Wall, Blake was able to emerge to contact his Soviet handlers.

The escape remained a mystery until Pottle and Randle went public with the story in 1989. When they were taken to court two years later, a sympathetic jury found them not guilty in defiance of the evidence. Blake was still living in Moscow in the early twentieth century.

▲ Double-agent George Blake had served only five years of a 42-year sentence when he broke out of prison and fled to the Soviet Union.

- Sterling is devalued; a loan from the International Monetary Fund (IMF) shores up Britain's finances
- The Plowden Report on primary schools recommends "child-centred learning"
- The Criminal Justice Act allows majority verdicts and suspended sentences
- Homosexual relations between consenting males over 21 are decriminalized
- Breathalyser tests are introduced to detect drunken drivers
- First cash-dispensing machine introduced in Britain
- Sir Edmund Compton is Britain's first Ombudsman
- The "Summer of Love" sees "Flower Power" styles fashionable
- Francis Chichester completes the first solo circumnavigation of the globe
- Books published this year include *The Naked Ape* by Desmond Morris and *The Third Policeman* by Flann O'Brien
- *The Mersey Sound* poetry anthology popularizes the Liverpool poets Roger McGough, Brian Patten and Adrian Henri
- British films this year include John Schlesinger's *Far From the Madding Crowd* and Joseph Losey's *Accident*
- The plays *Rosencrantz and Guildenstern are Dead* by Tom Stoppard, *The Homecoming* by Harold Pinter and *A Day in the Death of Joe Egg* by Peter Nichols open
- Richard Long's "sculpture" *A Line Made By Walking* introduces the concept of walking as an art form

CAMPBELL KILLED IN BLUEBIRD CRASH

▲ **Donald Campbell's pursuit of land and water speed records led to his untimely death when his Bluebird K7 disintegrated on Coniston Water.**

On January 4, 1967, 45-year-old Donald Campbell was killed when his turbo-jet hydroplane *Bluebird K7* took off at around 480 km/h (300 mph) during an attempt on the world waterspeed record. The boat somersaulted through the air before plunging into Coniston Water. Campbell's last words were: "She's going, she's going. I'm almost on my back ..."

Donald Campbell had emulated his famous father, Sir Malcolm Campbell, in competing for records both on land and water. In 1964 he set a land speed record of 648.7 km/h (403.1 mph) and a water speed record of 444.7 km/h (276.3 mph), becoming the only man to hold both records at the same time. At Lake Coniston, he was attempting to break through the 480 km/h (300 mph) barrier, a feat he would almost certainly have achieved but for the crash.

Bluebird disintegrated on hitting the surface of the lake and divers at the time failed to locate Campbell's remains. His body was not recovered until 2001.

STONES DRUG ARRESTS

On the night of February 12, 1967, police raided a house in Sussex owned by Rolling Stones guitarist Keith Richard. They arrested Richard, Stones lead singer Mick Jagger and art gallery owner Robert Fraser for possession of illegal drugs.

The impression that the police had decided to persecute the Rolling Stones because of their anti-authoritarian posture was confirmed when another member of the band, Brian Jones, was also arrested on a drugs charge after a further raid in May. Tried in late June, Jagger and Richard were sentenced to three months and a year in jail respectively.

The harsh sentences provoked protest from a most unexpected direction. William Rees-Mogg, editor of *The Times*, wrote a leading article headed "Who Breaks a Butterfly on a Wheel?" that denounced the proceedings as a breach of "tolerance and equity". Sensing the drift of opinion, the authorities released the two pending an appeal, which acquitted Richard and gave Jagger a conditional discharge.

The outcome of the trial showed what little chance authoritarians had of achieving a serious crackdown on rebellious youth in Sixties Britain. After the appeal verdict was announced, Jagger was flown off for a televised discussion with a respectful Rees-Mogg and leading churchmen. Pop artist Richard Hamilton produced a series of works based on a news photograph of Jagger and Fraser under arrest, entitled *Swingeing London*, one of which was bought by the Tate Gallery for the nation.

▲ **Mick Jagger and Keith Richards's arrest in a police raid inaugurated a dishonourable tradition of pop stars' brushes with the law over drugs.**

THE WRECK OF THE TORREY CANYON

At Easter 1967, Cornwall was the site of the world's first major oil-tanker disaster.

▲ The crippled oil tanker *Torrey Canyon* leaches tons of oil into the sea off Cornwall, polluting a long stretch of coastline.

On March 19, the tanker *Torrey Canyon*, carrying about 120,000 tons of crude oil, was attempting the difficult passage between Land's End and the Scilly Isles en route to the refinery at Milford Haven in south Wales.

Disaster struck when the tanker hit the Seven Stones reef and stuck fast, with a hole ripped in its hull. Oil began to flood out, carried by currents and the prevailing winds towards the Cornish coast, where it would pollute tourist beaches and destroy marine life.

The first response was to send Royal Naval vessels with thousands of gallons of detergent to spray on the oil slick. But within five days of the original accident the crude oil had spread out to cover approximately 1,800 square km (700 square miles) of ocean and had begun to drift ashore. Worse was to follow, for the wave-battered vessel then began to break up, releasing even more of its liquid cargo.

The British government decided on the radical step of dropping incendiary bombs and napalm on the stricken tanker. The aim was to set fire to the oil remaining in the tanker's hold and burn it off. To the humiliation of the Air Force commanders, in front of large crowds of Easter holidaymakers lining the Cornish cliffs – including Prime Minister Harold Wilson, who always holidayed in the Scillies – the bombers at first failed to hit their stationary target. The bombing was ultimately declared a success, but over 160 km (100 miles) of the Cornish coast had been polluted, requiring a massive clean-up operation.

The *Torrey Canyon* disaster gave fresh impetus to concerns about the environment that were mounting through the 1960s and would lead to the creation of Friends of the Earth in 1970 and Greenpeace the following year.

CHICHESTER SAILS SOLO AROUND THE WORLD

On May 28, 1967, 65-year-old Sir Francis Chichester sailed into Plymouth after a solo voyage around the world. His journey had taken nine months and one day, with a single stop at Sydney, Australia.

Chichester's yacht *Gipsy Moth IV* was escorted into harbour by hundreds of small boats and possibly as many as 250,000 people lined the shore to greet the yachtsman home. After 119 days at sea on the final leg from Sydney, Chichester had to walk with care after setting foot on land, but he was later described by a journalist as "looking as if he had just been away for a weekend". He told a press conference: "What I would like after four months of my own cooking is the best dinner from the best chef in the best surroundings and in the best company."

That July, Chichester was dubbed Sir Francis by Elizabeth II at Greenwich, using Sir Francis Drake's sword. His feat has been equalled or bettered many times since, but no subsequent yachtsman has had such an inspiring impact on the national mood as Chichester.

▲ Chichester's epic solo round-the-world voyage gave rise to comparisons with Britain's maritime achievements under Elizabeth I.

- Britain wins the Eurovision song contest with Sandie Shaw's "Puppet on a String"
- The BBC series *The Forsyte Saga* and ITV's *News At Ten* are first shown
- BBC2 begins limited colour broadcasting
- BBC radio replaces the Light, Home and Third programmes with Radios One, Two, Three and Four
- The Beatles release their first concept album, *Sergeant Pepper's Lonely Hearts Club Band*
- Songs of the year include Procul Harum's "A Whiter Shade of Pale", Donovan's "Mellow Yellow", and the Beatles' "All You Need Is Love", "Strawberry Fields Forever" and "Penny Lane"
- "Underground" magazine *OZ* is launched

JANUARY
- Jeremy Thorpe succeeds Jo Grimond as leader of the Liberal Party
- The British authorities impose a curfew in Aden after riots
- Death of Donald Campbell, attempting to break the water speed record

FEBRUARY
- Keith Richards and Mick Jagger of the Rolling Stones are arrested for alleged possession of drugs

MARCH
- Students stage a sit-in at the London School of Economics (LSE)
- The oil tanker *Torrey Canyon* runs aground off the coast of England

APRIL
- 100–1 outsider Foinavon wins the Grand National
- Nationalists foment unrest and violence in British-ruled Aden
- Labour loses heavily to the Conservatives in local elections

1967

THE SUMMER OF LOVE

The hippie subculture and its vague ideology – the rejection of individualism, work and private property, belief in "peace and love", the taking of hallucinogenic drugs, faith in the wisdom of the East – was imported into Britain from the United States. First developed by drop-outs in the Haight-Ashbury district of San Francisco, from the mid-1960s onwards it was spread by media coverage into an international youth movement.

The key moment for its importation to Britain can probably be dated to June 1965, when the American poet Alan Ginsberg headed a festival of poetry reading at London's Royal Albert Hall. Covered by television news cameras, the event attracted a packed audience. Cannabis was smoked, flowers handed out and poetry – mostly particularly bad – was recited. One line especially emphasized by Ginsberg, to the delight of his listeners, was "Tonite let's all make love in London".

By 1967 "Flower Power" and its attendant drugs culture had established a sufficient following to set the tone for large-scale open-air events. Britain's first pop festival was held at Woburn in August. That summer, London tinkled to the sound of cowbells worn around the neck and the chant of "Hare Krishna" first made itself heard in Oxford Street. Cults flourished, from Transcendental Meditation to druidic Earth-worship. The underground magazines *IT* and *OZ* were sold on the streets, with their novel "psychedelic" imagery. Thousands of young people set off on the overland trail to India, establishing

▲ **Hippies became the missionaries of the counter-culture, rejecting mainstream values in favour of "peace and love".**

outposts of hippiedom in Nepal, Goa and Afghanistan. The more business-minded made fortunes bringing back Indian fabrics or Afghan coats – the entrepreneurial spirit also flourished during the Summer of Love.

In 1967, this counter-culture world was inhabited by only a small minority of British people under 30. Most had not a whiff of marijuana, let alone a taste of an acid tab. Even at the Woburn festival, press photographers had to search around for young people to photograph in hippie regalia smoking dope – the majority were wearing nothing more exotic than jeans and drinking beer.

Most people participated in the Summer of Love – if at all – through media images, particularly of pop stars. George Melley cynically described the whole pop world as "dressing like mad prophets, and talking about love and vibrations and flying saucers".

With their long hair, droopy moustaches, granny glasses and experimentation with drugs, the Beatles were the world's most powerful advertisement for alternative style and culture. For the launch of their single "All You Need is Love" in June, they organized an international television link-up in the hope of spreading the benign but woolly philosophy of their guru, the Maharishi Mahesh Yogi.

The mass marketing of the Summer of Love inevitably diluted its message near to vanishing point. The record that represented the West Coast hippie scene to most of the world was Scott Mackenzie's dreamy "If You're Going to San Francisco (Be Sure to Wear Some Flowers in Your Hair)". The musical *Hair*, which opened off Broadway in October, was to show again how marketable an unthreatening version of the hippie vision could be.

The mood of the Summer of Love had its aesthetic successes, such as Procul Harum's Bach-based "Whiter Shade of Pale" and the first emergence of psychedelic band Pink Floyd. But it was the Beatles, as usual, who seemed to express its quintessence in the experimental single "Strawberry Fields" (accompanied by arguably the first pop video) and the first concept album, *Sergeant Pepper's Lonely Hearts Club Band*, with its celebrated cover designed by Pop artist Peter Blake and his wife. But the Summer of Love was also when the Beatles fairy story began to crack up. In August, while the Beatles were meditating with the Maharishi in Wales, their manager, Brian Epstein, died of an overdose. At the end of the year, their Christmas television film *Magical Mystery Tour* flopped.

In the United States, the issue of Vietnam gave the slogan "Make Love Not War" a real potency.

Many young people there saw a crossover between radical politics and hippie lifestyles. But in Britain the political side was restricted largely to a campaign to legalize cannabis. In July 1967 Paul McCartney organized a "Legalize Pot" rally in Hyde Park. He also paid for an advertisement in *The Times*, which declared the law against marijuana "immoral in principle and unworkable in practice". Signatories of the ad included not only the four Beatles and other predictable "alternative culture" figures, but MPs Tom Driberg and Brian Walden, novelist Graham Greene and Nobel Prize-winning scientist Francis Crick. It had no practical effect.

If the move to legalize the drug failed, it was largely because the authorities found it such a useful ground for harassment of cultural subversives such as the "underground" press. On the whole, though, in Britain conflict between the hippie-influenced counter-culture and the authorities

▲ Psychedelic band Pink Floyd enjoyed success in the late 1960s, tapping into a market that rejected conventional music.

▼ The Beatles join a meditation group under the Maharishi Mahesh Yogi, reflecting an interest in eastern philosophy in the 1960s.

never approached the extremes that were to occur in the United States. Although there were high-profile police raids and arrests, mostly based on breach of drug legislation or laws on pornography, the courts rarely followed through with substantial sentences. Nor did the behaviour of British members of the counter-culture reach the extremes seen in the communes of the American West Coast, breeding ground for serial killer Charles Manson and his "Family". In Britain, rebellious youth was never taken entirely seriously, even by itself.

The essentials of the Summer of Love – smoking dope, long hair, experiments in communal living and free love – expanded to involve a far larger proportion of young Britons over the following years. It reached its quantitative peak in the first half of the 1970s. But by that time media interest had moved on in search of to other novelties to pulicize.

GAY PLAYWRIGHT MURDERED

▲ Joe Orton (right) became one of Britain's most fashionable playwrights in the 1960s. He died dramatically at the hands of his lover, Keith Halliwell.

On the night of August 8, 1967, Joe Orton, one of England's most fashionable playwrights, was beaten to death with a hammer in his Islington flat. The murderer was Orton's long-term lover Kenneth Halliwell, who committed suicide with an overdose of pills after the killing.

Born in Leicester in 1933, Orton was another of the sons of the working class who made good in the Sixties. He met Halliwell when both were students at RADA in the early 1950s. Their joint creative efforts were unsuccessful for a decade, culminating in their imprisonment for subversive defacing of library books in 1962.

Orton's fortunes turned when his play *Entertaining Mr Sloane* was staged in May 1964. Its offbeat wit, casual violence and disturbing take on sexual relations provoked scandal as well as praise, but the playwright had made his mark. His next play, *Loot*, had a chequered history before its final version, premiered in London in September 1966, was received with rave reviews. A black farce, it caricatures the police in the person of the egregious Inspector Truscott and pours epigrammatic scorn upon every respected human sentiment. It made Orton the height of fashion and negotiations were opened for him to write a screenplay for the Beatles.

But Orton's fame led to the disintegration of his already shaky relationship with Halliwell. As his posthumously published diaries revealed, Orton was an aggressively promiscuous homosexual. To the tensions generated by this behaviour was added the increasing exclusion of Halliwell from Orton's burgeoning social life. Halliwell was in any case a disturbed individual. As a child, he had seen his mother die of a wasp sting and in his teens he found his father dead with his head in a gas oven. Feeling sidelined in every way from Orton's life, he resorted to murder and suicide.

THE POUND IN YOUR POCKET

On November 18, 1967, sterling was officially devalued by 14.3 per cent, falling from an exchange rate of $US2.80 to $US2.40. It was an overwhelming blow to the political prestige of Prime Minister Harold Wilson's Labour government, which had struggled to maintain sterling's value ever since taking office in October 1964.

In an effort to reassure the British public, Wilson told them in a television broadcast: "It does not mean, of course, that the pound here in Britain, in your pocket or purse or in your bank, has been devalued."

The Labour government had inherited a massive balance of payments crisis from its Conservative predecessors, Britain's exports being wholly inadequate to finance its imports. It was this endlessly debated "trade gap" that put downward pressure on sterling, officially held at the same level against the dollar since the aftermath of the Second World War.

In 1966, faced with around 5 per cent inflation and unemployment rising to almost half a million – regarded as crisis levels at the time – the government tried to impose a freeze on wages, prices and profits. The policy was intended, among other things, to lower

▲ Faced with rising unemployment and inflation, Wilson's government was forced into a politically humiliating devaluation of sterling.

imports by reducing spending power and boost exports by cutting costs. But it had only a limited effect. Trade union leaders endorsed the policy, but shop stewards opposed every attempt to block wage rises and there was a rash of unofficial strikes.

Devaluation had always been an alternative policy advocated by some Labour politicians as the quickest and most painless way of making British goods more competitive abroad. But there was no disguising the fact that it had been resorted to under duress after pressure in the international markets had become irresistible.

BRITAIN WITHDRAWS FROM ADEN

By the mid-1960s, Britain had given independence to all but a few far-flung remnants of its Empire. With a Labour government from 1964 keen to cut defence spending wherever possible, there was soon talk of withdrawing from all commitments "east of Suez". One of these was the port city of Aden and its hinterland, the South Arabian Federation.

The British garrison had been dealing with sporadic terrorist attacks in Aden since December 1963. In February 1966 the government announced that all British troops would be pulled out after Aden was granted independence in 1968. The announcement of Britain's imminent departure inspired the two would-be liberation organizations, the Front for the Liberation of Occupied South Yemen (FLOSY) and the National Liberation Front (NLF), to new levels of activity. More than 500 terrorist attacks took place in 1966, increasing to almost 300 a month in 1967. As casualties

rose, Britain decided to cut and run, advancing the date of its withdrawal to November 1967.

Even then, it was difficult to manage the withdrawal with any degree of dignity or pride. By the summer some areas of Aden, notably the city's Crater district, had become out of bounds for British forces. A mutiny by local police in June showed how far the

▲ Troops of the Argyll and Sutherland Highlanders were sent in to restore order in Aden in 1967.

disintegration of colonial control had gone. Honour was restored by the Argyll and Sutherland Highlanders, under the idiosyncratic command of Lieutenant-Colonel Colin Mitchell – a man whom the popular press nicknamed "Mad Mitch". In early July, in a demonstration of extraordinary bravado, the Argylls retook Crater without suffering a single casualty.

By the autumn FLOSY and the NLF were far more occupied with fighting one another over the future control of an independent South Yemen than they were with attacking the British. On November 30 the last of the British troops quit the colony in good order.

Journalist Bernard Levin wrote: "amid a skirl of pipes and a flurry of sand, Britain's troops left the Middle East, where so many of her sons had laid their bones, forever". He could not have foreseen that almost four decades later, British troops would be back in the Middle East, laying more of their bones in Iraq.

CRIME RATES SOAR

In February 1968 the Home Office launched an antitheft campaign with the slogan: "Look out! There's a thief about." There certainly was, as crime rates had almost doubled in the course of the decade. By the late 1960s Britain's prison population totalled around 30,000, compared with about 10,000 in the 1930s, yet the number of crimes committed just went on rising.

The crime wave was a challenge to pundits, since it occurred during a period of rising prosperity and increasing equality, defying the established liberal view that crime was the product of poverty

▲ The reassuring figure of the British bobby was not enough to stem a dramatic increase in crime during the 1960s.

and inequality. Obviously, the triumph of consumerism meant there were more goods to be stolen – the more cars, the more car theft. But it was hard to refute the argument of conservatives that some kind of break down in traditional morality and the social fabric was taking place.

Regardless of changes of government and economic ups and downs, the steep rise in crime continued through the next two decades. By 1990 the incidence of recorded crime was three times its 1968 level – and still no one could come up with a sure-fire way to tackle it.

ANTI-VIETNAM WAR VIOLENCE

On March 17, 1968, an anti-Vietnam War demonstration ended in violent clashes with police outside the American embassy in Grosvenor Square, London.

Attended by protesters variously numbered at between 10,000 and 80,000, the demonstration began peacefully with a rally in Trafalgar Square, addressed by speakers including actress Vanessa Redgrave and political activist Tariq Ali. After a march to Grosvenor Square, trouble started when some demonstrators attempted to storm the embassy building. Police reacted vigorously, charging the crowd on horseback.

Protestors fought back, throwing stones and using banners as clubs. Around 90 people were injured, about a quarter of them police officers. More than 200 arrests were made.

The degree of violence surprised most of those taking part, although it was in line with a widespread radicalization of political protest during this "year of revolt". Demonstrators were becoming aware that only violence would guarantee high-profile coverage for their cause on television and in the press. Violence was also chic – Mick Jagger, who was present at the demonstration, wrote a hit song about it called "Street Fightin' Man".

A further mass protest against the Vietnam War was organized the following October. On that occasion, with almost twice the number of demonstrators present, there was a widespread expectation of violence, but little occurred, probably because of the sheer scale of the police presence.

▲ A demonstration against the Vietnam War culminated in violent protests outside the American embassy in London's Grosvenor Square.

RIVERS OF BLOOD

▲ Enoch Powell makes his notorious "rivers of blood" speech that would cast him into Britain's political wilderness.

In 1968, race and immigration were key issues on the British political agenda. The Labour government had introduced a Race Relations Act to outlaw racial discrimination in employment and housing. On the other hand, in February 1968, Home Secretary James Callaghan rushed a new Immigration Act through parliament removing the right for Commonwealth citizens with British passports to enter Britain. The Act was a panic response to an influx of Kenyan Asians, who were being driven out of East Africa by the racist policies of the Kenyan government.

All British political parties, apart from the small newly formed National Front, were officially committed to racial harmony. But on April 20, 1968, Enoch Powell, a member of the Conservative shadow cabinet, made an extremist attack on the concept of a peaceful multiracial Britain.

Speaking in Birmingham, he expressed a vision of future racial conflict, using the sort of classical reference that came more naturally to him than to his audience: "As I look ahead I am filled with foreboding. Like the Roman I seem to see 'the river Tiber foaming with much blood'."

Simplified by headline writers as "rivers of blood", the speech caused a political sensation. Powell was sacked from the shadow cabinet by Tory leader Edward Heath. However, demonstrations by groups of workers, including dockers and Smithfields' meat porters, supported his views. Furthermore an opinion poll showed that as many as 75 per cent of the population broadly agreed with his views.

COLLAPSE OF RONAN POINT

On the morning of May 16, 1968, a corner of a 23-floor block of flats in Newham, East London, collapsed after an explosion caused by a gas leak. Although a relatively minor disaster, causing the deaths of four residents and injuring 17, it brought a halt to the policy of rehousing slum dwellers in tower blocks.

Made of prefabricated concrete panels bolted together, Ronan Point was the kind of cheap, rapidly built structure that had seemed to offer local councils an ideal solution to their need for affordable high-density housing. Since the start of the 1960s, thousands of similar blocks had been built in towns and cities across Britain. Although many tenants had at first been happy to move from run-down Victorian terraces into new homes in the sky, almost from the start there were complaints about social isolation and intermittently functioning lifts, as well as the ungracious impact of high-rise building on townscapes.

The Ronan Point disaster unleashed a pent-up torrent of criticism. Council tenants worried that tower blocks were unsafe and councillors were lambasted for allowing shoddy building standards to prevail. Conservationists devoted to the defence of the architectural heritage pronounced the definitive failure of modernism, with its projects for comprehensive redevelopment and idealized cities of glass, concrete and steel.

Ronan Point was rebuilt but had only a short life. It was pulled down in 1986, just 18 years after its completion. This fate it shared with many other council tower blocks, which by the 1980s were being demolished almost as rapidly as they had appeared.

▲ The collapse of the new Ronan Point tower-block ignited a fierce debate about the merits and safety of high-rise architecture.

- Songs of the year include "Hey Jude" by the Beatles, "Jumpin' Jack Flash" by the Rolling Stones and "Those Were the Days" by Mary Hopkin

JANUARY
- The "I'm Backing Britain" campaign is launched
- Left-wing Labour backbenchers rebel as the government introduces NHS prescription charges and spending cuts

FEBRUARY
- More than 3,000 East African Asians enter Britain during the month

MARCH
- The Commonwealth Immigrants Act comes into force
- George Brown resigns as Foreign Secretary after personal disagreements with Harold Wilson; Michael Stewart is his replacement
- Mauritius attains independence from Britain
- Anti-Vietnam War protesters battle with police outside the American embassy in Grosvenor Square, London

APRIL
- US millionaire Robert McCullough buys London Bridge
- Conservative politician Enoch Powell makes his "rivers of blood" anti-immigration speech
- Death of racing driver Jim Clark

1968

YEAR OF STUDENT PROTESTS

In 1968 student riots, sit-ins, demonstrations and protest movements took place across the world – in France, West Germany, Italy, Poland, Czechoslovakia, the United States, Mexico and Japan. Together they were an explosive expression of the anti-authoritarianism and idealism of 1960s youth. Except in Northern Ireland, where students actively challenged the injustices of a society based on Protestant ascendancy, Britain managed only a pale reflection of these dramatic events.

Yet Britain had much in common with countries such as France and West Germany, where would-be revolutionary activity was so much more intense. A rapid expansion of universities in the 1960s had made students a far less privileged group than in the past. Many were the first in their family actually to go to university. Only a small minority were heavily politicized, bent on world revolution – whether Trotskyist, Maoist or "New Left". But much larger numbers were at least vaguely critical of Western society, regarding it as oppressive, racist and militaristic. In addition, protests against the Vietnam War mobilized considerable numbers of otherwise apathetic students.

The difference in Britain was that the vast majority of students had a grudging respect for the country's political system, police and law courts. University authorities were rarely seriously at odds with the student body and an atmosphere of liberalism broadly reigned. Most young Sixties Britons were happy to sing along with the Beatles' anthem

▲ Although there were hotbeds of radicalism, British universities in 1968 saw far less protest than those in Europe.

"Revolution", with its catchy put-down: "If you go carrying pictures of Chairman Mao, You ain't going to make it with anyone anyhow."

Nonetheless, the minority of British student radicals was inspired to imitation by the sensational events in France in May 1968, when a spontaneous wave of revolt saw almost every university and school occupied by their students or pupils. At Essex University, one of the new Sixties foundations, a protest against the recruitment of students for war-related research led to the banning of three students, which in turn provoked a sit-in lasting three weeks. The London School of Economics (LSE) was a hotbed of agitation in intermittent ferment throughout the late 1960s. And Hornsey College of Art had its moment of fame when it was taken over by its students at the end of May, an occupation that lasted six weeks.

These essentially copycat gestures did not fool anyone into thinking that a revolutionary mood prevailed in Britain in 1968. Radicals were quite sharp enough to notice that the only spontaneous demonstrations by workers in Britain that year were in support of Enoch Powell's stance against "coloured" immigration.

BEST STARS IN UNITED EUROPEAN TRIUMPH

On May 29, 1968, Manchester United won the European Cup, beating Benfica of Portugal 4–1 after extra time. It was the first English club to win the competition, but not the first British club since Celtic had won the previous year.

Played at Wembley in front of a crowd of 100,000, the match was

slow to take fire. Captain Bobby Charlton gave United the lead early in the second half, but Benfica equalized and then almost won the game when star striker Eusebio forced a brilliant save from goalkeeper Alex Stepney. In extra time United ran away with the match after winger George

Best rounded the Benfica keeper to restore the lead. Further goals came from Brian Kidd and Bobby Charlton.

Coming ten years after the Munich air disaster, the victory was an emotional occasion. Manager Matt Busby declared himself "the proudest man in

England". He was a survivor of the crash, as were two of the players on the pitch, Bobby Charlton and Bill Foulkes.

But the star of the occasion was generally acknowledged to be European Footballer of the Year George Best, dubbed by the Portuguese "the footballing Beatle". Glamorous and supremely talented, Best was busy redefining what it meant to be a football star.

◀ **Manchester United's European Cup victory in 1968 was the first by an English club, and was to be the only one until 1977.**

He was the first British player to act out a celebrity lifestyle away from the pitch, from product endorsements to flash girlfriends. He might have survived all this but for his alcohol addiction, which soon brought his career at the top level to a premature close and eventually killed him.

Best was always unrepentant about seizing the opportunities the new world of the 1960s had to offer. One of his most famous remarks was: "I spent a lot of money on booze, birds and fast cars – the rest I just squandered."

SOUTH AFRICAN COLOUR BAN HITS CRICKET FOR SIX

In September 1968, politics and sport collided head-on when South African President B J Vorster cancelled a planned tour of his country by England cricketers. The reason for this gesture was the inclusion of a player in the England squad who was classified under South African apartheid rules as coloured.

Basil D'Oliveira had lived the early part of his life in Cape Town. As a "coloured", he was not permitted to play in first-class cricket, which was reserved for whites only. In 1960, cricket commentator John Arlott persuaded him to emigrate to England, where his career flourished. An immensely talented all-rounder, he was selected for the England national team in 1966 after becoming a British citizen.

In the summer of 1968, D'Oliveira performed outstandingly in the series against Australia, scoring 158 in the last Test match. But initially he was not selected to tour South Africa, evidently because the English cricketing establishment wished

to avoid a confrontation with the apartheid regime. As a compromise, he was made first substitute, and when one of the original choices dropped out through injury, he was added to the touring squad. D'Oliveira behaved with maturity throughout, quietly asserting his right to play cricket at the highest level while avoiding overt political comment.

The cancellation of the tour was a major step towards the sporting isolation of South Africa, which was to be enforced in subsequent years by an international boycott. No official England team played South Africa at cricket again until black majority rule was established in 1994. Tests between the two countries are now played for the Basil D'Oliveira Trophy.

▲ **Basil D'Oliveira became the centre of a sporting storm when South Africa sought to prevent him from playing cricket on racial grounds.**

- Voting age is lowered to 18 by the Representation of the People Act
- The Divorce Reform Act makes irretrievable breakdown of marriage the sole cause for divorce and introduces divorce by mutual consent after two years' delay
- The abolition of capital punishment is made permanent
- Australian media magnate Rupert Murdoch buys the *News of the World* and *Sun* newspapers
- Supersonic airliner Concorde makes its maiden flight
- The 50 new pence coin is introduced; it will replace the ten-shilling note
- British researchers achieve the first fertilization of human eggs in test tubes
- Books published this year include *The French Lieutenant's Woman* by John Fowles
- British films this year include Ken Russell's *Women in Love* and Richard Attenborough's *Oh! What a Lovely War*
- The Booker Prize is awarded for the first time, won by *Something To Answer For* by P H Newby
- First performance of *Eight Songs for a Mad King* by Peter Maxwell Davies
- New on television are *Civilisation*, presented by Sir Kenneth Clarke, and *Monty Python's Flying Circus*
- The mini-skirt is supplanted by the ankle-length "maxi"

CONCORDE GETS OFF THE GROUND

On March 2, 1969, the Anglo-French supersonic airliner Concorde made its maiden flight in Toulouse, France.

The British prototype, *Concorde 002*, followed with its maiden flight a month later. The idea for the airliner had first been floated in 1960. In November 1962, Britain and France had agreed to split the development costs, initially calculated at almost £200 million. By 1969, the estimated cost had risen to four times that figure.

The British and French governments claimed that they hoped to sell 400 Concordes at £10 million a piece when the aircraft came into service in 1974. But even while the maiden flights took place, severe doubts were being voiced about the aircraft's commercial viability.

Concorde was said to be too noisy to satisfy US environmental regulations and was felt to carry too small a payload to be commercially effective.

Meanwhile, in February 1969, Boeing flew the first 747 jumbo jet. Once again, Britain had displayed its technological brilliance, but it was the United States that had had the commercial acumen to back the right project.

▲ The supersonic Concorde was the fruit of a brilliant Anglo-French technological collaboration, but it never achieved commercial success.

KRAY TWINS ARE JAILED

On March 5, 1969, twin brothers Ronnie and Reggie Kray were sentenced to life imprisonment at the end of an extraordinary trial that exposed the sordid underworld of organized crime in London.

Through the 1960s, the Krays had employed protection rackets to build up an empire of nightclubs and casinos. Their ruthless use of intimidation extended their influence far beyond their original "patch" in the East End to Soho and Knightsbridge. They were part of the "Swinging London" scene, often to be found hobnobbing with celebrities and photographed by the ultra-fashionable David Bailey. Their associates included politicians and peers, notably Lord Boothby, whom Ronnie had met as a result of his homosexual proclivities.

Although both twins had served time in jail, they were mostly able to avoid prosecution because policemen were bought off and witnesses were too terrified to testify against them. Put on trial in 1965 for running a protection racket, they were found not guilty.

By 1968, however, a major police investigation had at last assembled a solid case against them. On May 8, in a series of raids across London, police arrested more than 20 members of the Kray gang, as well as the Kray twins themselves and their older brother Charlie. The three brothers and seven others were charged in connection with the murders of two fellow criminals, George Cornell and Jack "the Hat" McVitie.

Cornell was a thug who worked for a rival London gang, the Richardsons. A shooting war broke out between the two gangs in spring 1966. On April 9, Ronnie Kray walked into the Blind Beggar pub on the Whitechapel Road in London and shot Cornell in the head in front of customers and bar staff. McVitie was a minor member of the Kray "Firm" whose activities had got "out of order" as far as the Krays were concerned. In October 1967, he was stabbed to death by Reggie Kray in a house in Stoke Newington while Ronnie held him down. Charlie was convicted of helping to dispose of McVitie's body.

The judge sentenced the Kray twins to a minimum of 30 years in prison; their brother Charlie was given 10 years. The seven other accused were all sentenced to between two and 20 years in jail.

In a second trial the following month, the Kray twins were found not guilty of the murder of Frankie "Mad Axeman" Mitchell, but Reggie was convicted of helping Mitchell escape from prison two weeks before he was killed.

The Krays entered folklore, their career glamorized in numerous books, songs and a film. Ronnie Kray died in prison in 1995; Reggie Kray died less than a week after his release on compassionate grounds in 2000.

▲ **The jailing of the Kray brothers in 1968 marked the end of a reign of crime that had terrified the public and foxed the police.**

DEATH OF A ROLLING STONE

On the night of July 2–3, 1969, former Rolling Stone Brian Jones took a midnight dip in his swimming pool at his home Cotchford Farm in Hartfield, Sussex. In the early hours of the morning, his body was found floating in the pool. A doctor pronounced him dead at 3 am A coroner's court subsequently attributed his death to alcohol and drugs.

Jones had quit the Rolling Stones the previous June, saying: "I no longer see eye-to-eye with the others over the discs we are cutting." The Stones had hurriedly found a replacement, Mick Taylor, in time for a free open-air concert in Hyde Park scheduled for Saturday July 5. Reluctant to abandon the concert in the wake of Jones's death, Stones lead singer Mick Jagger decided to turn it into a tribute to his memory.

An estimated 250,000 fans turned up for the event. Jagger opened with a reading from Shelley's *Adonis*, accompanied by the release of a cloud of white butterflies. The 75-minute act that followed has become a rock music classic, largely because it was filmed for a Granada television documentary.

The occasion was anything but a display of pure peace and love. Hell's Angels provided heavy security and groups of skinheads roamed the periphery of the crowd looking for stray hippies to prey on. This atmosphere of edginess suited the Stones' image well enough, however, with a repertoire of numbers that included "Sympathy for the Devil" and "Street Fighting Man".

▲ **The original leader of the Stones, Brian Jones had been overshadowed by the emerging talents of Mick Jagger and guitarist Keith Richards.**

• The Beatle John Lennon stages "bed-ins for peace" with his wife Yoko Ono
• Albums released this year include *Abbey Road* by the Beatles and *Goodbye* by Cream
• Songs of the year include The Rolling Stones' "Honky Tonk Women", the Beatles' "Get Back", and Fleetwood Mac's "Albatross"

JANUARY
• Civil rights campaigners are attacked by Protestants at Burntollet Bridge, Northern Ireland
• More than 50 die as an airliner crashes into houses near Gatwick
• A government policy document *In Place of Strife* plans reform of industrial relations
• The government rejects a Wootton Committee recommendation to reduce penalties for possession of cannabis
• Student activists force temporary closure of the London School of Economics

FEBRUARY
• The Caribbean dependency of Antigua cuts links with Britain
• Women workers at Ford win equal pay with men
• Ulster Prime Minister Terence O'Neill suffers setbacks in Stormont elections
• Death of British-born actor Boris Karloff

MARCH
• The Kray twins are sentenced to life imprisonment
• The Beatle Paul McCartney marries Linda Eastman
• British troops restore control of Antigua
• Death of author John Wyndham

1969

NORTHERN IRELAND FALLS APART

On August 14–15, 1969, British troops were deployed on the streets of the Northern Ireland cities of Londonderry and Belfast to restore order after a savage outbreak of sectarian violence. They were expected to stay for a few months.

The violence had come about as the result of Protestant resistance to demands by Northern Ireland's Catholic minority for change. Ever since the division of Ireland in the 1920s, the North had been ruled by Protestant Unionists. Catholics not only had no share in political power but suffered widespread discrimination in areas such as housing and employment. The voting system was rigged to ensure Protestant control even in many localities with a Catholic

▲ **British troops erect barbed wire barricades in Belfast in an effort to keep the warring Protestant and Catholic communities apart.**

▲ **Elected as a Westminster MP at the age of 21, Bernadette Devlin became a powerful advocate of civil rights for Catholics.**

majority. In Londonderry, for example, more than 14,000 of the 23,000 voters were Catholic, yet the Unionists held a permanent majority on the city council through gerrymandered electoral districts. The effects of discrimination were worsened by economic decline – Northern Ireland had the highest unemployment and the worst housing in the United Kingdom.

After the election of a Labour government in Westminster in 1964, the Northern Ireland government came under pressure to reform. The Labour Party felt no sympathy with the Unionists, who were allies of the Conservatives. When Northern Ireland Prime Minister Captain Terence O'Neill showed signs of promoting mild change, however, he came under attack from Protestant extremists, of whom the most vociferous was the Reverend Ian Paisley. In 1966,

a group calling itself the Ulster Volunteer Force (UVF) murdered two Catholics in Belfast, the first sign of just how far some Protestants might be prepared to go in defence of the status quo.

In January 1967, Catholics formed the Northern Ireland Civil Rights Association to campaign for reform. Although denounced by Paisleyites as a front for the Irish Republican Army (IRA), it was in fact a largely respectable middle-class organization which wanted change within Northern Ireland, not unification with the Irish Republic. It was not until August 1968 that the movement staged the first of a series of civil rights marches. The Protestant reaction was not slow in coming. On October 5, civil rights marchers in Londonderry were brutally attacked by members of the overwhelmingly Protestant Royal Ulster Constabulary (RUC), provoking riots in Catholic areas of the city.

During 1968 the civil rights movement was joined by young student activists from Queen's University Belfast, who saw themselves as part of the worldwide movement of student revolt in that year. The students formed an organization called People's Democracy (PD). At the start of January 1969, a small but dedicated contingent of PD activists embarked on a march from Belfast to Londonderry. On January 4, at Burntollet Bridge, they were attacked by hundreds of club-wielding Protestants, some of them off-duty police auxiliaries. The force of RUC officers escorting the demonstration made no effort to protect the marchers, many of whom were severely beaten. News of this, captured by television cameras, sparked battles between the RUC and Catholics on the streets of Londonderry.

In the spring of 1969 the PD and the civil rights movement felt they had the wind in their sails. In April 21-year-old PD activist Bernadette Devlin was elected to the Westminster parliament as MP for Mid-Ulster. The youngest female MP ever elected to parliament, she made the Catholic case forcefully heard. But on into the summer tensions between Protestants and Catholics mounted unbearably as mutual fears came into play.

On August 12, the storm broke. The annual Protestant Apprentice Boys' parade, always a confrontational occasion, sparked rioting in Londonderry. Catholics in the Bogside district, with Bernadette Devlin prominent among them, threw up barricades. Catholic youths fought the RUC with stones and petrol bombs. Resisting repeated onslaughts in which the RUC used armoured cars and CS gas, and in which Protestant rioters fought side by

side with police, the Catholics kept control of the Bogside. The area was declared "Free Derry".

The troubles spread to other Northern Ireland towns and cities. In Armagh, B-Special police auxiliaries fired on a crowd, killing John Gallagher, a Catholic. As the situation deteriorated, the Stormont government reluctantly accepted the need for British troops to move in. The first soldiers were deployed in Londonderry on August 14 in an attempt to stop the fighting. However, that night even worse violence broke out in Belfast. Protestant extremists from Belfast's Shankill district rampaged through the Catholic Falls Road, burning houses and

attacking the inhabitants. The police joined in, driving armoured cars through the Falls and opening fire on blocks of flats with machine-guns. Eight people were killed, including a nine-year-old boy, and about 200 Catholic homes were destroyed by fire.

The following day, British troops arrived in force. Their mission was to restore order and protect the Catholic population. They were generally welcomed by the terrorized population in Catholic areas – British soldiers were photographed drinking cups of tea provided by friendly Catholic housewives. The British government assumed responsibility for security in Ulster and promised

reforms. When Home Secretary James Callaghan visited Ulster at the end of August, he received a rapturous welcome from Catholics. Paisley, meanwhile, described the British troops as "like the SS".

But the government had also felt bound to give Protestants a guarantee that Northern Ireland would remain part of the UK for as long as the majority in the province wished. Over the months ahead, reforms would be slow to arrive, while the British troops would become increasingly identified with the Protestant authorities. Instead of the end of a crisis, 1970 was to bring the beginning of a war.

▲ As the security situation in Ulster deteriorated in 1969, the sight of riot police firing tear gas became all too commonplace.

ISLE OF WIGHT MATCHES WOODSTOCK

In August 1969, the Isle of Wight was invaded by around 150,000 young people drawn to a three-day pop festival mounted by local promoters Ron and Ray Foulk. It was inevitably touted as Britain's answer to Woodstock, after the success of the massive American festival earlier the same month.

The big draw at the Isle of Wight was the promise of Bob Dylan on stage. The American superstar had not performed live for three years. Other bands included The Who, the Bonzo Dog Dooh Dah Band, Joe Cocker, the Edgar Broughton Band and The Moody Blues.

To general surprise, enough ferries were provided to transport the masses on to the island reasonably smoothly. Policing was low-key and a general atmosphere of goodwill reigned, at least until Dylan's performance. In return for a fee said to have totalled £38,000, he came on stage two hours late at 11 pm on the final evening and delivered a subdued, introverted performance that lasted under an hour. This caused a good deal of discontent.

In general, the festival was a gruelling experience for its audience. Richard Neville, editor of the underground magazine OZ, recalled: "The nights were freezing, the food ran out and the latrines stank. For the last hot dogs the queue was 300 yards long." Another audience member summed up the experience as: "inadequate toilet facilities; being very far away from the bands; pretending to oneself that one was having a good time, and occasionally having it ..."

None of this prevented the Isle of Wight festival being repeated the following year on an even larger scale. In 1970, around half a million people are believed to have turned up, making it the largest ever such event in Britain. But the occasion was marred by conflict between the organizers and anarchists determined to make it a free festival – entrance was priced at £3 – and proved a financial disaster for the Foulks. After it was over Ron Foulk announced: "This is the last festival, enough is enough".

▲ The influx of 150,000 pop fans to Britain's first large-scale festival on the Isle of Wight temporarily more than doubled the island's population.

CHAMPION YEAR FOR BRITISH SPORT

The summer of 1969 was a delight for British sports fans with sufficiently catholic taste to appreciate tennis, golf and motor racing. Anne Jones won the Wimbledon women's singles title, golfer Tony Jacklin triumphed in the Open championship, and Scottish driver Jackie Stewart took the Formula One world title. Jones, aged 30, was only the second Briton to win a Wimbledon singles title since the Second World War. Her opponent in the final on July 4 was the formidable American Billy-Jean King, who had defeated Jones in the final of the same competition in 1967. Jones lost the first set, but showed indomitable fighting qualities to take the next 6–3. She ran out the winner 6–2 in the final set, to the delight of the partisan Centre Court crowd.

Jacklin's victory in the Open at Royal Lytham and St Annes was the first for a British golfer since

Max Faulkner in 1951. Jacklin made his mark in the eyes of the general public when he sank the first televised hole-in-one at the 165-yard sixteenth at Royal St George's, Sandwich, in 1967. For a brief period in the late 1960s and early 1970s he was probably the best player in the world, winning the US Open in 1970 to cap his British triumph.

Unlike tennis and golf, motor racing had been dominated by the British through the 1960s, with drivers such as Graham Hill, Jim Clark and John Surtees. Jackie Stewart was a steady and professional driver at a time when

▲ **Tony Jacklin acknowledges the cheers of the crowd after he became the first British golfer to win the Open since 1951.**

the spirit of motor racing favoured deliberate risk taking. He was well known for his campaign for improvements in safety. In the 1969 season, driving a Matra-Ford car with a Cosworth engine, he formed a perfect partnership with his team manager Ken Tyrell. His lead in the championship became unbeatable when he won at Monza in September, in a race in which the front five cars crossed the finish line nose-to-tail within a second and a-half. Stewart went on to win the championship again in 1971 and 1973, before retiring at the height of his powers.

SIXTIES NOT SO SEXY

If the 1960s was famous for one thing, it was sex. This was the decade of the Pill, promiscuity, permissiveness and free love. Poet Philip Larkin even claimed in verse that "sexual intercourse began in 1963". Yet a survey conducted by social anthropologist Geoffrey Gorer in 1969 suggested that the message of sexual liberation had largely failed to penetrate the mores of the British population.

Gorer found that almost two-thirds of women who responded to his survey claimed to have been virgins when they married. Even of those who were not, the majority had had premarital intercourse only with the man they married. Nor did Gorer's male respondents make any large claims to being sexual adventurers: almost half married as virgins or having only had intercourse with their bride.

Gorer's finding also threw cold water on the idea that the availability of the Pill was transforming people's sex lives. According to his survey, 40 per cent of couples were using no form of birth control and less than

one in five married women was on the Pill.

Students, popularly believed to be devotees of wild promiscuity, were no exception to the relative conservatism of the nation's sexual behaviour. Another survey conducted in 1970 suggested that half of all female third-year

students at Durham University – presumably women aged 20 to 21 – were still virgins. Of course, traditional moralists could express outrage that half of these unmarried women were *not* virgins. But the statistics hardly represented the triumph of the "sexual revolution".

▲ **The popular and the public image of Sixties' youth, may have been of unbridled promiscuity, but surveys revealed a more conservative core.**

1970–1979

Whereas the 1960s are seen as a decade in which Britain redefined itself in terms of creativity, music and fashion, fun and style, the picture of Britain in the 1970s is dominated rather by images of disintegration and decline. Such broad-brush impressions are, of course, incapable of capturing the complexity of real life, but an unquestionable foundation of fact underlies this contrast between the 1970s and the preceding decade. The British economy had been performing poorly compared with its international competitors ever since the Second World War, but living standards and levels of employment had been buoyed up by the expansion of the world economy. From 1972 to 1973, the global economy ran on to the rocks and Britain suffered worse than most countries from the consequences. The brief age of full employment came to an end and the term "stagflation" had to be coined to describe simultaneous galloping inflation and falling output. With inflation rising to above 26 per cent, unemployment climbing above 1.5 million, and real incomes actually falling for two years in the mid-1970s, there were inevitable strains on the whole social structure.

The Conservative government elected in 1970 and the Labour regime that replaced it in 1974 in principle offered contradictory solutions. The Conservatives proposed a dose of free enterprise and tax cuts to stimulate growth. Labour championed increased state control over the economy and the redistribution of wealth from rich to poor. In practice, both parties were forced to adopt very similar emergency measures to tackle inflation and the decline in Britain's financial viability. Well before the election of Margaret Thatcher as Prime Minister in 1979, James Callaghan's Labour government had already abandoned the goal of full employment and had slashed government spending, putting national finances on a more stable basis at the expense of creating a new "underclass" of the jobless and impoverished.

The trade unions, often driven more by the militancy of their membership than by their leadership, were implacable in their pursuit of pay rises regardless of the consequences. National strikes by the coal miners in 1972 and 1974 led to power cuts and a three-day working week. The winter of 1978–79 brought a reprise of social chaos through public sector strikes. Both Conservative and Labour governments were fundamentally discredited by their failure to cope with the irresponsible exercise of power by the unions. Economic crisis encouraged political extremism. Both the right-wing National Front and left-wing Trotskyite groups gained a substantial following. Street battles far more brutal than anything seen in the supposedly revolutionary 1960s took place. Mainland Britain even briefly had its own home-grown terrorist movement in the Angry Brigade. In popular culture, from the middle of the decade punk styles of music and dress gave expression to a new mood of aggressive disaffection.

The crisis in Northern Ireland contributed to the darkening scene. Sectarian conflict bred a campaign of bombing and shooting by the Provisional IRA, designed to drive the British out of Ulster. More than 300 British soldiers were killed in Northern Ireland in the decade; at the peak of the Troubles in 1972, almost 500 people were killed there in a single year. The IRA's campaign spilled over on to the mainland, with bombings and assassinations in London and other cities. The British people had to learn for the first time to live under the permanent threat of terrorism. The intransigent rejection of compromise by Protestants in Northern Ireland blocked moves towards a political solution. Protestant terror groups came to match the IRA in the viciousness of their sectarian killings.

An entirely negative view of the 1970s, however, misses many positive aspects of the decade. The Women's Liberation movement flourished, achieving real gains in equality in the workplace and challenging age-old stereotypes in the home. The ecology movement took off, pressing for a more responsible attitude towards the exploitation of the Earth's resources. It could be argued that the sharp fall in the birth-rate during the decade was a positive development on an already overcrowded island. Looking to the future, Britain's entry into the European Community represented a necessary adjustment to the reality of a postcolonial world. And the coming onstream of North Sea oil offered the prospect of some relief for Britain's long-term balance of payments problem.

- Around 9 million working days are lost to strike action, the highest figure since 1926
- The Equal Pay Act gives women the right to the same pay and conditions as men for equivalent jobs, with effect from 1975
- The average price of a house in Britain is £4,874
- The Range Rover car is introduced
- The Open University is established
- Publication of the complete *New English Bible*, which is instant bestseller
- The *Sun* newspaper introduces its first topless "Page Three girl"
- Books published this year include *The Female Eunuch* by Germaine Greer, *The Atrocity Exhibition* by J G Ballard, *Troubles* by J G Farrell and *Crow* by Ted Hughes
- British films this year include David Lean's *Ryan's Daughter* and Joseph Losey's *The Go-Between*
- The sex revue *Oh! Calcutta!* opens in London
- David Hockney paints *Mr and Mrs Ossie Clark and Percy*
- The Beatles split up
- The rock opera *Tommy* by The Who is performed
- "Underground" band Soft Machine plays at the Proms
- Albums released this year include the Beatles' *Let It Be* and Eric Clapton's *Eric Clapton*
- Songs of the year include Mungo Jerry's "In the Summertime" and Black Sabbath's "Paranoid"

DEATH OF A PHILOSOPHER

▲ **Bertrand Russell's death robbed Britain both of one of its most respected philosophers and of a leading political activist and social reformer.**

On February 2, 1970, philosopher Bertrand Russell died at the age of 97. In accordance with his instructions, he was cremated at a private ceremony and his ashes were scattered over a hillside in Wales, the land of his birth.

Russell was the grandson of a Prime Minister, Earl Russell. Both of his parents died when he was a young child, and he was brought up by his austerely Victorian grandmother. His revolt against this upbringing made him a life-long advocate of the importance of sexual fulfilment and free love.

Russell's outstanding work in philosophy, which concerned the logical underpinnings of mathematics, was completed before the First World War. Its culminating achievement was *Principia Mathematica*, written with Alfred Whitehead and published between 1910 and 1913. His later philosophical works are not quite so highly regarded today, although his magisterial *History of Western Philosophy* (1945) became an international bestseller.

Russell's other career, as a political activist and radical social reformer, continued almost up until his death. Imprisoned briefly for pacifist agitation during the First World War, he scandalized conservative opinion in the 1920s and 1930s because of his unorthodox views on religion, education and sexual relationships. He was himself married four times, the painful complexity of his private life partly a result of attempts to live out his own theories.

From the late 1940s, Russell became obsessed with the need to avoid nuclear war, at one point going so far as to suggest a preemptive nuclear strike by the United States against the Soviet Union, to prevent the Soviets building up their own nuclear arsenal. His antinuclear commitment brought him to national prominence in the late 1950s and early 1960s as a leading figure in CND and, later, in the Committee of 100. In 1961, he was again imprisoned, for a week, for advocating civil disobedience.

Russell became increasingly anti-American in his old age and in the 1960s favoured support for guerrilla movements opposed to "US imperialism". He helped finance the establishment of an international tribunal to try the Americans for war crimes in Vietnam. Many found Russell's later political views lacking in coherence and intemperately expressed, but it was in tune with the spirit of his whole life to remain controversial to the last.

THE BEATLES SPLIT

When, in April 1970, Paul McCartney released his first solo album and announced he was leaving the Beatles, it was the culmination of a slow-motion break-up that had begun two and a half years earlier.

The group had never recovered from the death of their manager, Brian Epstein, in August 1967.

Since then, they had drifted apart, although the four still came together for recording sessions until well into 1969, producing some of their best music on the

White Album, *Abbey Road* and *Let It Be* albums.

Many looked to the personal relationships of Paul McCartney and John Lennon for the split. McCartney had met New York photographer Linda Eastman, while Lennon had become involved with New York-based Japanese performance artist Yoko Ono.

Meanwhile, Apple Records, the idealistic company the Beatles had set up to escape from the established music labels, had evolved from generosity into chaos. The four knew they needed a new business controller, but could not agree on who it should be. John, George and Ringo opted for New York accountant Allen Klein, while Paul wanted to rely on Eastman and Eastman, the New York law firm run by Linda's father. This business split led to acrimony and, ultimately, litigation.

It was an unhappy end for a band that would for ever symbolize the youthful, optimistic face of the 1960s. Nostalgia would continue to fuel rumours of a band reunion until Lennon's violent death in 1980 definitively closed the door on the Beatles era.

▶ **Paul and Linda McCartney. After leaving the Beatles, he became one of the top-selling solo artists of the 1970s.**

HEATH SAILS IN TO DOWNING STREET

In the general election held on June 18, 1970, the Conservatives achieved a surprise victory after opinion polls through most of the election campaign had predicted a clear win for the incumbent Labour government. Conservative leader Edward Heath found himself installed at 10 Downing Street with a fairly comfortable parliamentary majority – the Conservatives had 322 seats to Labour's 287.

Heath was the first Tory leader to have been elected by his party's MPs, instead of being appointed after consultations behind closed doors. He was also the first leader of the party to come from a lower-middle-class background, and to have been educated at a grammar school. But in his political stance he stood solidly with his immediate predecessors Macmillan and Home as a "One Nation" Tory, competing with Labour for the electoral middle ground.

The election was not fought on any complex ideological issues. Renegade Tory Enoch Powell referred to it as simply a choice between "the man with the pipe" (Wilson) and "the man with the yacht" (Heath, a well-known amateur sailor). But the Conservatives conducted a skilful campaign that deftly evaded issues such as Britain's entry into the European Community, on which they were bitterly divided. They instead concentrated on economic issues, exploiting the widespread impression that Labour had failed to manage the economy successfully or to master the trade unions, and had allowed inflation to rise out of control.

Heath did not contradict claims in Tory newspapers that a Conservative government would cut prices "at a stroke". At the same time, the Conservative manifesto stated that "we utterly reject the philosophy of compulsory wage control". This was a vote-winning pledge with trade unionists, who had been alienated from Labour by the Wilson government's imposition of legal restraints on pay rises. Exactly how prices would be cut without limiting wage rises was not explained. In practice, the Heath government soon found itself engaged in a crippling conflict with the trade unions, as holding down wages took centre stage in its economic policy.

▲ **As Prime Minister Edward Heath would steer Britain to EEC membership, but his conflict with the trade unions brought disaster.**

JANUARY
- Reduction of the voting age to 18 becomes law
- Thousands die in outbreak of Asian 'flu
- Violent anti-Vietnam War protests in Whitehall

FEBRUARY
- The government proposes forcing local authorities to introduce comprehensive schools
- Deaths of philosopher Bertrand Russell, Battle of Britain Fighter Command chief Hugh Dowding and cartoonist Henry Bateman

MARCH
- Rhodesia formally declares itself a republic
- Henry Cooper regains the British heavyweight boxing title
- British troops clash with Catholic rioters in Londonderry

APRIL
- 500 extra British troops are sent to Northern Ireland
- Chelsea win the FA Cup after a replay, beating Leeds 2–1

MAY
- The government lends money to the struggling Rolls-Royce engine company
- The South African cricket tour of England is cancelled after government pressure on the MCC
- England football captain Bobby Moore is held in Colombia on suspicion of theft

ENGLAND WORLD CUP BID FAILS

▲ **Expectations that England would repeat their 1966 World Cup Final proved to be unrealistic.**

Going to the 1970 World Cup finals in Mexico as reigning champions, England's footballers felt confident of their chances of retaining the Jules Rimet trophy. But their hopes were dashed in the cruellest fashion in the quarter-final against West Germany in Léon.

England suffered a setback even before the finals got under way, when team captain Bobby Moore was bizarrely implicated in the theft of a bracelet in Bogotá, Colombia. Moore was allowed to play in Mexico and eventually exonerated, but the event left a bad taste. Nonetheless, England performed well in the group stage, only losing to Brazil in a close-fought match distinguished by goalkeeper Gordon Banks's remarkable save from a Pelé header.

Banks was unfortunately ill for the quarter-final. His replacement, Peter Bonnetti, played a dismal role in England's defeat. Halfway through the second half England were ahead 2–0 and seemingly cruising to the semi-finals. Ageing star player Bobby Charlton was substituted to preserve his strength for the next match. But then Bonetti committed two errors that allowed the Germans to equalize. Germany went on to score the winning goal in extra time.

Given that Brazil, the eventual winners, were arguably the greatest side in World Cup history, it is perhaps unlikely that England would have won the tournament even if they had reached the final. But throwing away a 2–0 lead was a dismal way to go out. The defeat initiated a dreadful phase in English international football; England would not qualify for the World Cup finals again until 1982.

TYNAN PUTS SEX ON STAGE

The abolition of censorship on the British stage in 1968 opened the way for producers to attempt virtually unlimited sexual exhibitionism – although they could still be prosecuted for obscenity if a show was judged likely to "corrupt and deprave". One of the first tests of the new law was the erotic revue *Oh! Calcutta!*, which opened at the Round House in London on July 27, 1970.

The revue was staged by prominent critic Kenneth Tynan, who had been among the leaders of opinion arguing for the new freedom. It had first opened in New York in 1969, but the chances of prosecution in Britain seemed much higher. The show

▲ **Kenneth Tynan's erotic revue *Oh, Calcutta!* received widespread publicity from moral opponents of its staging.**

included a great deal of nudity, bawdy jokes of mixed quality, and self-consciously sophisticated sketches on sexual topics, some penned by famous literary figures. A campaign was mounted against it well before the London opening night. It was denounced in *The Times* as "the sort of exhibition of sexual voyeurism that used to be available to the frustrated and mentally warped in the side turnings of a certain kind of seaport".

With advance publicity of this kind, *Oh! Calcutta!* was always likely to be a massive box-office hit. The Attorney-General swiftly decided that there was "no reasonable likelihood" of a prosecution succeeding. Critics were lukewarm or dismissive, but the prurient public queued for a chance to witness the sexual barriers come down. *Oh! Calcutta!* transferred to the West End that autumn for a long run.

BRITAIN MEETS INTERNATIONAL TERROR

On September 6, 1970, 26-year-old Palestinian Leila Khaled and a Nicaraguan, Patrick Arguello, attempted to hijack an El Al airliner flying from Amsterdam to New York. The attempt was foiled by Israeli guards, who killed Arguello and overpowered Khaled. The airliner landed at Heathrow, and Khaled was delivered into British police custody.

The failed hijacking was part of a spectacular operation mounted by the Popular Front for the Liberation of Palestine (PFLP) in which three other airliners were also seized almost simultaneously. While Khaled waited in Ealing police station, over the following weeks an extraordinary drama was acted out in front of the world's television cameras. One of the hijacked airliners was blown up in Cairo; two others were flown to Dawson's Field, a remote airstrip in Jordan, where they were joined by yet another plane hijacked en route from Bahrain to London. On

▲ Palestinian Leila Khaled's hijacking of an El Al airliner finished without casualties as she was overpowered by guards.

12 September all three airliners at Dawson's Field were blown up.

The Palestinians still held dozens of British, Swiss, German and Israeli passengers and aircrew hostage. After frantic negotiations, agreement was reached for the release of terrorist prisoners in exchange for the hostages' safe return. The British government flew Khaled to freedom in Beirut at the end of September.

Prime Minister Edward Heath was much criticized for allegedly giving in to terrorist demands. Yet the whole event now appears startlingly civilized compared with what was to follow in subsequent years. Not a single passenger or crew member was killed in the hijackings. Khaled developed an enduring affection for Britain in her weeks of captivity, and returned to the country on several occasions in later years.

GREER SPEAKS FOR WOMEN

▲ Germaine Greer advocated a revolution in female attitudes towards men as well as in personal lives.

In October 1970, a book with the startling title *The Female Eunuch* appeared in Britain's bookshops. Written by Australian expatriate Germaine Greer, it marked for many British women the moment when Women's Liberation really began.

Greer had established herself on the London arts and journalism scene in the 1960s, writing for publications such as the "underground" magazine *OZ*. *The Female Eunuch* expressed the hostility to sexual repression, monogamy and the nuclear family that was a common thread in "counter-culture" thinking. But it differed from the ideology of the "sexual revolution" in its stress on men's alleged hatred of women. Greer attacked several literary favourites of the 1960s, including D H Lawrence and Henry Miller, denouncing the phallocentric sexism at the heart of their "liberated" attitudes.

Greer's book was a call for a revolution in women's personal lives and attitudes, rather than at the level of legislation. As such, it influenced an entire generation.

- Census gives UK population as 55.9 million
- Price inflation exceeds 10 per cent in the year to July 1971
- Working days lost to strike action exceed 10 million
- The Troubles in Northern Ireland cause the deaths of 173 people during the year
- Immigration Act further tightens restrictions on settlement in Britain by "New Commonwealth" immigrants
- Industrial Relations Act cracks down on unofficial strikes
- Environmental pressure group Greenpeace is founded
- British Lions win a rugby test series in New Zealand for first time
- Books published this year include *The Day of the Jackal* by Frederick Forsyth and *In A Free State* by V S Naipaul (Booker award winner)
- British films released this year include Stanley Kubrick's *A Clockwork Orange*, Ken Russell's *The Devils*, Nicolas Roeg's *Performance* (starring Mick Jagger) and John Schlesinger's *Sunday Bloody Sunday*
- Peter Brook directs radical staging of *A Midsummer Night's Dream*
- Musical *Jesus Christ Superstar* by Andrew Lloyd Webber and Tim Rice opens
- Albums released this year include "Sticky Fingers" by The Rolling Stones and "Imagine" by John Lennon

IBROX FOOTBALL DISASTER

On January 2. 1971, Ibrox Park in Glasgow was the scene of Britain's worst football crowd disaster until the 1989 Hillsborough tragedy. Sixty-six people died when crash barriers collapsed as fans were attempting to leave the stadium.

The match was a derby between Rangers and Celtic. With a few minutes of the game remaining, Celtic were in the lead, so

◄ **The antiquated design of many British football stadiums contributed to the Ibrox disaster in which 66 fans died.**

thousands of Rangers fans decided to leave the terraces early. It was as they packed into Stairway 13 that the tragedy occurred.

Initial reports suggested that the disaster was precipitated by a last-minute Rangers equalizer, which created chaos as many departing fans tried to return to the terraces. But a subsequent inquiry found that it was simply the crush of supporters all leaving at the same time that caused the barriers to buckle. Once people started to fall, the pressure of bodies from behind created an unstoppable avalanche.

THE ANGRY BRIGADE

On January 12, 1971, two bombs exploded outside the Hertfordshire home of the Secretary of State for Employment, Robert Carr. Although no one was injured, the windows and door at the front of the house were blown in and the minister's car was damaged. Responsibility for the attack was claimed by a group calling itself the Angry Brigade.

The evolution of a minority of student radicals into urban terrorists was an international phenomenon of the time. It produced the Red Brigades in Italy, the Baader-Meinhof group in Germany and the Weathermen in the United States. Like these groups, the Angry Brigade were young people living in the "alternative" society of communes and the "counter-culture" who had come to believe that only violence could trigger the revolutionary upheaval necessary to transform society.

The Angry Brigade carried out their first bombings in 1969, but these low-key efforts were dismissed as the work of cranks. The attack on Carr's home was a

different matter and set in motion a major police operation. The first breakthrough came on January 20, when Jake Prescott, an habitual criminal arrested on a drugs charge, boasted to cellmates about his part in the Carr bombing. By tracing Prescott's associates, police hoped to track down the terrorist cell.

The bombings continued into the summer, with attacks on the fashionable Biba department store in Kensington, on the home of the chairman of Ford UK, and on the apartment of Secretary of State for Trade and Industry, John Davies. The terrorists published a series of communiqués denouncing "politicians, the leaders, the rich, the big bosses" and calling for "power to the people".

On August 21 police raided a flat in Stoke Newington, north London, and found a cache of weapons and explosives. A dozen suspects were soon under arrest and the bombings ceased. In December 1972, after a trial lasting seven months, John Barker, James Greenfield, Anna Mendleson and Hilary Creek were

▲ **Supporters of the Angry Brigade protest outside the trial of members of the group who were accused of carrying out a bombing campaign.**

each sentenced to ten years imprisonment for conspiracy to cause explosions. The only other person found guilty was Prescott, sentenced to 15 years in prison after a separate trial.

THE POUND GOES DECIMAL

In February 1971, the time-honoured British institutions of the shilling, the florin, the sixpence and the half-crown were finally consigned to the dustbin of history as the new decimalized currency took over. No longer would foreigners be asked to puzzle over a system with 12 pence to the shilling and 20 shillings to the pound – or demand to know why pounds, shillings and pence should be written "L" "s" "d" for short.

A decision to keep the pound at its old value meant that the new penny, set at one-hundredth of a

pound, would be worth almost two and a half old pence.

The reception accorded to the new pennies was not improved by the failure to find a satisfactory way of referring to them. Without being able to say "ten pence", since this referred to the old currency, people resorted to the ugly reference "ten pee" – a pronunciation which has persisted ever since.

◀ **A thousand years of tradition ended when the pound went decimal in 1971, leading to the disappearance of traditional coins.**

OZ MAGAZINE ON TRIAL

In June 1971, the editors of *OZ* magazine, Richard Neville, Felix Dennis and Jim Anderson, were put on trial at the Old Bailey for "conspiring to corrupt the morals of liege subjects of Her Majesty the Queen by raising in their minds inordinate and lustful desires".

Neville had founded the original *OZ* magazine in his native Australia in 1963, setting up the British version in London four years later. Mostly sold on the streets rather than through shops, *OZ* was dedicated to a playful, lightweight version of cultural revolution, indulging in psychedelic colour schemes, nude photographs – supposedly sexually liberating rather than tackily pornographic – and wacky ideas of every kind.

In May 1970, Neville invited a group of adolescent schoolchildren to create a special edition of *OZ*. Marketed as the "School Kids Issue", it sported two naked women on the front page and included a cartoon strip showing Rupert Bear with a large erection. The implied conjunction of sex and children gave the magazine's enemies in the police Obscene

Publications Squad an ideal opportunity to make arrests.

The defendants took every opportunity to subvert the proceedings against them, turning up for the committal dressed in schoolgirl gymslips. Notable among those who rallied to their aid were John Lennon and Yoko Ono, who recorded a song to help finance the defence. Their lawyers included John Mortimer, a veteran of many 1960s obscenity trials. But the judge, Justice Michael Argyle, was

clearly determined they should be found guilty. The jury duly obliged and, on August 5, Argyle sentenced the defendants to prison terms ranging from nine to 15 months.

The sentences provoked an outcry and they were overturned on appeal. The defendants walked free, but Neville had by then tired of the magazine, which folded in 1973. He returned to Australia, while Dennis went on to become a publishing millionaire.

▲ **The defendants in the trial of the underground magazine *OZ* took every opportunity to satirize the proceedings against them.**

THATCHER ENDS FREE SCHOOL MILK

On June 14, 1971, the House of Commons approved a bill to end the provision of free milk at school to children over the age of seven. The controversial bill was pushed through by the Secretary of State for Education and Science, Margaret Thatcher.

Providing milk to schoolchildren was a health and welfare measure that had developed from early in the century. Once a vital counter to diseases of malnutrition, such as rickets, it had largely lost its rationale by the relatively prosperous 1960s. Harold Wilson's Labour government had abolished free milk in secondary schools in 1968. This did not, however, prevent Labour attacking the Thatcher bill, which extended the cut to primary schools.

Thatcher, like all the ministers in the Heath government, was under pressure to find spending cuts as the Conservatives struggled to fulfil election pledges to hold down taxes and public spending. In fact, overall her department singularly failed in this respect, since spending on education increased markedly. It was during Thatcher's tenure as Education Minister that the school leaving age was at last raised to 16 – a target set in the 1944 Education Act. She also, surprisingly considering her right-wing views, presided over a rapid expansion of the comprehensive school education system.

The school milk issue established Thatcher's reputation. The rest of her record in 1970 to 1974 was largely ignored. For years she would face the chant: "Thatcher, Thatcher, Milk Snatcher". From the point of view of her own career, this was entirely beneficial. It allowed her to present herself as a tough, hard-headed politician who would stop at nothing to keep public spending and inflation under control. It was on this basis that she would win the Tory party leadership in 1975.

▲ The ending of the provision of free milk to schoolchildren earned Margaret Thatcher the epithet "Thatcher the Milk Snatcher".

INTERNMENT IN NORTHERN IRELAND

At dawn on August 9, 1971, units of the British Army were sent into Catholic areas of Northern Ireland with orders to arrest 450 individuals suspected of supporting armed subversion. They were to be interned – held without charge or trial in special camps.

The British government had introduced internment reluctantly in the face of a deteriorating security situation. In the event, it only served to make matters worse.

When British soldiers had first arrived on the streets of Northern Ireland two years earlier, they had been largely welcomed by Catholics in the Protestant-ruled province. The first shots fired at British soldiers in October 1969 were from Protestant gunmen, outraged by drastic measures to reform the Protestant-dominated police. In the course of time, however, the British troops found themselves inevitably drawn into close cooperation with Northern Ireland's Protestant authorities, and thus into conflict with the Catholic population.

The alienation of the Catholics was exploited by the Provisional IRA, a recent breakaway from the long-established – and by this time relatively moderate – Irish Republican Army. The Provisionals were committed to achieving a united Ireland through armed struggle against the British "occupiers" and their Protestant allies. During the course of 1970, the Provisionals' ranks were swelled by a flood of recruits. With funding flowing in from sympathizers in the United States, the Provos began to arm themselves for an assault on British power.

On February 6, 1971, a British soldier, Gunner Robert Curtis, was shot by a Provisional sniper in Belfast: he was the first British fatality in the conflict. The Ulster government then declared that Northern Ireland was "at war with the Provisonal IRA". Many Catholic districts became in practice "no-go areas" for the British Army, as any army patrol would face, at best, rioters throwing bricks and petrol bombs, and – at worst – sniper fire.

From the security of these safe havens, the Provisionals launched a bombing campaign against commercial targets throughout the Province. By July, the number of bombings was approaching 100 a month.

Unable to contain the rapidly worsening situation, the British government acceded to demands from the head of the Northern Ireland government, Brian Faulkner, for the introduction of internment.

The implementation of this measure on August 9 was a political disaster. The Catholic areas rose in open revolt and fighting against the British Army spilled over into communal violence. Over the next two days, 23 people were killed and hundreds of buildings were burned out.

▲ **A soldier searches a Belfast civilian. Internment was one of the British government's more controversial policies in Northern Ireland.**

Many of the internees were subjected to interrogations that a commission of inquiry later admitted to be "ill-treatment". Fourteen prisoners were subjected to in-depth interrogation involving sensory deprivation. This was later condemned by the European Court of Human Rights as "inhuman and degrading". In effect, the British authorities had tainted themselves with arbitrary arrest and near-torture. And the net result was only to crank up the violence to a new pitch.

In the seven months before internment, 30 people died in the Northern Ireland Troubles. In the five months that followed, 143 lost their lives as the bombings, shootings and violence spiralled out of control.

HIROHITO VISITS THE QUEEN

▲ **The state visit of Japanese emperor Hirohito aroused widespread bitterness amongst those who remembered Japanese wartime atrocities.**

In October 1971 Japanese Emperor Hirohito began a state visit to Britain and was received by Elizabeth II at Buckingham Palace. However, the large crowds that turned out to line the streets of London were mostly silent and hostile, with some turning their backs as a potent gesture of disgust and protest.

In a remarkable recovery from its devastation at the end of the Second World War, Japan had established itself as the world's second-largest industrial power. But there remained widespread bitterness about Japanese war crimes. The survival of wartime Emperor Hirohito on the Japanese throne was a particular focus of resentment.

Survivors of Japanese prisoner-of-war camps were especially bitter about the effort to normalize relations with Japan, calling for a boycott of Japanese goods in protest at the Emperor's visit. Even the Queen felt unable entirely to gloss over the past. In welcoming her guest, she admitted: "We cannot pretend that relations between our two peoples have always been peaceful and friendly."

FROM BLOODY SUNDAY TO BLOODY FRIDAY

- 24 million working days are lost through strike action, the highest level since the General Strike
- Unemployment rises to almost one million
- The Troubles in Northern Ireland cause the deaths of 467 during the year
- The Jockey Club allows women jockeys to compete in races
- Books published this year include *Watership Down* by Richard Adams, *G* by John Berger (Booker prize winner) and *The Joy of Sex* by Alex Comfort
- British films this year include Alfred Hitchcock's *Frenzy* and Joseph Mankiewicz's *Sleuth*
- John Betjeman is appointed Poet Laureate
- The Tate Gallery purchases Carl Andre's *Equivalent VIII* minimalist brick sculpture
- First performance of Harrison Birtwistle's *Triumph of Time*
- Albums released this year include David Bowie's *The Rise and Fall of Ziggy Stardust and Spiders from Mars*, and the Rolling Stones' *Exile on Main Street*
- Songs of the year include Slade's "Mama Weer all Crazee Now" and "Amazing Grace" by the Royal Scots Dragoon Guards Band

▲ **British troops stationed in Belfast stand guard over Loyalist housing bombed by the IRA.**

The worst single year in the history of the Northern Ireland conflict had to be 1972. In the course of 12 months, a total of 467 people, including 103 British soldiers, lost their lives in the violence that convulsed the Province.

The year opened with the tragedy known as "Bloody Sunday". The predominantly Catholic Civil Rights Association had decided to mount a campaign of marches to protest against internment – a bold attempt to wrest back the initiative from the men of violence.

On January 30 a highly publicized march set off from the Creggan estate in Derry. When it was turned back from its planned route by an army barricade, a small number of rioters began throwing stones. British paratroopers pursued the rioters and opened fire near the Rossville Flats. Thirteen Catholic civilians were shot dead and another 12 wounded. The Widgery Tribunal, set up to investigate the event, admitted that "none of the deceased or wounded is proved to have been shot while handling a firearm or bomb".

Since it happened in full view of the media, the massacre caused a sensation around the world. In Dublin the British embassy was burned down. The Official IRA's response was a botched car-bombing at the Parachute Regiment's Aldershot barracks, which killed five cleaning women, a gardener and a Roman Catholic chaplain.

In Northern Ireland the Provisional IRA raised its terrorist campaign to a new pitch. Through the spring of 1972, bombings were a daily occurrence – in a single two-day period in mid-April, 40 explosive devices were planted across the Province. Although they were aimed at "economic targets", the bombs inevitably caused civilian deaths and horrific maimings. The security forces also suffered mounting casualties, chiefly from sniper fire. Not to be left out, Protestant paramilitaries stepped up their activities, targeting Catholics in a series of sectarian killings.

Desperate to regain control, on March 24, British Prime Minister Edward Heath suspended the Stormont government, taking over direct rule of the Province. The newly appointed Northern Ireland Secretary, William Whitelaw, and his military advisers were unable, in these early weeks, to reduce the level of violence. Solidly in control of Catholic districts of Belfast and Derry that were out of bounds for the security forces, the Provisionals felt confident that they could persuade the British to give up and go home.

▲ **Thousands attend the funeral of the 13 victims of Bloody Sunday on Creggan Hill in Belfast's Bogside.**

In June the Provisionals put out feelers for peace talks with the British government. Publicly, the government said that it would not enter into talks with terrorists, but privately they agreed to look for a deal.

On June 26, the Provisionals declared a truce and in the first week of July a delegation including Gerry Adams – released from internment so that he could take part – and Martin McGuiness met Whitelaw for secret talks in London. The meeting did not go badly, but on July 9 the ceasefire predictably broke down with a clash between Catholics and British troops on the streets of Belfast.

Over the following eight days, 15 British soldiers were killed in the Province. The bombing campaign was resumed with unparalleled ferocity, culminating on the afternoon of July 21 – the day later referred to as "Bloody Friday" – when 19 bombs exploded in Belfast city centre in an hour. Nine people were killed and 130 injured. Graphic television pictures depicting the maimed victims and the remains of bodies being scooped into plastic bags shocked viewers.

The horror of Bloody Friday lost the Provisionals much support among Northern Ireland Catholics and gave back the initiative to the British government. On July 31 the Army swept into the "no-go" areas in force, using armoured bulldozers to demolish barricades. They met little resistance.

Troops were permanently installed at strongpoints inside the Catholic districts. The loss of their safe havens was a serious blow to the Provisionals, and the level of bombings and shootings was almost halved in the following months; they would never again get close to driving the British out by force.

BRITAIN ENTERS EUROPE

▲ **Although decided by referendum, Britain's entry into the Common Market was bitterly opposed by many.**

The Six became the Ten when Britain, Ireland, Denmark and Norway signed the Treaty of Brussels on January 22, 1972, committing them to join the European Economic Community (EEC) on January 1, 1973. In the event, there were only nine, Norway having held a referendum in 1972 which rejected entry into Europe.

Many British people believed they too should have had a chance to vote on the issue – all opinion polls showed that a solid majority of the population opposed to EEC membership. There was already a controversial agreement among European leaders to progress towards a more complete European Union.

Britain's entry into Europe was a personal triumph for Edward Heath, Prime Minister since 1970. A fervent pro-European, he had been the chief negotiator when Britain first attempted to join the EEC, only to find British membership vetoed by France's

President Charles de Gaulle in 1963. De Gaulle vetoed another British application to join, initiated by Harold Wilson's Labour government, in 1967. It was only the French leader's fall from power in 1969 that opened the door to a fresh British approach.

Britain had negotiated special deals to maintain some of its privileged trading links with the Commonwealth. Nevertheless, both the Conservatives and Labour were split over the EEC. Generally, the Conservatives were more in favour of Europe than the socialists. The left wing of the Labour Party was opposed and, after Labour's election victory in 1974, forced Harold Wilson to call a referendum on membership. Held in 1975, this produced a large majority of around two to one in favour of Europe, partly in acknowledgement of a *fait accompli*, but also thanks to a lavishly funded campaign mounted by the pro-European lobby.

JANUARY
- Coal miners strike in pursuit of a 47 per cent pay rise
- Prime Minister Edward Heath signs the Treaty of Accession, formally joining the EEC
- 13 people are killed when troops open fire on a crowd in Londonderry – "Bloody Sunday"

FEBRUARY
- Irish protestors set fire to the British embassy in Dublin
- The miners strike ends after the grant of a substantial pay rise
- Seven people are killed when the Official IRA explodes a car bomb at the Aldershot barracks of the Parachute Regiment

MARCH
- Chancellor of the Exchequer Anthony Barber cuts taxes and raises public spending in the Budget
- The Stormont parliament is suspended; Northern Ireland comes under the direct rule of Secretary of State for Northern Ireland William Whitelaw

APRIL
- Rail workers begin a work-to-rule
- Terrorists explode more than 20 bombs in Northern Ireland in a two-day period

MAY
- Derby County win the Football League championship; Leeds United win the FA Cup
- The proposed settlement of the Rhodesian dispute is abandoned after a commission reports that the black majority in Rhodesia reject it
- Glasgow Rangers win the European Cup Winners' Cup, defeating Dynamo Moscow
- Deaths of the Duke of Windsor, former Edward VIII, of Poet Laureate Cecil Day-Lewis and actress Dame Margaret Rutherford

MINERS STRIKE BLACKS OUT BRITAIN

From its earliest days in office, the Conservative government of Edward Heath found itself at war with the trade union movement. Heath was determined to quash inflation, which was threatening to run totally out of control. He believed this could only be achieved by holding down wages in the public sector – the nationalized industries and public services. But public sector workers, under militant leadership, were determined to secure pay rises equal to or above price inflation. During 1971, electricity power workers and postal workers were among those who engaged in prolonged industrial action.

The situation was worsened by the government's Industrial Relations Act, introduced in 1971. This complex legislation was actually intended to strengthen the position of official trade unions, while cracking down on unofficial strike action led by shop stewards. But the Trade Union Congress (TUC) was deeply suspicious of any government regulation of union

▲ **Candle-lit evenings became a familiar experience during the 1972 Miner's strike, as blackouts were imposed across Britain.**

affairs and led a campaign of resistance to the new laws.

The government's confrontation with union power came to a climax in January 1972, when the National Union of Mineworkers (NUM) called the first nation-wide miners strike since the 1920s. The strike was conducted aggressively, with "flying pickets" blocking the movement of coal out of depots and into power stations. At Saltley Gate coke works in Birmingham, an estimated 15,000 militant miners intimidated police into closing the gates.

With Britain's largely coal-burning power stations running out of fuel, electricity blackouts were imposed across the country. By mid-February industry was operating on a three-day week to conserve power. Households grew accustomed to living by candlelight at night.

Rejecting the alternatives of using troops as strike-breakers or calling a general election, the government capitulated to the miners, who were granted pay rises of as much as 30 per cent. Power supplies were restored in early March. This demonstration of union power seriously undermined the government's prestige and inevitably encouraged more strikes in the future.

THE POULSON AFFAIR

▲ **John Poulson (above) was imprisoned for corruption. Politician Reginald Maudling fell from grace after revelations of his links with him.**

In July 1972 Reginald Maudling, the Home Secretary in the Conservative government and a potential Prime Minister, was obliged to resign after he was shown to be linked to Leeds property developer John Poulson, the subject of a police inquiry into corruption.

The Poulson case blew the lid off the cosy world of favours and bribery that had grown up during the years of rapid urban redevelopment in the 1960s.

A self-made millionaire, Poulson had created Europe's largest international architect's practice.

He was also at the centre of a web of corruption. Individuals such as Scottish Office civil servant George Pottinger and Newcastle Labour councillors T Dan Smith and Andy Cunningham received favours from Poulson, ranging from meals at the Dorchester hotel and suits from Savile Row tailors to Mediterranean cruises.

The scandal came to light when Poulson went bankrupt in 1972. At trials held in Leeds in 1973 and 1974, he was sentenced to prison terms of five and seven years, to run concurrently.

UGANDAN ASIANS ARRIVE

▲ The Asian community was crucial to Uganda's economy, which quickly faltered following their expulsion.

In early August 1972, Ugandan ruler General Idi Amin announced that he was expelling all of his country's Asian population, by some estimates numbering as many as 80,000 people. Introduced into East Africa by the British in the nineteenth century, the Asians were widely resented by black Africans because they constituted a business class with a generally higher standard of living. Amin's motivation for expelling them was simply the desire for plunder.

The majority of Ugandan Asians had British passports. Britain's Conservative government accepted its moral obligation to accept the Ugandan refugees and set up a Ugandan Resettlement Board to oversee their reception. But much of the British press, along with right-wing Conservatives such as Enoch Powell, responded to the prospect of a fresh influx of Asian immigrants with shock and outrage.

At the Conservative Party conference in October, Powell presented a motion highly critical of government immigration policy, but a counter-motion congratulating the government on its handling of the crisis was carried by a substantial majority. The failure of the Conservative Party to adopt a rigorous anti-immigration stance led to growing support for the extremist National Front over the following years.

About 30,000 Ugandan Asians arrived in Britain, many of them initially housed in disused army camps. The Ugandan Resettlement Board sought to ensure they were dispersed around the country, but they inevitably tended to gravitate towards areas with existing Asian communities. Showing great enterprise, many Ugandan Asians had soon established prosperous businesses in their new country, to the considerable benefit of the British economy as a whole.

BETJEMAN IS POET LAUREATE

In October 1972, John Betjeman was appointed Poet Laureate in succession to Cecil Day-Lewis. It was a popular choice but one that, by his own account, "dumbfounded" the poet himself.

Betjeman's poetry, often serious yet never taking itself seriously, was outrageously old-fashioned, yet consistently intelligent and funny. Both his *Collected Poems* and the autobiographical *Summoned by Bells* were bestsellers by the standard of poetry collections. But he was known to a wider public as a television personality, renowned for his campaigns to preserve historic buildings.

Betjeman proved no more successful than any other Poet Laureate at providing poetry for public occasions, but his appointment restored popular interest in the post. For once, the man in the street might actually know who the Poet Laureate was.

▲ John Betjeman's old-fashioned style and gentle wit struck a chord with the public. His appointment as Poet Laureate was a popular choice.

SEPTEMBER
- Northern Ireland athlete Mary Peters wins a gold medal for the pentathlon at the Munich Olympics
- An Icelandic gunboat attacks British trawlers at the start of the Cod War
- Death of Lord Fisher of Lambeth, former Archbishop of Canterbury

OCTOBER
- A fixed bank rate is replaced by a floating "minimum lending rate"

NOVEMBER
- The government institutes an emergency anti-inflation policy, starting with a 90-day freeze on wages, prices, rents and dividends
- Negotiations between Britain and Iceland on fishing rights collapse
- Death of author Sir Compton Mackenzie

DECEMBER
- The government announces a plan to revitalize the coal industry

1973

- The Provisional IRA begins a bombing campaign in mainland Britain
- Admission charges for national museums are introduced
- First commercial radio stations broadcast
- Books published this year include *The Honorary Consul* by Graham Greene and *Crash* by J G Ballard
- British films this year include Lindsay Anderson's *O Lucky Man!* and Nicolas Roeg's *Don't Look Now*
- New television series include *The World at War*
- New plays include Peter Shaffer's *Equus* and Alan Ayckbourn's *The Norman Conquests*
- Albums released this year include Mike Oldfield's *Tubular Bells* and Pink Floyd's *The Dark Side of the Moon*

JANUARY
- Britain formally joins the EEC

MARCH
- The Provisional IRA explodes bombs in central London
- Northern Ireland votes to maintain union with Britain in a referendum
- Death of playwright and composer Noel Coward

APRIL
- Phase Two of the government's anti-inflation policy limits wage rises to £1 per week plus 4 per cent

MAY
- Second-Division Sunderland win the FA Cup
- Prime Minister Heath describes the Lonrho mining company as the "unacceptable face of capitalism"

OIL CRISIS ROCKS BRITAIN

▲ **Saudi oil minister Sheikh Yamani became the public face of OPEC during the 1973 crisis, when the organization almost quadrupled oil prices.**

On October 6, 1973, on the Jewish holiday of Yom Kippur, Egyptian forces crossed the Suez Canal to attack Israeli troops occupying the Sinai desert. Britain was not a party to the ensuing conflict, known as the Yom Kippur War, but it precipitated a crisis in energy supplies that had a seismic effect on the British economy.

Like the rest of Western Europe, Britain had become heavily dependent on oil supplies from Arab countries in the Middle East. The British government correctly feared that the outbreak of war might lead to an economically crippling oil embargo. Britain joined with other European NATO countries in requesting the United States not to use bases in Europe for its operations in support of Israel. But remaining distant from the war was not sufficient to avoid its consequences.

Led by Saudi Arabia, the Arab oil producers united to use the "oil weapon" against the West. At the height of the war, they announced sharp reductions in oil production, steep price increases and a complete embargo on supplies to the United States and the Netherlands, the Western countries most closely associated with Israel. Although Britain thus escaped an embargo, it was faced with a scramble to secure oil that was now in short supply and increasingly expensive.

The government introduced measures to reduce petrol consumption and distributed petrol ration books. Queues developed outside petrol stations and panic buying exhausted supplies. The crisis deepened when – on November 12 – the National Union of Mineworkers imposed a ban on overtime working in support of a pay claim. The government responded by declaring a state of emergency and imposing energy-conservation measures, including a 80 km/h (50 mph) speed limit, and banning television broadcasts after 10.30 pm

The combined impact of the oil crisis and the miners' industrial action eventually led to the imposition of a three-day week in industry and, in 1974, to the fall of the Heath government. But spectacular as this short-term crisis may have been, the long-term effects of the rise in oil prices were more significant still. By March 1974 oil supplies were generally back to normal, but the price of crude oil had quadrupled. Through the Organization of the Petroleum Exporting Countries (OPEC), the oil producers worked to hold prices at their new level by regulating output.

As a consequence of this huge price hike, inflation surged in Britain and unemployment followed suit as the economy fell headlong into recession. The good times of the post war consumer boom were at an end. On the other hand, the new oil fields being explored in the North Sea were suddenly a potential source of profit to exploit. Britain was itself set to become an oil producer.

POLISH "CLOWN" BREAKS ENGLISH HEARTS

In 1973 England failed to qualify for the following year's football World Cup finals for the first time since entering the competition in 1950. The decisive match was played against Poland at Wembley on October 17. England went into the match needing a win to qualify for the finals. Tension was high, but so was confidence. Most pundits regarded England as a far better side than Poland. Brian

Clough, manager of Derby County, singled out goalkeeper Jan Tomaszewski as a weakness in the Polish team, describing him as a "clown".

In front of a capacity crowd, England did almost all the attacking, but they lacked the composure and patience to penetrate a committed Polish defence. A breakaway goal by Domarski gave Poland the lead against the run of play ten minutes into the second half. Allan Clarke equalized with a penalty eight minutes later, but Tomaszewski made a series of remarkable

▲ **Polish goalkeeper Tomaszewski was labelled a "clown", but his performance denied England a place in the World Cup Finals.**

saves to deny England a winning goal. The clown had the last laugh.

The result was a personal tragedy for England manager Sir Alf Ramsey. He was already at odds with most of the press and the football authorities – his request for league matches to be postponed on the Saturday four days before the Poland game had been turned down. Ramsey would not resign, but the following April he was sacked by the Football Association. It was shabby treatment for a man who had once brought England victory in the World Cup.

PRINCESS ANNE MARRIES

On November 14, 1973, 23-year-old Princess Anne became the first of the Queen's children to marry. Her bridegroom was Lieutenant Mark Phillips, an army officer she had met through her involvement in show-jumping. Phillips had won a gold medal in

the team event at the 1972 Munich Olympics, while Princess Anne was a gold medallist in European competition.

The wedding day was declared a national holiday, ensuring a vast crowd lined the route from Buckingham Palace to Westminster

Abbey. The bridegroom wore the ornate uniform of the 1st Queen's Dragoon Guards and the Princess was radiant in a Tudor-style high-collared wedding gown. Her two attendants were her youngest brother, nine-year-old Prince Edward, and her cousin Lady Sarah Armstrong-Jones.

The couple were generally agreed to be the picture of happiness. The warmth of the Princess's smiles throughout the wedding day contrasted with her sometimes severe demeanour on other occasions. The honeymoon began with a night at White House Lodge in Richmond Park, followed by a flight to Barbados to join the royal yacht for 18 days' cruising in the Atlantic and Pacific.

It was symptomatic of changing times that the fact of a prominent member of the royal family marrying a commoner occasioned little comment and no criticism. The fairytale wedding was not, however, followed by permanently happy marriage. The couple had two children, Peter and Zara, but were divorced in 1992, the first in a series of marital break-ups for the royal siblings.

▲ **Princess Anne and Captain Mark Phillips on the balcony of Buckingham Palace after their wedding in Westminster Abbey.**

- Government ministers Lord Lambton and Earl Jellicoe resign after admitting frequenting prostitutes

JUNE
- Elections for the new Northern Ireland Assembly

JULY
- Top professional tennis players boycott Wimbledon

AUGUST
- At least 50 die in a fire at the Summerland entertainment complex on the Isle of Man

SEPTEMBER
- Driver Jackie Stewart retires from motor racing
- Deaths of author J R R Tolkien and poet W H Auden

OCTOBER
- The Yom Kippur War between Israel and Arab states begins
- The Cod War between Britain and Iceland is ended by agreement
- Phase Three of the government's anti-inflation policy allows pay rises of 7 per cent

NOVEMBER
- The National Union of Miners declares an overtime ban
- The government declares a state of emergency to cope with the energy crisis
- A power-sharing Northern Ireland Executive Council is formed

DECEMBER
- A meeting at Sunningdale agrees on the formation of a Council of Ireland
- The government announces a three-day week with effect from the end of the year
- The Provisional IRA launches a Christmas bombing campaign in London
- Joseph Sieff, head of Marks & Spencer, survives an assassination attempt by Arab terrorists in London

1974

In the first half of the 1970s, the long postwar boom in the world economy came to an end. To people in the industrialized countries of the West, who had become accustomed to rising living standards and permanently low unemployment, the new reality of recession came as a psychological and political shock. In Britain the winter of 1973–74 was the point at which the postwar political consensus disintegrated under the impact of economic crisis.

Throughout 1973, pressures upon Edward Heath's Conservative government caused by the increasingly disturbed world economy mounted. The fixed exchange rate system that had brought stability to world markets since the war had to be abandoned, and prices of raw materials were rising fast. The increasing cost of Britain's imports fed into domestic price inflation

▲ Heath was unable to convince a wider public that he was right to force a confrontation with the miners. Here, students express their support for the strikers.

and widened the country's trade deficit, which reached a record £1.5 billion in the year.

The decision of the Arab oil states to reduce oil output and raise prices from October 1973 was a further turn of the screw. It might well have sufficed to sink the Heath government's chances of controlling inflation and avoiding mass unemployment. But a confrontation with the National Union of Mineworkers (NUM) over pay doomed an administration that already had its back to the wall.

The Heath government had not sought a confrontation with the trade unions. On the contrary, as a "One Nation" Tory committed to upholding the postwar consensus in British politics, Heath accepted that the unions had an important role to play and sought to cooperate with them. But the unions refused to play ball. To Heath's surprise, they refused to conform to the legal requirements of the 1971 Industrial Relations Act, leading to court proceedings against individual unions that soured the atmosphere. The unions also only cooperated fitfully with government efforts to combat inflation. By the autumn of 1973, Heath was convinced that any further concessions to inflationary wage demands would be disastrous.

▲ Edward Heath was not forced to call a general election, but he chose to do so on the issue of "Who Governs Britain?" The answer was that Heath did not.

On November 8, as the oil crisis began to bite, the NUM leadership voted for an overtime ban in response to an initial pay offer from the National Coal Board. Two weeks later, they rejected out of hand a revised offer of a pay rise of 13 per cent. With motorists already queuing for scarce petrol, Heath appealed to the NUM to call off industrial action in the national interest. When they refused, he took the offensive. On December 13 the Prime Minister declared that, to conserve energy supplies, a three-day working week would be instituted from the start of 1974. It was in effect a statement that should the miners go on strike, the government would fight them.

For the British public, the three-day week was in many ways a repeat of the experience of the previous miners strike in the winter of 1971–72. Candles were once more dug out of drawers for use when power was cut. Factory workers again enjoyed a four-day weekend. Office workers, who in precomputer days only used electricity for lighting and making tea, mostly continued to work five days a week, but on two days went home once it began to get dark.

The political situation was very different from 1972, however, in that the government had decided on a dramatic confrontation. For Heath it had become a question of "Who rules Britain?" Was it the government or the unions? After hesitations and negotiations through January, in early February 1974 the miners voted for an all-out strike and the government called a general election.

According to the opinion polls, Heath stood a fair chance of winning the election. However, the Conservative campaign did not go well. The government's own Pay Board announced that there was some justice in the miners' claim to be a "special case";

the director general of the Confederation of British Industries (CBI), Campbell Adamson, denounced the Industrial Relations Act for having "soured the industrial climate"; and rogue Tory Enoch Powell actually called on electors to vote for Labour, because it was more anti-European than the Conservatives.

Held on February 28, the election saw both major parties lose votes to the Liberals and the Scottish and Welsh Nationalists. The Conservatives won narrowly more votes than Labour – 37.8 per cent of votes cast to 37.2 per cent – but fewer seats in parliament. With Labour holding 301 seats and the Conservatives 297, no party had an overall majority. Heath attempted to make a deal with the Liberals that would have kept him in power, but on March 4 he had to admit failure. Labour leader

Harold Wilson was invited to form a government.

The Labour Party had chosen to campaigned on policies that committed it to a generous measure of egalitarianism. As shadow Chancellor of the Exchequer, in 1973 Denis Healey had memorably promised "to squeeze the rich until the pips squeak". Labour policies included punitive tax levels for high earners, subsidies to hold down food prices and a crackdown on "excessive" profits. There were Cabinet places for notable left-wingers such as Michael Foot and Tony Benn (as Anthony Wedgwood-Benn now styled himself).

The new administration ended the miners strike immediately by the simple expedient of paying up in full. Thoroughly content with a 35 per cent pay increase the miners went back to work.

A "social contract" was agreed between the government and the trade unions under which the unions agreed to exercise pay restraint in return for measures such as increased social benefits.

The performance of the Labour government impressed enough voters to secure re-election with a slender overall majority of four in October 1974. But the Wilson administration had no solution to Britain's economic problems. Inflation continued to rise steeply, driven by world prices, but also fuelled by high government spending. The trade deficit continued to run at an unsustainable level. In 1975 the government was forced to cut back on its spending plans and unemployment rose to levels not seen since the 1930s. Friction with the unions soon returned. The "British sickness" still remained to be cured.

▲ **After successfully running a minority government for eight months, Harold Wilson won a second general election in October 1974.**

- Price inflation for the year reaches 20 per cent; average wages rise by 26 per cent
- A major reorganization of local government is implemented: the counties of Rutland, Westmoreland, Cumberland and Huntingdonshire cease to exist
- The Methodist church ordains its first women ministers
- British Airways is formed by the merger of BOAC and BEA
- First McDonald's fast-food restaurant in Britain opens in south London
- The Covent Garden fruit and vegetable market in London moves to Nine Elms
- The Ceefax information service is introduced on BBC television
- Books published this year include *Tinker Tailor Soldier Spy* by John Le Carré and *High Windows* by Philip Larkin
- David Hockney designs sets for the Glyndebourne production of Stravinsky's opera *The Rake's Progress*
- Albums released this year include *Diamond Dogs* by David Bowie and *Band on the Run* by Paul McCartney and Wings

DC-10 AIR DISASTER

▲ **One of the engines of the Turkish Airlines DC-10 that crashed shortly after leaving Orly airport.**

On March 3, 1974, a Turkish Airlines DC-10 bound from Paris to London crashed only minutes after taking off from Orly airport. All 346 people on board were killed, making it the worst air disaster up to that time.

The aircraft broke up at an altitude of about 3,000 m (10,000 ft) and plunged into the Forest of Ermonville outside the town of Senlis. Parts of the wreckage were 11 km (7 miles) away and mutilated bodies were scattered over a wide area. Initial concerns that a terrorist bomb might have caused the crash proved false. The victims included a large number of English rugby supporters returning from a match in Paris.

The crash focused mounting concerns about air safety as both the number and size of airliners increased yearly – jumbo jets had come into service at the start of the decade. Only three years later, 583 people were killed in an air disaster at Tenerife.

PROTESTANTS BLOCK CHANGE IN ULSTER

In May 1974 a hopeful attempt at a political solution to the Northern Ireland crisis collapsed in the face of Protestant militancy. It would be more than 20 years before the stalemate thus created was broken again.

Successive British governments recognized that a return to a Protestant monopoly of power in Northern Ireland – as had existed prior to 1969 – was not a viable option. An alternative had to be found in power-sharing by representatives of both Protestant and Catholic communities. In June 1973 elections were held for a Northern Ireland assembly. The following November, a coalition government of Protestant and Catholic parties, headed by Brian Faulkner, was installed.

Sharing power with Catholics outraged Protestant diehards. They were even more appalled by the British government's recognition of an "Irish dimension" to the Northern Ireland problem.

In December 1973, at Sunningdale in Berkshire, the executive agreed to the creation of a Council of Ireland, which would give the Irish government a say in Northern Ireland affairs.

On May 14, 1974, the assembly ratified the Sunningdale agreement. That same evening, Harry Murray, a Belfast shop steward, announced that the Ulster Workers' Council (UWC) was calling a strike against the executive. Run

▲ **Northern Ireland Protestants brought down the power-sharing executive through barricades that paralyzed the province's economy.**

by a committee including hardline Loyalist politicians and the heads of Protestant paramilitary groups, the UWC effectively took over Northern Ireland. Barricades and roadblocks were erected across the Province, manned by armed paramilitaries. The UWC controlled power, food and fuel supplies. The British Army made no effort to intervene.

On May 25 Prime Minister Harold Wilson made an aggressive, blustering broadcast in which he denounced the Ulster Protestants as "people who spend their lives sponging on Westminster and British democracy and then systematically assault democratic methods". But unless it was ready to order the Army to take on the Protestants, the British government had no power to enforce its will. The assembly, the executive and Council of Ireland were abandoned, and the search for a political solution went back to square one.

FLIXBOROUGH CHEMICAL DISASTER

▲ The Flixborough chemical plant ablaze after a catastrophic explosion that killed 28 workers and destroyed nearby houses.

At 4.53 on the afternoon of June 10, 1974, a massive explosion occurred at a chemical plant at Flixborough, outside Scunthorpe on Humberside. The explosion killed 28 workers and devastated an entire village. People 6.5 km (4 miles) distant from the scene were buffeted by the blast. About 100 houses were wrecked and the factory itself was reduced to a twisted, blackened shell.

The Nypro plant was engaged in cyclohexane oxidation, a stage in the production of nylon. After a pipe feeding one of the reactors on the site developed a leak, a temporary pipe had been constructed to replace it. A leak from this pipe led to about 40 tons of gaseous cyclohexane escaping in a minute, until the vapour cloud ignited with devastating effect.

The main lesson drawn from the subsequent enquiry into the Flixborough disaster was that housing should be sited well away from chemical plants and other dangerous industrial locations as well.

THE DISAPPEARANCE OF LORD LUCAN

On the evening of November 7, 1974, Veronica, Countess Lucan, estranged wife of the 7th Earl of Lucan, stumbled into a pub near her Belgravia home in a distraught state. She claimed she had been attacked by her husband, who had murdered their children's nanny, Sandra Rivett. Thus began one of Britain's most enduring real-life mysteries.

Police found Rivett's body in the basement of Countess Lucan's home. She had been beaten to death. The Lucans' eldest daughter had been upstairs in the house during the killing, as were the couple's two other children. Her testimony appeared to confirm her mother's story. When the police went to Lord Lucan's flat, they found his passport and driving licence, but the earl himself had disappeared. A car that he had borrowed was found abandoned near Newhaven docks.

Lord Lucan, a descendant of the man who ordered the Charge of the Light Brigade at Balaclava, had led a troubled life. His marriage disintegrated after his wife began to suffer from severe depression. Separated, he fought for custody of the children and lost. He frittered away his fortune at the gambling tables and was heavily in debt.

The most likely explanation of the events of November 7 was that Lucan killed the nanny by mistake, believing, in the darkness of the basement, that she was his wife. In 1975, a coroner's court jury found that Lucan was guilty of his nanny's murder. But no criminal trial took place, because the suspect was never found.

Reported sightings of the missing earl began almost as soon as he disappeared and continued for 30 years. At one time, police were convinced he was living in South Africa, but the trail led nowhere. He was declared officially dead by the High Court in 1999, but another sighting was reported in Australia the following year. In 2003 it was alleged that Lucan had been living in Goa under the name of Barry Halpin, but this story, too, was swiftly discredited. His whereabouts, alive or dead, remain unknown.

▲ Lord Lucan's disappearance after the murder of his children's nanny sparked a mystery which remains unsolved to this day.

1974

IRA BLITZ ON BRITAIN

From 1973 onward, the Provisional IRA extended its campaign of bombing and shooting from Northern Ireland to mainland Britain. They set up "active service units", tight-knit groups of highly experienced personnel, to operate on the mainland. Attacks were primarily aimed at prestige targets or at off-duty soldiers.

Through 1974, the number and destructiveness of the bombings mounted alarmingly. On February 4 a bomb blew apart a coach carrying servicemen and their families along the M62 motorway, killing nine soldiers and three civilians. Westminster Hall, part of the Houses of Parliament, was bombed in June and the Tower of London in July. In October a bomb was left in a pub in Guildford frequented by soldiers; five people were killed, including four military personnel. The bombing of another soldiers' pub, this time in Woolwich, in early November left two dead. These were only the most notable in a spate of explosions during this period.

The bloody climax came in the Midlands in mid-November. On November 14 an IRA bomber, James McDade, was blown to bits by his own device, which he intended to plant at a Coventry telephone exchange. As IRA sympathizers gathered for McDade's funeral, the authorities announced that demonstrations in his memory were banned. Apparently in retaliation for this, on the evening of November 21 bombs were left in two crowded pubs in Birmingham city centre, the Mulberry Bush and the Tavern in the Town. A belated and inaccurate telephone warning left no chance for the pubs to be evacuated. In the ensuing explosions 21 people were killed and more than 180 injured, many seriously, in the carnage that resulted.

The Birmingham bombings triggered the passage of the Prevention of Terrorism Act, giving the police extensive new powers. Unfortunately, the police response to the bombing campaign had already been to arrest anyone they thought they could pin the bombings on and make sure the charges stuck by fair means or foul. The result was a series of major miscarriages of justice, while the terrorist campaign continued unabated into 1975.

▲ The wreckage of the Horse and Groom pub in Guildford after an IRA bomb devastated it, killing five people.

LABOUR MP FAKES SUICIDE

On November 20, 1974, John Stonehouse, Labour MP for Walsall North, disappeared during a visit to Miami, Florida. A pile of clothes on a beach was the only trace he left behind.

It was at first assumed that Stonehouse had taken a swim and accidentally drowned. When the dire state of his financial affairs was revealed, though, the case became one of suspected suicide. Obituaries were published detailing a career that had once promised great things – Stonehouse had been a minister in the 1960s Wilson government – but had latterly gone astray in increasingly dubious business dealings and a complex private life.

That Christmas Eve, however, police in Melbourne, Australia, arrested a man they had been trailing as a possible illegal immigrant. They were hoping that the individual, who gave his name as Donald Mildoon, would turn out to be murder suspect Lord Lucan. Instead, they had caught John Stonehouse.

The Labour MP had staged the phoney suicide to shake off a Department of Trade and Industry investigation that was closing in on various frauds he had perpetrated. He also intended to give his wife the slip. His new life in Australia was to be spent with his former secretary Sheila Buckley. As a long-term cover, he planned to adopt the identity of one of his constituents who had recently died.

The arrest of Stonehouse was the beginning of a lengthy legal battle. It was six months before the Australian authorities agreed to deport him to Britain. He was then held on remand in Brixton prison, while bizarrely remaining both a Labour MP and a Privy Counsellor. Indeed, his vote was theoretically of great importance

to the government, which was nursing the most slender of parliamentary majorities. When he left the Labour Party in April 1976, this technically made it a minority government.

After a lengthy and complex trial, Stonehouse was found guilty of theft, fraud and deception and sentenced to seven years in prison. In August 1976 he finally agreed to step down from his seat in parliament. After three years in Wormwood Scrubs, he was paroled on health grounds. He died of a heart attack in 1988.

◄ **Renegade MP John Stonehouse returns to Heathrow, after his attempt to fake suicide ended in arrest in Australia.**

MONTY PYTHON FLIES OFF TELEVISION

In November 1974 *Monty Python's Flying Circus* completed its fourth and final series on BBC television, although it was to enjoy a fruitful afterlife in the cinema.

The groundbreaking comedy was written and performed by John Cleese, Eric Idle, Graham Chapman, Terry Jones, Michael Palin and Terry Gilliam. All but the American Gilliam were Oxford or Cambridge graduates. Indeed, the programme was at heart quintessential Oxbridge comedy – all-male, interested in ideas and culture rather than people, and subversive in the most gentle and unthreatening way.

First broadcast at the back end of the BBC2 schedule in October 1969, *Monty Python* won a huge following attracting viewers by pushing content and format beyond all previously established limits. Freeing itself from the constraints of punch lines and even the vaguest respect for common sense, it was sillier –

or if you prefer, more surreal – than any comedy seen before. Its stream-of-consciousness linking of sketches, facilitated by Gilliam's inspired animation, allowed the team to put in anything that was funny and leave out all the boring bits.

The Pythons have been likened to the Beatles, which is fair in two

respects: they were a group of creative people with diverse and contrasting individual talents that complemented one another; and they had a substantial, if delayed, impact on the United States. It is largely thanks to *Monty Python* that many Americans to this day think of the British as especially gifted for comedy.

▲ The *Monty Python* team in the Tunisian desert to film *The Life of Brian*, a successful follow-up to their smash-hit television show.

- As a result of the falling birth rate, the UK population drops year-on-year for the first time since records have been kept
- Price inflation peaks in August at an annual rate of 26.9 per cent
- Number unemployed rises above 1.2 million
- Protestant and Catholic terrorists engage in a series of "tit-for-tat" revenge killings in Northern Ireland
- First North Sea oil is pumped ashore
- The Sex Discrimination Act outlaws discrimination in work, education and the supply of public services; its operation is monitored by an Equal Opportunities Commission
- State grants to "direct grant" schools are abolished
- "Bleepers" are introduced to alert people on the move to call their office
- Books published this year include *First Love, Last Rites* by Ian McEwan and *Hearing Secret Harmonies* by Anthony Powell, completing his 12-volume novel sequence *A Dance to the Music of Time*
- British films this year include Kevin Brownlow's *Winstanley*, Stanley Kubrick's *Barry Lyndon*, and Ken Russell's *Tommy*
- First performance of Steven Berkoff's play *East*
- New television series include *Fawlty Towers* and *The Sweeney*

TORIES ELECT WOMAN AS PARTY LEADER

On February 11, 1975, Conservative MPs elected Margaret Thatcher as leader of their party in succession to Edward Heath. That the Tories should choose a woman leader was a remarkable sign of the times – a triumph for the movement for Women's Liberation that was challenging male domination at all levels in the 1970s. But it was also evidence of the depth of feeling within the Conservative Party in favour of a fundamental change of direction.

The Heath government of 1970–74 had annoyed many Tory politicians and activists by what they saw as its abandonment of pure free-market capitalism, and its weakness in the face of the trade unions. A number of right-wing Conservatives, including Margaret Thatcher and Sir Keith Joseph, set up the Centre for Policy Studies (CPS) as a think-tank to devise alternative

▲ **Few expected Margaret Thatcher to succeed in her bid for the Tory leadership, but her strident views struck a chord with the party.**

strategies. The CPS worked out a new set of policies centred on strict control of the money supply, abandonment of the goal of full employment, welfare benefit cuts and a crackdown on union power.

Defeated twice in general elections in 1974, Heath was vulnerable to a leadership challenge. Sir Keith Joseph was at first the right wing's preferred candidate, but he made an ill-considered speech that seemed to suggest Britain's problems were caused by the poor's having too many children. The choice of the party's right-wingers then shifted to Margaret Thatcher.

Thatcher was widely regarded as merely a "stalking horse" put up to test the strength of anti-Heath feeling in the parliamentary party. But on February 4 she eliminated Heath in a straight fight by 130 votes to 119. In the second round a week later, her chief opponent as representative of the Tory moderates was William Whitelaw. She beat him by 146 votes to 79, with three other male contenders making little showing.

CREATOR OF JEEVES DIES

▲ **P G Wodehouse's novels established an enduring and largely unrealistic image of upper-class Englishness.**

Author Sir Pelham Grenville Wodehouse, known to his millions of admirers simply as P G Wodehouse, died on February 14, 1975, at the age of 93. His death came just six weeks after he had received a belated knighthood.

Although also a distinguished writer of song lyrics, Wodehouse is best known for his stylized novelistic fantasies of English upper-class life. His most famous creations were the hapless Bertie Wooster and his supercilious butler Jeeves, and Lord Emsworth, proud owner of prize pig the Empress of Blandings. Wodehouse's books bore no relation to the realities of contemporary English life, about which he was in any case poorly informed, since he lived abroad from 1924.

Interned by the Germans after they overran his French home in 1940, Wodehouse unwisely agreed to make light-hearted broadcasts from Berlin, an action which brought accusations of treason in the British press. Although no charges were brought against him, Wodehouse never again set foot in Britain, becoming an American citizen in 1955.

Wodehouse wrote 96 books in his prolific career. Asked how he did it, he quipped: "I just sit at a typewriter and curse a bit."

MYSTERY CRASH AT MOORGATE

▲ Rescuers carry away an injured passenger after the Moorgate tube disaster. The cause of the crash was never fully established.

On February 28, 1975, a disaster occurred on the London underground that has never been satisfactorily explained. At 8.46 am, a Northern Line train overran the platform at Moorgate station and accelerated into a dead-end tunnel. The train ran through a sand barrier and hit the brick wall at the end of the tunnel at around 65 km/h (40 mph). The front three carriages were mangled together in a mass of twisted wreckage. Rescue services worked throughout the day in appalling conditions to free survivors, the last to be brought out alive emerging at 10 pm In all, 43 people had died.

The driver, 55-year-old Leslie Newson, was among those killed. The investigation into the accident revealed that he had neither applied the brakes nor released the dead-man's switch, designed to stop the train if a driver fell unconscious. Newson had no problems with drugs or drink and no apparent motive for suicide. Every part of the Underground safety system, including brakes and signals, had been functioning perfectly.

In the wake of the accident all dead-end tunnels on the underground were equipped with automatic systems to brake any train driving into them.

ELM DISEASE BLIGHTS THE LANDSCAPE

During the 1970s, the British landscape celebrated in the works of artists such as John Constable and J M W Turner was changed for ever by an alliance between a fungus and a beetle, which destroyed a large majority of the country's elm trees.

Dutch elm disease was so called not because it originated in the Netherlands, but because it was first scientifically studied there. The disease was caused by the fungus *Ophiostoma ubni*, which was spread by bark beetles. It was first noticed in Britain in the 1920s, a far more virulent strain of the virus struck in 1967, possibly imported on a shipment of logs from the United States.

By the mid-1970s Dutch elm disease was raging across southern and central England, the heartlands of the English elm. About 20 million out of the 30 million elm trees in Britain were either dead or dying. There was no effective method of countering the disease, which cut off the water supply to the tree's leaves, denuding branches and eventually killing the whole tree by starvation.

The progress of the disease in East Anglia, Cornwall, northern England and Scotland was slower, but it continued to spread over following decades. By the end of the century, around 25 million elms had died across Britain.

▲ Crosses mark trees blighted by Dutch elm disease, a disease that wiped out 25 million trees in Britain, forever altering the landscape.

BRITAIN SUFFERS ECONOMIC CRISIS

In July 1975 inflation in Britain was running at an annual rate of 26 per cent. The apparently uncontrollable inflationary spiral was a result of the huge rise in oil prices during 1973–74, large wage rises dictated by powerful trade unions, and uncontrolled government spending. Public expenditure had increased from around 40 per cent of the country's Gross National Product (GNP) in the early 1960s to almost 60 per cent by 1975. Unemployment was still low by later standards, but rising fast – from virtually full employment at 2.6 per cent of the workforce in 1970 to 4.1 per cent in 1975. It would increase still further to 6.2 per cent by 1977.

Trying to master this difficult situation was the Labour government of Harold Wilson. In 1974 the government had tried to win union cooperation for voluntary wage restraint through a "social contract", offering improved social services and price controls in return for low pay rises. By July 1975, this was evidently not working, with wage demands in excess of 30 per cent commonplace. Chancellor of the Exchequer Denis Healey introduced compulsory wage controls, limiting wage rises to a maximum of £6 a week and freezing all incomes of £8,500 a year and above. Price controls were tightened and limits imposed on government spending.

The economic crisis led to a broader readjustment of government policies. Labour's programme before the February 1974 election had envisaged "a fundamental and irreversible shift in the balance of power and wealth in favour of working people". There was also a commitment to increasing the public sector of the economy. But by mid-1975 a retreat from such left-wing positions was under way. Tony Benn, the left-leaning Secretary of State for Industry, was moved to the less sensitive post of Energy Secretary because, in the words of his fellow minister Shirley Williams, he "had alarmed industrialists". Crudely, removing Benn was the price the government had to pay to secure the support of business in coping with the crisis.

Britain was forced later in the year to go to the International Monetary Fund (IMF) for a loan of over £1 billion. As a condition of the loan, the government was forced to impose further severe cuts in spending on health, education and all other social services. Ironically, the potential salvation of the British economy, North Sea oil, began to come ashore in 1975, but it would not be available in substantial quantities until the end of the decade.

▲ "What Crisis?" – Chancellor of the Exchequer Denis Healey (left) claims that Britain's economic problems are under control.

STREAKING CRAZE REACHES LORD'S

At 3.20 pm on August 4, 1975, on the fourth day of a test match between England and Australia, the slumbrous calm of Lord's cricket ground on a hot afternoon was enlivened by the sight of a long-haired young man clad only in plimsolls running towards the pitch. Captured live on television, the streaker hurdled both sets of stumps – by no means a risk-free enterprise – before police and officials could intervene.

Streaking had originated in the United States in the early 1970s. It made its first appearance in Britain at Twickenham in April

▲ Streaker, Michael Angelow, hurdles the stumps at Lords, an act that earned him enduring fame and a £25 fine.

1974, when 25-year-old Australian Michael O'Brien bared all during an England–France rugby match. The occasion generated a famous photograph of a policeman covering the bearded streaker's tackle with his helmet.

The Lord's streaker – the first to appear on television – was Michael Angelow, a cook in the merchant navy. He was fined £25 by magistrates, which he was apparently able to pay with the proceeds of the bet he won as a result of his exploit.

THE BALCOMBE STREET SIEGE

In the autumn of 1975, a Provisonal IRA terrorist cell in London was activated, and then embarked on a terror campaign across the capital. Among the targets of bombings were the London Hilton hotel, Green Park tube station and West End restaurants. Individuals were also targeted. On October 23 a bomb intended for Tory MP Hugh Fraser instead killed his neighbour, cancer expert Professor Gordon Hamilton-Fairley. On November 25 Ross McWhirter, creator of *The Guinness Book of Records*, was shot dead outside his home; he had annoyed the IRA by offering a £50,000 reward for information leading to the arrest of the bombers.

The terrorists' luck ran out on the evening of December 6, when they staged an armed attack on a restaurant in Mayfair. Driving away from the scene in a Ford Cortina, they were pursued by police. They abandoned their car near Balcombe Street in Marylebone and fled in to a block of flats. Carrying handguns, they broke into an apartment, taking the two occupants hostage. The

unfortunate couple were postal worker John Matthews and his wife Sheila, both in their 50s.

Armed police surrounded the block of flats and a protracted siege began. It lasted for six days. The police established that there were four IRA men inside the flat. Lengthy negotiations centred on their need for food, and concessions that could be extracted in return for supplying meals. By December 12, the terrorists had accepted that there was no escape. Mrs Matthews was released first. Then, with their

remaining hostage, the four gunmen emerged and surrendered to police.

Hugh Doherty, Martin O'Connell, Edward Butler and Harry Duggan were found guilty of six murders and duly sentenced to life imprisonment, to serve a recommended minimum of 30 years. While in custody awaiting trial, they hinted that they were also responsible for the Guildford and Woolwich pub bombings in 1974, but they were not tried for these offences and have never openly admitted to them. The four men were released in 1999 as part of the Good Friday agreement that brought an end to the IRA's campaign of violence.

▲ Police ran to ground an IRA cell responsible for a series of bombings and shootings in a Marylebone flat. The men surrendered after six days.

1976

NEWS IN BRIEF

- An abnormally hot summer and drought across Britain
- The government cuts spending to counter inflation and secure an IMF loan
- The bank rate peaks at 15 per cent
- The Race Relations Act makes it an offence to incite racial hatred; Commission for Racial Equality established
- Education Act compels local authorities still running grammar schools to prepare for comprehensive education
- The Concorde supersonic airliner begins commercial flights
- Conservative leader Margaret Thatcher is dubbed the "Iron Lady" by a Soviet newspaper
- The National Theatre building, designed by Denys Lasdun, opens in London on the South Bank of the Thames
- The National Exhibition Centre opens in Birmingham
- British films this year include Derek Jarman's *Sebastiane*, spoken in Latin
- First performance of David Edgar's play *Destiny*
- The punk music and fashion revolution begins with release of "Anarchy in the UK" by the Sex Pistols and "New Rose" by the Damned

HAROLD WILSON RESIGNS

On March 16, 1976, Britain's Labour Prime Minister Harold Wilson announced that he was resigning from office. The news came as a total surprise to insiders as well as to the general public. Despite awesome political problems, ranging from raging inflation and mounting unemployment to union militancy and IRA terrorism, there was no obvious reason why Wilson should have quit. He had won two general elections in 1974 and could have been expected to govern Britain for at least another three years.

Rumours were soon spreading that Wilson had been forced to go by a threat to reveal some scandal or secret about his past. It was later revealed that there had indeed been a plot to oust him, hatched by disgruntled MI5 officers. According to former MI5 officer Peter Wright's sensational book *Spycatcher*, published in 1986, the idea was to leak to the press secret files containing allegations against Wilson and some of his colleagues. According to the wildest theories circulating in secret service circles, endorsed by the paranoid American counter-intelligence chief James Angleton, Wilson was a full-blown Soviet agent. Angleton believed that Wilson's predecessor as Labour leader, Hugh Gaitskell, had been murdered by the KGB in 1963 so that they could get their man in the top post.

Unfortunately for the conspiracy theorists, there was not only no shred of truth in the allegations against Wilson, but also no connection between the MI5 plot and his resignation. In fact, the MI5 men did not carry through their plan – it was quashed by more senior officers.

It is now known that Wilson actually resigned because of the onset of Alzheimer's disease, which had begun to impair his faculties. Preferring to remain discreet about this, he spent a short spell performing useful duties in the House of Lords before retreating into private life. He was replaced as Prime Minister by James Callaghan, who led the government until the defeat of Labour in the 1979 elections.

▲ **Harold Wilson's resignation shocked Britain. Many believed that he was the victim of a secret service coup.**

THORPE CASE SCANDAL

In May 1976 Jeremy Thorpe, the leader of the British Liberal party since 1967, resigned in the face of what he described as "a sustained press witchhunt and campaign of denigration". The "witchhunt" concerned his relations with Norman Scott, usually described as an "unemployed male model". Scott had alleged that Thorpe seduced him as a young man, leading him into homosexuality. This allegation Thorpe hotly denied.

The issue might have been expected to fade from public attention after Thorpe's resignation and his replacement as Liberal leader by the clean-cut David Steele. But there was much more to the story than had immediately appeared. Police started to investigate an apparently unlikely allegation by Scott that Thorpe had plotted to have him murdered. Amazingly, enough evidence began to emerge to suggest that Scott's allegations should be taken seriously. In December 1978, a Devon magistrates court committed Thorpe and three associates for trial at the Old Bailey in London on the charge of conspiracy to murder.

The "trial of the century", as it was billed at the time, opened in May 1979. The jury heard the crown prosecutors assert that an airline pilot, Andrew Newton, had been paid £5,000 by Thorpe and three associates, George Deakin, David Holmes and John Le Mesurier, to kill Scott. The motive was the threat posed by Scott, an aggrieved ex-lover, to Thorpe's political career. It was alleged

that Newton had infact bodged the murder, succeeding only in shooting Scott's dog, a Great Dane called Rinka (hence the scandal is sometimes referred to as "Rinkagate").

The trial judge, Mr Justice Cantley, is generally agreed to have been heavily disposed in Thorpe's favour. In his summing-up, he emphasized the defendant's standing as "a

◀ **The court may have found him innocent, but Jeremy Thorpe's distinguished political career was demolished.**

Privy Counsellor, a former leader of the Liberal Party, and a national figure with a very distinguished public record". On June 22, after three days' deliberation, the jury found all the defendants not guilty. Thorpe claimed to be completely vindicated by the verdict, but he had been shown, at the very least, to have been involved with some shady characters in an unpleasant business, and his reputation and political career – he lost his seat at the next election – were left in tatters.

SUMMER OF HEAT AND DUST

In the 1970s nobody had heard of global warming and weather futurologists were inclined to speculate about a possible new ice age. So the hot, dry summer of 1976 came as a shock to long-established preconceptions about the British weather.

Starting on June 23, temperatures in southern England topped 32°C for 14 consecutive days. Even more striking than the temperature was the lack of rain. In July and August some parts of the West Country went for a month and a half without a drop of rain. Holidaymakers rejoiced and farmers wept under permanent sunshine and blue skies.

The summer drought came after an exceptionally dry winter – from October 1975 to August 1976, London had less than half its average rainfall. Forest and heath fires raged in the tinder-dry countryside. As the reservoirs emptied, mains water supplies failed in the most badly affected areas. In parts of the West Country, Wales and Yorkshire, people were forced to queue for water from tankers or standpipes. While much of the population

was delighted at basking in the hot sun, the government realized it was facing an unprecedented crisis. Early in August a Drought Act was passed imposing bans on the use of hosepipes and other water-saving measures. A dirty car became a symbol of patriotism; couples were urged to share a bath.

On August 24 Minister for Sport Denis Howell was appointed Minister in Charge of Drought Coordination. This move swiftly had the required effect. A week

after the "minister for drought" was installed, rain fell during a Test match at Lord's, drawing the loudest applause of the day from the crowd. Crisis measures remained in place into the autumn, but the weather was back to normal.

In its time, the summer of 1976 was an exceptional freak event. It was not until the 1990s that similar hot spells and the threat of drought became regular features of British life.

▲ **The exceptional summer of 1976 saw the country basking in an unbroken sunny spell for two months.**

COD WAR CRISIS

In June 1976 Britain and Iceland agreed to end the third of the "Cod Wars" that had brought these two essentially friendly nations absurdly close to armed conflict. The Cod Wars grew out of a worldwide phenomenon: the depletion of fish stocks as a result of overfishing. Between 1950 and 1970 world fish catches rose from 20 million tonnes to almost 70 million. For countries such as Iceland, heavily dependent on offshore fishing, the threat to livelihoods was acute.

Iceland's response to the fisheries crisis was unilaterally to extend its fishing limits – the distance from the Icelandic coast inside which only Icelandic fishing vessels were allowed to operate. The limits were extended from 7 km (4.5 miles) to 20 km (12 miles) in 1958, then to 50 km (31 miles) in 1972, and eventually to 320 km (200 miles) in 1975. Each time, Britain rejected the new limits, which cut ever deeper into the traditional fishing grounds of British trawlers.

The pattern of conflict in the three Cod Wars – 1958–61, 1972–73, and 1975–76 – was the same. British trawlers disregarding the new fishing limits were harassed by Icelandic gunboats, which cut their nets and sometimes sent boarding parties aboard. Britain responded by sending in Royal Navy vessels to protect its trawlers. The "warfare" largely consisted of attempts by British frigates or fishery protection vessels to manoeuvre between the gunboats and the trawlers they were harassing. This not infrequently led to collisions. In the third Cod War 15 out of the 20 British frigates deployed off Iceland were damaged in nine months.

The 1975–76 conflict was the most serious of the three, leading Iceland and Britain to break off diplomatic relations. At one point, an Icelandic gunboat, the *Thor*, actually fired a live round at British vessels. The agreement reached in June to end the dispute was largely favourable to Iceland. There was no escape for British fishermen from the trap of declining fish stocks and mounting international competition.

▲ **British trawlers prepare to enter Iceland's newly extended fishing zone, a hazardous venture during the Cod War years.**

NEW PM CALLAGHAN FACES FINANCIAL MELTDOWN

Except for the case of Winston Churchill in May 1940, it is probable that no British Prime Minister has taken office under more difficult circumstances than Jim Callaghan in 1976. Without a clear majority in parliament and thus dependent for survival on the tolerance of minority parties, his government faced a financial crisis that appeared intractable and a Labour Party that was threatening to split apart. The new Prime Minister's performance under these trying circumstances was remarkably assured.

After Harold Wilson's shock resignation, Callaghan won a Labour leadership contest in April 1976 with some ease, defeating left-winger Michael Foot in the second-round ballot by 176 votes to 137. A calm, cautious, pragmatic figure, he quickly established himself as a national leader in the Baldwin mode – reassuringly dull yet far sharper than he seemed. Crucially, he maintained good relations with trade union leaders, who trusted him more than they did any other Labour politician.

The acute financial crisis that Callaghan faced was the sorry consequence of years of high inflation, balance of trade deficits

and government overspending. Confidence in Britain among foreign investors was at rock bottom. During the summer of 1976, the value of sterling plummeted on foreign exchanges. Chancellor of the Exchequer Denis Healey had the thankless task of negotiating a second huge loan from the IMF. This time around £2.5 billion was needed. It could only be obtained in return for radical action to cut inflation and government spending.

In late September the fall of the pound was so critical that Healey, about to embark for a meeting with the IMF, was called back from Heathrow airport to shore up confidence. At this juncture, Callaghan made a

◀ **James Callaghan became PM in inauspicious circumstances, as the economy worsened and Britain had to negotiate emergency loans.**

keynote speech to the Labour Party conference. He laid out clearly the new realities of economic life in the troubled 1970s. "We used to think that you could spend your way out of recession and increase employment by cutting taxes and boosting government spending," he said. "I tell you with candour that that option no longer exists."

It was a statement that marked a transformation of British economic policy. The following December, a mini-Budget introduced spending cuts totalling £2.5 billion. It was inevitable that unemployment would rise as a result. But the IMF loan was secured and the country's finances stabilized. Despite rumblings about broken promises and the ditching of socialism, the Labour Party held together and the unions toed the line.

- The government introduces emergency measures to counter the drought
- West Indies cricketers trounce England 3–0 in the Test series; batsman Viv Richards scores 829 runs in four matches
- Violence breaks out during the annual Notting Hill carnival in London
- Death of actor Alastair Sim

SEPTEMBER
- Rioting prisoners wreck Hull prison
- British Trident and Yugoslav DC-9 collide in mid-air over Yugoslavia, killing 176
- Ian Smith accepts the principle of majority rule in Rhodesia
- The sterling crisis is acute; Prime Minister James Callaghan delivers a speech to the Labour Party conference announcing a sharp change in economic policy
- Death of Percy Shaw, inventor of "cat's eye" reflector pads

OCTOBER
- James Hunt wins the Formula One world championship
- Deaths of artist Edward Burra, actress Dame Edith Evans and philosopher Gilbert Ryle

NOVEMBER
- The government publishes a bill to create devolved parliaments in Scotland and Wales
- Death of architect Sir Basil Spence, designer of the new Coventry Cathedral

DECEMBER
- A mini-Budget makes spending cuts to meet conditions for the IMF loan
- Death of composer Benjamin Britten

DEATH OF BENJAMIN BRITTEN

The celebrated English composer Benjamin Britten died on December 4, 1976, at the age of 65. Britten first came to prominence in the 1930s, when he was often associated with the poet W H Auden – they notably provided the music and verse for the famous 1936 documentary film *Night Mail*. Britten was a pacifist and, like Auden, left for the United States at the start of Second World War.

Returning to England, Britten established his claim to be regarded as a major composer with the 1945 opera *Peter Grimes*. With this and a string of other music dramas, including *Billy Budd* and *The Turn of the Screw*, he almost single-handedly created a British operatic tradition. In 1962 his choral setting of the requiem

mass and poems by Wilfred Owen, *The War Requiem*, was premiered in Coventry Cathedral, recently rebuilt after its devastation by German bombs in 1940. The work was a popular and critical success, capturing the anti-war mood of the time. In his later years, Britten was increasingly preoccupied with the annual Aldeburgh Festival of which he was the presiding genius.

Britten's work reflected not only his pacifism, but also his homosexuality, though often in a veiled or allusive form. His life-long companion was the singer Peter Pears. Only six months before his death, Britten had been made a life peer.

▶ **Benjamin Britten's sustained brilliance as a composer was finally recognized with a life peerage just months before his death.**

NEWS IN BRIEF

- Average real incomes fall by 2 per cent in the year
- The basic rate of income tax is reduced from 35 per cent to 33 per cent
- Britain receives a large loan from the IMF
- The balance of payments moves into surplus
- Britain's oil production reaches 776,000 barrels a day
- The average price of a house in London tops £16,000
- The *Sun* overtakes the *Daily Mirror* as Britain's top-selling daily newspaper
- The Bullock Report on industrial democracy recommends appointment of worker-directors on boards of all large companies
- Books published this year include *A Time of Gifts* by Patrick Leigh Fermor and *The Ice Age* by Margaret Drabble
- Mike Leigh's television play *Abigail's Party* is broadcast
- Songs of the year include Wings' "Mull of Kintyre", the Sex Pistols' "God Save the Queen" and Julie Covington's "Don't Cry For Me Argentina"

JANUARY

- Former Labour minister Roy Jenkins becomes President of the EEC Commission
- Rhodesian leader Ian Smith rejects British proposals for Rhodesian independence
- Death of former Prime Minister Anthony Eden, Earl of Avon

DISASTER HIGHLIGHTS NORTH SEA OIL RISKS

In April 1977 the exploitation of the oil deposits beneath the North Sea produced its first ecological disaster. A blow-out occurred at a drilling platform, the Bravo rig, in Norway's Ekofisk Field when a valve was being changed. Oil gushed hundreds of metres into the air, as the workers on the platform were hastily evacuated. Over an eight-day period, more than 34 million litres (7.5 million gallons) of crude oil poured into the ocean, creating an oil slick 72.5 km (45 miles) long and 48 km (30 miles) wide. The gusher was eventually sealed by emergency teams using hydraulically operated rams.

There was no question of the oil spill causing any slowdown in the rush to develop North Sea oil production, however, spurred on by the world energy shortage since 1973. The first oil had come ashore in Britain in June 1975, and by 1977 776,000 barrels a day were being produced – a small quantity compared with more than 9 million barrels a day produced by the United States and Saudi Arabia, but far from insignificant.

▲ The massive expansion of oil production in the North Sea was not without its problems.

LIVERPOOL TRIUMPH IN ROME

▲ Liverpool's European Cup triumph was the start of a seven-year period in which the cup was won six times by English clubs.

On the evening of May 25, 1977, Liverpool initiated an exceptional period of English domination in the European Cup football competition with a victory over the German side Borussia Mönchengladbach in the Olympic Stadium in Rome.

Managed by Bob Paisley, Liverpool entered the month of May with the potential for a unique treble: the League championship, the FA Cup and the European Cup. They sewed up their second consecutive victory in the English league on May 15, but were beaten by Manchester United in the FA Cup final six days later.

In Rome, all eyes were on Liverpool striker Kevin Keegan, playing his last game for the club before transfer to German club Hamburg. He did not disappoint, performing outstandingly in a tight, gripping match. Liverpool were ahead at half-time through a goal by Terry McDermott, but Borussia equalized early in the second half. A Tommy Smith header restored Liverpool's advantage before Keegan was chopped down in the penalty box after running through the Borussia defence. Phil Neal converted the penalty to give Liverpool a 3–1 victory.

English clubs went on to win six of the following seven European Cup competitions. Liverpool won four times in this purple patch – in 1977, 1978, 1981 and 1984.

THE GRUNWICK STRIKE

In the summer of 1977, violent confrontations between pickets and police took place outside the Grunwick film processing plant in Brent, north London. The Grunwick strike became the focus for a national debate about union power and the use of picketing to uphold workers' rights.

Grunwick employed around 500 workers, a large proportion of them Asian women. Working conditions were bad and the women were typically paid £28 for a 40-hour week – the national average wage at the time was £72 a week. The strike began in the summer of 1976 when more than 100 workers were sacked for joining a trade union. Their determined maintenance of a picket outside the plant finally attracted national attention almost a year later, because of the brutal handling of some of the Asian women strikers by the police.

Grunwick's owner, George Ward, was a man of aggressive anti-union

▲ The violence at Grunwick became the focus for a national debate about union power and the use of picketing in worker disputes.

views, connected with the right-wing National Association for Freedom. He followed a policy of uncompromising resistance to the strike. In mid-June 1977 increasing numbers of young militants joined the Grunwick picket lines, attempting to stop "scab" labour being bussed into the plant. Local postal workers boycotted Grunwick, bringing its mail order business to a halt. On July 11 a "day of action" attracted more than 20,000 people to protest in front of the plant. There was fighting with police and numerous arrests.

The Grunwick confrontation came at a moment when the government, struggling against inflation, was especially determined to take a stand against workers' militancy. Although recognizing the justice of the strikers' case, ministers did not want to endorse mass picketing and intimidation. The case was referred to the newly established government conciliation service ACAS and then to a court of inquiry under Lord Scarman. Both of these found broadly in favour of the strikers, but Ward ignored their recommendations.

Without support from the government or the TUC, the strikers were doomed to defeat. By mid-November, mass picketing was at an end. The determined strikers ultimately abandoned their action in July 1978. No unions were allowed at Grunwick and there were no reinstatements of those who had been sacked.

ELIZABETH'S SILVER JUBILEE

▲ The Silver Jubilee of Queen Elizabeth II showed that Britain still had a taste for patriotic fervour, with street parties taking place in every town.

1977 was the 25th anniversary of the accession to the throne of Queen Elizabeth II. After some hesitation, the authorities, backed by the Conservative press, decided to make it an occasion for festivities.

The Silver Jubilee turned out to be a national party enjoyed by almost everyone. The celebrations began on June 6 with the lighting of a chain of bonfires around the British coast from Land's End to the Shetlands, in imitation of the beacons lit to warn of the Spanish Armada's arrival in 1588 under Queen Elizabeth I. There was a Thanksgiving Service in St Paul's Cathedral and a banquet in the Guildhall. But more important were the popular festivities at local level. Across Britain, neighbours organized street parties, with much food, drink and goodwill being consumed amid the waving of Union Jacks. It may not have been the unifying celebration of monarchy and traditional patriotism that some commentators wishfully described – after all, the Sex Pistols were near the top of the charts with their aggressive "God Save the Queen". But it was an impressive display of the continued existence of an underlying local community spirit in Britain, something most people had long thought was dead and gone.

1977

ANARCHY IN THE UK

JUNE
- Football fans damage the Wembley pitch after Scotland beat England 2–1
- Queen's Silver Jubilee is celebrated
- Violence during mass picketing outside Grunwick plant in Brent, London

JULY
- Virginia Wade wins the Wimbledon women's singles title, the first British winner since 1969
- *Gay News* is convicted of blasphemy after publishing controversial poem about Christ
- Don Revie quits as England football manager to coach the United Arab Emirates; Ron Greenwood replaces him
- Mass demonstration over Grunwick strike leads to battles with police
- International Cricket Conference threatens to ban players who appear in Kerry Packer's unofficial internationals

AUGUST
- England opener Geoffrey Boycott scores his hundredth first-class century in match against Australia at Headingley
- Queen visits Northern Ireland
- Anti-National Front demonstrators clash with police in Birmingham and London
- Scarman inquiry recommends reinstatement of sacked Grunwick workers, but its findings are ignored by Grunwick management

▲ "Don't know what I want, but I know how to get it …" – the Sex Pistols were viewed as the figureheads of the punk movement.

By the mid-1970s, the phase of hippie popular culture that had flowered in the second half of the 1960s – with its ethos of "peace and love", its search for spiritual fulfilment through drugs and Eastern mysticism, its hi-tech concept albums, and its millionaire rock superstars – had wilted. British youth and the British music and fashion scene were ready for something new and different: they found it in punk.

The true origins of punk lay in New York, where underground bands inspired by the example of Iggy Pop were creating a raw, hard-driven musical sound and exploring subversive sartorial modes, including ripped clothing and prominently displayed safety pins. An entrepreneurial English couple, agit-pop mastermind Malcolm McLaren and dress designer Vivienne Westwood, picked up on the New York scene and brought it to Britain, giving it their own twist. Through their clothes shop Sex in London's King's Road, McLaren met the young men who were to become the Sex Pistols.

Punk took off in Britain in 1976 through bands such as the Sex Pistols, the Damned, and the Clash. Their fast, primitive music was greeted as a return to the crude rebellious roots of rock'n'roll, a breath of fresh air after the "arty" rock of the hippie era. Political commentators hooked on the protest lyrics shouted over ear-splitting guitars presented punk as the expression of an alienated young generation confronted with a future on the dole. To punk's street following, gigs were a raucous, riotous explosion of misbehaviour.

In December 1976, the Sex Pistols scandalized conservative opinion by engaging in a foul-mouthed dispute with presenter Bill Grundy on early evening television. McLaren saw such confrontations as an opportunity to achieve commercial success while simultaneously subverting the system. They certainly succeeded in winning massive publicity, ensuring that punk would be the style of 1977.

Across the country, groups of young people, most with neither the ability nor the inclination to play music, climbed up on stage and called themselves bands – one of the best, the Adverts, performed a song appropriately called "One Chord Wonders". Performers adopted names such as Poly Styrene, Siouxsie and Dee Generate. The most extreme youth fashions ever seen flourished on the streets, from Mohican haircuts, Doc Martens, black rubbish sacks, and skin-piercing safety pins, to art-school-ironic chain-store kitsch.

Punks were, in principle, opposed to the established music business and independent labels sprang up to accommodate them. But bands such as X-Ray Spex and the Stranglers were soon appearing on *Top of the Pops*, comfortably being absorbed as the latest pop novelty in the endless and meaningless turnover of styles. The Sex Pistols were, as McLaren intended, less easily recuperated. Their single "God Save the Queen", provocatively released for the Silver Jubilee, was banned from radio and television, ensuring it would be a chart-topping hit.

By January 1978, when the Sex Pistols split up, punk was past its peak, although the next wave of performers – Elvis Costello, Blondie, Talking Heads – were heavily influenced by its example. The more extreme punk styles continued to survive as the uniform of a dwindling minority, eventually becoming a tourist attraction featured on postcards alongside Beefeaters, red telephone boxes and the British bobby.

PEACE PRIZE FOR THE PEACE PEOPLE

In October 1977 two Catholic women from Andersonstown, Belfast, were awarded the Nobel Peace Prize for their initiative in starting a grassroots peace movement in the Province. Betty Williams and Mairead Corrigan were, in fact, being belatedly awarded the prize for 1976, the award having been delayed through a technicality.

Williams and Corrigan started their peace initiative in August 1976 after three Catholic children in West Belfast, relatives of Corrigan, were killed by a Provisional IRA getaway car that was being pursued by an army patrol. They organized marches and rallies in which Protestant and Catholic women appeared side by side to protest against both Republican and Loyalist terrorism, braving attacks and abuse from sectarian mobs. Many former neighbours, long separated by the Troubles, reestablished contact across the sectarian divide.

The women's Ulster Peace Movement, later renamed the Peace People, attracted worldwide attention, and Williams and Corrigan became celebrities. But although the movement succeeded in temporarily reducing the level of

▲ **Betty Williams (left) and Mairead Corrigan (right) were awarded a Nobel Prize for their grassroots peace movement.**

violence in Northern Ireland, its long-term effects were limited by its lack of a political programme beyond the simple ideals of nonviolence, peace and justice.

DEATH OF A COMIC GENIUS

▲ **Silent star Charlie Chaplin in his best-loved character – the lovable tramp with a bowler hat and cane.**

On Christmas Day 1977, Charlie Chaplin, regarded by many as the greatest comic genius in the history of cinema, died at his home at Vevey in Switzerland, aged 88.

Born in London in 1889, Chaplin went into films in 1913 after learning his trade in the music halls of England. He soon invented the character of the Tramp, with bowler hat, baggy trousers and cane, becoming one of Hollywood's biggest stars. The advent of sound in films at the end of the 1920s inevitably checked his career, since his act was essentially pantomime and not adaptable to verbal repartee. His few films of the 1930s and 1940s, such as *Modern Times* and *The Great Dictator*, are widely admired, but he never recovered the popularity he had enjoyed in the silent-film era.

Chaplin was frequently a controversial figure. He married four times, always to a bride in her teens. His political views earned him the hostility of right-wing Americans, and in 1952, under pressure from McCarthyite witchhunters for alleged Communist affiliations, he vowed never to set foot in the United States again. He did return in 1972, however, to receive his second special Academy Award. He was knighted in 1975.

In a bizarre footnote to Chaplin's death, in March 1978 his coffin was stolen from Vevey cemetery, presumably in an effort to extort money from his family in exchange for the return of the body. The coffin and body were found in the nearby town of Noville two months later.

▲ **The exhumed coffin of Charlie Chaplin was found buried in a maize field close to his home on Lake Geneva.**

- Price inflation falls below 10 per cent for the first time in five years
- More than six per cent of the workforce is unemployed
- Trade union membership rises to over 13 million
- Nine million British people take holidays abroad in the year (1961: 4 million)
- Regular broadcasts of proceedings in the House of Commons begin; many listeners are disgusted by the childish behaviour of MPs
- The General Synod of the Church of England rejects the ordination of women
- Books published this year include *The Sea, The Sea* by Iris Murdoch, *The Human Factor* by Graham Greene and *The Cement Garden* by Ian McEwan
- British films this year include Alan Parker's *Midnight Express* and Martin Rosen's *Watership Down*
- First performances of David Hare's play *Plenty*, Harold Pinter's *Betrayal* and Andrew Lloyd Webber and Tim Rice's musical *Evita*
- New programmes on television include Dennis Potter's musical drama *Pennies from Heaven* and *The South Bank Show* presented by Melvyn Bragg
- Anna Ford becomes ITN's first woman newscaster
- Albums released this year include Elvis Costello's *This Year's Model* and the Jam's *All Mod Cons*
- Songs of the year include Kate Bush's *Wuthering Heights*, Police's *Roxanne* and the Boomtown Rats' *Rat Trap*

PRINCESS MARGARET DIVORCES

In May 1978, the Queen's sister, Princess Margaret, applied for a divorce from her husband, Lord Snowdon. It was the first royal divorce in Britain since Henry VIII separated from Catherine of Aragon in the sixteenth century.

Ironically, the issue of divorce had blighted Margaret's life in the 1950s, when she was pressured into renouncing the man she loved, Group Captain Peter Townsend, because his divorced state was unacceptable to the Church of England. Her marriage to the photographer Antony Armstrong-Jones, later Lord Snowdon, in 1960, at first seemed destined to succeed. As well as having two children, the couple enjoyed a lively social existence on the Sixties scene, mixing with fashionable show-business figures and others among the trendy elite.

By the 1970s, however, the marriage was on the rocks. In 1973, Princess Margaret met Roddy Llewellyn, an attractive and lively young man 17 years her junior. A failed landscape gardener, Llewellyn took to running a farm – described as a "commune" – in Wiltshire. Margaret visited him there and invited him to her property on the exclusive island of Mustique. In 1976 the *News of the World* published an "intimate" photograph of Llewellyn with Margaret in Mustique. Shortly after, Margaret and Lord Snowdon formally separated.

It was a sign of the times that the subsequent divorce in 1978 was granted quite casually. The Church of England professed itself sympathetic. Public opinion, however, was not. Margaret's relationship with a much younger man, as well as her self-indulgent lifestyle, brought outspoken criticism and severely affected the popularity she had enjoyed during the 1950s.

The relationship with Llewellyn lasted until 1981, when he married a fashion designer. Margaret's heavy smoking and drinking took their toll of her health, which declined rapidly through the 1980s. The whole sorry saga was the first sign that the romantic relationship between the British people and the royal family, carefully cultivated ever since Elizabeth II's accession to the throne, was about to enter a turbulent phase.

▲ **Princess Margaret's divorce in 1978 was the first in a series that would afflict the royal family over the next 25 years.**

DESPAIR FOR TARTAN ARMY IN ARGENTINA

In 1978, Scotland enjoyed the unprecedented experience of being the only British representative at the World Cup finals, controversially staged in military-ruled Argentina. Managed by the ebullient Ally MacLeod and including star players such as Kenny Dalgliesh and Graeme Souness, the Scots had high hopes of a successful tournament. There was even talk of winning the trophy.

Thousands of Scottish fans made the long journey to South America for the finals, but the Tartan Army soon lost its optimism. Drawn against Iran, Peru and the Netherlands in the group stage, Scotland got off to the worst possible start by losing 3–1 to Peru. After the match, Rangers

winger Willie Johnston failed a drug test, winning an unwanted place in the record books as the first player to be sent home from the World Cup finals for drug abuse.

Another spectacularly bad result – a 1–1 draw with World Cup novices Iran – left Scotland facing the near-impossible task of defeating the much-fancied Netherlands by a three-goal margin to qualify for the next round. The players rallied to the challenge in fine style. The score was 1–1 at half-time, and early in the second half bearded midfielder Archie Gemmill put Scotland ahead with a penalty. Gemmill scored again at around

70 minutes, this time jinking through the Dutch defence for one of the best individual goals ever seen at a World Cup finals. But the need for one more goal was too much for Scotland. Instead, the Netherlands scored and the match ended 3–2.

Having defeated a Dutch side that eventually made it to the final and was arguably the best in the tournament should have given Scottish fans satisfaction. But expectations had been raised too high and the early return home was viewed as a national humiliation, to be mulled over wherever Scotsmen met for many years to come.

▲ **Willie Johnston's expulsion from the World Cup was an additional humiliation for the Scottish side, which had badly underperformed.**

FIRST TEST-TUBE BABY BORN

At 11.47 pm on July 25, 1978, Louise Joy Brown was born at Oldham District General Hospital. A healthy baby weighing 2.6kg (5 lb 12 oz), she was the first person conceived outside of a human body.

The birth was the culmination of more than 12 years of research by Oldham gynaecologist Dr Patrick Steptoe, aided by Cambridge University physiologist Dr Robert Edwards. Steptoe had made it his mission to find some way of helping the many thousands of women who could not have children because of blocked Fallopian tubes. Their eggs were potentially fertile but could not descend to the uterus.

Steptoe's experiments showed how an egg extracted from the woman could be fertilized by sperm "in vitro" – in a test-tube or, more often, a dish. The most intractable problem proved to be returning the fertilized egg to the womb. By 1977, after around 80 attempts, Steptoe had still failed to make an egg implant successfully in the uterus.

Lesley and John Brown, a couple from Bristol, underwent the process of in vitro fertilization in November 1977. This time, thanks to a small change in procedure, successful implantation occurred. Because of last-minute worries about the mother's health, the baby was delivered by Caesarean section.

Along with worldwide praise for this British medical achievement,

there were many doubts expressed about such an "unnatural" birth. Some observers suggested that babies born in this way would experience long-term health or psychological problems. But Steptoe had the satisfaction of seeing in vitro fertilization become a standard medical procedure and was able to see Louise Brown grow into a healthy ten-year-old before his death in 1988.

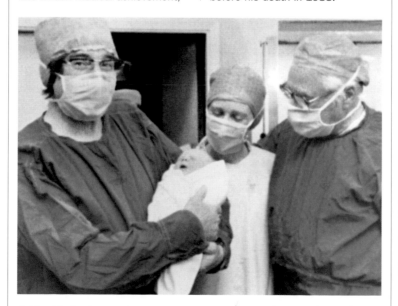

▲ **The birth of test-tube baby Louise Brown in 1978 marked the start of an era when many infertile couples could hope for a child.**

LIB-LAB PACT ABANDONED

▲ **David Steel's hope that his Liberals would have an influence on Labour government policy were never realized.**

From the spring of 1977, the loss of Labour MPs through by-election defeats and defections left James Callaghan's government without an overall parliamentary majority. The government survived on the sufferance of minority parties, especially the Liberals. A "Lib-Lab Pact" gave Callaghan sufficient assurance of consistent Liberal support to govern with confidence. The ending of the agreement in August 1978 marked the beginning of the end for his tenure of office.

The Liberals had first scented a possibility of a share in power in February 1974, when their candidates attracted over 19 per cent of the national vote and their MPs held the balance of power between Labour and the Conservatives at Westminster. Their leaders, however, turned down Edward Heath's offer of participation in a coalition government, a decision that many rank-and-file Liberals regarded as a fatal loss of nerve.

In May 1976 the Liberal Party was shaken by the alleged involvement of its leader Jeremy Thorpe in allegations relating to his relationship with Norman Scott, a former male model. The choice of the relatively uninspiring but absolutely upright David Steel as Thorpe's successor was a reaction to the scandal. Steel was not immensely popular with Liberal activists, but his responsible air reassured the public. It was in line with this image that he welcomed the chance to be seen to work with the government, supporting its efforts to overcome Britain's economic crisis.

In truth, the Liberals got very little out of Labour in return for supporting the government. What the Liberal Party desperately needed was the introduction of proportional representation in voting at general elections, but Callaghan had no intention of conceding this. In practice, the Liberals found themselves sharing the blame for some of the government's unpopular anti-inflationary measures and rising unemployment, although they could also claim some of the credit for reductions in inflation and the balance of payments.

Through 1978, pressure mounted on Steel from within his own party to abandon the pact and resume opposition to the government. In August, cooperation between the front benches of the Liberal and Labour parties was formally ended. This created a situation in which Callaghan was widely expected to call a general election. As well as facing difficulties in parliament, the government was heading for a renewed conflict with the trade unions, whose members were not willing to accept a newly imposed pay-rise limit of 5 per cent. Opinion polls suggested Labour might just win a snap election. But in September Callaghan defied all media predictions by proclaiming that he would delay calling an election until the following year.

The 1979 election was to prove a serious setback for the Liberals, whose share of the vote fell to 14 per cent. They were not helped by the trial of their former leader Thorpe for conspiracy to murder. But too close an identification with Labour had also clearly done them no good.

UMBRELLA ASSASSINATION

On September 15, 1978, a Bulgarian defector, Georgi Markov, died in a London hospital three days after being admitted with a high fever. An examination of his body revealed that there was a circular area on the back of his right thigh that showed signs of inflammation. At the centre of the inflamed area was a puncture mark about 2 mm in diameter. Under the skin doctors found a tiny metal sphere pierced with four minute holes. It was made of an alloy of platinum and iridium, a material mostly used in the aerospace industry. A coroner's inquest concluded that this metal pellet had been used to introduce poison into Markov's bloodstream, and that this was what had killed him.

Markov was an employee of Radio Free Europe and a well-known opponent of the Bulgarian communist regime of Todor Zhikov. The day before his admission to hospital, he had felt a sudden sharp pain in his thigh as he stood in a bus queue at Aldwych in central London. Turning around to see what had caused the pain, he saw a man running off. This was, it is now known, an agent of the Bulgarian secret service. He had stabbed Markov with the ferrule of his umbrella, which contained the poison-filled sphere.

Markov was not the only person attacked in this way. After his death, another Bulgarian exile, Vladimir Kostov, reported a similar incident in Paris the previous August. He had felt a sharp pain in his thigh one day when leaving the Métro, and this had been followed by a high fever – from which, however, he recovered. A medical examination revealed that Kostov had an identical perforated metal sphere under his skin. Doctors established that the poison used was ricin, a toxic derivative of castor oil.

▲ **Georgi Markov, the victim of a bizarre murder.**

VICIOUS BY NAME...

▲ **Former Sex Pistol Sid Vicious was found dead the morning after a party. He had taken a massive heroin overdose.**

On October 13, 1978, Nancy Spungen, girlfriend of the former Sex Pistols' bass player Sid Vicious, was found dead in the room the couple were sharing at New York's Chelsea hotel. She had died of stab wounds. Vicious was arrested, charged with second-degree murder, and taken to Riker's Island prison.

Born John Beverley in 1957, Vicious had been signed up for the Sex Pistols in March 1977. He was chosen by the band's manager Malcolm McLaren because his musical incompetence was matched by his talent for violent abuse. Vicious and Spungen shared a heroin habit, and their condition deteriorated after the break-up of the Pistols in early 1978. Vicious continued to perform intermittently, and had a hit with his shambolic performance of "My Way". The purpose of his American trip was to assemble a new act with Johnny Thunders, formerly drummer with punk band the New York Dolls.

No one knows what actually happened in the Chelsea hotel – probably Vicious himself did not know, given the quantities of heroin, barbiturates and alcohol he had consumed. But the event evidently left Vicious with no desire to go on living. He attempted suicide while inside Riker's Island prison. After his release on bail at the start of February 1979, his new girlfriend Michelle Robinson and his mother Ann Beverley threw a party, during which he collapsed. The following morning, he was found dead of a drug overdose.

- "Winter of discontent" brings strikes and unrest
- Unemployment rises sharply
- The price of oil doubles
- The minimum lending rate rises to 17 per cent
- The Education Act of 1976 is repealed, freeing local authorities in England and Wales from obligation to introduce comprehensive schools
- Books published this year include *Hitchhiker's Guide to the Galaxy* by Douglas Adams and *Smiley's People* by John Le Carré
- British films this year include Terry Jones's *Monty Python's Life of Brian*
- New plays include Martin Sherman's *Bent* and Peter Shaffer's *Amadeus*
- BBC television spy series *Tinker Tailor Soldier Spy* is broadcast
- Albums this year include The Clash's *London Calling* and Police's *Regatta de Blanc*
- Songs of the year include Elvis Costello's "Oliver's Army", Pink Floyd's "Another Brick in the Wall" and the Boomtown Rats' "I Don't Like Mondays"

THE WINTER OF DISCONTENT

▲ **Rubbish piles up in the street during the "Winter of Discontent". It was images such as this which brought down the Callaghan government.**

Prime Minister James Callaghan's decision not to hold a general election in September 1978 turned out in retrospect to have been one of the worst mistakes in modern British politics. What followed has gone down in history as the "winter of discontent" – after a Shakespeare-based headline in the *Sun* newspaper.

The Callaghan government had experienced considerable success in holding down wage rises to counter inflation, but there was mounting discontent among union members at wage levels. When Callaghan called for a 5 per cent limit on pay rises from the summer of 1978, the TUC ended its cooperation with government incomes policy and returned to "free collective bargaining", in which wage rises were set without guidelines being laid down by the government.

The winter crisis began when lorry drivers called a nationwide strike to begin at the start of the New Year. The country faced the prospect of failing food and fuel supplies. Under the circumstances, it was easy for journalists to make Callaghan's habitual unflappable air appear culpably complacent. When he returned from an international summit in Guadeloupe on January 10 looking tanned and relaxed, he was wrongly alleged to have said: "Crisis – what crisis?"

The lorry drivers were induced to return to work by pay rises of up to 20 per cent. This opened the floodgates for discontented public service workers to press their pay claims. A one-day national stoppage on January 22 was followed by a rash of local strikes by, among others, dustmen, health service workers, and gravediggers. Rubbish piled up in the streets, and schools closed for lack of support staff. Although a face-saving agreement with the trade unions was made in mid-February, the Callaghan government never recovered from the impression of chaos and incompetence that the "winter of discontent" created.

In the end, though, it was not strikes that brought down the Labour government but devolution. Since the ending of the Lib-Lab Pact, the government had been dependent for a majority on the support of Scottish Nationalists in the House of Commons. In referendums held in March, voters in Scotland and Wales failed to back a proposal that would have given them a measure of home rule. The government dropped its devolution legislation, and the Scottish Nationalists withdrew their support. On March 28 the government lost a vote of confidence in the Commons and was forced to call an election.

BLAIR PEACH KILLED BY POLICE

On April 23, 1979, clashes between police and antiracist demonstrators in Southall, west London, ended in the killing of a left-wing teacher, Blair Peach, beaten to death by police officers.

The Southall disturbances were one of a sequence of clashes in the late 1970s occasioned by the provocative behaviour of the right-wing National Front (NF) and the response of antiracist movements such as the Anti-Nazi League. With a general election campaign in progress, the NF chose to hold an election rally in Southall precisely because it was a district with a large Asian population. Despite protests and petitions by local residents, Home Secretary Merlyn Rees refused to ban the meeting. About 3,000 protestors – mostly local Asians and members of the Anti-Nazi League – turned out to demonstrate. There was a large police presence, including members of the Metropolitan Police's Special Patrol Group (SPG). Tasked with ensuring that the NF meeting went ahead, the police used aggressive tactics, driving vehicles at protesters and sending snatch squads into the crowd. Many demonstrators were injured, some seriously, and about 300 were arrested.

Blair Peach, a New Zealander who worked with special needs children in the East End, was a member of the Anti-Nazi League and the Socialist Workers Party. He was pursued by SPG officers in to a side street and beaten on the head with a heavy implement. He died the following day. Peach's funeral on June 13 was attended

▲ **Mourners carry the coffin of Blair Peach, killed during a protest against a National Front March. His killers were never prosecuted.**

by more than 10,000 people. He has since had a school named after him and been memorialized in other ways. But

no one was ever prosecuted for the killing, even though the police officers in the van that pursued him were subsequently identified

THATCHER ENTERS NO 10

▲ **Margaret and Denis Thatcher prepare to move into 10 Downing Street, which would be their home for the next decade.**

On May 4, 1979, Conservative leader Margaret Thatcher became Britain's first woman Prime Minister. She had guided the Tories to a substantial general election victory, with 44 per cent of the votes cast and 339 seats in the House of Commons, compared with Labour's 37 per cent vote share and 269 seats.

The Conservatives had taken the novel step of employing an advertising agency, Saatchi and Saatchi, to mastermind their propaganda during the election. A hoarding advertisement showing a dole queue, with the slogan "Labour isn't working", was especially effective – although unemployment was in fact low by the standards Britain would experience under the Thatcher government.

The election was a watershed in British politics. After a 15-year period in which Labour had been in power for all but four years, the

Conservatives were to rule for the next 18 years. What is more, they were to overturn many of the principles accepted by both parties since the Second World War, including the commitment to a welfare state and the acceptance of a "mixed economy", with a powerful state sector coexisting with private enterprise.

That such radical change would result from Thatcher's election was, however, at the time far from obvious. Celebrating her election, she piously declared to the media: "Where there is discord, may we bring harmony … where there is despair, may we bring hope." Her first government had no place for Edward Heath, but many of its members were what would later be called Conservative "wets" still committed to "One Nation" Toryism. The shape of a distinctively Thatcherite administration would take time to emerge.

EUROPEAN ELECTIONS

▲ **British members sat alongside colleagues, such as Jacques Chirac, as they faced the first direct elections to the European Parliament.**

The first direct elections to a European parliament were held on June 7, 1979. This should have been an epoch-making event in the progress away from a Europe of nation states, but the reaction of most voters across the Continent was boredom and indifference. This was especially true of Britain, suffering voting fatigue only a month after a general election. Less than one in three registered voters turned up at the polls. Most of those who did bother to vote backed the Tories, who won 60 of the 81 Euro-seats allotted to the United Kingdom. Labour took 17 seats, with one for the Scottish Nationalists and three going to Ulster Unionists. In Europe as a whole, however, victory went to social democrat parties.

Voters' lack of enthusiasm for Europe was shared by the new Prime Minister, Margaret Thatcher. By the end of the year, she had embarked on an aggressive campaign to cut Britain's contribution to the EEC budget. Thatcher made it clear that she would fight every attempt to chip away at British sovereignty.

MOUNTBATTEN KILLED BY IRA BOMB

On August 27, 1979, the Queen's cousin, Earl Mountbatten of Burma, was killed by the Provisional IRA. Lord Mountbatten was holidaying with his family in County Sligo, in the Irish Republic. A bomb was placed on board his boat, *Shadow V*, moored in Mullaghmore harbour. Shortly after he set out on a fishing trip with members of his family, the bomb was exploded by a terrorist with a radio remote-control.

Killed in the blast with Lord Mountbatten were his 15-year-old grandson, Nicholas Knatchbull, and a 15-year-old Irish boy, Paul Maxwell. His daughter, Lady Brabourne, her son Timothy, her husband Lord Brabourne, and her mother-in-law, the Dowager Lady Brabourne, were all seriously injured in the blast. The Dowager Lady Brabourne later died of her injuries.

On the same day, 18 British soldiers were killed at Warrenpoint in Northern Ireland, the biggest death toll suffered by the British Army in a single incident in the Province. The massacre occurred on a stretch of road separated from the Irish Republic by Carlingford Lough. Two bombs were exploded by remote control from across the Lough. Firing into the Irish Republic in an attempt to hit the terrorists responsible, the soldiers only succeeded in shooting dead an English tourist.

Most of the soldiers killed at Warrenpoint were members of the Parachute Regiment, the formation responsible for the killing of 13 Catholics on Bloody Sunday in 1972. After the events of August 27, a slogan painted on a wall in a Catholic area of Belfast read: "13 gone not forgotten, we got 18 and Mountbatten".

▲ The funeral of Earl Mountbatten of Burma, one of Britain's great war heroes and the most high-profile of all the IRA's victims.

THE QUEEN'S OWN SPY

▲ After a life at the very heart of the British establishment, Anthony Blunt was finally exposed as a former Soviet spy.

On November 21, 1979, Prime Minister Margaret Thatcher confirmed, in answer to a parliamentary question, that Sir Anthony Blunt, a leading art historian and Surveyor of the Queen's Pictures, had been a Soviet spy. His guilt had been strongly hinted at in a recent book, *The Climate of Treason*, by biographer Andrew Boyle. Blunt was promptly stripped of his knighthood, although this was the only penalty that befell him.

Blunt had been one of a group of upper-class students who were converted to communism while at Trinity College, Cambridge, in the 1930s, and recruited by Soviet intelligence. Two of the Cambridge spies, Donald MacLean and Guy Burgess, fled to the Soviet Union in 1951. A third, Kim Philby, was exposed in 1963. The following year, a tip-off led to the interrogation of Blunt, who had worked for MI5 during the Second World War. The wily aesthete did a deal with his interrogators, agreeing to tell them everything he knew – including his own part in the escape of Burgess and MacLean – in return for immunity from prosecution and total secrecy, allowing him to continue his distinguished career with an unblemished public reputation.

Blunt's eventual exposure was traceable to elements within MI5 who were unhappy that he had escaped punishment. The same MI5 officers, who included Peter Wright, the author of *Spycatcher*, were convinced that a fifth Soviet spy had worked in British intelligence, and that the Fifth Man was Sir Roger Hollis, the director-general of MI5 from 1956 to 1965. This startling allegation was, however, dismissed by Thatcher in 1981 as almost certainly untrue.

1980–1989

For Britain, the 1980s was dominated by a single personality: Margaret Thatcher. As Prime Minister throughout the decade, she won the adulation of her followers and the hatred of her enemies in equal measure. Yet during its first term, her administration achieved the unenviable feat of presiding over mass unemployment alongside rampant inflation. The Thatcher premiership might well have gone no further but for the Falklands War in 1982, victory in which allowed the Prime Minister to display her leadership skills to full effect. Along with a split in the Labour Party, its effects ensured Thatcher's re-election with a massive majority in 1983. This in turn opened the way for radical change, as she recast the country in her own image.

Thatcher may have genuinely believed that the threat of poverty and unemployment was a necessary spur to enterprise and ambition, and that the safety net of the welfare state undermined personal responsibility. The trend towards greater social equality that had prevailed ever since the Second World War was sharply reversed during her premiership by major cuts in taxation for the higher paid and reductions in benefits for the worst off. The "mixed economy", in which large state monopolies co-existed with a free market, was rapidly dismantled through "privatization", Thatcher's most lasting legacy. No institution — universities, hospitals, local councils or law courts — was sheltered from the government's radical drive to blow away the stuffy practices of the past with a cold bracing blast of competition and enterprise.

The Thatcher revolution naturally stimulated resistance, which was grist to the mill of a leader who revelled in conflict. Left-wingers who as recently as the 1970s had glimpsed a real possibility of turning Britain into some form of socialist workers' state, found themselves struggling against the tide of history. First, the trade union movement was excluded from the counsels of government, then it was crushed by legal curbs on industrial action and a ruthless deployment of police power to enforce industrial legislation. The defeat of the miners strike in 1984–85 was a decisive setback for the unions, brought on by a failure to assess the altered balance of forces and of willpower between workers and the government. Thatcher rode out riots in the inner cities, often with a strong racial element, which constituted an inarticulate protest against the society she was creating. She also survived the IRA, which had turned into a highly professional terrorist organization, and which almost succeeded in assassinating her at the Conservative Party conference in Brighton in 1984. Anti-nuclear protestors, who abounded after the decision to install US Cruise missiles in Britain, she simply dismissed as deluded stooges of the Soviet Union.

Britain became a more heartless society in the 1980s. At many levels, a sense of social solidarity which dated from the Second World War was replaced by personal ambition and competition. Life became more dynamic and enterprising, but much less secure. Of course, not even a leader as decisive as Thatcher could change a society as complex as Britain's in one clear direction. The tastelessly materialistic "yuppies", making quick fortunes out of the stock market and rising property prices, were definitely "Thatcher's children". So, in a different sense, were the increasingly desperate and violent members of the disadvantaged underclass, who terrorized decaying housing estates and rioted on the football terraces. But many of the cultural changes initiated in the 1950s and 1960s continued unabated. Divorce and illegitimacy rates continued to rise and — despite the onset of AIDS — young people partied with an extravagant decadence far surpassing that of the 1960s.

By the last years of the decade, Thatcher's hold on power was slipping. The Cabinet was a stage metaphorically littered with corpses, as wave after wave of ministers attracted their leader's ire or found her dominance intolerable. Even her government's core achievement, the restoration to health of the British economy, was called into question as inflation rose once more and the balance of payments deficit soared to record levels. As Prime Minister, Thatcher would not long survive the decade she so decisively dominated.

- Unemployment climbs above 2 million and inflation rises to 21 per cent as the government institutes monetarist economic policy
- Britain's oil exports exceed its oil imports
- The Employment Act curbs the power of trade unions, outlawing secondary picketing and requiring unions to ballot members before strikes
- The Housing Act gives council tenants the right to buy their homes cheaply
- The Companies Act makes "insider dealing" illegal
- The Campaign for Nuclear Disarmament (CND) revives, partly in response to a plan to station US Cruise missiles in Britain
- Simon Rattle becomes principal conductor of the Birmingham Symphony Orchestra
- Books published this year include *Rites of Passage* by William Golding
- New plays include Willy Russell's *Educating Rita*, Howard Brenton's *The Romans in Britain* and David Edgar's *Nicholas Nickleby*
- First performance of Oliver Knussen's opera *Where the Wild Things Are*
- Showing of the television documentary *Death of a Princess* outrages Saudi Arabia
- Albums released this year include Roxy Music's *Flesh and Blood* and The Police's *Zenyatta Mondatta*

DISASTER IN THE NORTH SEA

▲ The beleaguered rig *Alex Kielland* after it was towed into Stavangar Harbour for refloating.

On March 27, 1980, the *Alexander Kielland*, an oil platform owned by Phillips Petroleum, capsized in strong winds. It was the worst tragedy to hit the North Sea oil industry since production first became possible in 1975.

Based in Norwegian waters, the platform – used as a floating hotel – was turned on its back when hurricane-force gales hit the region. Many of the more than 200 men on board were cast into the North Sea; others were trapped inside. In spite of being a relatively busy shipping region – 20 vessels were within a radius of 80 km (50 miles) of the rig – the appalling weather conditions made rescue attempts very difficult, while the freezing waters of the northern North Sea made survival for more than a few hours unlikely. In the end, fewer than 100 men were saved.

An inquiry recorded that the collapse was a freak occurrence in unusually violent weather conditions, and was reluctant to make recommendations that would inhibit oil production. Oil was already becoming a crucial factor in the British economy. In the summer of 1980, Britain became for the first time a net exporter of oil, potentially offering a solution to the country's long-term balance of payments problem.

RHODESIA BECOMES ZIMBABWE

On April 18, 1980, Britain granted independence to Southern Rhodesia, its last colony in Africa. Renamed Zimbabwe, the independent state came under the rule of former guerrilla leader Robert Mugabe.

The founding of Zimbabwe brought to an end a saga that had begun with the illegal unilateral declaration of independence by Rhodesia's white minority leader Ian Smith in 1965. Ever since, British governments had vainly sought a path to legal independence for the country through a compromise between the white minority and the black majority.

Faced with a guerrilla war waged by the Patriotic Front (PF), an alliance between Mugabe's forces and those of Joshua Nkomo, Smith produced his own "internal settlement" under which anti-PF black politician Abel Muzorewa became Prime Minister in April 1979. But guerrilla activity continued to grow and the internal settlement did not win British recognition.

The Thatcher government elected in May 1979 was widely expected to favour the Rhodesian whites. Instead, Foreign Secretary Lord Carrington mounted a forceful

▲ The flag goes down on Empire. In April, 1980, Britain's last African colony, Rhodesia, became independent and was renamed Zimbabwe.

diplomatic initiative to pressure the whites into accepting majority rule. At the Lancaster House Conference in autumn 1979, all sides agreed on a plan for democratic elections which would lead to legal independence.

In December 1979, a British governor, Lord Soames, arrived in Rhodesia to take control of the colony while elections were held. A small Commonwealth Monitoring Force succeeded in policing a ceasefire that ensured reasonable freedom to vote, despite intimidation by armed men on both sides. The clear victory for Mugabe, regarded as the most radical candidate in the field by far, came as a shock both to the British government and to Rhodesian whites, but the result was accepted by all with reasonably good grace.

DEATH OF THE MAESTRO OF MYSTERY

April 29, 1980, saw the death of Alfred Hitchcock, Hollywood's king of suspense. He was 80 years old.

Born in London in 1899, Hitchcock joined the fledgling British film industry after studying engineering at the University of London. His first work was designing title cards. Quickly progressing, by 1925 he had directed his first feature film. The following year, he made *The Lodger*, about a man suspected of being Jack the Ripper. Leaving the audience on the edge of their seats until the very last frame, it was the first of more than 80 suspense-filled films Hitchcock would make during a distinguished 50-year career.

Hitchcock was one of the first great directors to understand the mechanics of film-making and how audiences could be manipulated. His hallmarks were surprise – "Always make the audience suffer as much as possible" – or a slow build-up of tension – "There is no terror in a bang, only in the anticipation of it."

In 1939, after establishing a world reputation with such classic British thrillers as *The Thirty Nine Steps* (1935) and *The Lady Vanishes* (1938), Hitchcock moved to Hollywood where his debut film, Daphne du Maurier's *Rebecca*, won him an Oscar. During the next 20 years, he made

▲ The king of suspense, Alfred Hitchcock, was responsible for many of the greatest Hollywood thrillers.

some of the greatest films of the period, including *Spellbound* (1945), *Strangers on a Train* (1951), *Rear Window* (1954) and *Vertigo* (1958).

An endearing characteristic of each of Hitchcock's films from 1940 onwards was a single fleeting cameo appearance, invariably away from the centre of action. His celebrity was such that audiences delighted in spotting the man who was, after all, the *true* star of his films. It was a view with which Hitchcock would also have agreed, having been famously quoted as saying "actors are like cattle"; when his star of the moment, Carole Lombard, took offence, his retort was: "What I said was, actors should be *treated* like cattle."

1980

STORMING THE EMBASSY

On April 30, 1980, the world of international terrorism came to London dramatically as five masked gunmen forced their way into the Iranian embassy, taking captive 19 hostages. Among the Iranian officials held at gun point were three Britons. A police cordon was immediately placed around the embassy.

The gunmen were identified as Iranian Arabs and issued a series of demands which included the release of political prisoners held by the Ayatollah Khomenei.

After tense negotiations, the kidnappers released five of the hostages. Over the days that followed, they grew increasingly impatient as no formal response came from Iran. They informed the British authorities that if their

▲ The siege of the Iranian embassy brought the SAS, with their motto "who dares wins", to the attention of the British public.

demands were not met, they would begin killing the hostages.

True to their word, on May 5 two hostages were shot. The response was a spectacular attack by the British Special Air Service (SAS), who abseiled into the embassy. Three of the five gunmen were killed instantly. All of the remaining hostages were safely released.

MOSCOW OLYMPICS

The 1980 Olympic Games, held in Moscow, were boycotted by the United States and many other nations in protest at the Soviet invasion of Afghanistan the previous December. Resisting pressure from the government, the British Olympic Association refused to join the boycott, allowing British athletes to enjoy their most successful games for years.

▲ Sebastian Coe celebrates a gold medal as he crosses the 1,500m finishing line, with Steve Ovett not far behind.

Scottish runner Allan Wells won the 100 m, the first Briton to do so since Harold Abrahams in 1924, and Daley Thompson fought off formidable Soviet competition to win the decathlon. The most gripping contest, however, was between middle-distance runners Sebastian Coe and Steve Ovett. Going into the games, Coe held the world record for the 800 m and shared the 1,500 m record with Ovett. In Moscow, Coe had to settle for silver behind Ovett in the 800 m, but took gold in the 1,500 m, with Ovett collecting the bronze medal.

American commentators tried to devalue medals won at Moscow, claiming the boycott had allowed second-string athletes to win. But statistics contradict this view, since 36 world records and 76 Olympic records were broken at the Games – hardly evidence of substandard performances.

THATCHER "NOT FOR TURNING"

During her second year in office, Prime Minister Margaret Thatcher came under intense pressure to change her economic policies, which seemed to be going disastrously wrong. Speaking at the Conservative conference on October 10, 1980, she stubbornly insisted that there would be no policy U-turn. In a phrase adapted from the title of a play by Christopher Fry, she told delegates: "The lady's not for turning."

At the time, her insistence on continuing with tight control of the money supply seemed politically suicidal. This monetarist policy and lack of government assistance for failing firms had brought closures of factories, mills and mines across the country. Output was falling and unemployment rocketed to the highest level in Western Europe. What is more, the chief aim of this tight money policy, to rein in inflation, completely failed. Price rises accelerated as they had in the mid-1970s, rising to above 20 per cent a year.

Mass unemployment and high inflation provoked criticism from all sides. No fewer than 364 economists signed a letter to *The Times* in March 1981 denouncing the government's economic policy. By then opinion polls showed a mere 27 per cent of electors intending to vote Conservative at the next election. Few would then have predicted that Thatcher would still be Prime Minister at the end of the decade.

▲ Mrs Thatcher's image as an unyielding conviction politician was underlined by her catchphrase "The lady's not for turning".

BEATLE MURDERED

▲ Tributes poured in from distraught fans after the shocking news of John Lennon's assassination.

On December 8, 1980, music fans the world over were stunned to hear the news that John Lennon, former member of the Beatles, the most famous pop group of all time, was dead. The 40-year-old musician had been returning from a recording session to his Manhattan apartment when he was shot four times from close range as he left his limousine.

The assassin was a 25-year-old fan named Mark Chapman. He had apparently stalked his idol for days, even at one point asking for an autograph. He did not resist arrest, nor give any reason for committing the murder. Chapman, although expected to plea insanity, admitted his guilt and in August 1981 he was sentenced to life imprisonment.

By the time the Beatles split in 1970, Lennon was already a well-established political protester, the peace "bed-ins" with his wife, the Japanese artist Yoko Ono, having made headline news the world over. His music had also taken a more political direction, with Lennon penning such popular anthems as "Give Peace a Chance" and "Imagine".

Alcohol, drugs and a well-publicized split with his wife kept him away from the music world during the second half of the 1970s. Reunited with Ono by 1980, Lennon's first album in half a decade, *Double Fantasy*, was released shortly before his death.

- Unemployment rises close to 3 million
- British Rail's new Advanced Passenger Train is withdrawn from service after technical hitches
- The Road Traffic Act makes the wearing of seat belts compulsory
- The Humber Bridge is completed, then the world's longest suspension bridge
- The NatWest Tower in the City of London, Europe's tallest building, is officially opened
- British Telecommunications (BT) is founded
- The London Docklands Development Corporation is set up
- *The Times* is bought by Australian Rupert Murdoch; "Tiny" Rowland, head of Lonrho, buys the *Observer*
- Books published this year include *Midnight's Children* by Salman Rushdie and *Lanark* by Alasdair Gray
- British films this year include Hugh Hudson's *Chariots of Fire* and Karel Reisz's *The French Lieutenant's Woman*
- New works by British sculptors include Tony Cragg's *Britain Seen from the North* and Richard Deacon's *If the Shoe Fits*
- The musical *Cats*, with music by Andrew Lloyd Webber, opens in London
- The television series *Brideshead Revisited* is broadcast
- Moira Stuart becomes Britain's first black woman newscaster

NEW POLITICAL PARTY FORMED

On January 25, 1981, four prominent members of the Labour Party resigned. In what they called the "Limehouse Declaration", former Cabinet ministers Roy Jenkins, Bill Rodgers, Shirley Williams and Dr David Owen made plain their view that the Labour Party was moving too far towards the political left. They went on to found the Social Democratic Party (SDP), the first significant new political party in Britain for almost 80 years.

The "gang of four" made their move after the election in November 1980 of the amiable but ineffectual left-winger Michael Foot as Labour leader. Foot was a passionate opponent of nuclear weapons and endorsed unilateral nuclear disarmament as official Labour policy. Pressure from the party rank and file committed Labour to a programme of state control of the economy, while left-wingers also secured an internal party reform which forced all sitting MPs to seek reselection by their local party members. More right-wing Labour MPs, unpopular with activists, faced being ousted.

The avowed aim of the Social Democrats was to promote a

centrist line that they felt was more in keeping with the desires of the public. The formal founding of the SDP took place on March 26, with Jenkins as party leader. Although it was hoped that it would attract moderate dissidents from both parties, of the 30 MPs who pledged allegiance, only one was a former Tory. Some SDP policies, such as electoral reform and European integration, overlapped with those of the Liberals and the two parties quickly formed what would become an uneasy alliance.

With Labour moving to the left and Mrs Thatcher leading an unpopular right-wing Conservative government, there was certainly room for a centre party in 1981. At first, the foundation of the SDP seemed thoroughly justified by its electoral success. In November, at the Crosby by-election, Shirley Williams was returned with a majority of 5,000 in a seat that the Tories had won by a clear 19,000 votes in 1979.

In practice, though, the only way that the SDP could succeed in the longer term was to supplant Labour as the principal opposition to the Conservatives. This in the end it failed to do, partly because Labour never moved so far to the left as to become unelectable. In practice, the main effect of the SDP was to ensure Thatcher's repeated re-election by splitting the vote against her.

▲ The founders of the Social Democratic Party pledged to "break the mould" of British politics.

IRISH HUNGER STRIKES

During 1981, there was a renewal of mass protest by Catholics in Northern Ireland. It was fuelled by a series of hunger strikes by inmates at the high-security Maze prison.

At the start of March 1981, Bobby Sands, a Sinn Fein candidate for the coming election, who was serving a sentence for a firearms offence, announced that he was on hunger strike in protest at his treatment by the British authorities. His demand – like that of other convicted members of the Irish Republican Army (IRA) – was that he should be treated as a political prisoner rather than a criminal. Two weeks later, Sands was joined on his protest by Francis Hughes, another convicted bomber.

The escalating hunger strikes within the Maze proved to be the focal point of a series of violent clashes between demonstrators and the British Army in Northern Ireland. The violence worsened on May 5, when, after 66 days of refusing food, Bobby Sands died,

▲ The death of hunger striker Bobby Sands (right) had a profound impact on Catholic opinion.

just weeks after winning a parliamentary seat. Hughes died a week later. Both were given IRA "military" burials. Eventually, a total of ten IRA inmates starved themselves to death, before the hunger strikes were called off in October.

The evident bravery and commitment of the men who died and the absoluteness of the Thatcher government's refusal to negotiate or make concessions of any kind had a profound effect on Catholic opinion in Northern Ireland. For the first time, Sinn Fein began to attract majority electoral support in some Catholic areas. In the long run, this was to shift the emphasis of the Republican struggle from the gun to the ballot box.

ENDGAME FOR THE YORKSHIRE RIPPER

On May 22, 1981, one of Britain's most notorious serial killers, Peter Sutcliffe, was found guilty of the murder of 13 women between 1975 and 1980. He was sentenced to life imprisonment, with a rider that he must serve at least 30 years.

Sutcliffe, a long-distance lorry driver, chose his victims by cruising the red-light districts of Bradford and Leeds. The violent nature of the murders – the victims, mostly prostitutes, were killed by hammer blows and then mutilated with a knife – quickly led police to deduce that they were the work of the same man. Long before Sutcliffe's discovery and arrest, the murderer had been christened "The Yorkshire Ripper" by the British media.

Sutcliffe was not an especially cunning criminal. The fact that he eluded the police for so long was more down to luck; during the massive police investigation of the murders he was even questioned once before being released. In the end, his capture was a simple matter of routine policing: he was stopped as a suspected kerb-crawler. Giving a false name, he failed a police check against his car registration and was arrested. He quickly confessed to the killings.

His trial began on May 5, 1981. Although his guilt was not a matter for dispute, his sanity was. Sutcliffe pleaded diminished responsibility, claiming that God had spoken to him, ordering him on a mission to rid the world of prostitutes. The jurors were unmoved by his claims.

▲ A retouched police photograph showing the likeness of Peter Sutcliffe at the wheel of his truck.

DISTURBED SUMMER

▲ **Black youths take to the streets of Brixton. London's Metropolitan Police were widely perceived as the "enemy".**

The summer of 1981 was a season of stark contrasts as the hysteria surrounding the forthcoming marriage of Prince Charles to Lady Diana Spencer was interrupted by periodic youth rioting in some of the country's poorest areas.

With unemployment having spiralled over the 2 million mark, the hardest-hit group were school leavers from minority cultures. The signs of trouble to come first emerged on April 11, 1981, when hundreds of predominantly black youths rampaged through the London suburb of Brixton. With the police powerless to react, the rioters looted and burned out dozens of shops and offices. In early July the focus of attention shifted to the Toxteth area of Liverpool, where a standoff resulted in more than 100 police injuries.

The rioting was seen as racially motivated by a Conservative government that always fell shy of making a connection between unemployment and crime. However, it served to highlight the alienation of a growing social grouping. By a peculiar quirk of fate, the zeitgeist of the summer of 1981 was captured succinctly in one of the season's biggest hits, "Ghost Town" by the Specials, an inter-racial pop group, which summed up the mood of the moment: "Government's left the youth on the shelf … people are getting angry."

BOTHAM WINS ASHES SERIES

The Test series against Australia in the summer of 1981 was one of the most unlikely England triumphs ever recorded, and it made flamboyant all-rounder Ian Botham a national hero.

Yet the series began dismally for Botham. He had been appointed England captain at the age of 24, a responsibility that weighed too heavily on his shoulders. In the first two Tests both his personal performance and that of the team were poor. Botham resigned the captaincy to avoid being sacked, and was replaced by Mike Brearley.

England went into the third Test at Leeds one match down. Late on the afternoon of the fourth day, they had been forced to follow on, and were 92 runs behind Australia with seven wickets lost. Bookmakers offered odds of 500–1 against an England win. But Botham was still at the wicket. Aided by the tail-enders, he battered the Australian bowling all around the ground. When England

▲ **Ian Botham's stature and skill with the bat and ball earned him the nickname "Beefy" and won an improbable Ashes victory for England.**

were finally all-out the following day, he was undefeated on 149. Australia required only 130 to win, but pace bowler Bob Willis completed the improbable victory by taking 8 for 43, shooting the Australians out for 111.

The cricketing madness continued in the next two tests. At Edgbaston, Botham once more turned certain Australian victory into defeat, with a bowling spell of five wickets for one run at the end of the match. At Old Trafford the all-rounder scored 118 in 123 minutes with six sixes to help England clinch the series 3–1. In Brearley's words, Botham had brought "the hunk and flavour of village cricket to the Test arena".

ROYAL EVENT OF THE DECADE

▲ It all seemed like a fairytale, but the wedding day of Charles and Diana was the prelude to an unhappy marriage.

July 29, 1981, was formally declared a public holiday throughout Great Britain in celebration of the marriage that day of the Prince of Wales to Lady Diana Spencer. The event was televised and watched by an audience numbering hundreds of millions throughout the world.

From his student days at Cambridge, the romances of the heir to the throne had always roused considerable interest. However, throughout 1980, rumours began to circulate of a growing relationship between the prince and 20-year-old Lady Diana Spencer. Demure, of aristocratic lineage and, above all, highly photogenic, Diana was rarely out of the public eye from the announcement of her engagement by Buckingham Palace on February 24, 1981, to her tragic death in August 1997.

Princess Diana was born in 1961 at Park House on the Queen's Sandringham estate. As a child, she often played with the Princes Andrew and Edward. She hardly excelled at school (she would later describe herself as "thick as a plank") and after a period spent at finishing school in Switzerland she returned to England to work as a kindergarten teacher.

The marriage took place in St Paul's Cathedral. Diana was resplendent in a pale ivory dress designed for her by the relatively unknown Elizabeth and David Emanuel. Her train flowed a full 7.5 m (25 ft) behind her as she took the four-minute walk up the aisle to the altar. Prince Charles wore the full dress uniform of a Royal Navy officer.

The marriage ceremony lasted an hour after which they drove in a gilded horse-drawn carriage back to Buckingham Palace. Tens of thousands basked in the summer sunshine, lining the streets to welcome the newlyweds.

At first, the royal marriage – which had been billed as a fairytale event – seemed as if it might have been a match made in heaven. Eleven months later, Diana gave birth to Prince William, second in the line of succession to the British throne. Two years later a second son, Prince Henry (known as Harry), was born.

As the decade progressed, rumours of a rift in the marriage were widely rumoured as the couple seemed to spend more and more time apart. Although there was a clear age gap, more significantly there seemed to be an insurmountable culture gap: the exuberant Diana with her love of parties, fashion and pop; and Charles the serious-minded angst-ridden critic of modern architecture with a penchant for long walks in the wilderness of the Scottish Highlands.

The problems became more acute for Princess Diana as she began to find the constant attentions of the world's press and paparazzi intrusive. Little wonder – by that time she was probably the most famous (and certainly the most photographed) woman in the world. It was clear that something, at some stage, was going to give.

AUGUST
- A tenth hunger striker dies in Northern Ireland
- A candidate representing dead hunger striker Bobby Sands wins the Fermanagh and South Tyrone by-election
- 13 oil workers are killed in a North Sea helicopter crash
- England's cricketers win the Ashes series against Australia 3–1
- Steve Ovett and Sebastian Coe break the world mile record three times in the month
- Death of actress Jessie Matthews, radio's Mrs Dale

SEPTEMBER
- The Liberal Party conference votes for electoral alliance with Social Democrats
- Denis Healey narrowly defeats Tony Benn in the election for the Labour Party deputy leadership
- The government announces plans to redevelop Liverpool's derelict South Dock
- British Honduras gains independence as Belize

OCTOBER
- IRA prisoners call off their hunger strike
- Norman Tebbit tells Tory Party conference that his father "got on his bike and looked for work"

NOVEMBER
- SDP member Shirley Williams overturns a Conservative majority of 19,000 to win the Crosby by-election
- Antigua and Barbuda gain independence from Britain

DECEMBER
- Arthur Scargill is elected leader of the National Union of Mineworkers

▲ The Royal Kiss. Prince Charles and his bride Princess Diana celebrate their marriage in the traditional manner.

1982

THE FALKLANDS WAR

On April 2, 1982, the people of Britain woke up to the unexpected news that one of its colonies, the Falkland Islands, had been invaded by Argentina. This heralded the beginning of a two-month war between the two countries that resulted in the deaths of around 1,000 Argentine and 255 British servicemen.

Situated 480 km (300 miles) off the southeast coast of Argentina, the Falklands had been a bone of contention between the British and the Argentines since the early nineteenth century. The British had surveyed the islands in 1690, naming them in honour of naval leader Viscount Falkland. After Argentina gained independence

▲ "The Empire Strikes Back". British troops prepare to embark on the long journey to liberate the Falkland Islands.

▲ A Royal Marine from Britain's task force stands guard over Argentinian soldiers captured at Goose Green.

from Spain in 1816, it made its own claim for sovereignty over what the South Americans referred to as Las Islas Malvinas. Nonetheless, by 1841 Britain had taken a firm hold over the Falklands. A British governor was appointed and Argentines were deported. By the end of the nineteenth century, a small community of around 2,000 Britons lived on the islands.

Throughout this time, Argentina continued to demand territorial rights. In 1964 it took its case to the United Nations. Argentina's claim was essentially based on a geographical proximity that none could deny. Britain countered, however, with the argument of self-determination – the population of the Falklands was British and – above all – wished to remain so.

The timing of the Argentine invasion was partly dictated by the country's internal politics. Its ruling military junta, headed by General Leopoldo Galtieri, badly needed a national cause to distract attention from a crumbling economy. But the Argentines had also been encouraged by the announced withdrawal of the Royal Navy's ice-patrol ship *Endurance* from the South Atlantic as part of the Conservative government's defence cuts. This gave the impression that Britain would not attempt a military response to any Argentine invasion.

Argentina's first move was to raise its flag on the remote island of South Georgia in mid-March. Then, on April 2, Galtieri's troops landed on East Falkland and quickly overran the force of 68 Royal Marines stationed at Port Stanley, the islands' only town. The British government instantly came under heavy criticism in parliament for having failed to defend the colony. Foreign Secretary Lord Carrington felt obliged to resign. Prime Minister Margaret Thatcher prepared an immediate military response. Amid a jingoistic fervour whipped up by the tabloid media, a Royal Navy task force departed for the Falklands. Its 13,000-km (8,000-mile) journey would take three weeks.

The first British success came in South Georgia, which was recaptured by a special force on April 25–26 – leading Thatcher to call on the British people to "rejoice, rejoice". On May 1, the main task force was attacked by Argentine aircraft. The following day, the Argentine cruiser *General Belgrano* was sunk by a British submarine as it sailed close to the war zone. More than 350 Argentine sailors drowned. The *Sun* newspaper reported the event with the triumphal headline "Gotcha!" However, some opposition MPs criticized the sinking of the *Belgrano*, as it had been 58 km (36 miles) outside

the maritime exclusion zone that Britain had declared around the Falklands. After the war ended, evidence indicated that the cruiser had, in fact, been sailing away from the war zone when the torpedoes were fired.

Two days after the sinking of the *Belgrano*, the Royal Navy task force suffered its first loss when the destroyer HMS *Sheffield* was sunk by an Exocet missile fired by an Argentine aircraft. It was the start of a prolonged air-sea battle in which Argentinian land-based warplanes sought to cripple the British fleet, which was defended by carrier-borne Harrier jets, anti-aircraft guns and missiles.

The failure of the British task force to achieve air superiority made the landing of troops a hazardous operation, but Marines and paratroopers began to go ashore at San Carlos on May 21. Three Royal Navy warships and a supply ship were sunk by air attack between May 21 and 25, as the Argentine Air Force did everything

▲ The landing ship *Sir Galahad* burns in Bluff Cove after an Argentinian air attack. Fifty-one Britons were killed in the attack.

in its power to disrupt the landings, but losses were fortunately small. What could have gone wrong was demonstrated later, when, on June 8, Argentine aircraft surprised two guards battalions attempting to land from troop ships at Bluff Cove, killing 51 men and seriously wounding 46 in a few minutes.

Once ashore, the British soldiers

displayed a level of training and equipment that gave them an overwhelming advantage over the largely conscript Argentine Army. Having lost their helicopters in the sinking of a transport vessel, the infantry had to advance on foot across difficult terrain. They captured settlements at Darwin and Goose Green after sharp fighting. On May 31 British forces reached the outskirts of Port Stanley, and then surrounded it. They launched a final offensive on June 11. Three days later, the 9,800 Argentine troops on the Falklands surrendered.

The defeat was a humiliation for Argentina. Four days after the end of the conflict, General Galtieri resigned. The military junta had suffered a serious loss of credibility, and the following year democracy returned to Argentina. In Britain the Falklands War proved to be a turning point for Margaret Thatcher. Before the war, her popularity ratings had fallen to their lowest point. But she basked in the Churchillian role of war leader and in the general election of June 1983 she was returned to government with a landslide majority. Her reputation as the "Iron Lady" was now established beyond all doubt.

▲ An Argentine bomb detonates HMS *Antelope*'s magazines. During the conflict, the Royal Navy lost five vessels.

- Unemployment rises above 3 million
- The value of the sterling pound falls below US $1.60
- The Barbican arts centre opens in London
- Television's Channel Four goes on air; it is criticized by the government for bad language and political bias
- Books published this year include Thomas Keneally's *Schindler's Ark*
- British films this year include Richard Attenborough's *Gandhi* and Peter Greenaway's *The Draughtsman's Contract*
- New television series include *The Boys From the Blackstuff* by Alan Bleasdale and *The Young Ones* (written by Ben Elton)
- Songs of the year include "Ebony and Ivory" by Paul McCartney and Stevie Wonder, and "Our House" by Madness

FEBRUARY
- Laker Airways collapses
- England cricketers stage a rebel tour of South Africa
- Death of artist Ben Nicholson

MARCH
- Argentines raise their flag on island of South Georgia
- Death of politician R A Butler (Lord Butler of Saffron Walden)

APRIL
- Argentine forces invade the Falkland Islands
- A Royal Navy Task Force sets sail for the Falklands
- British special forces recapture the island of South Georgia

THE SCOURGE OF UNEMPLOYMENT

▲ With dole queues growing, Norman Tebbit suggested that the unemployed should "get on their bikes" in search of work.

By the start of 1982, unemployment in Britain had shot above the 3 million mark, the first time such a figure had been known since the Depression of the 1930s. Since the Conservatives had come to power in mid-1979, the total number of people in employment had fallen by 2.3 million. Almost 1.5 million of these jobs had been lost in manufacturing – around one in five of all industrial jobs had disappeared.

The Thatcher government did not have a single clear view of the unemployment issue. On the one hand, it mounted schemes to create employment, but on the other it saw the high rate of joblessness as a way of applying downward pressure on wages and discouraging strikes. Secretary of State for Employment Norman Tebbit argued for a positive view of unemployment as a chance for workers to move to more productive areas of the economy. He famously reminded the current generation that his own father had responded to being out of work by "getting on his bike" to seek a job elsewhere.

If the government did relatively little to reduce unemployment, broadly accepted as a necessary side-effect of its radical drive to revive the British economy, it nonetheless did everything in its power to reduce the unemployment statistics. In the summer of 1982, being unemployed was redefined as not only being registered as seeking work, but also claiming benefit. To this cut in the figures was added – in 1983 – the exclusion of all people over 60. Taking into account the various attempts at massaging the statistics, many observers accepted that by mid-1983 the "true" level of unemployment had risen to more than 4 million.

CHARIOTS OF FIRE

The Best Picture award at the 1982 Oscars ceremony in Los Angeles went to a British film, *Chariots of Fire*. It was the brainchild of producer David Puttnam, who saw the film potential of the victories of athletes Harold Abrahams and Eric Liddell at the 1924 Olympics.

The film focuses on the personalities and motivations of the two runners – Abrahams, a Jew inspired by a desire to rebut anti-Semitism, and Liddel, a Scot whose religious faith would not allow him to run on a Sunday.

Chariots of Fire also won the awards for Best Costume Design, Best Original Score and Best Screenplay. Accepting the screenplay award, writer Colin Welland revived a warning cry first heard in North America at the time of the American Revolution: "The British are coming!"

▲ The tale of athletes Abrahams and Liddell struck a chord with a nation that two years before had thrilled to the Olympic golds of Coe and Ovett.

POPE MAKES HISTORIC VISIT

In May 1982 John Paul II became the first reigning pope to visit Britain. As he prayed alongside the Archbishop of Canterbury in Canterbury Cathedral, hopes were raised that the breach between the Church of England and Rome, opened up at the time of Henry VIII, might eventually be healed.

Every appearance by the Pope during his visit drew vast crowds, reflecting the impact his dynamic papacy had had since his election in 1978, but also curiosity about a man who had survived an assassination attempt the previous year. The visit was given added

▲ The visit of the first reigning Pope to set foot in Britain ignited hopes of a rapprochement between Anglican and Catholic churches.

significance by occurring at the height of the Falklands crisis. The Pope appealed for peace in the South Atlantic, a plea he repeated when visiting Argentina the following month.

In reality, John Paul's papacy was to turn out far less favourably disposed towards reconciliation with the Church of England than was initially expected. Moves towards a healing of the rift were blocked by the pope's conservative views on most social and religious issues, at a time when Anglicans were embracing many of the changes occurring in the modern world. The Church of England's acceptance in 1992 of the ordination of women proved of itself enough to end any chance of reversing the rift of the Reformation.

UP FROM THE DEEP

In a seminal event in the history of nautical archaeology, October 11, 1982, saw the climax of an incredible 17-year operation to raise a sixteenth-century British warship from its watery grave off the coast of the south of England.

Built in 1510, the 500-ton *Mary Rose* was known to have been one of Henry VIII's favourite vessels. It was thought to have been named after his favourite sister, Mary, and the emblem of the Tudor family, the rose.

The *Mary Rose* sank during an engagement with the French Navy during the Battle of Spithead. The French, while not formally at war with Britain, had launched an invasion of the Solent waters around the Isle of Wight. It was not, in fact, at the hands of French cannons that the *Mary Rose* perished with most of her crew of 500, but because of human error. It would seem that while attempting to turn, she took on water in the lowest row of gun

ports that had accidentally been left open after firing.

The wreck was first discovered by accident in 1836 when a local fisherman snagged his gear. A diving expedition led to the discovery of a number of bronze cannons. However, the modern story was largely the obsession of a man named Alexander McKee. He began searching for the wreck in 1966, discovering it four years later.

The operation cost an estimated £4 million to complete. The hull was successfully raised by drilling holes through the main structural timbers, into which huge metal backing plates were then bolted, allowing the strain of lifting to be spread evenly. Along with the *Mary Rose*, some 17,000 artifacts were discovered – a treasure-trove that provided a unique glimpse of Tudor England. The ship now stands on display in Portsmouth Harbour.

▲ After almost 500 years on the sea bed, the hull of Henry VIII's warship *Mary Rose* rises from its watery grave.

1983

- NHS hospitals are obliged to invite tenders from private contractors for cleaning and catering
- The £1 coin is introduced
- The wearing of car seat belts in front seats of vehicles is made compulsory
- First wheel clamps for illegally parked vehicles are introduced
- Early morning television broadcasts begin with the BBC's *Breakfast Time* and commercial television's *TV-AM*
- Books published this year include *Waterland* by Graham Swift and *Shame* by Salman Rushdie
- British films this year include Bill Forsyth's *Local Hero* and Richard Eyre's *The Ploughman's Lunch*
- Richard Attenborough's film *Gandhi* wins eight Oscars
- Albums released this year include David Bowie's *Let's Dance* and UB40's *Labour of Love*
- Songs of the year include "Every Breath You Take" by the Police and "Karma Chameleon" by Culture Club

JANUARY

- Michael Heseltine is appointed Secretary for Defence
- Franks Report clears the government of blame for failing to prevent the Argentine invasion of the Falklands

THATCHER'S LANDSLIDE

On June 9, 1983, British Prime Minister Margaret Thatcher won a second term in office, this time with a vastly increased majority in the House of Commons. The Conservatives won 397 seats, giving them an overall majority of 144. The landslide was remarkable in that only a year earlier opinion polls had shown Thatcher's government to be deeply unpopular.

The turnaround could be largely attributed to two factors. There was little doubt that Thatcher still basked in the afterglow of victory in the Falklands War of 1982. Evoking the memory of Winston Churchill's wartime leadership, she managed to stoke a nationalistic fervour that won her the support of many patriotic Britons who took pride in the success of their armed forces, and felt that

▲ **Margaret Thatcher's landslide election victory had seemed highly unlikely just a few years previously.**

national pride had been restored.

The Labour Party also played a spectacular part in its own defeat. Under the leadership of Michael Foot, Labour fell foul of in-fighting between its political wings. The founding of the Social Democratic Party by ex-Labour ministers split the anti-Conservative vote, with 25 per cent of votes cast for the Liberal–SDP alliance and 28 per cent for Labour, which had been damagingly portrayed by the pro-Thatcher media as dominated by the "Loony Left".

With such a majority in the House of Commons, the right-wing "Thatcher Revolution" was allowed to continue unopposed. It would take the Labour Party almost a decade to form an effective opposition, and another four years after that before it would at last win power again.

ALL CHANGE IN OPPOSITION

▲ **Liberal leader David Steel had hoped for a breakthrough at the election, but the SDP-Liberal Alliance won only 23 seats.**

The result of the 1983 general election was a disaster for the Labour Party. It was also a setback for the newly formed Social Democratic Party, which found the 25 per cent of the vote it had won in alliance with the Liberals translated into a mere 23 seats for the two parties in parliament. In the wake of the election, both Labour and the SDP decided on a change of leadership.

At the SDP, Roy Jenkins was replaced as leader by the more youthful Dr David Owen. A highly personable politician, Owen seemed the ideal man to woo the Tory-voting middle classes, but he was less well suited to eating further into Labour's traditional areas of support. He was to lead the SDP to a position to the right of the Liberals, thereby creating unsustainable strains in the centrist alliance.

Labour chose Neil Kinnock to replace the hapless Michael Foot. The election of Kinnock, a fiery and verbose Welshman, was at the time considered a confirmation of the domination of the left within the party. But with the relatively right-wing Roy Hattersley as his deputy, Kinnock devoted himself to restoring Labour's electoral credibility by reining in the party's left-wing activists. It was to prove a thankless task that would leave him the first Labour leader since Hugh Gaitskell never to become Prime Minister.

▲ **Neil Kinnock inherited a party riven by ideological dispute and much diminished in the House of Commons.**

GILLICK LOSES TEENAGE PILL CASE

▲ Victoria Gillick's anti-contraception campaign ignited a debate about the medical rights of children.

On July 26, 1983, anti-contraception campaigner Victoria Gillick lost a case in the High Court that would have banned doctors from prescribing the Pill to girls under 16 without parental consent. The case provoked a nationwide debate about teenage sexuality and parental authority.

Mrs Gillick applied to the court specifically to prevent contraceptives or advice on birth control being given to any of her five daughters, then aged from one to 13. Her counsel argued that providing contraceptives virtually amounted to aiding and abetting underage intercourse. The judge, Mr Justice Woolf, took the view that it was rather a way of palliating the consequences of illegal sex.

Claiming that large numbers of doctors were "actively encouraging children to be promiscuous", Mrs Gillick continued her campaign, winning the support of more than 200 MPs. The Court of Appeal subsequently found in her favour in December 1984, but this decision was reversed by the Law Lords the following year. What seemed to emerge most clearly from the public debate on this affair was that there was no reversing the relentless rise of sexual activity – legal or illegal – among teenagers, and that many people were deeply unhappy about this fact.

PARKINSON QUITS OVER AFFAIR

On October 14, 1983, during the annual Conservative Party conference, Cecil Parkinson, the Trade and Industry Secretary, resigned after revelations about his private life. Parkinson was one of Mrs Thatcher's closest political associates, widely credited with masterminding the general election victory the previous June.

A married man, Parkinson had had a long-term relationship with his secretary, Sara Keays. In early October he was forced to admit to the affair, which he declared a thing of the past. At that point, with the support of Thatcher, he clung on to his political office.

However, Keays was pregnant with Parkinson's child and in no mood to go quietly. She wrote a letter to The Times to "put the record straight".

According to Keays, her affair with Parkinson had been "a long-standing, loving relationship", which led her to believe that he would marry her once she was bearing his child. Although Parkinson made it clear he did not fully accept Keays's version of events, the scandal had reached a pitch that left him no choice but to go.

Parkinson succeeded in rescuing his marriage and returned to government as Energy Secretary in

▲ Tory minister Cecil Parkinson's tangled private life forced his resignation, despite the strong backing of Mrs Thatcher.

1987. But his public image was permanently tarnished. A dispute with Keays over maintenance payments for their child – who had learning difficulties and severe health problems – did nothing to restore his reputation.

CRUISE MISSILE PROTESTS

▲ **Demonstrators near the airbase at Greenham Common, which became a focus for protestors opposed to the deployment of US cruise missiles.**

On October 22, 1983, a rally to protest against nuclear weapons attracted more than 250,000 demonstrators to central London. The mass turnout underlined the re-emergence of a vociferous anti-nuclear movement in Britain, for the first time since the early 1960s.

The trigger for the revival of concern about nuclear war was the decision to update Britain's nuclear armoury and allow the United States to station Cruise missiles on British soil. The go-ahead for the installation of the missiles in Europe was the result of a complex debate within the NATO alliance. European members of NATO had become concerned that the Soviet Union's deployment of medium-range nuclear missiles might allow it to carry out a nuclear attack on Western Europe without involving the United States. Stationing US missiles in Europe would tie the Americans inextricably to the nuclear defence of the area. NATO leaders agreed at the same time to pursue arms limitation negotiations with the Soviets.

The subtleties of these military and diplomatic calculations were understandably lost upon those convinced that nuclear war threatened the destruction of life on Earth. Most members of the Campaign for Nuclear Disarmament (CND) saw the US Cruise missiles as making Britain a certain target for Soviet nuclear attack and rendering the country utterly subservient to the United States.

The two sites chosen for the Cruise missiles were Greenham Common in Berkshire and Molesworth in Cambridgeshire. In 1981 a group of women set up a peace camp outside the Greenham Common base and this became the chief focus of anti-nuclear protests. At times, large numbers of demonstrators would join the women in their permanent vigil, blockading the base.

Intermittent attempts by the authorities to eject the women were answered with considerable resistance.

The existence of the all-women camp, however, demonstrated one of the limitations of the anti-nuclear movement. It turned the protest into an assertion of feminism which alienated many people who might otherwise have backed CND. The prominent presence of left-wing extremists in the protests had a similar effect. Although the CND leadership did its best to broaden the movement to embrace respectable "Middle England", this effort largely failed.

Unlike in the 1960s, CND had the support of a major political party. The new Labour leader Neil Kinnock was one of the speakers at the October 22 rally, since his party had embraced unilateral nuclear disarmament in 1980. But the huge Conservative majority in parliament meant that this had no practical effect.

The Women's Peace Camp remained in existence for 19 years. In 1991 the Cruise missiles were finally withdrawn as a result of the thaw in relations with the Soviet Union under Mikhail Gorbachev.

▲ **Public opposition to American cruise missiles galvanized CND, which had been largely dormant since the 1960s.**

NILSEN CONFESSES TO MULTIPLE MURDERS

▲ Dennis Nilsen's career as a serial killer spanned five years, during which he killed up to 15 times before his arrest in 1983.

On October 24, 1983, homosexual civil servant Dennis Nilsen went on trial charged with six murders and two attempted murders. It is believed that he was responsible for at least nine other killings.

Nilsen started his career as a serial killer in 1978. He began taking young men he found attractive back to his garden flat in Willesden Green, north London, where he strangled them and cut up their bodies with a butcher's knife. Most of his victims were homeless or solitary homosexuals, living on the edge of society. They were not missed. When on occasion his murder attempts failed, the young men either did not contact the police or, if they did, were not believed.

Nilsen's killings might have continued indefinitely had he not moved to a new flat in Hornsey. This had no garden, making disposal of the dissected corpses far more difficult. He had killed three people at his new address when, in February 1983, fellow occupants of the house complained of blocked drains. Nilsen had been feeding body parts down the toilet. When rotting flesh was discovered by a plumber, the police were called. They found other human remains secreted in plastic bags around the flat.

Nilsen was sentenced to life imprisonment in November 1983 after the jury found him guilty by a majority verdict.

UPROAR OVER NUCLEAR BOMB FILM

On December 10, 1983, 15 million British television viewers tuned in to watch a controversial film about the aftermath of a nuclear bomb, three weeks after it had debuted in the United States. *The Day After* showed what might have followed after a Soviet nuclear attack on a small town in Kansas.

The film was strongly opposed by the British government which was firmly behind the idea of a nuclear deterrent. Defence Secretary Michael Heseltine claimed that the film gave a one-sided account of the nuclear issue and would play into the hands of the protest movements which proved such a headache to Conservative governments throughout the 1980s. Heseltine insisted that Yorkshire Television, which had bought the American-made film, gave the pro-nuclear defence an opportunity to put its case. The network agreed to a panel discussion but Heseltine pulled out when he discovered that Monsignor Bruce Kent, who was a prominent member of the Campaign for Nuclear Disarmament (CND), would also be joining the debate.

Some criticized the film's credibility. The British Medical Association said the scenes of a busy but orderly hospital dealing with the critical burns and injuries of thousands of survivors were unrealistic. As it argued, medical staff were just as likely to have been victims as civilians and hospitals would very quickly be overwhelmed to the point of chaos.

The fact that *The Day After* topped the viewing ratings on both sides of the Atlantic was an indication of the very real fear felt by many millions of ordinary people about the possibility of nuclear conflagration.

▲ What if the Soviets attacked Kansas? Nuclear devastation as shown in the controversial film *The Day After*.

1984

THE COAL MINERS' STRIKE

The origins of the coal miners strike of 1984–85 lay in an announcement by the National Coal Board (NCB) at the beginning of 1984. This stated that a number of so-called "uneconomic" mines were to be closed with a loss of 20,000 jobs. With a new round of pay talks between the National Union of Mineworkers (NUM) and the NCB about to start, the pit closures became part of the negotiations. While the NCB, under the tough leadership of American Ian MacGregor, was prepared to offer an overall 5.2 per cent pay increase, it was firmly resolved that the closures were not a matter for discussion.

Strike action began with local walk-outs at threatened pits such as Cortonwood, where miners stopped work on March 5. As strike action spread, the NUM's Marxist President Arthur Scargill called for nationwide industrial action. By mid-March 153 of Britain's 174 mines had shut down.

It was a strike for which the British government was well prepared. Prime Minister Margaret Thatcher had never forgotten the humiliation of a Conservative administration at the hands of the miners in 1973–74. She welcomed the chance of a return match, which she intended to win. Coal stocks at power stations had been carefully conserved in preparation for a confrontation. As coal now provided only one-fifth of Britain's energy needs, there were also effective plans for maintaining electricity supplies through the national grid even if coal ran out. In addition, new laws passed by the Thatcher government had given the authorities extensive

▲ The use of Britain's police force was brought into question during the miners' strike. Many saw them as more concerned with enforcing government policy than the law of the land.

powers to challenge strike action in the courts.

There was no doubt that most miners bitterly opposed the running down of their industry and were ready to fight to save it. However, the NUM leadership refused to hold a national ballot of mineworkers, as required by Thatcher's union legislation. As a result, less militant miners in Nottinghamshire and Kent refused to strike, even though most supported the aims of the industrial action. This split within the NUM was fatal to the minesworkers' cause.

The months that followed saw an eruption of violence, as "flying pickets" travelled from Wales and

Yorkshire, where support for the strike was strongest, to the pits of Nottinghamshire to put pressure on the strike-breaking "scabs". Their attempts to blockade the mines became increasingly heated and soon the police were ordered in to escort workers through the picket lines.

Violent clashes between strikers and police continued throughout the year. The most notorious confrontation occurred at the Orgreave coking plant in South Yorkshire on June 18. Thousands of pickets and police fought running battles. Seventy-two policemen and at least 51 miners were injured in a day of fierce fighting, sometimes known as the

"Battle of Orgreave". The police blamed the presence of Arthur Scargill for inflaming the mood of the pickets; while the NUM claimed, with some justification, that its basic right to picket was being openly violated by the police, who made liberal use of force against the strikers. Over the coming months, police cordons were placed on main roads around the country to turn away miners trying to join picket lines. It was the first time in the twentieth century that a British government had resorted to such draconian measures to intervene in a labour dispute. In all, more than 11,000 people were arrested in the course of the strike.

With the South Wales branch of the NUM refusing to pay fines handed out by the courts, on August 1 court action began for the seizure of the union's assets. The High Court eventually ruled that, because there had not been a national ballot of all union members, the miners strike was illegal. On October 25 the union's assets were seized. Without the ability to provide its members with strike pay, the union, it was thought, would have to call off the action.

With the onset of the winter months, more and more strikers found themselves financially unable to sustain their protest. By November almost a third of the pits were working again; by the beginning of February 1985, more than half of the miners had returned to work. The government was able to announce confidently that there would be no power cuts even if the strike continued. Although Scargill believed in a fight to the bitter end, it became clear that it was a battle that the

miners would never be able to win. On March 3, 1985, an NUM Special Delegate Committee voted by 98 to 91 to bring the year-long strike to an end. In a blaze of media attention, Prime Minister Thatcher hailed a "famous victory".

The failure of the strike was a disaster for the miners and the single most devastating event in the recent history of Britain's labour movement. It opened the way for further rounds of pit closures that reduced the coal

industry to a mere shadow of its former greatness. By 2005, only eight pits were still operating in Britain. The defeat also effectively neutered the power of the trade union movement. It not only showed that governments could no longer be intimidated by strike action, it also encouraged private companies to take an increasingly ruthless attitude towards striking employees. A fundamental shift in the balance of power between workers and employers, public or private, was under way.

▲ Defeated and demoralized, in March 1985 the striking miners finally returned to work.

NEWS IN BRIEF

- British Telecom is privatized
- Parliament approves GCSE exams, to be introduced in 1988
- The Data Protection Act regulates the use of computerized information
- The Committee of Inquiry headed by Dame Mary Warnock recommends controls on "test-tube baby" research
- "Genetic fingerprinting" is developed at the University of Leicester
- The Thames Flood Barrier is officially opened
- Robert Maxwell buys the Mirror newspaper group
- The term "yuppie" (young upwardly-mobile person) comes into general use
- Books published this year include *Money* by Martin Amis, *Flaubert's Parrot* by Julian Barnes, *The Wasp Factory* by Iain Banks and *Empire of the Sun* by J G Ballard
- Ted Hughes is appointed Poet Laureate
- Films this year include Roland Joffe's *The Killing Fields*, Michael Radford's *1984* and Malcolm Mowbray's *A Private Function*
- New television series include *The Jewel in the Crown* and *Spitting Image*
- Band Aid's single "Do They Know It's Christmas?" raises money for food aid to Africa
- Songs of the year include Frankie Goes to Hollywood's "Two Tribes" and George Michael's "Careless Whisper"

TORVILL AND DEAN

On Valentine's Day, February 14, 1984, British ice-skaters Jayne Torvill and Christopher Dean won the gold medal for ice-dancing at the winter Olympics in Sarajevo. Their sensual, pulsating interpretation of Ravel's *Bolero* brought the crowd to their feet and drew a maximum six points for artistic impression from all nine judges. It is generally recognized as one of the defining moments in sport and the dawn of a new era in ice dance.

Torvill and Dean's Olympic triumph was not a surprise. Ice-dancing together since 1975, they were already the holders of the World and European Championship titles, which they had won for four consecutive years. As a result of their victory in the Olympics, they were jointly voted BBC Sports Personality of the Year. The Nottingham pair went on to a lucrative commercial career starring in ice spectaculars and world tours. They retired in 1999.

▲ Jayne Torvill and Christopher Dean's stunning interpretation of Bolero thrilled British audiences and set new standards in ice dance.

POLICEWOMAN SHOT BY LIBYANS

On April 17, 1984, WPC Yvonne Fletcher was shot dead outside the Libyan embassy in St James's Square, London. The 25-year-old policewoman from Wiltshire was killed by machine-gun fire from within the embassy building.

Fletcher and other police officers – including her fiancé – were in the square to control a demonstration by exiled opponents of the Libyan government of Colonel Muammar Gaddafi. The staff of the embassy – or "Libyan People's Bureau" – included not only diplomats but young pro-Gaddafi radicals. They had given notice that they intended to react to the demonstration, but their use of firearms was totally unexpected.

The burst of gunfire from a first-floor window of the embassy was presumably aimed at the protesters. In all, 12 people were hit, but Fletcher was the only fatality. Shot in the stomach, she died in Westminster hospital just an hour later.

After the shooting, the Libyan embassy was surrounded by armed police and a siege began that lasted 11 days. The Libyan government responded with indignation, asserting the right of its embassy staff to diplomatic immunity. In retaliation, the British embassy in Tripoli was surrounded by armed soldiers. The stand-off ended with an agreement to allow the Libyan embassy staff to return to their country. Diplomatic relations between Britain and Libya were broken off and not resumed until 1999, when the Libyan government accepted "general responsibility" for the killing.

Fletcher was the first woman police officer murdered on duty in Britain. A memorial to her now stands in St James's Square.

▲ Yvonne Fletcher was the first British woman police officer to be killed on duty, shot dead outside the Libyan embassy.

LIGHTNING STRIKES MINSTER

In the early hours of the morning of July 9, 1984, York Minster, one of Britain's most famous historic buildings, was devastated by fire. Fire-fighters were helpless to combat a blaze that fed on medieval oak beams, bringing down the massive lead roof.

The fire was generally attributed to a bolt of lightning, as there had been electrical storms through the night. But was the lightning strike a manifestation of the wrath of God? Many observers were inclined to link the disaster to the consecration of a controversial theologian, the Rt Reverend David Jenkins, as Bishop of Durham, which had taken place in the Minster only three days before the fire. Jenkins's appointment had annoyed Church of England conservatives. They were most especially outraged by his rejection of the bodily resurrection of Christ – which Jenkins would later describe as a "conjuring trick with bones".

So had God destroyed the Minster as a mark of his disapproval? The Archbishop naturally dismissed the idea as "ridiculous". But its grip on the national imagination suggested that belief in divine intervention was more widespread than the sophisticated Church leaders would like to believe.

Fortunately, the Minster was well insured and offers of additional cash for rebuilding came from many sources. Reconstruction eventually took four years and cost more than £2 million.

▲ The lightning strike on York Minster was linked by some to the Bishop Jenkins's recent rejection of Christ's bodily resurrection.

DEATH OF A STAR

▲ Richard Burton rose from humble beginnings in the Welsh coalfields to become a film and stage colossus.

On August 5, 1984, actor Richard Burton died of a cerebral haemorrhage in Geneva, Switzerland. He was 58 years old.

Obituaries tended to lament Burton's life as an example of talent wasted, yet he had not done badly for a miner's son from the Welsh coalfields. The twelfth child of a Welsh-speaking family of 13, he was born Richard Walter Jenkins, in the village of Pontrhydyfen in 1925. Philip Burton, a teacher at his school in nearby Port Talbot, recognized and encouraged his acting ability. From the age of 16, the young actor adopted Burton's name.

After national service in the RAF, Burton's acting career blossomed in the late 1940s. Some memorable stage performances, notably in Christopher Fry's *The Lady's Not For Burning*, led to his first Hollywood film role in *My Cousin Rachel* in 1952. With his superb voice and magnetic physical presence, Burton excelled on stage rather than on screen. Yet he was increasingly drawn into the world of film stardom. His highly publicized affair with Elizabeth Taylor on the set of the epic *Cleopatra* in 1962 completed his ascension to superstar status. In the course of a stormy relationship, Burton and Taylor were twice married before their definitive divorce in 1976.

A heavy drinker, Burton went into early physical decline, yet still turned in the occasional high-quality performance, as in the film version of George Orwell's *1984*, released shortly after his death. He remained a Welsh patriot throughout his life and was buried in a red suit, in tribute to the colour of the dragon on his country's national flag.

BUDD RUNS FOR BRITAIN

▲ **Zola Budd's application for British nationality was rushed through to allow her to compete at the Olympics, but her bid for gold ended in tears.**

The most controversial appearance at the Los Angeles Olympics in August 1984 was that of 18-year-old South African-born runner Zola Budd. She not only evaded a ban on participation by athletes from her home country by taking British citizenship, but also clashed dramatically with one of the home nation's favourite competitors, Mary Decker.

Holder of the 5,000 metres world record, Budd was given a British passport in April 1984 after a campaign led by the *Daily Mail*. Citizenship was granted in less than a fortnight after her application was filed. Such special treatment for a white South African outraged anti-apartheid campaigners. The manoeuvre was specifically aimed at side-stepping the worldwide ban on sporting links with South Africa.

In the women's 3,000 m final, Budd came up against Mary Decker. Running barefoot as was her custom, she accidentally collided with Decker who tripped and left the track in tears. From that point on the American crowd systematically barracked Budd, destroying her concentration. She finished seventh.

More genuinely British athletes fared better. Sebastian Coe retained the 1,500 m Olympic title he had won in Moscow, beating fellow Briton Steve Cram into second place. The extraordinary Daley Thompson won his second consecutive gold in the pentathlon. The British national anthem was also played for Tessa Sanderson, who won a gold medal in the javelin.

THE BELGRANO LEAK

Controversy over the sinking of the Argentine cruiser *General Belgrano* dogged the Conservative government long after the end of the Falklands War. On August 18, 1984, a senior civil servant at the Ministry of Defence, Clive Ponting, was charged with breaking the Official Secrets Act by passing documents related to the affair to Labour MP Tam Dalyell.

"I did this because I believed that Ministers were not prepared to answer legitimate questions from an MP about a matter of considerable public concern simply in order to protect their own political positions," Ponting claimed.

Dalyell, who had been actively pursuing the case since the war, said the documents showed that the *Belgrano* had in fact reversed its course for home 11 hours before it was torpedoed by a British submarine. He argued that the sinking ended chances of a peaceful resolution to the conflict. Prime Minister Thatcher later replied that "the precise position and course of the *Belgrano* at the time were i rrelevant" and added that diplomatic action to reach a solution was "pursued vigorously".

Tam Dalyell praised Ponting's conduct, saying: "The civil servant who jeopardizes his own career for the public good is possibly the noblest Roman of them all."

Clive Ponting was tried and acquitted in February 1985.

▶ **Clive Ponting (right) broke the Official Secrets Act by leaking documents that suggested a government cover-up.**

THE BRIGHTON BOMBING

The morning of October 12 should have been a routine day during another Conservative Party conference. But breakfast news programmes were carrying a very different story that day, as Britain woke up to reports of the carnage created by an IRA bomb which had destroyed the main conference hotel.

The bomb, consisting of 10 kg (20 lb) of commercial explosive, went off at 2.54 am in a sixth-floor bathroom of Brighton's Grand hotel. Some guests plunged several floors as an entire section of the front of the hotel collapsed. Prime Minister Margaret Thatcher, working in the lounge of her suite on the text of her conference speech, escaped injury, but five people died.

No government ministers were killed, although the dead included popular MP Sir Anthony Berry and Roberta Wakeham, wife of the government Chief Whip. John Wakeham was himself pulled from

▲ The IRA bombing of the Grand Hotel could easily have resulted in the deaths of many members of the ruling British government.

the wreckage, as was Norman Tebbit, Secretary for Trade and Industry, among a total of 30 people who were admitted to hospital. Tebbit would not be able to return to the House of Commons until January the following year and his wife

Margaret was paralyzed from the neck down.

Margaret Thatcher won widespread praise when she still arrived punctually at the conference that morning. It was, she said, an attempt "to cripple Her Majesty's democratically elected government". In claiming responsibility for the attack, the IRA said: "Today we were unlucky, but remember – we have only to be lucky once: you will have to be lucky always."

The IRA bomber responsible for the attack was Patrick Magee. He had stayed at the hotel, using the name Roy Walsh, three weeks before the conference. He hid the bomb in a bathroom wall, with a timing device set to go off 24 days later. Magee was arrested in Glasgow in June 1985 and sentenced to spend at least 35 years in prison. He was, however, released in 1999 as a consequence of the Good Friday Agreement.

TELECOM SALE BONANZA

Although in principle devoted to "rolling back" the state sector of the economy, in her first term as Prime Minister, Margaret Thatcher made only limited progress in returning nationalized industries to the private sector. After her second election victory in 1983, however, the way was open for more radical change.

The true start of the privatization drive was the sell-off of 51 per cent of state-owned British Telecom in November 1984. It was not primarily an exercise in encouraging competitive free enterprise, since the company would still have a monopoly in some areas and be closely regulated by the state. The

main aims of the sell-off were to raise cash and broaden share ownership. A large-scale advertising campaign encouraged first-time investors to buy shares at flotation. The shares were priced so attractively that a profit was almost guaranteed.

The sale raised £4 billion, money that the government used to finance tax cuts. It also made money for investors. But it did not create the "share-owning democracy" of which Thatcher dreamed, since most people sold their shares for an instant profit.

▲ Privatization of state assets was a key part of the Tory programme; however its principal effect was to boost government coffers.

- The value of Sterling falls to $1.04, the lowest ever value against the US dollar
- The FTSE 100 Share Index tops 1,000 points for the first time
- The Crown Prosecution Service takes over responsibility for criminal prosecutions from the police
- A plan is announced to develop Canary Warf in London's Docklands as a large-scale complex of skyscrapers
- Canadian businessman Conrad Black takes control of Telegraph newspapers
- The British Antarctic Survey detects a hole in the ozone layer
- Screening is introduced to check blood donors for HIV infection
- The Saatchi Collection opens to the public in London
- Books published this year include *Hawksmoor* by Peter Ackroyd and *Oranges Are Not the Only Fruit* by Jeanette Winterson
- British films this year include Stephen Frears's *My Beautiful Laundrette* and Chris Bernard's *Letter to Brezhnev*
- First performance of Howard Brenton and David Hare's *Pravda*
- The musical *Les Misérables*, based on Victor Hugo's novel, opens in London
- First broadcast of the television soap opera *EastEnders*
- Albums released this year include the Smiths' *Meat Is Murder*, Dire Straits' *Brothers in Arms* and Tears for Fears' *Songs From the Big Chair*

TWIN SOCCER TRAGEDIES

May 1985 saw Britain's soccer season end on a tragic and bitter note as two unrelated incidents left almost 100 dead, close to 1,000 injured and the reputation of British football in tatters.

May 11 was supposed to be a day of celebration in the Yorkshire city of Bradford. It was the last game of the season and the home side, Bradford City, had already accumulated enough points to win the Third Division championship. A capacity crowd turned out to greet their local heroes.

The day turned to disaster shortly before half-time as a small fire broke out in one of the grandstands, creating panic among the fans who surged forward down the stand and over on to the football field. Within five minutes, the 76-year-old wooden stand was an inferno. In all, 56 fans were either burned to death or killed in the crush. Hundreds of others were seriously injured.

The disaster focused attention on the general state of some of Britain's football stadiums, especially among the lower divisions where grounds like Bradford City's had seen little change or improvement since the end of the war 40 years before.

It was an altogether more sinister disaster that struck less than four weeks later as reigning English champions Liverpool took on Juventus of Italy in the final of the European Cup. The game was held at the Heysel Stadium on the outskirts of Brussels in Belgium.

The organization surrounding the match on May 29 was notably poor. Policing was inadequate, the stadium was not equipped with closed-circuit television equipment and, worst of all, segregation of the rival supporters was badly organized. A large number of Liverpool fans were said to have been drunk on arrival and before the start of the game baiting between the two sets of fans grew increasingly hostile. When a group of Liverpool fans launched a charge at the Juventus area of one of the stands, the Italians tried to move out of the way. However, forced back against a concrete wall, they were faced with no way out. The wall quickly collapsed under the pressure, killing 39 and injuring more than 400. The fighting spilled on to the football field as the small police presence struggled to keep back the advancing Liverpool fans. The victims were almost all Juventus supporters.

English football had hit a new nadir. Even though football-related violence was actually no worse in Britain than it was in many other European countries, the phenomenon had become widely known as an "English Disease". It was a reputation exacerbated by the Heysel Stadium disaster.

Although the British government demanded a short, sharp solution to the problem, for all its tough rhetoric the only real outcome was the banning of the sale of alcohol at football matches. A compulsory identity card system was investigated but rejected as unworkable.

The implications were greater for the football teams themselves. The British Football Association, wanting to be seen to be taking a stand, immediately banned English clubs from the following season's European campaigns. In June UEFA, European football's governing body, extended this to an indefinite ban. It was the best part of a decade before an English presence was again seen in European football at club level.

▲ Fans look on as Bradford's stadium burns. Fifty-six fans died in the tragedy, which brought demands for Britain's football grounds to be upgraded.

LIVE AID

▲ Organizer Bob Geldof leads a chorus of the Live Aid anthem "Feed the World" in the finale to a bigger live event than Woodstock.

At midday on July 13, 1985, veteran English rock band Status Quo took the stage at London's Wembley Stadium. The opening chords of their famous anthem "Rockin' All Over The World" rang out, signalling the start of Live Aid, the most ambitious live music festival ever attempted.

The project had been initiated by Bob Geldof, the lead singer with top Irish band the Boomtown Rats. Geldof had been moved by the reports of the 1984 famine in Ethiopia and was unimpressed with the efforts of Western governments to relieve the crisis. His first move was the organization of the all-star Band Aid single "Feed The World". Released at Christmas 1984, with all profits going to the famine, "Feed The World" was already on the way to becoming the biggest-selling single of all time.

The Live Aid concerts took celebrity fundraising to a new height. In Britain and the United States, two huge concerts were planned to take place at the same time, with two-way video links joining Wembley Stadium in London to Philadelphia. Both broadcasts were transmitted live throughout the world, every network providing a credit card hotline for donations to be made.

The shows themselves were memorable, featuring stars from every generation of pop music, from Paul McCartney, Mick Jagger and Bob Dylan up to U2 and Madonna. Notable performances came from Queen, with flamboyant singer Freddie Mercury proving himself to be perhaps the greatest of rock's stadium showmen. The spectacle reached a stunning climax with all of the shows' stars taking the stage for a unique rendition of "Feed The World".

An astoundingly popular achievement, Live Aid raised more than £50 million for famine relief.

SINCLAIR C5 FLOPS

One of the most famous failures in the history of technological innovation was the Sinclair C5 electric vehicle. Hyped by its creator, Sir Clive Sinclair, as the future of road transport, it stayed in production for just seven months.

Sinclair had a superb track record as an innovator in electronic technology. He had been responsible for marketing the first British-designed pocket calculator in 1972 and one of the first personal computers, the ZX-81, in 1981. He sank a large part of the fortune thus amassed into the C5.

Costing only £399 and pollution-free, the C5 was unfortunately not an alternative to cars; it was a glorified tricycle. With a maximum speed of 24 km/h (15 mph), it was driven by a battery that, in cold weather, would last only for 10 km (6 miles) without recharging. It was open to the elements, and to the fumes of petrol-driven vehicles. And it was patently dangerous, pulling its occupant low down amid the wheels of passing traffic.

Launched in January 1985, the C5 was manufactured at a Hoover factory in Wales. Production ceased the following August. Only 17,000 of the vehicles were sold. The failed enterprise cost Sinclair more than £8 million.

▲ Technical prowess triumphed over commonsense in the design of the Sinclair C5, whose limited range made it an unappealing buy.

POLICEMAN HACKED TO DEATH

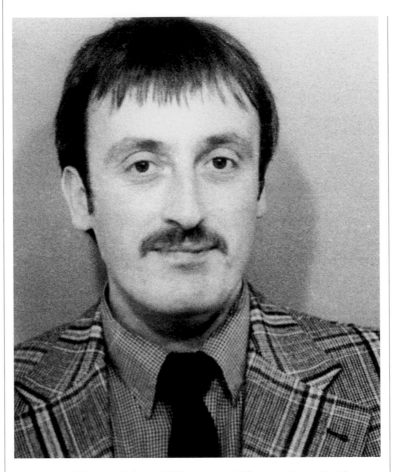

▲ PC Keith Blakelock's brutal killing was a chilling reminder that inner city Britain's social problems had not gone away.

On the night of October 6, 1985, PC Keith Blakelock, a 40-year-old father-of-three, was beaten and hacked to death by rioters on a housing estate in Tottenham, north London. It was the shocking climax of a chain of violent disturbances in Britain's most troubled inner-city areas.

The events superficially resembled the riots of the summer of 1981, with some of the same districts – Brixton in south London, Toxteth in Liverpool – featuring prominently. But the scale and intensity of the rioting was more extreme. The first disturbances, in the Handsworth district of Birmingham in early September, at first seemed an isolated incident. However, the shooting of a black woman, Cherry Groce, by police in Brixton on September 28, sparked a far larger conflagration. The incident occurred when armed police raided Mrs Groce's flat in search of her son Michael, an armed robbery suspect. A later inquiry established that the shooting, which left Mrs Groce crippled, was accidental. But the outrage felt by many black people in Brixton and elsewhere was fully understandable.

Protests outside Brixton police station were followed by riots throughout the district on the night after the shooting. The entire area was cordoned off by police as rioters set cars on fire and looted shops. Around 50 people were injured and one person, a photographer, was killed before the violence subsided. Within three days copy-cat riots had broken out in nearby Peckham and in Toxteth.

The Tottenham disturbances were the last, and worst, in the chain of riots. The trigger was in some ways similar to that in Brixton. Cynthia Jarrett, a black woman known to have a weak heart, died during a police raid on her home near the Broadwater Farm estate on October 5. The following day, police came under attack from housing-estate residents armed with bricks, knives and machetes.

Riot police were called in and rioters barricaded themselves into the estate. By nightfall police were facing petrol bombs and gunfire. PC Blakelock, a community policeman, entered the estate with a colleague to protect fire-fighters, who had come under attack while attempting to put out a blaze in a newsagents. He was surrounded by rioters, beaten to the ground and hacked to death with a machete.

After the killing, the rioting subsided and the estate was occupied by riot police. The police were naturally determined to identify and prosecute those who had murdered the police constable. As all too often in such cases, the desire for a "result" led to errors. Three men, Winston Silcott, Mark Braithwaite, and Engin Raghip, were charged with the crime and found guilty. In 1991, however, they were found not guilty on appeal, amid allegations that police evidence had been fabricated. No one else has ever been charged with the murder.

ANGLO-IRISH AGREEMENT

On November 15, 1985, Prime Minister Margaret Thatcher and her Irish counterpart Dr Garret FitzGerald signed a historic agreement that marked a major step on the long road to peace in Northern Ireland.

The accord gave the Irish government a consultative role in the affairs of Northern Ireland through an Intergovernmental Conference with a permanent secretariat. The Thatcher government made this concession in return for a more solid Irish commitment to co-operation on security. The Irish security forces were to act together with the British to clamp down on the IRA.

In a wider political perspective, the Agreement underlined the provisional nature of Britain's commitment to Northern Ireland. While reaffirming that the Province

▲ Margaret Thatcher and Garret FitzGerald sign the Anglo-Irish agreement, aimed at putting an end to decades of sectarian strife.

could not be unified with southern Ireland against the wishes of its population, it also made clear that unification would not be opposed by Britain if the majority in the north ever voted for it.

In the short term, the settlement was met with hostility by Unionists, who resented any involvement of

the Irish government in Ulster, and with coolness by Irish nationalists. But in the long run it suggested the possibility of a framework of goodwill, within which opposed political groups would be able to carry on their struggles for and against unification without recourse to violence.

DEATH OF PHILIP LARKIN

▲ Philip Larkin brought poetry to a wide audience, but spent most of his career as a librarian at the University of Hull.

On December 2, 1985, poet Philip Larkin died at the age of 63. The previous year he had turned down the post of Poet Laureate, offered to him on the death of Sir John Betjeman.

Larkin was brought up in Coventry, where his father – an

admirer of Hitler – was city treasurer. He later described his childhood as "a forgotten boredom", but was better pleased with life as a student at Oxford University, where he formed an enduring friendship with fellow writer Kingsley Amis.

Larkin first attracted notice as a poet in the 1950s, when he was regarded as a member of "The Movement" – poets who reacted against modernist obscurantism, and advocated the use of plain language and traditional verse forms. His most successful collection, *The Whitsun Weddings*, was published in 1964; it was followed by *High Windows* ten years later.

For most of his adult life, Larkin worked as a librarian at the University of Hull. He cultivated the persona of a shy and dull

individual, in deliberate contrast to the traditionally romantic view of the poet. His verse was often aggressively negative – he once wrote: "Deprivation is for me what daffodils were to Wordsworth." But his poetry attracted a wide readership because it often expressed sentiments that everyone understood in a direct, brutally humorous manner.

Larkin was honoured with a memorial service in Westminster Abbey, a ceremony accompanied by jazz, the music he loved. Since his death, his reputation has been tarnished by publication of his letters, which reveal him as outspokenly racist and tackily addicted to pornography. But phrases from his more memorable poems ("They fuck you up, your mum and dad …") have entered general usage.

- British Gas is privatized
- The London stock market is deregulated – known as the "Big Bang"
- The Local Government Act abolishes the GLC and other metropolitan councils
- The Public Order Act gives police new powers in dealing with demonstrations
- The Japanese company Nissan opens a car assembly plant in Sunderland
- The *Independent* newspaper is launched
- Richard Rodgers' Lloyds Building in the City of London is completed
- Books published this year include *An Artist of the Floating World* by Kazuo Ishiguro and *The Old Devils* by Kingsley Amis
- British films this year include Merchant and Ivory's *A Room with a View*, Bruce Robinson's *Withnail & I* and Derek Jarman's *Caravaggio*
- The musicals *Chess* (lyrics by Tim Rice) and *The Phantom of the Opera* (music by Andrew Lloyd Webber) open in London
- New television series include *Inspector Morse*, based on Colin Dexter's novels, and *The Singing Detective* by Dennis Potter
- Albums released this year include Billy Bragg's *Talking With the Taxman About Poetry* and Peter Gabriel's *So*
- Songs of the year include the Pet Shop Boys' "West End Girls" and the Communards' "Don't Leave Me This Way"

THE WESTLAND AFFAIR

On January 9, 1986, Defence Secretary Michael Heseltine stormed out of a Cabinet meeting at 10 Downing Street after a furious row with Margaret Thatcher. His dramatic resignation called into question the Prime Minister's style of leadership, described by her critics as

▲ **Michael Heseltine resigned over the Westland Affair. Mrs Thatcher would come to rue the loss of his talent and support.**

increasingly dictatorial.

The ministerial crisis blew up over the superficially insignificant question of who should buy the Yeovil-based Westland helicopter company. Heseltine favoured a bid from a European consortium, while the Trade and Industry Secretary Leon Brittan, with Thatcher's backing, supported a takeover by the American Sikorsky-Fiat group. The broader issue at stake concerned Britain's relationship with Europe. Heseltine wished to promote closer defence links with Europe, whereas the Prime Minister was suspicious of the Europeans and wanted to promote the "special relationship" with the United States.

The row exploded during the January 9 Cabinet meeting, when Thatcher told Heseltine that his public statements on Westland must be vetted by her officials. In his resignation statement Heseltine claimed that since no basis of trust existed between him and the Prime Minister, he could

not honourably remain in the government.

The sensation of Heseltine's impulsive departure from the Cabinet was reinforced by the revelation of "dirty tricks" by the Department of Trade and Industry during the Westland dispute. A fortnight after the Defence Secretary's resignation, Leon Brittan admitted authorizing the leak of a confidential document to the press containing criticism of Heseltine by the Attorney-General. Brittan was in his turn obliged to resign. Rumours abounded that the Prime Minister herself and her press secretary Bernard Ingham had also been involved in the leak.

In time, the crisis subsided and media interest moved on to other matters. But the elements that would ultimately break Mrs Thatcher's hold on power had been revealed – the deep divisions within her party over Europe and her alienation of ambitious colleagues who could not work under her authoritarian control.

THATCHER ABOLISHES GLC

On 31 March, 1986, England's six metropolitan authorities – the Greater London Council (GLC) and the metropolitan county councils of the West Midlands, Merseyside, Greater Manchester, Tyne and Wear, South Yorkshire and West Yorkshire – were abolished. It was the culmination of Mrs Thatcher's campaign against strong independent local government.

Labour-controlled metropolitan authorities had become centres of resistance to the Thatcher government, especially on Merseyside under the left-wing Militant activist Derek Hatton and in London under "Red Ken" Livingstone. The confrontation

between metropolitan and central government was especially striking in London as County Hall, home of the GLC, sat opposite parliament on the South Bank of the Thames. Livingstone had the city's rising unemployment figures displayed on a placard on top of the building.

The metropolitan councils had originally been set up by the Conservative Heath government in the 1970s. Their abolition was opposed by a minority within the Conservative Party, which abhorred the increase in the power of central government at the expense of local democracy. But Thatcher was unshakable in her will to destroy what she saw as

▲ **GLC Chairman Ken Livingstone had long been a thorn in the side of Mrs Thatcher, who solved the problem by abolishing his council.**

nests of financial profligacy and political subversion. The powers of the metropolitan authorities devolved to local boroughs. London became the only major city in the Western world without its own elected government.

FARMERS SUFFER CHERNOBYL FALL-OUT

▲ The Chernobyl nuclear plant in Ukraine, site of the world's worst nuclear accident, the effects of which were felt in Britain.

At the end of April 1985, a series of explosions at the Chernobyl nuclear power plant in the Soviet Republic of Ukraine released a cloud of radioactive material into the atmosphere. Winds carried the radioactive cloud westward across Europe. Around May 2 rainfall over some upland areas of Britain was found to contain radioactive caesium.

Monitors of the National Radiological Protection Board identified 9,000 hill farms in Cumbria, north Wales, southern Scotland, the Isle of Man and Northern Ireland as possible sources of a health risk. In June the movement and slaughter of sheep from affected areas was banned.

The crisis was a blow to hill farmers already struggling to scrape a living, although they eventually received financial compensation. The authorities insist that no damage to human health occurred in Britain. But 18 years later, a few hundred Welsh farms and some in Scotland were still finding a percentage of their lambs affected by radiation in the soil.

BRITISH GAS PRIVATIZED

By 1986 the government's drive to privatize nationalized industries was in full swing. To promote the sale of British Gas, the largest sell-off to date, the government financed an advertising campaign using the slogan: "If you see Sid, tell him ..." It succeeded in attracting 4.5 million investors to sign up for the shares.

British Gas was by all accounts a well-run, efficient and profitable state enterprise. The only justification for selling it – apart from a straightforward ideological commitment to privatization – was to raise short-term cash. The disposal of valuable assets at a knock-down price was criticized in the House of Lords by the ageing former Prime Minister Harold Macmillan, now the Earl of Stockton. In a haughtily patrician but memorable phrase, he condemned it as "selling the family silver".

But by the end of the year "Supermac" was dead and the "One Nation" Toryism he had embodied looked equally moribund. The sale of British Gas raised a massive £5.4 billion. Small investors quickly sold on their shares at a tidy profit, in an operation that was more a government handout than a stock market flutter. The mixed economy, combining state and private enterprise, which had existed since the Second World War was being rapidly dismantled and controls on unbridled capitalism abolished. There was no turning back the Thatcher revolution.

▲ "If you see Sid, tell him" was the memorable slogan that attracted 4.5 million investors to sign up for shares in the privatization of British Gas.

1986

ENGLAND BEATEN BY THE 'HAND OF GOD'

In 1986 England, Scotland and Northern Ireland qualified for the football World Cup finals, held in Mexico. Neither the Scots nor the Northern Irish made any significant impression on the tournament, but the English team had a turbulent time before being defeated in controversial fashion by Argentina in the quarter-finals.

The tournament commenced disastrously for England. In the group stage a 1–0 defeat at the hands of Portugal was followed by a goalless draw against lowly Morocco. In the course of the Morocco game, team captain Bryan Robson went off injured and Ray Wilkins, the player who took over his captain's armband, was sent off for throwing the ball at the referee. England were in crisis and the press had their knives out for manager Bobby Robson. But fortune turned in the last group match against Poland. England won 3–0 thanks to a hat-trick by Everton striker Gary Lineker, only recently established in the national team.

Qualifying second behind Morocco at the end of the group stage, England won their first knock-out game 3–0 against Paraguay, with two more goals from Lineker. This set up the quarter-final clash with Argentina, seen as a grudge match in the wake of the Falklands conflict.

The Argentine player Diego Maradona was widely regarded as the greatest footballer since Pelé, but he had little chance to shine in a hard-fought goalless first half. Shortly after the interval, however, Maradona scored with a blatant hand-ball. Fired up, he then ran through the England midfield and defence to score the best individual goal ever seen at a World Cup finals. Still, England had fight in them and Lineker scored from a cross by substitute John Barnes. But an equalizer narrowly eluded them.

After the match, Maradona attributed his first goal to "the hand of God". Argentina went on to win the World Cup. The only consolation for England was that Lineker took the Golden Boot award for most goals scored with six – Maradona could manage only five.

▲ **Maradona blatantly handles the ball into the goal to give Argentina a controversial win in the World Cup quarter-finals.**

DEATH OF SCULPTOR HENRY MOORE

On August 31, 1986, renowned sculptor Henry Moore died at his home in Much Hadham, Hertfordshire. In a long career, he had done more than any other individual to establish a British presence at the forefront of modern art.

Moore was born in 1898. The son of a mining engineer, he was brought up in a small terraced house in Castleford, Yorkshire. Although attracted to sculpture from the age of 11, Moore became a schoolteacher. It was only after serving as a conscript in the First World War that an ex-serviceman's grant enabled him to begin an art education.

Throughout his formative years as an artist he often worked alongside fellow sculptor Barbara Hepworth. Together they moved from the traditional illustrative style of sculpture still dominant in Britain to a more abstract modernism. Moore was influenced by the "primitive" sculptures of pre-Columbian America and tribal Africa, as well as Renaissance artists such as Michelangelo. Working in wood and stone, he also found inspiration in natural objects such as bones, driftwood, pebbles and shells.

In 1940 he was appointed an official war artist. His drawings of Londoners sheltering underground from German bombs during the Blitz much enhanced his reputation, especially in the United States. After the war, international recognition grew. His subject matter shifted to family groups and monumental reclining female figures cast in bronze. These large reassuringly peaceful sculptures were ideal for public commissions and began to appear in public spaces across the globe. He had to employ a team of assistants and came to command very high prices for his work.

Moore never lost his inventiveness or modernist capacity to puzzle or shock. Works such as the 1967 *Nuclear Energy*, apparently a fusion of a human skull and an atomic mushroom cloud, continued to challenge onlookers with their dense allusiveness and powerful physical presence. But Moore inevitably became an establishment figure in the eyes of new generations of sculptors struggling to emerge from the long shadow he cast.

The millions Moore made never

▲ **Henry Moore poses with two of his sculptures, *Woman* and *Falling Warrior*, characteristic of the monumental nature of his later works.**

changed his simple way of life. He poured the money into the Henry Moore Foundation, to promote the appreciation of sculpture and

preserve his works after his death. His remains were interred in the Artist's Corner of St Paul's Cathedral.

GOVERNMENT CAMPAIGN TO COUNTER AIDS

In November 1986 the government launched a £20 million publicity campaign to alert the British public to the threat of AIDS (Acquired Immune Deficiency Sydnrome). A leaflet about the disease was delivered to every household in Britain. This was backed up by an advertising campaign using the slogan "AIDS: Don't Die of Ignorance".

Some commentators regarded the campaign as rather belated, in that AIDS had been identified by the American medical establishment in 1981. By 1986, there were reckoned to be around 30,000 people infected with the HIV virus in Britain, although only 278 people were known to have died of AIDS.

The government campaign was a response to fears that the disease might be spreading from minority groups into the mass of the population. AIDS had first been identified among promiscuous gay men, and then also found concentrated among drug users who shared needles. The discovery that people were becoming HIV-positive as a result of infected blood transfusions had forced the introduction of screening programmes for blood donors.

The government leaflet said of AIDS: "Anyone can get it, gay or straight, male or female." This perhaps caused unnecessary alarm to grandmothers living a quiet life, but it struck at the complacency of young heterosexuals having unprotected sex in the belief that the "gay plague" was no concern of theirs. In the wake of the campaign, sales of condoms boomed.

▲ **Health Secretary Norman Fowler launches the government's "Don't Die of Ignorance" anti-AIDS campaign.**

1987

- House prices in London are rising at around 25 per cent a year
- 41 per cent of marriages in the UK now end in divorce
- The government announces the end of free dental check-ups and free eye tests
- The General Synod of the Church of England calls for compassion towards homosexuals, but invites them to repent
- Construction of the Channel Tunnel begins
- A scandal erupts over the removal of hundreds of children from their families in Cleveland, northeast England, by social workers pursuing allegations of sex abuse
- Books published this year include V S Naipaul's *Enigma of Arrival* and Margaret Drabble's *The Radiant Way*
- British films this year include David Leland's *Wish You Were Here*, Terry Jones's *Personal Services* and Richard Attenborough's *Cry Freedom*
- First performances of operas *The Electrification of the Soviet Union* by Nigel Osborne and *A Night at the Chinese Opera* by Judith Weir
- The drug ecstasy comes into widespread use among young people who dance to acid house music at "raves", frequently held in disused warehouses
- Albums released this year include U2's *The Joshua Tree*, Depeche Mode's *Music for the Masses* and George Michael's *Faith*

TERRY WAITE TAKEN HOSTAGE

By 1987 the benign bearded features of Terry Waite were a familiar sight on television news broadcasts. As personal envoy of the Archbishop of Canterbury, Dr Robert Runcie, Waite had established himself as a specialist in negotiation with the heads of anti-Western Muslim states and with Islamic terrorist groups. Basing his approach on the trust inspired by his religious commitment, through the 1980s he had succeeded in striking deals for the release of Western hostages. On January 20, 1987, however, Waite became a hostage himself.

Waite had gone to war-torn Beirut, Lebanon, in an effort to locate and free four hostages, including journalist John McCarthy, held by Islamic Jihad. He did not realize to what degree he had lost the confidence of the Islamic terrorists. At just this time the "arms for hostages" scandal was breaking in the United States, revealing how US Colonel Oliver North had arranged the supply of arms to Iran in return for the release of American hostages held in Lebanon. Waite had been compromised by the fall-out from this secret dealing.

Waite was seized when he turned up alone for a meeting with a Muslim contact who had promised to arrange for him to see the hostages. He was blindfolded and eventually incarcerated in an underground cell. He was kept in solitary confinement, although he managed to communicate with other hostages by tapping on the wall in code. His imprisonment lasted for 1,760 days until his release in November 1991.

▲ Terry Waite thought his role as a hostage negotiator gave him special protection, but his efforts to free others led to a captivity lasting 1,760 days.

193 DIE IN FERRY DISASTER

The roll-on-roll-off car ferry *Herald of Free Enterprise* left the Belgian port of Zeebrugge at about 7.00 pm on March 6, 1987, bound for Dover with around 650 passengers on board. Weather conditions were perfect, with good visibility and a calm sea.

Yet less than a kilometre out of the harbour, while still in shallow waters, the ship capsized and 193 passengers and crew died.

It later emerged that the ferry's bow doors had not been closed before leaving port. Once at sea, water poured into the ship, flooding the car decks and destabilizing the vessel, which turned over on its side. The disaster happened so close to shore that rescuers were soon on the scene. Teams of divers attempted to free people trapped in the submerged section of the ship. Survivors were hauled up through broken port-holes.

An inquiry into the disaster found that the ferry's owners, Townsend Thoresen, had been generally negligent in enforcing safety procedures. A coroner's court, however, blamed the individual failings of three crew members. In 1989 an unsuccessful attempt was made to prosecute the owners, by then renamed P&O European Ferries, for corporate manslaughter.

▲ The capsized *Herald of Free Enterprise* lies outside Zeebrugge Harbour; 193 perished when water flooded in through the bow doors.

THIRD THATCHER VICTORY

On June 11, 1987, Margaret Thatcher coasted effortlessly to a third consecutive general election victory. The Conservatives lost only 21 seats compared with their landslide win in 1983, and still had a working majority of 102.

The result reflected a widespread perception that the Thatcher government's handling of the economy had been a success. The balance of payments problem had been temporarily solved thanks to North Sea oil, inflation had come down, taxes had been cut, government finances were being put on a stable footing, and strikes were increasingly rare. Despite rising inequality and persistently high levels of unemployment, the majority of the population were better off than ever before.

For the future of British politics,

▲ Mrs Thatcher poses with Soviet President Mikhail Gorbachev shortly before her third landslide general election victory.

the most important contest at the election was between Labour and the SDP–Liberal Alliance. In 1983 it had seemed as if the Alliance might replace Labour as the main opposition force. But in 1987, led by Neil Kinnock, Labour took 31 per cent of the vote to 23 per cent for the Alliance. Labour's problems were only too evident. Their core

base in the old industrial areas was fast shrinking. They won no seats in the prosperous south of England, save in run-down parts of London. But they still commanded support as the party of the NHS and state education.

The election was a disaster for the Alliance. As usual with centre parties, they were split between appealing to voters to the left of them and voters to the right. The "two Davids", Liberal leader David Steel and SDP leader David Owen, were constantly at odds. In the wake of the election, a majority of SDP members voted to join the Liberals in a new Social and Liberal Democrat Party. The SDP, which had set out to "break the mould" of British politics, inglorously faded from the scene in 1990 after a mere nine years of existence.

HUNGERFORD MASSACRE

On August 19, 1987, 27-year-old gun enthusiast Michael Ryan went on a shooting spree that left 16 people dead and 15 seriously wounded. The massacre took place in the peaceful market town of Hungerford in Berkshire, an almost surreal setting for one of Britain's worst ever mass murders.

A member of several gun clubs, Ryan owned a perfectly legal armoury of automatic rifles, pistols and shotguns. One of the weapons he used on his rampage was a Kalashnikov AK-47. He began by abducting and shooting a woman who was picnicking with her children in Savernake Forest. He then drove to his Hungerford home, shooting up a petrol station en route. After setting his own house ablaze, Ryan roamed the streets on

foot, opening fire at random.

The first police officers sent to respond to emergency calls were unarmed. One of them, PC Roger Brereton, was among those shot dead. Ryan was eventually surrounded inside a secondary

school, which was deserted for the summer holidays. Police negotiators attempted to persuade him to surrender, but early in the evening he shot himself. One of his last statements to police was: "I wish I'd stayed in bed."

▲ Michael Ryan's fatal shooting spree at Hungerford led to a clamour for stronger gun control in Britain.

THE GREAT GALE

▲ The wreckage of a car crushed by a tree during the hurricane-force winds that hit the southeast of England.

In the early hours of October 16, 1987, the southeast of Great Britain was hit by hurricane-force winds, causing widespread devastation and millions of pounds' worth of damage. Amid collapsing trees and flying debris, 17 people were known to have died and hundreds were injured. It was the worst storm to hit Britain since records began.

With railway lines blocked by fallen trees, many train services were out of action for almost a week, causing widespread disruption for London commuters.

The winds, which were measured at over 177 km/h (110 mph), came as something of a shock to the British public, even though 36 hours beforehand weather centres in Holland had accurately predicted what would happen. It was a major embarrassment for Britain's Meteorological Office, whose well-known weather man Michael Fish confidently reported on national television that "there is no chance of a hurricane." The official explanation was that "the storm built up over an area of sea with little shipping" and hence was not monitored carefully.

Although insurance companies were hit heavily, a price tag could not be put on some of the damage. In the Chelsea Physic Garden, rare trees, some dating as far back as 1673, were snapped like twigs. It was estimated that the Royal Botanical Gardens at Kew would take at least 30 years to recover from the damage. As an official put it: "It looks as if a giant has just stepped across the garden."

Apart from tree surgeons, glaziers and roofing contractors, who flourished in the aftermath, the only other group that might have taken advantage of the pandemonium were ornithologists who could have spotted several species of rare birds blown hundreds of kilometres inland.

BLACK MONDAY

October 19, 1987, saw the worst ever day on the London stock exchange as £50 billion was wiped off the value of shares in a single day's trading. That fateful day, commonly known as "Black Monday", represented a 10 per cent fall in the market.

The drop was even more dramatic in New York where the Dow Jones industrial average fell by more than 500 points, leaving shares worth an average of 22.6 per cent less than they had been at the start of the day. Even at its worst, the October 1929 collapse that ushered in the Great Depression only managed a 13

▲ Traders were overwhelmed by a huge wave of selling orders on "Black Monday", as the stock market fell by 10 per cent in a single day.

per cent fall over a single day.

The trauma felt by the world's stock markets brought a sudden ending to a five-year bull market, one which had seen a 350 per cent rise in share prices. Although it did not trigger a second depression as some analysts had feared – by the end of October, half of the losses had been recouped – October 19, 1987, is widely viewed as the end of the 1980s boom. A recession slowly followed which lasted into the early years of the next decade.

Black Monday was not a result of one single factor. Like its precursor 50 years earlier, stocks and shares had become overvalued. The crises in London and other markets were a direct consequence of panic on Wall Street.

Of concern to investors was the United States' continuing trade deficit and inability to balance its budget. Some also blamed the advent of computerized trading systems which they argued had turned the stock market into one great unpredictable gamble.

As with all sudden market downturns, it was the smaller companies that were hit the hardest. The well-established stocks were quickly able to regain ground as investors bought at bargain low prices in the reasonably sure knowledge that they would be a reliable long-term bet.

POPPY DAY BOMBING

November 8, 1987 will be remembered as the day that the IRA carried out one of its most callous bombings in Northern Ireland. At a Remembrance Day parade in the small town of Enniskillen a bomb was detonated, killing 11 and injuring 60. Among the victims were a number of women and children.

The bombing followed reports that the IRA had restructured its organization into a number of small semi-autonomous service groups. The change was thought to have followed a number of successful intelligence operations, making crucial information leaks less likely.

The horror of the carnage reported in the media brought widespread condemnation from all sides of the community. Sensing the outrage, some, like Bishop Brian Hannon, sought a positive outcome: "I hope the Enniskillen massacre will be a catalyst for peace within Northern Ireland." The IRA, however, remained resolute that there was no peace. As its tersely worded statement read: "The British Army did not leave Ireland after Bloody Sunday."

It was a poignant event in the history of the "Irish question", signalling a stepping up of violent protest by the IRA. However, it also

▲ The Enniskillen bombing shocked communities on both sides of the Irish question, but the violence continued.

saw a resurgence of a vocal cross-community opposition to terrorist activities by either side. Also poignantly, the funeral of the victims was held on November 15, two years to the day that the governments of London and Dublin had signed an agreement giving the south a consultative role in the running of Ulster. It had been hoped that such a concession to the nationalists in the north would be taken as an act of good faith. Such optimism was in vain.

This was merely the latest in a succession of unsuccessful attempts to solve a problem whose resolution would never seem able to satisfy both the Loyalist and nationalist communities.

DEATH ON THE ROCK

- Base interest rates rise from 8 per cent to more than 12 per cent during the year; price inflation tops 6 per cent
- Chancellor of the Exchequer Nigel Lawson cuts the basic rate of income tax to 25 per cent and establishes a single higher rate of 40 per cent
- The Licensing Act allows pubs to open from 11 am. to 11 pm from Monday to Saturday
- The Education Reform Act introduces a national curriculum and testing of children at four "key stages"; schools can "opt out" of the control of local education authorities
- Children sit GCSE exams for the first time
- The government bans Sinn Fein politicians' voices from being heard on television or radio
- The Tate Collection opens a new gallery in Liverpool's redeveloped Albert Dock
- Books published this year include *A Brief History of Time* by Stephen Hawking, *The Satanic Verses* by Salman Rushdie and *The Swimming Pool Library* by Alan Hollinghurst
- British films this year include Peter Greenaway's *Drowning By Numbers*, Charles Crichton's *A Fish Called Wanda* and Terence Davies's *Distant Voices, Still Lives*
- Museum of the Moving Image opens on London's South Bank

On March 7, 1988, three IRA terrorists were gunned down at point-blank range by plain-clothed members of the Special Air Service (SAS). The incident took place in Gibraltar, the tiny British possession on the southern Mediterranean coast of Spain. The three victims, two of whom had already served long prison sentences for terrorist activities, were Sean Savage, Daniel McCann and "commander" Mairead Farrell.

British intelligence had known that an IRA service unit was at work in Gibraltar. Information they had discovered led them to believe that they were planning to bomb a local changing the guard ceremony. Indeed, the day after the shooting, a white Renault car rented by the terrorists was discovered with 63.5 kg (140 lb) of plastic explosive concealed in it. Had the plot succeeded, the lives of up to 50 soldiers who would have been involved in the parade could have been endangered.

There was some controversy as to whether there had been any genuine attempt to capture the suspects. The official report claimed that when challenged, the two men and one woman made as if to escape, so that, given their high-risk status and the fact that they may have been armed, a shoot-to-kill policy was the only option. A local witness, however, reported that the terrorists were given no warning before the shooting, making the incident little more than an authorized execution. A number of later media reports tended to confirm this latter view, even though there was very little real public sympathy for the fates of the three victims.

A week later, the "Death on the Rock" saga, as it became known, took a further twist. In the eyes of the IRA, its three "soldiers" had died on active service and thus, on March 16, they had a military-style funeral. The Belfast cemetery service was an emotionally charged affair, attended by a crowd of 5,000. The British army had chosen not to police the event. As the three bodies were being lowered into the ground a lone gunman emerged, lobbing grenades and shooting indiscriminately into the crowd. Three were killed and 50 injured. Eventually the man was brought

▲ Mourners for three IRA terrorists killed by the British SAS in Gibraltar take cover behind a gravestone as a Protestant gunman, Michael Stone, fires into the crowd.

down and given a severe beating before the police intervened.

The incident was unusual in that both nationalists and Loyalists were traditionally scrupulous in their observation of sectarian funerals. It later transpired that the Protestant gunman had been working alone. He had apparently tried on a number of occasions to join the loyalist Ulster Defence Association (UDA) but had been turned down. He was believed to have been on drugs at the time of the attack.

Three days later, a further related incident took place that would send shock waves throughout the whole of Britain. Two British soldiers in their car found themselves inadvertently caught up in the midst of an IRA parade. The mood of the crowd was suspicious and ill tempered hardly surprising after the funeral shooting. It was here, and in the full glare of television cameras, that the two luckless corporals, Derek Wood and Robert Howes, were pulled out of their car and lynched. They were beaten unconscious, stripped and taken away to nearby wasteland, where they were shot dead.

It was not known why the two soldiers were even there. Although the IRA claimed that they were on a reconnaissance mission, the British Army maintained that they were not on active duty.

The heightened paramilitary activity on both sides of the Troubles since the Enniskillen bombing of November 1987 looked poised to continue indefinitely. The peace agreements unsuccessfully brokered in 1985 by Margaret Thatcher and the Irish Prime Minister Garrett Fitzgerald were now dead and buried, and the IRA was preparing to step up its "war" outside Northern Ireland, carrying it to mainland Great Britain.

PIPER ALPHA OIL-RIG BLAZE

▲ **The explosion on the Piper Alpha platform was the worst ever offshore oil disaster.**

On July 6, 1988, there was an escape of flammable liquefied gas at the Piper Alpha oil rig some 190 km (120 miles) off the northeast coast of Scotland. The disaster that followed cost the lives of 167 men.

Owned by Occidental Petroleum, the oil and gas platform was the largest and oldest in the North Sea. That day, there were 225 men on board. The leak occurred in the late evening, setting off an explosion when the flammable gas ignited. A second, far larger explosion followed about 20 minutes later. As fire engulfed the platform, many workers were asphyxiated by toxic fumes. Others slid down pipes or jumped hundreds of metres into the water, which was itself ablaze with burning oil. Some of those saved by rescue boats and helicopters were severely burned.

Texan oilwell-fire specialist Red Adair was brought in a week later to put out the blaze. An inquiry into the disaster, headed by Lord Cullan, was strongly critical of maintenance procedures and safety standards on the rig. A court later found two workers guilty of negligence, although this finding has been hotly contested.

The Piper Alpha catastrophe remains the worst ever offshore oil disaster. The enforcement of better safety procedures in its wake has almost certainly helped avert a repetition of the event, although oil companies are still frequently accused of skimping on safety in the pursuit of profit.

CHARLES TAKES ON THE ARCHITECTS

▲ **Prince Charles's strongly worded invectives against "the horrors" of modern architecture were bitterly resented by many.**

Prince Charles emerged in the 1980s as a campaigner against modernism in architecture. It was a surprising role for an heir to the throne to adopt, but one that did not breach rules barring members of the royal family from partisan comment on political issues.

The prince's concerns were first publicly formulated in an address to the Royal Institute of British Architects in 1984, in which he referred to a proposed modern tower block as "a giant glass stump". He proved his influence when plans for an extension to the National Gallery were changed after he described the original design as "like a monstrous carbuncle on the face of a much-loved and elegant friend".

In October 1988, the prince took the unprecedented step of writing and presenting a television documentary, broadcast in the BBC's *Omnibus* series. He was shown travelling down the Thames by boat and denouncing the modernist buildings he passed on his journey – the National Theatre he described as like "a nuclear power station". He praised buildings that exhibited a human scale and blended with their natural and built environment.

Although many architects reacted scornfully to the prince's amateur intervention in their professional sphere, his views undoubtedly corresponded with those of much of the British public. His influence gave a definite boost to architects working in pastiches of British vernacular styles.

▲ **The National Theatre on London's South Bank, a building Prince Charles described as like "a nuclear power station".**

BAN ON SPYCATCHER FAILS

On October 13, 1988, the government conceded defeat in a long legal battle to prevent publication of *Spycatcher*, a book by former MI5 officer Peter Wright.

Subtitled "the candid autobiography of a senior intelligence officer", *Spycatcher* gave an insider's account of the history of the British intelligence services in the post-Second World War era. Much of it was an interesting but unsensational description of the electronic bugging techniques that were Wright's speciality. The most dramatic "revelations" were speculative and unproven, including the allegations that Roger Hollis, director-general of MI5 from 1956 to 1965, was a Soviet spy and that MI5 officers had conspired against Harold Wilson when he was Prime Minister.

The government was bizarrely persistent in pursuit of a ban on the book. Since Wright was living in Tasmania, he was out of reach of British law. Although the book was published in Australia in 1985, it was banned in Britain and the government used "gagging orders" against British newspapers that attempted to publish excerpts.

▲ **Peter Wright (centre) at the launch of his book *Spycatcher*, an event the British government had fought long to prevent.**

The government also took legal action in Australia to have the book banned there.

The Australian court case dragged on into 1987. At one point, a hapless senior civil servant, Sir Robert Armstrong, was obliged to admit that his government had been "economical with the truth" in presenting its case. By the time the British application to have the book banned was rejected, it had already sold almost half a million copies in the United States.

The decision of the Law Lords to authorize the book's publication in Britain in October 1988 was in effect a recognition of a fait accompli. The essence of the book's contents was by then known to all. *Spycatcher* made the canny Wright a millionaire before he died in 1995.

LOCKERBIE BOMBING

The small Scottish border town of Lockerbie found itself at the centre of a major terrorist incident on December 21, 1988, as a Boeing 747 jumbo jet travelling from London to New York exploded, falling from the sky. All 259 crew and passengers on board Pan-Am Flight 103 died and another 11 people on the ground were killed by the debris.

The wings and a section of fuselage struck Sherwood Crescent in Lockerbie, creating a large crater and damaging a score of houses. Several of them were totally destroyed. Cars travelling along the nearby A74(M) were scorched by the fireball. Other wreckage was spread over an area of more than 2,000 sq km (800 sq miles)

Investigators analyzing the wreckage were quickly able to deduce that the disaster had been caused by a bomb hidden inside a cassette-player in a suitcase on board the aircraft. The immediate suspects were

▲ The wreckage of Pan Am Flight 103 lies strewn around the small Scottish border town of Lockerbie. In 2001 Libyan agent Abdel Baset al-Magrahi was found guilty of carrying out the terrorist attack.

terrorists from Iran – the bombing was believed to be revenge for the downing of an Iranian passenger jet by a US warship that July. But in the end, the trail of evidence led to Libya.

In the early 1990s the US government publicly named two Libyan nationals whom it suspected of being responsible for

the crime. Libyan leader Colonel Gaddafi at first refused to extradite them, but in 1998 he agreed that the suspects could be tried in the Netherlands, under Scottish law, and with a Scottish judge presiding. Abdelbaset Ali Mohmed al-Megrahi was jailed for life in January 2001, but his alleged accomplice was found not guilty.

BIG BANG BOOK IS BEST-SELLER

The bestselling new book of 1988 was a demanding work on physics and cosmology by a severely disabled Cambridge University scientist. The book was *A Brief History of Time* and the author Stephen Hawking.

One of the world's leading theoretical physicists, Hawking had pursued his work despite being afflicted with motor neurone disease since the age of 21. Almost totally paralyzed, he was only able to speak and operate a computer through a range of technological devices. Inevitably, some of the

fascination of his book lay in its writer's disability.

A Brief History of Time centred on a description of the Big Bang in which our universe began. It also discoursed on other areas of cosmology such as the strange behaviour of black holes. Although intended as a popularization, the book eschewed neither mathematics nor abstruse topics such as superstring theory.

How many of the purchasers of *A Brief History of Time* actually read the book from cover to cover is unknown. But its popularity undoubtedly reflected a belief that

▲ Stephen Hawking brought theoretical physics to the masses with his bestseller *A Brief History of Time.*

scientists such as Hawking had the answers to the big questions about life and the universe. The book remained in the *Sunday Times* bestseller list for four years and sold more than 9 million copies worldwide.

SEPTEMBER
- Addressing the Council of Europe in Bruges, Mrs Thatcher describes moves towards European political and economic union as "folly"

OCTOBER
- Death of car designer Sir Alec Issigonis, creator of the Morris Minor and the Mini

NOVEMBER
- The government announces its intention of privatizing water and electricity services
- Scottish Nationalists win a shock victory in the Govan by-election
- Students protest at the proposed introduction of student loans to replace grants

DECEMBER
- 34 die when two crowded commuter trains crash in Clapham, south London
- A terrorist bomb explodes on a Boeing 747 over Lockerbie in Scotland; 259 passengers and crew are killed, as well as 11 people on the ground

1989

- Britain has a record trade deficit of £20 billion; the base interest rate rises to 15 per cent
- Sky television launches satellite television
- Plans for a high-speed rail link between the Channel Tunnel and London are shelved
- Books published this year include *The Remains of the Day* by Kazuo Ishiguro and *London Fields* by Martin Amis
- British films this year include Richard Branagh's *Henry V* and Peter Greenaway's *The Cook The Thief His Wife and her Lover*
- First performance of John Tavener's *The Protecting Veil*
- Albums released this year include New Order's *Technique* and the Stone Roses' *The Stone Roses*

JANUARY
- 47 die when a British Midlands airliner crashes on the M1 motorway

FEBRUARY
- Lawyer Pat Finucane is shot dead in Northern Ireland
- Iran issues a fatwa calling for the death of author Salman Rushdie

APRIL
- 96 die in the Hillsborough football disaster
- Jockey Peter Scudamore achieves a record 200th win in a National Hunt season
- Death of novelist Daphne du Maurier

BLASPHEMY OR FREE SPEECH?

An extraordinary series of events began to unfold on February 14, 1989, as the author Salman Rushdie found himself the object of a death threat from Islamic fundamentalists. Rushdie's "crime" was the publication of his third novel, *The Satanic Verses*, in which a fictional character was interpreted by some as satirizing the prophet Mohammed. Under Islamic law this represents blasphemy punishable by death. It was the Ayatollah Khomeini, the revolutionary Islamic leader of Iran, who announced the fatwa – the call for Rushdie's execution.

Published in summer 1988, *The Satanic Verses* was quickly condemned by British Muslim leaders. By the new year the protests had spread throughout the Islamic world, with violent demonstrations taking place in Pakistan that left six dead and almost 100 injured.

Few doubted that Khomeini's threat was a serious matter. A reward of £3 million was even offered to the executioner. Rushdie had no choice but to go into hiding. Despite government protests, the Ayatollah refused to lift the death sentence. Most Western governments condemned the action as an attempt to suppress free speech.

Although an award-winning novelist, the Anglo-Indian Rushdie was barely known to the ordinary public until this time. Ironically, *The Satanic Verses* became an international bestseller, reaching a far wider public than the minority audience to whom Rushdie's books usually appealed.

▲ Novelist Salman Rushdie's *Satanic Verses* provoked uproar in the Islamic world and led to a call for his death.

Rushdie, however, was unable to take much joy from his high profile. It was not until the late 1990s that he was able to emerge from hiding.

HILLSBOROUGH DISASTER

The tragedies of May 1985 that had seen 56 deaths in a blaze at Bradford and 39 the same month at Belgium's Heysel Stadium sent a message to the world that all was not well with the state of English football.

The quick-fix solutions offered by the football authorities to deter direct intervention by the British government largely involved treating football fans like potentially dangerous animals. Policing was increased and at football grounds all over the country wire fences were erected to prevent violence spilling over on to the field. On April 15, 1989, the short-sightedness of this policy was laid bare in a catastrophe that resulted in 96 fans being crushed to death.

The game was an FA Cup semi-final between Liverpool and Nottingham Forest. As was traditional, the match was held in a neutral venue – in this case, the Hillsborough Stadium in Sheffield, South Yorkshire. The problems began a few minutes before the start of the match as police took the decision to relieve the intense crowd pressure that had built up outside the stadium by opening the gates and letting Liverpool fans in without checking their tickets. This quickly created a problem of

▲ Ninety-five fans died at Hillsborough in a disaster that showed quick-fix solutions had done little to solve the problems of Britain's ageing stadiums.

overcrowding as Liverpool supporters surged forward to find a good view. Six minutes into the game, panic set in, forcing people forward and crushing them against the concrete and steel fencing.

The aftermath turned into a major controversy as blame was sought. Most put the blame on poor policing. The *Sun* newspaper had its own ideas, running under the headline "The Truth", a story documenting the allegedly appalling behaviour of Liverpool fans. Creating outrage, to this day the *Sun* remains widely boycotted throughout Liverpool.

An official investigation into the Hillsborough disaster conducted by Lord Justice Taylor controversially concluded that the deaths were accidental. In spite of the apparently defensive and evasive reactions of senior officers during the inquiry, South Yorkshire police were cleared of responsibility. Lord Justice Taylor also commented critically on the poor state of sporting arenas in Britain, in particular those – like most used in football then – in which most spectators were forced to stand. By enforcing all-seater stadiums, the sequence of events that resulted in the Hillsborough tragedy could not recur. While this move was not wholly popular with regular football supporters, for whom standing on the terraces was a part of the sport's great tradition, it was overwhelmingly responsible for the gentrification of football that took place during the next decade.

GUILDFORD FOUR CLEARED OF IRA BOMBING

On October 19, 1989, the Court of Appeal quashed the convictions of the four people jailed for the bombing of a Guildford pub in 1974. The case was one of the worst miscarriages of justice in recent British history.

The pub bombing, which killed five people – four of them soldiers – occurred at the height of the IRA terror campaign on the British mainland. Despite not being IRA members, Gerard Conlon, Patrick Armstrong, Carole Richardson and Paul Hill were arrested by Surrey police and confessed to the crime. Hill and Armstrong were also charged with another pub bombing in Woolwich.

The successful appeal followed an investigation by Avon and Somerset police, which found that the original notes of the confessions had been doctored by police officers. Since the police had lied about this matter, the court accepted that their entire evidence was unreliable. The Guildford Four claimed that the confessions were false and had been extracted under duress.

Conlon, Armstrong and Richardson were released immediately. Conlon told reporters:

▲ Gerard Conlon, one of the "Guildford Four" following his release after serving 14 years for an IRA bombing of which he was cleared.

"I have been in prison for something I did not do. I am totally innocent." Hill was still held on another murder charge, but he was soon freed on bail and was cleared of the remaining charge in 1994.

The successful appeal led to the re-examination of other cases from the same period. The convictions of the Maguire Seven, directly related to those of the Guildford Four, were quashed in 1991. In the same year, the six men convicted of the Birmingham pub bombings in November 1974 were exonerated.

1990–1999

The last decade of the millennium opened with the downfall of Prime Minister Margaret Thatcher. She was ousted from power by a coup within her own party, but the discontent among Tories with her leadership reflected her waning popularity in the country at large. Her successor, John Major, won a surprising general election victory in 1992, despite an economic recession. It was an election the Conservatives would probably have done better to lose. Internal differences over Europe tore the party apart, while the Tories' image was further besmirched by revelations of "sleaze", both financial and sexual. Meanwhile, the 1992 election defeat at last spurred Labour to embrace fundamental change. Under Tony Blair, socialism was consigned to the dustbin of history and "New Labour" emerged as the friend of business and enterprise.

Ironically, the much-reviled Major government achieved remarkable success in its management of the British economy. The failure to maintain an artificially high exchange rate for sterling led to a sharp depreciation of the pound that in turn stimulated exports. By the middle of the decade, recession had been replaced by rapid growth and both unemployment and inflation were falling. Thanks to the overwhelming Labour general election victory in 1997, this economic recovery was inherited by Labour Chancellor of the Exchequer Gordon Brown. He showed great skill in maintaining the health of the economy, adeptly avoiding any of the exchange rate crises or panics in the City of London that had hamstrung previous Labour administrations.

The economy was not the only area in which the Labour government built upon the success of its predecessor. In Northern Ireland John Major's government achieved significant progress in breaking the political stalemate that seemed to have condemned the Province to living with terrorism for ever. But it was Labour's Northern Ireland Secretary Mo Mowlam who won the assent of the men of violence on both sides to a peace process that only their support could make work. The much-trumpeted Good Friday Agreement of 1998 did not resolve Northern Ireland's political and social difficulties at a stroke, but, except for the scattered actions of a few rogue elements, it did bring an end to large-scale terrorist attacks. After three decades and more than 3,000 deaths, this was a considerable achievement.

The notable innovations of the Blair government after 1997 came mostly in the sphere of constitutional reform. The long-mooted idea of granting a measure of autonomous government to Scotland and Wales became a reality at last in 1999. Since the Labour Party initially dominated the new assemblies in both countries, the emergence of sharp conflict between the national parliaments and central government remained a future risk rather than a current problem. Reform of the Westminster parliament meant that the House of Lords ceased to be primarily an assembly of hereditary peers. But radical reform of the electoral system – which might have made the composition of the House of Commons more accurately reflect voters' wishes – did not materialize.

The nature of changes outside the narrow world of politics was more difficult to pin down. The communications revolution sweeping the world hit Britain with full force, with personal computers and mobile phones becoming commonplace. From around the middle of the decade, a somewhat spurious sense of renewed optimism was embodied in an upsurge of British pop music, fashion and the arts. The rebranding of the nation as "Cool Britannia" by New Labour propagandists did not convince many, but Britain's multi-cultural cities certainly saw an expansion of leisure activities that gave an impression of youthful creativity. Respect for traditional authority was at a low ebb, reflected as much in cynical attitudes to politicians as in increasingly negative treatment of the royal family in the popular press. Some tried to find evidence of a more caring Britain in the emotional reaction to the death of the Princess of Wales in 1997, but British society was equally characterized by racist violence and rising crime levels. The Labour government made some progress in improving the situation of the poorest through advantageous changes for those in low-paid work and stealthily increased taxation for the better-off. But Britain remained a markedly less egalitarian place than it had been 20 years earlier.

- The British economy enters recession with six consecutive months of falling output
- Inflation rises above 10 per cent – higher than when Mrs Thatcher came to power in 1979
- Introduction of the poll tax provokes riots and passive resistance
- The National Health Service and Community Care Act creates an "internal market" in the NHS
- The trial for fraud and other crimes of businessmen involved in the Guinness takeover of Distillers
- Stephen Hendry wins the World Professional Snooker Championship at the age of 21
- Books published this year include *Possession* by A S Byatt and *The Buddha of Suburbia* by Hanif Kureishi
- British films this year include Mike Leigh's *Life is Sweet*
- Albums released this year include George Michael's *Listen Without Prejudice Vol 1* and the Happy Mondays' *Pills 'n' Thrills and Bellyaches*
- Songs of the year include Elton John's "Sacrifice" and Sinead O'Connor's "Nothing Compares 2U"

GLASGOW IS CITY OF CULTURE

The selection of Glasgow as European City of Culture for 1990 provoked more than a few expressions of disbelief, especially at the other end of the M8 where the citizens of Edinburgh prided themselves on their cultural superiority. The cynics were proved wrong, however, as Glasgow successfully transformed its image from that of a tough, decaying industrial town to a major destination for cultural tourism.

A key moment in the Glasgow renaissance was the opening of the Burrell Collection in 1983, a world-class museum and art gallery constructed in Pollok Park to display the collection donated to the city by ship owner Sir William Burrell. The Glasgow Garden Festival of 1988 was another landmark, turning the desolate Princes Dock in Govan into a

▲ **The opening of the Burrell Collection in 1983 marked a cultural renaissance for Glasgow.**

horticultural paradise that attracted 3 million visitors. The "year of culture" achieved similar success on a far grander scale, with more than 600 theatrical productions and more than 1,900 exhibitions staged.

Glasgow's experience showed how playing the culture card could effect an economic regeneration for an old industrial city. Ten years after the "year of culture", the city was attracting around 4 million tourist visitors a year. There were more Glaswegians working in the tourist industry than had ever worked in ship-building, once the city's prime source of employment.

In some ways, the changes in Glasgow epitomized major developments throughout the UK, which had brought about a shift from an economy centred on industrial production to one in which service industries predominated. City centres were changing from primarily places of work to principally places of leisure. But it was also a sign of a specifically Scottish growth in national pride and cultural energy, which found expression politically in growing support for the Scottish Nationalist Party.

POLL TAX LEADS TO VIOLENCE

The most unpopular measure of Margaret Thatcher's 11-year period as UK Prime Minister was the "community charge", universally known as the "poll tax", devised to replace local rates. Its introduction in England and Wales in April 1990, a year after it had come into force in Scotland, caused widespread disturbances in many areas and culminated in serious rioting in central London.

Under the old rating system, local government revenue had been raised from householders on the basis of the size of their property. In a rough-and-ready way, the rates tended to take more money from the well-off and less from the poor. The poll tax, in principle, imposed a standard charge for every adult in a given local government area, irrespective of his or her income – although there were reductions for those on benefit. It was backed up by draconian laws to prevent non-payment. The level of the tax was

officially set by local councils, but in fact it was manipulated by the government under complex rules that – or so it seemed to some – ensured that flagship Conservative councils such as Wandsworth were able to set astonishingly low levels.

Disturbances started in early March, as crowds of protesters gathered at town halls across the country, where the level of the local poll tax was being fixed. In some places, including Bristol and the London districts of Brixton and Hackney, there were serious clashes with police. On Saturday March 31, an estimated 300,000 people gathered in Trafalgar Square to protest against the poll tax and hear calls from speakers for a campaign of civil disobedience to make the new tax uncollectable. The rally was ending when police pushed forward in force to clear the crowd. Missiles were thrown and a chaotic melee ensued. Small groups of demonstrators started fires and ran amok through shopping streets, smashing windows and terrifying passers-by. Scattered fighting continued through the evening. More than 300 people were arrested.

▶ **A large Trafalgar Square rally against the the poll tax degenerated into scenes of violence and destruction.**

THE SUPERGUN AFFAIR

Early in 1990 MI6 and other European intelligence agencies received reports that key machine parts for a long-range artillery piece were about to be exported from Britain to Iraq. This "supergun" was an experimental weapon capable of firing a 91-cm (36-in) diameter shell, fitted with a conventional, biological or even

▲ **The piping at the heart of the "supergun" scandal. The exporters claimed it was an oil pipe when it was clearly a gun barrel.**

nuclear warhead, to distances in excess of 320 km (200 miles). Complicating matters further, on April 2 the gun's maverick Canadian designer, Dr Gerald Bull, was mysteriously killed in Brussels. The finger of suspicion pointed at Mossad, the Israeli secret service, whose government feared that Iraq was planning to use the gun against Israel.

During the Iran–Iraq War, an arms embargo had been imposed on the warring nations. Despite some later relaxation of the embargo terms, the intelligence agencies decided to prevent the supergun's export. On April 11 British customs officials seized at the port of Teesside crates which were described as containing "petroleum piping", which was, in fact, parts of the supergun barrel. A week later a British driver was arrested in Athens when his truck

was found to be loaded with supergun parts. Finally, in May, Italian authorities impounded more parts for the gun in the port of Naples.

While these arrests were being made, there was confusion over who had given authorization for British companies to work on the order. The company that had made the barrel parts, Sheffield Forgemasters, claimed that it was not breaking any arms embargo. A spokesman for the company said that "after the initial approach was made by someone on behalf of the Iraqis, the company was given the green light by the Department of Trade and Industry".

The precise role of the British authorities in this whole, murky business was to develop into the "Arms for Iraq" scandal that bedevilled the Conservative government during the 1990s.

GASCOIGNE WEEPS AS ENGLAND LOSE

On July 4, 1990, in the Stadio delle Alpi in Turin, England were defeated by Germany in a penalty shoot-out in the semi-finals of the football World Cup. It was only England's second appearance in a World Cup semi-final, the other being when they had won the trophy in 1966.

England started the finals unconvincingly, scraping through the group stage with a 1–0 win against Egypt and draws against Ireland and the Netherlands. Even so, they did better than Scotland, who lost their opening match to Costa Rica and went home early despite a subsequent win against Sweden.

England progressed to the semi-finals with tightly contested extra-time wins against Belgium and Cameroon. By the time of the Germany match, English fans had two new heroes in David Platt and – more especially – Paul Gascoigne. The stocky Geordie's openly emotional nature attracted as much attention as his flashes of creative brilliance.

When the semi-final went into extra time at 1–1, Gascoigne received his second yellow card of the finals for a bad tackle. It meant that if England had qualified for the final he could not have played. Gascoigne burst into tears, an image that became the most lasting memory of the tournament, provoking debate about current notions of masculinity and stimulating an unprecedented level of female interest in the sport.

The 1990 World Cup finals marked a decisive moment in the relationship between the English people and football. The endemic violence exhibited by English football fans in the 1980s and the sporadic disasters to which the sport was prone – from Bradford and the Heysel Stadium to Hillsborough – had led to serious debate about whether English football had a future at all. England's World Cup odyssey and its emotional climax rendered football fashionable and opened the way for a transformation of the finances of the English professional game.

▲ Paul Gascoigne's emotional outburst, as he realized he wouldn't be playing in the final, is an enduring memory for many fans.

THATCHER STANDS ALONE IN EUROPE

In one of her last international appearances as Prime Minister, at the European Community Summit in Rome in October 1990, Margaret Thatcher made plain her opposition to the direction in which the EC was heading. She dismissed plans for a European Central Bank and for an eventual European single currency as "cloud cuckoo land". It was a stance that left Britain isolated in Europe and Mrs Thatcher at odds with leading members of her own government.

Throughout the 1980s, the Prime Minister had led the more pro-European of the two major political parties. Whereas it had become Labour policy to withdraw from Europe, the majority of Conservatives, influenced by the views of big business, looked favourably upon closer economic links with the EC. But there was also a tendency in the Tory Party – and in the thinking of Mrs Thatcher – that feared the loss of national independence to a faceless bureaucracy in Brussels.

Progress within the EC towards economic and political integration brought tension between these conflicting views to breaking point.

IRELAND 1990

In 1986, Mrs Thatcher signed the Single European Act, which opened the way for progress to economic union. Yet in September 1988, in a keynote speech delivered in Bruges, she forcefully expressed her fear of a "European super-state exercising a new dominance from Brussels". This ambivalence continued into 1990. Thatcher suprisingly approved Britain's joining of the Exchange Rate Mechanism, which linked the value of European

◄ **Although opposed to Europe, Mrs Thatcher signed the European Single Act, opening the way for a progressive European union.**

currencies and was designed to prepare the way for monetary union. Yet at the same time, she made clear her abhorrence of abandoning the pound in favour of a European currency.

The disagreement within the Conservative Party over Europe ruined Thatcher's relationship with key pro-European figures, including Michael Heseltine, Sir Geoffrey Howe and Nigel Lawson, and thus contributed directly to her fall from power. It would continue to plague her successor, John Major, who was to face implacable opposition from the anti-European wing of the party.

NOVEMBER

• Deputy Prime Minister Sir Geoffrey Howe resigns; his resignation speech is a bitter attack on Mrs Thatcher
• Mrs Thatcher fails to win sufficient votes to defeat a Conservative leadership challenge from Michael Heseltine in a first-round ballot; she withdraws from the contest
• John Major heads the second-round Conservative leadership ballot and becomes Prime Minister
• Death of writer and broadcaster Malcolm Muggeridge

DECEMBER

• The last wall of chalk separating the two ends of the Channel tunnel is broken

SADDAM HOLDS BRITISH HOSTAGES

At the start of August 1990, Iraqi forces occupied Kuwait. Faced with a hostile response from the international community to this blatant act of aggression, Iraq's leader Saddam Hussein decided to use captured foreign nationals as a shield against a counter-attack and a bargaining chip in negotiations.

Among the 5,000 foreigners seized by the Iraqis during the invasion, many were British citizens. Saddam ordered them to be distributed around the country at power stations, dams, factories, arms dumps and other sites that could be the target of air attack. This human shield would, he hoped, deter the Americans and their allies from air strikes. With a sinister mix of threat and supposed reassurance, Saddam appeared with some of his British "guests" on television, even attempting to ruffle the hair of an extremely uncomfortable five-year-old.

As Britain participated in US-led preparations for a UN-authorized

military campaign to drive the Iraqis out of Kuwait, fears for the hostages' safety were acute. In early September Saddam released the women and children, but hundreds of British men remained in captivity. Former Conservative Prime Minister Edward Heath, an advocate of a negotiated settlement with Iraq, flew to Baghdad in mid-October for talks with Saddam aimed at securing the hostages' release. Thirty-three

of the sick and elderly were allowed to return to Britain as a result of this initiative.

Some 500 British citizens were still held in Iraq when, on December 10, Saddam ordered the wholesale repatriation of foreign nationals. Whatever the reason for this sudden change of heart, it was a profound relief for the relatives of those being held, as well as for the hostages themselves.

▲ **Saddam Hussein plays host to a terrified young British hostage during an event staged for television cameras in the run-up to the 1990 Gulf War.**

1990 END OF THE THATCHER ERA

On November 28, 1990, Margaret Thatcher resigned as Britain's Prime Minister after an extraordinary 11 years in office – the longest period served in 10 Downing Street by any Prime Minister in the twentieth century. She had won three consecutive general elections, but had ultimately failed to convince her party that she could win a fourth.

Born in Grantham in 1925, the daughter of a grocer, Thatcher became Conservative MP for Finchley in 1959. She was Secretary of State for Education and Science in Edward Heath's government from 1970 to 1974, earning the rhyming epithet

▲Chancellor of the Exchequer Nigel Lawson resigned from office after disagreements with Margaret Thatcher on her attitude towards Europe.

▲ Margaret Thatcher dominated the government of Britain during the 1980s like no other politician of the twentieth century.

"Milk-Snatcher" from her political opponents for her abolition of free school milk. In 1975 she defeated Heath in a contest for the Tory Party leadership, supported by the right of the party. Heath never forgave her.

The novelty of a woman party leader soon wore off, however, as Thatcher's abrasive style denied any link between the stereotypical qualities of her sex and her political persona. Her fervent anti-Communism soon saw her branded by Moscow as the "Iron Lady". In the run-up to the 1979 general election, her aggressive attitude towards the trade unions won her support from many voters appalled by the chaos of the "winter of discontent".

In her first speech as Prime Minister, on May 4, 1979, Thatcher said: "Where there is discord, may we bring harmony". But this was not to be the style of her rule. She embarked on a radical transformation of the British economy, making savage cuts in public spending and accepting mass unemployment as the price that had to be paid for financial stability and improved competitiveness. Her first term in office appeared a disaster, with rising unemployment matched by rampant inflation as whole sectors of British industry went under. But the Falklands War in 1982 gave her a chance to turn the political tide. Her Falklands triumph, plus the split in the Labour Party between old Labour and new Social Democrats, were the keys to her 1983 election victory.

The degree to which Thatcher achieved her political objectives was remarkable. She broke the power of the unions, especially through the brutal defeat of the miners strike in 1984. She began a vast programme of "privatization" that dismantled the state sector of industry and introduced millions of people to share ownership. She radically reduced government borrowing and savaged much of the welfare state. She cut income tax, especially for high earners. Despite the persistence of mass unemployment, a permanent feature of the Thatcher years, enough people felt she had given them new opportunities and prosperity to bring her a third election victory in 1987.

Over time, though, Thatcher's overbearing style as Prime Minister alienated many of her most able Tory colleagues. Most spectacular was her clash with Defence Secretary Michael Heseltine in January 1986, when Heseltine stormed out of a Cabinet meeting after being bluntly overruled by Thatcher in the Westland helicopter affair. The nub of the Westland affair, apart from a clash of personalities, was Heseltine's preference for closer links with Europe, opposed by Thatcher. In October 1989 Thatcher's anti-European views also led to a showdown with her Chancellor of the Exchequer, Nigel Lawson. The central issue was whether Britain should belong to the European Monetary System (EMS), a step towards a single European currency. Lawson was committed to the EMS, but found his policy undermined by Thatcher's personal economic adviser, Professor Sir Alan Walters. After a stand-up row with the Prime Minister, Lawson stormily resigned from office. He was replaced by John Major.

The Lawson affair led directly to the first formal challenge to Thatcher's leadership. A backbencher, Sir Anthony Meyer, stood against her as a token candidate to test the party's mood. Sixty Tory MPs failed to vote for her, a sufficient revolt to open up the prospect of a much more serious leadership challenge in the near future.

Thatcher's hold on power could hardly have been shaken, however, without the poll tax fiasco. The Prime Minister was one of the few people in Britain who felt the new community charge, introduced in April 1990, was a fair improvement on the old rates. The government's popularity plummeted. Local elections in May brought an 11 per cent swing to Labour. In October the Liberal Democrats scored a shock by-election victory in Eastbourne, considered one of the safest Tory seats in the country. Ominously, the economy was also in trouble, with inflation heading above 10 per cent – higher than it had been when Thatcher came to power in 1979. This was a particular blow to a Pime Minister who had consistently made "beating inflation" a major plank of her policy platform.

At the start of November, the Deputy Prime Minister, Sir Geoffrey Howe, hitherto one of Thatcher's most loyal followers, resigned over European policy. His resignation speech in the House of Commons on November 13 was a sensational attack on the Prime Minister. The day after, Michael Heseltine announced that he was challenging for the party leadership.

In the first round of voting by Tory MPs on November 20, 152 backed Heseltine and 204 voted for Thatcher. Under the rules of the contest, this was four votes short of the total she needed for outright victory. Thatcher's immediate response was to announce that she would fight on. Behind the scenes, however, it was made plain to her that if she stood in the second round of the ballot, she could expect to be comprehensively defeated.

On November 22, commenting "It's a funny old world", she withdrew from the contest. Her favoured candidate, John Major, won the leadership contest on the third ballot and duly took over as Prime Minister. He went on to lead the Conservatives to their fourth election victory in a row, albeit a narrow one, in 1992.

▲ "It's a funny old world" – still extremely popular among Tory voters, Margaret Thatcher was baffled by her political demise.

1991

- Prime Minister John Major launches a Citizen's Charter in the drive to improve public services
- The government proposes a council tax to replace the poll tax from 1993
- Bank of Credit and Commerce International (BCCI) collapses after large-scale fraud
- TESSA tax-free savings schemes come into operation
- Many NHS hospitals become self-governing "trusts"
- Headteachers in primary schools resist publication of the results of the first compulsory tests of seven-year-olds
- 22 English football clubs agree to break away from the Football League and form the FA Premiership (effective from August 1992)
- Stansted airport opens, its terminal designed by Sir Norman Foster
- The Sainsbury Wing extension to the National Gallery opens, designed by US architect Robert Venturi
- Books published this year include Pat Barker's *Regeneration* and Martin Amis's *Time's Arrow*
- British films this year include Peter Greenaway's *Prospero's Books*, Anthony Minghella's *Truly, Madly, Deeply* and Peter Medak's *Let Him Have It*
- Harrison Birtwistle's opera *Sir Gawain and the Green Knight* has its first performance
- Alan Bennett's play *The Madness of King George III* opens
- New television series include *The Darling Buds of May* and *Prime Suspect*

In response to Iraq's invasion of Kuwait in August 1990, a coalition led by the United States and empowered by the United Nations sent large-scale military forces to Saudi Arabia. By the start of 1991, the Allies were able to deploy more than 500,000 ground troops, 3,600 tanks and 1,750 aircraft. The bulk of this force came from the United States, but Britain was among more than 30 other coalition countries providing substantial contingents, with around 40,000 men deployed on land, air and sea.

The key to Allied strategy in the Gulf lay in exploiting overwhelming air superiority. From the night of January 16–17, 1991, Iraq was subjected to a series of devastating air attacks in which RAF Tornado fighter-bombers played a leading role. Unable to match the Allies, the Iraqi Air Force flew its aircraft to Iran, where the authorities impounded them. But Iraqi anti-aircraft guns and missiles posed a serious threat to Allied aircraft. In all, six Tornadoes were shot down in the course of the conflict. Pilot Flight-Lieutenant John Peters and Navigator Adrian Nicol, who baled out of their stricken Tornado on the first night of the campaign, were captured by the Iraqis, tortured and paraded on Iraqi television.

By mid-February the coalition was preparing to initiate a land offensive. Air attacks "softened up" Iraqi troops, with special attention being given to "degrading" Iraq's elite Republican Guard. The belligerent coalition commander, General Norman Schwarzkopf, planned to send a strong force of US Marines, supported by Arab units, into Kuwait and pin down the Iraqi forces around Kuwait City. Meanwhile, the bulk of the Allied forces, spearheaded by US and British armoured formations, would secretly move westward and swing round behind Kuwait, destroy the Republican Guard and cut off the remaining Iraqi forces.

In the early hours of February 24, Allied forces advanced, meeting little resistance. So complete was Allied domination that the rate of advance was dictated by the speed of the main battle tanks leading the attack. The only Iraqi response was to set fire to the oil fields in Kuwait. Thousands of Iraqis were killed by the Allied armour and aviation, and tens of thousands more soon began to surrender. The heaviest single loss for British forces was ironically due to "friendly fire". Nine soldiers died when US aircraft attacked British armoured vehicles, mistaking them for Iraqis.

The Allies called a halt to the conflict at 8 am local time on February 28 – precisely 100 hours after the start of the land offensive. The Iraqi Army had ceased to exist as a fighting force. British losses in the war were initially given as 24 dead, although 47 dead was later proposed as more accurate. Either way, it was very far short of the thousands of casualties feared at the outset of the conflict. The victory was, however, a partial one. Stopping short of an advance on Baghdad, the coalition fatefully left Saddam in power.

▲ **Prime Minster John Major addresses British troops before they take part in the campaign to expel Iraqi forces from Kuwait.**

IRA MORTARS FIRED AT DOWNING STREET

At 10 o'clock on the morning of February 7, 1991, Prime Minister John Major was chairing a session of the War Cabinet at 10 Downing Street. They were discussing the progress of the conflict with Iraq when the windows of the room were blown in by an explosion in the garden outside. Clambering back out from under the table where they had instinctively taken cover, startled ministers found they had survived the most audacious IRA assassination bid since the 1984 Brighton bombing.

The attack on Downing Street was delivered from a white Ford transit van that had parked in Whitehall minutes earlier. Three mortar bombs were fired from inside the van through a concealed opening in its roof. The one that did the damage hit a tree about 15 m (50 ft) from the room where the Cabinet meeting was being held. The other two went harmlessly off target. The IRA man who had driven the van escaped from the scene on the pillion of a motorbike ridden by an accomplice.

John Major commanded admiration for the coolness of his behaviour throughout. His first comment to his Cabinet colleagues was apparently: "I think we had better start again somewhere else." The event was celebrated by Irish nationalists in a song called Downing Street, containing the lyrics: "Now at No. 10 it's like Crossmaglen ... while you hold Ireland. It's not safe down the street where you live."

▲ The IRA's mortar bomb attack on 10 Downing Street narrowly failed to wipe out the entire British government.

DEATH OF MARGOT FONTEYN

Celebrated ballerina Dame Margot Fonteyn died in Panama City on February 21, 1991, at the age of 71. She is universally acknowledged as one of the finest dancers of the twentieth century.

Born in Reigate, Surrey, in 1919, Fonteyn was plain Margaret Hookham until the demands of a stage career required a more exotic name. Her prodigious talent was recognized at an early age. She was attracting admiring attention at the Vic-Wells ballet at the age of 16, and soon became choreographer Frederick Ashton's favourite female lead. By the 1950s she was an international celebrity, her eloquent but understated performances striking many foreigners as the essence of Englishness.

▲ Margot Fonteyn's career spanned more than half a century, during which she became one of ballet's most acclaimed dancers.

In 1956 her life took a more exotic turn when she married Panamanian diplomat Roberto Arias. This brought her into contact with the drama and violence of Latin American political life. In 1959 she was briefly arrested in Panama for complicity in a coup attempt mounted by her husband. Five years later, Arias was shot by a political opponent and permanently disabled.

By then Fonteyn's career had achieved an unexpected late flowering through her pairing with the young Soviet defector Rudolf Nureyev. Their performances in ballets such as choreographer Kenneth MacMillan's Romeo and Juliet in 1966 have become the stuff of legend. Fonteyn retired from the stage in the 1970s after a career spanning 40 years.

- A free concert by tenor Luciano Pavarotti attracts an audience of 150,000 to Hyde Park
- Albums released this year include the KLF's The White Room and Primal Scream's Screamadelica
- Comic magazine Viz sells more than a million copies per issue

JANUARY
- The RAF participates in a US-led air offensive against Iraq in Operation Desert Storm
- Death of yachtsman Sir Alec Rose

FEBRUARY
- The IRA fires mortar bombs at 10 Downing Street
- British ground forces participate in the defeat of Iraqi forces in Kuwait
- Death of ballerina Dame Margot Fonteyn

MARCH
- The Birmingham Six are released after the Appeal Court finds their conviction for the 1974 IRA pub bombings "unsatisfactory"
- A 21–19 victory over France at Twickenham gives England's rugby team victory in the Five Nations' championship
- Ulster Unionists agree to participate in talks with Nationalists and the Irish government on the future of Northern Ireland

APRIL
- Prime Minister John Major outlines a plan for a "safe haven" for Kurds in Iraq
- Dr George Carey is enthroned as Archbishop of Canterbury in succession to Dr Robert Runcie
- Welsh golfer Ian Woosnam wins the US Masters golf tournament
- Deaths of novelist Graham Greene and film director Sir David Lean

BRITAIN'S FIRST ASTRONAUT GOES INTO SPACE

On May 18, 1991, Britain's first astronaut blasted off from the Baikonur cosmodrome in Soviet Kazakhstan on board a Soyuz spacecraft. She was 27-year-old Sheffield-born chemist Helen Sharman.

Sharman had been working as a food technologist for a chocolate company when, in June 1989, she heard a radio advertisement that changed her life. It declared: "Astronaut wanted – no experience necessary." Sharman was among 13,000 people who responded to the ad. She won through and was sent to a cosmonaut training centre in Moscow for 18 months of gruelling preparation.

Known as Project Juno, the space flight was supposed to be financed by British businesses, but little support was forthcoming. As the Conservative government was not interested in promoting a flight

▲ Food technologist Helen Sharman answered a radio ad to become the first Briton in space on board the Soviet space station *Mir*.

on board a Soviet spacecraft, the Soviet Union ended up providing much of the funding itself.

Sharman spent eight days on board the space station *Mir*, carrying out the usual "research" used to justify space journeys – one of her projects was to show that pansies grew in weightless conditions. She returned to Earth safely in a capsule that parachuted down in Central Asia.

Sharman's flight made Britain the only country to have a woman as its first representative in space. Although she was awarded an OBE, her achievement was celebrated with only the faintest fanfare, but she went on to have a successful career as a lecturer and broadcaster.

MYSTERIOUS DEATH OF NEWSPAPER TYCOON

On November 5, 1991, the flamboyant publishing tycoon Robert Maxwell was found dead in

▲ Many still believe that Robert Maxwell committed suicide when he realized that his business empire was about to fall.

the Atlantic off the Canary Islands. He had been holidaying on board his yacht *Lady Ghislaine*. Since he disappeared from the deck in the early hours of the morning, he is suspected of having committed suicide, although the death may have been accidental.

Born in Czechoslovakia, Maxwell was a self-made millionaire who was often criticized for using sharp practices to expand his business empire. His response to criticism and revelations about his colourful life often involved a ruthless resort to libel lawyers, which made him much feared by investigative journalists. In politics he supported the Labour Party, and was a Labour MP from 1964 to 1970.

The revelation of the state of Maxwell's business empire in the wake of his death certainly showed there was ample motive for him to have killed himself. Owner of newspapers such as the *Daily Mirror* and New York's *Daily News*, Maxwell had made labyrinthine business arrangements that concealed massive debts and heavy losses. In the months before he died, his creditors were closing in on him and he was engaged in a desperate struggle to prevent his empire going under. He had recently fraudulently taken £440 million from his employees' pension fund to stave off bankruptcy.

Within a month of his death, his companies were in receivership and his business affairs were under investigation by the Serious Fraud Squad. His sons, Ian and Kevin, were cleared of fraud charges in 1996 after a long and expensive prosecution.

AIDS DEATHS CONTINUE

On November 24, 1991, singer Freddie Mercury, who made Queen one of the most successful rock bands of the 1970s, died of AIDS. The response to his death showed how attitudes towards AIDS – and homosexuality – were evolving.

In the early 1990s the number of people in Britain being diagnosed with HIV infection was running at around 2,500 a year. Once blood transfusions had been rendered safe by screening, homosexuals and intravenous drug users were left as by far the largest categories of those infected. The large-scale spread of the disease to heterosexuals – predicted in the 1980s – did not occur in Britain, in contrast to the experience in Africa and other parts of the developing world.

Under the circumstances, a

▲ The highly publicized death of rock star Freddie Mercury raised public awareness and sympathy for AIDS sufferers.

reversal of the well-established trend towards increased acceptance of homosexuality might have been expected. But Mercury, a flamboyant bisexual, had won widespread praise for publicly acknowledging that he had tested HIV-positive. Far from alienating the public, his death from the disease provoked a wave of public sympathy and heavy sales of Queen backlist records.

Mercury's death was followed by that of other prominent figures such as dancer Rudolf Nureyev (1993) and film-maker Derek Jarman (1994). For them, too, there was public sympathy rather than condemnation. If anything, AIDS raised the profile of gay sex and made it seem more discussable as a health context. AIDS deaths in Britain peaked at about 1,700 in 1994.

HOSTAGES FREED

One of the most hopeful developments of 1991 was the freeing of almost all the hostages from Western countries being held by Islamic fundamentalist militants in the Lebanon. The most prominent of these was Terry Waite, who had been kidnapped in Beirut in January 1987 while acting as a roving ambassador for the Archbishop of Canterbury – ironically, while on a mission to negotiate the release of other hostages.

In August 1991 journalist John McCarthy, who had been held in Beirut for more than five years, was released and reported that Waite was still alive and well. The release of the Archbishop of Canterbury's representative followed on November 18. The last American hostage, Terry Anderson, who had

been held since March 1985, flew home in early December.

The hostages all had appalling stories to tell of how they had

been treated, often kept for long periods in solitary confinement and darkness, under the constant threat of execution.

▲ After five years in captivity in the Lebanon, British journalist John McCarthy finally arrives back on home soil.

NOVEMBER

- England lose to Australia in the final of the rugby World Cup at Twickenham
- Newspaper publisher Robert Maxwell drowns off the Canary Islands
- The Quorn hunt is banned from National Trust land after allegations of cruelty by the hunt's masters
- An outbreak of sectarian violence leaves ten dead in two days in Belfast
- Terry Waite is released after almost five years as a hostage in Beirut
- Freddie Mercury, lead singer of the rock group Queen, dies of AIDS

DECEMBER

- Robert Maxwell's business empire collapses; the Mirror newspaper group goes into receivership
- Britain and other EC members meeting at Maastricht agree on closer European political union
- Death of cricket commentator John Arlott

1992

- Base interest rates temporarily rise to 15 per cent in a sterling crisis
- The number of people killed in the Northern Ireland conflict since 1969 now exceeds 3,000
- The government announces the phasing out of CFCs, harmful to the ozone layer, by 1995
- The General Synod of the Church of England votes to allow women to be ordained as priests
- Polytechnics are raised in status, becoming universities
- Lloyds insurance market declares huge losses
- The magazine *Punch* ceases publication after more than 150 years in existence
- Books published this year include *Fever Pitch* by Nick Hornby, *Hideous Kinky* by Esther Freud and *The English Patient* by Michael Ondaatje
- British films this year include Sally Potter's *Orlando*, James Ivory's *Howards End* and Neil Jordan's *The Crying Game*
- Damien Hirst's sculpture of a shark in formaldehyde, *The Physical Impossibility of Death in the Mind of Someone Living*, is shown at the Young British Artists exhibition at the Saatchi Gallery
- Albums released this year include P J Harvey's *Dry* and Aphex Twin's *Selected Ambient Works 85–92*

THE MAASTRICHT TREATY

On February 7, 1992, representatives of Britain and the other member states of the European Community signed the Treaty on European Union, known as the Maastricht Treaty after the Dutch town in which the signing took place. The treaty committed the member states to European Monetary Union (EMU) and eventual political integration. There was to be a single currency (referred to at the time as the Ecu), a European Central Bank, and common foreign and defence policies. After a number of setbacks, including an initial defeat for the proposals in a referendum in Denmark, the treaty came into force in November 1993. The European Community was renamed the European Union.

Implementation of the treaty was never going to be straightforward for Britain. The country had joined the Exchange Rate Mechanism (ERM) in 1990, which was intended as the first step on the road to a European single currency. The ERM kept the exchange value of

▲ John Major's handshake with French President Mitterand belied discord over Britain's role in Europe.

European national currencies broadly in line with one another. However, when Britain adhered to the system the value of sterling was set too high in relation to stronger European currencies such as the German Deutsche Mark.

In September 1992 fierce speculation against sterling on the international money markets threatened to force the currency below its lowest allowable ERM valuation. Committed to remaining in the ERM at all costs, the Treasury resorted to panic measures, including a hike in interest rates from 10 to 15 per cent and the expenditure of billions

of pounds of Britain's foreign reserves to support sterling. Yet on September 16 Britain was nonetheless forced to pull out of the ERM and allow the pound to float freely downward. The crisis fundamentally undermined popular confidence in John Major's recently re-elected government, but paved the way for an export-led economic boom based on the drop in the value of the pound, which made Britain's exports more competitive.

From the time of its withdrawal from the ERM, Britain was placed at a distance from the mainstream of progress towards monetary union, an alienation that was increased by the hostility of some political groups, particularly on the right of the Conservative Party, to any further progress towards European integration. It was typical that, when Europe officially became a single market without frontiers on January 1, 1993, Britain was one of four states that retained the right to demand that European travellers show their passports on entry.

HOPKINS TRIUMPHS AT THE OSCARS

Welsh actor Anthony Hopkins was the star of the Hollywood Academy Awards ceremony on March 30, 1992. He won the coveted Oscar for Best Actor for his role as the sinister Dr Hannibal "the Cannibal" Lecter in *The Silence of the Lambs*. He dominated the film despite being on screen for little more than a quarter of an hour. It was the third consecutive Best Actor award for British performers, coming after Oscars for Daniel Day-Lewis in 1990 and Jeremy Irons in 1991.

Hopkins was born in 1937 in Margam, Port Talbot, not far from the birthplace of Richard Burton. He was a dominant presence on the London stage from the 1960s onward, but was much slower to establish himself in cinema. His appearance in *The Silence of the Lambs* brought superstar status.

As well as reprising the role of Lecter, since 1992 Hopkins has notably appeared as the butler Stevens in *The Remains of the Day* and as President Richard Nixon in the eponymous film. He was knighted in 1993.

▲ Long established as a stage actor, Anthony Hopkins's role as Hannibal Lecter in *The Silence of the Lambs* won him an Oscar.

MAJOR WINS ELECTION

After the downfall of Margaret Thatcher in 1990, the Labour Party hoped and expected that its long period out of office would soon come to an end. Thatcher's replacement, John Major, was an uncharismatic figure who seemed ill-suited to rebuild the Conservative Party's popularity. The poll tax, the main cause of Thatcher's downfall, was hastily ditched, but many Tories entered the 1992 general election with a tacit conviction that the time had come for the other side to have a chance to bat.

Opinion polls during the run-up to the election consistently foretold a Labour win. Labour leader Neil Kinnock allowed himself to be the focus of a triumphalist campaign that doubtless irritated many voters with its complacency. More were alienated by the honesty of Labour's shadow chancellor of the exchequer, the prudent John Smith, who spelled out exactly what tax increases would be needed to finance Labour's programme.

In the election on April 9, the Conservatives polled almost 42 per cent of the votes cast to Labour's 34 per cent, giving the Tories an adequate Commons majority of 21. Shocked and humiliated by his second consecutive general election defeat, Neil Kinnock resigned as Labour party leader. John Smith was chosen to replace him.

▲ **Confounding the predictions of some pollsters, John Major won a fourth successive term in office for the Conservative Party.**

ARTIST FRANCIS BACON DIES

On April 28, 1992, Francis Bacon, Britain's most internationally renowned painter, died at the age of 82.

Born in Ireland to English parents, Bacon received neither a formal education nor an artistic training. As an asthmatic homosexual transvestite and masochist, he was at odds with his home background and escaped in the 1920s to a shiftless life in London and Europe. Discovering a fascination with art, he took up painting and had his first solo show in 1934.

Bacon's breakthrough came in 1945 when works including the famous *Studies for Three Figures at the Base of a Crucifixion* were exhibited in London. Their violent extremism was taken to express the human predicament in a war-torn world. In the 1950s his renown was confirmed by paintings such as the "screaming popes" – versions of a portrait by Velazquez. He specialized in tortured distortions of the human form.

Bacon remained a familiar figure in London's Soho drinking clubs up to his death. Addicted to alcohol, gambling and working-class men, he ran through money at a fearsome rate, but still left an estate worth £11 million.

▶ **Francis Bacon was the quintessential outsider, but his art won him acceptance and international renown.**

JANUARY
• An IRA bomb kills eight Protestant building workers employed at a British Army base in Northern Ireland

FEBRUARY
• Britain signs the Treaty on European Union and the Maastricht Final Act
• Liberal Democrat leader Paddy Ashdown admits to a past affair with his secretary; his standing in opinion polls rises

MARCH
• The Duke and Duchess of York officially separate
• England lose to Pakistan in the final of the cricket World Cup in Melbourne

APRIL
• The Conservatives win the general election with a reduced majority
• Neil Kinnock resigns as leader of the Labour Party
• A massive IRA bomb devastates the Baltic Exchange in the City of London, killing three and injuring around 100 people
• Princess Anne is divorced from Captain Mark Phillips
• Betty Boothroyd is elected first woman Speaker of the House of Commons
• Deaths of artist Francis Bacon and comedians Frankie Howerd and Benny Hill

MAY
• Leeds United win the Football League championship; Liverpool win the FA Cup
• Demonstrators protest at the unveiling of a statue of Sir Arthur "Bomber" Harris in Whitehall

OLYMPIC GOLD FOR BRITONS

▲ **Sally Gunnell performs a lap of honour after her victory in the Olympic 400m hurdles.**

The 1992 summer Olympic Games were held in Barcelona, Spain. Although it was not an outstanding tournament overall from a British point of view, a number of individual performances had a memorable impact.

Foremost among these was Linford Christie's victory in the 100 m. Aged 32, the Jamaica-born athlete was by a clear four years the oldest man ever to win gold at the distance. He was also only the third Briton to win the event, his predecessors being Harold Abrahams in 1924 and Alan Wells in 1980. The following year, Christie would become the only athlete to hold the Olympic, World, European and Commonwealth 100 metres titles simultaneously.

Other British successes were Sally Gunnell, who won gold in the 400 m hurdles, and Chris Boardman, whose victory in the 4,000 m individual pursuit was the first for a British cyclist at the Olympics since 1920. Less noticed at the time was the achievement of rower Steve Redgrave, with Matthew Pinsent, who won a gold medal in the coxless pairs. It was Redgrave's third gold in consecutive Olympics. He would go on to repeat the feat in 1996 and 2000 to achieve a British record of five consecutive golds.

ANGLICANS APPROVE WOMEN PRIESTS

On November 11, 1992, the General Synod of the Church of England passed the Priests (Ordination of Women) Measure. After 20 years of debate within the Anglican Church, women were at last to be allowed to join the priesthood.

The new measure was approved by around two-thirds of the clerical and lay members of the Synod, who had responded to an appeal by the Archbishop of Canterbury, Dr George Carey, to "take the risk of faith". But a large part of the minority opposed to women priests felt very deeply on the subject. Conservative politician Ann Widdecombe immediately announced she was leaving the Church of England, and her

▲ **Dragging the Church into the twentieth century: the decision to allow women priests was by no means universally popular.**

colleague, Minister of Agriculture John Gummer, resigned from his lay membership of the Synod, saying the decision was without "authority of scripture or tradition".

The Anglican leadership bent over backwards to accommodate the discontented, agreeing that bishops could refuse the ordination of women within their own dioceses. "Episcopal visitors", dubbed "flying bishops" in the press, would be available for those who disagreed with their own bishop's line on women priests. Efforts to form a breakaway church came to nothing though many Anglican priests, both married and unmarried, moved to the Catholic Church, and the measure received royal assent in November 1993.

THE QUEEN'S HORRIBLE YEAR

In her televised message to the nation broadcast on Christmas Day, the Queen described 1992 as her "annus horribilis". The royal year had been marked by the separations of the Prince and Princess of Wales and the Duke and Duchess of York, and by a fire that had destroyed part of Windsor Castle. In a measured understatement, the Queen said: "1992 is not a year on which I shall look back with undiluted pleasure."

Much of the Queen's sorrow arose from the rapidly deteriorating relationship between the royal family and the press. The disintegrating marriages of the Queen's children were like blood in the water to the sharks of the tabloid newspapers. The "royals" found themselves being treated with no more respect than any other celebrities.

Prince Andrew, the Duke of York, was on the face of it a credit to his family and nation. As a career naval officer, he had performed creditably in the frontline during the Falklands War. His marriage to the boisterous Sarah Ferguson in 1986 seemed set to introduce a breath of fresh air into the stuffiness of royal circles. But "Fergie" soon came under cruel media criticism for her weight and dress sense, while the couple were rarely together because of the demands of naval service. An official separation was announced

▲ The fire that devastated Windsor Castle was the result of an electrical fault in the private chapel.

in March 1992 after the Duchess became involved in an alleged extramarital relationship. To compound the damage, in August the *Daily Mirror* published photos of "Fergie" topless with a "financial adviser", John Bryan, kissing her toes.

The marriage of the Prince and Princess of Wales had also once been hailed by the popular press as a fairytale come true. By 1992 it was apparent that all was far from well with the couple, but the publication in the summer of Andrew Morton's biography of the princess, entitled *Diana: Her True Story*, caused a sensation. The picture it painted was of Diana being grossly mistreated by her husband and his family, driving her to repeated suicide attempts. It also became clear during the year that she had been involved in at least one extramarital liaison, after the publication of intimate tapes in which the word "squidgy" was used as a term of endearment. The private lives of members of the royal family had not provided such sensational copy for journalists since the time of George IV.

On top of the embarrassment heaped upon her by her children, the Queen had to endure a thoroughly upsetting accident. On the night of November 20, Windsor Castle was seriously damaged by a fire that started in the Royal Chapel. More than 200 fire-fighters took 15 hours to subdue the blaze, which damaged about 100 rooms. Restoration costs were estimated at around £40 million. It had indeed been a horrible year.

SEPTEMBER
- The *Sun* alleges a relationship between Princess Diana and James Hewitt
- Sterling is withdrawn from the European Exchange Rate Mechanism after speculators undermine its value
- England midfielder Paul Gascoigne makes his debut for Italian side Lazio
- Heritage Secretary David Mellor resigns after allegations about his private life

OCTOBER
- The government announces the closure of 31 coal mines, but is forced to cancel or defer the closures after protests

NOVEMBER
- Fire causes extensive damage to Windsor Castle

DECEMBER
- IRA bombs explode in Manchester, injuring more than 60 people
- The Prince and Princess of Wales separate
- Princess Anne marries Commander Tim Laurence
- In her Christmas speech the Queen describes the year as an "annus horribilis"

1993

NEWS IN BRIEF

- The economic recession ends; unemployment and inflation fall
- The Community Care Act reforms treatment of the mentally ill, introducing "care in the community"
- The Child Support Agency is set up to force absent fathers to provide financial support for their children
- Books published this year include *Trainspotting* by Irvine Welsh and *A Suitable Boy* by Vikram Seth
- British films this year include Mike Leigh's *Naked*, Ken Loach's *Raining Stones* and James Ivory's *The Remains of the Day*
- Rachel Whiteread wins the Turner Prize for *House*, a concrete cast of the inside of a house in London's East End
- Albums released this year include Blur's *Modern Life is Rubbish* and Jamiroquai's *Emergency on Planet Earth*

JANUARY
- The European Community single market comes into operation
- Newspapers publish transcripts of an intimate conversation between the Prince of Wales and Camilla Parker Bowles

FEBRUARY
- Ranulph Fiennes and Michael Stroud complete the first crossing of Antarctica on foot
- Two-year-old James Bulger is murdered in Liverpool
- Death of footballer Bobby Moore

THE JAMES BULGER MURDER CASE

On February 12, 1993, two-year-old James Bulger disappeared from a busy shopping precinct in Bootle, Liverpool, where he had gone with his mother. Four days later his body was found alongside a railway line 5 km (3 miles) away. Security cameras in the precinct had captured the moment when he was abducted, showing him being led away by two older children. Ten days after the killing, two ten-year-old boys, Robert Thompson and Jon Venables, were charged with kidnapping and murder.

The case provoked a wave of moral outrage. When the two boys appeared at a local court, they were assailed by a furious crowd, forcing the authorities to shift the hearings to a court in Preston.

▲ A final sighting of two-year-old James Bulger taken by shopping mall security cameras shortly after his abduction.

Politicians leaped forward to proclaim a breakdown in society. Home Secretary Kenneth Clarke spoke of "a loss of purpose and a loss of values" and introduced a new kind of custodial sentence for child offenders. Prime Minister John Major declared a "crusade against crime" and said society should "condemn a little more and understand a little less".

The boys, tried in an adult court, were found guilty in November and sentenced to be detained "during Her Majesty's pleasure". The trial judge suggested this should mean a minimum of eight years, the Lord Chief Justice upped this to ten years and the new Home Secretary, Michael Howard, intervened to order the boys to serve at least 15 years.

As emotions cooled, more rational voices made themselves heard, suggesting that children who committed atrocious crimes were in a very real sense as much victims as those who suffered at their hands. In June 1997, the Law Lords upheld an Appeal Court ruling that Howard had exceeded his powers in raising the boys' minimum sentence to 15 years.

IRA BOMBINGS HIT HOME

In the spring of 1993, an IRA bombing campaign in mainland Britain was in full swing, as the terrorists continued their policy of trying to make the cost of staying in Northern Ireland unacceptably high for the British government and people. On March 20 two quite small devices were left in litter bins in a shopping centre in Warrington, Cheshire. Exploding in the middle of the day, they killed two children, Jonathan Ball, aged three, and Timothy Parry, aged 12. About 50 other people were injured, some of them gravely.

The childrens' deaths aroused widespread condemnation. The IRA tried to distance itself from the consequences of its action, laying the blame for the deaths "squarely at the door of the British authorities who deliberately failed to act on precise and adequate warnings". This version of events was indignantly rejected by the police. A swiftly assembled group called "Peace Initiative 93" responded to the bombing by organizing peace rallies which were attended by thousands in London, Dublin and Belfast.

The IRA had no intention of calling off its campaign, however. On Saturday April 24 a huge bomb was left in a truck in Bishopsgate, in the heart of the City of London. When it exploded it not only killed a passer-by and injured 40 others, but also wrecked the prestigious office building of the Hong Kong and Shanghai Bank, the NatWest Tower and several other office blocks. Damage was estimated at around £1 billion.

The Bishopsgate bomb represented the first time that the IRA had managed to deliver a serious blow to the British economy. Large-scale security measures, including permanent police roadblocks at weekends, were put in place in the City in an effort to make a repetition of such an attack on one of the world's major financial centres impossible.

▶ **Members of the public lay wreaths to commemorate the deaths of two children, killed by an IRA bomb attack in Warrington, Cheshire.**

THE QUEEN PAYS HER TAXES

▲ **The subject of an increasingly critical press, the Queen sought to regain popularity by announcing she would pay income tax.**

By 1993, for the first time in the twentieth century, there seemed a chance that republicanism could take root in Britain as the popularity of the royal family plummeted in the wake of highly publicized scandals. As one way of deflecting criticism, the Queen took steps to make the monarchy less of a burden upon the taxpayer.

From April 1993 the royal family renounced many of their financial privileges. Henceforth, the Queen would pay income tax on her personal earnings and capital gains tax on income from her investments like any other individual. The Prince of Wales also agreed to pay full tax on his income from the Duchy of Cornwall, in 1993 estimated at £3 million a year. At the same time, all the royal family except the Queen, Prince Philip and the Queen Mother would cease to receive payments from the Civil List, the £7.9 million of public

money received by the Queen every year for the fulfilment of her state duties. Instead, the costs of the public duties of junior members of the royal family would be met by the Queen.

The Queen also reacted to a public outcry over plans for the government to pay the £40 million bill to repair Windsor Castle, damaged by fire the previous November. Instead, the Queen agreed to open Buckingham Palace to tourists in the summer months and use the funds raised thereby to pay for the repairs.

Supporters of the monarchy hoped that these measures would be adequate to reduce public pressure on the royal family and to show that the Queen was in touch with public opinion. Critics, however, continued to feel that more than superficial financial concessions would be needed to restore confidence in the Windsors and the system they represented.

MARCH
• IRA bombs kill two children in Warrington

APRIL
• After two false starts, the Grand National is declared void
• An IRA truck bomb devastates the City of London

MAY
• The Chancellor of the Exchequer Norman Lamont is sacked in a government reshuffle
• Manchester United win the FA Premiership in its first season

JUNE
• Deaths of racing driver James Hunt and author Sir William Golding

JULY
• The government loses a vote on the Maastricht Treaty in the House of Commons, but wins a vote of confidence

AUGUST
• Buckingham Palace state apartments opened to the public

OCTOBER
• Prime Minister John Major says it is time to "get back to basics"

NOVEMBER
• The Maastricht Treaty comes into force; the EC is now the EU
• Graham Taylor resigns as England football manager after the team fails to qualify for the World Cup finals

DECEMBER
• Irish Prime Minister Albert Reynolds and John Major issue the Downing Street Declaration, pointing the way to a future Northern Ireland peace settlement

- The Channel Tunnel is officially opened
- The National Lottery is established
- Sunday trading is liberalized
- The Criminal Justice and Public Order Act is passed, restricting the rights of protesters and the right to silence
- The coal industry and railways are privatized
- Rover, the last British-owned car company, is sold to the German firm BMW
- VAT is imposed on domestic gas and electricity supplies
- The homosexual age of consent is lowered from 21 to 18
- Books published this year include *Captain Corelli's Mandolin* by Louis de Bernières, *Birdsong* by Sebastian Faulks and *How Late It Was, How Late* by James Kerman
- British films released this year include Danny Boyle's *Shallow Grave* and Mike Newell's *Four Weddings and a Funeral*
- Damien Hirst curates an art exhibition entitled "Some Went Mad, Some Ran Away" at the Serpentine Gallery, London
- Albums released this year include Portishead's *Dummy*, Oasis's *Definitely Maybe* and Blur's *Parklife*
- Songs of the year include Wet Wet Wet's "Love is All Around" and Take That's "Sure"

BACK TO BASICS REBOUNDS ON MAJOR

In January 1994 Tim Yeo, Minister for the Environment, resigned from the government after admitting that he had fathered an illegitimate child in an extramarital relationship with a Tory councillor, Julia Stent. It was the first sign of a creeping problem that was to be a thorn in the flesh of John Major's administration – the failure of individual politicians to live up to a high standard of personal morality.

In October 1993, in search of a theme that would give a sense of direction to his government, John Major had made a speech in which he declared: "It is time ... to get back to basics: to self-discipline and respect for the law; to consideration for others; to accepting responsibility for yourself and your family ..." Although it was not what Major intended, the key phrase "back to basics" was taken to refer above all to individual morality, placing a premium upon marital fidelity and financial honesty. Not unnaturally, the public took a dim view of politicians who preached to them in this manner and yet themselves indulged in precisely the sort of behaviour they professed to castigate.

Yeo's resignation was followed in February by the grotesque death of promising Tory MP Stephen Milligan, which was apparently caused by erotic auto-asphyxiation. There was much sympathy for Milligan, but the case hardly graced the image of a party dedicated to family values. More harmful were mounting allegations of Conservative MPs accepting money in return for raising specific issues in parliament. The "cash for questions" issue saw two Tory MPs suspended from parliament in 1995.

As time went on, revelations of sexual or financial misdeeds by Conservative politicians turned into a veritable avalanche. In the run-up to the 1997 general election, Major was faced with allegations of Tories indulging in both homosexual and heterosexual affairs, as well as a "sleaze" scandal concerning MPs Neil Hamilton and Tim Smith. Rarely can any catchphrase have been as thoroughly regretted as "back to basics" was by John Major.

▲ Tory MP Neil Hamilton's career ended over allegations he had taken cash to ask questions in the Commons.

▲ A rising star of the Tory party, Stephen Milligan died in tragic circumstances involving erotic auto-asphyxiation.

CROMWELL STREET: MURDER MOST FOUL

On February 24, 1994, Gloucestershire police began digging up the garden of 25 Cromwell Street, Gloucester. What they found there would reveal one of the most gruesome serial murder cases ever recorded in Britain.

The occupants of the Cromwell Street house were builder Fred West and his wife Rosemary. Police had become concerned about the disappearance of the Wests' daughter Heather. It was her body that they were expecting to find. But it was soon evident that at least two sets of human remains were buried in the garden.

Under arrest, West quickly confessed to other killings. Police uncovered more remains around the house, mostly in the cellar. Later, bodies were also found in a field outside Gloucester and at the Wests' former home in another part of the city.

Since the 1970s, the Wests had run a peculiar household, in which young drifters were often made welcome. West was obsessively interested in sex and engaged in diverse sexual practices, from intercourse with his own offspring to voyeuristic observation of his wife engaged in prostitution. He also often had sex with the young women who found a home in his house. The killings had taken place either in the course of sadistic sex sessions or in sudden explosions of violence against those who

▲ **Fred West hanged himself in prison, but his wife, Rosemary, was sentenced for her involvement in the serial killings.**

crossed or threatened him.

West eventually confessed to the killing of 12 named young women, mostly in the 1970s, but later told police that he had, in fact, murdered 20 more. The victims included Shirley Robinson, murdered while pregnant with West's child; Lucy Partington, an Exeter University undergraduate, picked up by the Wests at a bus stop in 1973 and never seen alive again; a Swiss hitch-hiker; and Heather West, murdered when she was 16.

Fred West was never brought to trial. On New Year's Day 1995, he was found hanged in his cell in Winson Green prison, After his suicide, Rosemary West was tried for ten of the murders. She was found guilty and sentenced to life imprisonment in November 1995.

THE CHANNEL TUNNEL

Britain effectively ceased to be an island on May 6, 1994, when the Queen and French President François Mitterrand inaugurated the Channel Tunnel rail link between the south coast of England and the Continent. Running under the English Channel for 50 km (31 miles), it was one of the largest engineering projects ever carried out, and cost around £10 billion. The Queen travelled on a Eurostar train to Coquelles in France, where she met President Mitterrand. She then travelled back to Britain with the President in the royal Rolls-Royce on Le Shuttle.

An under-Channel tunnel link to the European mainland had frequently been proposed in the past, but had fallen foul of British insularity. In 1907, for example, a parliamentary bill to allow a rail tunnel to be built was withdrawn after military experts declared it a

defence risk. This time round, the continental invaders feared by Britons were mostly disease, especially in the form of rabid foxes, and illegal immigrants. Another main plank of opposition to the Tunnel was the issue of safety, particularly its vulnerability to terrorist attack.

Prime Minister Margaret Thatcher was not a person to allow objectors much scope, however. Construction of the Tunnel began in November 1987, and three

years later workers from the two sides met in the middle. The project went massively over budget and there were some bitter disputes between the constructors and the Eurotunnel company that was footing the bill.

In the end, the only part of the project not completed in the twentieth century was the building of a high-speed rail link to a special terminal in London. A terminal at St Pancras is due for completion in 2007.

▲ **No longer an island – the two tunnels that link Britain to the mainland of Europe.**

1994

BLAIR REPLACES SMITH AS LABOUR LEADER

▲ **Mourners at John Smith's funeral. The Labour leader's untimely demise led to the election of Tony Blair.**

On May 12, 1994, John Smith, the leader of the Labour Party, died suddenly of a heart attack at the age of 55. He had been elected party leader in July 1992, after the resignation of Neil Kinnock in the wake of that year's Conservative election victory. Smith was a solid politician who had tackled his task to rebuild Labour with honesty, intelligence and humour. Even his best friends, however, would not have described him as charismatic.

In the leadership contest which followed Smith's death, the main contenders appeared to be Gordon Brown and Tony Blair. Brown was persuaded to support Blair's candidacy, and the contest was eventually fought out between Blair and John Prescott, a bluff and hearty representative of the old Labour tradition. Young and smart, Blair presented himself as the advocate for a fundamental modernization of the party, involving abandoning many of the shibboleths of the past. He won the leadership election in July by a comfortable margin, becoming, at 41, Labour's youngest-ever leader. Prescott was elected deputy leader.

Blair's promise to his followers was simple and straightforward: he would put Labour back where it belonged, "in government again". Twenty years after they had last won a general election, Labour members would prove themselves prepared to support any policy change that would achieve that desired end.

ARISE SIR BOBBY

On June 10, 1994, England and Manchester United footballer Bobby Charlton was knighted by the Queen. It was recognition of an exceptional career and an outstanding sporting personality.

Charlton was born in Ashington, Northumberland, in 1937. He joined Manchester United as a teenager, scoring twice on his first-team debut in 1956. Playing initially as a winger, his speed established his place in manager Matt Busby's talented young side, known as the Busby Babes. He survived the traumatic experience of the 1958 Munich air crash to become the hub around which the Manchester United side was rebuilt.

Charlton's footballing career peaked in the 1960s. He perfected the role of deep-lying centre-forward, which gave full rein both to his creative passing game and his powerful long-range shooting. He was a key member of the England side that won the World Cup in 1966, and he captained Manchester United in their famous European championship victory of 1968, scoring twice in the final against Benfica.

Charlton's last match for England was in their defeat by West Germany in the 1970 World Cup finals. He left Manchester United in 1973, remaining on the pitch as player-manager of Preston North End for another two seasons. His career statistics are awesome: 247 goals for Manchester United in 754 appearances, plus 106 England caps and a record 49 goals for his country. But he is also admired for his modesty and decency, which stood in stark contrast to many other footballers of his era.

▲ **It took 28 years for Bobby Charlton's role in England's World Cup triumph in 1966 to be recognized by a knighthood.**

BRITAIN GAMBLES ON LOTTERY

▲ **By the end of the decade, the British National Lottery was estimated to have created more than 1,000 new millionaires.**

Britain's first National Lottery draw was held on November 19. Seven people shared the £15.8 million prize. An estimated 25 million people bought tickets, well over half the country's adult population. About one third of the £45 million take was allocated to a fund that would provide money for selected good causes.

The franchise to run the National Lottery had been won by Camelot, a consortium that intended to make a substantial profit out of the business. This choice was severely criticized by Virgin boss Richard Branson, who had proposed instead a non profit making UK Lottery Foundation for the franchise.

Criticism of the lottery fever that swept the country came chiefly from religious leaders. Ordinary punters were more critical of the use to which their involuntary contributions to charity were put, such as the payment of £12 million to the Churchill family for Sir Winston Churchill's personal archives.

DEATH OF AN ANGRY MAN

Playwright John Osborne died on Christmas Eve, 1994, at the age of 65. He had long ceased to be at the forefront of fashion, but was acknowledged as a man who had helped propel the British stage into the modern era.

Born in London in 1929, Osborne by his own account suffered an unhappy and stifling childhood, overshadowed by the death of his father when he was 12. His lower-middle-class upbringing, which he reviled venomously in his autobiography, left him with a fund of rage against the world, upon which he drew heavily in adult life.

By the early 1950s Osborne was an actor-manager working with various provincial repertory companies. His early plays were performed in regional theatres before *Look Back in Anger* was accepted in 1956 by the newly formed English Stage Company for performance at the Royal Court. The ranting misogynistic tirades of Osborne's anti-hero Jimmy Porter were hailed by progressive critics as the authentic voice of protest. His follow-up play, *The Entertainer*, interpreted as an allegory of the British Empire in decay, confirmed his standing as the quintessential 1950s Angry Young Man.

At the start of the 1960s, Osborne was a familiar bearded figure at the front of anti-nuclear protests. He was a member of the Committee of 100, set up as a radical alternative to CND, and was duly arrested for carrying out acts of civil disobedience. His plays, however, increasingly failed to lend themselves to left-wing political interpretation. *Luther*, first performed in 1961, was a complex and heavyweight success, but Osborne's prestige waned as critics and audiences found the point of his plays harder to see.

From the 1970s Osborne's work is generally accepted to have declined. The playwright himself wrote that he had become "a spokesman for no one but myself ... cruelly abusive, unable to be coherent about my despair". His death was caused by diabetes.

▲ **John Osborne was the classic 1950s Angry Young Man. By the time of his death in 1994, his prestige had greatly waned.**

- The Nolan Committee Inquiry into parliamentary standards recommends new rules for MPs to avoid financial corruption
- Excessively high earnings of executives in privatized industries are widely criticized
- The drought and hot summer lead to water shortages, especially in Yorkshire
- The Skye Bridge opens, connecting the island with the mainland
- Plans to expand sections of the M25 London orbital motorway to 14 lanes are scrapped after protests
- Books published this year include *The Unconsoled* by Kazuo Ishiguro and *The Information* by Martin Amis
- Irish poet Seamus Heaney wins the Nobel Prize for Literature
- Films this year include Nick Park's animation *A Close Shave*
- Albums released this year include Pulp's *Different Class*, Radiohead's *The Bends* and Oasis's *(What's The Story) Morning Glory?*
- Songs of the year include Blur's "Country House", Pulp's "Common People", Suede's "Beautiful Ones" and Oasis's "Roll With It"

LEESON BRINGS DOWN BARINGS BANK

On February 24, 1995, senior managers at Barings Bank in London realized that they were facing ruinous losses amounting to £860 million as a result of speculative and fraudulent trading by Nick Leeson, general manager of the bank's Singapore office. Deposits, including £1 million belonging to the Prince's Trust, were immediately frozen as chief executives sought a buyer for Britain's oldest merchant bank.

Realizing that the writing was on the wall, the 28-year-old "boy wonder" from Watford had fled Singapore the previous evening, faxing his resignation and apologies from Kuala Lumpur, Malaysia, the next day. He and his wife Lisa then flew to Kota Kinabalu in Borneo, where they enjoyed a few days at a luxury "Shangri-La" resort before attempting to return to England on March 2 via Frankfurt, where German police were awaiting their arrival and arrested Leeson.

Appointed general manager and head trader of Barings Futures

Singapore in late 1992, Leeson was a well-known figure on the trading floor of the Singapore futures exchange, where he was known as the man with the Midas touch. He reported unprecedented profits of £28.5 million in 1994, which chairman Peter Baring, described as "pleasantly surprising". But it was all an illusion. In fact, Leeson had accrued losses of £208 million by December 1994, which he was able to conceal in an account none of his bosses knew about because he controlled both the trading floor operations and the back-office settlements in Singapore.

On January 17, 1995, disaster struck in the form of the Kobe earthquake, which sent the Nikkei index tumbling and Leeson's losses into freefall. He entered fictitious trades between the accounts in order to create fictitious profits, invented debts owed to Barings Futures and borrowed money illegally to fund ever more desperate bets in a bid to recover his soaring debts.

The Dutch bank ING bought Barings for £1 on March 5, but promised to inject £660 million of new capital. Nick Leeson went on trial in Singapore on December 2. Convicted of fraud, he spent four years in a Singapore jail.

▲ Nick Leeson's speculation fraud might have gone unnoticed but for the Nikkei index collapse that followed the Kobe earthquake.

SINN FEIN BECOMES RESPECTABLE

In March 1995 Gerry Adams's bid to achieve respectability for Sinn Fein, the Republican party he led, received a marked boost from a triumphant visit to the United States. As Sinn Fein was generally recognized to be the political wing of the terrorist IRA, it had previously always been shunned by mainstream politicians. President Bill Clinton, however, not only invited Adams to lunch at the White House but treated him to a warm handshake that acknowledged his newfound role as a peacemaker.

Adams was widely credited with having persuaded the Republican movement that the way forward in Northern Ireland lay in a negotiated settlement. The announcement of a "complete cessation of military operations" by the IRA on August 31, 1994,

▲ Presented as the new face of Irish republicanism, Sinn Fein leader Gerry Adams chats with US President Bill Clinton.

had been greeted in many quarters as meaning peace after 25 years of war in Ulster. Irish Prime Minister Albert Reynolds said at the time: "As far as we are concerned, the long nightmare is over". Others were more cautious. British Prime Minister John Major continued to insist that the IRA had to disarm before it could be included in peace talks.

In February 1995 Major and the new Irish Prime Minister, John Bruton, came up with an agreed framework for peace in Northern Ireland. It included proposals for a legislative assembly in the Province, and renunciation by the Irish Republic of its historic claim to Ulster. The framework was broadly welcomed by Sinn Fein, but the issue of the

decommissioning of IRA arms blocked further progress towards all-party talks. The election of David Trimble as the new leader of the Ulster Unionists in September was, at the time, seen as another blow to the peace process, since Trimble was noted as a hardliner opposed to making concessions to the Republicans.

Despite numerous predictions to the contrary, however, the ceasefire held and in November 1995, after some prodding from the United States, a "two-track" approach was adopted to shift the stalled negotiations. The question of disarming terrorists was to be left to a commission under US Senator George Mitchell. Meanwhile, Sinn Fein would be included in preliminary peace talks. The deal allowed Clinton to pay a triumphant visit to Ulster at the end of the month and repeat his handshake with Adams on the Falls Road.

BLAIR CREATES NEW LABOUR

On April 29, 1995, Labour leader Tony Blair achieved a revolution in his party that had eluded his predecessors since Hugh Gaitskell in the 1950s. By an overwhelming majority, delegates to a special conference in Westminster voted to ditch the notorious Clause Four of the party's constitution, which committed Labour to nationalization of the economy.

Blair's determination to sacrifice this Labour sacred cow was a dramatic indication of the direction in which he intended to take the party. Generations of Labour leaders had paid only lip-service to Clause Four, but its continued existence had been a guarantor for the left of the long-term commitment to socialism.

The readiness of Labour members to back Blair's new direction was based on the perception that, after four consecutive general election defeats, "Old Labour" was simply unelectable. They wanted the Labour Party back in power, come what may. Although eyebrows were raised when Blair courted the favour of newspaper magnate Rupert Murdoch or made speeches in praise of business entrepreneurs, many assumed that once elected he would change his tune.

But the demise of Clause Four in fact signalled the Labour leadership's embrace of the free market and their genuine acceptance that capitalist enterprise was the key to future

prosperity. To the outrage of many Labour stalwarts, Tony Blair's Labour really would be "New".

▲ Media magnate Rupert Murdoch's *Sun* newspaper switched its allegiance to Tony Blair's New Labour.

BATTLE OF THE BRITPOP BANDS

▲ Blur were cast as the nice guys in the media-staged "battle of the bands", which the groups were more than happy to play along with.

▲ Oasis were declared the losers by the press in the "battle", but both they and Blur had won out from the publicity.

When the editors of the *Oxford English Dictionary* were asked in 1995 which new word best exemplified the current year, they chose "Britpop". Bands such as Blur, Oasis, Suede and Pulp recreated the self-conscious pride in British pop music that had existed in the 1960s, becoming briefly the focus for a wider sense of reawakening in the national culture.

The decade of "Swinging London" was the cultural reference point for Britpop bands, who revived the guitar-based sound, tuneful songwriting and flat English accents of the Beatles, The Who, the Kinks and the Rolling Stones. As always in this arena, there was a certain time-lag between the appreciation of the new scene by dedicated music fans, which could be dated back to at least 1993, and its later emergence into general public consciousness.

The peak of the Britpop boom came in the summer of 1995, when a scrupulously staged "battle of the bands" between Blur and Oasis grabbed the newspaper headlines. In another clear homage to the 1960s, the Oasis brothers Noel and Liam Gallagher were groomed as the rough, rude Rolling Stones, while Blur were cast as the altogether nicer Beatles. The two bands released simultaneous singles, "Roll with It" and "Country House" respectively, and newspaper front pages dutifully tracked their sales, eventually declaring Blur the winners by a short head.

By the following year, Britpop was already on the wane, but it had staked a renewed claim for Britain to be recognized as a world centre of music, fashion and artistic inventiveness.

TEENAGE DEATH BLAMED ON ECSTASY

In November 1995 the dangers of the drug ecstasy made headline news as a result of the death of Essex teenager Leah Betts. The girl went into a coma after taking an ecstasy tablet at her eighteenth birthday party. She died five days later in Broomfield Hospital, Chelmsford.

Leah's father was a former Metropolitan Police Drugs Squad officer and her stepmother gave drugs advice to schools. They decided to go public with their private grief in an effort to persuade other young people not to take ecstasy. A publicity campaign was subsequently mounted with the slogan:

▲ Leah Betts's death after taking an ecstasy pill ignited fears about the spread of the new drug amongst British youth.

"Sorted: Just one ecstasy tablet killed Leah Betts."

The reality of her tragic death was, however, not so simple. An inquest revealed that she had in fact died through drinking too much water. She had consumed around seven litres in an hour and a half, apparently in response to health warnings about dehydration, said to be a risk for young people taking part in "raves". Excess water consumption had led to a fatal cerebral oedema.

The news stories and publicity campaign undoubtedly heightened parental fears about ecstasy. They did not appreciably reduce the use of the drug by the young.

DIANA APPEALS TO THE HEART

On November 20, 1995, the Princess of Wales gave a candid interview on BBC television's *Panorama* programme. Her revelations rolled her marriage further down the road to divorce and took the unpopularity of the monarchy to a new pitch.

Interviewed by journalist Martin Bashir, Diana spoke of her adultery with her riding instructor James Hewitt and of her husband's involvement with Camilla Parker Bowles. "There were three of us in this marriage," she commented, which made it "a bit crowded". She spoke of her depression and bulimia, and of advice given to the

▲ Diana's appearance on "Panorama" was a calculated attempt to win public sympathy over the plight of her marriage.

prince to have her "put in a home of some sort".

The entire performance, watched by an audience of 15 million viewers, indicated the princess's new-found mastery of an emotional and confessional mode that had wide popular appeal. Her declared desire to be "queen of people's hearts" was a direct challenge to the actual Queen, whose command of her subject's emotional allegiance was looking distinctly shaky.

A month after the interview, the Queen publicly called on the royal couple to divorce. Clearly, the continuation of the marriage could only bring further damage to the royal family. The divorce decree was eventually granted in August 1996.

DAMIEN HIRST WINS TURNER PRIZE

In November 1995 the prestigious Turner Prize for contemporary art was awarded to Damien Hirst, a key figure in the group of "Young British Artists" that enjoyed the patronage of advertising millionaire Charles Saatchi. The award was based on an exhibition called "Some Went Mad, Some Ran Away", which Hirst had curated and which included many of his own provocative works.

Hirst was best known for his use of animal carcasses or dead fish, preserved in formaldehyde and exhibited in glass cases. These works were given sentimental or metaphysical titles such as *Away From the Flock* (a sheep), *Mother and Child, Divided* (a cow and a calf cut in half in separate cases) and *The Physical Impossibility of Death in the Mind of Someone Living* (a shark).

Hirst's work stood squarely in the tradition of avant-garde art designed to attract attention to itself by shocking the bourgeoisie – although the artist claimed to be using shock effects "to make aspects of life and death visible". The Turner award drew inevitable criticism from traditionalists. Conservative politician Norman Tebbit dismissed Hirst's exhibits as "lumps of dead animals" and Brian Sewell, art critic of the *Evening Standard*, described them as "no more interesting than a stuffed pike over a pub door".

Whether admired or reviled, however, Hirst indisputably raised the public profile of British art, helping to put "Britart" on the map alongside "Britpop".

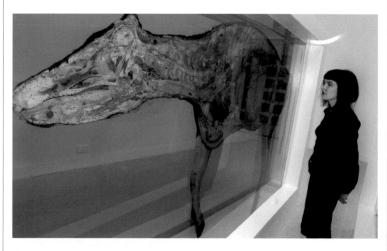

▲ Damian Hirst's use of animal carcasses in his art prompted one Tory minister to describe his work as " lumps of dead animals".

1996

- Private companies take over the running of British rail services and the railway network
- The Downey Inquiry is set up to investigate "cash-for-questions" allegations against Conservative MPs
- Defections by Conservative MPs and by-election losses mean the government no longer has a majority in parliament
- New Severn Crossing Bridge opened
- The Globe Theatre, a reproduction of the original Shakespearean building, opens in London
- The Euro '96 football tournament is held in England
- Books published this year include *Ecstasy* by Irvine Welsh and *Last Orders* by Graham Swift
- British films this year include Danny Boyle's *Trainspotting* and Mike Leigh's *Secrets and Lies*
- British fashion designers Alexander McQueen and John Galliano attain international prominence
- The television series *Our Friends in the North* is broadcast
- Albums released this year include Suede's *Coming Up* and Fatboy Slim's *Better Living Through Chemistry*
- Songs of the year include the Spice Girls' "Wannabe" and "2 Become 1"

IRA RESUMES BOMBING

▲ Towering over London's Docklands, Canary Wharf was severely damaged by the bomb that signalled an end to the IRA ceasefire.

On February 10, 1996, the IRA ceasefire that had held since August 1994 came spectacularly to an end with a devastating attack in east London. In the early evening, a massive bomb exploded outside South Quays station on the Isle of Dogs, in the heart of the Docklands redevelopment area. It caused damage over a wide area, killed two people and injured many more, most of them cut by flying glass from blown-out windows. As proof that this was not an isolated incident, a week later a bomb blew up on a bus in central London, killing the terrorist who had been using the bus to carry the bomb to its target.

The new IRA campaign on the British mainland was based chiefly on the use of large bombs to hit symbolic or economic targets. In April two devices even larger than the Docklands bomb were positioned to blow up Hammersmith Bridge over the Thames in west London, but failed to explode. Next it was the turn of Manchester. On June 15 a huge explosion devastated the city centre, injuring hundreds of people and causing damage to property on a scale not seen before from the IRA in Britain.

The renewal of the IRA bombing campaign led to the automatic exclusion of Sinn Fein, the IRA's political wing, from all-party talks on the future of Northern Ireland. The British government had made the cessation of violence an absolute precondition for Sinn Fein's involvement. In May, however, to the government's embarrassment, Gerry Adams's party won 17 seats in elections to the all-party forum where the talks were to take place.

The refusal to allow Sinn Fein representatives to take their seats in the forum, although understandable, rendered the talks largely futile, since it excluded a group without whose agreement peace could not be established. Eventually, the election of a new government in Britain in 1997 unjammed the peace process and brought about a renewed IRA ceasefire.

FIRST MAMMALS CLONED

In March 1996 researchers at the Roslin Institute, Edinburgh, put on show a pair of healthy adult sheep produced by cloning. It was a triumph for the Roslin team headed by Dr Ian Wilmut, but raised serious ethical issues for the future.

The sheep, named Megan and Morag, were cloned using genetic material from differentiated embryo cells. By taking the nucleus of a cell from one lamb, placing this into the emptied egg cell of another, and then implanting the combined cells in

▲ Dolly the sheep, the first mammal cloned from an adult cell, raised the frightning possibility of one day repeating the process in humans.

a ewe to act as a surrogate mother, the researchers were able to produce an exact copy – in effect, an identical twin – of the donor lamb. Later that year, the Roslin team succeeded in cloning a lamb, called Dolly, using a cell from an adult sheep.

The immediate practical goal of the cloning research was to develop animals with special characteristics to be used for various medical purposes. But Dr Wilmut was inevitably asked if the cloning of human beings was on the horizon. His response was that "if we wished to be able to do it, one day we would be able to ..."

MASSACRE AT DUNBLANE

Just before 9.30 am on the morning of March 13, 1996, a former Scout leader, Thomas Hamilton, walked into a primary school in the Scottish town of Dunblane, a bespectacled figure wearing a dark woolly hat and ear muffs. He was armed with four guns – two 9 mm Browning self-loading pistols and two .357 Smith and Wesson revolvers – and 743 rounds of ammunition.

Hamilton then entered the gymnasium, where a class of five-and six-year-olds were waiting to start their exercises. Also in the room was the class's teacher, Gwen Mayor, a part-time teacher, Eileen Harrild, and an assistant, Mary Blake. Using one of his Brownings, Hamilton first shot the adults, killing Mayor and wounding the others. He then opened fire on the children, walking around the room to pick them off as they attempted to take cover. After about four minutes, he fired a volley into another classroom, then put a Smith and Wesson in his mouth and pulled the trigger. Hamilton had fired 105 rounds, killing 16 children and injuring 11 others. Only one of the class of 28 in the gymnasium escaped physically unscathed.

Hamilton's motivation for mass murder seems to have been his sense of grievance at frequent complaints about his behaviour around children. A 43-year-old bachelor, in 1973 he had been dismissed as a Scout leader, a rebuff that rankled with him so

▲ A community in shock – grief-stricken parents await news of the shooting at Dunblane Primary School.

bitterly more than 20 years later that he wrote a letter of complaint about it to the Queen only days before the massacre. He had also mentioned the Dunblane school specifically in complaints about what he claimed were unjustified slurs on his character.

The sense of shock and outrage at the murders increased as more was revealed about the killer. It was asked why, for 20 years, he had been allowed to run boys' clubs despite so much evidence of his unsuitability. Even more extraordinary was his possession of a gun licence: the weapons he used in the attack were all fully legal. An inquiry chaired by Lord Cullen uncovered the fact that in November 1991 Detective Sergeant Paul Hughes had written

a memo to Deputy Chief Constable Douglas McMurdo describing Hamilton as an "unsavoury character and unstable personality" who had an "extremely unhealthy interest" in young boys and should not have a firearms certificate. McMurdo took no action and renewed Hamilton's licence in 1992, then again in 1995, when he was given approval for two more weapons. Criticized by the Cullen Inquiry, McMurdo resigned from the police force.

A direct consequence of the Dunblane massacre was a ban on the personal ownership of handguns in Britain. Reacting to public opinion, MPs eventually passed a measure even stronger than the recommendations of Lord Cullen's report.

MAY

- The former Conservative leader of Westminster City Council, Dame Shirley Porter, is accused of misconduct by the district auditor
- Manchester United do the "double", winning the Premiership title and the FA Cup
- Elections are held in Northern Ireland for a 110-seat forum to discuss a peace settlement; Sinn Fein take 15 per cent of the total vote
- The Duke and Duchess of York are divorced
- Death of actor John Pertwee

JUNE

- An IRA bomb devastates the centre of Manchester
- 78 anti-European Conservative MPs call for a referendum on the European Union
- England lose to Germany in a penalty shoot-out in the semi-final of the Euro '96 football tournament at Wembley

JULY

- An Orange parade returning from Drumcree Church through Portadown in Northern Ireland is blocked by the Army and RUC, then allowed to proceed; rioting occurs throughout the Province

AUGUST

- Britain wins only one gold medal at the Atlanta Olympics, for rowers Steve Redgrave and Matthew Pinsent
- The Prince and Princess of Wales are divorced
- Deaths of fashion designer Ossie Clark and jet engine inventor Sir Frank Whittle

BRITISH BEEF SUCCUMBS TO MAD COW PANIC

On March 20, 1996, Health Secretary Stephen Dorrell admitted in parliament that there was a possible link between "mad cow disease" – bovine spongiform encephalopathy (BSE) – in cattle

▲ Minister for Agriculture John Gummer places his faith firmly in British beef.

and a new strain of the potentially fatal Creutzfeld-Jakob disease (CJD) in humans. It was the end of a long battle by the government to deny any health risk to humans associated with BSE, which had developed in British herds in the 1980s, probably through the practice of feeding cows on offal from slaughtered animals.

Five days after Dorrell's sensational statement, the European Commission imposed a worldwide ban on exports of British beef. The meat was also shunned by many British consumers and dropped by major outlets such as McDonald's. Prices fell to rock bottom, with catastrophic results

for British beef farmers. The government belatedly attempted to restore confidence by a cull of millions of cattle considered to be most at risk, but this was too late, as reports of individuals dying of CJD began to feature regularly in the press, and some experts refused to rule out a major epidemic.

The following years seemed to prove that the degree of panic over BSE had been exaggerated, with around 150 people recognized as having died of new variant CJD by 2006. But the faith of the public in the Conservative government had been severely undermined by its perceived readiness to take risks with the nation's health.

SPICE GIRLS POWER

From the appearance of their first single "Wannabe" in the summer of 1996, the Spice Girls were a pop music phenomenon, dominating sales charts worldwide. The all-female British band proved ephemeral, but nonetheless culturally significant.

The Spice Girls were a manufactured group, assembled in response to an advertisement and precisely honed for appeal to a mass youth market. They were calculatedly diverse in ethnic and cultural origins, a diversity spelled out in a silly set of nicknames: Posh Spice (Victoria Adams), Scary Spice (Melanie Brown), Ginger Spice (Geri Halliwell), Baby Spice (Emma Bunton) and Sporty Spice (Melanie Chisholm). Their music, written for them, was supremely catchy.

Their "ideology" was also one calculated for its market. The Spice Girls allegedly stood for "Girl Power", a combination of

▲ The Spice Girls were a manufactured band, carefully crafted to appeal to a mass youth market.

self-confident independence with unabashed sex appeal and a thirst for pleasure. This was a stance with which the mass of young women, relaxed inheritors of the victories of 1970s feminism, wholeheartedly identified. It also, of course, appealed to most young men.

As well as signalling a new phase in what has been lamely dubbed "postfeminism", the Spice Girls continued the self-conscious

rebranding of Britain begun by the Britpop bands. One of their most notorious outfits consisted of sexy Union Jack dresses. They were major contributors to "Cool Britannia" – the publicity agents' vision of Britain in the 1990s as young, hip, fun and creative.

The brief reign of the Spice Girls ended in 1998 after the departure of Geri Halliwell. They are reckoned to have sold around 45 million albums and 16 million singles.

CHARLES AND DIANA DIVORCE

On August 28, 1996, the 15-year marriage of the Prince and Princess of Wales was brought to an end with a decree absolute rubber-stamped at Somerset House in London.

The divorce was granted on the grounds that the couple had been officially separated since December 1992 – although adultery could have been cited, given that both parties had publicly admitted to it.

Charles and Diana's parting was the second royal divorce of the year, as the Duke and Duchess of York had already received their decree absolute in May.

The Queen had suggested publicly in December 1995 that the Prince and Princess of Wales would do well to divorce, hoping that this would stem the seemingly endless tide of revelations about the couple's unhappy private life. There was immediate speculation that the Prince of Wales might plan to marry his long-term companion Camilla Parker Bowles, herself divorced the previous year.

▶ **Tabloid revelations about the state of the royal marriage resulted in widespread public sympathy for Princess Diana.**

THE McLIBEL CASE

In December 1996 the longest libel trial in British legal history came to an end. Popularly known as the "McLibel case", it was brought by McDonald's, one of the world's largest multinational corporations, against two almost penniless ecology campaigners who had distributed leaflets critical of the fast-food chain. In 1990 McDonald's told Dave Morris, Helen Steel and three other campaigners that they must either apologize or face legal action. To the corporation's astonishment, Morris and Steel not only refused to retract the allegations made in their leaflet but fought a two-and-a-half-year action in the High Court.

The case was heard without a jury, at McDonald's request. The judge delivered his detailed verdict in June 1997, when he predictably found in favour of the corporation. He allowed that the two campaigners had proved that McDonald's was "culpably responsible" for cruelty to animals and exploited children, but they had not proved, on the other hand, allegations that the corporation was destroying rainforests, causing food poisoning or creating starvation in the Third World.

McDonald's had spent an estimated £10 million on an action that had brought them nothing but ridicule.

▲ **For many, the case of McDonald's versus Morris and Steel brought the words "sledgehammer" and "nut" to mind.**

SEPTEMBER
• Jockey Frankie Dettori rides a record seven winners in one day at Ascot
• Police arrest several IRA suspects and shoot one dead in raids on houses in London
• Death of comedian Leslie Crowther

OCTOBER
• Driver Damon Hill wins the Formula One world championship
• The Ministry of Defence admits that soldiers were exposed to harmful chemicals during the Gulf War
• Death of actress Beryl Reid

NOVEMBER
• A section of the Channel Tunnel is devastated by fire
• The Stone of Scone is returned to Scotland
• Outbreak of an E. coli infection in Scotland
• Death of actor Michael Bentine

DECEMBER
• Three infants, three mothers and a teacher are injured in a machete attack on school in Wolverhampton
• Deaths of comedian Willie Rushton and jazz musician Ronnie Scott

1997

NEWS IN BRIEF

- The new parliament includes 119 women MPs
- The Labour government gives the Bank of England power to set base interest rates
- The government levies a £5 billion "windfall" tax on privatized utilities
- New British Library opens at St Pancras
- Many building societies, including Alliance & Leicester, Halifax and the Woolwich, are floated on the London Stock Exchange, following the example set by Abbey National in 1989
- Books published this year include *Enduring Love* by Ian McEwan and *Harry Potter and the Philosopher's Stone* by J K Rowling
- British films this year include Peter Cattaneo's *The Full Monty*, Gary Oldman's *Nil By Mouth* and Ian Softley's *The Wings of the Dove*
- The "Sensation" exhibition by Young British Artists shows at the Royal Academy
- Sculptor David Mach completes his *Train*, made out of 185,000 bricks
- Channel Five and the BBC's News 24 channel begin broadcasting
- The Teletubbies appear on children's television
- Albums released this year include the Spice Girls' *Spiceworld*, Radiohead's *OK Computer* and the Verve's *Urban Hymns*
- Songs of the year include Elton John's "Candle in the Wind 1997", Robbie Williams's "Angels" and the Verve's "Bittersweet Symphony"

BLAIR AND NEW LABOUR SWEEP TO POWER

The United Kingdom general election of May 1, 1997, was a political earthquake. Not only did a Labour government come to power after 18 years of Conservative rule, but it did so with the largest parliamentary majority for any party since the Second World War. With 419 seats in the House of Commons to 165 for the Conservatives, Labour leader Tony Blair was almost certain to govern for the next five years.

Labour had captured 45 per cent of the votes cast to 31 per cent for the Conservatives. The scale of the Labour victory was magnified in terms of seats won both by the "first-past-the-post" electoral system and by tactical voting by Labour and Liberal-Democrat supporters, who generally backed whichever candidate was most likely to beat the Tories in a given constituency. The Lib-Dems won 17 per cent of the vote, which converted into an impressive 46 seats in the Commons. Liberal leader Paddy Ashdown was prepared broadly to support the new government, giving Labour an even more assured Commons majority.

The election victory was a personal triumph for Tony Blair who, at the age of 43, became Britain's youngest Prime Minister for 185 years. It was the culmination of his three-year drive to establish "New Labour" as an electoral force capable of defeating the Tories. In the process he had slaughtered Labour's sacred cows at an astonishing rate, embracing most aspects of the Thatcher revolution, from the privatization of nationalized industries to low direct taxation, tight limits on union power and the culture of "enterprise". Yet he had done so without splitting the party – indeed, Labour had shown an impressively unified front during the election. Blair had been rewarded with the support of media mogul Rupert Murdoch and many other prominent business figures, including Virgin boss Richard Branson.

The election was a painful debacle for the Conservatives. John Major, personally far more popular than his party, resigned as Tory leader as soon as the result was known. Defeat was the logical conclusion to accumulating damage from splits and scandals over the previous two years. The party had become deeply divided on its policy towards Europe and more than 70 "Eurosceptic" Tory MPs had been in more or less

▲ **Tony Blair swept to power under the banner "New Labour, New Britain". In practice, this meant a sharp shift away from the party's traditional socialist policies.**

permanent revolt against their own government on the issue. The government had also been weakened by setbacks such as the "Arms for Iraq" affair, which had brought searing criticism of senior ministers from the Scott Inquiry in February 1996, and the "mad cow" disease crisis which revealed powerful evidence of ministerial mishandling. Above all, the Conservative government had failed to distance itself from the misdeeds of a small number of Tory MPs, including Neil Hamilton, accused of accepting cash in return for asking parliamentary questions.

The defeat of Hamilton by an anti-sleaze candidate, journalist Martin Bell, was one of the highlights of a notably dramatic election night. Other prominent losers included the Defence Secretary Michael Portillo, beaten by a political beginner, Stephen Twigg, and former minister David Mellor, who lost his seat in Putney largely through the intervention of millionaire Sir James Goldsmith and his anti-European Referendum Party. In Northern Ireland, Sinn Fein leaders Gerry Adams and Martin McGuiness were elected to Westminster. Most notable of all, however, was the number of women elected – 119 in all, more than 100 of them Labour.

On winning the election, Blair told voters: "You have put your trust in me and I intend to repay that trust." Gordon Brown, appointed Chancellor of the Exchequer, immediately stressed the new government's financial rectitude by handing over control of interest rates to the Bank of England. Remarkably, a Labour victory was followed by a rise in share prices. Only time would tell whether New Labour really stood for anything – if the earthquake was more apparent than real.

THE RISE OF THE ECO-WARRIORS

▲ **Environmentalists occupy a treetop during the protests against proposals to cut down a forest to make way for the Newbury bypass.**

In 1990s Britain no new motorway, bypass, or airport extension could be planned and built without a prolonged battle between well-organized, dedicated environmental protesters – the "eco-warriors" – and the authorities. During 1996, the most attention-grabbing protest tactic, used especially on the proposed route of the Newbury bypass in Berkshire, was to take to the trees. Protesters lived in tree houses connected by walkways, preventing road-builders clearing the route until a difficult and dangerous process of eviction had been completed.

In January 1997 a new obstructive tactic succeeded in winning extensive media coverage. Five protesters planning to block construction of a Honito-to Exeter link road at Fairmile in east Devon decided to dig a network of tunnels under the proposed route. They intended to live underground, day and night, defying bailiffs to find a way of evicting them. Attracted by the bravery and sheer oddity of the protest, the media quickly turned the five into celebrities. With their jokey nicknames, such as "Animal", "Muppet Dave" and "Swampy", they provided newsmen with excellent copy.

The underground protest lasted seven days, before tunnelling experts brought in by the bailiffs reached most of the protesters. Swampy, whose real name was Daniel Hooper, was the last to emerge, coming out voluntarily. He became the main focus of later media interest as he proceeded to dig in again at the site of another protest, against the building of a second runway at Manchester airport.

Although in one sense the media exploited Swampy, feeding him into the celebrity machine – he even appeared on BBC2's satirical show *Have I Got News For You* – in another sense it was the eco-warriors who exploited the media. As Swampy said to journalists after the Fairmile eviction: "If I had just written a letter to my MP, would you lot be here? Think not."

1997

THE DEATH OF DIANA

In the early hours of the morning of August 31, 1997, a Mercedes carrying the Princess of Wales and her companion Dodi Fayed crashed into a concrete pillar in an underpass in Paris at high speed. Dodi Fayed and the driver of the car, Henri Paul, were killed instantly. The princess died at the hospital of La Pitié Salpetrière after a failed attempt to revive her. A bodyguard, Trevor Rees-Jones, survived the crash, though with very serious injuries.

At the time of her death, Diana was probably the most prominent celebrity in the world. Since her divorce from Prince Charles in 1996, she had never been out of the public eye, attracting attention

▲ During the grieving that followed her death, floral tributes to the "People's Princess" could be found in public places throughout Britain.

▲ Happier times: the Prince and Princess of Wales enjoying a holiday in Spain with their young sons William and Harry.

equally for her support of humanitarian causes, such as AIDS charities and the campaign to ban landmines, and for her glamour, enhanced by a dazzling succession of haute couture frocks. Her relationship with Dodi Fayed, son of the owner of Harrods in London, Egyptian-born Mohamed Al Fayed, had been the talk of the tabloids throughout the summer.

None the less, few people were prepared for the astonishing wave of public grieving that swept Britain in the following week. Only Prime Minister Tony Blair immediately caught the appropriate tone. Speaking on the morning of the accident, he said: "She was the People's Princess and that is how she will stay … in our hearts and our memories for ever." Millions of people clearly agreed. The area in front of the gates of Kensington Palace, the princess's London home, became a vast shrine to her memory – a sea of floral tributes interspersed with poems, personal

mementos, candles and cards. Mourners queued for hours to sign books of condolence in St James's Palace. Similar scenes were repeated on a smaller scale in many parts of the country.

With the sense of mourning came also a tide of anger. This was partly directed at the press. It was known that the Mercedes had been pursued by press photographers – the paparazzi – on motorbikes. Diana's brother, Earl Spencer, expressed a widely held view in his bitter statement immediately after the crash: "I always believed the press would kill her in the end, but not even I could believe they would take such a direct hand in her death."

Anger was also directed at the royal family, who were believed by Diana's admirers to have treated her shabbily, and whose response to the tragedy was widely regarded as grudging and inadequate. Prince Charles flew to Paris to bring back Diana's body, which was taken to the Chapel Royal at St James's Palace. He then returned to Balmoral, where the royal family, including his sons, chose to grieve in private. The newspapers were soon expressing popular discontent at the lack of a public gesture from the Queen. The royal family were forced to issue a statement saying they were "hurt by suggestions that they are indifferent to the country's sorrow". On Friday, September 5, some of the damage was repaired, with a walkabout by the Queen and other royals among mourners in London, and a televised address by the Queen in which she praised Diana as "a gifted human being".

Popular feeling dictated that there must be a state funeral for the princess – by no means a foregone conclusion for the divorced wife of the heir to the throne. It took place in London on Saturday, September 6. A silent procession from Kensington Palace to Westminster Abbey was followed by a service of great drama and pathos. Earl Spencer delivered a stinging attack on the press and the royal family for their treatment of Diana, a speech that drew applause from part of the congregation and the huge crowd outside the Abbey. Singer Elton John, a friend of the princess, sang a new version of his song "Candle in the Wind", dedicated to her and guaranteed to be one of the biggest-selling records of all time. When it was all over, the princess's remains were driven along flower-strewn roads to the Spencer family home at Althorp, to be buried on an island in a lake.

Meanwhile, the story of the events of the fatal night had begun to emerge in more detail, without resolving the mysteries surrounding the crash. Princess Diana and Dodi Fayed had dined at the Ritz hotel, owned by Dodi's father. The Mercedes' driver, Henri Paul, was not a trained chauffeur,

▲ A simple tribute from the Princes William and Harry. At her funeral Princess Diana's brother, Earl Spencer, vowed to help raise the children in the way she would have wanted.

but deputy head of security at the Ritz. Blood tests appeared to reveal that he had been drinking heavily before taking the wheel. Paparazzi on motorbikes had indeed buzzed around the vehicle, but the only evidence of a collision was with a mysterious white Fiat. The inevitable conspiracy theories began to circulate, with the open encouragement of Mohamed Al Fayed, attributing the death to a plot by the British Secret Service and the royal family. Evidence for this was totally lacking.

The extreme public mourning for Diana was such a striking phenomenon that many people saw in it evidence of some fundamental change in the emotions and attitudes of the British people. Tony Blair was far from alone in claiming that a more caring, compassionate society was emerging, evidenced by the reaction to Diana's death and encouraged by her example. Certainly, early contributions to her memorial fund were running at more than £100,000 a day.

In the end, however, the most durable effect of the event seems to have been, rather surprisingly, a revival of respect and affection for the royal family. They had learnt the lesson that a more popular image was needed. The Queen was soon to be seen visiting pubs and signing footballs, while Prince Charles jollied along with female pop stars. Opinion polls soon showed that their popularity was rising to the highest levels for many years.

▲ An enduring image of Princess Diana with a young African girl, a landmine victim, during her final campaign to ban the use of landmines.

PROGRESS TOWARDS PEACE IN IRELAND

▲ **Throughout the history of the Troubles, the vast majority of the people of Northern Ireland had declared their desire for peace.**

JUNE

- William Hague is elected leader of the Conservative Party, defeating Kenneth Clarke in the third-round ballot
- Tony Blair opts to continue the Conservative government's project for a Millennium Dome
- Former Tory minister Jonathan Aitken is disgraced after his libel case against the *Guardian* and Granada Television television collapses
- Ownership of handguns is banned

JULY

- Britain hands over Hong Kong to China
- Gordon Brown's first Budget sees sharp increases in health and education spending
- The Orange Parade in Drumcree is followed by Nationalist riots and demonstrations across Northern Ireland
- The IRA declares a new ceasefire
- Death of financier Sir James Goldsmith

AUGUST

- Princess Diana is killed in a car crash in Paris

SEPTEMBER

- Scots vote overwhelmingly in favour of devolution; the Welsh support devolution by a tiny majority
- Six die when an express train collides with a freight train near Southall station
- Sinn Fein and Ulster Unionists participate in all-party talks in Northern Ireland
- European golfers win the Ryder Cup at Valderrama

In September 1997 all-party talks on the future of Northern Ireland got under way with the participation of both Sinn Fein, the political wing of the IRA, and the Ulster Unionists, the main Protestant party. This remarkable step forward for the peace process was due in large measure to the new British government elected the previous May.

One of Prime Minister Tony Blair's first speeches after taking office set the agenda, reassuring Unionists that a united Ireland was not a serious option, but offering to talk to all sides, despite the lack of a ceasefire by the IRA. The appointment of Mo Mowlam as Northern Ireland Secretary brought intelligence, directness and evident goodwill to the process.

In the summer of 1997, it appeared that Northern Ireland was heading back into chaos. The decision to allow the annual Drumcree Orange Parade to pass through a Catholic area of Portadown on July 6 sparked Republican riots and bombings across the Province. A breakthrough, however, came almost immediately afterwards. First, Loyalists agreed to re-route marches to avoid Catholic districts, a major concession in the context of Northern Ireland sectarian tensions. Then, on July 19, the IRA announced a resumption of the 1994 ceasefire which they had abandoned 18 months earlier. The path to the peace talks was open.

DEVOLUTION UNDER WAY

During the 1997 election campaign, New Labour had promised major constitutional reforms, and once in power they proved true to their word. In September referendums asked Scottish and Welsh voters to approve the setting up of national assemblies that would give them a considerable measure of control over their own affairs. The Scots were also asked whether they wanted their assembly to have the power to alter tax levels, a power not offered to the Welsh.

In Scotland the prospect of devolution excited considerable enthusiasm. There had been deep resentment at the treatment of Scotland by successive Conservative governments over the previous 18 years; as a result, the Tories did not win a single seat north of the border in the general election. Scottish Secretary Donald Dewar led a high-profile campaign for a convincing "yes-yes" vote, with the active assistance of the Scottish Nationalists. On a reasonable turnout of electors, 73.4 per cent voted in favour of a Scottish Assembly and 63.5 per cent approved that assembly having tax-varying powers. This scale of success could not be repeated in Wales, where the population was far more sceptical about devolution. In the event, the government managed to drum up a "yes" vote in Wales only by the

▲ **For many Scots voters, the referendum victory was the first step along the path to complete independence.**

narrowest of margins – a mere 6,721 votes.

It was generally agreed that the existence of a Welsh Assembly would change little, but Scotland was another matter. The new parliament, which would meet in Edinburgh in 1999, marked the biggest change in Anglo-Scottish relations for 300 years. It was intended to have control of domestic matters such as health and education, while foreign policy and defence remained in the hands of Westminster. But once a democratically elected parliament was in place clearly expressing the will of the Scottish people, what was to stop it extending its powers if it so wished – the same process that had recently led to the break-up of the Soviet Union and Yugoslavia? The Scottish Nationalist leader Alex Salmond was certain that devolution would prove to be the first step towards total independence for Scotland; Tony Blair asserted that it would strengthen the Union. The issue remained open.

"SENSATION" EXHIBITION CAUSES SENSATION

A major exhibition of work by young British artists, all from the Saatchi Collection, opened at the Royal Academy in London on September 18, 1997. The exhibition was called "Sensation" and fully lived up to its name.

Pre-publicity ensured long queues from the first day of the show. Visitors were warned at the entrance that they might find some of the works displayed "distasteful". Many did. The exhibition contained images and objects that the BBC described as "explicit pornography" as well as much that was simply bizarre.

Works on show included Damien Hirst's *A Thousand Years*, a cruel but ingenious installation in which maggots bred in a cow's head hatched into flies and were then electrocuted. Tracey Emin, an artist most famous for having once appeared drunk on television, exhibited her unmade bed and a tent embroidered inside with a comprehensive list of the names of her many lovers. The room containing Jake and Dinos Chapman's sculptures of children with genitals attached to their faces was restricted to over-18s.

Most outrage was caused by two images considered more specifically offensive, rather than just generally odd or tasteless. One was Chris Ofili's allegedly blasphemous picture of the Virgin Mary surrounded by images of female genitalia. The other was Marcus Harvey's *Myra*, a large-scale portrait of serial killer Myra Hindley made out of children's hand-prints. The exhibition was picketed by the mother of one of Hindley's victims and protestors threw ink and eggs at the portrait, forcing its temporary withdrawal for cleaning.

Some 300,000 people paid to see the exhibition. The public didn't know whether it was art, but they did know it wasn't boring.

▲ **The portrait of Myra Hindley caused particular revulsion amongst those who claimed the exhibition transgressed the bounds of good taste.**

- An EU report says 23 per cent of British families are headed by a single parent
- The government introduces a "New Deal" offering subsidies to employers who give jobs to long-term unemployed aged 18–24
- Unemployment falls to 1.4 million, its lowest level since 1980
- The £2 coin goes into circulation
- The government decides that the Viagra anti-impotence pill will not be available on demand on the NHS
- Lieutenant Sue Moore and Lieutenant Melanie Rees are the first women to command Royal Navy warships
- Books published this year include *Birthday Letters* by Ted Hughes and *The Restraint of Beasts* by Magnus Mills
- British films this year include Guy Ritchie's *Lock, Stock and Two Smoking Barrels*, Peter Howitt's *Sliding Doors*, and Shekar Kapur's *Elizabeth*
- David Hare's play *The Blue Room*, performed in London, includes a nude scene for Hollywood actress Nicole Kidman
- Anthony Gormley's statue *Angel of the North* is erected alongside the A1 at Gateshead
- Albums released this year include Talvin Singh's *OK* and Pulp's *This Is Hardcore*
- Songs of the year include All Saints' "Never Ever" and Billie Piper's "Because We Want To"
- Melanie Blatt of girl-group All Saints sets the fashion for clothes that bare pregnancy "bumps"

GEORGE MICHAEL OUTED

On April 7, 1998, British pop singer George Michael was charged with performing a "lewd act" in a Beverly Hills public convenience, witnessed by an undercover police officer. A Los Angeles court later sentenced him to 81 days' community service and a fine of £500.

Shortly after he was charged, Michael announced on television that he was currently in a homosexual relationship. He told CNN: "I have not been in a relationship with a woman for almost ten years." Michael had originally been marketed as a heterosexual heart throb with the

▲ **In spite of the tabloid headlines, George Michael's "outing" has had little adverse impact on his popularity.**

pop duo Wham! and was at pains to state that, at that time, his relationships were with women.

Michael's discomfiture served to highlight the continuing problems of gay life at the end of the twentieth century. Despite the generally liberated atmosphere prevailing in Western countries, many gays still preferred to remain in the closet. Their difficulties were emphasized again later in the year in Britain, when government ministers Peter Mandelson and Nick Brown were pursued by the tabloid press with allegations of homosexuality. Gay liberation still had a long way to go.

THE GOOD FRIDAY PEACE AND THE OMAGH BOMB

On Good Friday, April 10, 1998, agreement was reached on a comprehensive peace settlement in Northern Ireland. Although rejected by some Unionists and derided by many political commentators, the Good Friday Agreement was the best chance for an end to the Ulster Troubles since their escalation in the 1960s.

At the start of 1998, few people held out any great hopes for the all-party peace talks that had begun the previous September. But the British and Irish governments were unrelenting in their drive for an agreement. Prime Minister Tony Blair had shown how far he was prepared to go in December 1997 when he had invited a Sinn Fein delegation, headed by Gerry Adams, to talks in Downing Street – the first time Irish Republicans had set foot there since 1921. Northern Ireland Secretary Mo Mowlam went even further the following January

by entering the Maze prison for talks with convicted Loyalist terrorists, who were threatening to veto the peace process. When the IRA were shown to have carried out a killing in breach of their ceasefire in February, Sinn Fein was banned from the

talks for a paltry two weeks.

Only two days before Good Friday, which had been set as the deadline for agreement to be reached, it still seemed unlikely that all sides could strike an accord. The arrival of Blair and his Irish opposite number, Bertie

▲ **Irish Prime Minister Bertie Ahern and Tony Blair's Good Friday Agreement could not wholly end the violence.**

▲ A renegade group of Republican terrorists murdered over 28 people in the Omagh bombing, shattering hopes that the killing was over.

Ahern, at the talks, plus the intervention of President Bill Clinton by telephone, eventually pushed the Northern Ireland parties into overcoming their many doubts and reservations. The agreement provided for an Ulster parliament elected by proportional representation and a power-sharing executive committee. Various bodies would be channels for co-operation with the Irish Republic. Terrorist prisoners were all to be released within two years. The key issue of the decommissioning of terrorist weapons was fudged.

After the agreement was reached, Blair said: "I hope that the burden of history can at long last be lifted from our shoulders." It was an ambitious hope in a country so saturated in historic conflicts. Optimism rose, however, as successive hurdles were overcome. Ulster Unionist leader David Trimble and Sinn Fein's Gerry Adams both persuaded their own parties to back the agreement. Although other Unionist groups rejected the peace deal and the Protestant community was clearly deeply divided on the issue, in a referendum held in May the people of Northern Ireland overwhelmingly approved the

agreement, with 71 per cent voting in favour. Mo Mowlam triumphantly proclaimed: "They have voted to take the gun out of politics."

Elections for the new assembly were held in June and David Trimble became First Minister of the new Northern Ireland executive. But opposition from dissident Unionists remained fierce. As in the previous year, the annual Drumcree Orange Parade at Portadown in July was turned into a mass display of Protestant intransigence. As Orangemen confronted security forces ordered to stop the march passing through a Catholic area, a widespread breakdown of order in Ulster was predicted. But at the height of the confrontation, three young boys, Richard, Mark and Jason Quinn, were burned to death in a Loyalist petrol-bomb attack on their home. The horror was too great, and support for the Drumcree confrontation melted away.

The Quinn family massacre was soon dwarfed, however, by the Omagh bombing of August 15, the worst single outrage in the whole of the Northern Ireland conflict. A car bomb exploded in Market Street, Omagh's main thoroughfare, at 3.10 on a busy

Saturday afternoon. Because of a confused telephone warning, police had cleared the wrong area. Twenty-eight people were killed and more than 200 injured. The dead included three generations of the same family – a grandmother, mother and daughter. Yet the reaction to this massacre, caused by a Republican splinter group called the Real IRA, only proved how far the peace process had come. Gerry Adams denounced the attack, following up with a statement that violence must be "a thing of the past, over, done with and gone". Public revulsion was so great that the Real IRA were forced to announce the suspension of their terrorist campaign.

In October it was announced that First Minister David Trimble and Social Democratic and Labour Party leader John Hume had been awarded the Nobel Peace Prize. Trimble cautiously commented: "There is an element of prematurity about this." The failure of terrorists to disarm remained a major obstacle to the full implementation of the peace agreement. But at least, for the first time in many years, there was hope in Northern Ireland.

OWEN HERO AT WORLD CUP

▲ Michael Owen's equalizer in England's second-round tie against Argentina was in vain, as the South Americans won on penalties.

The football World Cup finals were held in France in June and July 1998, with both England and Scotland competing. Strong fears of hooliganism expressed in many quarters before the event were at least partly realized, although Britain was far from solely to blame. If there were serious disturbances involving drunken England supporters in Marseilles, an even worse rampage by Germans followed in Lens. Despite the attention devoted to these incidents – with Prime Minister Tony Blair calling on employers to sack convicted hooligans – for most people it was the football that mattered.

Football fever gripped both England and Scotland. On match days streets were empty and normal life came to a halt. Both home teams performed creditably. Scotland gave the holders, Brazil, a close call in the opening match of the finals, before making their traditional exit at the end of the first round. England won through to a dramatic second-round tie against Argentina, illuminated by a spectacular individual goal from 18-year-old Michael Owen, the youngest player to appear for England in the twentieth century. The match was marred by the harsh sending off of midfielder David Beckham for petty retaliation early in the second half. Reduced to ten men, England fought a lion-hearted rearguard action, but eventually lost on penalties.

HEREDITARY PEERS TO GO

In October 1998 the Labour leader in the House of Lords, Baroness Jay of Paddington, announced that the government intended to abolish the right of hereditary peers to sit in the upper house of the UK parliament. She described the possession of political power by right of birth as "glaringly unfair and glaringly outdated".

The government faced a crucial difficulty in its effort to reform the Lords: the ability of peers to delay any legislation abolishing their powers. Of the 1,165 members of the House of Lords, 475 were committed Tory supporters, as against 176 for Labour. Among hereditary peers, 302 were

► Over 500 years of tradition ended when hereditary peers lost their right to legislate, in an effort to reform the Lords

committed Tories and 18 regularly supported Labour.

In an effort to smooth the path of reform legislation, in January 1999 the government accepted a compromise under which 92 of the 751 hereditary peers would be allowed to remain in a "transition House" while a Royal Commission decided exactly what formula a new Upper House should follow. Most hereditary peers duly lost their seats the following November.

The Royal Commission chaired by Lord Wakeham reported in January 2000, but its proposal for a mix of elected and appointed seats in the Upper House failed to provide the basis for agreement on further reform. Even after the third consecutive Labour election victory in 2005, reform of the House of Lords remained on the agenda, but its final form was still unresolved.

GENERAL PINOCHET ARRESTED

On October 17, 1998, the 82-year-old former Chilean dictator General Augusto Pinochet was arrested in a private London hospital, where he was recovering from back surgery. The arrest was at the official request of two Spanish judges, Baltasar Garzon and Manuel Garcia Castellon, who had been investigating the disappearance or death of hundreds of Spanish nationals in Chile during the general's 17-year rule. They wanted Pinochet extradited to Spain to stand trial. The Swiss, Belgian and French authorities subsequently filed their own requests for extradition.

Pinochet came to power in Chile in a military coup against the democratically elected left-wing government of Salvador Allende in 1973. The seizure of power was followed by thousands of well-documented cases of human rights abuses, including the killing of at least 3,000 people and the widespread use of torture. In 1990 Chile returned to democracy and Pinochet stepped down as President.

Ironically, Pinochet was an admirer of Britain, making annual visits to London to lunch at Fortnum and Mason and visit Madame Tussaud's. Former Prime Minister Margaret Thatcher was a great admirer of the general, who regularly sent her chocolates and flowers on her birthday, and had

▲ **Protestors outside the London clinic where former Chilean President Pinochet was arrested at the request of a Spanish judge.**

been to her house for tea. Along with other leading Conservatives, including the current party leader William Hague, Mrs Thatcher voiced her criticism of the proposed extradition, arguing variously that Pinochet had helped Britain during the Falklands War and that he was basically a good man who had prevented Chile falling under a communist dictatorship. The British government stuck to the official line that the request for extradition was a purely legal matter, although individual ministers were more outspoken. Trade and Industry Secretary Peter Mandelson said

that the idea of a brutal dictator claiming immunity from prosecution as a former head of state "would be pretty gut-wrenching stuff" for most people.

On October 28 the High Court upheld the view that Pinochet enjoyed immunity as a former head of state and declared his detention illegal. An appeal to the House of Lords produced a dramatic reversal of this decision, however, with the Law Lords voting 3–2 to allow extradition proceedings to continue. This decision, endorsed by Home Secretary Jack Straw, was subsequently undermined by the revelation that one of the Law Lords, Lord Hoffman, was associated with Amnesty International, an organization that had submitted evidence against Pinochet and campaigned in favour of his extradition.

Sitting without Hoffman, in March 1999 the Law Lords repeated the pro-extradition ruling with some modification. Extradition proceedings were stopped some months later, however, when the Home Secretary ruled that Pinochet was too ill to stand trial. The former dictator returned to Chile in March 2000 after being held under house arrest in Britain for over 16 months. Despite this outcome, the Pinochet case clearly marked another step forward for those in Britain keen to see respect for human rights enforced by international law.

- The FTSE 100 stock market index rises above 6,000 (compared with 4,000 at the start of 1997)
- The base interest rate falls to 5 per cent, the lowest in 22 years
- The government indicates that it favours joining the single European currency "if economic conditions are right"
- The Budget announces abolition of tax relief on mortgages, but lowers income tax, introducing a 10p tax band for low earners
- A national minimum wage comes into effect, set at £3.60 an hour
- Official statistics show that two in five of all births in England and Wales now occur outside marriage
- A health scare leads to the removal of Genetically Modified (GM) foods from sale; the government is forced to severely restrict the growing of GM crops
- 24 million Britons own mobile phones by the year's end
- The London Eye wheel is raised on London's South Bank
- Andrew Motion is appointed Poet Laureate
- British films this year include John Madden's *Shakespeare in Love*, Damien O'Donnell's *East is East* and Roger Michell's *Notting Hill*
- The ITV nightly news programme *News At Ten* is replaced by earlier and later news broadcasts; the change attracts much criticism
- Albums released this year include Travis's *The Man Who* and Charlotte Church's *Voice of an Angel*

REPORT CONDEMNS POLICE RACISM

The report of the official inquiry into the murder of black teenager Stephen Lawrence, published in February 1999, constituted a damning indictment of the Metropolitan Police. Written by Sir William Macpherson, it described the police investigation of the killing as marred by "professional incompetence, institutional racism, and a failure of leadership by senior officers".

▲ The parents of black teenager Stephen Lawrence. The investigation into his murder led to accusations of institutional racism against the Met Police.

Lawrence was stabbed to death at a bus stop in an unprovoked racist attack in April 1993. Although five white youths believed to be responsible for the murder were identified, the slowness and incompetence of the initial police investigation made it impossible subsequently to secure a conviction against them. Only the determination of the Lawrence parents to see justice done kept the issue alive.

Two internal police inquiries failed to find any cause for concern in the case. When Labour were elected to power in 1997, however, Home Secretary Jack Straw set up a public inquiry. The recommendations of the Macpherson Report were far-reaching, ranging from outlawing racist statements in private conversations to changing the "double-jeopardy" law that made it impossible to try someone twice for the same offence, even if new evidence was available.

WAR IN EUROPE

On March 24, 1999, the combined air forces of NATO launched the first of a series of bombing raids against targets in Serbia. Prime Minister Tony Blair was prominent in advocating and justifying the air campaign, NATO's first offensive against a sovereign state in its 50-year history.

The war was provoked by Serb Prime Minister Slobodan Milosevic's refusal to halt his program of "ethnic cleansing" in the Serbian province of Kosovo. Ninety per cent of the population of Kosovo were ethnic Albanians and only 10 per cent Serbs. In the mid-1990s a Kosovo Liberation Army (KLA) initiated a guerrilla campaign against the Serbian authorities. From 1998 Milosevic unleashed the Serbian Army upon the Kosovans. Hundreds of thousands of ethnic Albanians were forced to flee their homes. As towns and villages were razed, reports from the region suggested that ethnic genocide was in progress.

In January–February 1999 a six-nation "contact group", including Britain and the United States, held talks at Rambouillet, France, with the Serb and Kosovan leaders. Agreement was reached on Kosovan autonomy inside the Serb Republic, but Milosevic would not agree to the stationing of a NATO peacekeeping force in Kosovo. Serbia's rejection of the peace agreement triggered the NATO offensive.

NATO's strategy of debilitating Serbia's military machine through continuous air raids was widely criticized. There was no United Nations mandate for the bombing, which some claimed made the campaign illegal. However, Tony Blair vigorously defended the armed intervention. Writing in the American magazine *Newsweek*, he declared: "We are fighting not for territory but for values, for a new internationalism where the brutal repression of whole ethnic groups will no longer be tolerated."

Many military strategists asserted that only a costly land invasion by NATO troops would succeed in removing Serbian forces from Kosovo. Yet in Britain and the United States – the two strongest supporters of the air campaign – were proved right in their faith in air power. Although the campaign, which continued for more than two months, was marred by incidents such as the accidental bombing of a refugee convoy and the destruction of the Chinese embassy in Belgrade, it did achieve its objective.

In June 1999 Serbia accepted a peace deal jointly proposed by Russia and the European Union. Serbian forces withdrew from Kosovo and the province was occupied by an international force under NATO command. The Kosovan Albanian refugees, more than a million of whom had fled to

▲ **British troops enter a town in Kosovo, after a sustained NATO bombing campaign forced Serbian forces to withdraw from the province.**

escape Serbian massacres and NATO bombing, were able to return to their homes. This had been achieved without a single NATO combat fatality.

Restoring any semblance of order and security to Kosovo proved a predictably difficult task. The NATO-commanded forces soon uncovered shocking evidence of

massacres of Kosovan Albanians carried out by Serb militias, which gave considerable retrospective justification to the NATO campaign. Whatever their critics might say, US and British leaders believed the Kosovo War had been a success, showing that military intervention could be an effective way of achieving political aims.

BOMBER STRIKES THRICE

▲ **David Copeland, whose nail-bombs brought terror to London's gay, Asian and West Indian communities.**

Late on the afternoon of Saturday, April 17, 1999, a nail bomb exploded in the busy heart

of Brixton, south London. It was the start of a brief but murderous one-man bombing campaign that spread terror across the capital.

The Brixton bombing, which injured around 50 people, was followed by a second explosion a week later in Brick Lane, east London. Since Brixton was famous for its West Indian population and Brick Lane for its Asians, the attacks seemed certain to be aimed at racial minorities. Early on the evening of Friday, April 30, another nail bomb exploded in the Admiral Duncan pub in Soho's Old Compton Street, this time killing three people and injuring 65. The pub was mostly frequented by gays, although a pregnant woman was among the dead.

By the time of the third

explosion, police had identified the bomber on CCTV footage from the site of the Brixton bombing and released his picture to the public. A tip-off from a man who recognized the CCTV image led police to the Hampshire home of 22-year-old David Copeland. His room was decorated with Nazi regalia and crammed with weapons and explosives.

Copeland had been a member of the right-wing British National Party (BNP), before joining the even more extreme National Socialist Movement. Police were, however, at pains to stress that he had acted alone and the government resisted pressure for a general crackdown on right-wing extremist groups. Copeland was sentenced to six terms of life imprisonment.

THE MURDER OF TELEVISION GOLDEN GIRL

▲ The motive for television presenter Jill Dando's murder remains a mystery.

Monday, April 26, 1999, saw Britain's television-viewing public reeling with shock as the news emerged that Jill Dando, one of the country's most popular presenters, had been murdered outside her home in west London.

Neighbours had heard a scream and found the 37-year-old slumped on the doorstep of her terraced house in Fulham. By the time she had been taken to nearby Charing Cross hospital, she was dead. After an autopsy, it was established that she had been shot through the head at point-blank range.

Dando had started her career on a local newspaper in her home town of Weston-super-Mare, on the west coast of England. She progressed through regional broadcasting to a regular place on the BBC's national news network. Her public fame, however, came more from her work with the television programmes *Holiday* and *Crimewatch*, the latter a popular show in which members of the public were invited to help the police solve difficult, often violent, crimes.

Dando's murder brought tributes from colleagues who viewed her as both a consummate professional and someone whose character had been unchanged by celebrity. Her popularity ensured that her baffling murder touched the public more than the death of any other figure since that of Diana, Princess of Wales in August 1997.

A particularly sad irony was that in spite of an increasingly successful career, her personal life had until recent times been less than settled. This seemed about to change with the announcement of a proposed autumn marriage to gynaecologist Alan Farthing.

The motives for Jill Dando's murder remain a mystery. Some suggested that it might have been retribution for the NATO bombing of Serbian television buildings. Others considered that it may have been connected with Dando's role on *Crimewatch*. Indeed the calculated and professional manner in which she was murdered – a single silenced shot from a 9 mm pistol – had all the hallmarks of a contract killing. However, Barry George, a loner obsessed with guns and celebrity, was convicted of the crime in 2001.

▲ A police cordon surrounds Jill Dando's Fulham house: her killing took place in broad daylight on her own doorstep.

QUEEN OPENS SCOTTISH PARLIAMENT

On July 1, 1999, the Queen officially opened the Scottish parliament in Edinburgh's Assembly Hall. She described it as "a moment rare in the life of any nation when we step across the threshold of a new constitutional age". This seemed to be no exaggeration, for the Scots had been without their own elected assembly since the union of England and Scotland in 1707.

The Queen received a warm welcome from Scots, who lined the route of the royal procession in

▲ When the Queen opened the Scottish parliament in 1999, it was the first time the country had had its own elected assembly since 1707.

large numbers. The St Andrew's Saltire, Scotland's national flag, flew alongside the Union flag in a gesture that encapsulated the aspirations of devolution – to reconcile Scottish nationalism with membership of the United Kingdom. The only discordant note was struck by a handful of Irish Republican demonstrators brandishing placards who jumped over safety barriers as the royal party passed.

Scotland's first devolved government, a coalition of Labour and the Liberal Democrats, was headed by First Minister Donald Dewar. In his speech at the opening ceremony, he stressed that the parliament was as much about national identity as about legislative powers. He told his fellow Scots: "This is about who we are."

Dewar was destined to serve as First Minister for less than 18 months before dying of a brain haemorrhage. By then the parliament had already proved it was going to be a turbulent chamber for debate with a real influence on Scottish life. The huge cost of the new Holyrood parliament building, belatedly completed in 2004, was heavily criticized by thrifty Scots, but a Scotland without its own parliament had become almost unthinkable.

- Unknown Scottish golfer Paul Lawrie wins the Open championship at Carnoustie
- Death of Conservative politician William Whitelaw (Viscount Whitelaw of Penrith)

AUGUST
- Charles Kennedy is elected leader of the Liberal Democrats

SEPTEMBER
- Death of Conservative MP and diarist Alan Clark

OCTOBER
- Two commuter trains are involved in a head-on collision outside London's Paddington station, killing 31 people
- Peter Mandelson replaces Mo Mowlam as Northern Ireland Secretary

NOVEMBER
- Australians vote to keep the Queen as head of state
- Prime Minister Tony Blair's 45-year-old wife Cherie announces she is pregnant
- Death of author and performer Quentin Crisp

DECEMBER
- In Northern Ireland a power-sharing executive is set up under First Minister David Trimble, fulfilling the terms of the Good Friday Agreement

PADDINGTON RAIL CRASH

When Britain's railways were privatized by John Major's Conservative government, critics alleged that the pursuit of profit would lead to a decline in safety standards. These predictions seemed fulfilled by a rail crash on October 5, 1999, that killed 31 people and injured more than 400, many of them badly burned.

The accident took place at Ladbroke Grove, outside London's Paddington station, at 8.09 am. A First Great Western 125 express train from Cheltenham, travelling at high speed, ran head-on into a Thames Trains Turbo that had just left Paddington. Hundreds of passengers were trapped in the wreckage of the express, parts of which were engulfed by fire.

The accident happened because the driver of the Turbo, who had been in his job for two weeks, failed to stop at a red signal light.

An inquiry into the disaster criticized Railtrack, the company responsible for the rail network, for failing to react to repeated warnings about poorly positioned and confusing signals. The train operators were censured for inadequate training of drivers and the failure to install automatic systems to stop trains passing signals at danger. Even if the problems had been inherited from British Rail, little had been done to remedy them.

▲ The Paddington rail crash, in which 31 people died, led to the censuring of rail companies for inadequate safety measures.

2000 —

The new millennium opened with no great expectations of a transformation for the better in life during the century ahead. If anything, voices prophesying doom dominated the British media, with prominent predictions of long-term global catastrophe through global warming and the destruction of the environment. Pessimism about the future was soon justified, though from a direction that few had anticipated. The co-ordinated terrorist attacks on the United States on September 11, 2001, put Islamic extremism at the centre of the world stage. They were followed by US-led invasions of Afghanistan and Iraq in which Britain participated as America's most loyal ally. Through placing Britain "shoulder to shoulder" with the United States in the "war on terror", Prime Minister Tony Blair set off a series of political storms that his government weathered in parliament, but that sharply divided the country. Official predictions that a major terrorist outrage in Britain was sure to follow the US attacks were proved sadly correct when London's transport network was attacked by British Muslim suicide bombers in July 2005.

Re-elected twice in the new millennium, Blair confirmed a dominance of the British political scene similar to that achieved by Margaret Thatcher in the 1980s. Like her's, Blair's style of government was presidential, and had little in common with the tradition of collective Cabinet decision-making. Like Thatcher, he was loathed and admired in almost equal measure. Once dismissed by his critics as a media-savvy vote-winner with no profound political beliefs, Blair revealed himself to be a complex and in some ways enigmatic figure. His readiness to use military force and his close alliance with US President George Bush – a thoroughly unpopular figure in Britain – were damaging to his control over his own party and to his standing in the country. Yet he stuck to his chosen foreign policy with absolute conviction.

In some areas the policies of New Labour continued those of preceding Conservative governments. There was no turning back from competition, consumer choice and the free market as principles to be applied to all areas of national life. On the other hand, far more money was made available for the National Health Service and state schools, after long years of relative neglect. Chancellor of the Exchequer Gordon Brown's tax and benefits policies achieved a discreet but significant shift in favour of the worse-off. Yet the insecurity that came with greater enterprise and competition continued to disrupt people's lives. Fewer people had jobs for life and for many work meant low pay for long hours. But unemployment and inflation were stabilized at a sustainable level, giving the basic economic indicators a sedate predictability.

The integration of Britain into a global economy and global communications was an ineluctable fact of life. The place of national identity and national boundaries in the globalized world was an ever-present issue. It was at the forefront in the ongoing debate about Britain's adherence to the European Union, with every move towards greater economic integration or political unification meeting stiff resistance. It lay behind varied attitudes towards Britain's ever more multi-racial and multi-cultural society, whose increasing diversity raised enduring questions about the meaning of being British. The tens of thousands of asylum-seekers and illegal immigrants making their way to the country – reaching about one per cent of the population according to official estimates – were a physical manifestation of the wider world pressing upon Britain's shores.

Many of Britain's problems at the start of the new millennium were in fact the downside of decades of solid progress. Concerns about the nation's health were focused not on poverty and deprivation but on excess consumption – children were too fat, adults drank too much. An ageing population – the triumph of a century of medical advances, improved nutrition and housing – threatened a major financial crisis, because pension provision had been based on lower life expectancy. Even the influx of immigrants, legal or illegal, was an acknowledgement of the availability of jobs in Britain and, to a degree, the attractiveness of the British way of life. Britain had lost its Empire and had to adjust to a lesser role upon the world stage. But a national culture characterized by creativity, tolerance and decency could still potentially contribute to meeting the global challenges of the twenty-first century.

BRITAIN GREETS A NEW MILLENNIUM

On the night of December 31, 1999–January 1, 2000, the beginning of the third millennium and of the twenty-first century was greeted with what some journalists described as the biggest party the planet had ever seen. Britons played their part fully in the worldwide celebrations, inspiring Prime Minister Tony Blair to speak of a "real sense of confidence and optimism" on the threshold of the new millennium. Cynical journalists, however, had long been sharpening their knives to attack the London centrepiece of Britain's celebrations: the Millennium Dome.

The desire to mark the new millennium's advent had inspired a host of new projects across Britain, many of them financed by the Millennium Commission's distribution of cash from the National Lottery. Innovations were especially striking in London, where a huge sightseeing wheel, the London Eye, was erected opposite the Houses of Parliament and a former power station at Bankside was refurbished – to popular acclaim – as the Tate Modern art museum. These successes, however, were offset by the problematic Dome.

Originally conceived by John Major's Conservative administration, the Dome project was adopted by New Labour in 1997. It was to offer a mixture of popular entertainment and instructive exhibits, rather in the spirit of the 1951 Festival of Britain. By a near miracle, the structure was ready for its opening night on December 31, 1999, but the event proved a public relations disaster when important opinion-formers had to queue in the cold for hours because of security checks. Several million ordinary people who lined the Thames probably had a better time, although a somewhat chaotic fireworks show fell short of fulfilling the organizers' promise of a "river of fire".

Meant, with absurd optimism, to attract 12 million visitors in a year, the Dome was soon in financial crisis as the required numbers failed to materialize and the project had to be bailed out with fresh cash in May and September. Strangely, most people

▲ On New Year's Eve 1999, more than 200,000 people packed Edinburgh's streets to mark the Hogmanay celebrations.

who actually went to the Dome said they enjoyed it. And there were lots of them – 6.5 million by the time it closed at the end of the year. But this could not prevent the Dome being dubbed a national disaster by a hostile press and becoming a severe embarrassment for the government.

Dire warnings that the new millennium might usher in global chaos proved predictably unfounded. Computer experts had worked up a fever of excitement about the "millennium bug" – a failure of some computer systems to recognize the year 2000 as a possible date. This, it was asserted, could lead to a breakdown of water, energy and food supplies. Massive sums were spent by the government and private companies to counter the threat. But the bug turned out to be a damp squib. The worst that could be said, as the new millennium got under way, was that life looked very much the same as it had before.

▲ The Millennium Dome was the centrepiece of the government's programme to mark the coming of 2000.

LIVINGSTONE BACK AS LONDON MAYOR

The restoration of city government to London – abolished by Margaret Thatcher in 1986 – should have been a popular triumph for the Labour government. Instead, the election of a mayor and London assembly turned into a humiliation for the Prime Minister and a triumph for one of his most consistent left-wing critics, Ken Livingstone.

It was apparent as soon as the mayoral contest began that "Red Ken", a broadly popular figure well remembered from his time as head of the Labour-run Greater London Council in the 1980s, would be the likely winner. Yet Tony Blair could not accept the prospect of a left-winger becoming London Mayor. A rigged selection process ensured that former Secretary of State for Health Frank Dobson was adopted as Labour's candidate. After some hesitation, Livingstone decided to stand as an independent and was duly expelled from the Labour Party.

The Conservatives, meanwhile, had their own problems. Their original choice for mayoral candidate, Lord Archer, withdrew after being forced to admit to rigging an alibi to win a libel suit. He was replaced by Steven Norris, a liberal Tory well-judged to attract support from wavering London voters.

In the election on May 4, 2000, Livingstone won almost 40 per cent of first-preference votes and 58 per cent once second-preference votes were reallocated, well ahead of Norris. Dobson attracted only a humiliating 13 per cent of first-preference votes.

In practice, Livingstone's radicalism proved to have grown less fiery over the years. Despite conflict with the government over the future of the London Underground system, he was readmitted to the party in time to win re-election as official Labour mayoral candidate in 2004.

▲ Expelled from the Labour Party, Ken Livingstone still managed to win convincingly to become London's first elected Mayor.

58 DEAD IN FREEZER LORRY

In the early hours of the morning of 19 June, 2000, customs officers at Dover opened the back of a sealed freezer truck that had arrived in the English port on a ferry from Zeebrugge in Belgium. Behind a cargo of tomatoes they discovered a pile of twisted corpses – 54 men and four women, all suffocated in the airless container. Only two men were found alive.

The 60 men and women who had entered the truck at Rotterdam, in the Netherlands, were all illegal immigrants from villages in southeastern China. They had paid thousands of pounds to criminal gangs known as "snakeheads", which organized the long clandestine journey across Asia and Europe to the Channel coast. The refrigerated truck was the last stage that would have brought them to their goal – Britain, seen as a land of opportunity by economic migrants fleeing the poverty of the developing world. The Chinese would have survived the Channel crossing but for the truck driver's decision to close the only air vent, because he was afraid noises from inside might alert the authorities. He had also turned off the refrigeration unit, despite it

▲ The death of 58 Chinese migrants who suffocated in a lorry container highlighted the growth of human trafficking.

being a very hot summer day, causing the temperature in the truck to rise to an intolerable level.

The deaths highlighted the mounting worldwide traffic in human beings, described by one expert as having replaced drugs as the most lucrative trade for criminal gangs. It was reckoned that around 400,000 people were entering the European Union illegally every year. The Dutch truck driver, Perry Wacker, was subsequently convicted of manslaughter by a British court, while other members of the gang that organized the human shipment were jailed in the Netherlands. But no one believed the illegal traffic would do anything but increase, as long as there remained huge disparities of wealth between different parts of the globe and ever tighter restrictions on legal immigration to the richer countries.

DEATH OF SARAH PAYNE

▲ **The family of the murdered eight-year-old Sarah Payne release balloons to mark the ninth birthday she never saw.**

On July 1, 2000, eight-year-old Sarah Payne went missing while out playing with her siblings at Kingston Gorse, Sussex. Her disappearance led to a nationwide search. Sarah's parents Sara and Michael Payne appeared repeatedly on television to appeal for her safe return. The search ended tragically with the discovery of Sarah's body on July 17, quite close to the place where she had been abducted.

Roy Whiting, a local man on the sex offenders register, was arrested and eventually convicted of the crime after 18 months of painstaking work by forensic scientists. He was sentenced to life imprisonment in December 2001. Whiting had a previous conviction for abducting an eight-year-old in 1995, a crime for which he had served little over two years in prison.

Sarah Payne's parents, in alliance with the *News of the World*, mounted a campaign for "Sarah's Law", which would give parents the right to know the identity of sex offenders living in their area. The high-profile campaign attracted widespread support. A petition with 700,000 signatures was presented to Home Secretary Jack Straw, and the Paynes were invited to meet Tony Blair. Less encouragingly, in the wake of the tragedy, mobs gathered sporadically to attack the homes of alleged paedophiles at locations across Britain.

CONCORDE CRASH

▲ **The catastrophic crash of an Air France Concorde in 2000 heralded the end for the pioneering supersonic jet.**

On July 25, 2000, an Air France Concorde supersonic airliner crashed shortly after taking off from Paris's Charles de Gaulle airport, killing the 109 passengers and crew on board. The crash marked the beginning of the end for the prestigious Anglo-French aircraft.

A fire broke out under the wing of the Concorde even before it left the ground, but too late to abort the take-off. The pilot attempted in vain to nurse the aircraft to another Paris airport. After three minutes in the air, trailing flames and smoke, it came down near the town of Gonesse, demolishing a hotel. Miraculously, only four people on the ground were killed.

Air France and British Airways Concordes were grounded pending an investigation into the cause of the accident. It was discovered that one of the Concorde's tyres had struck a piece of metal debris shed by another airliner on the runway. The metal shredded off rubber from the tyre, and this struck the fuel tanks in the bottom of the wing, making a hole from which highly flammable kerosene sprayed out.

French and British Concordes returned to service in 2001, with modifications that included reinforced fuel tanks. But the crash had reminded everyone that Concorde was an ageing aircraft with – it emerged – a disturbing record of faults, major and minor. Two years later, the airlines decided that the cost of keeping their Concordes operational could no longer be justified and they were pensioned off to become museum pieces. The brief era of supersonic passenger flight was over.

THE PERFECT OLYMPICS

The Millennium Olympic Games, held in Sydney, Australia, ended on October 1, 2000, amid a deluge of praise for both the spirit and organization of the event. Juan Antonio Samaranch, President of the International Olympic Committee, declared that the Olympics "could not have been better". This was an opinion certainly shared by the Great Britain team, which won as many gold medals in Australia as in the previous three Olympics combined.

The British successes came generally in the less eye-catching events, with three sailing golds for Shirley Robertson, Ben Ainsley and Iain Percy, and others for shooter Richard Faulds and cyclist Jason Queally. Steve Redgrave won rowing gold for the fifth consecutive Olympics, a British record that earned him a knighthood. In field events Jonathan Edwards, almost as well known for his devout Christian belief as for his outstanding athletic prowess, took the gold medal in the triple jump, while Denise Lewis won the heptathlon despite a foot injury.

Victories on the final day for heavyweight boxer Audley Harrison and for Stephanie Cook in the women's modern pentathlon took the British tally to 11 gold medals, along with 10 silver and seven bronze. The only major

▲ **Britain's Jonathan Edwards celebrates winning the gold medal in the men's triple jump at the Millennium Olympics in Sydney.**

disappointment was the failure of much-liked distance runner Paula Radcliffe to win the 10,000 m, despite leading the field for most of the race.

The British success was to some degree attributed to funding from the National Lottery, which had allowed the team to compete on more equal terms with countries used to putting more of their money into sport. It showed what British sportsmen and women might be capable of with the right support.

OCTOBER
- Four people die and more than 100 are injured when a GNER train crashes at high speed at Hatfield, Hertfordshire; the crash was caused by a broken rail
- England football manager Kevin Keegan resigns as his team appear likely not to qualify for the 2002 World Cup finals
- Scottish First Minister Donald Dewar dies suddenly; his place is taken by Henry McLeish
- Seven leading Conservative politicians admit to having smoked cannabis in their youth
- Death of gang leader Reggie Kray

NOVEMBER
- An attempt to steal diamonds being exhibited in London's Millennium Dome is foiled by police
- 10-year-old Damilola Taylor is murdered by a gang in Peckham, south London
- Deaths of novelist Sir Malcolm Bradbury and historian Sir Steven Runciman

DECEMBER
- Virgin boss Richard Branson fails to take over the National Lottery
- Outgoing US President Clinton visits Northern Ireland.
- Britain and the world's other leading industrial countries agree to write off the debts of the world's 20 poorest states
- Death of Liverpool poet Adrian Henri

- A census estimates the UK population at 58.8 million; 21 per cent of the population is over 60
- Almost 4.9 million – 8.3 per cent of the total UK population – were born abroad (1951: 4.2 per cent)
- The minimum wage is raised to £4.10 an hour
- The Child Poverty Action Group reports the number of children living in poverty has fallen by 1.2 million since Labour took power
- The Eden Project near St Austell, Cornwall, opens to the public
- The Gateshead Millennium Bridge opens across the Tyne at Newcastle
- Books published this year include *Atonement* by Ian McEwan and *Fury* by Salman Rushdie
- British films this year include Sharon Maguire's *Bridget Jones's Diary* and Chris Columbus's *Harry Potter and the Philosopher's Stone*
- Albums released this year include Gorillaz' *Gorillaz* and Super Furry Animals' *Rings Around the World*

FOOT AND MOUTH CLOSES DOWN RURAL BRITAIN

On 20 February, 2001, foot and mouth disease was discovered in pigs at an abattoir in Essex. They were traced back to the Burnside Farm at Heddon-on-the-Wall in Northumbria. By the time the diseased pigs were identified, animals had already been infected at more than 40 other farms across Britain, as well as some in continental Europe. It was an especially virulent strain of the disease – one that had first been noted in India in 1990 and was probably brought into Britain in illegally imported meat.

When the disease was discovered, the immediate government response was hesitant and insufficient. A nationwide ban on the movement of animals was instituted, but not quickly enough. A cull of animals in infected areas also got off to a slow start as the veterinary service was overwhelmed by the scale of an outbreak that stretched from Devon to Dumfriesshire. Eventually, however, the government took measures that were draconian enough by any standards. The Army was brought in to speed up the cull and tens of thousands of slaughtered animals burned in mass funeral pyres. In the worst-affected areas, such as Cumbria and Devon, farmers became virtual prisoners on their farms and footpaths were closed to ramblers. Much of the countryside was effectively shut down.

By the time the last case was verified, at a farm in Cumbria on 30 September, there had been a total of 2,030 animals identified as suffering from foot and mouth. About 6 million sheep, cows, pigs and other livestock had been slaughtered – one in eight of all British farm animals. Many voices were raised in protest at the policy of controlling the disease through mass slaughter, calling instead for mass vaccination.

Whereas farmers received generous compensation for livestock killed, the real losers were people in the rural tourist industry. Footpath closures and the association of the countryside with diseased animals and funeral pyres meant that country hotels and bed-and-breakfasts stood empty through the year. The epidemic – by far the worst that Britain had ever seen – was not officially declared over until January 2002.

▲ The outbreak of foot and mouth led to the mass slaughter of cattle.

SECOND TERM FOR BLAIR

The general election held on 7 June, 2001, confirmed the seismic shift in British politics that had taken place with the triumph of Tony Blair and New Labour in 1997. After four years in power, New Labour were able to stage a repeat performance of their landslide victory, taking 413 seats compared with 166 for the Conservatives and 52 for the Liberal Democrats. This was despite the ravages of foot and mouth disease through much of the countryside – a crisis that caused Blair to postpone the election date, originally planned for early May – and the ridicule heaped on the government over the Millennium Dome.

According to many political commentators, the true victor in

▲ Tony's Blair's second landslide election victory saw the lowest voter turnout since the First World War.

the election was apathy. Only 59 per cent of the electorate bothered to vote, the lowest turnout since 1918 and sharply down from the 71 per cent turnout in 1997. The election seemed a foregone conclusion from the start, with all pollsters accurately predicting another Blair landslide. There were only a few moments when the campaign came to life, notably when Deputy Prime Minister John Prescott punched a man who had thrown an egg at him – a rare moment of spontaneity from a politician that probably earned Prescott more sympathy than condemnation. Despite the lack of popular enthusiasm shown by the low turnout, Blair was justified in calling the result "an historic moment for the Labour Party". He was the first Labour leader ever to achieve two consecutive terms in office with a working majority in the House of Commons. For Conservative leader William Hague the result was a personal disaster. He immediately resigned, precipitating another acrimonious Tory leadership contest, from which Iain Duncan Smith emerged as the unlikely winner.

ASIAN YOUTHS RIOT

On July 7–8, 2001, the Yorkshire city of Bradford was racked by rioting on a scale not seen in Britain since the 1980s. The troubles drew attention to the existence of a racially segregated society in some northern cities, where communities of Pakistani and Bangladeshi origin had become cut off from wider British society. Rioting in Bradford and elsewhere expressed the simmering discontent of British-born Asian youths who felt alienated both from their own traditional community leaders and from the police.

The first serious riots of the year occurred in Oldham at the end of May. Other clashes followed in Burnley and Leeds before the worst outbreak exploded in Bradford. The pattern was always the same: Asian youths responded violently to provocation by white racists and were then involved in battles with riot police.

The Bradford disturbances began with an Anti-Nazi League counter-demonstration against a meeting of right-wing extremists. Soon, Asian youths were engaged in running battles with police,

▲ Riots in Yorkshire and Lancashire towns with large Asian populations drew the spotlight onto a community which felt alienated.

throwing bottles, bricks and petrol-bombs. The Manningham district of Bradford was worst affected. Cars and buildings were set on fire and shops looted. At least 200 people were injured and police arrested 36 people, including both whites and Asians.

By coincidence, the report of an inquiry headed by Lord Ouseley into race relations in Bradford was published a week after the riots. The Ouseley Report painted a picture of a city in which segregation promoted by white racists and tolerated by local authorities had been embraced equally by Muslim traditionalists, who preferred to keep their children separate from Western society. Although Asians made up around 20 per cent of the city's population, many schools were more or less exclusively Asian or white. Insensitive policing and social deprivation were also blamed for exacerbating tensions.

2001

JUNE

- Tony Blair is elected Prime Minister for a second term, retaining his massive parliamentary majority
- Chancellor Gordon Brown says the government will take a "cautious and considered" approach to joining the European single currency
- Tim Henman loses in the Wimbledon men's singles semi-final for the third time in four years
- Death of actress Joan Sims

JULY

- Barry George is found guilty of the murder of the television presenter Jill Dando
- Race riots rock the city of Bradford with clashes between whites, Asians and police
- Author and Conservative politician Lord Archer is found guilty of perjury

AUGUST

- Paul Burrell, formerly butler to Princess Diana, is charged with theft of some of her possessions
- Deaths of social reformer Lord Longford and astronomer Sir Fred Hoyle

SEPTEMBER

- England's footballers defeat Germany 1–5 in a World Cup qualifier in Munich
- The government declares solidarity with the United States after Islamic terrorists strike targets in New York and Washington, DC, killing around 3,000 people
- Iain Duncan Smith defeats Kenneth Clarke in a run-off vote to become the new leader of the Conservative Party

LORD ARCHER JAILED FOR PERJURY

On July 19, 2001, Lord Archer – millionaire, bestselling novelist, life peer and one-time leading Conservative politician – was found guilty of perjury and perverting the course of justice. It was a spectacular downfall for a man who less than two years previously had been preparing to stand as Tory candidate in the election for Mayor of London.

The case related to a libel case that Archer brought against the *Daily Star* in 1987. Then Deputy Chairman of the Conservative Party, he successfully sued the newspaper for alleging that he had had sex with a prostitute. The trial judge invited ridicule by commenting on the "fragrance" of Archer's wife Mary, which apparently made a sordid liaison with a prostitute unlikely. The *Daily Star* was forced to pay £500,000 in damages.

In 1999, however, a former friend of Archer, Ted Francis, informed the *News of the World* that Archer had asked him to concoct a false alibi for use in the libel case. Although this alibi had never been used in court, the revelation was sufficient to persuade the Conservatives to drop Archer as mayoral candidate and to lead to Archer's trial at the Old Bailey.

In a bizarre gesture typical of his attention-seeking personality, while the case was in progress Archer appeared in a West End play he had written, called *The Accused*. The novelty of the play was that each evening the audience was asked to vote on whether Archer's stage character was innocent or guilty. Thus he was on trial at the Old Bailey during the day and on stage at night.

Archer was sentenced to four years in prison, but was released on probation in July 2003 after being subjected to a remarkably lax form of confinement. He retained his life peerage, since there was no precedent for rescinding one, but was not readmitted to the Conservative ranks.

▲ **Lord Archer's colourful career ended in shame as he was convicted of perjury and perverting the course of justice in a previous libel case.**

BRITAIN SIGNS GREENHOUSE GAS ACCORD

On July 22, 2001, the representatives of 178 countries, including Britain, agreed on a programme to cut emissions of carbon dioxide and other "greenhouse gases" in order to – so it was hoped – stem the rising tide of global warming. The agreement, an updated version of the 1997 Kyoto Protocol, was reached at the end of a long and difficult meeting in Bonn, Germany, after a final unbroken 48 hours of haggling and horse-trading.

The British government, which had been a prime mover in pushing for fulfilment of the Kyoto accord, committed itself to cutting the country's carbon dioxide emissions by 20 per cent by 2012. Much of the effort to achieve this target was to be focused on developing renewable energy resources such as wind-farms, which at the time provided less than one per cent of Britain's energy. It was probably not uncorrected to the government's enthusiasm for renewable energy that Britain was set once more to become a net importer of oil and natural gas in the latter part of the decade, after a quarter-century as a net exporter.

Although governments were almost certainly in good faith in adhering to the accord, it was soon apparent that many would have difficulty achieving the emission reductions agreed. In this Britain was no exception. The failure of the British government to persuade its American ally to join in the fight against global warming also undermined the effectiveness of the agreement.

By the middle of the decade, plans to build wind-farms in some of the most beautiful stretches of British countryside were running into resistance, particularly when the

▲ Greenpeace activists protest at an Essex oil refinery against President Bush's refusal to sign the Kyoto Accord.

awesome scale of the wind power needed to generate significant amounts of electricity began to be widely appreciated. The government even floated the idea of reviving a large-scale nuclear power programme in the desperate search for clean renewable energy. The targeted 20 per cent cut in emissions by 2012 showed no sign of being achieved.

BRITAIN "SHOULDER TO SHOULDER" WITH AMERICA

On the morning of September 11, 2001, four airliners on American domestic flights were hijacked by Islamic terrorists. Two of the aircraft were flown into the twin towers of the World Trade Center in Manhattan. Another hit the Pentagon building in Washington DC, while the fourth crashed outside Pittsburgh, Pennsylvania, after a struggle between passengers and the hijackers. Some 3,000 people died in these concerted acts of mass terrorism. From that day the world entered a significantly different era – the era of the "war on terror" and the "clash of civilizations".

The reaction of Prime Minister Tony Blair to the events in the United States was immediate and unequivocal. On the evening of the same day, he declared that Britain stood "shoulder to shoulder with our American friends". In his opinion, it was "not a battle between the United States and terrorism, but between the free and democratic world and terrorism".

▲ A Westminster Abbey service for the victims of 9/11 reflected the solidarity which the British people felt towards the USA.

Although other NATO countries, including France and Germany, also expressed solidarity with the United States, it was in altogether more guarded terms. Blair established himself as President Bush's closest and most reliable ally in the "war on terror". In October Britain confirmed its commitment in action by providing forces to support the US onslaught on Afghanistan, which was the principal base for the al-Qaeda terrorist network.

Blair's stance was praised by some as brave and principled, but criticized by others as foolhardy in making Britain a prime target for Islamic terrorists. The authorities made it clear that they expected a major Islamic terrorist attack to occur in Britain sooner or later and that nothing could be done to prevent it.

- Share prices fall steeply as new technology stocks slump
- Serious concerns arise over the ability of company pension funds to meet their commitments
- The Nationality, Immigration and Asylum Act tightens rules on asylum seekers entering Britain
- As Chief Secretary to the Treasury, Paul Boateng is the first black Cabinet minister
- The Falkirk Wheel boat lift is opened, linking the Forth & Clyde and Union canals
- Books published this year include *Fingersmith* by Sarah Waters and *London Orbital* by Iain Sinclair
- British films this year include Chris Columbus's *Harry Potter and the Chamber of Secrets* and Gurinder Chadha's *Bend it Like Beckham*
- *The Osbournes*, a television programme about the home life of British rock star Ozzy Osbourne, is a hit in the United States.
- Albums released this year include Coldplay's *A Rush of Blood to the Head* and The Corals' *The Corals*
- Popular songs this year include Will Young's "Anything Is Possible" and Sugababes' "Freak Like Me"

BRITAIN CLINGS TO THE POUND

▲ **Fireworks explode around a massive euro symbol as Europe celebrates its new currency.**

From January 1, 2002, the euro became the everyday currency of 12 of the 15 countries of the European Union. But while other national currencies laden with patriotic symbolism were consigned to the dustbin of history, the pound sterling remained in circulation. Britain – along with Denmark and Sweden – chose to stay outside the euro zone.

The issue of membership of the single currency had split the British government, with Prime Minister Tony Blair broadly in favour, but Chancellor Gordon Brown opposed. Blair saw adherence to the single currency as primarily a political move that would place Britain at the centre of the European Union. Brown adopted the stance that whether to go in or stay out of the euro zone

was a pragmatic economic issue – a question of what was in the "long-term national economic interest". The Chancellor set five economic "tests" that had to be passed before it would be acceptable for Britain to join the euro zone.

The Prime Minister raised expectations that a referendum would be held on euro membership. Public opinion, which stood solidly against abandoning the pound, would be "educated" by the government to achieve a "yes" vote. But, since the Chancellor's five criteria for euro membership were not met – and never looked likely to be – the issue of a referendum could be indefinitely postponed.

There was more than simple-minded nationalism in British doubts about the euro. Because of Britain's stable economic performance since the mid-1990s, confidence in the current management of the economy was high. With inflation and unemployment under control, why embark on a major change that might rock the boat?

QUEEN MOTHER DIES AT 101

On March 30, 2002, Queen Elizabeth the Queen Mother died in her sleep at the age of 101. She had been in an increasingly frail condition since contracting a chest infection the previous Christmas. Her death occurred at the Royal Lodge at Windsor, in the middle of the afternoon.

Born Elizabeth Bowes-Lyon at the dawn of the twentieth century, she had married the Duke of York, the brother of the heir to the throne, in 1923. It was only through Edward VIII's abdication in 1936 that her husband came to the throne as George VI. As Queen, she won the hearts of the British people by her stoicism during the Second World War. After the King's death in 1952, and the accession

of the new Queen, the title Queen Mother was created in recognition of her "devoted service to Britain and the Empire".

The Queen Mother's body lay in state for four days in Westminster Hall, where hundreds of thousands of mourners queued to pay their last respects. The funeral was held in Westminster Abbey, from where the coffin was taken to her final resting place, alongside her husband in the royal chapel at Windsor.

Coming after the demise of her younger daughter, Princess Margaret, in mid-February, the Queen Mother's death inevitably cast a shadow over what was intended to be a year of royal celebration – the Golden Jubilee of Queen Elizabeth's reign. The round

of parties, walkabouts, fireworks displays and concerts nonetheless went ahead in May and June, and were counted a notable success. Both the mourning and the celebrations demonstrated convincingly the enduring popularity of the royal family.

▲ **The Queen Mother's four grandsons stand vigil at the four corners of the dais as her coffin lies in state in Westminster Hall, London.**

MAY DAY PROTESTS

Protests by a variety of left-wing and anarchist groups under the banner of "anti-capitalism" had become an established feature of life at the start of the twenty-first century. The events of May 1, 2002, in London were an indicator of both the strength and weakness of the anti-capitalist movement.

Because of previous May Day disturbances in 2000 and 2001, the police deployed resources on an impressive scale to block any possible violence. The centre of London was occupied by around 5,000 police, while a sophisticated operations room monitored the movements of demonstrators. Many shops and businesses in the capital were boarded up.

Yet the number of anti-capitalist protesters was in fact quite small, far less than those attending a mainstream TUC-organized event in Trafalgar Square. Protests were largely peaceful, although localized skirmishes between riot police and a handful of anarchists broke out late in the day.

The impact of the anti-capitalist protests, however, far exceeded the numbers involved. Their ability to focus media attention inevitably gave currency to ideas that might otherwise have remained marginalized in public debate.

▲ Anti-capitalist May Day protests had become almost a feature in London's calendar, and those of 2002 were largely peaceful.

FOREIGNER TAKES ENGLAND TO WORLD CUP FINALS

The England team's presence at the World Cup finals held in June 2002 in Japan and South Korea came as a pleasant surprise for their long-suffering fans. Eighteen months earlier, they had seemed almost certain to fail to qualify, joining the other UK national teams on the sidelines of international football. But the appointment of a Swedish manager, Sven-Goran Eriksson, to lead the squad brought a dramatic change in fortunes, with a sensational 1–5 away win against Germany helping secure the longed-for qualification.

Eriksson's appointment was in its way a significant indicator of the changes occurring in the early twenty-first-century world. The principles of globalization and the free market were eroding national boundaries in football as much as in other areas. By 2002 almost half of the players in the FA Premiership were from outside the UK, while major clubs such as Arsenal and Liverpool had foreign coaches. Appointing a foreigner to lead the England team recognized the decreasing relevance of nationalism in the contemporary world – although since the World Cup was a contest between national sides, the situation was uncomfortably paradoxical.

In a competition where many top teams underperformed, England seemed at one point in with a chance, despite injuries that hampered key players David Beckham and Michael Owen. Victory over arch-rivals Argentina carried England through the first stage and provoked an outbreak of

▲ After initial high hopes, Sven-Goran Eriksson could only steer the team as far as a World Cup quarter-final defeat.

football fever at home. But in the quarter-finals Brazil, the eventual winners, proved too skilful for the tiring English.

QUEEN CELEBRATES GOLDEN JUBILEE

On June 4, 2002, the fiftieth anniversary of the Queen's accession to the throne was celebrated in spectacular style with a day-long series of events that attracted around a million people to central London. It was an opportunity for reflection upon the changes that half a century had wrought in British life and on the recently revived popularity of the monarchy following some difficult years.

The festivities began the previous evening with a pop music concert held in the gardens of Buckingham Palace. The audience of 12,000 people, who had won tickets in a national ballot, watched performances by a string of pop legends, including Sir Elton John, Sir Paul McCartney and Tom Jones, as well as current top acts such as S Club 7. The concert was rounded off with a spectacular fireworks display.

The celebrations continued next morning with a royal procession from Buckingham Palace to St Paul's Cathedral where a Thanksgiving Service was held. The Queen then went for lunch at the Guildhall, while a carnival parade was staged in the streets. Involving around 20,000 people, the parade was led by a Hell's Angel biker, followed by a West Indian steel band and the world's largest gospel choir. The Queen returned to Buckingham Palace to greet the vast crowd in The Mall from the palace balcony and to witness a fly-past of historic aircraft, including Concorde.

It was noticeable during the celebrations that – apart from the Queen herself – the warmest popular reception was accorded to Prince William and Prince Harry. Despite occasional negative publicity, the emergence of the young princes into public life had on the whole been a key factor in restoring a positive tone to the royal image. The Queen summed up her own reaction to the Golden Jubilee in the three words "gratitude, respect and pride."

▲ The enthusiastic celebrations for the Queen's Golden Jubilee went some way to erasing bitter memories of some difficult years for the royal family.

BRITAIN'S WORST SERIAL KILLER

In July 2002 a public inquiry, chaired by High Court judge Dame Janet Smith, found that convicted murderer Dr Harold Shipman had been responsible for killing between 215 and 260 people over a 23-year period. He ranked as the worst serial killer in British history and possibly the worst in the world.

Born in Nottingham in 1946, Shipman was deeply affected by his mother's death from cancer when he was 17. He trained as a doctor and began practising as a GP in Todmorden, West Yorkshire, in the mid-1970s. His career looked set for an early end when he became addicted to pain-killing drugs, but after treatment he returned to general practice, moving to Hyde, Greater Manchester.

It is now known that right back to his time as a trainee doctor, Shipman had been murdering patients who were elderly or terminally ill, or to whom he took a dislike. He usually killed them with an injection of a drug such as diamorphine. As a doctor and father of four, he appeared a respectable and upright member of society, and when suspicions were raised about the death of one of his patients in 1985, police

made no serious investigation.

In early 1998 he appeared likely to escape prosecution again, when suspicions raised by a fellow GP were again dismissed by police after a superficial inquiry. But the murder of 81-year-old ex-Mayoress Kathleen Grundy in June 1998 was his undoing. The dead woman's daughter, solicitor Angela Woodruff, became concerned when a will was found leaving all Mrs

◀ **Harold Shipman abused his position of trust as a local GP to murder scores of his elderly and vulnerable patients.**

Grundy's money to Shipman. Mrs Grundy's body was exhumed the following August. A series of other exhumations over subsequent months confirmed Shipman's guilt. He was jailed for life in January 2000 for the murder of 15 of his patients and the forging of Mrs Grundy's will.

Shipman hanged himself in Wakefield prison in January 2004. A final revised report of the public inquiry published a year after his death concluded that he had been responsible for at least 250 murders.

NOVEMBER
• The trial of Paul Burrell, the former butler to Princess Diana, collapses when the Queen reveals that she was aware that he was taking some of Diana's possessions.
• Fire-fighters strike in pursuit of a 40 per cent pay rise
• Former MI5 officer David Shayler is jailed for six months for passing classified information to the *Mail on Sunday*
• Deaths of singer Lonnie Donegan, murderer Myra Hindley and film director Karel Reisz

DECEMBER
• British newspapers print revelations about the relationship between Cherie Blair, "lifestyle guru" Carole Caplin and Caplin's friend Australian fraudster Peter Foster
• The Red Cross-run centre for illegal immigrants at Sangatte, near the mouth of the Channel Tunnel, is closed
• Deaths of Clash guitarist Joe Strummer and novelist Mary Wesley

BLAIR TURNS THE SCREW ON IRAQ

On September 24, 2002, Prime Minister Tony Blair recalled the House of Commons from recess to hear him speak on the subject of the weapons of mass destruction (WMDs) allegedly being developed by Iraqi dictator Saddam Hussein. It was the beginning of a personal crusade by the Prime Minister to persuade the British people and politicians that the overthrow of Saddam was essential to Britain's national security.

Blair's statement to the House was based on a 50-page dossier drawn up by the Joint Intelligence Committee, which was released to the press on the same day. The conclusion of the intelligence assessment was, in Blair's words, that "Saddam's weapons of mass destruction programme is active, detailed and growing." Iraq was alleged to possess chemical and biological weapons and to be trying to develop nuclear weapons.

The abandonment of WMD programmes had been a prime condition of the ceasefire agreement imposed on Saddam at the end of the 1991 Gulf War.

Since the war, however, the Iraqi dictator had played cat and mouse with UN weapons inspectors. Repeated UN resolutions demanding compliance with unfettered inspection of weapon sites and research facilities had failed to produce a satisfactory result, as had UN economic sanctions and occasional punitive strikes by US aircraft and missiles.

While describing this situation as intolerable, Blair was careful to state: "No one wants military conflict." The official goal of Britain and the United States at this stage was to seek action through the United Nations to end the stalemate on WMDs and produce "regime change" in Iraq. How this could be achieved without war was, however, hard to see.

▲ **Tony Blair addresses the House of Commons which had been recalled from the summer recess for an all-day debate on Iraq.**

- Temperatures reach the highest ever recorded in Britain at 38.5°C (101.3°F)
- Attempts to limit the entry of asylum seekers brings the government into conflict with the courts
- A traffic "congestion charge" is introduced in London
- Books published this year include *The Curious Incident of the Dog in the Night-Time* by Mark Haddon, *Brick Lane* by Monica Ali and *Harry Potter and the Order of the Phoenix* by J K Rowling
- British films released this year include Richard Curtis's *Love Actually*
- Albums this year include the Darkness's *Permission to Land* and Radiohead's *Hail to the Thief*
- Songs of the year include David Sneddon's "Stop Living the Lie" and Girls Aloud's "Sound of the Underground"

JANUARY

- Britain sends 26,000 troops to the Gulf
- A police officer is killed during a counter-terrorist raid in Manchester
- Traces of the lethal toxin ricin are found when six suspected terrorists are arrested in London
- Shoe-bomber Richard Reid is sentenced to life imprisonment in the United States
- Death of politician Lord Jenkins

SHOE-BOMBER FOILED

On January 30, 2003, British citizen Richard Reid was found guilty of terrorism in a federal court in Boston, Massachusetts. He was sentenced to life in prison for attempting to blow up an airliner in mid-Atlantic using explosives hidden in his shoe.

Reid boarded American Airlines Flight 63 bound from Paris to Miami on December 22, 2001. He had been prevented from boarding the same flight the previous day by security officials who had found his behaviour suspicious. Over the Atlantic, Reid was spotted by a flight attendant trying to light a match on his shoe. He was restrained after a struggle and sedated.

The bizarre form that Reid's attempted bombing took, as well as his dishevelled appearance, at first suggested the incident was the work of an eccentric loner. But

▲ **Richard Reid was sentenced to life in prison for attempting to blow up a trans-Atlantic flight using explosives hidden in his shoe.**

on investigation the shoe bomb turned out to be a sophisticated device quite capable of blowing a hole in the aircraft's hull. Although the details remained obscure, it appeared that Reid had direct links with Islamic terrorist organizations.

From a British point of view, however, the most striking aspect of the case was that Reid had been born and reared in Britain. He came from Bromley in south London, the son of an English mother and a Jamaican father. After leaving school, he fell into a life of petty crime. It was in a young offenders' institution that he converted to Islam. His involvement in Islamic extremism is presumed to have developed at mosques in Brixton and Finsbury Park – the latter the fief of radical Muslim cleric Abu Hamza.

Britain's counter-terrorist effort was focused on the threat posed by extremists from the Muslim countries of the Middle East. But home-grown terrorists were to prove harder to spot and far more dangerous.

CONGESTION CHARGE
MAKES DRIVERS PAY

The density of traffic in central London had been an issue since at least 1903, when a Royal Commission was appointed to seek solutions to the congestion that was threatening to bring the capital to a halt. The boldest, and most controversial, attempt at a solution was initiated a century after that inquiry, with the imposition of a charge on drivers entering the city centre.

The "congestion charge" was introduced on February 17, 2003. Anyone driving a private vehicle into or around the City of London and the West End had to pay a £5 fee. The scheme depended

▶ **In a bold attempt to tackle traffic volume, London became the first major city to introduce congestion charging.**

on modern surveillance technology, linking 230 cameras to a computerized number-plate recognition system and to the national register of car ownership. Drivers who failed to pay on the day faced a stiff penalty charge.

The man behind the scheme was London Mayor Ken Livingstone. He contended that the charge would make drivers transfer to public transport or bicycles, which would lower pollution levels and improve journey times on unclogged roads. Most of the income from the charge was to be used to put more buses on the roads.

An official report on the effect of the congestion charge in its first six months in operation showed that the number of cars driving in central London was down by 60,000, or around 30 per cent. Average journey times had been cut by 15 per cent. Whether the charge adversely affected shops and other businesses in central London was a matter of dispute.

As the first major city to introduce congestion charging, London's experiment was watched with interest by city governments around the world. There was no rush by other cities in Britain to follow suit, however. At first, Leeds, Cardiff, Manchester, Birmingham, Bristol and Edinburgh all expressed interest, but a sense that congestion charging would be highly unpopular dowsed initial enthusiasm.

Livingstone's re-election as Mayor in 2004 ensured that London's congestion charge would stay in place, and probably be extended. The charge was increased to £8 in 2005 and a doubling of the congestion zone was planned for 2007.

HARRY POTTER FASTEST BESTSELLER EVER

At one minute past midnight on Saturday, 21 June, 2003, the most hyped book in publishing history went on sale simultaneously across the world.

Thousands of people queued for hours to be first to get their hands on *Harry Potter and the Order of the Phoenix*, the fifth of J K Rowling's phenomenally successful school-for-wizards series. The book immediately broke all previous records for speed of sale. In Britain alone 1.8 million people – more than one in 30 of the population – bought the weighty 766-page tome on its first day in the shops. There were comparable scenes of Pottermania across the globe – in Singapore and Taiwan, Chicago and Nairobi.

The book's publisher, Bloomsbury, had cleverly exploited what could have been a commercially disastrous gap of three years from publication of the previous volume, *Harry Potter and the Goblet of Fire*. The long delay was used to build up suspense about the content, or even the very appearance, of another chunk of

▲ J K Rowling's tales of schoolboy sorcery injected a little magic into the lives of millions of young (and not so young) fans worldwide.

the saga. The release of two Harry Potter films in the meantime helped increase expectation to fever pitch. The author and publisher went to extraordinary lengths to prevent leaking of the details of the new novel's plot before the moment of publication.

Rowling began writing the Harry Potter series as an impoverished single parent in the 1990s. Desperate to make a living, she was delighted in 1997 when Bloomsbury offered her a £2,500 advance for *Harry Potter and the Philosopher's Stone*. The publication of the latest volume was set to make her the richest woman in Britain and one of the richest in the world.

2003

In March 2003 Britain joined with the United States in an invasion of Iraq. It was Britain's most controversial military action since the Suez Crisis of 1956. The invasion was opposed by many within Prime Minister Tony Blair's own party and government. It gave rise to mass anti-war demonstrations in Britain and around the globe. Yet Blair insisted that the action was necessary for future peace and security and would serve the interests of democracy and freedom.

The prime mover behind the invasion was the Bush administration in the United States. President Bush and his advisers believed that, in the new world situation following the 9/11 terrorist attacks, it was no longer possible to tolerate the existence of foreign governments openly hostile to the United States which were capable of developing weapons of mass destruction (WMDs). Iraq's dictator, Saddam Hussein, was an obvious target for "regime change". He was widely believed to have failed to destroy all WMDs and facilities designed to produce such weapons, as required by the ceasefire agreement that ended the 1991 Gulf War. This non-compliance could be interpreted as providing grounds for military action to remove him from power.

Backed by Britain, in November 2002 the United States persuaded the UN Security Council to pass Resolution 1441, requiring Iraq to prove that it had given up all WMDs or face "serious consequences". When Saddam responded by allowing UN weapons inspectors to return to Iraq, the United States was forced to resort

▲ **When American-led land forces finally entered Iraq in March 2003, they initially met far stiffer resistance than expected.**

to increasingly tenuous arguments as it pressed for a second UN resolution authorizing military action against Iraq.

As the prospect of war drew closer, Britons were drawn into a passionate debate about the rights and wrongs of the Iraq issue. Blair was tireless in his efforts to persuade MPs and the British people to back the drive to war, but there were severe doubts both inside and outside parliament about the wisdom and legality of an invasion without UN authorization. On February 15 the Stop the War Coalition organized a protest march in London that attracted more than a million people. With the Conservative Party broadly supporting the war, a government defeat on the issue in parliament was always unlikely, but the Liberal Democrats and a large number of Labour MPs were unshakably opposed to military action. After a debate on February

26, more than 120 Labour MPs voted against the government.

Blair was also tirelessly engaged on the international scene. A far more convincing speaker than President Bush, he set himself the task of shifting world opinion in favour of an invasion. However, most of Britain's European allies, including France and Germany, remained unconvinced. Spain was the only major European power that joined Britain in wholesale support of the US stance. The opposition of France and Russia, permanent members of the UN Security Council with a right of veto, made it certain by mid-March that no second UN resolution backing military action would be forthcoming. The United States and Britain were thus left with the choice of invading Iraq without UN authorization – which might be considered an act of aggression under international law – or backing down.

Blair's decision to commit Britain to the conflict suggested real personal conviction, for there was no doubt it entailed enormous political risks. Many of his government colleagues doubted the wisdom of the path the Prime Minister had chosen. Chancellor Gordon Brown expressed only the most formal and distant support for the war. On March 17, as troops were readied for action, Robin Cook, former Foreign Secretary and current Leader of the House, resigned from the Cabinet. His resignation speech was a ringing attack on "the commitment of troops in a war that has neither international agreement nor domestic support".

On March 20 US and British ground forces invaded Iraq from the south, while bombs and missiles struck targets in Baghdad and elsewhere. More than 45,000 British servicemen were committed to the invasion. The aerial bombardment of the Iraqi capital fulfilled a declared US policy of "shock and awe". On the ground there was some stiff fighting, especially during a difficult period when sandstorms temporarily obliterated the coalition's overwhelming technological advantage. But once the weather cleared, armoured forces loyal to Saddam were swept aside. By the middle of April, the Americans had occupied Baghdad, the British had captured the southern city of Basra, and US military chiefs declared "major combat operations" over.

The military triumph had been striking, both in its speed and the relatively low level of military and civilian casualties – relative, that is, to dire predictions before the event. But its aftermath was not at all what Blair and Bush had hoped for. Little thought had been given to coping with the chaos that victory brought in its wake. Iraqis turned to looting on a grand scale as soldiers with no clear orders looked on passively. The provision

▲ **The toppling of Saddam Hussein's statue marked a symbolic end to the reign of Iraq's dictator.**

▼ **After his capture in December 2003, video images of an apparently disoriented Saddam Hussein were shown on television worldwide.**

of essential services and supplies was slow to develop as military imperatives were given priority. British troops found themselves attempting to maintain order among a restive Shia population that showed evident relief at the downfall of the hated Saddam, but equally had no love for the Western invaders.

The biggest problem for Blair, in terms of the political situation at home, was the failure to find Iraqi WMDs or facilities for producing them. Political rows were soon raging over whether the Prime Minister had misled the public. Had he ever, in fact, believed that Iraq had such weapons at all? Already under attack within his own party, Blair was thrown further on to the defensive in July when Dr David Kelly, a weapons expert involved in this fierce dispute, committed suicide.

By that time the security situation in Iraq was deteriorating rapidly. Although British troops did not face the kind of guerrilla campaign waged against the Americans further north, they suffered losses to mob violence and isolated terrorist attacks. The capture of the fugitive Saddam in mid-December did not herald a halt to the guerrilla attacks and suicide bombings. Blair's declared goal of a democratic, pro-Western Iraq looked remote as 2003 ended.

TERRORISM AND PROTESTS AS BUSH VISITS BRITAIN

On November 20, 2003, during a four-day state visit to Britain by President George Bush, Islamic suicide bombers attacked two British targets in Istanbul, Turkey. Once more the crude violence of terrorism was able to overshadow the deliberations of world leaders, the pomp of state ceremony – and the anti-war protests of Western liberals.

President Bush arrived in Britain on November 18 amid unprecedented security, which closed down much of central London. An entourage numbering hundreds – most of them armed – accompanied the President to guarantee his safety. The bad impression created by the perhaps excessive level of security threatened to be compounded by a mass demonstration against the war in Iraq. Tony Blair's assertion that "it was precisely the right time for President Bush to be visiting this country" was regarded by most journalists as merely putting a brave face on a public relations disaster – even if opinion polls revealed that far more British people approved of the visit than opposed it.

The Istanbul bombers struck on the third morning of the state visit – as anti-war demonstrators were gathering in London. First, a truck laden with explosives rammed into the British consulate. Then, minutes later, the offices of the London-based HSBC Bank were hit. At least 27 people were killed and 450 injured. Among the dead was the British Consul-General Roger Short. The worst of the carnage was at the bank, where the bodies of the dead and injured were strewn across the street and among the wreckage of the building. Two synagogues in Istanbul had been the target of bombing attacks only five days earlier.

At a press conference held immediately after the news of the attacks came through, Prime Minister Blair eloquently made a powerful defence of Anglo-American policy. He argued that success in creating "a free, democratic and stable Iraq" would destroy "the wretched and backward philosophy of these terrorists". In response to the suggestion that the United States and Britain had brought the terrorist attacks on themselves by their policies, the Prime Minister stated: "America did not attack al-Qaeda on September 11. Al-Qaeda attacked America, and in doing so, attacked not just America but the way of life of all people who believe in tolerance and freedom, justice and peace."

The "Stop Bush" anti-war demonstration was unquestionably large, attracting at least 100,000 people. But the news of the suicide bomb attacks in Istanbul stole the protesters' thunder to a degree. Their gesture of toppling a papier mâché statue of President Bush in Trafalgar Square – in satirical imitation of the toppling of Saddam's statue in Baghdad – was left looking a trifle lame alongside graphic television images of the devastation caused by the bombings in Istanbul.

▲ Demonstrators protesting against George Bush's London visit pull down an effigy of the US President.

ENGLAND WIN RUGBY WORLD CUP

On November 22, 2003, England won the rugby World Cup for the first time ever, defeating reigning champions Australia 20–17 at home in Sydney. Played in drizzling rain, the game was watched by a crowd of 83,000, along with a television audience that numbered 14.5 million in Britain alone.

The final was not a great exhibition of rugby, but for

nail-biting excitement and cliff-hanging drama it could hardly have been bettered. Australia started the game brightly and scored first, but the English forwards soon got the upper hand and by half-time England were ahead 14–5. The Australians then staged a tremendous comeback. Trailing 11–14 with seconds of normal time to go, Australia converted a penalty to level the scores and take the game into extra time. The scores were

► **Jonny Wilkinson's kicking won England the coveted trophy.**

again even at 17–17 as the end of extra time drew near, when England fly-half Jonny Wilkinson kicked a perfect drop-goal to claim the Webb Ellis Trophy for his side.

On December 8 a victory parade through central London brought the capital to a halt, with some 750,000 fans lining the streets. England captain Martin Johnson described the reception the squad received as "absolutely mind-blowing". It was the first time that rugby players had enjoyed the same kind of celebrity status as soccer players in England.

SOHAM MURDERS TRIAL ENDS IN GUILTY VERDICT

▲ **Ian Huntley had been the subject of a series of prior allegations that should have precluded his employment as a school caretaker.**

On December 17, 2003, school caretaker Ian Huntley was sentenced to life imprisonment for the murder of two Cambridgeshire schoolgirls. Holly Wells and Jessica Chapman, both aged ten, disappeared after straying from a family barbecue in their home village of Soham on August 4, 2002.

As a nationwide search was mounted, Huntley came forward to say that, on the day of their disappearance, he had seen the girls walk past the house he shared with his girlfriend, Maxine Carr. Suspicion of Huntley led police to search the local school which the girls attended, and where Huntley and Carr both worked. On a second search, police found the partly burned remains of the girls' football shirts in a dustbin. Huntley and Carr were arrested on August 17. Later that day, a walker discovered the girls' bodies in a ditch near Lakenheath airbase in Suffolk.

When he came to trial, Huntley admitted that the girls had died in his house and that he had disposed of their bodies and clothing. But he alleged that the two deaths had been accidental. Despite the implausibility of this story, his performance on the witness stand was so effective that the jury took five days to reach a majority guilty verdict. Carr was convicted of conspiring to pervert the course of justice.

It subsequently emerged that Huntley had faced a prior string of allegations of rape, indecent assault and underage sex. Police in Humberside, where Huntley previously lived, had identified him as a "serial sex attacker", but the report had been deleted from their records. Cambridgeshire police had failed to vet Huntley's application to work in the school. The system supposed to protect children from predators such as Huntley was revealed to be a shambles.

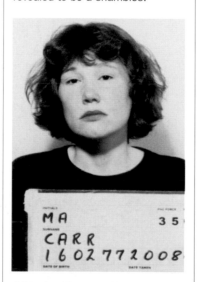

▲ **Maxine Carr was found guilty of trying to conceal Ian Huntley's guilt in murdering schoolgirls Holly Wells and Jessica Chapman.**

HUTTON INQUIRY ACCUSED OF "WHITEWASH"

- First NHS hospitals become foundation trusts
- The Children Act outlaws smacking children in England and Wales if it causes bruising
- The Pensions Commission warns that 12 million Britons have inadequate pension provision
- The new Scottish parliament building at Holyrood is completed, costing ten times its original budget
- Books published include *The Line of Beauty* by Alan Hollinghurst and *Cloud Atlas* by David Mitchell
- British films this year include Mike Leigh's *Vera Drake* and Edgar Wright's *Shaun of the Dead*
- A warehouse fire destroys part of the Saatchi art collection
- Songs of the year include Franz Ferdinand's "Take Me Out" and Band Aid 20's "Do They Know It's Christmas?"

JANUARY
- Serial killer Harold Shipman hangs himself in prison
- The Higher Education Bill, providing for university "top-up" fees, passes its second reading by five votes in the House of Commons

MARCH
- Tony Blair meets Libyan leader Muammar Gaddafi in Tripoli

APRIL
- Tony Blair announces that a referendum will be held on a European Constitution

▲ **Government weapons expert Dr David Kelly, whose suicide was at the centre of the Hutton inquiry. Tony Blair was cleared of all wrongdoing.**

The report of the Hutton Inquiry, published on January 28, 2004, was eagerly anticipated by opponents of Prime Minister Tony Blair. It was widely expected to deliver a damning judgement on his conduct in the run-up to the invasion of Iraq and during the later events surrounding the death of government weapons expert Dr David Kelly. But the report cleared the Prime Minister and his entourage of all wrongdoing, leading to accusations of a "whitewash".

The background to the inquiry was the bitter controversy over the government's justification for the Iraq invasion. A dossier on Iraq prepared by the Joint Intelligence Committee (JIC) and published by the government in September 2002 stated that Iraq had weapons of mass destruction (WMDs), some of which could be deployed within 45 minutes. The subsequent failure to find WMDs in Iraq led to allegations that the government had deliberately misled parliament and the British people.

Dr Kelly had been involved in preparing intelligence on Iraqi weaponry. Although he agreed with the conclusion that Iraq possessed WMDs, he felt that the government had exaggerated intelligence findings in the September dossier, particularly through the prominence given to the "45-minute claim". In May 2003 Dr Kelly privately expressed his concerns to a BBC journalist, Andrew Gilligan. The journalist then made a radio broadcast and wrote a newspaper article accusing the government, and specifically Blair's media chief Alastair Campbell, of "sexing up" the intelligence report.

Gilligan's allegations, picked up by other journalists, provoked a furious public row. The government and Campbell demanded a retraction from the BBC, which the BBC refused to make. In early July Dr Kelly was identified in newspapers as Gilligan's source. After the government confirmed this identification, on July 17 the weapons expert committed suicide.

In an effort at damage limitation, the government immediately ordered Lord Hutton to carry out an inquiry into the circumstances surrounding Dr Kelly's death. Through August and September 74 witnesses testified to the inquiry, including Blair and Campbell. The 750-page report that resulted almost totally exonerated the government.

Lord Hutton found that the government was not responsible for Dr Kelly's suicide, although it could have handled the matter more sensitively. Nor was the government guilty of distorting the JIC's dossier – it had only taken legitimate steps to stress elements it felt worthy of attention. By contrast, Hutton was severely critical of the BBC, which he said had made serious accusations without adequately checking the facts and had failed to respond seriously to requests from the government for a retraction. In the wake of the report, BBC director-general Greg Dyke was forced to resign.

The anti-Blair press on the right and left dismissed the report as a whitewash, although they could find no fault with its factual conclusions. The real complaint was that it had failed to investigate the whole issue of the validity of the government's claims about Iraqi WMDs, something Hutton dismissed as simply outside the scope of his inquiry.

CHINESE WORKERS DROWNED

On the evening of February 5, 2004, at least 21 Chinese workers were drowned while cockle-picking on sandbanks in Morecambe Bay, northwest England. The tragedy drew public attention to the existence of a hidden world of ruthlessly exploited immigrant labour existing on the margins of British society.

Morecambe Bay is notorious for its fast-moving tides and treacherous quicksands, but its sand and mud banks are rich in cockles, shellfish that command a good price on the European market. The Chinese, almost all from villages in Fujian province, were mostly illegal immigrants or asylum seekers who had had their applications turned down. Impoverished and without

▲ The death of 20 Chinese cocklers at Morecambe Bay exposed the hidden world of exploited illegal immigrants.

legal status, they were fed and equipped by a gangmaster who set them to work on the cockle-beds.

The evening of the tragedy, the Chinese were trapped between the rising tide and floodwaters from rivers feeding into the bay. Rescue services were too late to save them. Twenty-one men were identified as having drowned, although at least two more unidentified individuals are thought to have died. One of the workers succeeded in contacting his home village on his mobile phone as the waters rose around him.

In March 2006 Lin Liangren, the Chinese gangmaster responsible for the cockle harvesting operation, was convicted of manslaughter by gross negligence. But it was correctly pointed out that overall responsibility had to lie with a system that put so many immigrant workers outside the protection of the law.

FLASH FLOOD AT BOSCASTLE

On August 16, 2004, the picturesque coastal village of Boscastle in north Cornwall was devastated by a flash flood after over 7 cm (2.7 in) of rain fell in two hours. Astonishingly, although the village was packed with residents and holiday visitors, there was only one injury – a broken thumb.

Up to 2 million tonnes of water swept down the valley where the village is located, tossing cars around like toys and devastating buildings and bridges. Seven rescue helicopters were mobilized to lift people off the roofs of houses and cars. In all, some 60 buildings were flooded, four of them demolished by the force of the water. More than 30 cars were carried out to sea on the flood, with 80 others wrecked.

The spectacular disaster fed concerns about the allegedly increasing menace of flooding

across Britain. According to the government Environment Agency, around 2 million British homes were at risk from floods, as a result of climate change and unwise new building. On the other hand, a

remarkable coincidence drew attention to the perennial nature of flooding: the devastation of Boscastle occurred 52 years to the day after the infamous Lynmouth flash flood of 1952.

▲ The devastation of Boscastle by a flash flood underlined the risks faced by coastal communities in the face of climate change.

NEW SOLO YACHTING RECORD

British yachtswoman Ellen MacArthur entered the record books on February 7, 2005 when she crossed the finishing line of her solo round-the-world voyage in 71 days, 14 hours, 18 minutes and 33 seconds. The Derbyshire-born 28-year-old beat the record set by Frenchman Francis Joyon in 2004 by 33 hours. As she sailed into Falmouth harbour accompanied by a flotilla of boats, including the navy patrol boat HMS *Severn*, she commented: "This is the moment when we all realize that we've done it, that we've actually achieved it."

Much of the 44,011-km (27,348-mile) journey was gruelling. MacArthur battled high winds and difficult seas, having to make repairs to the mast and generators of her 23 m (75 ft)

▲ **Ellen MacArthur celebrates as she sails into Falmouth Bay, Cornwall, after completing her solo round-the-world journey.**

B&Q trimaran. However, she praised her boat – nicknamed Moby: "She has been the most incredible boat. She's a fighter, a boat that will not let you down." MacArthur, who was made a dame, signalled that this would not be the last sailing challenge she undertook. "There are lots of other records out there. The transatlantic record is almost certainly something I'll be aiming for, and maybe round Britain and Ireland solo," she said.

- The Home Office estimates that more than 500,000 illegal immigrants are living in Britain
- The Civil Partnership Act allows single-sex couples to have the same status as married couples
- The government announces a plan to introduce ID cards
- New licensing laws allow pubs and clubs in England to apply for licenses for 24-hour drinking
- London wins the right to stage the 2012 Olympics
- 56 people are killed by four suicide bombings in London carried out by Islamic terrorists
- Television chef Jamie Oliver mounts an effective campaign to improve the quality of school dinners
- Books published this year include *Never Let Me Go* by Kazuo Ishiguro and *Saturday* by Ian McEwan
- Films this year include Kirk Jones's *Nanny McPhee* and Nick Park's *Wallace & Gromit: The Curse of the Were-Rabbit*
- Live 8 concerts pressure governments into action to end poverty in Africa
- BBC2 broadcasts the controversial musical *Jerry Springer – the Opera*, despite the threat of blasphemy prosecution from Christian groups
- Albums released this year include Antony & the Jonsons's *I Am a Bird Now* and The Kaiser Chiefs' *Employment*

CHARLES AND CAMILLA WED

▲ **The wedding of the Prince of Wales and Camilla Parker-Bowles set a seal on a relationship that dated back almost four decades.**

On April 9, 2005, the Prince of Wales married his long-term companion Camilla Parker Bowles in a civil wedding at Windsor's Guildhall. After the low-key ceremony, the couple returned to Windsor Castle for a service of blessing led by the Archbishop of Canterbury and a reception attended by 800 celebrities, dignitaries and members of the royal family. The Queen made a speech in which she praised her son for overcoming "terrible obstacles". She said: "I am very proud and wish them well."

Born in 1947, Mrs Parker Bowles was married to a cavalry officer until her divorce in 1995 and has two children. The prince first met her in 1970 and their close relationship was one of the causes of the break-up of his marriage to Princess Diana. After the princess's death in 1997, the prince's relationship with Mrs Parker Bowles became gradually more public and the couple had been living together at Clarence House for some years before the engagement was announced in February 2005.

Although the engagement excited media debate about the legal and constitutional implications of the heir to the throne marrying a divorcee, opinion polls showed the British public as torn between indifference and sympathy towards the couple.

Through her second marriage Mrs Parker Bowles became the Duchess of Cornwall. If Charles becomes king, her preferred title will be Princess Consort, rather than Queen.

BLAIR WINS RECORD THIRD TERM

On May 5, 2005, Tony Blair became the first Labour leader to win three consecutive general elections. Although the government's overall majority in parliament was reduced to 66, it was still adequate to ensure Labour a further full term in power.

The election gave Labour 356 seats in the House of Commons, compared with 198 seats for the Conservatives, although the difference in the share of the popular vote between the two main parties was quite slender – 35 per cent for Labour as against 32 per cent for the Tories. The Liberal Democrats performed well, taking 62 seats with 22 per cent of the vote, but their goal of becoming the main opposition party

remained well out of reach.

Efforts by opponents of the war in Iraq to make the conflict the focus of the election were only sporadically successful. In the Bethnal Green and Bow constituency, former Labour MP George Galloway, standing for the anti-war Respect Party, defeated the sitting Labour MP Oona King by winning the support of the large local Muslim community. In Blair's Sedgefield constituency Reg Keys, the father of a soldier killed in Iraq, stood as an anti-war candidate and won 10 per cent of the vote.

But none of this could shake the scale of Blair's achievement, as a man who 11 years earlier had taken over a party that had been out of power for 15 years and was

▲ **Although Tony Blair remained Prime Minister, many wondered when Gordon Brown would succeed him.**

widely regarded as unelectable. The real threat to Blair for the future lay not in electoral disillusionment, but in discontent within his own party.

LIVE 8 CAMPAIGNS AGAINST POVERTY

▲ **Bob Geldof's reprise of his Live Aid event 20 years before drew the same predictable chorus of policy promises from politicians.**

On the twentieth anniversary of the famous Live Aid festival, singer Bob Geldof returned to the task of marshalling pop stars to contribute to the war on poverty with Live 8. This consisted of simultaneous concerts held in Hyde Park, London, and nine other

locations around the world on July 2, 2005. It was intended to pressure the leaders of the G8 states, meeting at Gleneagles, Perthshire, the following week, into various economic measures in favour of the world's poorest countries, most of them in Africa.

The concerts attracted vast

crowds, who were subjected to a barrage of anti-poverty propaganda between and during songs. For music connoisseurs, the highlight in Hyde Park was probably an appearance by Pink Floyd, a band not seen together for many years. A number of celebrities could not refrain from posturing, gratuitous swearing by Madonna being an example. Even so, the event was generally judged an excellent feel-good occasion.

The concerts were followed four days later by a 200,000-strong protest march in Edinburgh, ending in another music-fest. The G8 leaders, with a canny eye to their electorates, expressed themselves wholly in favour of Live 8's generous sentiments and respectful of Geldof's insights into the workings of the world economy. They agreed a debt cancellation programme even before the event, and at Gleneagles promised to double aid to Africa by 2010.

JANUARY

• Britain and 25 other countries pledge more than $3 billion to aid reconstruction after the Indian Ocean tsunami disaster

• Prince Harry is photographed in a Nazi uniform at a fancy dress party

• England win the cricket Test series against South Africa 2–1

FEBRUARY

• Ellen MacArthur sails solo around the world in record time

• Three British soldiers found guilty of abusing prisoners in Iraq are sent to military prison

• A ban on hunting mammals with a full pack of hounds comes into force in England and Wales, outlawing fox-hunting

• Death of Amnesty International founder Peter Benenson

MARCH

• Wales complete a Grand Slam in the rugby Six Nations tournament

• The Controversial Prevention of Terrorism Act is passed, giving the Home Secretary the right to impose "control orders" restricting the movements of terrorist suspects

APRIL

• The Prince of Wales marries Camilla Parker Bowles

• Liverpool win European Championship, defeating AC Milan on penalties

2005

SUICIDE BOMBERS HIT LONDON

On July 7, 2005, London suffered its worst ever terrorist attack as four suicide bombers struck the city's transport network. Three bombs were detonated within 50 seconds of each other at around 8.50 am on Underground trains close to King's Cross, Aldgate and Edgware Road stations. The fourth bomb exploded almost an hour later on the upper deck of a bus near Tavistock Square, ripping the roof off the vehicle. Carried out at the height of the morning rush hour, the explosions caused carnage, killing at least 56 people (including the bombers) and injuring around 700 others. With tragic irony, the bombings occurred at a moment when Londoners were filled with a special pride in their city, which the previous day had won the right to stage the summer Olympic Games in 2012.

The London authorities had been preparing for a major terrorist attack ever since the 9/11 attack on New York in 2001. The

▲ Police examine the remains of the bus that was blown up near Tavistock Square, killing 13 people.

▲ An injured passenger from the Edgware Road explosion is helped to safety.

emergency services carried out an impeccable operation under the most testing of circumstances. Terrified passengers trapped on the Tube in smoke and darkness were led to safety while efforts were made to tend the injured, some of whom had suffered dreadful mutilation. Then the arduous tasks of sifting forensic evidence amid the wreckage and retrieving bodies from the deep tunnels got under way. As the dead were identified, it became evident that they reflected the wide mix of nationalities and ethnic groups found in contemporary London, ranging from an Afghan refugee to young Polish women and

including a number of Muslims.

The style of the attacks, reminiscent of the 2004 bombings of commuter trains in Madrid, immediately cast suspicion upon the Islamic terrorist network of al-Qaeda. A group calling itself al-Qaeda in Europe claimed responsibility for the bombings, but although the perpetrators were clearly Islamic extremists, it remained uncertain what their links might be to any wider organization or whether there was an experienced "mastermind" behind the operation.

At the time of the attacks, Prime Minister Tony Blair was in Edinburgh, hosting a summit of G8

countries. Praising the "stoicism and resilience" of Londoners, he insisted that Britain "would not be intimidated". London Mayor Ken Livingstone, still in Singapore after London's Olympic bid, described the bombings as an attack on "the noble and admirable vision" of a multicultural city. Muslim community leaders joined in condemnation of the attacks, though some commentators were soon insisting that Blair's support for the US-led invasion of Iraq was to blame for putting Britain in the firing line.

Over the following days, as London struggled to return to normal life, the four bombers were identified by police as British citizens. Three were Asians from Leeds: Hasib Hussain, Mohammed Sidique Khan and Shehzad Tanweer; the fourth was a West Indian convert to Islam, Jamal Lindsay. None of them was known to the police as a suspected terrorist. Police found a bomb factory at a location they raided in Leeds and also discovered bombs in a car parked outside Luton station, through which three of the men had passed on their way south to London. CCTV footage revealed them to be ordinary-looking young men carrying rucksacks on their backs, in which their homemade bombs were packed.

The authorities warned that any number of similar terrorist cells could be in place and that further attacks were to be expected. These fears were fulfilled exactly two weeks later, on July 21. In what was clearly an attempt to repeat the July 7 attacks, terrorists again attempted to explode three devices on Underground trains and one on a bus. Fortunately, this time all the bombs failed to explode when the detonators were activated, and the perpetrators fled from the scene, no doubt surprised and disorientated to find themselves still alive.

This second wave of attacks triggered a massive manhunt as police hastened to find the would-be bombers before they could strike again. The London streets were awash with armed police officers expecting further suicide attacks at any moment. The day after the failed bombings, plain-clothes police officers followed a suspect into the Underground station at Stockwell, in south London, and shot him eight times in the head, believing he was about to trigger an explosion. The man turned out to be an innocent young Brazilian, Jean Charles de Menezes, who lived in the same block of flats as a known terrorist suspect. Despite this disastrous mistake, the authorities confirmed

▲ **A CCTV image of bomber Hasib Hussain at Luton train station on the morning of July 7 (left), and the photograph from his driving licence.**

a policy of shoot-to-kill in the case of suspected suicide bombers.

Within a week of the failed bombings, the police were closing in on the men they believed to be responsible. CCTV pictures of the men had been released and

information from the public, along with the tracing of mobile phone calls, enabled the police to track down the wanted fugitives. In a series of raids by armed police, three of the bomb suspects were arrested in Britain: Yasin Hassan Omar was picked up in Birmingham after being shot by a police stun-gun; Muktar Said Ibrahim and Ramzi Mohammed were arrested after the siege of a block of flats in the north Kensington area of west London. The fourth suspect, Osman Hussain, was traced to Italy, where he had travelled by Eurostar without being detected. He was arrested in Rome. The suspects were Muslims from east Africa who had lived for many years in Britain. More than a dozen other arrests were also made in connection with the bombings.

There were no illusions that the arrests constituted an end to the bombing campaign. Mayor Ken Livingstone stated that the terrorist threat was set to continue not just for years, but for decades to come. This was to be the new normality of London life.

Thursday 7th July 2005 - A devastating day - Innocent people have lost their lives, the injured will suffer this tragedy forever. Families and friends are in absolute agony.
You will never be forgotten and the cowards responsible will be caught, but sadly this will not bring you back to us.
We shall always remember that You are the "GREAT" that makes GREAT BRITAIN
Forever in our thoughts
Lauren

▲ **Floral tributes lie outside Edgware Road Underground station, as police patrol near by on July 11, 2005.**

2005

LONDON TO STAGE OLYMPICS

On July 6, 2005, the International Olympic Committee (IOC) announced that London would host the 2012 Olympic Games. London's victory after a two-year campaign was a surprise, since Paris had from the outset appeared the most likely city to win.

Initially, Londoners had shown little enthusiasm for staging the Games, but the London bid gathered momentum with the support of Mayor Ken Livingstone and, after some hesitation, Prime Minister Tony Blair. Bid leader Lord Sebastian Coe campaigned tirelessly, overcoming doubts about London's dated transport infrastructure and limited existing sports facilities. The bid centred around construction of an all-new Olympic park on waste ground in a run-down part of Stratford.

The IOC gathered in Singapore for the decisive vote. London engaged in some powerful last-minute lobbying, with sports stars such as footballer David Beckham deploying their prestige. Blair made an influential visit before heading home for the G8 summit at Gleneagles. But the crucial factor was London's final presentation, in which Lord Coe stressed the impact the Olympics would have on the social and sporting development of the city's youthful multi-racial population. With Moscow, New York and Madrid eliminated, Paris and London were left head-to-head in the last round of voting. London's winning margin was 54 to 50.

If Londoners had been lukewarm about the bid initially, there was no

▲ Cynicism gave way to celebration as London was chosen as the venue for the 2012 Olympics.

mistaking the pride and joy with which they responded to this victory. The Tube and bus bombings the following day temporarily dampened spirits, but in the longer term staging the Olympics promised to be a major step in the regeneration of the British capital.

ENGLAND GOES CRICKET CRAZY

▲ England's wait to win the Ashes had stretched to almost 20 years, and the joy of the English cricket team (and their hair) was extravagant.

In the summer of 2005, England and Australia played an Ashes Test series that, for sheer drama, was regarded by many experts as the best ever. Almost the entire nation – including many people with only the sketchiest idea of the rules of the game – was caught up in an outbreak of cricket fever.

Expectation was high before the series began, as England were reckoned to have a chance of beating Australia for the first time since 1987. Australia won the first match of the series with ease, but England took victory in the second Test at Edgbaston by two runs, the closest margin in Ashes history. The next match was a nail-biting draw, with the last Australian pair at the wicket when time ran out. England totally dominated the fourth Test at Trent Bridge, yet a final innings collapse meant they scraped home with only three wickets to spare. After further heart-stopping moments, England secured the draw they needed in the final Test for a 2–1 series victory.

The series made a popular hero of England all-rounder Andrew Flintoff and filled a new generation of youngsters with enthusiasm for the sport. But ironically, the cricketing authorities had sold the rights to televise future Tests to a satellite television channel, creating the prospect of only a minority of young people being able to watch cricket in the future.

PINTER WINS NOBEL PRIZE

In 2005 English playwright Harold Pinter was awarded the Nobel Prize for Literature. It was a prize almost certainly awarded in recognition of his anti-American political views as well as of the quality of his writing for stage and screen.

Pinter was born in Hackney, east London, in 1930. He had his first major success in the theatre in 1960 with *The Caretaker*. Along with his earlier, and originally unsuccessful, play *The Birthday Party*, it established the verbal style and situations that would enter dictionaries as "Pinteresque" – frequent pauses, an air of underlying menace, and characters lacking in consistent motivation or identity.

From the 1970s political

▲ Late in his career, playwright Harold Pinter turned his savage wit to denunciations of American foreign policy.

commitment became central to Pinter's life and work. He frequently denounced the United States for supporting right-wing dictatorships and spreading the use of torture. His denunciations spread to Prime Minister Tony Blair after the NATO intervention in Kosovo in 1999. He opposed this and the subsequent invasions of Afghanistan and Iraq, describing Blair as a mass murderer and likening the United States to Nazi Germany.

Suffering from throat cancer, Pinter was not able to travel to Sweden, but he delivered his acceptance speech by satellite link. It was, as expected, a savage attack upon the lies and oppression allegedly perpetrated by the leaders of Britain and the United States.

FUEL DEPOT EXPLODES

Shortly after 6 am on Sunday, December 11, 2005, the Hertfordshire town of Hemel Hempstead was rocked by a huge explosion at the Buncefield oil depot. The disaster was described as possibly the largest incident of its kind ever witnessed in Europe in peacetime.

The depot, located on the outskirts of the town near Junction 8 of the M1 motorway, supplied fuel to Heathrow, Gatwick and Luton airports. More than 20 of its massive oil tanks, each capable of holding 3 million gallons of fuel, were ignited by the blast. Two smaller explosions followed as the fire spread.

The initial explosion was reportedly heard as far away as the Netherlands and northern France, a phenomenon attributed partly to weather conditions. Houses close to the depot had their windows and doors blown in. Around 2,000 residents were

evacuated as hundreds of fire-fighters moved in to contain the blaze. A plume of dense smoke, clearly visible on satellite photos, spread across southern England.

Remarkably, only two people were seriously injured and no one was killed. By December 13 fire-fighters had mastered the blaze, blanketing tank after tank with

foam. There were fears of health effects from air pollution and of damage to local waterways, but on the whole the incident passed with remarkably little harmful effect.

Suggestions that a terrorist attack or other sabotage was responsible for the explosion were dismissed by police. The most probable cause was the igniting of a fuel vapour leak.

▲ An explosion at the Buncefield oil depot spread a pollution cloud far across southern England, sparking fears of widespread damage to health.

- The number of British service personnel who have died in Iraq rises above 100
- The government stocks up on a vaccine to counter avian flu amid mounting fears of a pandemic
- New legislation bans smoking in offices, pubs, restaurants and clubs, with effect from summer 2007
- The shortage of gas supplies leads to a sharp rise in prices for domestic consumers
- A drought threatens the southeast of England after a dry winter
- Animators Nick Park and Steve Box win their fourth Oscar, with *Wallace & Gromit: The Curse of the Were-Rabbit* taking the Academy Award for Best Animated Feature

JANUARY

- The Liberal Democrat leader Charles Kennedy resigns after admitting to a serious drink problem
- A row erupts over the employment of alleged paedophiles in schools
- Respect MP George Galloway is criticized for appearing on the reality TV show *Celebrity Big Brother*
- A bottle-nosed whale dies after being stranded in the Thames in central London
- Deaths of Labour politician Lord Merlyn-Rees and gardening writer Christopher Lloyd

KENNEDY OUT AND "MING" IS IN

▲ Sir Menzies Campbell celebrates his election as Liberal Democrat leader, flanked by losing candidates Simon Hughes (right) and Chris Huhne.

On January 7, 2006, Liberal Democrat leader Charles Kennedy was forced to resign by a revolt within his own parliamentary party. Under Kennedy's leadership the Liberals had gained greater electoral success than at any time since the 1920s, winning 62 parliamentary seats in 2005. But senior colleagues felt he was not exploiting the party's new-found strength with sufficient energy.

Kennedy's personal weak spot, which enabled the challenge to his leadership to succeed, was alcohol. After repeated denials, on January 5 he was forced into a public admission of his drink problem. At a hastily organized press conference, he stated that he had sought "professional help" and that his drinking days were over. But when 25 MPs announced they would refuse to serve on the Lib Dem front-bench under him, Kennedy was obliged to resign.

The subsequent Lib Dem leadership election produced its own drama, as one candidate, Simon Hughes, was forced after much evasion to admit to homosexual tendencies. The contest was won by Sir Menzies "Ming" Campbell, a 64-year-old former Olympic athlete, thus bucking the recent trend toward electing younger party leaders.

Campbell faced a serious task coping with the centre party's eternal dilemma – how to attract Labour voters who felt their party was too right-wing, while at the same time appealing to Conservative voters seeking a "safe" alternative to Labour. The emergence of David Cameron as a liberal-leaning Conservative leader in 2005 constituted a direct threat to the progress the Liberals had made over previous years at the Tories' expense. Campbell would also have to combat the impression that leading Liberals were the sort of people liable to have skeletons in their cupboards.

HUNDREDTH BRITISH SOLDIER DIES IN IRAQ

On January 31, 2006, Gordon Pritchard, a 31-year-old corporal in the Scots Dragoon Guards and the father of three children, became the hundredth member of the British armed forces to die in Iraq since the 2003 invasion.

Corporal Pritchard was killed by a remote controlled bomb which devastated an army patrol in the port town of Umm Qasr. Ironically, Tony Blair, the architect of Britain's military involvement in Iraq, had been photographed with Pritchard during a visit to British troops the previous month.

Of the 100 British fatalities, 77

▲ Corporal Gordon Pritchard of the Royal Scots Dragoon Guards, the unfortunate victim of a roadside bomb in southern Iraq.

were defined as deaths in action, the other soldiers dying of natural causes. Thirty-three of the combat deaths were sustained in the initial invasion, the other 44 during almost three years of occupation.

There were signs that the security situation in predominantly Shia southern Iraq was deteriorating – another soldier, Lance Corporal Allan Douglas, had been shot by a sniper the day before Corporal Pritchard's death. Shia militants backed by Iran were increasing their attacks on British forces, in the broader context of a slide towards the long-feared civil war between the Sunnis and the Shia in Iraq.

JAIL FOR "PREACHER OF HATE"

On February 7, 2006, Muslim extremist cleric Abu Hamza was sentenced to seven years in prison after being found guilty on six charges of soliciting to murder and five other offences. Hamza's conviction showed the determination of the British authorities to crack down on Islamic radical propagandists.

Born in Egypt in 1958, Hamza moved to Britain in his early 20s. At some point in his chequered career he lost both hands and one eye in an explosion, possibly while making a bomb. In 1997, he became imam of a mosque in Finsbury Park, north London, which became a hotbed of Islamic extremism. His inflammatory preaching denounced atheists, Christians, Jews, homosexuals and most aspects of modern Western society. He spoke repeatedly of the need for killing and for sacrifice, stating that "the dignity of Muslims will not be regained unless with

blood". In 2003, Hamza was expelled from the mosque, but continued to address his followers outside its doors.

Sentencing Hamza, the judge, Mr Justice Hughes, said the cleric had "commended suicide bombing" and encouraged young Muslims to kill. Terrorists once associated with the Finsbury Park mosque included Richard Reid, who tried to blow up an airliner with a shoe-bomb, and Kamel Bourgass, who murdered a policeman and was convicted in 2004 of plotting to use ricin in terror attacks on London.

In the wake of the Hamza case, the government succeeded in pushing through parliament a controversial clause in its new anti-terrorism legislation banning the glorification of terrorism. The government's position, as expressed by the Chancellor, Gordon Brown, was that there should be no tolerance for "preachers of hate".

▲ **Abu Hamza preaches his inflammatory message to the faithful in the street after being expelled from Finsbury Park mosque in 2003.**

THIRD OSCAR FOR CLAY HEROES

In any list of British contributions to modern popular culture, animated clay-model heroes Wallace and Gromit deserve a prominent place. Their first full-length movie *Wallace & Gromit: The Curse of the Were-Rabbit* was voted Best Animated Feature at the Hollywood Academy Awards in March 2006. It was the third Oscar for the comedy duo and the fourth for their creator, Nick Park, and Bristol-based animation studio Aardman Animations.

The international success of the ever-optimistic, cheese-loving inventor and his faithful pooch began with Oscar-winning animated shorts *The Wrong Trousers* (1993)

▲ **Nick Park and Steve Box share the Oscar for *Wallace & Gromit in the Curse of the Were-Rabbit*.**

and *A Close Shave* (1995). The pair have undergone real-life adventures, too. In 1995, Park left the two clay figures in a New York taxi, sparking a man-hunt until the

cabbie returned them unharmed. In October 2005, a fire at Aardman's Bristol plant destroyed many of the models for the Wallace and Gromit movies.

Park's movies are produced by the time-consuming process of stop-animation, with clay models repositioned minutely between the shooting of each individual frame. It is largely thanks to Park that this antiquated animation technique has survived against the rise of computer animation. Although Park's movies are now made for Disney's Dreamworks, they have remained as unmistakably British as Wallace's beloved Wensleydale cheese.

INDEX

CREDITS

The publishers would like to thank the following sources for their kind permission to reproduce the images in this book:

AKG Images: 154

The Bridgeman Art Library: 18 tr

Corbis Images: 25 b, 25 t, 28 t, 119 t, 125 m, 127 t, 133 t, 139 tl, 141 t, 167 tl, 316, 318 m, 353, 355 b, /Austrian Archives: 103 b, /Assignments Photographers/Bryn Colton: 290 t, 319 t, /BBC: 98 b, /Bettmann: 24 b, 53 tl, 54 t, 54 tr, 62 t, 69 b, 73 b, 74 t, 77 t, 83 t, 84 t, 85 b, 86 tr, 88 t, 90, 96 b, 97, 98 t, 99 b, 101 t, 101 br, 104 b, 105, 110 t, 110 b, 115 tl, 116 t, 122, 138 t, 145 b, 147 b, 149 t, 182 t, 187 b, 203 t, 207 t, 211 t, 214, 217 l, 218 b, 220 t, 220 b, 222, 232, 234 t, 236, 237 t, 249, 253 b, 283, 287 b, 293, 294 t, 296 b, 303 t, /Michael Brennan: 222 t, /EPA: 287 t, /EPA/Gerry Penny: 372, /Robert Estall: 91 t, /Lynn Goldsmith: 275 b, /Tim Graham: 272, 277 b, 354, 285 b, /Hulton-Deutsch Collection: 8, 33 t, 39 bl, 54 b, 59, 60 t, 66 t, 69 t, 72 b, 76, 77 b, 79 b, 81 b, 82 b, 85 t, 86 tl, 87 b, 88 t, 91 t, 94 t, 94 b, 95, 101 bl, 102 t, 102 b, 104 t, 107 , 107 t, 107 b, 113 t, 114 b, 117 b, 118 t, 123 t, 125 b, 126, 129 b, 130, 135 ml, 136, 138 b, 139 tr, 139 b, 141 b, 143 t, 144 t, 145 t, 147 t, 149 b, 184 b, 185 t, 190 t, 190 b, 196, 197, 198 , 200 t, 202, 203 b, 205 b, 215 b, 218 t, 221 b, 226, 231 , 267 t, 284 t, 295 b, 304, /Douglas Kirkland: 301 b, /Milepost 92 1/2/Colin Garratt: 146, /The Military Picture Library/Yves Debay: 330, /Museum of Flight: 73 t, /Reuters: 359, 363 b, /Reuters/David Bebber: 384, /Reuters/Dan Chung: 385 m, /Reuters/Handout: 275 b, /Reuters/Kevin Lamarque: 328 b, /Reuters/Kai PFaffenbach: 376 t, /Reuters/Hugo Philpott: 381, /Michael St.Maur Sheil: 53 t, /John Springer Collection: 133 b, 137 b, 219 t, /Sygma/Maher Attar: 312 t, /Sygma /B.B.C Panorama/Tim Graham: 347 t, /Sygma/William Campbell: 282 t, /Sygma/Lional Derimais: 320 t, /Sygma/Michel Vauris Gravos: 278, /Sygma/Kent News & Picture: 369 b, /Sygma/Polak Matthew: b, 339 t, 348, /Sygma/Mercury Press: 338, /Sygma/Patrick Robert: 383 t, /Selwyn Tait: 254 b, /Underwood & Underwood: 67 b, 72 t, 80

Empics: 183 b, 325 t, 328 t, 365 t, /AP: 192, 199 t, 206, 209 t, 209 b, 225 b, 242 t, 260 b, 289 b, 327 b,383 b, /AP/Odd Anderen: 388 b, /AP/Max Desfor: 144 b, /AP/Kevork Djansezian: 395, /AP/Max Nash: 392 t, /AP/Null: 208 t, /AP/Roberto Pfeil: 326, /AP/Toshihiko Sato: 370 b, /Canadian Press: 378, /Martin Cleaver: 291 t, /Ross Kinnaird: 320 t, 263, 284 b, 302, /Jeff Moore/allactiondigital.com: 394 t, /PA: 63 b, 199 b, 201 b, 208 t, 212 t, 213, 217 r, 229 t, 231 t, 234 t, 245 t, 247 b, 253 t, 255, 257 t, 261 t, 265 t, 273 t, 274, 288, 289 t, 290 b, 294 b, 296 t, 300 b, 303 b, 305, 306, 308, 309 b, 311 b, 312 b, 313 b, 317, 331 t, 331 b, 332 b, 333 t, 337, 340 r, 343 b, 346 b, 350 b, 351 t, 358 b, 360 t, 361, 365 b, 375 b, 376 b, 379 b, 385 b, 389 t, /PA/Chris Bacon: 327 t, 349, 357 b, /PA/Adam Butler: 333 b, /PA/David Cheskin: 368 t, /PA/Willliam Conran: 373 t, /PA/Gareth Copley: 392 b, /PA/Derek Cox: 368 b, /PA/Ben Curtis: 364 t, 366, /PA/Sean Dempsey: 322, 329, 352, 358 t, 374, /PA/Matt Dunham: 366, /PA/John Giles: 340 l, 342 t, 387 t, /PA/Johnny Green: 386, /PA/Fiona Hanson: 332 t, 346 t, 347 b, 355 b, 364 b, /PA/Martyn Hayhow: 279 t, 339 b, /PA/Hertfordshire Police: 393 b, /PA/Owen Humphreys: 373 t, /PA/Chris Ison: 388 t, /PA/Jim James: 335 t, 350 t, /PA/Peter Jordan: 345 b, 351 b, 362, /PA/Martin Keene: 342 t, /PA/Croft Malcolm: 328 t, /PA/Paul McErlane: 356, /PA/Tim Ockenden: 334, /PA/Stefan Rousseau: 369 t, /PA/Michael Stephens: 343 t, 357 , /PA/John Stillwell: 321, 393 t, /PA/Kirsty Wigglesworth: 370 t, /PA/Yui Wok: 389 b, /Peter Robinson: 268 b, /Neal Simpson: 371, 377 b, /SMG: 244 t, /Wilfred Witters: 300 t, 360 t

Getty Images: 58 b, 176, 187 t, 215 t, 248 t, 336 t, 379 t, 380 t, /AFP: 313 t, /AFP/Adrian Dennis: 390 t, /AFP/M.O.D: 387 b, 394 b, /AFP/Gerry Penny: 375 t, /Erich Auerbach: 267 b, /Scott Barbour: 380 b, /Arthur Barrett: 37 t, /Herbert

Barraud/Rischgitz: 27 t, /Danial Berehulak: 391 b, /George C. Beresford: 21 b, /Blank Archives: 219 t, /Bongarts: 310, /Gareth Cattermole: 390 b, /Central Press: 29 b, 39 tr, 47 t, 51 t, 64 t, 64 b, 71 t, 84 b, 99 t, 124 b, 194 b, 204 t, 229 t, 250 b, 271 t, 271 b, 291 b, /Central Press/Hulton Archive: 36t, /Central Press/Roger Jackson: 241 b, 252, /Central Press/Norman Potter: 170, 36 t, /Central Press/Dennis Oulds: 245 b, /Colin Davey: 298, /Curt Gunther/BIPs: /Davis: 51 b, /Evening Standard: 134 b, 184 t, 211 b, 241 t, 244 b, 259 b, 263 b, 269 t, /Evening Standard/Mike Lawn: 277 t, /Evening Standard/Mike Lloyd: 258, /Evening Standard/Harry Thompson: 204 b, /Express/John Downing: 188, 212 b, /Fox Photos: 68 b, 87 tl, 88 br, 100 b, 119 b, 200 b, 228 t, 259 b, 269 b, 279 b, /Fox Photos/Mike Barnes: 242 b, /Fox Photos/Derek Berwin: 195 b, /Fox Photos/Cattani: 220 m, /Fox Photos/J.Hardman: 189 b, /Fox Photos/Hulton Archive: 178 t, /Fox Photos/Mike Lawn: 238/9, /Fox Photos/R. H.Lesesne: 93 b, /Fox Photos/M.McNeill: 142, /Fox Photos/Reg Speller: 121 b, 189 t, 191 b, /Hulton Archive/F.A.Swaine: 28 b, /General Photographic Agency: 34, 43 t, 271 bl, /Edward Gooch: 39 tl, /Tim Graham: 318 t, /Charles Hewitt: 103 t, /Maurice Hibberd: 261 b, /Hulton Archive: 10 t, 10 b, 11 b, 11 t, 12 tl, 12 m, 13 t, 14 t, 15, 16 t, 17 b, 18 bl, 18 br, 19, 20 b, 22 b, 23, 26 t, 27 b, 30 b, 31 t, 32 t, 32 b, 35 tr, 35 b, 36 b, 37 b, 38 t, 40, 41 t, 41 b, 42 t, 43 b, 44 t, 44 b, 45 t, 45 b, 46 t, 46 b, 47 b, 49 t, 49 b, 50 t, 55 t, 58 t, 63 mr, 63 tl, 65 t, 65 b, 67 t, 70, 78 t, 81 t, 88 bl, 91 b, 92, 93 t, 111 b, 112, 113 b, 115 b, 116 b, 118 b, 120 t, 120 b, 123 b, 124 t, 127 m, 127 b, 129 t, 130 t, 131 t, 131 b, 135 t, 135 br, 156, 159, 160 t, 160 b, 161, 162, 163, 164, 167 tr, 168, 169, 173, 175 b, 175 t, 178 b, 179, 182 b, 183 t, 186 b, 201 t, 205 t, 221 t, 235, 240, 247 t, 262, 265 b, 268 t, 292 t, 294 m, 299, 302 b, 305, 309 t, 315, 341 b, 354 t, /Hulton Archive/Mills: 22 t, /Hulton Archive/Platt Collection: 270, /Hulton Archive/Graham Wiltshire: 260 t, /Imagno: 60 b, /IOC/Allsport: 26 b, /R.Jones: 243 b, /Keystone: 114 t, 75 t, 83 b, 100 t, 111 t, 117 t, 128 t, 128 b, 134 t, 137 t, 143 b, 148, 186 t, 196 t, 207 b, 224, 225 t, 227 t, 251 t, 251 b, 256 t, 264, 273 b, 285 t, /Keystone/Ron Case/: 185 b, /Keystone/Jim Gray: 227 b, /Keystone/Hulton Archive: 158, /Keystone/Douglas Miller: 257 t, /Keystone/Chris Ware: 311 t, /David Levenson: 280, /Three Lions: 17 t, /London Stereoscopic Company: 14 b, /Met Police: 391 t, /Miller: 140, /Ernest H.Mills: 21 t, /Mirrorpix: 382, /Fred Morley: 115 tr, /Picture Post: 121 t, /Patrick Riviere: 318 b, /Dave Rogers: 385 t, /Sasha: 56/57, 86 b, /Frank Tewkesbury: 256 b, /Reinhold Thiele: 30 t, /Time Life Pictures/Bill Eppridge: 223 t, /Time Life Pictures/David Lees: 195 t, /Time Life Pictures/Mansell: 10 b, 13 b, 16 b, 48 t, 79 t, /Time Life Pictures/Terry Smith: 319 b, /Time Life Pictures/Terrence Spencer: 335 b, /Topical Press Agency: 20 t, 24 t, 31 b, 35 t, 35 tr, 38 t, 39 br, 42 t, 48 b, 50 b, 53 b, 55 b, 68 t, 75 b, 78 b, /Topical Press Agency/E.Bacon: 71 b, /Topical Press Agency/A.R.Coster: 87 tr, /Topical Press Agency/H.F.Davis: 74 b, /Topical Press Agency/David Savill: 96 t, /Topical Press Agency/Stringer: 52, /Topical Press Agency/Walshe: 61 t, 61 b, 62 b, /Sion Touhig: 377 t, /Graham Turner: 276, /John Williams/BIPs: 237 b

The Guardian Newspapers Ltd 1981: /John Hobber: 288 b

Rex Features: /SIPA PRESS: 254 t, /Fox Photos/Reg Speller: 191 br

Topfoto.co.uk: 29 t, 66 b, 82 t, 89, 108, 132, 191 tl, 194 t, 210, 223 b, 228 b, 231 b, 233 t, 233 b, 243 t, 248 b, 250 t, 266, 282 t, 282 t, 292, 293 t, 297 t, 301 t, 307 t, 314 t, 314 b, 324, /AP: 345 t, /ARPL: 198 b, /Henry Grant: 216, /PA: 297 t, 309 b, 325 b, 341 t, 344, /Rosie Scott-Taggart: 246, /UPPA: 286, 295 t, 307 b

Every effort has been made to acknowledge correctly and contact the source and/or copyright holder of each picture and Carlton Books Limited apologizes for any unintentional errors or omissions which will be corrected in future editions of this book.